Getting Started with Containerization

Reduce the operational burden on your system by automating and managing your containers

Gabriel N. Schenker
Hideto Saito
Hui-Chuan Chloe Lee
Ke-Jou Carol Hsu

BIRMINGHAM - MUMBAI

Getting Started with Containerization

First published: March 2019

Production reference: 1260319

Published by Packt Publishing Ltd.
Livery Place
35 Livery Street
Birmingham
B3 2PB, UK.

ISBN 978-1-83864-570-0

www.packtpub.com

`mapt.io`

Mapt is an online digital library that gives you full access to over 5,000 books and videos, as well as industry leading tools to help you plan your personal development and advance your career. For more information, please visit our website.

Why subscribe?

- Spend less time learning and more time coding with practical eBooks and Videos from over 4,000 industry professionals

- Improve your learning with Skill Plans built especially for you

- Get a free eBook or video every month

- Mapt is fully searchable

- Copy and paste, print, and bookmark content

Packt.com

Did you know that Packt offers eBook versions of every book published, with PDF and ePub files available? You can upgrade to the eBook version at `www.packt.com` and as a print book customer, you are entitled to a discount on the eBook copy. Get in touch with us at `customercare@packtpub.com` for more details.

At `www.packt.com`, you can also read a collection of free technical articles, sign up for a range of free newsletters, and receive exclusive discounts and offers on Packt books and eBooks.

Contributors

About the authors

Gabriel N. Schenker has more than 25 years of experience as an independent consultant, architect, leader, trainer, mentor, and developer. Currently, Gabriel works as Senior Curriculum Developer at Confluent after coming from a similar position at Docker. Gabriel has a Ph.D. in Physics, and he is a Docker Captain, a Certified Docker Associate, and an ASP Insider. When not working, Gabriel enjoys time with his wonderful wife Veronicah and his children.

Hideto Saito has around 20 years of experience in the computer industry. In 1998, while working for Sun Microsystems Japan, he was impressed by Solaris OS, OPENSTEP, and Sun Ultra Enterprise 10000 (also known as StarFire). He then decided to pursue UNIX and macOS operating systems.
In 2006, he relocated to southern California as a software engineer to develop products and services running on Linux and macOS X. He was especially renowned for his quick Objective-C code when he was drunk. He is also an enthusiast of Japanese anime, drama, and motorsports, and loves Japanese Otaku culture.

Hui-Chuan Chloe Lee is a DevOps and software developer. She has worked in the software industry on a wide range of projects for over five years. As a technology enthusiast, she loves trying and learning about new technologies, which makes her life happier and more fulfilling. In her free time, she enjoys reading, traveling, and spending time with the people she loves.

Ke-Jou Carol Hsu has three years of experience working as a software engineer and is currently a PhD student in the area of computer systems. Not only involved programming, she also enjoys getting multiple applications and machines perfectly working together to solve big problems. In her free time, she loves movies, music, cooking, and working out.

Packt is searching for authors like you

If you're interested in becoming an author for Packt, please visit
`authors.packtpub.com` and apply today. We have worked with thousands of
developers and tech professionals, just like you, to help them share their insight with
the global tech community. You can make a general application, apply for a specific
hot topic that we are recruiting an author for, or submit your own idea.

Table of Contents

Preface

This Learning Path introduces you to the world of containerization with an overview of Docker fundamentals and a quick brush up on how Kubernetes works with containers. Starting with creating Kubernetes clusters and running applications with proper authentication and authorization, you'll learn how to create high-availability Kubernetes clusters on Amazon Web Services (AWS), and also learn how to use kubeconfig to manage different clusters. Whether it is learning about Docker containers, Docker images, and Docker Compose, or building a continuous delivery pipeline for your application, this Learning Path equips you with all the right tools and techniques to get started with containerization.

By the end of this Learning Path, you will have hands-on experience of working with Docker containers and orchestrators, such as SwarmKit and Kubernetes.

This Learning Path includes content from the following Packt products:

- Learn Docker - Fundamentals of Docker 18.x by Gabriel N. Schenker
- Kubernetes Cookbook - Second Edition by Hideto Saito, Hui-Chuan Chloe Lee, and Ke-Jou Carol Hsu

Who this book is for

This Learning Path is designed for system administrators, operations engineers, DevOps engineers, and developers who are interested in getting started with Docker and Kubernetes. Though you do not need any prior experience with Docker, it will help you to have basic knowledge of Kubernetes and containers.

What this book covers

Chapter 1, *What Are Containers and Why Should I Use Them?*, focuses on the software supply chain and the friction within it. It then presents containers as a means to reduce this friction and add enterprise-grade security on top of it. In this chapter, we also look into how containers and the ecosystem around them are assembled. We specifically point out the distinction between the upstream OSS components (Moby) that form the building blocks of the downstream products of Docker and other vendors.

`Chapter 2`, *Setting up a Working Environment*, discusses in detail how to set up an ideal environment for developers, DevOps engineers, and operators that can be used when working with Docker containers.

`Chapter 3`, *Working with Containers*, teaches how start, stop, and remove containers. The chapter also teaches how to inspect containers to retrieve additional metadata. Furthermore, it introduces how to run additional processes and how to attach to the main process in an already running container. It also shows how to retrieve logging information from a container that is produced by the processes running inside it.

`Chapter 4`, *Creating and Managing Container Images*, introduces the different ways to create container images, which serve as templates for containers. It introduces the inner structure of an image and how it is built.

`Chapter 5`, *Data Volumes and System Management*, introduces data volumes that can be used by stateful components running in containers. The chapter also introduces system-level commands that are used to gather information about Docker and the underlying OS, as well as commands to clean the system from orphaned resources. Finally, it introduces the system
events generated by the Docker engine.

`Chapter 6`, *Distributed Application Architecture*, introduces the concept of a distributed application architecture and discusses the various patterns and best practices that are required to run a distributed application successfully. Finally, it discusses the additional requirements that need to be fulfilled to run such an application in production.

`Chapter 7`, *Single-Host Networking*, introduces the Docker container networking model and its single-host implementation in the form of the bridge network. The chapter introduces the concept of software-defined networks (SDNs) and how they are used to secure containerized applications. Finally, it introduces how container ports can be opened to the public and thus how to make containerized components accessible from the outside world.

`Chapter 8`, *Docker Compose*, introduces the concept of an application consisting of multiple services, each running in a container, and how Docker Compose allows us to easily build, run, and scale such an application using a declarative approach.

`Chapter 9`, *Orchestrators*, introduces the concept of orchestrators. It teaches why orchestrators are needed and how they work. The chapter also provides an overview of the most popular orchestrators and explores a few of their pros and cons.

Chapter 10, *Introduction to Docker Swarm*, introduces Docker's native orchestrator called SwarmKit. It elaborates on all the concepts and objects SwarmKit uses to deploy and run a distributed, resilient, robust, and highly available application in a cluster on-premise, or in the cloud. The chapter also introduces how SwarmKit ensures secure applications using SDNs to isolate containers and secrets to protect sensitive information.

Chapter 11, *Zero Downtime Deployments and Secrets*, teaches how to deploy services or applications onto a Docker swarm with zero downtime and automatic rollback capabilities. It also introduces secrets as a means to protect sensitive information.

Chapter 12, *Building Your Own Kubernetes Cluster*, explains how to build your own Kubernetes cluster with various deployment tools and run your first container on it.

Chapter 13, *Walking through Kubernetes Concepts*, covers both basic and advanced concepts we need to know about Kubernetes. Then, you will learn how to combine them to create Kubernetes objects by writing and applying configuration files.

Chapter 14, *Playing with Containers*, explains how to scale your containers up and down and perform rolling updates without affecting application availability. Furthermore, you will learn how deploy containers for dealing with different application workloads. It will also walk you through best practices of configuration files.

Chapter 15, *Building High-Availability Clusters*, provides information on how to build High Availability Kubernetes master and etcd. This will prevent Kubernetes components from being the single point of failure.

Chapter 16, *Building Continuous Delivery Pipelines*, talks about how to integrate Kubernetes into an existing Continuous Delivery pipeline with Jenkins and private Docker registry.

Chapter 17, *Building Kubernetes on AWS*, walks you through AWS fundamentals. You will learn how to build a Kuberentes cluster on AWS in few minutes.

Chapter 18, *Advanced Cluster Administration*, talks about important resource management in Kubernetes. This chapter also goes through other important cluster administration, such as Kubernetes dashboard, authentication, and authorization.

To get the most out of this book

Ideally you have access to a laptop or personal computer with Windows 10 Professional or a recent version of Mac OS X installed. A computer with any popular Linux OS installed works too. If you're on a Mac you should install Docker for Mac and if you're on Windows then install Docker for Windows. You can download them from here: `https://www.docker.com/community-edition`.

If you are on an older version of Windows or are using Windows 10 Home edition, then you should install Docker Toolbox. You can find the Docker Toolbox here: `https://docs.docker.com/toolbox/toolbox_install_windows/`.

On the Mac, use the Terminal application, and on Windows, use a PowerShell console to try out the commands you will be learning. You also need a recent version of a browser such as Google Chrome, Safari or Internet Explorer. Of course you will need internet access to download tools and container images that we are going to use and explore in this book.

Starting with `Chapter 12`, *Building Your Own Kubernetes Cluster*, we use at least three servers with a Linux-based OS to build all of the components in Kubernetes. From scalability point of view, we recommend you start with three servers in order to scale out the components independently and push your cluster to the production level.

Download the example code files

You can download the example code files for this book from your account at `www.packt.com`. If you purchased this book elsewhere, you can visit `www.packt.com/support` and register to have the files emailed directly to you.

You can download the code files by following these steps:

1. Log in or register at `www.packt.com`.
2. Select the **SUPPORT** tab.
3. Click on **Code Downloads & Errata**.
4. Enter the name of the book in the **Search** box and follow the onscreen instructions.

Once the file is downloaded, please make sure that you unzip or extract the folder using the latest version of:

- WinRAR/7-Zip for Windows
- Zipeg/iZip/UnRarX for Mac
- 7-Zip/PeaZip for Linux

The code bundle for the book is also hosted on GitHub at `https://github.com/PacktPublishing/Getting-Started-with-Containerization`. In case there's an update to the code, it will be updated on the existing GitHub repository.

We also have other code bundles from our rich catalog of books and videos available at `https://github.com/PacktPublishing/`. Check them out!

Conventions used

There are a number of text conventions used throughout this book.

`CodeInText`: Indicates code words in text, database table names, folder names, filenames, file extensions, pathnames, dummy URLs, user input, and Twitter handles. Here is an example: "Next is the actual command we want to execute in the given context, which is `run`."

A block of code is set as follows:

```
$ docker container run alpine echo "Hello World"
```

Bold: Indicates a new term, an important word, or words that you see onscreen. For example, words in menus or dialog boxes appear in the text like this. Here is an example: "To start the installation, click on the **Get Docker for Mac (Edge)** button and follow the instructions."

 Warnings or important notes appear like this.

 Tips and tricks appear like this.

Get in touch

Feedback from our readers is always welcome.

General feedback: If you have questions about any aspect of this book, mention the book title in the subject of your message and email us at `customercare@packtpub.com`.

Errata: Although we have taken every care to ensure the accuracy of our content, mistakes do happen. If you have found a mistake in this book, we would be grateful if you would report this to us. Please visit `www.packt.com/submit-errata`, selecting your book, clicking on the Errata Submission Form link, and entering the details.

Piracy: If you come across any illegal copies of our works in any form on the Internet, we would be grateful if you would provide us with the location address or website name. Please contact us at `copyright@packt.com` with a link to the material.

If you are interested in becoming an author: If there is a topic that you have expertise in and you are interested in either writing or contributing to a book, please visit `authors.packtpub.com`.

Reviews

Please leave a review. Once you have read and used this book, why not leave a review on the site that you purchased it from? Potential readers can then see and use your unbiased opinion to make purchase decisions, we at Packt can understand what you think about our products, and our authors can see your feedback on their book. Thank you!

For more information about Packt, please visit `packt.com`.

1
What Are Containers and Why Should I Use Them?

This first chapter of this book will introduce you to the world of containers and their orchestration. The book starts from the beginning, assuming no prior knowledge in the area of containers, and will give you a very practical introduction into the topic.

In this chapter, we are focusing on the software supply chain and the friction within it. We then present containers as a means to reduce this friction and add enterprise-grade security on top of it. In this chapter, we also look into how containers and the ecosystem around them are assembled. We specifically point out the distinction between the upstream **Operations Support System** (**OSS**) components, united under the code name Moby, that form the building blocks of the downstream products of Docker and other vendors.

The chapter covers the following topics:

- What are containers?
- Why are containers important?
- What's the benefit for me or for my company?
- The Moby project
- Docker products
- The container ecosystem
- Container architecture

After completing this module, you will be able to:

- Explain in a few simple sentences to an interested layman what containers are, using an analogy such as physical containers
- Justify to an interested layman why containers are so important, using an analogy such as physical containers versus traditional shipping, or apartment homes versus single family homes, and so on
- Name at least four upstream open source components that are used by the Docker products, such as Docker for Mac/Windows
- Identify at least three Docker products

Technical requirements

This chapter is a theoretical introduction into the topic. Therefore, there are no special technical requirements for this chapter.

What are containers?

A software container is a pretty abstract thing and thus it might help if we start with an analogy that should be pretty familiar to most of the readers. The analogy is a shipping container in the transportation industry. Throughout history, people have been transporting goods from one location to another by various means. Before the invention of the wheel, goods would most probably have been transported in bags, baskets, or chests on the shoulders of the humans themselves, or they might have used animals such as donkeys, camels, or elephants to transport them.

With the invention of the wheel, transportation became a bit more efficient as humans would built roads on which they could move their carts along. Many more goods could be transported at a time. When we then introduced the first steam-driven machines, and later gasoline driven engines, transportation became even more powerful. We now transport huge amounts of goods in trains, ships, and trucks. At the same time, the type of goods became more and more diverse, and sometimes complex to handle.

In all these thousands of years, one thing did not change though, and that was the necessity to unload the goods at the target location and maybe load them onto another means of transportation. Take, for example, a farmer bringing a cart full of apples to a central train station where the apples are then loaded onto a train, together with all the apples from many other farmers. Or think of a winemaker bringing his barrels of wine with a truck to the port where they are unloaded, and then transferred to a ship that will transport the barrels overseas.

This unloading from one means of transportation and loading onto another means of transportation was a really complex and tedious process. Every type of good was packaged in its own way and thus had to be handled in its own way. Also, loose goods risked being stolen by unethical workers, or goods could be damaged in the process.

Then, there came the container, and it totally revolutionized the transportation industry. The container is just a metallic box with standardized dimensions. The length, width, and height of each container is the same. This is a very important point. Without the world agreeing on a standard size, the whole container thing would not have been as successful as it is now.

Now, with standardized containers, companies who want to have their goods transported from A to B package those goods into these containers. Then, they call a shipper which comes with a standardized means for transportation. This can be a truck that can load a container or a train whose wagons can each transport one or several containers. Finally, we have ships that are specialized in transporting huge amounts of containers. The shippers never need to unpack and repackage goods. For a shipper, a container is a black box and they are not interested in what is in it nor should they care in most cases. It is just a big iron box with standard dimensions. The packaging of goods into containers is now fully delegated to the parties that want to have their goods shipped, and they should know best on how to handle and package those goods.

Since all containers have the same standardized shape and dimensions, the shippers can use standardized tools to handle containers, that is, cranes that unload containers, say from a train or a truck, and load them onto a ship or vice versa. One type of crane is enough to handle all the containers that come along over time. Also, the means of transportation can be standardized, such as container ships, trucks, and trains.

Because of all this standardization, all the processes in and around shipping goods could also be standardized and thus made much more efficient than they were before the age of containers.

I think by now you should have a good understanding of why shipping containers are so important and why they revolutionized the whole transportation industry. I chose this analogy purposefully, since the software containers that we are going to introduce here fulfill the exact same role in the so-called software supply chain as shipping containers do in the supply chain of physical goods.

In the old days, developers would develop a new application. Once that application was completed in the eyes of the developers, they would hand this application over to the operations engineers that were then supposed to install it on the production servers and get it running. If the operations engineers were lucky, they even got a somewhat accurate document with installation instructions from the developers. So far so good, and life was easy.

But things got a bit out of hand when in an enterprise, there were many teams of developers that created quite different types of applications, yet all needed to be installed on the same production servers and kept running there. Usually, each application has some external dependencies such as which framework it was built on or what libraries it uses and so on. Sometimes, two applications would use the same framework but in different versions that might or might not be compatible between each other. Our operations engineer's life became much harder over time. They had to be really creative on how they could load their ship, which is of course their servers with different applications without breaking something.

Installing a new version of a certain application was now a complex project on its own and often needed months of planning and testing. In other words, there was a lot of friction in the software supply chain. But these days, companies rely more and more on software and the release cycles become shorter and shorter. We cannot afford anymore to just have a new release maybe twice a year. Applications need to be updated in a matter of weeks or days, or sometimes even multiple times per day. Companies that do not comply risk going out of business due to the lack of agility. So, *what's the solution?*

A first approach was to use **virtual machines** (**VMs**). Instead of running multiple applications all on the same server, companies would package and run a single application per VM. With it, the compatibility problems were gone and life seemed good again. Unfortunately, the happiness didn't last for long. VMs are pretty heavy beasts on their own since they all contain a full-blown OS such as Linux or Windows Server and all that for just a single application. This is as if in the transportation industry you would use a gigantic ship just to transport a truck load of bananas. What a waste. That can never be profitable.

The ultimate solution to the problem was to provide something much more lightweight than VMs but also able to perfectly encapsulate the goods it needed to transport. Here, the goods are the actual application written by our developers plus (and this is important) all the external dependencies of the application, such as framework, libraries, configurations, and more. This holy grail of a software packaging mechanism was the Docker container.

Developers use Docker containers to package their applications, frameworks, and libraries into them, and then they ship those containers to the testers or to the operations engineers. For the testers and operations engineers, the container is just a black box. It is a standardized black box, though. All containers, no matter what application runs inside them, can be treated equally. The engineers know that if any container runs on their servers, then any other containers should run too. And this is actually true, apart from some edge cases which always exist.

Thus, Docker containers are a means to package applications and their dependencies in a standardized way. Docker then coined the phrase—*Build, ship and run anywhere.*

Why are containers important?

These days, the time between new releases of an application become shorter and shorter, yet the software itself doesn't become any simpler. On the contrary, software projects increase in complexity. Thus, we need a way to tame the beast and simplify the software supply chain.

We also hear every day how much more cyber crimes are on the rise. Many well-known companies are affected by security breaches. Highly sensitive customer data gets stolen, such as social security numbers, credit card information, and more. But not only customer data is compromised, sensitive company secrets are also stolen.

Containers can help in many ways. First of all, Gartner has found in a recent report that applications running in a container are more secure than their counterparts not running in a container. Containers use Linux security primitives such as Linux kernel namespaces to sandbox different applications running on the same computers and **control groups** (cgroups), to avoid the noisy neighbor problem where one bad application is using all available resources of a server and starving all other applications.

Due to the fact that container images are immutable, it is easy to have them scanned for known vulnerabilities and exposures, and in doing so, increase the overall security of our applications.

Another way we can make our software supply chain more secure when using containers is to use **content trust**. Content trust basically ensures that the author of a container image is who they pretend to be and that the consumer of the container image has a guarantee that the image has not been tampered with in transit. The latter is known as a **man-in-the-middle** (**MITM**) attack.

All that I have just said is of course technically also possible without using containers, but since containers introduce a globally accepted standard, it makes it so much easier to implement those best practices and enforce them.

OK, but security is not the only reason why containers are important. There are other reasons:

One of them is the fact that containers make it easy to simulate a production-like environment, even on a developer's laptop. If we can containerize any application, then we can also containerize, say, a database such as Oracle or MS SQL Server. Now, everyone who has ever had to install an Oracle database on a computer knows that this is not the easiest thing to do and it takes a lot of space away on your computer. You wouldn't want to do that to your development laptop just to test whether the application you developed really works end to end. With containers at hand, I can run a full-blown relational database in a container as easily as saying 1, 2, 3. And when I'm done with testing, I can just stop and delete the container and the database is gone without leaving a trace on my computer.

Since containers are very lean compared to VMs, it is not uncommon to have many containers running at the same time on a developer's laptop without overwhelming the laptop.

A third reason why containers are important is that operators can finally concentrate on what they are really good at, provisioning infrastructure, and running and monitoring applications in production. When the applications they have to run on a production system are all containerized, then operators can start to standardize their infrastructure. Every server becomes just another Docker host. No special libraries of frameworks need to be installed on those servers, just an OS and a container runtime such as Docker.

Also, the operators do not have to have any intimate knowledge about the internals of the applications anymore since those applications run self-contained in containers that ought to look like black boxes to the operations engineers, similar to how the shipping containers look to the personnel in the transportation industry.

What's the benefit for me or for my company?

Somebody once said that today, every company of a certain size has to acknowledge that they need to be a software company. Software runs all businesses, period. As every company becomes a software company, there is a need to establish a software supply chain. For the company to remain competitive, their software supply chain has to be secure and efficient. Efficiency can be achieved through thorough automation and standardization. But in all three areas, security, automation, and standardization, containers have shown to shine. Large and well-known enterprises have reported that when containerizing existing legacy applications (many call them traditional applications) and establishing a fully automated software supply chain based on containers, they can reduce the cost used for maintenance of those mission-critical applications by a factor of 50 to 60% and they can reduce the time between new releases of these traditional applications by up to 90%.

That said, the adoption of container technology saves these companies a lot of money, and at the same time it speeds up the development process and reduces the time to market.

The Moby project

Originally, when the company Docker introduced Docker containers, everything was open source. Docker didn't have any commercial products at this time. The Docker engine which the company developed was a monolithic piece of software. It contained many logical parts, such as the container runtime, a network library, a RESTful API, a command-line interface, and much more.

Other vendors or projects such as Red Hat or Kubernetes were using the Docker engine in their own products, but most of the time they were only using part of its functionality. For example, Kubernetes did not use the Docker network library of the Docker engine but provided its own way of networking. Red Hat in turn did not update the Docker engine frequently and preferred to apply unofficial patches to older versions of the Docker engine, yet they still called it the **Docker engine**.

Out of all these reasons and many more, the idea emerged that Docker had to do something to clearly separate the Docker open source part from the Docker commercial part. Furthermore, the company wanted to prevent competitors from using and abusing the name Docker for their own gains.

This was the main reason why the Moby project was born. It serves as the umbrella for most of the open source components Docker developed and continues to develop. These open source projects do not carry the name Docker in them anymore.

Part of the Moby project are components for image management, secret management, configuration management, and networking and provisioning, to name just a few. Also, part of the Moby project are special Moby tools that are, for example, used to assemble components into runnable artifacts.

Some of the components that technically would belong to the Moby project have been donated by Docker to the **Cloud Native Computing Foundation** (**CNCF**) and thus do not appear in the list of components anymore. The most prominent ones are `containerd` and `runc` which together form the container runtime.

Docker products

Docker currently separates its product lines into two segments. There is the **Community Edition** (**CE**) which is closed source yet completely free, and then there is the **Enterprise Edition** (**EE**) which is also a closed source and needs to be licensed on a yearly basis. The enterprise products are backed by 24 x 7 support and are supported with bug fixes much longer than their CE counterparts.

Docker CE

Part of the Docker community edition are products such as the Docker Toolbox, Docker for Mac, and Docker for Windows. All these three products are mainly targeting developers.

Docker for Mac and Docker for Windows are easy-to-install desktop applications that can be used to build, debug, and test Dockerized applications or services on a Mac or on Windows. Docker for Mac and Docker for Windows are complete development environments which deeply integrated with their respective hypervisor framework, networking, and filesystem. These tools are the fastest and most reliable way to run Docker on a Mac or on Windows.

Under the umbrella of the CE, there are also two products that are more geared towards operations engineers. Those products are Docker for Azure and Docker for AWS.

For example, with Docker for Azure, which is a native Azure application, you can set up Docker in a few clicks, optimized for and integrated to the underlying Azure **Infrastructure as a Service** (**IaaS**) services. It helps operations engineers to accelerate time to productivity in building and running Docker applications in Azure.

Docker for AWS works very similar but for Amazon's cloud.

Docker EE

The Docker EE consists of the two products **Universal Control Plane** (**UCP**) and **Docker Trusted Registry** (**DTR**) that both run on top of Docker Swarm. Both are Swarm applications. Docker EE builds on top of the upstream components of the Moby project and adds enterprise-grade features such as **role-based access control** (**RBAC**), multi tenancy, mixed clusters of Docker Swarm and Kubernetes, web-based UI, and content trust, as well as image scanning on top of it.

The container ecosystem

There has never been a new technology introduced in IT that penetrated the landscape so quickly and so thoroughly than containers. Any company that doesn't want to be left behind cannot ignore containers. This huge interest in containers from all sectors of the industry has triggered a lot of innovation in this sector. Numerous companies have specialized in containers and either provide products that build on top of this technology or build tools that support it.

Initially, Docker didn't have a solution for container orchestration thus other companies or projects, open source or not, tried to close this gap. The most prominent one is Kubernetes which was initiated by Google and then later donated to the CNCF. Other container orchestration products are Apache Mesos, Rancher, Red Hat's Open Shift, Docker's own Swarm, and more.

More recently, the trend goes towards a service mesh. This is the new buzz word. As we containerize more and more applications, and as we refactor those applications into more microservice-oriented applications, we run into problems that simple orchestration software cannot solve anymore in a reliable and scalable way. Topics in this area are service discovery, monitoring, tracing, and log aggregation. Many new projects have emerged in this area, the most popular one at this time being Istio, which is also part of the CNCF.

Many say that the next step in the evolution of software are functions, or more precisely, **Functions as a Service** (**FaaS**). Some projects exist that provide exactly this kind of service and are built on top of containers. One prominent example is OpenFaaS.

We have only scratched the surface of the container ecosystem. All big IT companies such as Google, Microsoft, Intel, Red Hat, IBM, and more are working feverishly on containers and related technologies. The CNCF that is mainly about containers and related technologies, has so many registered projects, that they do not all fit on a poster anymore. It's an exciting time to work in this area. And in my humble opinion, this is only the beginning.

Container architecture

Now, let's discuss on a high level how a system that can run Docker containers is designed. The following diagram illustrates what a computer on which Docker has been installed looks like. By the way, a computer which has Docker installed is often called a Docker host, because it can run or host Docker containers:

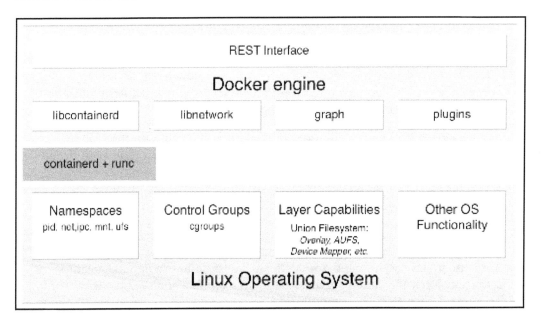

High-level architecture diagram of the Docker engine

In the preceding diagram, we see three essential parts:

- On the bottom, we have the Linux operating system
- In the middle dark gray, we have the container runtime
- On the top, we have the Docker engine

Containers are only possible due to the fact that the Linux OS provides some primitives, such as namespaces, control groups, layer capabilities, and more which are leveraged in a very specific way by the container runtime and the Docker engine. Linux kernel namespaces such as **process ID** (**pid**) namespaces or **network** (**net**) namespaces allow Docker to encapsulate or sandbox processes that run inside the container. Control groups make sure that containers cannot suffer from the noisy neighbor syndrome, where a single application running in a container can consume most or all of the available resources of the whole Docker host. Control groups allow Docker to limit the resources, such as CPU time or the amount of RAM that each container gets maximally allocated.

The container runtime on a Docker host consists of `containerd` and `runc`. `runc` is the low-level functionality of the container runtime and `containerd`, which is based on `runc`, provides the higher-level functionality. Both are open source and have been donated by Docker to the CNCF.

The container runtime is responsible for the whole life cycle of a container. It pulls a container image (which is the template for a container) from a registry if necessary, creates a container from that image, initializes and runs the container, and eventually stops and removes the container from the system when asked.

The Docker engine provides additional functionality on top of the container runtime, such as network libraries or support for plugins. It also provides a REST interface over which all container operations can be automated. The Docker command-line interface that we will use frequently in this book is one of the consumers of this REST interface.

Summary

In this chapter, we looked at how containers can massively reduce the friction in the software supply chain and on top of that, make the supply chain much more secure.

In the upcoming chapter, we will familiarize ourselves with containers. We will learn how to run, stop, and remove containers and otherwise manipulate them. We will also have a pretty good overview over the anatomy of containers. For the first time, we're really going to get our hands dirty and play with these containers, so stay tuned.

Questions

Please solve the following questions to assess your learning progress:

1. Which statements are correct (multiple answers are possible)?
    1. A container is kind of a lightweight VM
    2. A container only runs on a Linux host
    3. A container can only run one process
    4. The main process in a container always has PID 1
    5. A container is one or more processes encapsulated by Linux namespaces and restricted by cgroups
2. Explain to an interested layman in your own words, maybe using analogies, what a container is.
3. Why are containers considered to be a game changer in IT? Name three to four reasons.
4. What does it mean when we claim: *If a container runs on a given platform then it runs anywhere...*? Name two to three reasons why this is true.
5. True or False: *Docker containers are only really useful for modern greenfield applications based on microservices*. Please justify your answer.
6. How much does a typical enterprise save when containerizing their legacy applications?
    1. 20%
    2. 33%
    3. 50%
    4. 75%
7. Which two core concepts of Linux are containers based on?

Further reading

Here is a list of links that lead to more detailed information regarding topics we have discussed in this chapter:

- *Docker overview* at `https://docs.docker.com/engine/docker-overview/`
- *The Moby project* at `https://mobyproject.org/`
- *Docker products* at `https://www.docker.com/get-docker`
- *Cloud Native Computing Foundation* at `https://www.cncf.io/`
- *containerd – industry standard container runtime* at `https://containerd.io/`

Setting up a Working Environment 2

In the last chapter, we learned what Docker containers are and why they're important. We learned what kinds of problem containers solve in a modern software supply chain.

In this chapter, we are going to prepare our personal or working environment to work efficiently and effectively with Docker. We will discuss in detail how to set up an ideal environment for developers, DevOps, and operators that can be used when working with Docker containers.

This chapter covers the following topics:

- The Linux command shell
- PowerShell for Windows
- Using a package manager
- Choosing a code editor
- Docker Toolbox
- Docker for Mac and Docker for Windows
- Minikube

After completing this chapter, you will be able to do the following:

- Use an editor on your laptop that is able to edit simple files such as a Dockerfile or a `docker-compose.yml` file
- Use a shell such as Bash on Mac and PowerShell on Windows to execute Docker commands and other simple operations, such as navigating the folder structure or creating a new folder
- Install Docker for Mac or Docker for Windows on your computer

- Execute simple Docker commands such as `docker version` or `docker container run` on your Docker for Mac or Docker for Windows
- Successfully install Docker Toolbox on your computer
- Use `docker-machine` to create a Docker host on VirtualBox
- Configure your local Docker CLI to remote access a Docker host running in VirtualBox

Technical requirements

For this chapter, you will need a laptop or a workstation with either macOS or Windows, preferably Windows 10 Professional, installed. You should also have free internet access to download applications and the permission to install those applications on your laptop.

The Linux command shell

Docker containers were first developed on Linux for Linux. It is thus natural that the primary command-line tool used to work with Docker, also called a shell, is a Unix shell; remember, Linux derives from Unix. Most developers use the Bash shell. On some lightweight Linux distributions, such as Alpine, Bash is not installed and consequently one has to use the simpler Bourne shell, just called **sh**. Whenever we are working in a Linux environment, such as inside a container or on a Linux VM, we will use either `/bin/bash` or `/bin/sh`, depending on their availability.

Although macOS X is not a Linux OS, Linux and OS X are both flavors of Unix and thus support the same types of tools. Among those tools are the shells. So, when working on a Mac, you will probably be using the Bash shell.

In this book, we expect from the reader a familiarity with the most basic scripting commands in Bash, and PowerShell if you are working on Windows. If you are an absolute beginner, then we strongly recommend that you familiarize yourself with the following cheat sheets:

- *Linux Command Line Cheat Sheet* by Dave Child at `http://bit.ly/2mTQr8l`
- *PowerShell Basic Cheat Sheet* at `http://bit.ly/2EPHxze`

PowerShell for Windows

On a Windows computer, laptop, or server, we have multiple command-line tools available. The most familiar is the command shell. It has been available on any Windows computer for decades. It is a very simple shell. For more advanced scripting, Microsoft has developed PowerShell. PowerShell is very powerful and very popular among engineers working on Windows. On Windows 10, finally, we have the so-called **Windows Subsystem for Linux**, which allows us to use any Linux tool, such as the Bash or Bourne shells. Apart from this, there also exist other tools that install a Bash shell on Windows, for example, the Git Bash shell. In this book, all commands will use Bash syntax. Most of the commands also run in PowerShell.

Our recommendation for you is thus to either use PowerShell or any other Bash tool to work with Docker on Windows.

Using a package manager

The easiest way to install software on a Mac or Windows laptop is to use a good package manager. On a Mac, most people use **Homebrew** and on Windows, **Chocolatey** is a good choice.

Installing Homebrew on a Mac

Installing Homebrew on a Mac is easy; just follow the instructions at `https://brew.sh/`.

The following is the command to install Homebrew:

```
/usr/bin/ruby -e "$(curl -fsSL
https://raw.githubusercontent.com/Homebrew/install/master/install)"
```

Once the installation is finished, test whether Homebrew is working by entering `brew --version` in the Terminal. You should see something like this:

```
$ brew --version
Homebrew 1.4.3
Homebrew/homebrew-core (git revision f4e35; last commit 2018-01-11)
```

Now, we are ready to use Homebrew to install tools and utilities. If we, for example, want to install the Vi text editor, we can do so like this:

```
$ brew install vim
```

This will then download and install the editor for you.

Installing Chocolatey on Windows

To install the Chocolatey package manager on Windows, please follow the instructions at https://chocolatey.org/ or just execute the following command in a PowerShell Terminal that you have run as administrator:

```
PS> Set-ExecutionPolicy Bypass -Scope Process -Force; iex ((New-Object
System.Net.WebClient).DownloadString('https://chocolatey.org/install.p
s1'))
```

Once Chocolatey is installed, test it with the command choco without additional parameters. You should see output similar to the following:

```
PS> choco
Chocolatey v0.10.3
```

To install an application such as the Vi editor, use the following command:

```
PS> choco install -y vim
```

The -y parameter makes sure that the installation happens without asking for reconfirmation. Please note that once Chocolatey has installed an application, you need to open a new PowerShell window to use it.

Choosing a code editor

Using a good code editor is essential to working productively with Docker. Of course, which editor is the best is highly controversial and depends on your personal preference. A lot of people use Vim, or others such as Emacs, Atom, Sublime, or **Visual Studio (VS)** Code, to just name a few. If you have not yet decided which editor is best suited for you, then I highly recommend that you try VS Code. This is a free and lightweight editor, yet it is very powerful and is available for Mac, Windows, and Linux. Give it a try. You can download VS Code from https://code.visualstudio.com/download.

But if you already have a favorite code editor, then please continue using it. As long as you can edit text files, you're good to go. If your editor supports syntax highlighting for Dockerfiles and JSON and YAML files, then even better.

Docker Toolbox

Docker Toolbox has been available for developers for a few years. It precedes the newer tools such as Docker for Mac and Docker for Windows. The toolbox allows a user to work very elegantly with containers on any Mac or Windows computer. Containers must run on a Linux host. Neither Windows or Mac can run containers natively. Thus, we need to run a Linux VM on our laptop, where we can then run our containers. Docker Toolbox installs VirtualBox on our laptop, which is used to run the Linux VMs we need.

As a Windows user, you might already be aware that there exists so-called Windows containers that run natively on Windows. And you are right. Recently, Microsoft has ported the Docker engine to Windows and it is now possible to run Windows containers directly on a Windows Server 2016 without the need for a VM. So, now we have two flavors of containers, Linux containers and Windows containers. The former only run on Linux host and the latter only run on a Windows Server. In this book, we are exclusively discussing Linux containers, but most of the things we learn also apply to Windows containers.

Let's use `docker-machine` to set up our environment. Firstly, we list all Docker-ready VMs we have currently defined on our system. If you have just installed Docker Toolbox, you should see the following output:

List of all Docker-ready VMs

The IP address used might be different in your case, but it will be definitely in the `192.168.0.0/24` range. We can also see that the VM has Docker version `18.04.0-ce` installed.

If, for some reason, you don't have a default VM or you have accidentally deleted it, you can create it using the following command:

```
$ docker-machine create --driver virtualbox default
```

The output you should see looks as follows:

```
$ docker-machine create --driver virtualbox default
Running pre-create checks...
Creating machine...
(default) Copying /Users/gabriel/.docker/machine/cache/boot2docker.iso to /Users/gabriel/.docker/machine/
machines/default/boot2docker.iso...
(default) Creating VirtualBox VM...
(default) Creating SSH key...
(default) Starting the VM...
(default) Check network to re-create if needed...
(default) Waiting for an IP...
Waiting for machine to be running, this may take a few minutes...
Detecting operating system of created instance...
Waiting for SSH to be available...
Detecting the provisioner...
Provisioning with boot2docker...
Copying certs to the local machine directory...
Copying certs to the remote machine...
Setting Docker configuration on the remote daemon...
Checking connection to Docker...
Docker is up and running!
To see how to connect your Docker Client to the Docker Engine running on this virtual machine, run: docke
r-machine env default
$
```

Creating the VM called default in VirtualBox

To see how to connect your Docker client to the Docker Engine running on this virtual machine, run the following command:

```
$ docker-machine env default
```

Once we have our VM called default ready, we can try to SSH into it:

```
$ docker-machine ssh default
```

When executing the preceding command, we are greeted by a boot2docker welcome message.

Type docker --version in the Command Prompt as follows:

```
docker@default:~$ docker --version
Docker version 17.12.1-ce, build 7390fc6
```

Now, let's try to run a container:

```
docker@default:~$ docker run hello-world
```

This will produce the following output:

Running the Docker Hello World container

Docker for Mac and Docker for Windows

If you are using a Mac or have Windows 10 Professional installed on your laptop, then we strongly recommend that you install Docker for Mac or Docker for Windows. These tools give you the best experience when working with containers. Note, older versions of Windows or Windows 10 Home edition cannot run Docker for Windows. Docker for Windows uses Hyper-V to run containers transparently in a VM but Hyper-V is not available on older versions of Windows nor is it available in the Home edition.

Installing Docker for Mac

Navigate to the following link to download Docker for Mac at `https://docs.docker.com/docker-for-mac/install/`.

 There is a stable version and a so-called edge version of the tool available. In this book, we are going to use some newer features and Kubernetes, which at the time of writing are only available in the edge version. Thus, please select this version.

To start the installation, click on the **Get Docker for Mac (Edge)** button and follow the instructions.

Once you have successfully installed Docker for Mac, please open a Terminal. Press *command + spacebar* to open Spotlight and type `terminal`, then hit *Enter*. The Apple Terminal will open as follows:

```
                  gabriel — gabriel@Anubis — ~ — zsh — 80×24
Last login: Sat Feb  3 12:49:33 on ttys003
→  ~
```

Apple Terminal window

Type `docker --version` in the Command Prompt and hit *Enter*. If Docker for Mac is correctly installed, you should get an output similar to the following:

```
$ docker --version
Docker version 18.02.0-ce-rc2, build f968a2c
```

To see whether you can run containers, enter the following command into the Terminal and hit *Enter*:

```
$ docker run hello-world
```

If all goes well, your output should look something like the following:

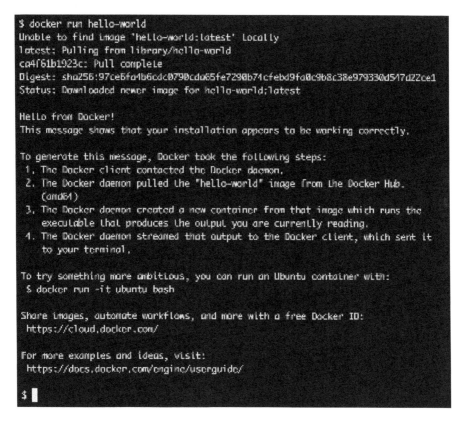

Running the Hello World container on Docker for Mac

Congratulations, you are now ready to work with Docker containers.

Installing Docker for Windows

Note, you can only install Docker for Windows on Windows 10 Professional or Windows Server 2016 since it requires Hyper-V, which is not available on older Windows versions or on the Home edition of Windows 10. If you are using Windows 10 Home or an older version of Windows, you will need to stick with Docker Toolbox.

Navigate to the following link to download Docker for Windows at `https://docs.docker.com/docker-for-windows/install/`.

 There is a stable version and a so-called edge version of the tool available. In this book, we are going to use some newer features and Kubernetes, which at the time of writing are only available in the edge version. Thus, please select this version.

To start the installation, click on the **Get Docker for Windows (Edge)** button and follow the instructions.

With Docker for Windows, you can develop, run, and test Linux containers and Windows containers. In this book, though, we are only discussing Linux containers.

Once you have successfully installed Docker for Windows, open a PowerShell window and type `docker --version` in the Command Prompt. You should see something like the following:

```
PS> docker --version
Docker version 18.04.0-ce, build 3d479c0
```

Using docker-machine on Windows with Hyper-V

If you have Docker for Windows installed on your Windows laptop, then you also have Hyper-V enabled. In this case, you can't use Docker Toolbox since it uses VirtualBox, and Hyper-V and VirtualBox cannot coexist and run at the same time. In this case, you can use `docker-machine` with the Hyper-V driver.

Open a PowerShell console as an administrator. Install `docker-machine` using Chocolatey as follows:

```
PS> choco install -y docker-machine
```

Create a VM called `boot2docker` in Hyper-V with the following command:

```
PS> docker-machine create --driver hyperv --hyperv-virtual-switch "My
Internal Switch" boot2docker
```

Note, you must run the preceding command in administrator mode or it will fail.

You should see the following output generated by the preceding command:

```
Running pre-create checks...
(boot2docker) Image cache directory does not exist, creating it at
C:\Users\Docker\.docker\machine\cache...
(boot2docker) No default Boot2Docker ISO found locally, downloading
the latest release...
(boot2docker) Latest release for github.com/boot2docker/boot2docker is
v18.01.0-ce
....
....
Checking connection to Docker...
Docker is up and running!
To see how to connect your Docker Client to the Docker Engine running
on this virtual machine, run: C:\Program Files\Doc
ker\Docker\Resources\bin\docker-machine.exe env boot2docker
```

To see how to connect your Docker client to the Docker Engine running on this virtual machine, run the following:

```
C:\Program Files\Docker\Docker\Resources\bin\docker-machine.exe env
boot2docker
```

Listing all VMs generated by `docker-machine` gives us the following output:

```
PS C:\WINDOWS\system32> docker-machine ls
NAME            ACTIVE   DRIVER   STATE    URL                SWARM
DOCKER          ERRORS
boot2docker     -        hyperv   Running  tcp://[...]:2376
v18.01.0-ce
```

Now, let's SSH into our `boot2docker` VM:

```
PS> docker-machine ssh boot2docker
```

You should be greeted by the welcome screen.

We can test the VM by executing our `docker version` command, which is shown as follows:

```
$ docker version
Client:
 Version:        18.03.0-ce-rc4
 API version:    1.37
 Go version:     go1.9.4
 Git commit:     fbedb97
 Built: Thu Mar 15 07:33:28 2018
 OS/Arch:        darwin/amd64
 Experimental:   false
 Orchestrator:   swarm

Server:
 Engine:
  Version:       18.03.0-ce-rc4
  API version:   1.37 (minimum version 1.12)
  Go version:    go1.9.4
  Git commit:    fbedb97
  Built:         Thu Mar 15 07:42:29 2018
  OS/Arch:       linux/amd64
  Experimental: true
$
```

Version of the Docker client (CLI) and server

This is definitely a Linux VM, as we can see on the `OS/Arch` entry, and has Docker `18.03.0-ce-rc4` installed.

Minikube

If you cannot use Docker for Mac or Windows or, for some reason, you only have access to an older version of the tool that does not yet support Kubernetes, then it is a good idea to install Minikube. Minikube provisions a single-node Kubernetes cluster on your workstation and is accessible through **kubectl**, which is the command-line tool used to work with Kubernetes.

Installing Minikube on Mac and Windows

To install Minikube for Mac or Windows, navigate to the following link at `https://kubernetes.io/docs/tasks/tools/install-minikube/`.

Follow the instructions carefully. If you have the Docker Toolbox installed, then you already have a hypervisor on your system since the Docker Toolbox installer also installed VirtualBox. Otherwise, I recommend that you install VirtualBox first.

If you have Docker for Mac or Windows installed, then you already have `kubectl` installed with it, thus you can skip that step too. Otherwise, follow the instructions on the site.

Finally, select the latest binary for Minikube for Mac or Windows and install it. For Mac, the latest binary is called `minikube-darwin-amd64` and for Windows it is `minikube-windows-amd64`.

Testing Minikube and kubectl

Once Minikube is successfully installed on your workstation, open a Terminal and test the installation. First, we need to start Minikube. Enter `minikube start` at the command line. The output should look like the following:

```
Starting local Kubernetes v1.9.0 cluster...
Starting VM...
Downloading Minikube ISO
 142.22 MB / 142.22 MB [————————————————————————————] 100.00% 0s
Getting VM IP address...
Moving files into cluster...
Downloading localkube binary
 162.41 MB / 162.41 MB [————————————————————————————] 100.00% 0s
 0 B / 65 B [---------------------------------------------]  0.00%
 65 B / 65 B [————————————————————————————————————————] 100.00% 0sSetting up certs...
Connecting to cluster...
Setting up kubeconfig...
Starting cluster components...
Kubectl is now configured to use the cluster.
Loading cached images from config file.
$
```

Starting Minikube

Now, enter `kubectl version` and hit *Enter* to see something like the following screenshot:

Determining the version of the Kubernetes client and server

If the preceding command fails, for example, by timing out, then it could be that your `kubectl` is not configured for the right context. `kubectl` can be used to work with many different Kubernetes clusters. Each cluster is called a context. To find out which context `kubectl` is currently configured for, use the following command:

```
$ kubectl config current-context
minikube
```

The answer should be `minikube`, as shown in the preceding output. If this is not the case, use `kubectl config get-contexts` to list all contexts that are defined on your system and then set the current context to `minikube` as follows:

```
$ kubectl config use-context minikube
```

The configuration for `kubectl`, where it stores the contexts, is normally found in `~/.kube/config`, but this can be overridden by defining an environment variable called `KUBECONFIG`. You might need to unset this variable if it is set on your computer.

For more in-depth information about how to configure and use Kubernetes contexts, consult the link at `https://kubernetes.io/docs/concepts/configuration/organize-cluster-access-kubeconfig/`.

Assuming Minikube and `kubectl` work as expected, we can now use `kubectl` to get information about the Kubernetes cluster. Enter the following command:

```
$ kubectl get nodes
NAME        STATUS    ROLES     AGE       VERSION
minikube    Ready     <none>    47d       v1.9.0
```

Evidently, we have a cluster of one node, which in my case has Kubernetes `v1.9.0` installed on it.

Summary

In this chapter, we set up and configured our personal or working environment so that we can productively work with Docker containers. This equally applies for developers, DevOps, and operations engineers. In that context, we made sure that we use a good editor, have Docker for Mac or Windows installed, and can also use `docker-machine` to create VMs in VirtualBox or Hyper-V which we can use to run and test containers.

In the next chapter, we're going to learn all the important facts about containers. For example, we will explore how we can run, stop, list, and delete containers, but more than that, we will also dive deep into the anatomy of containers.

Questions

On the basis of your reading of this chapter, please answer the following questions:

1. What is `docker-machine` used for? Name three to four scenarios.
2. True or false? With Docker for Windows, one can develop and run Linux containers.
3. Why are good scripting skills (such as Bash or PowerShell) essential for a productive use of containers?
4. Name three to four Linux distributions on which Docker is certified to run.
5. Name all the Windows versions on which you can run Windows containers.

Further reading

Consider the following link for further reading:

- *Run Docker on Hyper-V with Docker Machine at* `http://bit.ly/2HGMPiI`

3
Working with Containers

In the previous chapter, you learned how to optimally prepare your working environment for the productive and frictionless use of Docker. In this chapter, we are going to get our hands dirty and learn everything that is important to work with containers. Here are the topics we're going to cover in this chapter:

- Running the first container
- Starting, stopping, and removing containers
- Inspecting containers
- Exec into a running container
- Attaching to a running container
- Retrieving container logs
- Anatomy of containers

After finishing this chapter you will be able to do the following things:

- Run, stop, and delete a container based on an existing image, such as NGINX, busybox, or alpine
- List all containers on the system
- Inspect the metadata of a running or stopped container
- Retrieve the logs produced by an application running inside a container
- Run a process such as `/bin/sh` in an already-running container.
- Attach a Terminal to an already-running container
- Explain in your own words to an interested layman the underpinnings of a container

Technical requirements

For this chapter, you should have installed Docker for Mac or Docker for Windows. If you are on an older version of Windows or are using Windows 10 Home Edition, then you should have Docker Toolbox installed and ready to use. On macOS, use the Terminal application, and on Windows, a PowerShell console to try out the commands you will be learning.

Running the first container

Before we start, we want to make sure that Docker is installed correctly on your system and ready to accept your commands. Open a new Terminal window and type in the following command:

```
$ docker -v
```

If everything works correctly, you should see the version of Docker installed on your laptop output in the Terminal. At the time of writing, it looks like this:

```
Docker version 17.12.0-ce-rc2, build f9cde63
```

If this doesn't work, then something with your installation is not right. Please make sure that you have followed the instructions in the previous chapter on how to install Docker for Mac or Docker for Windows on your system.

So, you're ready to see some action. Please type the following command into your Terminal window and hit return:

```
$ docker container run alpine echo "Hello World"
```

When you run the preceding command the first time, you should see an output in your Terminal window similar to this:

```
Unable to find image 'alpine:latest' locally
latest: Pulling from library/alpine
2fdfe1cd78c2: Pull complete
Digest: sha256:ccba511b...
Status: Downloaded newer image for alpine:latest
Hello World
```

Now that was easy! Let's try to run the very same command again:

```
$ docker container run alpine echo "Hello World"
```

The second, third, or nth time you run the preceding command, you should see only this output in your Terminal:

```
Hello World
```

Try to reason about why the first time you run a command you see a different output than all the subsequent times. But don't worry if you can't figure it out, we will explain the reasons in detail in the following sections of the chapter.

Starting, stopping, and removing containers

You have successfully run a container in the previous section. Now we want to investigate in detail what exactly happened and why. Let's look again at the command we used:

```
$ docker container run alpine echo "Hello World"
```

This command contains multiple parts. First and foremost, we have the word `docker`. This is the name of the Docker **command-line interface** (**CLI**), which we are using to interact with the Docker engine that is responsible to run containers. Next, we have the word `container`, which indicates the context we are working with. As we want to run a container, our context is the word `container`. Next is the actual command we want to execute in the given context, which is `run`.

Let me recap—so far, we have `docker container run`, which means, *Hey Docker, we want to run a container....*

Now we also need to tell Docker which container to run. In this case, this is the so-called `alpine` container. Finally, we need to define what kind of process or task shall be executed inside the container when it is running. In our case, this is the last part of the command, `echo "Hello World"`.

Maybe the following figure can help you to get a better approach to the whole thing:

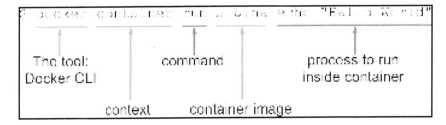

Anatomy of the docker container run expression

Now that we have understood the various parts of a command to run a container, let's try to run another container with a different process running inside it. Type the following command into your Terminal:

```
$ docker container run centos ping -c 5 127.0.0.1
```

You should see output in your Terminal window similar to the following:

```
Unable to find image 'centos:latest' locally
latest: Pulling from library/centos
85432449fd0f: Pull complete
Digest: sha256:3b1a65e9a05...
Status: Downloaded newer image for centos:latest
PING 127.0.0.1 (127.0.0.1) 56(84) bytes of data.
64 bytes from 127.0.0.1: icmp_seq=1 ttl=64 time=0.022 ms
64 bytes from 127.0.0.1: icmp_seq=2 ttl=64 time=0.019 ms
64 bytes from 127.0.0.1: icmp_seq=3 ttl=64 time=0.029 ms
64 bytes from 127.0.0.1: icmp_seq=4 ttl=64 time=0.030 ms
64 bytes from 127.0.0.1: icmp_seq=5 ttl=64 time=0.029 ms

--- 127.0.0.1 ping statistics ---
5 packets transmitted, 5 received, 0% packet loss, time 4103ms
rtt min/avg/max/mdev = 0.021/0.027/0.029/0.003 ms
```

What changed is that, this time, the container image we're using is `centos` and the process we're executing inside the `centos` container is `ping -c 5 127.0.0.1`, which pings the loopback address for five times until it stops.

Let's analyze the output in detail:

- The first line is as follows:

```
Unable to find image 'centos:latest' locally
```

This tells us that Docker didn't find an image named `centos:latest` in the local cache of the system. So, Docker knows that it has to pull the image from some registry where container images are stored. By default, your Docker environment is configured such as that images are pulled from the Docker Hub at `docker.io`. This is expressed by the second line, as follows:

```
latest: Pulling from library/centos
```

- The next three lines of output are as follows:

```
85432449fd0f: Pull complete
Digest: sha256:3b1a65e9a05...
Status: Downloaded newer image for centos:latest
```

This tells us that Docker has successfully pulled the image `centos:latest` from the Docker Hub.

All the subsequent lines of the output are generated by the process we ran inside the container, which is the ping tool in this case. If you have been attentive so far, then you might have noticed the keyword `latest` occurring a few times. Each image has a version (also called a tag), and if we don't specify a version explicitly, then Docker automatically assumes it as latest.

If we run the preceding container again on our system, the first five lines of the output will be missing since, this time, Docker will find the container image cached locally and thus won't have to download it first. Try it out and verify what I just told.

Running a random quotes container

For the subsequent sections of this chapter, we need a container that runs continuously in the background and produces some interesting output. That's why, we have chosen an algorithm that produces random quotes. The API that produces those free random quotes can be found at `https://talaikis.com/random_quotes_api/`.

Now the goal is to have a process running inside a container that produces a new random quote every five seconds and outputs the quote to STDOUT. The following script will do exactly that:

```
while :
do
    wget -qO- https://talaikis.com/api/quotes/random
    printf 'n'
```

```
    sleep 5
done
```

Try it in a Terminal window. Stop the script by pressing *Ctrl+ C*. The output should look similar to this:

```
{"quote":"Martha Stewart is extremely talented. Her designs are
picture perfect. Our philosophy is life is messy, and rather than
being afraid of those messes we design products that work the way we
live.","author":"Kathy Ireland","cat":"design"}

{"quote":"We can reach our potential, but to do so, we must reach
within ourselves. We must summon the strength, the will, and the faith
to move forward – to be bold – to invest in our
future.","author":"John Hoeven","cat":"faith"}
```

Each response is a JSON-formatted string with the quote, its author, and its category.

Now, let's run this in an `alpine` container as a daemon in the background. For this, we need to compact the preceding script into a one-liner and execute it using the `/bin/sh -c "..."` syntax. Our Docker expression will look as follows :

```
$ docker container run -d --name quotes alpine \
    /bin/sh -c "while :; do wget -qO-
https://talaikis.com/api/quotes/random; printf '\n'; sleep 5; done"
```

In the preceding expression, we have used two new command-line parameters, `-d` and `--name`. The `-d` tells Docker to run the process running in the container as a Linux daemon. The `--name` parameter in turn can be used to give the container an explicit name. In the preceding sample, the name we chose is `quotes`.

If we don't specify an explicit container name when we run a container, then Docker will automatically assign the container a random but unique name. This name will be composed of the name of a famous scientist and and adjective. Such names could be `boring_borg` or `angry_goldberg`. Quite humorous our Docker engineers, *isn't it?*

One important takeaway is that the container name has to be unique on the system. Let's make sure that the quotes container is up and running:

```
$ docker container ls -l
```

This should give us something like this:

Listing the last run container

The important part of the preceding output is the STATUS column, which in this case is Up 16 seconds. That is, the container has been up and running for 16 seconds now.

Don't worry if the last Docker command is not yet familiar to you, we will come back to it in the next section.

Listing containers

As we continue to run containers over time, we get a lot of them in our system. To find out what is currently-running on our host, we can use the container list command as follows:

```
$ docker container ls
```

This will list all currently-running containers. Such a list might look similar to this:

List of all containers running on the system

By default, Docker outputs seven columns with the following meanings:

Column	Description
Container ID	The unique ID of the container. It is a SHA-256.
Image	The name of the container image from which this container is instantiated.
Command	The command that is used to run the main process in the container.
Created	The date and time when the container was created.

Status	The status of the container (created, restarting, running, removing, paused, exited, or dead).
Ports	The list of container ports that have been mapped to the host.
Names	The name assigned to this container (multiple names are possible).

If we want to list not only the currently running containers but all containers that are defined on our system, then we can use the command-line parameter `-a` or `--all` as follows:

```
$ docker container ls -a
```

This will list containers in any state, such as `created`, `running`, or `exited`.

Sometimes, we want to just list the IDs of all containers. For this, we have the parameter `-q`:

```
$ docker container ls -q
```

You might wonder where this is useful. I show you a command where it is very helpful right here:

```
$ docker container rm -f $(docker container ls -a -q)
```

Lean back and take a deep breath. Then, try to find out what the preceding command does. Don't read any further until you find the answer or give up.

Right: the preceding command deletes all containers that are currently defined on the system, including the stopped ones. The `rm` command stands for remove, and it will be explained further down.

In the previous section, we used the parameter `-1` in the list command. Try to use Docker help to find out what the `-1` parameter stands for. You can invoke help for the list command as follows:

```
$ docker container ls -h
```

Stopping and starting containers

Sometimes, we want to (temporarily) stop a running container. Let's try this out with the quotes container we used previously. Run the container again with this command:

```
$ docker container run -d --name quotes alpine \
    /bin/sh -c "while :; do wget -qO-
https://talaikis.com/api/quotes/random; printf '\n'; sleep 5; done"
```

Now, if we want to stop this container then we can do so by issuing this command:

```
$ docker container stop quotes
```

When you try to stop the quotes container, you will probably note that it takes a while until this command is executed. To be precise, it takes about 10 seconds. *Why is this the case?*

Docker sends a Linux SIGTERM signal to the main process running inside the container. If the process doesn't react to this signal and terminate itself, Docker waits for 10 seconds and then sends SIGKILL, which will kill the process forcefully and terminate the container.

In the preceding command, we have used the name of the container to specify which container we want to stop. But we could also have used the container ID instead.

How do we get the ID of a container? There are several ways of doing so. The manual approach is to list all running containers and find the one that we're looking for in the list. From there, we copy its ID. A more automated way is to use some shell scripting and environment variables. If, for example, we want to get the ID of the quotes container, we can use this expression:

```
$ export CONTAINER_ID = $(docker container ls | grep quotes | awk
'{print $1}')
```

Now, instead of using the container name, we can use the variable $CONTAINER_ID in our expression:

```
$ docker container stop $CONTAINER_ID
```

Once we have stopped the container, its status change to Exited.

If a container is stopped, it can be started again using the `docker container start` command. Let's do this with our quotes container. It is good to have it running again, as we'll need it in the subsequent sections of this chapter:

```
$ docker container start quotes
```

Removing containers

When we run the `docker container ls -a` command, we can see quite a few containers that are in status `Exited`. If we don't need these containers anymore, then it is a good thing to remove them from memory, otherwise they unnecessarily occupy precious resources. The command to remove a container is:

```
$ docker container rm <container ID>
```

Another command to remove a container is:

```
$ docker container rm <container name>
```

Try to remove one of your exited containers using its ID. Sometimes, removing a container will not work as it is still running. If we want to force a removal, no matter what the condition of the container currently is, we can use the command-line parameter `-f` or `--force`.

Inspecting containers

Containers are runtime instances of an image and have a lot of associated data that characterizes their behavior. To get more information about a specific container, we can use the `inspect` command. As usual, we have to provide either the container ID or name to identify the container of which we want to obtain the data. So, let's inspect our sample container:

```
$ docker container inspect quotes
```

The response is a big JSON object full of details. It looks similar to this:

```
[
```

```
    {
        "Id": "c5c1c68c87...",
        "Created": "2017-12-30T11:55:51.223271182Z",
        "Path": "/bin/sh",
        "Args": [
            "-c",
            "while :; do wget -qO-
https://talaikis.com/api/quotes/random; printf '\n'; sleep 5; done"
        ],
        "State": {
            "Status": "running",
            "Running": true,
            ...
        },
        "Image": "sha256:e21c333399e0...",
        ...
        "Mounts": [],
        "Config": {
            "Hostname": "c5c1c68c87dd",
            "Domainname": "",
            ...
        },
        "NetworkSettings": {
            "Bridge": "",
            "SandboxID": "2fd6c43b6fe5...",
            ...
        }
    }
]
```

The output has been shortened for readability.

Please take a moment to analyze what you got. You should see information such as:

- The ID of the container
- The creation date and time of the container
- From which image the container is built and so on

Many sections of the output, such as Mounts or NetworkSettings don't make much sense right now, but we will certainly discuss those in the upcoming chapters of the book. The data you're seeing here is also named the **metadata** of a container. We will be using the inspect command quite often in the remainder of the book as a source of information.

Sometimes, we need just a tiny bit of the overall information, and to achieve this, we can either use the **grep tool** or a **filter**. The former method does not always result in the expected answer, so let's look into the latter approach:

```
$ docker container inspect -f "{{json .State}}" quotes | jq
```

The $-f$ or $--filter$ parameter is used to define the filter. The filter expression itself uses the **Go template** syntax. In this example, we only want to see the state part of the whole output in the JSON format.

To nicely format the output, we pipe the result into the jq tool:

```
{
  "Status": "running",
  "Running": true,
  "Paused": false,
  "Restarting": false,
  "OOMKilled": false,
  "Dead": false,
  "Pid": 6759,
  "ExitCode": 0,
  "Error": "",
  "StartedAt": "2017-12-31T10:31:51.893299997Z",
  "FinishedAt": "0001-01-01T00:00:00Z"
}
```

Exec into a running container

Sometimes, we want to run another process inside an already-running container. A typical reason could be to try to debug a misbehaving container. *How can we do this?* First, we need to know either the ID or the name of the container, and then we can define which process we want to run and how we want it to run. Once again, we use our currently-running quotes container and we run a shell interactively inside it with the following command:

```
$ docker container exec -i -t quotes /bin/sh
```

The flag $-i$ signifies that we want to run the additional process interactively, and $-t$ tells Docker that we want it to provide us with a TTY (a terminal emulator) for the command. Finally, the process we run is /bin/sh.

If we execute the preceding command in our Terminal, then we will be presented with a new prompt. We're now in a shell inside the quotes container. We can easily prove that by, for example, executing the `ps` command, which will list all running processes in the context:

```
# / ps
```

The result should look somewhat similar to this:

```
/ # ps
PID   USER      TIME    COMMAND
    1 root      0:00 /bin/sh -c while :; do wget -q0- https://talaikis.com/api
   85 root      0:00 /bin/sh
  110 root      0:00 sleep 5
  111 root      0:00 ps
```

List of Processes running inside the quotes Container

We can clearly see that the process with `PID 1` is the command that we have defined to run inside the quotes container. The process with `PID 1` is also named the main process.

Leave the container by entering `exit` at the prompt. We cannot only execute additional processes interactive in a container. Please consider the following command:

```
$ docker container exec quotes ps
```

The output evidently looks very similar to the preceding output:

```
$ docker container exec quotes ps
PID   USER      TIME    COMMAND
    1 root      0:00 /bin/sh -c while :; do wget -q0- https://talaikis.com/api
  570 root      0:00 sleep 5
  571 root      0:00 ps
$
```

List of Processes running inside the quotes Container

We can even run processes as daemon using the flag -d and define environment variables using the -e flag variables as follows:

```
$ docker container exec -it \
    -e MY_VAR="Hello World" \
    quotes /bin/sh
# / echo $MY_VAR
Hello World
# / exit
```

Attaching to a running container

We can use the `attach` command to attach our Terminal's standard input, output, and error (or any combination of the three) to a running container using the ID or name of the container. Let's do this for our quotes container:

```
$ docker container attach quotes
```

In this case, we will see every five seconds or so a new quote appearing in the output.

To quit the container without stopping or killing it, we can press the key combination *Ctrl+P Ctrl+Q*. This detaches us from the container while leaving it running in the background. On the other hand, if we want to detach and stop the container at the same time, we can just press *Ctrl+C*.

Let's run another container, this time an Nginx web server:

```
$ docker run -d --name nginx -p 8080:80 nginx:alpine
```

Here, we run the Alpine version of Nginx as a daemon in a container named `nginx`. The `-p 8080:80` command-line parameter opens port 8080 on the host for access to the Nginx web server running inside the container. Don't worry about the syntax here as we will explain this feature in more detail in the `Chapter 7`, *Single-Host Networking*.

Let's see whether we can access Nginx, using the `curl` tool and running this command:

```
$ curl -4 localhost:8080
```

If all works correctly, you should be greeted by the welcome page of Nginx:

```
<html>
<head>
<title>Welcome to nginx!</title>
<style>
    body {
        width: 35em;
        margin: 0 auto;
        font-family: Tahoma, Verdana, Arial, sans-serif;
    }
</style>
</head>
<body>
<h1>Welcome to nginx!</h1>
<p>If you see this page, the nginx web server is successfully
installed and
working. Further configuration is required.</p>

<p>For online documentation and support please refer to
<a href="http://nginx.org/">nginx.org</a>.<br/>
Commercial support is available at
<a href="http://nginx.com/">nginx.com</a>.</p>

<p><em>Thank you for using nginx.</em></p>
</body>
</html>
```

Now, let's attach our Terminal to the `nginx` container to observe what's happening:

```
$ docker container attach nginx
```

Once you are attached to the container, you first will not see anything. But now open another Terminal, and in this new Terminal window, repeat the `curl` command a few times, for example, using the following script:

```
$ for n in {1..10}; do curl -4 localhost:8080; done
```

You should see the logging output of Nginx, which looks similar to this:

```
172.17.0.1 - - [06/Jan/2018:12:20:00 +0000] "GET / HTTP/1.1" 200 612
"-" "curl/7.54.0" "-"
172.17.0.1 - - [06/Jan/2018:12:20:03 +0000] "GET / HTTP/1.1" 200 612
"-" "curl/7.54.0" "-"
```

```
172.17.0.1 - - [06/Jan/2018:12:20:05 +0000] "GET / HTTP/1.1" 200 612
"-" "curl/7.54.0" "-"
...
```

Quit the container by pressing *Ctrl+C*. This will detach your Terminal and, at the same time, stop the `nginx` container.

To clean up, remove the `nginx` container with the following command:

```
$ docker container rm nginx
```

Retrieving container logs

It is a best practice for any good application to generate some logging information that developers and operators alike can use to find out what the application is doing at a given time, and whether there are any problems to help pinpoint the root cause of the issue.

When running inside a container, the application should preferably output the log items to STDOUT and STDERR and not into a file. If the logging output is directed to STDOUT and STDERR, then Docker can collect this information and keep it ready for consumption by a user or any other external system.

To access the logs of a given container, we can use the `docker container logs` command. If, for example, we want to retrieve the logs of our `quotes` container, we can use the following expression:

```
$ docker container logs quotes
```

This will retrieve the whole log produced by the application from the very beginning of its existence.

 Stop, wait a second—this is not quite true, what I just said. By default, Docker uses the so-called `json-file` logging driver. This driver stores the logging information in a file. And if there is a file rolling policy defined, then `docker container logs` only retrieves what is in the current active log file and not what is in previous, rolled files that might still be available on the host.

If we want to only get a few of the latest entries, we can use the `-t` or `--tail` parameter, as follows:

```
$ docker container logs --tail 5 quotes
```

This will retrieve only the last five items the process running inside the container produced.

Sometimes, we want to follow the log that is produced by a container. This is possible when using the parameter `-f` or `--follow`. The following expression will output the last five log items and then follow the log as it is produced by the containerized process:

```
$ docker container logs --tail 5 --follow quotes
```

Logging drivers

Docker includes multiple logging mechanisms to help us get information from running containers. These mechanisms are named **logging drivers**. Which logging driver is used can be configured at the Docker daemon level. The default logging driver is `json-file`. Some of the drivers that are currently supported natively are:

Driver	Description
none	No log output for the specific container is produced.
json-file	This is the default driver. The logging information is stored in files, formatted as JSON.
journald	If the journals daemon is running on the host machine, we can use this driver. It forwards logging to the journald daemon.
syslog	If the syslog daemon is running on the host machine, we can configure this driver, which will forward the log messages to the syslog daemon.
gelf	When using this driver, log messages are written to a **Graylog Extended Log Format** (GELF) endpoint. Popular examples of such endpoints are Graylog and Logstash.
fluentd	Assuming that the fluentd daemon is installed on the host system, this driver writes log messages to it.

If you change the logging driver, please be aware that the `docker container logs` command is only available for the `json-file` and `journald` drivers.

Using a container-specific logging driver

We have seen that the logging driver can be set globally in the Docker daemon configuration file. But we can also define the logging driver on a container by container basis. In the following example, we are running a `busybox` container and use the `--log-driver` parameter to configure the `none` logging driver:

```
$ docker container run --name test -it \
    --log-driver none \
    busybox sh -c 'for N in 1 2 3; do echo "Hello $N"; done'
```

We should see the following:

```
Hello 1
Hello 2
Hello 3
```

Now, let's try to get the logs of the preceding container:

```
$ docker container logs test
```

The output is as follows:

```
Error response from daemon: configured logging driver does not support
reading
```

This is to be expected, since the `none` driver does not produce any logging output. Let's clean up and remove the `test` container:

```
$ docker container rm test
```

Advanced topic – changing the default logging driver

Let's change the default logging driver of a Linux host. The easiest way to do this is on a real Linux host. For this purpose, we're going to use Vagrant with an Ubuntu image:

```
$ vagrant init bento/ubuntu-17.04
$ vagrant up
$ vagrant ssh
```

Once inside the Ubuntu VM, we want to edit the Docker daemon configuration file. Navigate to the folder /etc/docker and run vi as follows:

```
$ vi daemon.json
```

Enter the following content:

```
{
  "Log-driver": "json-log",
  "log-opts": {
    "max-size": "10m",
    "max-file": 3
  }
}
```

Save and exit Vi by first pressing *Esc* and then typing :w:q and finally hitting the *ENTER* key.

The preceding definition tells the Docker daemon to use the json-log driver with a maximum log file size of 10 MB before it is rolled, and the maximum number of log files that can be present on the system is 3 before the oldest file gets purged.

Now we have to send a `SIGHUP` signal to the Docker daemon so that it picks up the changes in the configuration file:

```
$ sudo kill -SIGHUP $(pidof dockerd)
```

Note that the preceding command only reloads the config file and does not restart the daemon.

Anatomy of containers

Many individuals wrongly compare containers to VMs. However, this is a questionable comparison. Containers are not just lightweight VMs. OK then, *what is the correct description of a container?*

Containers are specially encapsulated and secured processes running on the host system.

Containers leverage a lot of features and primitives available in the Linux OS. The most important ones are **namespaces** and **cgroups**. All processes running in containers share the same Linux kernel of the underlying host operating system. This is fundamentally different compared with VMs, as each VM contains its own full-blown operating system.

The startup times of a typical container can be measured in milliseconds, while a VM normally needs several seconds to minutes to startup. VMs are meant to be long-living. It is a primary goal of each operations engineer to maximize the uptime of their VMs. Contrary to that, containers are meant to be ephemeral. They come and go in a quick cadence.

Let's first get a high-level overview of the architecture that enables us to run containers.

Architecture

Here, we have an architectural diagram on how this all fits together:

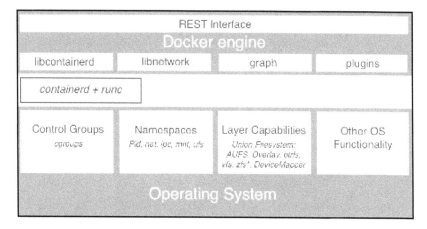

High level architecture of Docker

On the lower part of the the preceding figure, we have the Linux operating system with its cgroups, namespaces, and layer capabilities as well as other functionality that we do not need to explicitly mention here. Then, there is an intermediary layer composed of **containerd** and **runc**. On top of all that now sits the Docker engine. The Docker engine offers a RESTful interface to the outside world that can be accessed by any tool, such as the Docker CLI, Docker for Mac, and Docker for Windows or Kubernetes to just name a few.

Let's now describe the main building blocks in a bit more detail.

Namespaces

Linux namespaces had been around for years before they were leveraged by Docker for their containers. A namespace is an abstraction of global resources such as filesystems, network access, process tree (also named PID namespace) or the system group IDs, and user IDs. A Linux system is initialized with a single instance of each namespace type. After initialization, additional namespaces can be created or joined.

The Linux namespaces originated in 2002 in the 2.4.19 kernel. In kernel version 3.8, user namespaces were introduced and with it, namespaces were ready to be used by containers.

If we wrap a running process, say, in a filesystem namespace, then this process has the illusion that it owns its own complete filesystem. This of course is not true; it is only a virtual FS. From the perspective of the host, the contained process gets a shielded subsection of the overall FS. It is like a filesystem in a filesystem:

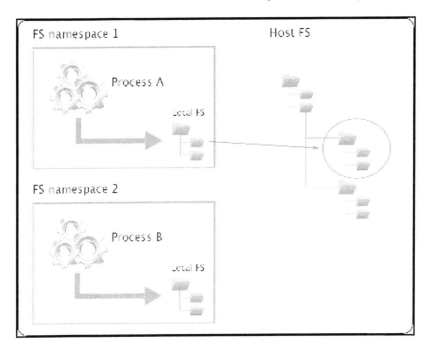

The same applies for all the other global resources for which namespaces exist. The user ID namespace is another example. Having a user namespace, we can now define a user jdoe many times on the system as long at it is living in its own namespace.

The PID namespace is what keeps processes in one container from seeing or interacting with processes in another container. A process might have the apparent PID **1** inside a container, but if we examine it from the host system, it would have an ordinary PID, say **334**:

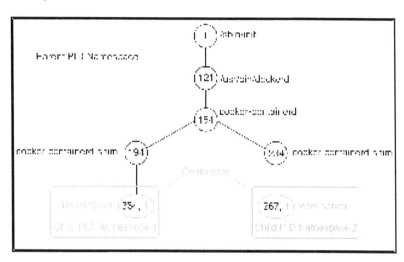

Process tree on a Docker host

In a given namespace, we can run one to many processes. That is important when we talk about containers, and we have experienced that already when we executed another process in an already-running container.

Control groups (cgroups)

Linux cgroups are used to limit, manage, and isolate resource usage of collections of processes running on a system. Resources are CPU time, system memory, network bandwidth, or combinations of these resources, and so on.

Engineers at Google have originally implemented this feature starting in 2006. The cgroups functionality was merged into the Linux kernel mainline in kernel version 2.6.24, which was released in January 2008.

Using cgroups, administrators can limit the resources that containers can consume. With this, one can avoid, for example, the classical *noisy neighbor* problem, where a rogue process running in a container consumes all CPU time or reserves massive amounts of RAM and, as such, starves all the other processes running on the host, whether they're containerized or not.

Union filesystem (UnionFS)

The UnionFS forms the backbone of what is known as container images. We will discuss container images in detail in the next chapter. At this time, we want to just understand a bit better what a UnionFS is and how it works. UnionFS is mainly used on Linux and allows files and directories of distinct filesystems to be overlaid and with it form a single coherent file system. In this context, the individual filesystems are called branches. Contents of directories that have the same path within the merged branches will be seen together in a single merged directory, within the new, virtual filesystem. When merging branches, the priority between the branches is specified. In that way, when two branches contain the same file, the one with the higher priority is seen in the final FS.

Container plumbing

The basement on top of which the Docker engine is built; we can also call it the **container plumbing** and is formed by the two component—**runc** and **containerd**.

Originally, Docker was built in a monolithic way and contained all the functionality necessary to run containers. Over time, this became too rigid and Docker started to break out parts of the functionality into their own components. Two important components are runc and containerd.

Runc

Runc is a lightweight, portable container runtime. It provides full support for Linux namespaces as well as native support for all security features available on Linux, such as SELinux, AppArmor, seccomp, and cgroups.

Runc is a tool for spawning and running containers according to the **Open Container Initiative** (**OCI**) specification. It is a formally specified configuration format, governed by the **Open Container Project** (**OCP**) under the auspices of the Linux Foundation.

Containerd

Runc is a low-level implementation of a container runtime; containerd builds on top of it, and adds higher-level features, such as image transfer and storage, container execution, and supervision, as well as network and storage attachments. With this, it manages the complete life cycle of containers. Containerd is the reference implementation of the OCI specifications and is by far the most popular and widely-used container runtime.

Containerd has been donated to and accepted by the CNCF in 2017. There exist alternative implementations of the OCI specification. Some of them are rkt by CoreOS, CRI-O by RedHat, and LXD by Linux Containers. However, containerd at this time is by far the most popular container runtime and is the default runtime of Kubernetes 1.8 or later and the Docker platform.

Summary

In this chapter, you learned how to work with containers that are based on existing images. We showed how to run, stop, start, and remove a container. Then, we inspected the metadata of a container, extracted the logs of it, and learned how to run an arbitrary process in an already-running container. Last but not least, we dug a bit deeper and investigated how containers work and what features of the underlying Linux operating system they leverage.

In the next chapter, you're going to learn what container images are and how we can build and share our own custom images. We're also discussing the best practices commonly used when building custom images, such as minimizing their size and leveraging the image cache. Stay tuned!

Questions

To assess your learning progress please answer the following questions:

1. What are the states of a container?
2. Which command helps us to find out what is currently running on our host?
3. Which command is used to list the IDs of all containers?

Further reading

The following articles give you some more information related to the topics we discussed in this chapter:

- *Docker container* at `http://dockr.ly/2iLBV2I`
- *Getting started with containers* at `http://dockr.ly/2gmxKWB`
- *Isolate containers with a user namespace* at `http://dockr.ly/2gmyKdf`
- *Limit container's resources* at `http://dockr.ly/2wqN5Nn`

4
Creating and Managing Container Images

In the previous chapter, we learned what containers are and how to run, stop, remove, list, and inspect them. We extracted the logging information of some containers, ran other processes inside an already running container, and finally we dived deep into the anatomy of containers. Whenever we ran a container, we created it using a container image. In this chapter, we will be familiarizing ourselves with these container images. We will learn in detail what they are, how to create them, and how to distribute them.

This chapter will cover the following topics:

- What images are?
- Creating images
- Sharing or shipping images

After completing this chapter, you will be able to do the following:

- Name three of the most important characteristics of a container image
- Create a custom image by interactively changing the container layer and committing it
- Author a simple Dockerfile using keywords such as `FROM`, `COPY`, `RUN`, `CMD`, and `ENTRYPOINT` to generate a custom image
- Export an existing image using `docker image save` and import it into another Docker host using `docker image load`
- Write a two-step Dockerfile that minimizes the size of the resulting image by only including the resulting artifacts (binaries) in the final image

What are images?

In Linux, everything is a file. The whole operating system is basically a filesystem with files and folders stored on the local disk. This is an important fact to remember when looking at what container images are. As we will see, an image is basically a big tarball containing a filesystem. More specifically, it contains a layered filesystem.

The layered filesystem

Container images are templates from which containers are created. These images are not just one monolithic block, but are composed of many layers. The first layer in the image is also called the base layer:

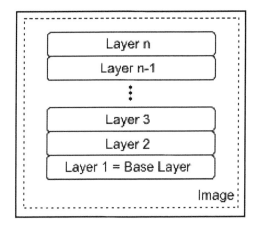

The image as a stack of layers

Each individual layer contains files and folders. Each layer only contains the changes to the filesystem with respect to the underlying layers. Docker uses a union filesystem—as discussed in Chapter 3, *Working with Containers*—to create a virtual filesystem out of the set of layers. A storage driver handles the details regarding the way these layers interact with each other. Different storage drivers are available that have advantages and disadvantages in different situations.

The layers of a container image are all immutable. Immutable means that once generated, the layer cannot ever be changed. The only possible operation affecting the layer is the physical deletion of it. This immutability of layers is important because it opens up a tremendous amount of opportunities, as we will see.

In the following image, we can see what a custom image for a web application using Nginx as a web server could look like:

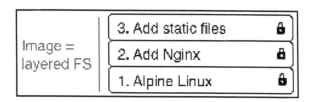

A sample custom image based on Alpine and Nginx

Our base layer here consists of the Alpine Linux distribution. Then, on top of that, we have a layer where Nginx is added on top of Alpine. Finally, the third layer contains all the files that make up the web application, such as HTML, CSS, and JavaScript files.

As has been said previously, each image starts with a base image. Typically, this base image is one of the official images found on Docker Hub, such as a Linux distro, Alpine, Ubuntu, or CentOS. However, it is also possible to create an image from scratch.

 Docker Hub is a public registry for container images. It is a central hub ideally suited for sharing public container images.

Each layer only contains the delta of changes in regard to the previous set of layers. The content of each layer is mapped to a special folder on the host system, which is usually a subfolder of `/var/lib/docker/`.

Since layers are immutable, they can be cached without ever becoming stale. This is a big advantage, as we will see.

The writable container layer

As we have discussed, a container image is made of a stack of immutable or read-only layers. When the Docker engine creates a container from such an image, it adds a writable container layer on top of this stack of immutable layers. Our stack now looks as follows:

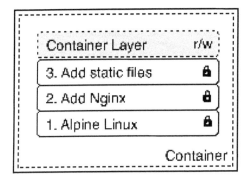

The writable container layer

The container layer is marked as read/write. Another advantage of the immutability of image layers is that they can be shared among many containers created from this image. All that is needed is a thin, writable container layer for each container:

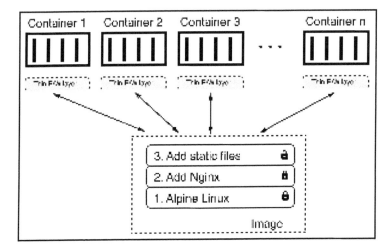

Multiple containers sharing the same image layers

This technique, of course, results in a tremendous reduction of resources that are consumed. Furthermore, this helps to decrease the loading time of a container since only a thin container layer has to be created once the image layers have been loaded into memory, which only happens for the first container.

Copy-on-write

Docker uses the copy-on-write technique when dealing with images. Copy-on-write is a strategy of sharing and copying files for maximum efficiency. If a layer uses a file or folder that is available in one of the low-lying layers, then it just uses it. If, on the other hand, a layer wants to modify, say, a file from a low-lying layer, then it first copies this file up to the target layer and then modifies it. In the following figure, we can see a glimpse of what this means:

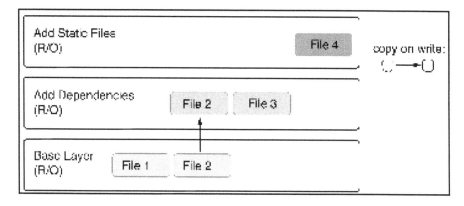

Copy-on-write

The second layer wants to modify **File 2**, which is present in the base layer. Thus, it copied it up and then modified it. Now, let's say that we're sitting in the top layer of the preceding figure. This layer will use **File 1** from the base layer and **File 2** and **File 3** from the second layer.

Graph drivers

Graph drivers are what enable the union filesystem. Graph drivers are also called storage drivers and are used when dealing with the layered container images. A graph driver consolidates the multiple image layers into a root filesystem for the mount namespace of the container. Or, put differently, the driver controls how images and containers are stored and managed on the Docker host.

Docker supports several different graph drivers using a pluggable architecture. The preferred driver is overlay2 followed by overlay.

Creating images

There are three ways to create a new container image on your system. The first one is by interactively building a container that contains all the additions and changes one desires and then committing those changes into a new image. The second and most important way is to use a Dockerfile to describe what's in the new image and then build this image using that Dockerfile as a manifest. Finally, the third way of creating an image is by importing it into the system from a tarball.

Now, let's look at these three ways in detail.

Interactive image creation

The first way we can create a custom image is by interactively building a container. That is, we start with a base image that we want to use as a template and run a container of it interactively. Let's say that this is the `alpine` image. The command to run the container would then be as follows:

```
$ docker container run -it --name sample alpine /bin/sh
```

By default, the alpine container does not have the `ping` tool installed. Let's assume we want to create a new custom image that has `ping` installed. Inside the container, we can then run the following command:

```
/ # apk update && apk add iputils
```

This uses the Alpine package manager `apk` to install the `iputils` library, of which `ping` is a part. The output of the preceding command should look as follows:

```
fetch
http://dl-cdn.alpinelinux.org/alpine/v3.7/main/x86_64/APKINDEX.tar.gz
fetch
http://dl-cdn.alpinelinux.org/alpine/v3.7/community/x86_64/APKINDEX.ta
r.gz
v3.7.0-50-gc8da5122a4 [http://dl-cdn.alpinelinux.org/alpine/v3.7/main]
v3.7.0-49-g06d6ae04c3
[http://dl-cdn.alpinelinux.org/alpine/v3.7/community]
OK: 9046 distinct packages available
(1/2) Installing libcap (2.25-r1)
(2/2) Installing iputils (20121221-r8)
Executing busybox-1.27.2-r6.trigger
OK: 4 MiB in 13 packages
```

Now, we can indeed use `ping`, as the following snippet shows:

```
/ # ping 127.0.0.1
PING 127.0.0.1 (127.0.0.1) 56(84) bytes of data.
64 bytes from 127.0.0.1: icmp_seq=1 ttl=64 time=0.028 ms
64 bytes from 127.0.0.1: icmp_seq=2 ttl=64 time=0.044 ms
64 bytes from 127.0.0.1: icmp_seq=3 ttl=64 time=0.049 ms
^C
--- 127.0.0.1 ping statistics ---
3 packets transmitted, 3 received, 0% packet loss, time 2108ms
rtt min/avg/max/mdev = 0.028/0.040/0.049/0.010 ms
```

Once we have finished our customization, we can quit the container by typing `exit` at the prompt. If we now list all containers with `docker container ls -a`, we can see that our sample container has a status of `Exited`, but still exists on the system:

```
$ docker container ls -a | grep sample
eff7c92a1b98    alpine    "/bin/sh"    2 minutes ago      Exited (0)
...
```

If we want to see what has changed in our container in relation to the base image, we can use the `docker container diff` command as follows:

```
$ docker container diff sample
```

The output should present a list of all modifications done on the filesystem of the container:

```
C /bin
C /bin/ping
```

```
C /bin/ping6
A /bin/traceroute6
C /etc/apk
C /etc/apk/world
C /lib/apk/db
C /lib/apk/db/installed
C /lib/apk/db/lock
C /lib/apk/db/scripts.tar
C /lib/apk/db/triggers
C /root
A /root/.ash_history
C /usr/lib
A /usr/lib/libcap.so.2
A /usr/lib/libcap.so.2.25
C /usr/sbin
C /usr/sbin/arping
A /usr/sbin/capsh
A /usr/sbin/clockdiff
A /usr/sbin/getcap
A /usr/sbin/getpcaps
A /usr/sbin/ipg
A /usr/sbin/rarpd
A /usr/sbin/rdisc
A /usr/sbin/setcap
A /usr/sbin/tftpd
A /usr/sbin/tracepath
A /usr/sbin/tracepath6
C /var/cache/apk
A /var/cache/apk/APKINDEX.5022a8a2.tar.gz
A /var/cache/apk/APKINDEX.70c88391.tar.gz
C /var/cache/misc
```

In the preceding list, A stands for *added*, and C for *changed*. If we had any deleted files, then those would be prefixed with D.

We can now use the `docker container commit` command to persist our modifications and create a new image from them:

```
$ docker container commit sample my-alpine
sha256:44bca4141130ee8702e8e8efd1beb3cf4fe5aadb62a0c69a6995afd49c2e7419
```

With the preceding command, we have specified that the new image shall be called `my-alpine`. The output generated by the preceding command corresponds to the ID of the newly generated image. We can verify this by listing all images on our system, as follows:

```
$ docker image ls
```

We can see this image ID (shortened) as follows:

```
REPOSITORY TAG       IMAGE ID      CREATED             SIZE
my-alpine  latest    44bca4141130  About a minute ago  5.64MB
...
```

We can see that the image named `my-alpine`, has the expected ID of `44bca4141130` and automatically got a tag `latest` assigned. This happens since we did not explicitly define a tag ourselves. In this case, Docker always defaults to the tag `latest`.

If we want to see how our custom image has been built, we can use the `history` command as follows:

```
$ docker image history my-alpine
```

This will print the list of layers our image consists of:

```
IMAGE           CREATED         CREATED BY      SIZE
COMMENT
44bca4141130    3 minutes ago   /bin/sh         1.5MB
e21c333399e0    6 weeks ago     /bin/sh -c #... 0B
<missing>       6 weeks ago     /bin/sh -c #... 4.14MB
```

The first layer in the preceding list is the one that we just created by adding the `iputils` package.

Using Dockerfiles

Manually creating custom images as shown in the previous section of this chapter is very helpful when doing exploration, creating prototypes, or making feasibility studies. But it has a serious drawback: it is a manual process and thus is not repeatable or scalable. It is also as error-prone as any task executed manually by humans. There must be a better way.

This is where the so-called Dockerfile comes into play. The Dockerfile is a text file that is usually literally called Dockerfile. It contains instructions on how to build a custom container image. It is a declarative way of building images.

Declarative versus imperative:

In computer science, in general and with Docker specifically, one often uses a declarative way of defining a task. One describes the expected outcome and lets the system figure out how to achieve this goal, rather than giving step-by-step instructions to the system on how to achieve this desired outcome. The latter is the imperative approach.

Let's look at a sample Dockerfile:

```
FROM python:2.7
RUN mkdir -p /app
WORKDIR /app
COPY ./requirements.txt /app/
RUN pip install -r requirements.txt
CMD ["python", "main.py"]
```

This is a Dockerfile as it is used to containerize a Python 2.7 application. As we can see, the file has six lines, each starting with a keyword such as FROM, RUN, or COPY. It is a convention to write the keywords in all caps, but that is not a must.

Each line of the Dockerfile results in a layer in the resulting image. In the following image, the image is drawn upside down compared to the previous illustrations in this chapter, showing an image as a stack of layers. Here, the base layer is shown on top. Don't let yourself be confused by this. In reality, the base layer is always the lowest layer in the stack:

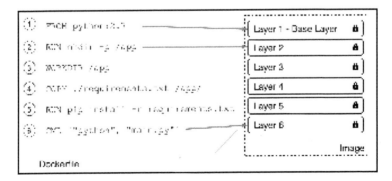

The relation of Dockerfile and layers in an image

Now let's look at the individual keywords in more detail.

The FROM keyword

Every Dockerfile starts with the FROM keyword. With it, we define which base image we want to start building our custom image from. If we want to build starting with CentOS 7, for example, we would have the following line in the Dockerfile:

```
FROM centos:7
```

On Docker Hub, there are curated or official images for all major Linux distros, as well as for all important development frameworks or languages, such as Python, Node JS, Ruby, Go, and many more. Depending on our need, we should select the most appropriate base image.

For example, if I want to containerize a Python 2.7 application, I might want to select the relevant official python:2.7 image.

If we really want to start from scratch, we can also use the following statement:

```
FROM scratch
```

This is useful in the context of building super minimal images that only, for example, contain a single binary, the actual statically linked executable, such as Hello-World. The scratch image is literally an empty base image.

FROM scratch is a no-op in the Dockerfile, and as such does not generate a layer in the resulting container image.

The RUN keyword

The next important keyword is RUN. The argument for RUN is any valid Linux command, such as the following:

```
RUN yum install -y wget
```

The preceding command is using the CentOS package manager yum to install the wget package into the running container. This assumes that our base image is CentOS or RHEL. If we had Ubuntu as our base image, then the command would look similar to the following:

```
RUN apt-get update && apt-get install -y wget
```

It would look like this because Ubuntu uses `apt-get` as a package manager. Similarly, we could define a line with RUN like this:

```
RUN mkdir -p /app && cd /app
```

We could also do this:

```
RUN tar -xJC /usr/src/python --strip-components=1 -f python.tar.xz
```

Here, the former creates a /app folder in the container and navigates to it, and the latter untars a file to a given location. It is completely fine, and even recommended, for you to format a Linux command using more than one physical line, such as this:

```
RUN apt-get update \
  && apt-get install -y --no-install-recommends \
    ca-certificates \
    libexpat1 \
    libffi6 \
    libgdbm3 \
    libreadline7 \
    libsqlite3-0 \
    libssl1.1 \
  && rm -rf /var/lib/apt/lists/*
```

If we use more than one line, we need to put a backslash (\) at the end of the lines to indicate to the shell that the command continues on the next line.

Try to find out what the preceding command does.

The COPY and ADD keywords

The COPY and ADD keywords are very important since, in the end, we want to add some content to an existing base image to make it a custom image. Most of the time, these are a few source files of, say, a web application or a few binaries of a compiled application.

These two keywords are used to copy files and folders from the host into the image that we're building. The two keywords are very similar, with the exception that the ADD keyword also lets us copy and unpack TAR files, as well as provide a URL as a source for the files and folders to copy.

Let's look at a few examples of how these two keywords can be used:

```
COPY . /app
COPY ./web /app/web
COPY sample.txt /data/my-sample.txt
ADD sample.tar /app/bin/
ADD http://example.com/sample.txt /data/
```

In the preceding lines of code:

- The first line copies all files and folders from the current directory recursively to the /app folder inside the container image
- The second line copies everything in the web subfolder to the target folder, /app/web
- The third line copies a single file, sample.txt, into the target folder, /data, and at the same time, renames it to my-sample.txt
- The fourth statement unpacks the sample.tar file into the target folder, /app/bin
- Finally, the last statement copies the remote file, sample.txt, into the target file, /data

Wildcards are allowed in the source path. For example, the following statement copies all files starting with sample to the mydir folder inside the image:

```
COPY ./sample* /mydir/
```

From a security perspective, it is important to know that by default, all files and folders inside the image will have a **user ID** (**UID**) and a **group ID** (**GID**) of 0. The good thing is that for both ADD and COPY, we can change the ownership that the files will have inside the image using the optional --chown flag, as follows:

```
ADD --chown=11:22 ./data/files* /app/data/
```

The preceding statement will copy all files starting with the name web and put them into the /app/data folder in the image, and at the same time assign user 11 and group 22 to these files.

Instead of numbers, one could also use names for the user and group, but then these entities would have to be already defined in the root filesystem of the image at /etc/passwd and /etc/group respectively, otherwise the build of the image would fail.

The WORKDIR keyword

The WORKDIR keyword defines the working directory or context that is used when a container is run from our custom image. So, if I want to set the context to the /app/bin folder inside the image, my expression in the Dockerfile would have to look as follows:

```
WORKDIR /app/bin
```

All activity that happens inside the image after the preceding line will use this directory as the working directory. It is very important to note that the following two snippets from a Dockerfile are not the same:

```
RUN cd /app/bin
RUN touch sample.txt
```

Compare the preceding code with the following code:

```
WORKDIR /app/bin
RUN touch sample.txt
```

The former will create the file in the root of the image filesystem, while the latter will create the file at the expected location in the /app/bin folder. Only the WORKDIR keyword sets the context across the layers of the image. The cd command alone is not persisted across layers.

The CMD and ENTRYPOINT keywords

The CMD and ENTRYPOINT keywords are special. While all other keywords defined for a Dockerfile are executed at the time the image is built by the Docker builder, these two are actually definitions of what will happen when a container is started from the image we define. When the container runtime starts a container, it needs to know what the process or application will be that has to run inside this container. That is exactly what CMD and ENTRYPOINT are used for—to tell Docker what the start process is and how to start that process.

Now, the differences between CMD and ENTRYPOINT are subtle, and honestly most users don't fully understand them or use them in the intended way. Luckily, in most cases, this is not a problem and the container will run anyway; it's just the handling of it that is not as straightforward as it could be.

To better understand how to use the two keywords, let's analyze what a typical Linux command or expression looks like—for example, let's take the `ping` utility as an example, as follows:

```
$ ping 8.8.8.8 -c 3
```

In the preceding expression, `ping` is the command and `8.8.8.8 -c 3` are the parameters to this command. Let's look at another expression:

```
$ wget -O - http://example.com/downloads/script.sh
```

Again, in the preceding expression, `wget` is the command and `-O - http://example.com/downloads/script.sh` are the parameters.

Now that we have dealt with this, we can get back to CMD and ENTRYPOINT. ENTRYPOINT is used to define the command of the expression while CMD is used to define the parameters for the command. Thus, a Dockerfile using `alpine` as the base image and defining `ping` as the process to run in the container could look as follows:

```
FROM alpine:latest
ENTRYPOINT ["ping"]
CMD ["8.8.8.8", "-c", "3"]
```

For both ENTRYPOINT and CMD, the values are formatted as a JSON array of strings, where the individual items correspond to the tokens of the expression that are separated by whitespace. This the preferred way of defining CMD and ENTRYPOINT. It is also called the **exec** form.

Alternatively, one can also use what's called the **shell** form, for example:

```
CMD command param1 param2
```

We can now build an image from the preceding Dockerfile, as follows:

```
$ docker image build -t pinger .
```

Then, we can run a container from the `pinger` image we just created:

```
$ docker container run --rm -it pinger
PING 8.8.8.8 (8.8.8.8): 56 data bytes
64 bytes from 8.8.8.8: seq=0 ttl=37 time=19.298 ms
64 bytes from 8.8.8.8: seq=1 ttl=37 time=27.890 ms
64 bytes from 8.8.8.8: seq=2 ttl=37 time=30.702 ms
```

The beauty of this is that I can now override the CMD part that I have defined in the Dockerfile (remember, it was ["8.8.8.8", "-c", "3"]) when I create a new container by adding the new values at the end of the docker container run expression:

```
$ docker container run --rm -it pinger -w 5 127.0.0.1
```

This will now cause the container to ping the loopback for 5 seconds.

If we want to override what's defined in the ENTRYPOINT in the Dockerfile, we need to use the --entrypoint parameter in the docker container run expression. Let's say we want to execute a shell in the container instead of the ping command. We could do so by using the following command:

```
$ docker container run --rm -it --entrypoint /bin/sh pinger
```

We will then find ourselves inside the container. Type exit to leave the container.

As I already mentioned, we do not necessarily have to follow best practices and define the command through ENTRYPOINT and the parameters through CMD, but we can instead enter the whole expression as a value of CMD and it will work:

```
FROM alpine:latest
CMD wget -O - http://www.google.com
```

Here, I have even used the **shell** form to define the CMD. But what does really happen in this situation where ENTRYPOINT is undefined? If you leave ENTRYPOINT undefined, then it will have the default value of /bin/sh -c, and whatever is the value of CMD will be passed as a string to the shell command. The preceding definition would thereby result in entering following process to run inside the container:

```
/bin/sh -c "wget -O - http://www.google.com"
```

Consequently, /bin/sh is the main process running inside the container, and it will start a new child process to run the wget utility.

A complex Dockerfile

We have discussed the most important keywords commonly used in Dockerfiles. Let's look at a realistic and somewhat complex example of a Dockerfile. The interested reader might note that it looks very similar to the first Dockerfile that we presented in this chapter. Here is the content:

```
FROM node:9.4
RUN mkdir -p /app
WORKDIR /app
COPY package.json /app/
RUN npm install
COPY . /app
ENTRYPOINT ["npm"]
CMD ["start"]
```

OK, so what is happening here? Evidently, this is a Dockerfile that is used to build an image for a Node.js application; we can deduce this from the fact that the base image node:9.4 is used. Then the second line is an instruction to create a /app folder in the filesystem of the image. The third line defines the working directory or context in the image to be this new /app folder. Then, on line four, we copy a package.json file into the /app folder inside the image. After this, on line five, we execute the npm install command inside the container; remember, our context is the /app folder and thus, npm will find the package.json file there that we copied on line four.

After all Node.js dependencies are installed, we copy the rest of the application files from the current folder of the host into the /app folder of the image.

Finally, on the last two lines, we define what the startup command shall be when a container is run from this image. In our case, it is npm start, which will start the Node application.

Building an image

In your home directory, create a FundamentalsOfDocker folder and navigate to it:

```
$ mkdir ~/FundamentalsOfDocker
$ cd ~/FundamentalsOfDocker
```

In the preceding folder, create a `sample1` subfolder and navigate to it:

```
$ mkdir sample1 && cd sample1
```

Use your favorite editor to create a file called `Dockerfile` inside this sample folder with the following content:

```
FROM centos:7
RUN yum install -y wget
```

Save the file and exit your editor.

Back in the Terminal, we can now build a new container image using the preceding Dockerfile as a manifest or construction plan:

```
$ docker image build -t my-centos .
```

Please note that there is a period at the end of the preceding command. This command means that the Docker builder is creating a new image called `my-centos` using the Dockerfile that is present in the current directory. Here, the period at the end of the command stands for *current directory*. We could also write the preceding command as follows, with the same result:

```
$ docker image build -t my-centos -f Dockerfile .
```

But we can omit the `-f` parameter, since the builder assumes that the Dockerfile is literally called `Dockerfile`. We only ever need the `-f` parameter if our Dockerfile has a different name or is not located in the current directory.

The preceding command gives us this (shortened) output:

```
Sending build context to Docker daemon 2.048kB
Step 1/2 : FROM centos:7
7: Pulling from library/centos
af4b0a2388c6: Pull complete
Digest:
sha256:2671f7a3eea36ce43609e9fe7435ade83094291055f1c96d9d1d1d7c0b986a5
d
Status: Downloaded newer image for centos:7
---> ff426288ea90
Step 2/2 : RUN yum install -y wget
---> Running in bb726903820c
Loaded plugins: fastestmirror, ovl
Determining fastest mirrors
 * base: mirror.dal10.us.leaseweb.net
 * extras: repos-tx.psychz.net
 * updates: pubmirrors.dal.corespace.com
```

```
Resolving Dependencies
--> Running transaction check
---> Package wget.x86_64 0:1.14-15.el7_4.1 will be installed
...
Installed:
wget.x86_64 0:1.14-15.el7_4.1
Complete!
Removing intermediate container bb726903820c
---> bc070cc81b87
Successfully built bc070cc81b87
Successfully tagged my-centos:latest
```

Let's analyze this output:

- First, we have the following line:

  ```
  Sending build context to Docker daemon 2.048kB
  ```

  The first thing the builder does is package the files in the current build context, excluding the files and folder mentioned in the .dockerignore file, if present, and sends the resulting .tar file to the Docker daemon.

- Next, we have the following lines:

  ```
  Step 1/2 : FROM centos:7
  7: Pulling from library/centos
  af4b0a2388c6: Pull complete
  Digest: sha256:2671f7a...
  Status: Downloaded newer image for centos:7
  ---> ff426288ea90
  ```

  The first line tells us which step of the Dockerfile the builder is currently executing. Here, we only have two statements in the Dockerfile, and we are on step 1 of 2. We can also see what the content of that section is. Here is the declaration of the base image, on top of which we want to build our custom image. What the builder then does is pull this image from Docker Hub if it is not already available in the local cache. The last line of the preceding snippet indicates which ID the just-built layer gets assigned by the builder.

- Now, follows the next step. I have shortened it even more than the preceding one to concentrate on the essential part:

```
Step 2/2 : RUN yum install -y wget
---> Running in bb726903820c
...
...
Removing intermediate container bb726903820c
---> bc070cc81b87
```

Here, again, the first line indicates to us that we are in step 2 of 2. It also shows us the respective entry from the Dockerfile. On line two, we can see `Running in bb726903820c`, which tells us that the builder has created a container with `ID bb726903820c` inside, which it executes the `RUN` command. We have omitted the output of the `yum install -y wget` command in the snippet since it is not important in this section. When the command is finished, the builder stops the container, commits it to a new layer, and then removes the container. The new layer has `ID bc070cc81b87`, in this particular case.

- At the very end of the output, we encounter the following two lines:

```
Successfully built bc070cc81b87
Successfully tagged my-centos:latest
```

This tells us that the resulting custom image has been given the ID `bc070cc81b87`, and has been tagged with the name `my-centos:latest`.

So, *how does the builder work, exactly?* It starts with the base image. From this base image, once downloaded into the local cache, it creates a container and runs the first statement of the Dockerfile inside this container. Then, it stops the container and persists the changes made in the container into a new image layer.

The builder then creates a new container from the base image and the new layer, and runs the second statement inside this new container. Once again, the result is committed to a new layer. This process is repeated until the very last statement in the Dockerfile is encountered. After having committed the last layer of the new image, the builder creates an ID for this image and tags the image with the name we provided in the `build` command:

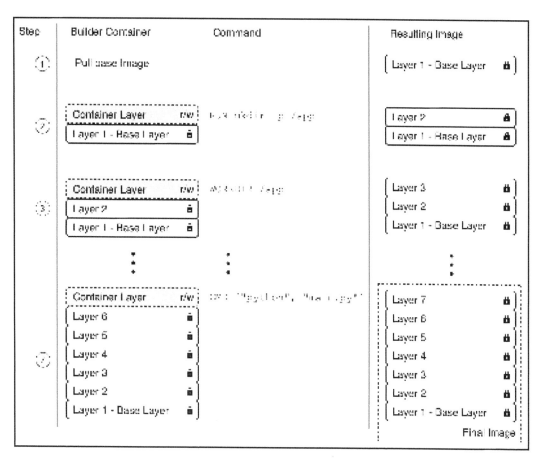

The image build process visualized

Multistep builds

To demonstrate why a Dockerfile with multiple build steps is useful, let's make an example Dockerfile. Let's take a `Hello World` application written in C. Here is the code found inside the `hello.c` file:

```
#include <stdio.h>
int main (void)
{
  printf ("Hello, world!\n");
  return 0;
}
```

Now, we want to containerize this application and write this Dockerfile:

```
FROM alpine:3.7
RUN apk update &&
apk add --update alpine-sdk
RUN mkdir /app
WORKDIR /app
COPY . /app
RUN mkdir bin
RUN gcc -Wall hello.c -o bin/hello
CMD /app/bin/hello
```

Now, let's build this image:

```
$ docker image build -t hello-world .
```

This gives us a fairly long output, since the builder has to install the Alpine SDK, which, among other tools, contains the C++ compiler we need to build the application.

Once the build is done we can list the image and see its size shown as follows:

```
$ docker image ls | grep hello-world
hello-world       latest      e9b...      2 minutes ago      176MB
```

With a size of 176 MB, the resulting image is way too big. In the end, it is just a `Hello World` application. The reason for it being so big is that the image not only contains the `Hello World` binary, but also all the tools to compile and link the application from the source code. But this is really not desirable when running the application, say, in production. Ideally, we only want to have the resulting binary in the image and not a whole SDK.

It is precisely for this reason that we should define Dockerfiles as multistage. We have some stages that are used to build the final artifacts and then a final stage where we use the minimal necessary base image and copy the artifacts into it. This results in very small images. Have a look at this revised Dockerfile:

```
FROM alpine:3.7 AS build
RUN apk update && \
    apk add --update alpine-sdk
RUN mkdir /app
WORKDIR /app
COPY . /app
RUN mkdir bin
RUN gcc hello.c -o bin/hello

FROM alpine:3.7
COPY --from=build /app/bin/hello /app/hello
CMD /app/hello
```

Here, we have a first stage with an alias build that is used to compile the application, and then the second stage uses the same base image `alpine:3.7`, but does not install the SDK, and only copies the binary from the build stage, using the `--from` parameter, into this final image.

Let's build the image again as follows:

```
$ docker image build -t hello-world-small .
```

When we compare the sizes of the images, we get the following output:

```
$ docker image ls | grep hello-world
hello-world-small    latest    f98...    20 seconds ago    4.16MB
hello-world          latest    469...    10 minutes ago    176MB
```

We have been able to reduce the size from 176 MB down to 4 MB. This is reduction in size by a factor of 40. A smaller image size has many advantages, such as a smaller attack surface area for hackers, reduced memory and disk consumption, faster startup times of the corresponding containers, and a reduction of the bandwidth needed to download the image from a registry, such as Docker Hub.

Dockerfile best practices

There are a few recommended best practices to consider when authoring a Dockerfile, which are as follows:

- First and foremost, we need to consider that containers are meant to be ephemeral. By ephemeral, we mean that a container can be stopped and destroyed and a new one built and put in place with an absolute minimum of setup and configuration. That means that we should try hard to keep the time that is needed to initialize the application running inside the container at a minimum, as well as the time needed to terminate or clean up the application.

- The next best practice tells us that we should order the individual commands in the Dockerfile so that we leverage caching as much as possible. Building a layer of an image can take a considerable amount of time, sometimes many seconds or even minutes. While developing an application, we will have to build the container image for our application multiple times. We want to keep the build times at a minimum.

When we're rebuilding a previously built image, the only layers that are rebuilt are the ones that have changed, but if one layer needs to be rebuilt, all subsequent layers also need to be rebuilt. This is very important to remember. Consider the following example:

```
FROM node:9.4
RUN mkdir -p /app
WORKIR /app
COPY . /app
RUN npm install
CMD ["npm", "start"]
```

In this example, the `npm install` command on line five of the Dockerfile usually takes the longest. A classical Node.js application has many external dependencies, and those are all downloaded and installed in this step. This can take minutes until it is done. Therefore, we want to avoid running `npm install` each time we rebuild the image, but a developer changes their source code all the time during development of the application. That means that line four, the result of the `COPY` command, changes all the time and this layer has to be rebuilt each time. But as we discussed previously, that also means that all subsequent layers have to be rebuilt, which in this case includes the `npm install` command.

To avoid this, we can slightly modify the Dockerfile and have the following:

```
FROM node:9.4
RUN mkdir -p /app
WORKIR /app
COPY package.json /app/
RUN npm install
COPY . /app
CMD ["npm", "start"]
```

What we have done here is that, on line four, we only copy the single file that the `npm install` command needs as a source, which is the `package.json` file. This file rarely changes in a typical development process. As a consequence, the `npm install` command also has to be executed only when the `package.json` file changes. All the remaining, frequently changed content is added to the image after the `npm install` command.

- A further best practice is to keep the number of layers that make up your image relatively small. The more layers an image has, the more the graph driver needs to work to consolidate the layers into a single root filesystem for the corresponding container. Of course, this takes time, and thus the fewer layers an image has, the faster the startup time for the container can be.

But *how can we keep our number of layers low?* Remember that in a Dockerfile, each line that starts with a keyword, such as FROM, COPY, or RUN, creates a new layer. The easiest way to reduce the number of layers is to combine multiple individual RUN commands into a single one—for example, say that we had the following in a Dockerfile:

```
RUN apt-get update
RUN apt-get install -y ca-certificates
RUN rm -rf /var/lib/apt/lists/*
```

We could combine these into a single concatenated expression, as follows:

```
RUN apt-get update \
    && apt-get install -y ca-certificates \
    && rm -rf /var/lib/apt/lists/*
```

The former will generate three layers in the resulting image, while the latter only creates a single layer.

The next three best practices all result in smaller images. Why is this important? Smaller images reduce the time and bandwidth needed to download the image from a registry. They also reduce the amount of disk space needed to store a copy locally on the Docker host and the memory needed to load the image. Finally, smaller images also means a smaller attack surface for hackers. Here are the best practices mentioned:

- The first best practice that helps to reduce the image size is to use a `.dockerignore` file. We want to avoid copying unnecessary files and folders into an image to keep it as lean as possible. A `.dockerignore` file works in exactly the same way as a `.gitignore` file, for those who are familiar with Git. In a `.dockerignore` file, we can configure patterns to exclude certain files or folders from being included in the context when building the image.
- The next best practice is to avoid installing unnecessary packages into the filesystem of the image. Once again, this is to keep the image as lean as possible.
- Last but not least, it is recommended that you use multistage builds so that the resulting image is as small as possible and only contains the absolute minimum needed to run your application or application service.

Saving and loading images

The third way to create a new container image is by importing or loading it from a file. A container image is nothing more than a tarball. To demonstrate this, we can use the `docker image save` command to export an existing image to a tarball:

```
$ docker image save -o ./backup/my-alpine.tar my-alpine
```

The preceding command takes our `my-alpine` image that we previously built and exports it into a `./backup/my-alpine.tar` file.

If, on the other hand, we have an existing tarball and want to import it as an image into our system, we can use the `docker image load` command as follows:

```
$ docker image load -i ./backup/my-alpine.tar
```

Sharing or shipping images

To be able to ship our custom image to other environments, we need to first give it a globally unique name. This action is often called tagging an image. We then need to publish the image to a central location from which other interested or entitled parties can pull it. These central locations are called **image registries**.

Tagging an image

Each image has a so-called **tag**. A tag is often used to version images, but it has a broader reach than just being a version number. If we do not explicitly specify a tag when working with images, then Docker automatically assumes we're referring to the *latest* tag. This is relevant when pulling an image from Docker Hub, for example:

```
$ docker image pull alpine
```

The preceding command will pull the `alpine:latest` image from the Hub. If we want to explicitly specify a tag, we do so like this:

```
$ docker image pull alpine:3.5
```

This will now pull the `alpine` image that has been tagged with `3.5`.

Image namespaces

So far, you have been pulling various images and haven't worried so much about where those images originated from. Your Docker environment is configured so that, by default, all images are pulled from Docker Hub. We also only pulled so-called official images from the Docker Hub, such as `alpine` or `busybox`.

Now it is time to widen our horizon a bit and learn about how images are namespaced. The most generic way to define an image is by its fully qualified name, which looks as follows:

```
<registry URL>/<User or Org>/<name>:<tag>
```

Let's look at this in a bit more detail:

- `<registry URL>`: This is the URL to the registry from which we want to pull the image. By default, this is `docker.io`. More generally, this could be `https://registry.acme.com`.

Other than Docker Hub, there are quite a few public registries out there that you could pull images from. The following is a list of some of them, in no particular order:

- Google at `https://cloud.google.com/container-registry`
- Amazon AWS at `https://aws.amazon.com/ecr/`
- Microsoft Azure at `https://azure.microsoft.com/en-us/services/container-registry/`
- Red Hat at `https://access.redhat.com/containers/`
- Artifactory at `https://jfrog.com/integration/artifactory-docker-registry/`

- `<User or Org>`: This is the private Docker ID of either an individual or an organization defined on Docker Hub, or any other registry for that matter, such as `microsoft` or `oracle`.
- `<name>`: This is the name of the image that is often also called a repository.
- `<tag>`: This is the tag of the image.

Let's look at an example:

```
https://registry.acme.com/engineering/web-app:1.0
```

Here, we have an image, `web-app`, that is tagged with version `1.0` and belongs to the `engineering` organization on the private registry at `https://registry.acme.com`.

Now, there are some special conventions:

- If we omit the registry URL, then Docker Hub is automatically taken
- If we omit the tag, then `latest` is taken
- If it is an official image on Docker Hub, then no user or organization namespace is needed

A few samples in tabular form are as follows:

Image	Description
alpine	Official `alpine` image on Docker Hub with the `latest` tag.
ubuntu:16.04	Official `ubuntu` image on Docker Hub with the `16.04` tag or version.

`microsoft/nanoserver`	`nanoserver` image of Microsoft on Docker Hub with the `latest` tag.
`acme/web-api:12.0`	`web-api` image version `12.0` associated with the `acme` org. The image is on Docker Hub.
`gcr.io/gnschenker/sample-app:1.1`	`sample-app` image with the `1.1` tag belonging to an individual with the `gnschenker` ID on Google's container registry.

Official images

In the preceding table, we mentioned *official image* a few times. This needs an explanation. Images are stored in repositories on the Docker Hub registry. Official repositories are a set of repositories that are hosted on Docker Hub and are curated by individuals or organizations that are also responsible for the software that is packaged inside the image. Let's look at an example of what that means. There is an official organization behind the Ubuntu Linux distro. This team also provides official versions of Docker images that contain their Ubuntu distros.

Official images are meant to provide essential base OS repositories, images for popular programming language runtimes, frequently used data storage, and other important services.

Docker sponsors a team whose task it is to review and publish all those curated images in public repositories on Docker Hub. Furthermore, Docker scans all official images for vulnerabilities.

Pushing images to a registry

Creating custom images is all well and good, but at some point, we want to actually share or ship our images to a target environment, such as a test, QA, or production system. For this, we typically use a container registry. One of the most popular and public registries out there is Docker Hub. It is configured as a default registry in your Docker environment, and it is the registry from which we have pulled all our images so far.

On a registry, one can usually create personal or organizational accounts. For example, my personal account at Docker Hub is `gnschenker`. Personal accounts are good for personal use. If we want to use the registry professionally, then we probably want to create an organizational account, such as `acme`, on Docker Hub. The advantage of the latter is that organizations can have multiple teams. Teams can have differing permissions.

To be able to push an image to my personal account on Docker Hub, I need to tag it accordingly. Let's say I want to push the latest version of `alpine` to my account and give it a tag of `1.0`. I can do this in the following way:

```
$ docker image tag alpine:latest gnschenker/alpine:1.0
```

Now, to be able to push the image, I have to log in to my account:

```
$ docker login -u gnschenker -p <my secret password>
```

After a successful login, I can then push the image:

```
$ docker image push gnschenker/alpine:1.0
```

I will see something similar to this in the terminal:

```
The push refers to repository [docker.io/gnschenker/alpine]
04a094fe844e: Mounted from library/alpine
1.0: digest: sha256:5cb04fce... size: 528
```

For each image that we push to Docker Hub, we automatically create a repository. A repository can be private or public. Everyone can pull an image from a public repository. From a private repository, one can only pull an image if one is logged in to the registry and has the necessary permissions configured.

Summary

In this chapter, we have discussed in detail what container images are and how we can build and ship them. As we have seen, there are three different ways that an image can be created—either manually, automatically, or by importing a tarball into the system. We also learned some of the best practices commonly used when building custom images.

In the next chapter, we're going to introduce Docker volumes that can be used to persist the state of a container, and we will also introduce some helpful system commands that can be used to inspect the Docker host more deeply, work with events generated by the Docker daemon, and clean up unused resources.

Questions

Please try to answer the following questions to assess your learning progress:

1. How will you create a Dockerfile that inherits from Ubuntu version 17.04, and that installs ping and runs ping when a container starts. The default address to ping will be 127.0.0.1.
2. How will you create a new container image that uses alpine:latest and installs curl. Name the new image my-alpine:1.0.
3. Create a Dockerfile that uses multiple steps to create an image of a Hello World app of minimal size, written in C or Go.
4. Name three essential characteristics of a Docker container image.
5. You want to push an image named foo:1.0 to your jdoe personal account on Docker Hub. Which of the following is the right solution?

    1. ```
       $ docker container push foo:1.0
       ```
    2. ```
       $ docker image tag foo:1.0 jdoe/foo:1.0
       $ docker image push jdoe/foo:1.0
       ```
    3. ```
       $ docker login -u jdoe -p <your password>
       $ docker image tag foo:1.0 jdoe/foo:1.0
       $ docker image push jdoe/foo:1.0
       ```
    4. ```
       $ docker login -u jdoe -p <your password>
       $ docker container tag foo:1.0 jdoe/foo:1.0
       $ docker container push jdoe/foo:1.0
       ```
    5. ```
       $ docker login -u jdoe -p <your password>
       $ docker image push foo:1.0 jdoe/foo:1.0
       ```
       ```

Further reading

The following list of references gives you some material that dives more deeply into the topic of authoring and building container images:

- *Best practices for writing Dockerfiles at* `http://dockr.ly/22WiJiO`
- *Using multistage builds at* `http://dockr.ly/2ewcUY3`
- *About Storage drivers at* `http://dockr.ly/1TuWndC`
- *Graphdriver plugins at* `http://dockr.ly/2eIVCab`
- *User-guided caching in Docker for MAC at* `http://dockr.ly/2xKafPf`

Data Volumes and System Management

5

In the last chapter, we learned how to build and share our own container images. Particular focus was put on how to build images that are as small as possible by only containing artifacts that are really needed by the containerized application.

In this chapter, we are going to learn how we can work with stateful containers, that is containers that consume and produce data. We will also learn how to keep our Docker environment clean and free from unused resources. Last but not least, we will be looking into the stream of events that a Docker engine is producing.

Here is a list of the topics we're going to discuss:

- Creating and mounting data volumes
- Sharing data between containers
- Using host volumes
- Defining volumes in images
- Obtaining exhaustive Docker system information
- Listing resource consumption
- Pruning unused resources
- Consuming Docker system events

After working through this chapter, you will be able to:

- Create, delete, and list data volumes
- Mount an existing data volume into a container
- Create durable data from within a container using a data volume

- Share data between multiple containers using data volumes
- Mount any host folder into a container using data volumes
- Define the access mode (read/write or read-only) for a container when accessing data in a data volume
- List the amount of space consumed by Docker resources on a given host, such as images, containers, and volumes
- Free your system from unused Docker resources, such as containers, images, and volumes
- Display Docker system events in a console in real time

Technical requirements

For this chapter, you need either Docker Toolbox installed on your machine or access to a Linux VM running Docker on your laptop or in the cloud. There is no code accompanying this chapter.

Creating and mounting data volumes

All meaningful applications consume or produce data. Yet containers are preferably meant to be stateless. How are we going to deal with this? One way is to use Docker volumes. Volumes allow containers to consume, produce, and modify state. Volumes have a life cycle that goes beyond the life cycle of containers. When a container that uses a volume dies, the volume continues to exist. This is great for the durability of state.

Modifying the container layer

Before we dive into volumes, let's first discuss what's happening if an application in a container changes something in the filesystem of the container. In this case, the changes are all happening in the writable container layer. Let's quickly demonstrate this by running a container and execute a script in it that is creating a new file:

```
$ docker container run --name demo \
    alpine /bin/sh -c 'echo "This is a test" > sample.txt'
```

The preceding command creates a container named `demo` and inside this container creates a file called `sample.txt` with the content `This is a test`. The container exits after this but remains in memory available for us to do our investigations. Let's use the `diff` command to find out what has changed in the container's filesystem in relation to the filesystem of the image:

```
$ docker container diff demo
```

The output should look like this:

```
A /sample.txt
```

Evidently a new file, `A`, has been added to the filesystem of the container as expected. Since all layers that stem from the underlying image (`alpine` in this case) are immutable, the change could only happen in the writeable container layer.

If we now remove the container from memory, its container layer will also be removed and with it all the changes will be irreversibly deleted. If we need our changes to persist even beyond the lifetime of the container, this is not a solution. Luckily, we have better options in the form of Docker volumes. Let's get to know them.

Creating volumes

Since, at this time, when using Docker for Mac or Windows containers are not running natively on OS X or Windows but rather in a (hidden) VM created by Docker for Mac and Windows, it is best we use `docker-machine` to create and use an explicit VM running Docker. At this point, we assume that you have Docker Toolbox installed on your system. If not, then please go back to Chapter 2, *Setting up a Working Environment,* where we provide detailed instructions on how to install Toolbox.

Use `docker-machine` to list all VMs currently running in VirtualBox:

```
$ docker-machine ls
```

If you do not have a VM called `node-1` listed then create one:

```
$ docker-machine create --driver virtualbox node-1
```

If you have a VM called `node-1` but it is not running then please start it:

```
$ docker-machine start node-1
```

Now that everything is ready, SSH into this VM called `node-1`:

```
$ docker-machine ssh node-1
```

You should be greeted by a **boot2docker** welcome image .

To create a new data volume, we can use the `docker volume create` command. This will create a named volume which can then be mounted into a container and be used for persistent data access or storage. The following command creates a volume, `my-data` using the default volume driver:

```
$ docker volume create my-data
```

The default volume driver is the so-called local driver which stores the data locally in the host filesystem. The easiest way to find out where the data is stored on the host is by using the `inspect` command on the volume we just created. The actual location can differ from system to system and so, this is the safest way to find the target folder:

```
$ docker volume inspect my-data
[
    {
        "CreatedAt": "2018-01-28T21:55:41Z",
        "Driver": "local",
        "Labels": {},
        "Mountpoint": "/mnt/sda1/var/lib/docker/volumes/my-
data/_data",
        "Name": "my-data",
        "Options": {},
        "Scope": "local"
    }
]
```

The host folder can be found in the output under `Mountpoint`. In our case, when using `docker-machine` with a LinuxKit-based VM running in VirtualBox, the folder is `/mnt/sda1/var/lib/docker/volumes/my-data/_data`.

The target folder often is a protected folder and we thus might need to use `sudo` to navigate to this folder and execute any operations in it. In our case, we do not need to use `sudo`:

```
$ cd /mnt/sda1/var/lib/docker/volumes/my-data/_data
```

If you are using Docker for Mac to create a volume on your laptop and then do a `docker volume inspect` on the volume you just created, the `Mountpoint` is shown as `/var/lib/docker/volumes/my-data/_data`. But you will discover that there is no such folder on the Mac. The reason is that the path is in relation to the hidden VM that Docker for Mac uses to run containers. At this time, containers cannot run natively on OS X. The same applies to volumes created with Docker for Windows.

There are other volume drivers available from third parties in the form of plugins. We can use the `--driver` parameter in the `create` command to select a different volume driver. Other volume drivers use different types of storage systems to back a volume, such as cloud storage, NFS drives, software-defined storage and more.

Mounting a volume

Once we have created a named volume, we can mount it into a container. For this, we can use the `-v` parameter in the `docker container run` command:

```
$ docker container run --name test -it \
    -v my-data:/data alpine /bin/sh
```

The preceding command mounts the `my-data` volume to the `/data` folder inside the container. Inside the container, we can now create files in the `/data` folder and then exit:

```
# / cd /data
# / echo "Some data" > data.txt
# / echo "Some more data" > data2.txt
# / exit
```

If we navigate to the host folder that contains the volume data and list its content, we should see the two files we just created inside the container:

```
$ cd /mnt/sda1/var/lib/docker/volumes/my-data/_data
$ ls -l
total 8
-rw-r--r-- 1 root root 10 Jan 28 22:23 data.txt
-rw-r--r-- 1 root root 15 Jan 28 22:23 data2.txt
```

We can even try to output the content of say, the second file:

```
$ cat data2.txt
```

Let's try to create a file in this folder from the host and then use the volume with another container:

```
$ echo "This file we create on the host" > host-data.txt
```

Now, let's delete the `test` container and run another one based on CentOS. This time we are even mounting our volume to a different container folder, `/app/data`:

```
$ docker container rm test
$ docker container run --name test2 -it \
    -v my-data:/app/data \
    Centos:7 /bin/bash
```

Once inside the CentOS container, we can navigate to the folder `/app/data` where we have mounted the volume to and list its content:

```
# / cd /app/data
# / ls -l
```

As expected, we should see these three files:

```
-rw-r--r-- 1 root root 10 Jan 28 22:23 data.txt
-rw-r--r-- 1 root root 15 Jan 28 22:23 data2.txt
-rw-r--r-- 1 root root 32 Jan 28 22:31 host-data.txt
```

This is the definitive proof that data in a Docker volume persists beyond the lifetime of a container, and also that volumes can be reused by other, even different containers from the one that used it first.

It is important to note that the folder inside the container to which we mount a Docker volume is excluded from the union filesystem. That is, each change inside this folder and any of its subfolders will not be part of the container layer, but persisted in the backing storage provided by the volume driver. This fact is really important since the container layer is deleted when the corresponding container is stopped and removed from the system.

Removing volumes

Volumes can be removed using the `docker volume rm` command. It is important to remember that removing a volume destroys the containing data irreversibly and thus is to be considered a dangerous command. Docker helps us a bit in this regard as it does not allow us to delete a volume that is still in use by a container. Always make sure before you remove or delete a volume that you either have a backup of its data or you really don't need this data anymore.

The following command deletes our `my-data` volume that we created earlier:

```
$ docker volume rm my-data
```

After executing the preceding command, double-check that the folder on the host has been deleted.

To remove all running containers to clean up the system, run the following command:

```
$ docker container rm -f $(docker container ls -aq)
```

Sharing data between containers

Containers are like sandboxes for the applications running inside them. This is mostly beneficial and wanted in order to protect applications running in different containers from each other. That also means that the whole filesystem visible to an application running inside a container is private to this application and no other application running in a different container can interfere with it.

At times though, we want to share data between containers. Say an application running in container A produces some data that will be consumed by another application running in container B. *How can we achieve this?* Well I'm sure you've already guessed it—we can use Docker volumes for this purpose. We can create a volume and mount it to container A as well as to container B. In this way, both applications A and B have access to the same data.

Now, as always when multiple applications or processes concurrently access data, we have to be very careful to avoid inconsistencies. To avoid concurrency problems, such as race conditions, we ideally have only one application or process that is creating or modifying data, while all other processes concurrently accessing this data only read it. We can enforce a process running in a container to only be able to read the data in a volume by mounting this volume as read only. Have a look at the following command:

```
$ docker container run -it --name writer \
    -v shared-data:/data \
    alpine /bin/sh
```

Here we create a container called `writer` which has a volume, `shared-data`, mounted in default read/write mode. Try to create a file inside this container:

```
# / echo "I can create a file" > /data/sample.txt
```

It should succeed. Exit this container and then execute the following command:

```
$ docker container run -it --name reader \
    -v shared-data:/app/data:ro \
    ubuntu:17.04 /bin/bash
```

And we have a container called `reader` that has the same volume mounted as **read-only** (**ro**). Firstly, make sure you can see the file created in the first container:

```
$ ls -l /app/data
total 4
-rw-r--r-- 1 root root 20 Jan 28 22:55 sample.txt
```

And then try to create a file:

```
# / echo "Try to break read/only" > /app/data/data.txt
```

It will fail with the following message:

```
bash: /app/data/data.txt: Read-only file system
```

Let's exit the container by typing `exit` at the Command Prompt. Back on the host, let's clean up all containers and volumes:

```
$ docker container rm -f $(docker container ls -aq)
$ docker volume rm $(docker volume ls -q)
```

Once this is done, exit the `docker-machine` VM by also typing `exit` at the Command Prompt. You should be back on your Docker for Mac or Windows. Use `docker-machine` to stop the VM:

```
$ docker-machine stop node-1
```

Using host volumes

In certain scenarios, such as when developing new containerized applications or when a containerized application needs to consume data from a certain folder produced, say, by a legacy application, it is very useful to use volumes that mount a specific host folder. Let's look at the following example:

```
$ docker container run --rm -it \
    -v $(pwd)/src:/app/src \
    alpine:latest /bin/sh
```

The preceding expression interactively starts an `alpine` container with a shell and mounts the subfolder `src` of the current directory into the container at `/app/src`. We need to use `$(pwd)` (or `'pwd'` for that matter) which is the current directory, as when working with volumes we always need to use absolute paths.

Developers use these techniques all the time when they are working on their application that runs in a container, and want to make sure that the container always contains the latest changes they make to the code, without the need to rebuild the image and rerun the container after each change.

Let's make a sample to demonstrate how that works. Let's say we want to create a simple static website using Nginx as our web server. First, let's create a new folder on the host where we will put our web assets, such as HTML, CSS, and JavaScript files and navigate to it:

```
$ mkdir ~/my-web
$ cd ~/my-web
```

Then we create a simple web page like this:

```
$ echo "<h1>Personal Website</h1>" > index.html
```

Now, we add a Dockerfile which will contain the instructions on how to build the image containing our sample website. Add a file called Dockerfile to the folder with this content:

```
FROM nginx:alpine
COPY . /usr/share/nginx/html
```

The Dockerfile starts with the latest Alpine version of Nginx and then copies all files from the current host directory into the containers folder, `/usr/share/nginx/html`. This is where Nginx expects web assets to be located. Now let's build the image with the following command:

```
$ docker image build -t my-website:1.0 .
```

And finally, we run a container from this image. We will run the container in detached mode:

```
$ docker container run -d \
  -p 8080:80 --name my-site\
  my-website:1.0
```

Note the -p 8080:80 parameter. We haven't discussed this yet but we will do it in detail in Chapter 7, *Single-Host Networking*. At the moment, just know that this maps the container port 80 on which Nginx is listening for incoming requests to port 8080 of your laptop where you can then access the application. Now, open a browser tab and navigate to http://localhost:8080/index.html and you should see your website which currently consists only of a title, Personal Website.

Now, edit the file index.html in your favorite editor to look like this:

```
<h1>Personal Website</h1>
<p>This is some text</p>
```

And save it. Then refresh the browser. OK, that didn't work. The browser still displays the previous version of the index.html which consists only of the title. So let's stop and remove the current container, then rebuild the image, and rerun the container:

```
$ docker container rm -f my-site
$ docker image build -t my-website:1.0 .
$ docker container run -d \
    -p 8080:80 --name my-site\
    my-website:1.0
```

This time when you refresh the browser the new content should be shown. Well, it worked, but there is way too much friction involved. Imagine you have to do this each and every time that you make a simple change in your website. That's not sustainable.

Now is the time to use host-mounted volumes. Once again, remove the current container and rerun it with the volume mount:

```
$ docker container rm -f my-site
$ docker container run -d \
    -v $(pwd):/usr/share/nginx/html \
    -p 8080:80 --name my-site\
    my-website:1.0
```

Now, append some more content to the index.html and save it. Then refresh your browser. You should see the changes. And this is exactly what we wanted to achieve; we also call this an edit-and-continue experience. You can make as many changes in your web files and always immediately see the result in the browser without having to rebuild the image and restart the container containing your website.

It is important to note that the updates are now propagated bi-directionally. If you make changes on the host they will be propagated to the container and vice versa. Also important is the fact that when you mount the current folder into the container target folder, `/usr/share/nginx/html`, the content that is already there is replaced by the content of the host folder.

Defining volumes in images

If we go for a moment back to what we have learned about containers in `Chapter 3`, *Working with Containers,* then we have this: the filesystem of each container when started is made up of the immutable layers of the underlying image plus a writable container layer specific to this very container. All changes that the processes running inside the container make to the filesystem will be persisted in this container layer. Once the container is stopped and removed from the system, the corresponding container layer is deleted from the system and irreversibly lost.

Some applications, such as databases running in containers, need to persist their data beyond the lifetime of the container. In this case they can use volumes. To make things a bit more explicit let's look at a concrete sample. MongoDB is a popular open source document database. Many developers use MongoDB as a storage service for their applications. The maintainers of MongoDB have created an image and published it on Docker Hub which can be used to run an instance of the database in a container. This database will be producing data that needs to be persisted long term. But the MongoDB maintainers do not know who uses this image and how it is used. So they have no influence over the `docker container run` command with which the users of the database will start this container. *How can they now define volumes?*

Luckily, there is a way of defining volumes in the Dockerfile. The keyword to do so is VOLUME and we can either add the absolute path to a single folder or a comma-separated list of paths. These paths represent folders of the container's filesystem. Let's look at a few samples of such volume definitions:

```
VOLUME /app/data
VOLUME /app/data, /app/profiles, /app/config
VOLUME ["/app/data", "/app/profiles", "/app/config"]
```

The first line defines a single volume to be mounted at /app/data. The second line defines three volumes as a comma-separated list and the last one defines the same as the second line, but this time the value is formatted as a JSON array.

When a container is started, Docker automatically creates a volume and mounts it to the corresponding target folder of the container for each path defined in the Dockerfile. Since each volume is created automatically by Docker, it will have an SHA-256 as ID.

At container runtime, the folders defined as volumes in the Dockerfile are excluded from the union filesystem and thus any changes in those folders do not change the container layer but are persisted to the respective volume. It is now the responsibility of the operations engineers to make sure that the backing storage of the volumes is properly backed up.

We can use the docker image inspect command to get information about the volumes defined in the Dockerfile. Let's see what MongoDB gives us. First, we pull the image with the following command:

```
$ docker image pull mongo:3.7
```

Then we inspect this image and use the --format parameter to only extract the essential part from the massive amount of data:

```
$ docker image inspect \
   --format='{{json .ContainerConfig.Volumes}}' \
    mongo:3.7 | jq
```

Which will return the following result:

```
{
"/data/configdb": {},
"/data/db": {}
}
```

Evidently, the Dockerfile for MongoDB defines two volumes at /data/configdb and /data/db.

Now, let's run an instance of MongoDB as follows:

```
$ docker run --name my-mongo -d mongo:3.7
```

We can now use the `docker container inspect` command to get information about the volumes that have been created, among other things. Use this command to just get the volume information:

```
$ docker inspect --format '{{json .Mounts}}' my-mongo | jq
```

The expression should output something like this:

```
[
  {
    "Type": "volume",
    "Name": "b9ea0158b5...",
    "Source": "/var/lib/docker/volumes/b9ea0158b.../_data",
    "Destination": "/data/configdb",
    "Driver": "local",
    "Mode": "",
    "RW": true,
    "Propagation": ""
  },
  {
    "Type": "volume",
    "Name": "5becf84b1e...",
    "Source": "/var/lib/docker/volumes/5becf84b1.../_data",
    "Destination": "/data/db",
    "Driver": "local",
    "Mode": "",
    "RW": true,
    "Propagation": ""
  }
]
```

Note that the values of the `Name` and `Source` fields have been trimmed for readability. The `Source` field gives us the path to the host directory where the data produced by the MongoDB inside the container will be stored.

Obtaining Docker system information

Whenever we need to troubleshoot our system, the commands presented in this section are essential. They provide us with a lot about the Docker engine installed on the host and about the host operating system. Let's first introduce the `docker version` command. It provides abundant information about the Docker client and server that your current configuration is using. If you enter the command in the CLI, you should see something similar to this:

```
$ docker version
Client:
 Version:       18.04.0-ce
 API version:   1.37
 Go version:    go1.9.4
 Git commit:    3d479c0
 Built: Tue Apr 10 18:13:16 2018
 OS/Arch:       darwin/amd64
 Experimental:  true
 Orchestrator:  swarm

Server:
 Engine:
  Version:      18.04.0-ce
  API version:  1.37 (minimum version 1.12)
  Go version:   go1.9.4
  Git commit:   3d479c0
  Built:        Tue Apr 10 18:23:05 2018
  OS/Arch:      linux/amd64
  Experimental: true
$
```

Version Information about Docker

In my case, I can see that on both client and server, I am using version `18.04.0-ce-rc2` of the Docker engine. I can also see that my orchestrator is Swarm and more.

Now to clarify what the client and what the server is, let's look at the following diagram:

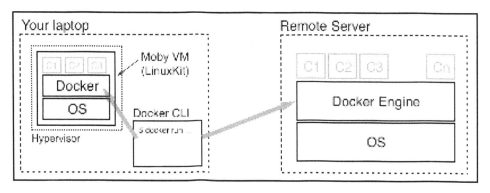

CLI accessing different Docker Hosts

You can see that the client is the little CLI through which we send Docker commands to the remote API of the Docker host. The Docker host is the container runtime which hosts the containers and might run on the same machine as the CLI, or it might run on a remote server, on-premise or in the cloud. We can use the CLI to manage different servers. We do this by setting a bunch of environment variables such as `DOCKER_HOST`, `DOCKER_TLS_VERIFY`, and `DOCKER_CERT_PATH`. If these environment variables are not set on your working machine and you're using Docker for Mac or Windows then that means that you are using the Docker engine that runs on your machine.

The next important command is the `docker system info` command. This command provides information about what mode the Docker engine is operating in (swarm mode or not), what storage driver is used for the union filesystem, what version of the Linux kernel we have on our host, and much more. Please have a careful look at the output generated by your system when running the command. Analyze what kind of information is shown:

```
$ docker system info
Containers: 1
 Running: 0
 Paused: 0
 Stopped: 1
Images: 70
Server Version: 18.04.0-ce
Storage Driver: overlay2
 Backing Filesystem: extfs
 Supports d_type: true
 Native Overlay Diff: true
Logging Driver: json-file
Cgroup Driver: cgroupfs
Plugins:
 Volume: local
 Network: bridge host ipvlan macvlan null overlay
 Log: awslogs fluentd gcplogs gelf journald json-file logentries splunk syslog
Swarm: inactive
Runtimes: runc
Default Runtime: runc
Init Binary: docker-init
containerd version: 773c489c9c1b21a6d78b5c538cd395416cc50f88
runc version: 4fc53a81fb7c994640722ac585fa9ca548971871
init version: 949e6fa
Security Options:
 seccomp
  Profile: default
Kernel Version: 4.9.87-linuxkit-aufs
Operating System: Docker for Mac
OSType: linux
Architecture: x86_64
CPUs: 4
Total Memory: 1.952GiB
Name: linuxkit-025000000001
ID: WV5X:CY7N:IHTP:SWJ7:T5SW:P5QM:MFYU:MMGV:5S0H:RALF:57DN:QH7Y
Docker Root Dir: /var/lib/docker
Debug Mode (client): false
Debug Mode (server): true
 File Descriptors: 22
 Goroutines: 42
 System Time: 2018-04-21T12:08:17.9628687
 EventsListeners: 2
HTTP Proxy: gateway.docker.internal:3128
HTTPS Proxy: gateway.docker.internal:3129
Registry: https://index.docker.io/v1/
Labels:
Experimental: true
Insecure Registries:
 127.0.0.0/8
Live Restore Enabled: false
```

Output of the Command docker system info

Listing resource consumption

Over time, a Docker host can accumulate quite a bit of resources such as images, containers, and volumes in memory and on disk. As in every good household, we should keep our environment clean and free unused resources to reclaim space. Otherwise, there will come the moment when Docker does not allow us to add any more new resources, meaning actions such as pulling an image can fail due to lack of available space on disk or in memory.

The Docker CLI provides a handy little `system` command that lists how much resources currently are used on our system and how much of this space can possibly be reclaimed. The command is:

```
$ docker system df
```

If you execute this command on your system, you should see an output similar to this:

```
TYPE             TOTAL   ACTIVE   SIZE       RECLAIMABLE
Images           21      9        1.103GB    845.3MB (76%)
Containers       14      11       9.144kB    4.4kB (48%)
Local Volumes 14         14       340.3MB    0B (0%)
Build Cache               0B      0B
```

The last line in the output, the `Build Cache`, is only displayed on newer versions of Docker. This information has been added recently. The preceding output is explained as follows:

- In my case, the output tells me that on my system I am currently having 21 images locally cached of which 9 are in active use. An image is considered to be in active use if currently at least one running or stopped container is based on it. These images occupy 1.1 GB disk space. Close to 845 MB can technically be reclaimed since the corresponding images are not currently used.

- Further, I have 11 running containers on my system and three stopped ones for a total of 14 containers. I can reclaim the space occupied by the stopped containers which is 4.4 kB in my case.

- I also have 14 active volumes on my host that together consume about 340 MB of disk space. Since all volumes are in use, I cannot reclaim any space at this time.

- Finally, my `Build Cache` is currently empty and thus of course I cannot reclaim any space there too.

If I want even more detailed information about the resource consumption on my system, I can run the same command in verbose mode using the −v flag:

```
$ docker system df -v
```

This will give me a detailed list of all images, containers, and volumes with their respective size. A possible output could look like this:

Verbose output of the system resources consumed by Docker

This verbose output should give us enough detailed information to make an informed decision as to whether or not we need to start cleaning up our system, and which parts we might need to clean up.

Pruning unused resources

Once we have concluded that some clean up is needed Docker provides us with so-called pruning commands. For each resource, such as images, containers, volumes, and networks there exists a `prune` command.

Pruning containers

In this section we want to regain unused system resources by pruning containers. Let's start with this command:

```
$ docker container prune
```

The preceding command will remove all containers from the system that are not in `running` status. Docker will ask for confirmation before deleting the containers that are currently in `exited` or `created` status. If you want to skip this confirmation step you can use the `-f` (or `--force`) flag:

```
$ docker container prune -f
```

Under certain circumstances, we might want to remove all containers from our system, even the running ones. We cannot use the `prune` command for this. Instead we should use a command, such as the following combined expression:

```
$ docker container rm -f $(docker container ls -aq)
```

Please be careful with the preceding command. It removes all containers without warning, even the running ones! Please, before you proceed look at the preceding command again in detail and try to explain what exactly happens and why.

Pruning images

Next in line are images. If we want to free all space occupied by unused image layers we can use the following command:

```
$ docker image prune
```

After we reconfirm to Docker that we indeed want to free space occupied by unused image layers, those get removed. Now I have to specify what we mean when talking about unused image layers. As you recall from the previous chapter, an image is made up of a stack of immutable layers. Now, when we are building a custom image multiple times, each time making some changes in, say, the source code of the application for which we're building the image, then we are recreating layers and previous versions of the same layer become orphaned. *Why is this the case?* The reason is that layers are immutable, as discussed in detail in the previous chapter. Thus, when something in the source that is used to build a layer is changed, the very layer has to be rebuilt and the previous version will be abandoned.

On a system where we often build images, the number of orphaned image layers can increase substantially over time. All these orphaned layers are removed with the preceding `prune` command.

Similar to the `prune` command for containers, we can avoid Docker asking us for a confirmation by using the force flag:

```
$ docker image prune -f
```

There is an even more radical version of the image `prune` command. Sometimes we do not just want to remove orphaned image layers but all images that are not currently in use on our system. For this, we can use the `-a` (or `--all`) flag:

```
$ docker image prune --force --all
```

After execution of the preceding command, only images that are currently used by one or more containers will remain in our local image cache.

Pruning volumes

Docker volumes are used to allow for persistent access of data by containers. This data can be important and thus the commands discussed in this section should be applied with special care.

If you know that you want to reclaim space occupied by volumes and with it irreversibly destroy the underlying data, you can use the following command:

```
$ docker volume prune
```

This command will remove all volumes that are not currently in use by at least one container.

 This is a destructive command and cannot be undone. You should always create a backup of the data associated with the volumes before you delete them except when you're sure that the data has no further value.

To avoid system corruption or malfunctioning applications, Docker does not allow you to remove volumes that are currently in use by at least one container. This applies even to the situation where a volume is used by a stopped container. You always have to remove the containers that use a volume first.

A useful flag when pruning volumes is the `-f` or `--filter` flag which allows us to specify the set of volumes which we're considering for pruning. Look at the following command:

```
$ docker volume prune --filter 'label=demo'
```

This will only apply the command to volumes that have a `label` with the `demo` value. The filtering flag format is `key=value`. If there is more than one filter needed, then we can use multiple flags:

```
$ docker volume prune --filter 'label=demo' --filter 'label=test'
```

The filter flag can also be used when pruning other resources such as containers and images.

Pruning networks

The last resource that can be pruned are networks. We will discuss networks in detail in `Chapter 7`, *Single-Host Networking*. To remove all unused networks, we use the following command:

```
$ docker network prune
```

This will remove the networks on which currently no container or service is attached. Please don't worry about networks too much at this time. We will come back to them and all this will make much more sense to you.

Pruning everything

If we just want to prune everything at once without having to enter multiple commands, we can use the following command:

```
$ docker system prune
```

The Docker CLI will ask us for a confirmation and then remove all unused containers, images, volumes, and networks in one go and in the right order.

Once again, to avoid Docker asking us for a confirmation, we can just use the force flag with the command.

Consuming Docker system events

The Docker engine, when creating, running, stopping, and removing containers and other resources such as volumes or networks, produces a log of events. These events can be consumed by external systems, such as some infrastructure services that use them to make informed decisions. An example of such a service could be a tool that creates an inventory of all containers that are currently running on the system.

We can hook ourselves into this stream of system events and output them, for example in a terminal, by using the following command:

```
$ docker system events
```

This command is a blocking command. Thus, when you execute it in your terminal session the according session is blocked. Therefore, we recommend that you always open an extra window when you want to use this command.

Assuming we have executed the preceding command in an extra terminal window, we can now test it and run a container like this:

```
$ docker container run --rm alpine echo "Hello World"
```

The output produced should look like this:

```
2018-01-28T15:08:57.318341118-06:00 container create
8e074342ef3b20cfa73d17e4ef7796d424aa8801661765ab5024acf166c6ecf3
(image=alpine, name=confident_hopper)

2018-01-28T15:08:57.320934314-06:00 container attach
8e074342ef3b20cfa73d17e4ef7796d424aa8801661765ab5024acf166c6ecf3
(image=alpine, name=confident_hopper)

2018-01-28T15:08:57.354869473-06:00 network connect
c8fd270e1a776c5851c9fa1e79927141a1e1be228880c0aace4d0daebccd190f
(container=8e074342ef3b20cfa73d17e4ef7796d424aa8801661765ab5024acf166c
6ecf3, name=bridge, type=bridge)

2018-01-28T15:08:57.818494970-06:00 container start
8e074342ef3b20cfa73d17e4ef7796d424aa8801661765ab5024acf166c6ecf3
(image=alpine, name=confident_hopper)

2018-01-28T15:08:57.998941548-06:00 container die
8e074342ef3b20cfa73d17e4ef7796d424aa8801661765ab5024acf166c6ecf3
(exitCode=0, image=alpine, name=confident_hopper)

2018-01-28T15:08:58.304784993-06:00 network disconnect
c8fd270e1a776c5851c9fa1e79927141a1e1be228880c0aace4d0daebccd190f
```

```
(container=8e074342ef3b20cfa73d17e4ef7796d424aa8801661765ab5024acf166c
6ecf3, name=bridge, type=bridge)

2018-01-28T15:08:58.412513530-06:00 container destroy
8e074342ef3b20cfa73d17e4ef7796d424aa8801661765ab5024acf166c6ecf3
(image=alpine, name=confident_hopper)
```

In this output, we can follow the exact life cycle of the container. The container is created, started, and then destroyed. If the output generated by this command is not to your liking you can always change it by using the `--format` parameter. The value of the format has to be written using the Go template syntax. The following sample outputs the type, image, and action of the event:

```
$ docker system events --format 'Type={{.Type}}
Image={{.Actor.Attributes.image}} Action={{.Action}}'
```

If we run the exact same container `run` command as before, the output generated now looks like this:

```
Type=container    Image=alpine       Action=create
Type=container    Image=alpine       Action=attach
Type=network      Image=<no value> Action=connect
Type=container    Image=alpine       Action=start
Type=container    Image=alpine       Action=die
Type=network      Image=<no value> Action=disconnect
Type=container    Image=alpine       Action=destroy
```

Summary

In this chapter, we have introduced Docker volumes that can be used to persist states produced by containers and make it durable. We can also use volumes to provide containers with data originating from various sources. We have learned how to create, mount and use volumes. We have learned various techniques of defining volumes such as by name, by mounting a host directory, or by defining volumes in a container image.

In this chapter, we have also discussed various system-level commands that either provide us with abundant information to troubleshoot a system, or to manage and prune resources used by Docker. Lastly, we have learned how we can visualize and potentially consume the event stream generated by the container runtime.

Questions

Please try to answer the following questions to assess your learning progress:

1. How will you create a named data volume with a name, for example `my-products`, using the default driver?
2. How will you run a container using the image `alpine` and mount the volume `my-products` in read-only mode into the /data container folder?
3. How will you locate the folder which is associated with the volume `my-products` and navigate to it? Also, how will you create a file, `sample.txt` with some content?
4. How will you run another `alpine` container to which you mount the `my-products` volume to the `/app-data` folder, in read/write mode? Inside this container, navigate to the `/app-data` folder and create a `hello.txt` file with some content.
5. How will you mount a host volume, for example `~/my-project`, into a container?
6. How will you remove all unused volumes from your system?
7. How will you determine the exact version of the Linux kernel and of Docker running on your system?

Further reading

The following articles provide more in-depth information:

*   Use volumes at `http://dockr.ly/2EUjTml`
*   Manage data in Docker at `http://dockr.ly/2EhBpzD`
*   Docker volumes on PWD at `http://bit.ly/2sjIfDj`
*   Containers—clean up your house at `http://bit.ly/2bVrCBn`
*   Docker system events at `http://dockr.ly/2BlZmXY`

6
Distributed Application Architecture

In the previous chapter, we learned how we can use Docker volumes to persist created or modified state, as well as share data between applications running in containers. We also learned how to work with events generated by the Docker daemon and clean up unused resources.

In this chapter, we introduce the concept of a distributed application architecture and discuss the various patterns and best practices that are required to run a distributed application successfully. Finally, we will discuss the additional requirements that need to be fulfilled to run such an application in production.

In this chapter, we will cover the following topics:

- What is a distributed application architecture?
- Patterns and best practices
- Running in production

After finishing this chapter, you will be able to do the following:

- Name at least four characteristics of a distributed application architecture
- Name at least four patterns that need to be implemented for a production-ready distributed application

What is a distributed application architecture?

In this section, we are going to explain in detail what we mean when we talk about a distributed application architecture. First, we need to make sure that all words or acronyms we use have a meaning and that we are all talking the same language.

Defining the terminology

In this and the subsequent chapters, we will talk a lot about concepts that might not be familiar to everyone. To make sure we all talk the same language, let's briefly introduce and describe the most important of these concepts or words:

VM	Acronym for virtual machine. This is a virtual computer.
Node	Individual server used to run applications. This can be a physical server, often called **bare metal**, or a VM. A node can be a mainframe, supercomputer, standard business server, or even a Raspberry Pi. Nodes can be computers in a company's own data center or in the cloud. Normally, a node is part of a cluster.
Cluster	Group of nodes connected by a network used to run distributed applications.
Network	Physical and software-defined communication paths between individual nodes of a cluster and programs running on those nodes.
Port	Channel on which an application such a web server listens for incoming requests.
Service	This, unfortunately, is a very overloaded term and its real meaning depends on the context in which it is used. If we use the term *service* in the context of an application such as an application service, then it usually means that this is a piece of software that implements a limited set of functionality which is then used by other parts of the application. As we progress through this book, other types of services that have a slightly different definition will be discussed.

Naively said, a distributed application architecture is the opposite of a monolithic application architecture, but it's not unreasonable to look at this monolithic architecture first. Traditionally, most business applications have been written in such a way that the result can be seen as one single, tightly coupled program that runs on a named server somewhere in a data center. All its code is compiled into a single binary or a few very tightly coupled binaries that need to be co-located when running the application. The fact that the server, or more general host, on which the application is running has a well-defined name or static IP address is also important in this context. Let's look at the following diagram to illustrate this type of application architecture a bit more clearly:

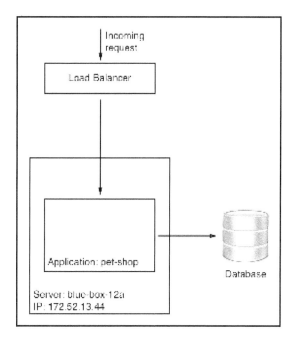

Monolithic application architecture

In the preceding figure, we see a server named **blue-box-12a** with an IP address of `172.52.13.44` running an application called **pet-shop**, which is a monolith consisting of a main module and a few tightly coupled libraries.

Now, let's look at the following figure:

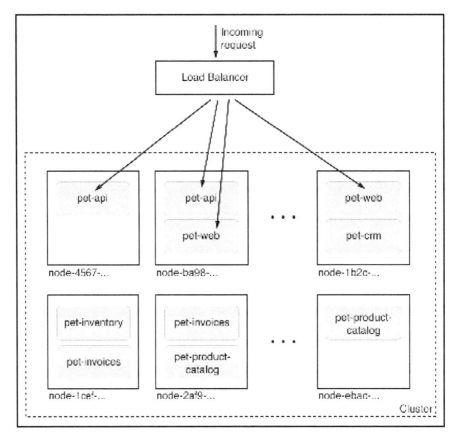

Distributed application architecture

Here, all of a sudden, we don't have only a single named server anymore, but we have a lot of them and they don't have human-friendly names, but rather some unique IDs that can be something like a **universal unique identifier** (**UUID**). The pet shop application, all of a sudden, also does not consist of a single monolithic block anymore but rather of a plethora of interacting yet loosely coupled services such as **pet-api**, **pet-web**, and **pet-inventory**. Furthermore, each service runs in multiple instances in this cluster of servers or hosts.

You might be wondering why we are discussing this in a book about Docker containers, and you are right to ask. While all the topics we're going to investigate apply equally to a world where containers do not (yet) exist, it is important to realize that containers and container orchestration engines help to address all the problems in a much more efficient and straightforward way. Most of the problems that used to be very hard to solve in a distributed application architecture become quite simple in a containerized world.

Patterns and best practices

A distributed application architecture has many compelling benefits, but it has also one very significant drawback compared to a monolithic application architecture - the former is way more complex. To tame this complexity, the industry has come up with some important best practices and patterns. In the following sections, we are going to look into some of the most important ones in more detail.

Loosely coupled components

The best way to address a complex subject has always been to divide it into smaller sub problems that are more manageable. As an example, it would be insanely complex to build a house in one single step. It is much easier to build the house up from simple parts that are then combined into the final result.

The same also applies to software development. It is much easier to develop a very complex application if we divide this application into smaller components that interoperate and together make up the overall application. Now, it is much easier to develop these components individually if they are only loosely coupled to each other. What this means is that component A makes no assumptions about the inner workings of, say, components B and C, but is only interested in how it can communicate with those two components across a well-defined interface. If each component has a well-defined and simple public interface through which communication with the other components in the system and the outside world happens, then this enables us to develop each component individually, without implicit dependencies to other components. During the development process, other components in the system can be replaced by stubs or mocks to allow us to test our component.

Stateful versus stateless

Every meaningful business application creates, modifies, or uses data. Data is also called state. An application service that creates or modifies persistent data is called a stateful component. Typical stateful components are database services or services that create files. On the other hand, application components that do not create or modify persistent data are called stateless components.

In a distributed application architecture, stateless components are much simpler to handle than stateful components. Stateless components can be easily scaled up and scaled down. They can also be quickly and painlessly torn down and restarted on a completely different node of the cluster—all this because they have no persistent data associated with them.

Given that fact, it is helpful to design a system in a way that most of the application services are stateless. It is best to push all the stateful components to the boundary of the application and limit their number. Managing stateful components is hard.

Service discovery

As we build applications that consist of many individual components or services that communicate with each other, we need a mechanism that allows the individual components to find each other in the cluster. Finding each other usually means that one needs to know on which node the target component is running and on which port it is listening for communication. Most often, nodes are identified by an IP address and a port, which is just a number in a well-defined range.

Technically, we could tell **Service A**, which wants to communicate with a target, **Service B**, what the IP address and port of the target are. This could happen, for example, through an entry in a configuration file:

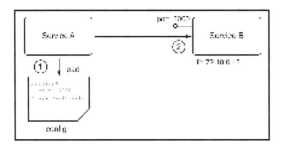

Components are hardwired

While this might work very well in the context of a monolithic application that runs on one or only a few well-known and curated servers, it totally falls apart in a distributed application architecture. First of all, in this scenario, we have many components, and keeping track of them manually becomes a nightmare. It is definitely not scalable. Furthermore, Service A typically should or will never know on which node of the cluster the other components run. Their location may not even be stable as component B could be moved from node X to another node Y, due to various reasons external to the application. Thus, we need another way in which Service A can locate Service B, or any other service for that matter. What is most commonly used is an external authority that is aware of the topology of the system at any given time. This external authority or service knows all the nodes and their IP addresses that currently pertain to the cluster; it knows all services that are running and where they are running. Often, this kind of service is called a **DNS service**, where **DNS** stands for **Domain Name System**. As we will see, Docker has a DNS service implemented as part of the underlying engine. Kubernetes also uses a DNS service to facilitate communication between components running in the cluster:

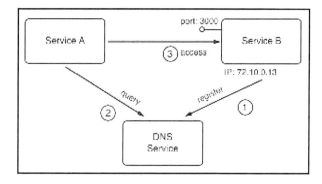

Components consult an external locator service

In the preceding figure, we see how Service A wants to communicate with Service B. But it can't do this directly; it has to first query the external authority, a registry service, here called a **DNS Service**, about the whereabouts of Service B. The registry service will answer with the requested information and hand out the IP address and port number with which Service A can reach Service B. Service A then uses this information and establishes communication with Service B. Of course, this is a naive picture of what's really happening on a low level, but it is a good picture to understand the architectural pattern of service discovery.

Routing

Routing is the mechanism of sending packets of data from a source component to a target component. Routing is categorized into different types. One uses the so-called OSI model (see reference in the *Further reading* section of this chapter) to distinguish between different types of routing. In the context of containers and container orchestration, routing at layers 2, 3, 4, and 7 is relevant. We will dive into more detail about routing in the subsequent chapters. Here, let's just say that layer 2 routing is the most low-level type of routing, which connects a MAC address to a MAC address, while layer 7 routing, which is also called application-level routing, is the most high-level one. The latter is, for example, used to route requests having a target identifier that is a URL such as `example.com/pets` to the appropriate target component in our system.

Load balancing

Load balancing is used whenever Service A requests a service from Service B, but the latter is running in more than one instance, as shown in the following figure:

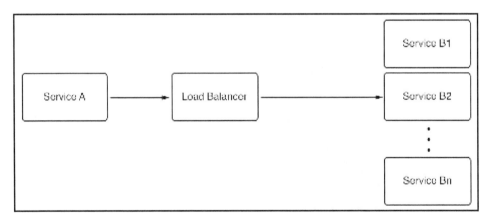

Request of Service A load balanced to Service B

If we have multiple instances of a service such as Service B running in our system, we want to make sure that every, of those instances gets an equal amount of workload assigned to it. This task is a generic one, which means that we don't want the caller to have to do the load balancing, but rather an external service that intercepts the call and takes over the part of deciding to which of the target service instances to forward the call. This external service is called a **load balancer**. Load balancers can use different algorithms to decide how to distribute the incoming calls to the target service instances. The most common algorithm used is called round robin. This algorithm just assigns requests in a repetitive way, starting with instance 1 then 2 until instance n. After the last instance has been served, the load balancer starts over with instance number 1.

Defensive programming

When developing a service for a distributed application, it is important to remember that this service is not going to be standalone, but is dependent on other application services or even on external services provided by third parties, such as credit card validation services or stock information services, to just name two. All these other services are external to the service we are developing. We have no control over their correctness or their availability at any given time. Thus, when coding, we always need to assume the worst and hope for the best. Assuming the worst means that we have to deal with potential failures explicitly.

Retries

When there is a possibility that an external service might be temporarily unavailable or not responsive enough, then the following procedure can be used. When the call to the other service fails or times out, the calling code should be structured in such a way that the same call is repeated after a short wait time. If the call fails again, the wait should be a bit longer before the next trial. The calls should be repeated up until a maximum number of times, each time increasing the wait time. After that, the service should give up and provide a degraded service, which could mean to return some stale cached data or no data at all, depending on the situation.

Logging

Important operations in a service should always be logged. Logging information needs to be categorized to be of a real value. A common list of categories is debug, info, warning, error, and fatal. Logging information should be collected by a central log aggregation service and not be stored on an individual node of the cluster. Aggregated logs are easy to parse and filter for relevant information.

Error handling

As mentioned earlier, each application service in a distributed application is dependent on other services. As developers, we should always expect the worst and have appropriate error handling in place. One of the most important best practices is to fail fast. Code the service in such a way that unrecoverable errors are discovered as early as possible and, if such an error is detected, have the service fail immediately. But don't forget to log meaningful information to STDERR or STDOUT, which can be used by developers or system operators later to track malfunctions of the system. Also, return a helpful error to the caller, indicating as precisely as possible why the call failed.

One sample of fail fast is to always check the input values provided by the caller. *Are the values in the expected ranges and complete?* If not, then do not try to continue processing, but immediately abort the operation.

Redundancy

A mission-critical system has to be available all the time, around the clock, 365 days a year. Downtime is not acceptable, since it might result in a huge loss of opportunities or reputation for the company. In a highly distributed application, the likelihood of a failure of at least one of the many involved components is non-neglectable. One can say that the question is not whether a component will fail, but rather when a failure will occur.

To avoid downtime when one of the many components in the system fails, each individual part of the system needs to be redundant. This includes the application components as well as all infrastructure parts. What that means is that if we, say, have a payment service as part of our application, then we need to run this service redundantly. The easiest way to do that is to run multiple instances of this very service on different nodes of our cluster. The same applies, say, for an edge router or a load balancer. We cannot afford for this to ever go down. Thus the router or load balancer must be redundant.

Health checks

We have mentioned various times that in a distributed application architecture, with its many parts, failure of an individual component is highly likely and it is only a matter of time until it happens. For that reason, we run every single component of the system redundantly. Proxy services then load balance the traffic across the individual instances of a service.

But now there is another problem. *How does the proxy or router know whether a certain service instance is available or not?* It could have crashed or it could be unresponsive. To solve this problem, one uses so-called health checks. The proxy, or some other system service on behalf of the proxy, periodically polls all the service instances and checks their health. The questions are basically *Are you still there? Are you healthy?* The answer of each service is either *Yes* or *No*, or the health check times out if the instance is not responsive anymore.

If the component answers with *No* or a timeout occurs, then the system kills the corresponding instance and spins up a new instance in its place. If all this happens in a fully automated way, then we say that we have an auto-healing system in place.

Circuit breaker pattern

A **circuit breaker** is a mechanism that is used to avoid a distributed application going down due to a cascading failure of many essential components. Circuit breakers help to avoid one failing component tearing down other dependent services in a domino effect. Like circuit breakers in an electrical system, which protect a house from burning down due to the failure of a malfunctioning plugged-in appliance by interrupting the power line, circuit breakers in a distributed application interrupt the connection from Service A to Service B if the latter is not responding or is malfunctioning.

This can be achieved by wrapping a protected service call in a circuit breaker object. This object monitors for failures. Once the number of failures reaches a certain threshold, the circuit breaker trips. All subsequent calls to the circuit breaker will return with an error, without the protected call being made at all:

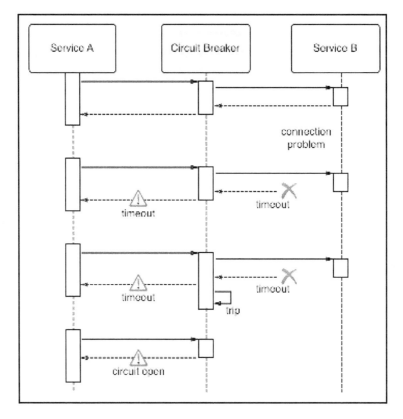

Circuit breaker pattern

Running in production

To successfully run a distributed application in production, we need to consider a few more aspects beyond the best practices and patterns presented in the preceding sections. One specific area that comes to mind is introspection and monitoring. Let's go through the most important aspects in detail.

Logging

Once a distributed application is in production, it is not possible to debug it. But how can we then find out *what exactly is the root cause of a malfunction of the application that has been reported by a user?* The solution to this problem is to produce abundant and meaningful logging information. Developers need to instrument their application services in such a way that they output helpful information, such as when an error happens or a potentially unexpected or unwanted situation is encountered. Often, this information is output to STDOUT and STDERR, from where it is then collected by system daemons that write the information to local files or forward it to a central log aggregation service.

If there is sufficient information in the logs, developers can use those logs to track down the root cause of errors in the system that have been reported.

In a distributed application architecture, with its many components, logging is even more important than in a monolithic application. The paths of execution of a single request through all the components of the application can be very complex. Also, remember that the components are distributed across a cluster of nodes. Thus, it makes sense to log everything of importance and to each log entry add things such as the exact time when it happened, the component in which it happened, and the node on which the component ran, to name just a few. Furthermore, the logging information should be aggregated in a central location so that it is readily available for developers and system operators to analyze.

Tracing

Tracing is used to find out how an individual request is funneled through a distributed application and how much time is spent overall for the request and in every individual component. This information, if collected, can be used as one of the sources for dashboards that show the behavior and health of the system.

Monitoring

Operators like to have dashboards showing live key metrics of the system, which show them the overall health of the application in one glance. These metrics can be non-functional metrics such as memory and CPU usage, number of crashes of a system or application component, health of a node, and so on, as well as functional and thus application-specific metrics such as the number of checkouts in an ordering system or the number of items out of stock in an inventory service.

Most often, the base data used to aggregate the numbers that are used for a dashboard are extracted from logging information. This can either be system logs, which will mostly be used for non-functional metrics, and application-level logs, for functional metrics.

Application updates

One of the competitive advantages for a company is to be able to react in a timely manner to changing market situations. Part of this is to be able to quickly adjust an application to fulfill new and changed needs or to add new functionality. The faster we can update our applications, the better. Many companies these days roll out new or changed features multiple times per day.

Since application updates are so frequent, these updates have to be non-disruptive. We cannot allow the system to go down for maintenance when upgrading. It all has to happen seamlessly and transparently.

Rolling updates

One way of updating an application or an application service is to use rolling updates. The assumption here is that the particular piece of software that has to be updated runs in multiple instances. Only then can we use this type of update.

What happens is that the system stops one instance of the current service and replaces it with an instance of the new service. As soon as the new instance is ready, it will be served traffic. Usually, the new instance is monitored for some time to see whether or not it works as expected and, if it does, the next instance of the current service is taken down and replaced by a new instance. This pattern is repeated until all service instances have been replaced.

Since there are always a few instances running at any given time, current or new, the application is operational all the time. No downtime is needed.

Blue-green deployments

In blue-green deployments, the current version of the application service, called *blue*, handles all the application traffic. We then install the new version of the application service, called *green*, on the production system. The new service is not yet wired with the rest of the application.

Once green is installed, one can execute smoke tests against this new service and, if those succeed, the router can be configured to funnel all traffic that previously went to blue to the new service, green. The behavior of green is then observed closely and, if all success criteria are met, blue can be decommissioned. But if, for some reason, green shows some unexpected or unwanted behavior, the router can be reconfigured to return all traffic to blue. Green can then be removed and fixed, and a new blue-green deployment can be executed with the corrected version:

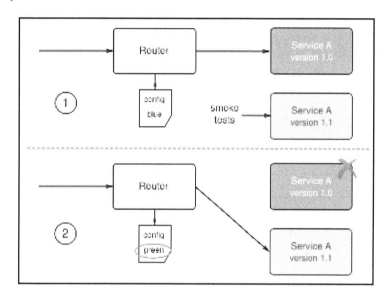

Blue-green deployment

Canary releases

Canary releases are releases where we have the current version of the application service and the new version installed on the system in parallel. As such, they resemble blue-green deployments. At first, all traffic is still routed through the current version. We then configure a router so that it funnels a small percentage, say 1%, of the overall traffic to the new version of the application service. The behavior of the new service is then monitored closely to find out whether or not it works as expected. If all the criteria for success are met, then the router is configured to funnel more traffic, say 5% this time, through the new service. Again, the behavior of the new service is closely monitored and, if it is successful, more and more traffic is routed to it until we reach 100%. Once all traffic is routed to the new service and it has been stable for some time, the old version of the service can be decommissioned.

Why do we call this a canary release? It is named after the coal miners who would use canary birds as an early warning system in the mines. Canary birds are particularly sensitive to toxic gas and if such a canary bird died, the miners knew they had to abandon the mine immediately.

Irreversible data changes

If part of our update process is to execute an irreversible change in our state, such as an irreversible schema change in a backing relational database, then we need to address this with special care. It is possible to execute such changes without downtime if one uses the right approach. It is important to recognize that, in such a situation, one cannot deploy the code changes that require the new data structure in the data store at the same time as the changes to the data. Rather, the whole update has to be separated into three distinct steps. In the first step, one rolls out a backward-compatible schema and data change. If this is successful, then one rolls out the new code in the second step. Again, if that is successful, one cleans up the schema in the third step and removes the backwards-compatibility:

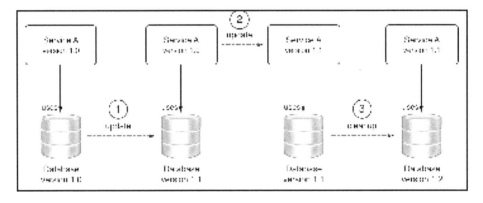

Rolling out an irreversible data or schema change

Rollback

If we have frequent updates to our application services that run in production, sooner or later there will be a problem with one of those updates. Maybe a developer, while fixing a bug, introduced a new one, which was not caught by all the automated, and maybe manual, tests, so the application is misbehaving and it is imperative that we roll back the service to the previous good version. In this regard, a rollback is a recovery from a disaster.

Again, in a distributed application architecture, it is not a question of whether a rollback will ever be needed, but rather when a rollback will have to occur. Thus we need to absolutely be sure that we can always roll back to a previous version of any service that makes up our application. Rollbacks cannot be an afterthought but have to be a tested and proven part of our deployment process.

If we are using blue-green deployments to update our services, then rollbacks should be fairly simple. All we need to do is switch the router from the new green version of the service back to the previous blue version.

Summary

In this chapter, we learned what a distributed application architecture is and what patterns and best practices are helpful or needed to successfully run a distributed application. Lastly, we discussed what is needed in addition to run such an application in production.

In the next chapter, we will dive into networking limited to a single host. We're going to discuss in detail how containers living on the same host can communicate with each other and how external clients can access containerized applications if necessary.

Questions

Please answer the following questions to assess your understanding of this chapter's content.

1. When and why does every part in a distributed application architecture have to be redundant? Explain in a few short sentences.
2. Why do we need DNS services? Explain in 3 to 5 sentences.
3. What is a circuit breaker and why is it needed?
4. What are some important differences between a monolithic application and a distributed or multi-service application?
5. What is a blue-green deployment?

Further reading

The following articles provide more in-depth information:

- *CircuitBreaker* at `http://bit.ly/1NU1sgW`
- *The OSI model explained* at `http://bit.ly/1UCcvMt`
- *BlueGreenDeployment* at `http://bit.ly/2r2IxNJ`

Single-Host Networking 7

In the last chapter, we learned about the most important architectural patterns and best practices that are used when dealing with a distributed application architecture.

In this chapter, we will introduce the Docker container networking model and its single-host implementation in the form of the bridge network. This chapter also introduces the concept of software-defined networks and how they are used to secure containerized applications. Finally, it demonstrates how container ports can be opened to the public and thus make containerized components accessible to the outside world.

This chapter will contain the following topics:

- The container network model
- Network firewalling
- The bridge network
- The host network
- The null network
- Running in an existing network namespace
- Port management

After completing this module, you will be able to do the following:

- Draft the container networking model—along with all the essential components onto a whiteboard
- Create and delete a custom bridge network
- Run a container attached to a custom bridge network
- Inspect a bridge network

- Isolate containers from each other by running them on different bridge networks
- Publish a container port to a host port of your choice

Technical requirements

For this chapter, the only thing you will need is a Docker host that is able to run Linux containers. You can use your laptop with either Docker for Mac or Windows or Docker Toolbox installed.

The container network model

So far, we have worked with single containers. But in reality, a containerized business application consists of several containers that need to collaborate to achieve a goal. Therefore, we need a way for individual containers to communicate with each other. This is achieved by establishing pathways that we can use to send data packets back and forth between containers. These pathways are called **networks**. Docker has defined a very simple networking model, the so-called **container network model** (**CNM**), to specify the requirements that any software that implements a container network has to fulfill. The following is a graphical representation of the CNM:

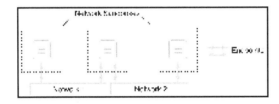

The Docker container network model

The CNM has three elements—sandbox, endpoint, and network:

- **Sandbox:** The sandbox perfectly isolates a container from the outside world. No inbound network connection is allowed into the sandboxed container. Yet, it is very unlikely that a container will be of any value in a system if absolutely no communication with it is possible. To work around this, we have element number two, which is the endpoint.

- **Endpoint:** An endpoint is a controlled gateway from the outside world into the network's sandbox that shields the container. The endpoint connects the network sandbox (but not the container) to the third element of the model, which is the network.
- **Network:** The network is the pathway that transports the data packets of an instance of communication from endpoint to endpoint, or ultimately from container to container.

It is important to note that a network sandbox can have zero to many endpoints, or, said differently, each container living in a network sandbox can either be attached to no network at all or it can be attached to multiple different networks at the same time. In the preceding image, the middle of the three network sandboxes is attached to both networks 1 and 2 through a respective endpoint.

This networking model is very generic and does not specify where the individual containers that communicate with each other run over a network. All containers could, for example, run on one and the same host (local) or they could be distributed across a cluster of hosts (global).

Of course, the CNM is just a model describing how networking works among containers. To be able to use networking with our containers, we need real implementations of the CNM. For both local and global scope, we have multiple implementations of the CNM. In the following table, we give a short overview of the existing implementations and their main characteristics. The list is in no particular order:

Network	Company	Scope	Description
Bridge	Docker	Local	Simple network based on Linux bridges allowing networking on a single host
Macvlan	Docker	Local	Configures multiple layer 2 (that is, MAC) addresses on a single physical host interface
Overlay	Docker	Global	Multinode-capable container network based on **Virtual Extensible LAN (VXLan)**
Weave Net	Weaveworks	Global	Simple, resilient, multihost Docker networking
Contiv Network Plugin	Cisco	Global	Open source container networking

All network types not directly provided by Docker can be added to a Docker host as a plugin.

Network firewalling

Docker has always had the mantra of security first. This philosophy had a direct influence on how networking in a single and multihost Docker environment was designed and implemented. Software-defined networks are easy and cheap to create, yet they perfectly firewall containers that are attached to this network from other non-attached containers, and from the outside world. All containers that belong to the same network can freely communicate with each other, while others have no means to do so:

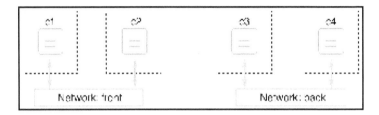

Docker networks

In the preceding image, we have two networks called **front** and **back**. Attached to the front network, we have containers **c1** and **c2**, and attached to the back network, we have containers **c3** and **c4**. **c1** and **c2** can freely communicate with each other, as can **c3** and **c4**. But **c1** and **c2** have no way to communicate with either **c3** or **c4**, and vice versa.

Now what about the situation where we have an application consisting of three services, **webAPI**, **productCatalog**, and **database**? We want webAPI to be able to communicate with productCatalog, but not with the database, and we want productCatalog to be able to communicate with the database service. We can solve this situation by placing webAPI and the database on different networks and attach productCatalog to both of these networks, as shown in the following image:

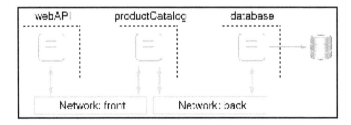

Container attached to multiple networks

Since creating SDNs is cheap, and each network provides added security by isolating resources from unauthorized access, it is highly recommended that you design and run applications so that they use multiple networks and run only services on the same network that absolutely need to communicate with each other. In the preceding example, there is absolutely no need for the web API component to ever communicate directly with the database service, so we have put them on different networks. If the worst-case scenario happens and a hacker compromises the web API, they have no ability to access the database from there without first also hacking the product catalog service.

The bridge network

The Docker bridge network is the first implementation of the container network model that we're going to look at in detail. This network implementation is based on the Linux bridge. When the Docker daemon runs for the first time, it creates a Linux bridge and calls it `docker0`. This is the default behavior, and can be changed by changing the configuration. Docker then creates a network with this Linux bridge and calls the network bridge. All the containers that we create on a Docker host and that we do not explicitly bind to another network leads to Docker automatically attaching to this bridge network.

To verify that we indeed have a network called `bridge` of type `bridge` defined on our host, we can list all networks on the host with the following command:

```
$ docker network ls
```

This should provide an output similar to the following:

Listing of all Docker networks available by default

In your case, the IDs will be different, but the rest of the output should look the same. We do indeed have a first network called `bridge` using the driver `bridge`. The scope being `local` just means that this type of network is restricted to a single host and cannot span across multiple hosts. In a later chapter, we will also discuss other types of networks that have a global scope, meaning they can span whole clusters of hosts.

Now, let's look a little bit deeper into what this bridge network is all about. For this, we are going to use the Docker `inspect` command:

```
$ docker network inspect bridge
```

When executed, this outputs a big chunk of detailed information about the network in question. This information should look like the following:

```
C:\Users\admin>docker network inspect bridge
[
    {
        "Name": "bridge",
        "Id": "3b08c1c711ada84ae859c4bed48b5af1f45b68db89356ca5045dc7ee8672e946",
        "Created": "2018-04-09T09:47:29.9424652Z",
        "Scope": "local",
        "Driver": "bridge",
        "EnableIPv6": false,
        "IPAM": {
            "Driver": "default",
            "Options": null,
            "Config": [
                {
                    "Subnet": "172.17.0.0/16",
                    "Gateway": "172.17.0.1"
                }
            ]
        },
        "Internal": false,
        "Attachable": false,
        "Ingress": false,
        "ConfigFrom": {
            "Network": ""
        },
        "ConfigOnly": false,
        "Containers": {},
        "Options": {
            "com.docker.network.bridge.default_bridge": "true",
            "com.docker.network.bridge.enable_icc": "true",
            "com.docker.network.bridge.enable_ip_masquerade": "true",
            "com.docker.network.bridge.host_binding_ipv4": "0.0.0.0",
            "com.docker.network.bridge.name": "docker0",
            "com.docker.network.driver.mtu": "1500"
        },
        "Labels": {}
    }
]
```

Output generated when inspecting the Docker bridge network

We have already seen the ID, Name, Driver, and Scope values when we listed all the networks, so that is nothing new. But let's have a look at the **IP address management (IPAM)** block. IPAM is software that is used to track IP addresses that are used on a computer. The important part in the IPAM block is the Config node with its values for Subnet and Gateway. The subnet for the bridge network is defined by default as 172.17.0.0/16. This means that all containers attached to this network will get an IP address assigned by Docker that is taken from the given range, which is 172.17.0.2 to 172.17.255.255. The 172.17.0.1 address is reserved for the router of this network whose role in this type of network is taken by the Linux bridge. One can expect that the very first container that will be attached to this network by Docker will get the 172.17.0.2 address. All subsequent containers will get a higher number; the following image illustrates this fact:

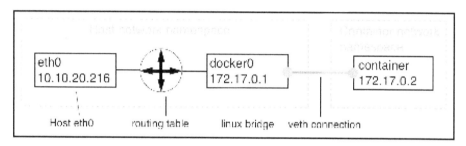

The bridge network

In the preceding image, we can see the network namespace of the host, which includes the host's eth0 endpoint, which is typically a NIC if the Docker host runs on bare metal or a virtual NIC if the Docker host is a VM. All traffic to the host comes through eth0. The Linux bridge is responsible for the routing of the network traffic between the host's network and the subnet of the bridge network.

By default, only traffic from the egress is allowed, and all ingress is blocked. What this means is that while containerized applications can reach the internet, they cannot be reached by any outside traffic. Each container attached to the network gets its own **virtual ethernet** (**veth**) connection with the bridge. This is illustrated in the following image:

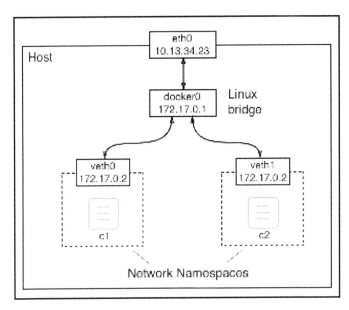

Details of the bridge network

The preceding image shows us the world from the perspective of the host. We will explore how the situation looks from within a container later on in this section.

We are not limited to just the `bridge` network, as Docker allows us to define our own custom bridge networks. This is not just a feature that is nice to have, but it is a recommended best practice to not run all containers on the same network, but to use additional bridge networks to further isolate containers that have no need to communicate with each other. To create a custom bridge network called `sample-net`, use the following command:

```
$ docker network create --driver bridge sample-net
```

If we do this, we can then inspect what subnet Docker has created for this new custom network as follows:

```
$ docker network inspect sample-net | grep Subnet
```

This returns the following value:

```
"Subnet": "172.18.0.0/16",
```

Evidently, Docker has just assigned the next free block of IP addresses to our new custom bridge network. If, for some reason, we want to specify our own subnet range when creating a network, we can do so by using the `--subnet` parameter:

```
$ docker network create --driver bridge --subnet "10.1.0.0/16" test-
net
```

To avoid conflicts due to duplicate IP addresses, make sure you avoid creating networks with overlapping subnets.

Now that we have discussed what a bridge network is and how one can create a custom bridge network, we want to understand how we can attach containers to these networks. First, let's interactively run an Alpine container without specifying the network to be attached:

```
$ docker container run --name c1 -it --rm alpine:latest /bin/sh
```

In another Terminal window, let's inspect the `c1` container:

```
$ docker container inspect c1
```

In the vast output, let's concentrate for a moment on the part that provides network-related information. It can be found under the NetworkSettings node. I have it listed in the following output:

Network settings section of the container metadata

In the preceding output, we can see that the container is indeed attached to the bridge network since the NetworkID is equal to 026e65..., which we can see from the preceding code is the ID of the bridge network. We can also see that the container got the IP address of 172.17.0.4 assigned as expected and that the gateway is at 172.17.0.1. Please note that the container also had a MacAddress associated with it. This is important as the Linux bridge uses the Mac address for routing.

So far, we have approached this from the outside of the container's network namespace. Now, let's see how the situation looks when we're not only inside the container, but inside the container's network namespace. Inside the `c1` container, let's use the `ip` tool to inspect what's going on. Run the `ip addr` command and observe the output that is generated as follows:

Container namespace as seen by the IP tool

The interesting part of the preceding output is the number `19`, the `eth0` endpoint. The `veth0` endpoint that the Linux bridge created outside of the container namespace is mapped to `eth0` inside the container. Docker always maps the first endpoint of a container network namespace to `eth0`, as seen from inside the namespace. If the network namespace is attached to an additional network, then that endpoint will be mapped to `eth1`, and so on.

Since at this point we're not really interested in any endpoint other than `eth0`, we could have used a more specific variant of the command, which would have given us the following:

```
/ # ip addr show eth0
195: eth0@if196: <BROADCAST,MULTICAST,UP,LOWER_UP,M-DOWN> mtu 1500
qdisc noqueue state UP
    link/ether 02:42:ac:11:00:02 brd ff:ff:ff:ff:ff:ff
    inet 172.17.0.2/16 brd 172.17.255.255 scope global eth0
       valid_lft forever preferred_lft forever
```

In the output, we can also see what MAC address (`02:42:ac:11:00:02`) and what IP (`172.17.0.2`) have been associated with this container network namespace by Docker.

We can also get some information about how requests are routed by using the `ip route` command:

```
/ # ip route
default via 172.17.0.1 dev eth0
172.17.0.0/16 dev eth0 scope link src 172.17.0.2
```

This output tells us that all traffic to the gateway at `172.17.0.1` is routed through the `eth0` device.

Now, let's run another container called `c2` on the same network:

```
$ docker container run --name c2 -d alpine:latest ping 127.0.0.1
```

The `c2` container will also be attached to the `bridge` network, since we have not specified any other network. Its IP address will be the next free one from the subnet, which is `172.17.0.3`, as we can readily test:

```
$ docker container inspect --format "{{.NetworkSettings.IPAddress}}" c2
172.17.0.3
```

Now, we have two containers attached to the `bridge` network. We can try to inspect this network once again to find a list of all containers attached to it in the output.:

```
$ docker network inspect bridge
```

The information is found under the `Containers` node:

The containers section of the output of docker network inspect bridge

Once again, we have shortened the output to the essentials for readability.

Now, let's create two additional containers, c3 and c4, and attach them to the test-net. For this, we use the --network parameter:

```
$ docker container run --name c3 -d --network test-net \
    alpine:latest ping 127.0.0.1
$ docker container run --name c4 -d --network test-net \
    alpine:latest ping 127.0.0.1
```

Let's inspect network test-net and confirm that the containers c3 and c4 are indeed attached to it:

```
$ docker network inspect test-net
```

This will give us the following output for the Containers section:

Containers section of the command docker network inspect test-net

The next question we're going to ask ourselves is whether the two c3 and c4 containers can freely communicate with each other. To demonstrate that this is indeed the case, we can exec into the container c3:

```
$ docker container exec -it c3 /bin/sh
```

Once inside the container, we can try to ping container c4 by name and by IP address:

```
/ # ping c4
PING c4 (10.1.0.3): 56 data bytes
64 bytes from 10.1.0.3: seq=0 ttl=64 time=0.192 ms
64 bytes from 10.1.0.3: seq=1 ttl=64 time=0.148 ms
...
```

The following is the result of the ping using the IP address of the container c4:

```
/ # ping 10.1.0.3
PING 10.1.0.3 (10.1.0.3): 56 data bytes
64 bytes from 10.1.0.3: seq=0 ttl=64 time=0.200 ms
64 bytes from 10.1.0.3: seq=1 ttl=64 time=0.172 ms
...
```

The answer in both cases confirms to us that the communication between containers attached to the same network is working as expected. The fact that we can even use the name of the container we want to connect to shows us that the name resolution provided by the Docker DNS service works inside this network.

Now we want to make sure that the bridge and the test-net networks are firewalled from each other. To demonstrate this, we can try to ping the c2 container from the c3 container, either by its name or by its IP address:

```
/ # ping c2
ping: bad address 'c2'
```

The following is the result of the ping using the IP address of the target container c2 instead:

```
/ # ping 172.17.0.3
PING 172.17.0.3 (172.17.0.3): 56 data bytes
^C
--- 172.17.0.3 ping statistics ---
43 packets transmitted, 0 packets received, 100% packet loss
```

The preceding command remained hanging and I had to terminate the command with *Ctrl+C*. From the answer to pinging c2, we can also see that the name resolution does not work across networks. This is the expected behavior. Networks provide an extra layer of isolation, and thus security, to containers.

Earlier, we learned that a container can be attached to multiple networks. Let's attach a `c5` container to the `sample-net` and `test-net` networks at the same time:

```
$ docker container run --name c5 -d \
    --network sample-net \
    --network test-net \
    alpine:latest ping 127.0.0.1
```

We can then test that `c5` is reachable from the `c2` container similar to when we tested the same for containers `c4` and `c2`. The result will show that the connection indeed works.

If we want to remove an existing network, we can use the `docker network rm` command, but note that one cannot accidentally delete a network that has containers attached to it:

```
$ docker network rm test-net
Error response from daemon: network test-net id 863192... has active
endpoints
```

Before we continue, let's clean up and remove all containers:

```
$ docker container rm -f $(docker container ls -aq)
```

Then we remove the two custom networks that we created:

```
$ docker network rm sample-net
$ docker network rm test-net
```

The host network

There exist occasions where we want to run a container in the network namespace of the host. This can be necessary when we need to run some software in a container that is used to analyze or debug the host network's traffic. But keep in mind that these are very specific scenarios. When running business software in containers, there is no good reason to ever run the respective containers attached to the host's network. For security reasons, it is strongly recommended that you do not run any such container attached to the host network on a production or production-like environment.

That said, *how can we run a container inside the network namespace of the host?* Simply by attaching the container to the `host` network:

```
$ docker container run --rm -it --network host alpine:latest /bin/sh
```

If we now use the `ip` tool to analyze the network namespace from within the container, we will see that we get exactly the same picture as we would if we were running the `ip` tool directly on the host. For example, if I inspect the `eth0` device on my host, I get this:

```
/ # ip addr show eth0
2: eth0: <BROADCAST,MULTICAST,UP,LOWER_UP> mtu 1500 qdisc pfifo_fast
state UP qlen 1000
    link/ether 02:50:00:00:00:01 brd ff:ff:ff:ff:ff:ff
    inet 192.168.65.3/24 brd 192.168.65.255 scope global eth0
        valid_lft forever preferred_lft forever
    inet6 fe80::c90b:4219:ddbd:92bf/64 scope link
        valid_lft forever preferred_lft forever
```

Here, I find that `192.168.65.3` is the IP address that the host has been assigned and that the MAC address shown here also corresponds to that of the host.

We can also inspect the routes to get the following (shortened):

```
/ # ip route
default via 192.168.65.1 dev eth0 src 192.168.65.3 metric 202
10.1.0.0/16 dev cni0 scope link src 10.1.0.1
127.0.0.0/8 dev lo scope host
172.17.0.0/16 dev docker0 scope link src 172.17.0.1
...
192.168.65.0/24 dev eth0 scope link src 192.168.65.3 metric 202
```

Before I let you go on to the next section of this chapter, I want to once more point out that the use of the `host` network is dangerous and needs to be avoided if possible.

The null network

Sometimes, we need to run a few application services or jobs that do not need any network connection at all to execute the task. It is strongly advised that you run those applications in a container that is attached to the `none` network. This container will be completely isolated, and thus safe from any outside access. Let's run such a container:

```
$ docker container run --rm -it --network none alpine:latest /bin/sh
```

Once inside the container, we can verify that there is no `eth0` network endpoint available:

```
/ # ip addr show eth0
ip: can't find device 'eth0'
```

There is also no routing information available, as we can demonstrate by using the following command:

```
/ # ip route
```

This returns nothing.

Running in an existing network namespace

Normally, Docker creates a new network namespace for each container we run. The network namespace of the container corresponds to the sandbox of the container network model we described earlier on. As we attach the container to a network, we define an endpoint that connects the container network namespace with the actual network. This way, we have one container per network namespace.

Docker provides an additional way to define the network namespace in which a container runs. When creating a new container, we can specify that it should be attached to or maybe we should say included in the network namespace of an existing container. With this technique, we can run multiple containers in a single network namespace:

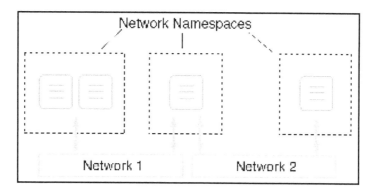

Multiple containers running in a single network namespace

In the preceding image, we can see that in the leftmost network namespace, we have two containers. The two containers, since they share the same namespace, can communicate on localhost with each other. The network namespace (and not the individual containers) is then attached to **Network 1**.

This is useful when we want to debug the network of an existing container without running additional processes inside that container. We can just attach a special utility container to the network namespace of the container to inspect. This feature is also used by Kubernetes when it creates a pod. We will hear more about Kubernetes and pods in subsequent chapters of this book.

Now, let's demonstrate how this works. First, we create a new bridge network:

```
$ docker network create --driver bridge test-net
```

Next, we run a container attached to this network:

```
$ docker container run --name web -d --network test-net nginx:alpine
```

Finally, we run another container and attach it to the network of our web container:

```
$ docker container run -it --rm --network container:web alpine:latest
/bin/sh
```

Specifically, note how we define the network: --network container:web. This tells Docker that our new container shall use the same network namespace as the container called web.

Since the new container is in the same network namespace as the web container running Nginx, we're now able to access Nginx on localhost! We can prove this by using the wget tool, which is part of the Alpine container, to connect to Nginx. We should see the following:

```
/ # wget -qO - localhost
<!DOCTYPE html>
<html>
<head>
<title>Welcome to nginx!</title>
...
</html>
```

Note that we have shortened the output for readability. Please also note that there is an important difference between running two containers attached to the same network and two containers running in the same network namespace. In both cases, the containers can freely communicate with each other, but in the latter case, the communication happens over localhost.

To clean up the container and network we can use the following command:

```
$ docker container rm --force web
$ docker network rm test-net
```

Port management

Now that we know how we can isolate or firewall containers from each other by placing them on different networks, and that we can have a container attached to more than one network, we have one problem that remains unsolved. *How can we expose an application service to the outside world?* Imagine a container running a web server hosting our webAPI from before. We want customers from the internet to be able to access this API. We have designed it to be a publicly accessible API. To achieve this, we have to, figuratively speaking, open a gate in our firewall through which we can funnel external traffic to our API. For security reasons, we don't just want to open the doors wide, but to have only a single controlled gate through which traffic flows.

We can create such a gate by mapping a container port to an available port on the host. We're also calling this container port to publish a port. Remember, the container has its own virtual network stack, as does the host. Therefore, container ports and host ports exist completely independently, and by default have nothing in common at all. But we can now wire a container port with a free host port and funnel external traffic through this link, as illustrated in the following image:

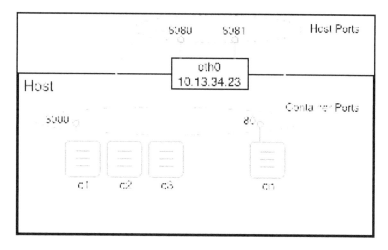

Mapping container ports to host ports

But now it is time to demonstrate how one can actually map a container port to a host port. This is done when creating a container. We have different ways of doing so:

- First, we can let Docker decide which host port our container port shall be mapped to. Docker will then select one of the free host ports in the range of 32xxx. This automatic mapping is done by using the $-P$ parameter:

```
$ docker container run --name web -P -d nginx:alpine
```

The preceding command runs an Nginx server in a container. Nginx is listening at port 80 inside the container. With the $-P$ parameter, we're telling Docker to map all the exposed container ports to a free port in the 32xxx range. We can find out which host port Docker is using by using the `docker container port` command:

```
$ docker container port web
80/tcp -> 0.0.0.0:32768
```

The Nginx container only exposes port 80, and we can see that it has been mapped to the host port 32768. If we open a new browser window and navigate to `localhost:32768`, we should see the following screenshot:

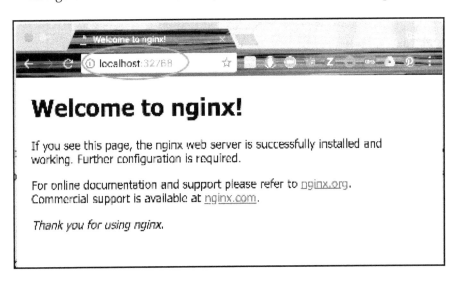

The welcome page of Nginx

- An alternative way to find out which host port Docker is using for our container is to inspect it. The host port is part of the `NetworkSettings` node:

```
$ docker container inspect web | grep HostPort
32768
```

- Finally, the third way of getting this information is to list the container:

```
$ docker container ls
CONTAINER ID     IMAGE             ...     PORTS
NAMES
56e46a14b6f7     nginx:alpine      ...     0.0.0.0:32768->80/tcp
web
```

Please note that in the preceding output, the `/tcp` part tells us that the port has been opened for communication with the TCP protocol, but not for the UDP protocol. TCP is the default, and if we want to specify that we want to open the port for UDP, then we have to specify this explicitly. The `0.0.0.0` in the mapping tells us that traffic from any host IP address can now reach the container port `80` of the `web` container.

Sometimes, we want to map a container port to a very specific host port. We can do this by using the parameter-p (or `--publish`). Let's look at how this is done with the following command:

```
$ docker container run --name web2 -p 8080:80 -d nginx:alpine
```

The value of the `-p` parameter is in the form of `<host port>:<container port>`. Therefore, in the preceding case, we map container port `80` to host port `8080`. Once the `web2` container runs, we can test it in the browser by navigating to `localhost:8080`, and we should be greeted by the same Nginx welcome page that we saw in the previous example that dealt with automatic port mapping.

When using the UDP protocol for communication over a certain port, then the `publish` parameter will look like `-p 3000:4321/udp`. Note that if we want to allow communication with both TCP and UDP protocols over the same port, then we have to map each protocol separately.

Summary

In this chapter, we have learned about how containers running on a single host can communicate with each other. First, we looked at the CNM that defines the requirements of a container network and then we looked at several implementations of the CNM, such as the bridge network. We then looked at how the bridge network functions in detail and also what kind of information Docker provides us with about the networks and the containers attached to those networks. We also learned about adopting two different perspectives, from both outside and inside the container.

In the next chapter, we're going to introduce Docker Compose. We will learn about creating an application that consists of multiple services, each running in a container, and how Docker Compose allows us to easily build, run, and scale such an application using a declarative approach.

Questions

To assess your skills, please try to answer the following questions:

1. Name the three core elements of the **container network model** (**CNM**).
2. How will you create a custom bridge network called for example, frontend?
3. How will you run two nginx:alpine containers attached to the frontend network.
4. For the frontend network, get the following:
    1. IPs of all attached containers.
    2. The subnet associated with the network.
5. What is the purpose of the host network?
6. Name one or two scenarios where the use of the host network is appropriate.
7. What is the purpose of the none network?
8. In what scenarios should the none network be used?

Further reading

Here are some articles that describe the topics presented in this chapter in more detail:

- *Docker networking overview* at http://dockr.ly/2sXGzQn
- *Container networking* at http://dockr.ly/2HJfQKn
- What is a Bridge at https://bit.ly/2HyC3Od
- *Use bridge networks* at http://dockr.ly/2BNxjRr
- *Use Macvlan networks* at http://dockr.ly/2ETjy2x
- *Networking using the host network* at http://dockr.ly/2F4aI59

8
Docker Compose

In the previous chapter, we learned a lot about how container networking works on a single Docker host. We introduced the **Container Network Model** (**CNM**), which forms the basis of all networking between Docker containers, and then we dove deep into different implementations of the CNM, specifically the bridge network.

This chapter introduces the concept of an application consisting of multiple services, each running in a container, and how Docker Compose allows us to easily build, run, and scale such an application using a declarative approach.

The chapter covers the following topics:

- Demystifying declarative versus imperative
- Running a multi-service application
- Scaling a service
- Building and pushing an application

After completing this chapter, the reader will be able to do the following:

- Explain in a few short sentences the main differences between an imperative and declarative approach for defining and running an application
- Describe in their own words the difference between a container and a Docker Compose service
- Author a Docker Compose YAML file for a simple multi-service application
- Build, push, deploy, and tear down a simple multi-service application using Docker Compose
- Use Docker Compose to scale an application service up and down

Demystifying declarative versus imperative

Docker Compose is a tool provided by Docker that is mainly used where one needs to run and orchestrate containers running on a single Docker host. This includes but is not limited to development, **continuous integration** (**CI**), automated testing, and manual QA.

Docker Compose uses files formatted in YAML as input. By default, Docker Compose expects these files to be called `docker-compose.yml`, but other names are possible. The content of a `docker-compose.yml` is said to be a *declarative* way of describing and running a containerized application potentially consisting of more than a single container.

So, *what is the meaning of declarative?*

First of all, *declarative* is the antonym of *imperative*. Well, that doesn't help much. Now that I have introduced another definition, I need to explain both of them:

- **Imperative:** It's a way in which we can solve problems by specifying the exact procedure which has to be followed by the system.

  If I tell a system such as the Docker daemon imperatively how to run an application then that means that I have to describe step by step what the system has to do and how it has to react if some unexpected situation occurs. I have to be very explicit and precise in my instructions. I need to cover all edge cases and how they need to be treated.

- **Declarative:** It's a way in which we can solve problems without requiring the programmer to specify an exact procedure to be followed.

  A declarative approach means that I tell the Docker engine what my desired state for an application is and it has to figure out on its own how to achieve this desired state and how to reconcile it if the system deviates from it.

Docker clearly recommends the declarative approach when dealing with containerized applications. Consequently, the Docker Compose tool uses this approach.

Running a multi-service app

In most cases, applications do not consist of only one monolithic block, but rather of several application services that work together. When using Docker containers, each application service runs in its own container. When we want to run such a multi-service application, we can of course start all the participating containers with the well-known `docker container run` command. But this is inefficient at best. With the Docker Compose tool, we are given a way to define the application in a declarative way in a file that uses the YAML format.

Let's have a look at the content of a simple `docker-compose.yml` file:

```
version: "3.5"
services:
  web:
    image: fundamentalsofdocker/ch08-web:1.0
    ports:
      - 3000:3000
  db:
    image: fundamentalsofdocker/ch08-db:1.0
    volumes:
      - pets-data:/var/lib/postgresql/data

volumes:
  pets-data:
```

The lines in the file are explained as follows:

- `version`: In this line, we specify the version of the Docker Compose format we want to use. At the time of writing, this is version 3.5.
- `services`: In this section, we specify the services that make up our application in the `services` block. In our sample, we have two application services and we call them `web` and `db`:
  - `web`: The `web` service is using the image `fundamentalsofdocker/ch08-web:1.0` from the Docker Hub and is publishing container port `3000` to the host port, also `3000`.
  - `db`: The `db` service, on the other hand, is using the image `fundamentalsofdocker/ch08-db:1.0`, which is a customized PostgreSQL database. We are mounting a volume called `pets-data` into the container of the `db` service.
- `volumes`: The volumes used by any of the services have to be declared in this section. In our sample, this is the last section of the file. The first time the application is run, a volume called `pets-data` will be created by Docker and then, in subsequent runs, if the volume is still there, it will be reused. This could be important when the application, for some reason, crashes and has to be restarted. Then, the previous data is still around and ready to be used by the restarted database service.

Navigate to the subfolder `ch08` of the `labs` folder and start the application using Docker Compose:

```
$ docker-compose up
```

If we enter the preceding command, then the tool will assume that there must be a file in the current directory called `docker-compose.yml` and it will use that one to run. In our case, this is indeed the case and the application will start. We should see the output as follows:

```
$ docker-compose up
Creating network "ch08_default" with the default driver
Creating volume "ch08_pets-data" with default driver
Pulling web (fundamentalsofdocker/ch08-web:1.0)...
1.0: Pulling from fundamentalsofdocker/ch08-web
605ce1bd3f31: Pull complete
d9c1bb10879c: Pull complete
d610c8516793: Pull complete
bf3a86e46185: Pull complete
f082b7c3a97c: Pull complete
188adc417c9f: Pull complete
ad8771290e5e: Pull complete
Digest: sha256:d797862735281334e8f9bbf700ecb39bece12873956e5b77dc5e6431e9126a8
Status: Downloaded newer image for fundamentalsofdocker/ch08-web:1.0
Pulling db (fundamentalsofdocker/ch08-db:1.0)...
1.0: Pulling from fundamentalsofdocker/ch08-db
ff3a5c916c97: Pull complete
a503b44e1ce0: Pull complete
211706713093: Pull complete
8df57d533c71: Pull complete
7858f71c02fb: Pull complete
55a8ef17ba59: Pull complete
3fb44f73d373: Pull complete
65cad41156b3: Pull complete
5492a5bead70: Pull complete
ac3385cd756f: Pull complete
Digest: sha256:eb5364a418bf7072de3e992517cad4ce8c55725a1cdfcd18e1c04ea2ec2a7356
Status: Downloaded newer image for fundamentalsofdocker/ch08-db:1.0
Creating ch08_db_1 ... done
Creating ch08_web_1 ... done
Attaching to ch08_db_1, ch08_web_1
```

Running the sample application, part 1

```
db_1    |   done
db_1    | server started
web_1   | listening at 0.0.0.0:3000
db_1    | CREATE DATABASE
db_1    |
db_1    | CREATE ROLE
db_1    |
db_1    |
db_1    | /usr/local/bin/docker-entrypoint.sh: running /docker-entrypoint-initdb.d/init-db.sql
db_1    | CREATE TABLE
db_1    | ALTER TABLE
db_1    | ALTER ROLE
db_1    | INSERT 0 1
db_1    | INSERT 0 1
db_1    | INSERT 0 1
db_1    | INSERT 0 1
db_1    | INSERT 0 1
db_1    | INSERT 0 1
db_1    | INSERT 0 1
db_1    | INSERT 0 1
db_1    | INSERT 0 1
db_1    | INSERT 0 1
db_1    | INSERT 0 1
db_1    | INSERT 0 1
db_1    |
db_1    |
db_1    | waiting for server to shut down....2018-03-21 12:52:40.709 UTC [34] LOG:  received fast shutdown
 request
db_1    | 2018-03-21 12:52:40.711 UTC [34] LOG:  aborting any active transactions
db_1    | 2018-03-21 12:52:40.712 UTC [34] LOG:  worker process: logical replication launcher (PID 41) exi
ted with exit code 1
db_1    | 2018-03-21 12:52:40.712 UTC [36] LOG:  shutting down
db_1    | 2018-03-21 12:52:40.737 UTC [34] LOG:  database system is shut down
db_1    |   done
db_1    | server stopped
db_1    |
db_1    | PostgreSQL init process complete; ready for start up.
db_1    |
db_1    | 2018-03-21 12:52:40.817 UTC [1] LOG:  listening on IPv4 address "0.0.0.0", port 5432
db_1    | 2018-03-21 12:52:40.817 UTC [1] LOG:  listening on IPv6 address "::", port 5432
db_1    | 2018-03-21 12:52:40.821 UTC [1] LOG:  listening on Unix socket "/var/run/postgresql/.s.PGSQL.543
2"
db_1    | 2018-03-21 12:52:40.832 UTC [49] LOG:  database system was shut down at 2018-03-21 12:52:40 UTC
db_1    | 2018-03-21 12:52:40.835 UTC [1] LOG:  database system is ready to accept connections
```

Running the sample application, part 2

The preceding output is explained as follows:

- In the first part of the output, we can see how Docker Compose pulls the two images that constitute our application. This is followed by the creation of a network ch08_default and a volume ch08_pets-data, followed by the two containers ch08_web_1 and ch08_db_1, one for each service, web and db. All the names are automatically prefixed by Docker Compose with the name of the parent directory, which in this case is called ch08.

- After that, we see the logs produced by the two containers. Each line of the output is conveniently prefixed with the name of the service, and each service's output is in a different color. Here, the lion's share is produced by the database and only one line is from the web service.

We can now open a browser tab and navigate to localhost:3000/pet. We should be greeted by a nice cat image and some additional information about the container it came from, as shown in the following screenshot:

The sample application in the browser

Refresh the browser a few times to see other cat images. The application selects the current image randomly from a set of 12 images whose URLs are stored in the database.

As the application is running in interactive mode and thus the Terminal where we ran Docker Compose is blocked, we can cancel the application by pressing *Ctrl+C*. If we do so, we will see the following:

```
^CGracefully stopping... (press Ctrl+C again to force)
Stopping ch08_web_1 ... done
Stopping ch08_db_1 ... done
```

We will notice that the database service stops immediately while the web service takes about 10 seconds to do so. The reason for this being that the database service listens to and reacts to the SIGTERM signal sent by Docker while the web service doesn't, and thus Docker kills it after 10 seconds.

If we run the application again, the output will be much shorter:

Output of docker-compose up

This time, we didn't have to download the images and the database didn't have to initialize from scratch, but it was just reusing the data that was already present in the volume pets-data from the previous run.

We can also run the application in the background. All containers will run as daemons. For this, we just need to use the -d parameter, as shown in the following code:

```
$ docker-compose up -d
```

Docker Compose offers us many more commands than just `up`. We can use it to list all services that are part of the application:

```
$ docker-compose ps
    Name              Command              State          Ports
------------------------------------------------------------------------
ch08_db_1      docker-entrypoint.sh postgres    Up      5432/tcp
ch08_web_1     /bin/sh -c node src/server.js    Up      0.0.0.0:3000->3000/tcp
$
```

Output of docker-compose ps

This command is similar to `docker container ls`, with the only difference being that it only lists containers that are part of the application.

To stop and clean up the application, we use the `docker-compose down` command:

```
$ docker-compose down
Stopping ch08_web_1 ... done
Stopping ch08_db_1 ... done
Removing ch08_web_1 ... done
Removing ch08_db_1 ... done
Removing network ch08_default
```

If we also want to remove the volume for the database, then we can use the following command:

```
$ docker volume rm ch08_pets-data
```

Why is there a `ch08` *prefix in the name of the volume?* In the `docker-compose.yml` file, we have called the volume to use `pets-data`. But as we have already mentioned, Docker Compose prefixes all names with the name of the parent folder of the `docker-compose.yml` file plus an underscore. In this case, the parent folder is called `ch08`.

Scaling a service

Now, let's, for a moment, assume that our sample application has been live on the web and become very successful. Loads of people want to see our cute animal images. So now we're facing a problem since our application has started to slow down. To counteract this problem, we want to run multiple instances of the web service. With Docker Compose, this is readily done.

Running more instances is also called scaling up. We can use this tool to scale our `web` service up to, say, three instances:

```
$ docker-compose up --scale web=3
```

If we do this, we are in for a surprise. The output will look similar to the following screenshot:

Output of docker-compose --scale

The second and third instances of the web service fail to start. The error message tells us why: we cannot use the same host port more than once. When instances 2 and 3 try to start, Docker realizes that port `3000` is already taken by the first instance. *What can we do?* Well, we can just let Docker decide which host port to use for each instance.

If, in the `ports` section of the `compose` file, we only specify the container port and leave out the host port, then Docker automatically selects an ephemeral port. Let's do exactly this:

1. First, let's tear down the application:

   ```
   $ docker-compose down
   ```

2. Then, we modify the `docker-compose.yml` file to look as follows:

   ```
   version: "3.5"
   services:
     web:
       image: fundamentalsofdocker/ch08-web:1.0
       ports:
         - 3000
     db:
   ```

```
image: fundamentalsofdocker/ch08-db:1.0
volumes:
  - pets-data:/var/lib/postgresql/data

volumes:
  pets-data:
```

3. Now, we can start the application again and scale it up immediately after that:

```
$ docker-compose up -d
$ docker-compose scale web=3
Starting ch08_web_1 ... done
Creating ch08_web_2 ... done
Creating ch08_web_3 ... done
```

4. If we now do a docker-compose ps, we should see the following screenshot:

```
$ docker-compose ps
     Name              Command            State            Ports
-----------------------------------------------------------------------------
ch08_db_1      docker-entrypoint.sh postgres   Up      5432/tcp
ch08_web_1     /bin/sh -c node src/server.js   Up      0.0.0.0:32769->3000/tcp
ch08_web_2     /bin/sh -c node src/server.js   Up      0.0.0.0:32771->3000/tcp
ch08_web_3     /bin/sh -c node src/server.js   Up      0.0.0.0:32770->3000/tcp
$
```

Output of docker-compose ps

5. As we can see, each service has been associated to a different host port. We can try to see whether they work, for example, using curl. Let's test the third instance, ch08_web_3:

```
$ curl -4 localhost:32770
Pets Demo Application
```

The answer, Pets Demo Application, tells us that, indeed, our application is still working as expected. Try it out for the other two instances to be sure.

Building and pushing an application

We can also use the `docker-compose build` command to just build the images of an application defined in the underlying `compose` file. But to make this work, we'll have to add the build information to the `docker-compose` file. In the folder, we have a file, `docker-compose.dev.yml`, which has those instructions already added:

```
version: "3.5"
services:
  web:
    build: web
    image: fundamentalsofdocker/ch08-web:1.0
    ports:
      - 3000:3000
  db:
    build: database
    image: fundamentalsofdocker/ch08-db:1.0
    volumes:
      - pets-data:/var/lib/postgresql/data

volumes:
  pets-data:
```

Please note the `build` key for each service. The value of that key indicates the context or folder where Docker is expecting to find the Dockerfile to build the corresponding image.

Let's use that file now:

```
$ docker-compose -f docker-compose.dev.yml build
```

The `-f` parameter will tell the Docker Compose application which compose file to use.

To push all images to Docker Hub, we can use `docker-compose push`. We need to be logged in to Docker Hub so that this succeeds, otherwise we get an authentication error while pushing. Thus, in my case, I do the following:

```
$ docker login -u fundamentalsofdocker -p <password>
```

Assuming the login succeeds, I can then push the following code:

```
$ docker-compose -f docker-compose.dev.yml push
```

The preceding command pushes the two images to the account `fundamentalsofdocker` on Docker Hub. You can find these two images at the URL: `https://hub.docker.com/u/fundamentalsofdocker/`.

Summary

In this chapter, we introduced the tool `docker-compose`. This tool is mostly used to run and scale multi-service applications on a single Docker host. Typically, developers and CI servers work with single hosts and those two are the main users of Docker Compose. The tool is using YAML files as input that contain the description of the application in a declarative way.

The tool can also be used to build and push images among many other helpful tasks. The code accompanying this chapter can be found in `labs/ch08`.

In the next chapter, we are going to introduce orchestrators. An **orchestrator** is an infrastructure software that is used to run and manage containerized applications in a cluster and it makes sure that these applications are in their desired state at all the time.

Questions

To assess your learning progress please answer the following questions:

1. How will you use `docker-compose` to run an application in daemon mode?
2. How will you use `docker-compose` to display the details of the running service?
3. How will you scale up a particular web service to say, three instances?

Further reading

The following links provide additional information on the topics discussed in this chapter:

- *The official YAML website* at http://www.yaml.org/
- *Docker Compose documentation* at http://dockr.ly/1FL2VQ6
- *Compose file version 3 reference* at http://dockr.ly/2iHUpeX

9
Orchestrators

In the previous chapter, we introduced Docker Compose, a tool that allows us to work with multi-service applications that are defined in a declarative way on a single Docker host.

This chapter introduces the concept of orchestrators. It teaches why orchestrators are needed and how they work conceptually. This chapter will also provide an overview of the most popular orchestrators and names a few of their pros and cons.

In this chapter, we will cover the following topics:

- What are orchestrators and why do we need them?
- The tasks of an orchestrator
- Overview of popular orchestrators

After finishing this chapter you will be able to:

- Name three to four tasks an orchestrator is responsible for
- List two to three of the most popular orchestrators
- Explain to an interested layman in your own words and with appropriate analogies why we need container orchestrators

What are orchestrators and why do we need them?

In `Chapter 6`, *Distributed Application Architecture*, we learned which patterns and best practices are commonly used to successfully build, ship, and run a highly distributed application. Now, if our highly distributed application is containerized, then we're facing the exact same problems or challenges that a non-containerized distributed application faces. Some of these challenges are those discussed in `Chapter 6`, *Distributed Application Architecture*, service discovery, load balancing, scaling, and so on.

Similar to what Docker did with containers—standardizing the packaging and shipping of software with the introduction of containers—we would like to have some tool or infrastructure software that handles all or most of the challenges mentioned. This software turns out to be what we call orchestrators or, as we also call them, orchestration engines.

If what I just said doesn't make much sense to you yet, then let's look at it from a different angle. Take an artist who plays an instrument. They can play wonderful music to an audience all on their own, just the artist and their instrument.

But now take an orchestra of musicians. Put them all in a room, give them the notes of a symphony, ask them to play it, and leave the room. Without any director, this group of very talented musicians would not be able to play this piece in harmony; it would more or less sound like a cacophony. Only if the orchestra has a conductor who orchestrates the group of musicians will the resulting music of the orchestra be enjoyable to our ears:

A container orchestrator is like the conductor of an orchestra

Instead of musicians, we now have containers, and instead of different instruments, we have containers that have different requirements to the container hosts to run. And instead of the music being played in varying tempi, we have containers that communicate with each other in particular ways and have to scale up and scale down. In this regard, a container orchestrator has very much the same role as a conductor in an orchestra. It makes sure that the containers and other resources in a cluster play together in harmony.

I hope you can now see more clearly what a container orchestrator is and why we need one. Assuming that you confirm this question, we can now ask ourselves how the orchestrator is going to achieve the expected outcome, namely to make sure all the containers in the cluster play with each other in harmony. Well, the answer is, the orchestrator has to execute very specific tasks, similar to the way in which the conductor of an orchestra also has a set of tasks they execute in order to tame and at the same time elevate the orchestra.

The tasks of an orchestrator

So, what are the tasks that we expect an orchestrator worth its money to execute for us? Let's look at them in detail. The following list shows the most important tasks that, at the time of writing, enterprise users typically expect from their orchestrator.

Reconciling the desired state

When using an orchestrator, one tells it in a declarative way how one wants it to run a given application or application service. We learned what *declarative* versus *imperative* means in `Chapter 8`, *Docker Compose*. Part of this declarative way of describing the application service we want to run is elements such as which container image to use, how many instances to run of this service, which ports to open, and more. This declaration of the properties of our application service is what we call the *desired state*.

So, when we now tell the orchestrator the first time to create such a new application service based on the declaration, then the orchestrator makes sure to schedule as many containers in the cluster as requested. If the container image is not yet available on the target nodes of the cluster where the containers are supposed to run, then the scheduler makes sure they're downloaded from the image registry first. Next, the containers are started with all the settings, such as networks to which to attach, or ports to expose. The orchestrator works as hard as it can to exactly match in reality in the cluster what it got in our declaration.

Once our service is up and running as requested, that is, it is running in the desired state, then the orchestrator continues to monitor it. Each time the orchestrator discovers a discrepancy between the actual state of the service and its desired state, it again tries its best to reconcile the desired state.

What could such a discrepancy between the actual and desired states of an application service be? Well, let's say one of the replicas of the service, that is, one of the containers, crashes due to, say, a bug, then the orchestrator will discover that the actual state differs from the desired state in the number of replicas: there is one replica missing. The orchestrator will immediately schedule a new instance to another cluster node, which replaces the crashed instance. Another discrepancy could be that there are too many instances of the application service running, if the service has been scaled down. In this case, the orchestrator will just randomly kill as many instances as needed to achieve parity between the actual and the desired number of instances. Another discrepancy could be when the orchestrator discovers that there is an instance of the application service running a wrong (maybe old) version of the underlying container image. By now, you should get the picture, right?

Thus, instead of us actively monitoring our application's services running in the cluster and correcting any deviation from the desired state, we delegate this tedious task to the orchestrator. This works very well, if we use a declarative and not an imperative way of describing the desired state of our application services.

Replicated and global services

There are two quite different types of services that we might want to run in a cluster managed by an orchestrator. They are **replicated** and **global** services. A replicated service is a service which is required to run in a specific number of instances, say 10. A global service, in turn, is a service that is required to have an instance running on every single worker node of the cluster. I have used the term *worker node* here. In a cluster managed by an orchestrator, we typically have two types of nodes, **managers** and **workers**. A manager node is usually exclusively used by the orchestrator to manage the cluster and does not run any other workload. Worker nodes, in turn, run the actual applications.

So, the orchestrator makes sure that, for a global service, an instance of it is running on every single worker node, no matter how many there are. We do not need to care about the number of instances, but only that on each node it is guaranteed to run a single instance of the service.

Once again, we can fully rely on the orchestrator to take care of this feat. In a replicated service, we will always be guaranteed to find the exact desired number of instances, while for a global service, we can be assured that on every worker node, there will always run exactly one instance of the service. The orchestrator will always work as hard as it can to guarantee this desired state.

In Kubernetes, a global service is also called a daemon set.

Service discovery

When we describe an application service in a declarative way, we are never supposed to tell the orchestrator on which cluster nodes the different instances of the service have to run. We leave it up to the orchestrator to decide which nodes best fit this task.

It is, of course, technically possible to instruct the orchestrator to use very deterministic placement rules, but this would be an anti-pattern and is not recommended at all.

So, if we now assume that the orchestration engine has complete and free will as to where to place individual instances of the application service and, furthermore, that instances can crash and be rescheduled by the orchestrator to different nodes, then we will realize that it is a futile task for us to keep track of where the individual instances are running at any given time. Even better, we shouldn't even try to know this since it is not important.

OK, you might say, but what about if I have two services, A and B, and Service A relies on Service B; *shouldn't any given instance of Service A know where it can find an instance of Service B?*

There I have to say loudly and clearly—no, it shouldn't. This kind of knowledge is not desirable in a highly distributed and scalable application. Rather, we should rely on the orchestrator to provide us the information we need to reach other service instances we depend on. It is a bit like in the old days of telephony, when we could not directly call our friends but had to call the phone company's central office, where some operator would then route us to the correct destination. In our case, the orchestrator plays the role of the operator, routing a request coming from an instance of Service A to an available instance of Service B. This whole process is called **service discovery**.

Routing

We have learned so far that in a distributed application, we have many interacting services. When Service A interacts with Service B, it happens through the exchange of data packets. These data packets need to somehow be funneled from Service A to Service B. This process of funneling the data packets from a source to a destination is also called **routing**. As authors or operators of an application, we do expect the orchestrator to take over this task of routing. As we will see in later chapters, routing can happen on different levels. It is like in real life. Suppose you're working in a big company in one of their office buildings. Now, you have a document that needs to be forwarded to another employee of the company. The internal post service will pick up the document from your outbox and take it to the post office located in the same building. If the target person works in the same building, the document can then be directly forwarded to that person. If, on the other hand, the person works in another building of the same block, the document will be forwarded to the post office in that target building, from where it is then distributed to the receiver through the internal post service. Thirdly, if the document is targeted at an employee working in another branch of the company located in a different city or even country, then the document is forwarded to an external postal service such as UPS, which will transport it to the target location, from where, once again, the internal post service takes over and delivers it to the recipient.

Similar things happen when routing data packets between application services running in containers. The source and target containers can be located on the same cluster node, which corresponds to the situation where both employees work in the same building. The target container can be running on a different cluster node, which corresponds to the situation where the two employees work in different buildings of the same block. Finally, the third situation is when a data packet comes from outside of the cluster and has to be routed to the target container running inside the cluster.

All these situations and more have to be handled by the orchestrator.

Load balancing

In a highly available distributed application, all components have to be redundant. That means that every application service has to be run in multiple instances so that if one instance fails, the service as a whole is still operational.

To make sure that all instances of a service are actually doing work and not just sitting around idle, one has to make sure that the requests for service are distributed equally to all the instances. This process of distributing workload among service instances is called **load balancing**. Various algorithms exist for how the workload can be distributed. Usually, a load balancer works using the so-called round robin algorithm, which makes sure that the workload is distributed equally to the instances using a cyclic algorithm.

Once again, we expect the orchestrator to take care of load balancing requests from one service to another or from external sources to internal services.

Scaling

When running our containerized, distributed application in a cluster managed by an orchestrator, we also want an easy way to handle expected or unexpected increases in workload. To handle an increased workload, we usually just schedule additional instances of a service that is experiencing this increased load. Load balancers will then automatically be configured to distribute the workload over more available target instances.

But in real-life scenarios, the workload varies over time. If we look at a shopping site such as Amazon, it might have a high load during peak hours in the evening, when everyone is at home and shopping online; it may experience extreme loads during special days such as Black Friday; and it may experience very little traffic early in the morning. Thus, services need to not just be able to scale up, but also to scale down when the workload goes down.

We also expect orchestrators to distribute the instances of a service in a meaningful way when scaling up or down. It would not be wise to schedule all instances of the service on the same cluster node, since if that node goes down, the whole service goes down. The scheduler of the orchestrator, which is responsible for the placement of the containers, needs to also consider not placing all instances into the same rack of computers, since if the power supply of the rack fails, again the whole service is affected. Furthermore, service instances of critical services should even be distributed across data centers to avoid outages. All these decisions and many more are the responsibility of the orchestrator.

Self-healing

These days, orchestrators are very sophisticated and can do a lot for us to maintain a healthy system. Orchestrators monitor all containers running in the cluster and they automatically replace crashed or unresponsive ones with new instances. Orchestrators monitor the health of cluster nodes and take them out of the scheduler loop if a node becomes unhealthy or is down. A workload that was located on those nodes is automatically rescheduled to different available nodes.

All these activities where the orchestrator monitors the current state and automatically repairs the damage or reconciles the desired state lead to a so-called **self-healing** system. We do not, in most cases, have to actively engage and repair damage. The orchestrator will do this for us automatically.

But there are a few situations that the orchestrator cannot handle without our help. Imagine a situation where we have a service instance running in a container. The container is up and running and, from the outside, looks perfectly healthy. But the application inside is in an unhealthy state. The application did not crash, it just is not able to work as designed anymore. *How could the orchestrator possibly know about this without us giving it a hint?* It can't! Being in an unhealthy or invalid state means something completely different for each application service. In other words, the health status is service dependent. Only the authors of the service or its operators know what health means in the context of a service.

Now, orchestrators define seams or probes, over which an application service can communicate to the orchestrator in what state it is. Two fundamental types of probe exist:

- The service can tell the orchestrator that it is healthy or not
- The service can tell the orchestrator that it is ready or temporarily unavailable

How the service determines either of the preceding answers is totally up to the service. The orchestrator only defines how it is going to ask, for example, through an HTTP GET request, or what type of answers it is expecting, for example, OK or NOT OK.

If our services implement logic to answer the preceding health or availability questions, then we have a truly self-healing system, since the orchestrator can kill unhealthy service instances and replace them with new healthy ones, and it can take service instances that are temporarily unavailable out of the load balancer's round robin.

Zero downtime deployments

These days, it gets harder and harder to justify a complete downtime for a mission-critical application that needs to be updated. Not only does that mean missed opportunities, but it can also result in a damaged reputation for the company. Customers using the application are just not ready to accept such an inconvenience anymore and will turn away quickly. Furthermore, our release cycles get shorter and shorter. Where, in the past, we would have one or two new releases per year, these days, a lot of companies update their applications multiple times a week or even multiple times per day.

The solution to that problem is to come up with a zero downtime application update strategy. The orchestrator needs to be able to update individual application services batch-wise. This is also called **rolling updates**. At any given time, only one or a few of the total number of instances of a given service are taken down and replaced by the new version of the service. Only if the new instances are operational and do not produce any unexpected errors or show any misbehavior will the next batch of instances be updated. This is repeated until all instances are replaced with their new version. If, for some reason, the update fails, we expect the orchestrator to automatically roll the updated instances back to their previous version.

Other possible zero downtime deployments are so-called canary releases and blue-green deployments. In both cases, the new version of a service is installed in parallel with the current, active version. But initially, the new version is only accessible internally. Operations can then run smoke tests against the new version and when the new version seems to be running just fine, then, in the case of blue-green deployment, the router is switched from the current blue to the new green version. For some time, the new green version of the service is closely monitored and, if everything is fine, the old blue version can be decommissioned. If, on the other hand, the new green version does not work as expected, then it is only a matter of setting the router back to the old blue version to achieve a complete rollback.

In the case of a canary release, the router is configured in such a way that it funnels a tiny percentage, say 1%, of the overall traffic through the new version of the service, while 99% of the traffic is still routed through the old version. The behavior of the new version is closely monitored and compared to the behavior of the old version. If everything looks good, then the percentage of the traffic funneled through the new service is slightly increased. This process is repeated until 100% of the traffic is routed through the new service. If the new service has run for a while and everything looks good, then the old service can be decommissioned.

Most orchestrators support at least the rolling update type of zero downtime deployment out of the box. Blue-green and canary releases are often quite easy to implement.

Affinity and location awareness

Sometimes, certain application services require the availability of dedicated hardware on the nodes they run on. For example I/O-bound services require cluster nodes with an attached high-performance **solid-state drive (SSD)**, or some services require an **Accelerated Processing Unit (APU)**. Orchestrators allow us to define node affinities per application service. The orchestrator will then make sure that its scheduler only schedules containers on cluster nodes that fulfill the required criteria.

Defining an affinity to a particular node should be avoided; this would introduce a single point of failure and thus compromise high availability. Always define a set of multiple cluster nodes as the target for an application service.

Some orchestration engines also support what is called **location awareness** or **geo-awareness**. What this means is that one can request the orchestrator to equally distribute instances of a service over a set of different locations. One could, for example, define a label `datacenter` with the possible values `west`, `center`, and `east` and apply the label to all cluster nodes with the value that corresponds to the geographical region in which the respective node is located. Then, one instructs the orchestrator to use this label for geo-awareness of a certain application service. In this case, if one requests nine replicas of the service, the orchestrator would make sure that three instances are deployed to nodes in each of the three data centers, west, center, and east.

Geo-awareness can even be defined hierarchically; for example, one can have a data center as the top-level discriminator, followed by the availability zone and then the server rack.

Geo-awareness or location awareness is used to decrease the probability of outages due to power supply failures or data center outages. If the application instances are distributed across server racks, availability zones, or even data centers, it is extremely unlikely that everything goes down at once. One region will always be available.

Security

These days, security in IT is a very hot topic. Cyberwarfare is at an all-time high. Most high-profile companies have been victims of hacker attacks, with very costly consequences. One of the worst nightmares of each **chief information officer** (**CIO**) or **chief technology officer** (**CTO**) is to wake up in the morning and hear in the news that their company has become a victim of a hacker attack and that sensitive information has been stolen or compromised.

To counter most of these security threats, we need to establish a secure software supply chain and enforce security defense in depth. Let's look at some of the tasks one can expect from an enterprise-grade orchestrator.

Secure communication and cryptographic node identity

First and foremost, we want to make sure that our cluster managed by the orchestrator is secure. Only trusted nodes can join the cluster. Each node that joins the cluster gets a cryptographic node identity, and all communication between the nodes must be encrypted. For this, nodes can use **mutual transport layer security** (**MTLS**). To authenticate nodes of the cluster with each other, certificates are used. These certificates are automatically rotated periodically or on request to protect the system in case a certificate is leaked.

The communication that happens in a cluster can be separated into three types. One talks about communication planes. There are **management**, **control**, and **data** planes:

- The management plane is used by the cluster managers or masters to, for example, schedule service instances, execute health checks, or create and modify any other resources in the cluster, such as data volumes, secrets, or networks.
- The control plane is used to exchange important state information between all nodes of the cluster. This kind of information is, for example, used to update the local IP tables on clusters which are used for routing purposes.
- The data plane is where the application services communicate with each other and exchange data.

Normally, orchestrators mainly care about securing the management and control plane. Securing the data plane is left to the user, yet the orchestrator may facilitate this task.

Secure networks and network policies

When running application services, not every service needs to communicate with every other service in the cluster. Thus, we want the ability to sandbox services from each other and only run those services in the same networking sandbox that absolutely need to communicate with each other. All other services and all network traffic coming from outside of the cluster should have no possibility of accessing the sandboxed services.

There are at least two ways in which this network-based sandboxing can happen. We can either use a **software-defined network** (**SDN**) to group application services or we can have one flat network and use network policies to control who does and does not have access to a particular service or group of services.

Role-based access control (RBAC)

One of the most important tasks, next to security, an orchestrator must fulfill to make it enterprise ready is to provide role-based access to the cluster and its resources. RBAC defines how subjects, users, or groups of users of the system, organized into teams and so on, can access and manipulate the system. It makes sure that unauthorized personnel cannot do any harm to the system nor see any resources available in the system they're not supposed to know of or see.

A typical enterprise might have user groups such as Development, QA, and Prod, and each of those groups can have one to many users associated with it. John Doe, the developer, is a member of the Development group and, as such, can access resources dedicated to the development team, but he cannot access, for example, the resources of the Prod team, of which Ann Harbor is a member. She, in turn, cannot interfere with the Development team's resources.

One way of implementing RBAC is through the definition of **grants**. A grant is an association between a subject, a role, and a resource collection. Here, a role is comprised of a set of access permissions to a resource. Such permissions can be to create, stop, remove, list, or view containers; to deploy a new application service; to list cluster nodes or view the details of a cluster node; and many more.

A resource collection is a group of logically related resources of the cluster, such as application services, secrets, data volumes, or containers.

Secrets

In our daily life, we have loads of secrets. Secrets are information that is not meant to be publicly known, such as the username and password combination you use to access your online bank account, or the code to your cell phone or your locker at the gym.

When writing software, we often need to use secrets, too. For example, we need some certificate to authenticate our application service with some external service we want to access, or we need a token to authenticate and authorize our service when accessing some other API. In the past, developers, for convenience, have just hardcoded those values or put them in clear text in some external configuration files. There, this very sensitive information has been accessible to a broad audience that in reality should never have had the opportunity to see those secrets.

Luckily, these days, orchestrators offer what's called secrets to deal with such sensitive information in a highly secure way. Secrets can be created by authorized or trusted personnel. The values of those secrets are then encrypted and stored in the highly available cluster state database. The secrets, since they are encrypted, are now secure at rest. Once a secret is requested by an authorized application service, the secret is only forwarded to the cluster nodes that actually run an instance of that particular service, and the secret value is never stored on the node but mounted into the container in a `tmpfs` RAM-based volume. Only inside the respective container is the secret value available in clear text.

We already mentioned that the secrets are secure at rest. Once they are requested by a service, the cluster manager or master decrypts the secret and sends it over the wire to the target nodes. *So, what about the secrets being secure in transit?* Well, we learned earlier that the cluster nodes use MTLS for their communication, thus the secret, although transmitted in clear text, is still secure since data packets will be encrypted by MTLS. Thus, secrets are secure at rest and in transit. Only services that are authorized to use secrets will ever have access to those secret values.

Content trust

For added security, we want to make sure that only trusted images run in our production cluster. Some orchestrators allow us to configure a cluster so that it can only ever run signed images. Content trust and signing images is all about making sure that the authors of the image are the ones that we expect them to be, namely our trusted developers or, even better, our trusted CI server. Furthermore, with content trust, we want to guarantee that the image we get is fresh and not an old and maybe vulnerable image. And finally, we want to make sure that the image cannot be compromised by malicious hackers in transit. The latter is often called a **man-in-the-middle** (**MITM**) attack.

By signing images at the source and validating the signature at the target, we can guarantee that the images we want to run are not compromised.

Reverse uptime

The last point I want to discuss in the context of security is reverse uptime. *What do we mean by that?* Imagine that you have configured and secured a production cluster. On this cluster, you're running a few mission-critical applications of your company. Now, a hacker has managed to find a security hole in one your software stacks and has gained root access to one of your cluster nodes. That alone is already bad enough but, even worse, this hacker could now mask their presence on this node they are root on the machine, after all, and then use it as a base to attack further nodes of your cluster.

Root access in Linux or any Unix-type operating system means that one can do anything on this system. It is the highest level of access that someone can have. In Windows, the equivalent role is that of an Administrator.

But *what if we leverage the fact that containers are ephemeral and cluster nodes are quickly provisioned, usually in a matter of minutes if fully automated?* We just kill each cluster node after a certain uptime of, say, 1 day. The orchestrator is instructed to drain the node and then exclude it from the cluster. Once the node is out of the cluster, it is torn down and replaced by a freshly provisioned node.

That way, the hacker has lost their base and the problem has been eliminated. This concept is not yet broadly available, though, but to me it seems to be a huge step towards increased security and, as far as I have discussed it with engineers working in this area, it is not difficult to implement.

Introspection

So far, we have discussed a lot of tasks that the orchestrator is responsible for and that it can execute in a completely autonomous way. But there is also the need for human operators to be able to see and analyze what's currently running on the cluster and in what state or health the individual applications are. For all this, we need the possibility of introspection. The orchestrator needs to surface crucial information in a way that is easily consumable and understandable.

The orchestrator should collect system metrics from all the cluster nodes and make it accessible to the operators. Metrics include CPU, memory and disk usage, network bandwidth consumption, and more. The information should be easily available on a node-per-node basis, as well in an aggregated form.

We also want the orchestrator to give us access to logs produced by service instances or containers. Even more, the orchestrator should provide us `exec` access to each and every container if we have the correct authorization to do so. With `exec` access to containers, one can then debug misbehaving containers.

In highly distributed applications, where each request to the application goes through numerous services until it is completely handled, tracing requests is really important task. Ideally, the orchestrator supports us in implementing a tracing strategy or gives us some good guidelines to follow.

Finally, human operators can best monitor a system when working with a graphical representation of all the collected metrics and logging and tracing information. Here, we are speaking about dashboards. Every decent orchestrator should offer at least some basic dashboard with a graphical representation of the most critical system parameters.

But human operators are not all that concerned about introspection. We also need to be able to connect external systems with the orchestrator to consume this information. There needs to be an API available, over which external systems can access data such as cluster state, metrics, and logs and use this information to make automated decisions, such as creating pager or phone alerts, sending out emails, or triggering an alarm siren if some thresholds are exceeded by the system.

Overview of popular orchestrators

At the time of writing, there are many orchestration engines out there and in use. But there are a few clear winners. The number one spot is clearly held by Kubernetes, which reigns supreme. A distant second is Docker's own SwarmKit, followed by others such as Apache Mesos, AWS **Elastic Container Service** (**ECS**), or Microsoft **Azure Container Service** (**ACS**).

Kubernetes

Kubernetes was originally designed by Google and later donated to the **Cloud Native Computing Foundation** (**CNCF**). Kubernetes was modeled after Google's proprietary Borg system, which has been running containers on supermassive scale for years. Kubernetes was Google's attempt to go back to the drawing board and completely start over and design a system that incorporates all the lessons learned with Borg.

Contrary to Borg, which is proprietary technology, Kubernetes was open sourced early on. This was a very wise choice by Google, since it attracted a huge number of contributors from outside of the company and, over only a couple of years, an even more massive ecosystem evolved around Kubernetes. One can rightfully say that Kubernetes is the darling of the community in the container orchestration space. No other orchestrator has been able to produce so much hype and attract so many talented people willing to contribute in a meaningful way to the success of the project as a contributor or an early adopter.

In that regard, Kubernetes in the container orchestration space to me looks very much like what Linux has become in the server operating system space. Linux has become the de facto standard of server operating systems. All relevant companies, such as Microsoft, IBM, Amazon, RedHat, and even Docker, have embraced Kubernetes.

And there is one thing that cannot be denied: Kubernetes was designed from the very beginning for massive scalability. After all, it was designed with Google Borg in mind.

One negative aspect that one could voice against Kubernetes is that it is complex to set up and manage, at least at the time of writing. There is a significant hurdle to overcome for newcomers. The first step is steep. But once one has worked with this orchestrator for a while, it all makes sense. The overall design is carefully thought through and executed very well.

In the newest release of Kubernetes, 1.10, whose **general availability** (**GA**) was in March 2018, most of the initial shortcomings compared to other orchestrators such as Docker Swarm have been eliminated. For example, security and confidentiality is now not only an afterthought, but an integral part of the system.

New features are implemented at a tremendous speed. New releases are happening every 3 months or so, more precisely, about every 100 days. Most of the new features are demand-driven, that is, companies using Kubernetes to orchestrate their mission-critical applications can voice their needs. This makes Kubernetes enterprise ready. It would be wrong to assume that this orchestrator is only for start-ups and not for risk-averse enterprises. The contrary is the case. *On what do I base this claim?* Well, my claim is justified by the fact that companies such as Microsoft, Docker, and RedHat, whose clients are mostly big enterprises, have fully embraced Kubernetes and provide enterprise-grade support for it if it is used and integrated into their enterprise offerings.

Kubernetes supports both Linux and Windows containers.

Docker Swarm

It is well-known that Docker popularized and commoditized software containers. Docker did not invent containers, but standardized them and made them broadly available, not least by offering the free image registry Docker Hub. Initially, Docker focused mainly on the developer and the development life cycle. But companies that started to use and love containers soon also wanted to use containers, not just during development or testing of new applications, but also to run those applications in production.

Initially, Docker had nothing to offer in that space, so other companies jumped into that vacuum and offered help to the users. But it didn't take long and Docker recognized that there was a huge demand for a simple yet powerful orchestrator. Docker's first attempt was a product called classic Swarm. It was a standalone product that enabled users to create a cluster of Docker host machines that could be used to run and scale their containerized applications in a highly available and self-healing way.

The setup of a classic Docker Swarm, though, was hard. A lot of complicated manual steps were involved. Customers loved the product but struggled with its complexity. So Docker decided it could do better. It went back to the drawing board and came up with SwarmKit. SwarmKit was introduced at DockerCon 2016 in Seattle and was an integral part of the newest version of the Docker engine. Yes, you got that right, SwarmKit was and still is to this day an integral part of the Docker engine. Thus, if you install a Docker host, you automatically have SwarmKit available with it.

SwarmKit was designed with simplicity and security in mind. The mantra was and still is that it has to be almost trivial to set up a swarm, and the swarm has to be highly secure out of the box. Docker Swarm operates on the assumption of least privilege.

Installing a complete, highly available Docker Swarm is literally as simple as starting with a `docker swarm init` on the first node in the cluster, which becomes the so-called leader, and then a `docker swarm join <join-token>` on all other nodes. The `join-token` is generated by the leader during initialization. The whole process takes less that 5 minutes on a Swarm with up to 10 nodes. If it is automated, it takes even less time.

As I already mentioned, security was top on the list of must-haves when Docker designed and developed SwarmKit. Containers provide security by relying on Linux kernel namespaces and cgroups as well as Linux syscall whitelisting (seccomp) and the support of Linux capabilities and the **Linux security module** (**LSM**). Now, on top of that, SwarmKit adds MTLS and secrets that are encrypted at rest and in transit. Furthermore, Swarm defines the so-called **container network model** (**CNM**), which allows for SDNs that provide sandboxing for application services running on the swarm.

Docker SwarmKit supports both Linux and Windows containers.

Apache Mesos and Marathon

Apache **Mesos** is an open source project and was originally designed to make a cluster of servers or nodes look like one single big server from the outside. Mesos is software that makes the management of computer clusters simple. Users of Mesos should not have to care about individual servers, but just assume they have a gigantic pool of resources to their disposal, which corresponds to the aggregate of all the resources of all the nodes in the cluster.

Mesos, in IT terms, is already pretty old, at least compared to the other orchestrators. It was first publicly presented in 2009. But at that time, of course, it wasn't designed to run containers since Docker didn't even exist yet. Similar to what Docker does with containers, Mesos uses Linux cgroups to isolate resources such as CPU, memory, or disk I/O for individual applications or services.

Mesos is really the underlying infrastructure for other interesting services built on top of it. From the perspective of containers specifically, **Marathon** is important. Marathon is a container orchestrator running on top of Mesos which is able to scale to thousands of nodes.

Marathon supports multiple container runtimes, such as Docker or its own Mesos containers. It supports not only stateless but also stateful application services, for example, databases such as PostgreSQL or MongoDB. Similar to Kubernetes and Docker SwarmKit, it supports many of the features described earlier in this chapter, such as high availability, health checks, service discovery, load balancing, and location awareness, to just name some of the most important ones.

Although Mesos and, to a certain extent, Marathon are rather mature projects, their reach is relatively limited. It seems to be most popular in the area of big data, that is, to run data crunching services such as Spark or Hadoop.

Amazon ECS

If you are looking for a simple orchestrator and have already heavily bought into the AWS ecosystem, then Amazon's ECS might be the right choice for you. It is important to point out one very important limitation of ECS: if you buy into this container orchestrator, then you lock yourself into AWS. You will not be able to easily port an application running on ECS to another platform or cloud.

Amazon promotes its ECS service as a highly scalable, fast container management service that makes it easy to run, stop, and manage Docker containers on a cluster. Next to running containers, ECS gives direct access to many other AWS services from the application services running inside the containers. This tight and seamless integration with many popular AWS services is what makes ECS compelling for users who are looking for an easy way to get their containerized applications up and running in a robust and highly scalable environment. Amazon also provides its own private image registry.

With AWS ECS, you can use Fargate to have it fully manage the underlying infrastructure so that you can concentrate exclusively on deploying containerized applications and do not have to care about how to create and manage a cluster of nodes. ECS supports both Linux and Windows containers.

In summary, ECS is simple to use, highly scalable, and well-integrated with other popular AWS services, but it is not as powerful as, say, Kubernetes or Docker SwarmKit and it is only available on Amazon AWS.

Microsoft ACS

Similar to what we said about ECS, we can claim the same for Microsoft's ACS. It is a simple container orchestration service that makes sense if you are already heavily invested in the Azure ecosystem. I should say the same as I have pointed out for Amazon ECS: if you buy into ACS, then you lock yourself in to the offerings of Microsoft. It will not be easy to move your containerized applications from ACS to any other platform or cloud.

ACS is Microsoft's container service, which supports multiple orchestrators such as Kubernetes, Docker Swarm, and Mesos DC/OS. With Kubernetes becoming more and more popular, the focus of Microsoft has clearly shifted to that orchestrator. Microsoft has even rebranded its service and called it **Azure Kubernetes Service** (**AKS**) to put the focus on Kubernetes.

AKS manages, for you, a hosted Kubernetes or Docker Swarm or DC/OS environment in Azure, so you can concentrate on the applications you want to deploy and don't have to care about configuring infrastructure. Microsoft, in its own words, claims the following:

> *AKS makes it quick and easy to deploy and manage containerized applications without container orchestration expertise. It also eliminates the burden of ongoing operations and maintenance by provisioning, upgrading, and scaling resources on demand, without taking your applications offline.*

Summary

This chapter demonstrated why orchestrators are needed in the first place and how they conceptually work. It pointed out which orchestrators are the most prominent ones at the time of writing and discussed the main commonalities and differences between the various orchestrators.

The next chapter will introduce Docker's native orchestrator, called SwarmKit. It will elaborate on all the concepts and objects SwarmKit uses to deploy and run a distributed, resilient, robust, and highly available application in a cluster on-premises or in the cloud.

Questions

Answer the following questions to assess your learning progress:

1. Why do we need an orchestrator? Name two to three reasons.
2. Name three to four typical responsibilities of an orchestrator.
3. Name at least two container orchestrators, as well as the main sponsor behind them.

Further reading

The following links provide some deeper insight to orchestration-related topics:

- *Kubernetes - production-grade orchestration at* https://kubernetes.io/
- *Docker Swarm Mode overview at* https://docs.docker.com/engine/swarm/
- *Mesosphere - container orchestration services at* http://bit.ly/2GMpko3
- *Containers and orchestration explained at* http://bit.ly/2DFoQgx

Introduction to Docker Swarm

10

In the last chapter, we introduced orchestrators. Like a conductor in an orchestra, an orchestrator makes sure that all our containerized application services play together nicely and contribute harmoniously to a common goal. Such orchestrators have quite a few responsibilities, which we have discussed in detail. Finally, we have provided a short overview of the most important container orchestrators on the market.

This chapter introduces Docker's native orchestrator, **SwarmKit**. It elaborates on all the concepts and objects SwarmKit uses to deploy and run a distributed, resilient, robust, and highly available application in a cluster on-premise or in the cloud. The chapter also introduces how SwarmKit ensures secure applications by using a **software defined network (SDN)** to isolate containers. Additionally, this chapter demonstrates how to install a highly available Docker Swarm in the cloud. It introduces the routing mesh which provides layer-4 routing and load balancing. Finally, it demonstrates how to deploy a first application consisting of multiple services onto the swarm.

These are the topics we are going to discuss in this chapter:

- Architecture
- Swarm nodes
- Stacks, services, and tasks
- Multi-host networking
- Creating a Docker Swarm
- Deploying a first application
- The swarm routing mesh

After completing this chapter, you will be able to:

- Sketch the essential parts of a highly available Docker Swarm on a whiteboard
- Explain in two or three simple sentences to an interested layman what a (swarm) service is
- Create a highly available Docker Swarm in AWS consisting of three manager and two worker nodes
- Successfully deploy a replicated service such as Nginx on a Docker Swarm
- Scale up and down a running Docker Swarm service
- Retrieve the aggregated log of a replicated Docker Swarm service
- Write a simple stack file for a sample application consisting of at least two interacting services
- Deploy a stack into a Docker Swarm

Architecture

The architecture of a Docker Swarm from a 30,000-foot view consists of two main parts—a raft consensus group of an odd number of manager nodes, and a group of worker nodes that communicate with each other over a gossip network, also called the **control plane**. The following figure illustrates this architecture:

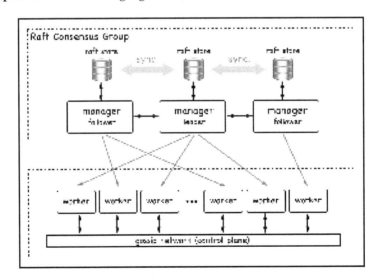

High-level architecture of a Docker Swarm

The manager nodes manage the swarm whilst the worker nodes execute the applications deployed into the swarm. Each manager has a complete copy of the full state of the swarm in its local raft store. Managers communicate with each other in a synchronous way and the raft stores are always in sync.

The workers, on the other hand, communicate with each other asynchronously for scalability reasons. There can be hundreds if not thousands of worker nodes in a swarm. Now that we have a high-level overview of what a Docker Swarm is, let's describe all the individual elements of a Docker Swarm in more detail.

Swarm nodes

A swarm is a collection of nodes. We can classify a node as a physical computer or **virtual machine** (**VM**). Physical computers these days are often referred to as *bare metal*. People say *we're running on bare metal* to distinguish from running on a VM.

When we install Docker on such a node, we call this node a **Docker host**. The following figure illustrates a bit better what a node and what a Docker host is:

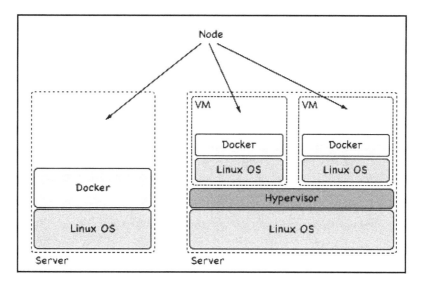

Bare metal and VM type Docker Swarm nodes

To become a member of a Docker Swarm, a node must also be a Docker host. A node in a Docker Swarm can have one of two roles. It can be a manager or it can be a worker. Manager nodes do what their name implies; they manage the swarm. The worker nodes in turn execute application workload.

Technically, a manager node can also be a worker node and thus run application workload, although that is not recommended, especially if the swarm is a production system running mission critical applications.

Swarm managers

Each Docker Swarm needs to have at least one manager node. For high availability reasons we should have more than one manager node in a swarm. This is especially true for production or production-like environments. If we have more than one manager node then these nodes work together using the **Raft consensus protocol**. The Raft consensus protocol is a standard protocol that is often used when multiple entities need to work together and always need to agree with each other as to which activity to execute next.

To work well, the Raft consensus protocol asks for an odd number of members in what is called the **consensus group**. Thus we should always have 1, 3, 5, 7, and so on manager nodes. In such a consensus group there is always a leader. In the case of Docker Swarm, the first node that starts the swarm initially becomes the leader. If the leader goes away then the remaining manager nodes elect a new leader. The other nodes in the consensus group are called **followers**.

Now let's assume that we shut down the current leader node for maintenance reasons. The remaining manager nodes will elect a new leader. When the previous leader node comes back online he will now become a follower. The new leader remains the leader.

All the members of the consensus group communicate in a synchronous way with each other. Whenever the consensus group needs to make a decision, the leader asks all followers for agreement. If a majority of the manager nodes give a positive answer then the leader executes the task. That means if we have three manager nodes then at least one of the followers has to agree with the leader. If we have five manager nodes then at least two followers have to agree.

Since all manager follower nodes have to communicate synchronously with the leader node to make a decision in the cluster, the decision-making process gets slower and slower the more manager nodes we have forming the consensus group. The recommendation of Docker is to use one manager for development, demo, or test environments. Use three manager nodes in small to medium size swarms, and use five managers in large to extra large swarms. To use more than five managers in a swarm is hardly ever justified.

Manager nodes are not only responsible for managing the swarm but also for maintaining the state of the swarm. *What do we mean by that?* When we talk about the state of the swarm we mean all the information about it—for example, *how many nodes are in the swarm, what are the properties of each node, such as name or IP address.* We also mean what containers are running on which node in the swarm and more. What, on the other hand, is not included in the state of the swarm is data produced by the application services running in containers on the swarm. This is called application data and is definitely not part of the state that is managed by the manager nodes:

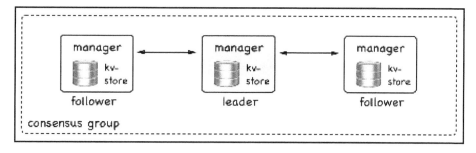

A swarm manager consensus group

All the swarm state is stored in a high performance key-value store (**kv-store**) on each manager node. That's right, each manager node stores a complete replica of the whole swarm state. This redundancy makes the swarm highly available. If a manager node goes down, the remaining managers all have the complete state at hand.

If a new manager joins the consensus group then it synchronizes the swarm state with the existing members of the group until it has a complete replica. This replication is usually pretty fast in typical swarms but can take a while if the swarm is big and many applications are running on it.

Swarm workers

As we mentioned earlier, a swarm worker node is meant to host and run containers that contain the actual application services we're interested in running on our cluster. They are the workhorses of the swarm. In theory, a manager node can also be a worker. But, as we already said, this is not recommended on a production system. On a production system we should let managers be managers.

Worker nodes communicate with each other over the so-called control plane. They use the gossip protocol for their communication. This communication is asynchronous, which means that at any given time not all worker nodes must be in perfect sync.

Now you might ask—*what information do worker nodes exchange?* It is mostly information that is needed for service discovery and routing, that is, information about which containers are running on with nodes and more:

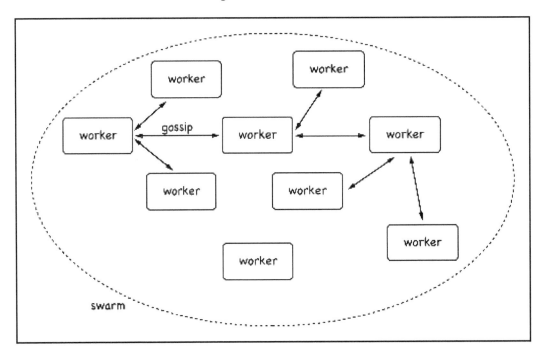

Worker nodes communicating with each other

In the preceding figure, you can see how workers communicate with each other. To make sure the gossiping scales well in a large swarm, each worker node only synchronizes its own state with three random neighbors. For those who are familiar with the Big-O notation, that means that the synchronization of the worker nodes using the gossip protocol scales with O(0).

Worker nodes are kind of passive. They never actively do something other than run the workloads that they get assigned by the manager nodes. The worker makes sure, though, that it runs these workloads to the best of its capabilities. Further down in this chapter we will get to know more about exactly what workloads the worker nodes are assigned by the manager nodes.

Stacks, services, and tasks

When using a Docker Swarm versus a single Docker host, there is a paradigm change. Instead of talking of individual containers that run processes, we are abstracting away to services that represent a set of replicas of each process, and like through become highly available. We also do not speak anymore of individual Docker hosts with well known names and IP addresses to which we deploy containers; we'll now be referring to clusters of hosts to which we deploy services. We don't care about an individual host or node anymore. We don't give it a meaningful name; each node rather becomes a number to us. We also don't care about individual containers and where they are deployed anymore—we just care about having a desired state defined through a service. We can try to depict that as shown in the following figure:

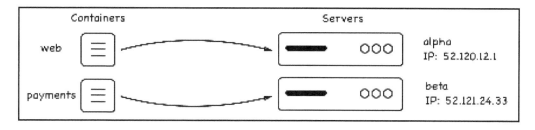

Containers are deployed to well known servers

Instead of deploying individual containers to well known servers like the preceding one, where we deploy container **web** to server **alpha** with IP address 52.120.12.1, and container **payments** to server **beta** with IP 52.121.24.33, we switch to this new paradigm of services and swarms (or, more generally, clusters):

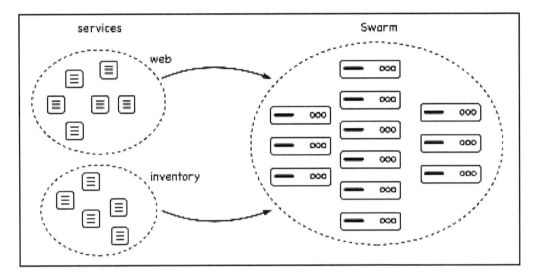

Services are deployed to swarms

In the preceding figure, we see that a service **web** and a service **inventory** are both deployed to a swarm that consists of many nodes. Each of the services has a certain number of replicas; six for web and five for inventory. We don't really care on which node the replicas will run, we only care that the requested number of replicas is always running on whatever nodes the swarm scheduler decides to put them on.

Services

A swarm service is an abstract thing. It is a description of the desired state of an application or application service that we want to run in a swarm. The swarm service is like a manifest describing such things as the:

- Name of the service
- Image from which to create the containers
- Number of replicas to run
- Network(s) that the containers of the service are attached to
- Ports that should be mapped

Having this service manifest the swarm manager, then, makes sure that the described desired state is always reconciled if ever the actual state should deviate from it. So, if for example one instance of the service crashes, then the scheduler on the swarm manager schedules a new instance of the service on a node with free resources so that the desired state is reestablished.

Task

We have learned that a service corresponds to a description of the desired state in which an application service should be at all times. Part of that description was the number of replicas the service should be running. Each replica is represented by a task. In this regard, a swarm service contains a collection of tasks. On Docker Swarm, a task is the atomic unit of deployment. Each task of a service is deployed by the swarm scheduler to a worker node. The task contains all the necessary information that the worker node needs to run a container based off the image, which is part of the service description. Between a task and a container there is a one-to-one relation. The container is the instance that runs on the worker node, while the task is the description of this container as a part of a swarm service.

Stack

Now that we have a good idea about what a swarm service is and what tasks are, we can introduce the stack. A stack is used to describe a collection of swarm services that are related, most probably because they are part of the same application. In that sense, we could also say that a stack describes an application that consists of one to many services that we want to run on the swarm.

Typically, we describe a stack declaratively in a text file that is formatted using YAML and that uses the same syntax as the already-known Docker compose file. This leads to the situation where people sometimes say that a stack is described by a `docker-compose` file. A better wording would be—a stack is described in a stack file that uses similar syntax to a `docker-compose` file.

Let's try to illustrate the relationship between stack, services, and tasks in the following figure and connect it with the typical content of a stack file:

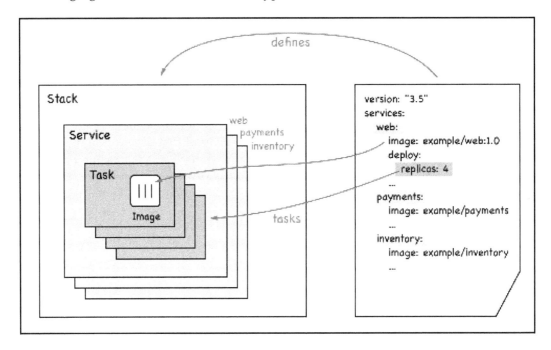

Diagram showing the relationship between stack, services and tasks

In the preceding figure, we see on the right-hand side a declarative description of a sample stack. The stack consists of three services called **web**, **payments**, and **inventory**. We also see that the service **web** uses the image **example/web:1.0** and has four replicas.

On the left-hand side of the figure, we see that the stack embraces the three services mentioned. Each service in turn contains a collection of tasks, as many as there are replicas. In the case of the service **web** we have a collection of four tasks. Each task contains the name of the image from which it will instantiate a container once the task is scheduled on a swarm node.

Multi-host networking

In Chapter 7, *Single-Host Networking*, we discussed how containers communicate on a single Docker host. Now, we have a swarm that consists of a cluster of nodes or Docker hosts. Containers that are located on different nodes need to be able to communicate with each other. There are many techniques that can help one achieve this goal. Docker has chosen to implement an overlay network driver for Docker Swarm. This overlay network allows containers attached to the same **overlay network** to discover each other and freely communicate with each other. The following is a schema for how an overlay network works:

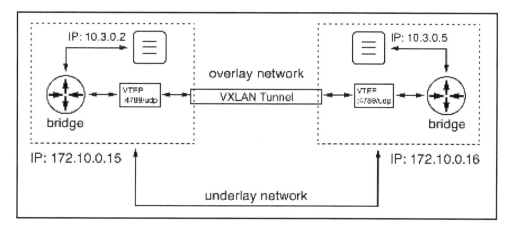

Overlay network

We have two nodes or Docker hosts with the IP addresses 172.10.0.15 and 172.10.0.16. The values we have chosen for the IP addresses are not important; what is important is that both hosts have a distinct IP address and are connected by a physical network (a network cable), which is called the underlay network.

On the node on the left-hand side we have a container running with the IP address 10.3.0.2 and on the node on the right-hand side another container with the IP address 10.3.0.5. Now, the former container wants to communicate with the latter. *How can this happen?* In Chapter 7, *Single-Host Networking*, we saw how this works when both containers are located on the same node; by using a Linux bridge. But Linux bridges only operate locally and cannot span across nodes. So, we need another mechanism. Linux VXLAN comes to the rescue. VXLAN has been available on Linux since way before containers were a thing.

When the left-hand container sends a data packet, the bridge realises that the target of the packet is not on this host. Now, each node participating in an overlay network gets a so-called **VXLAN Tunnel Endpoint** (**VTEP**) object, which intercepts the packet (the packet at that moment is an OSI layer 2 data packet), wraps it with a header containing the target IP address of the host that runs the target container (this makes it now an OSI layer 3 data packet), and sends it over the VXLAN tunnel. The VTEP on the other side of the tunnel unpacks the data packet and forwards it to the local bridge, which in turn forwards it to the target container.

The overlay driver is included in the SwarmKit and is in most cases the recommended network driver for Docker Swarm. There are other multi-node-capable network drivers available from third-parties that can be installed as plugins to each participating Docker host. Certified network plugins are available from the Docker store.

Creating a Docker Swarm

Creating a Docker Swarm is almost trivial. It is so easy that it seems unreal if one knows what an orchestrator is all about. But it is true, Docker has done a fantastic job in making swarms simple and elegant to use. At the same time, Docker Swarm has been proven in use by large enterprises to be very robust and scalable.

Creating a local single node swarm

So, enough fancying, let's demonstrate how one can create a swarm. In its most simple form, a fully functioning Docker Swarm consists only of a single node. If you're using Docker for Mac or Windows, or even if you're using Docker Toolbox, then your personal computer or laptop is such a node. Thus, we can start right there and demonstrate some of the most important features of a swarm.

Let's initialize a swarm. On the command-line, just enter the following command:

```
$ docker swarm init
```

And after an incredibly short time you should see something like the following screenshot:

Output of the docker swarm init command

Our computer is now a swarm node. Its role is that of a manager and it is the leader (of the managers, which makes sense since there is only one manager at this time). Although it took only a very short time to finish the `docker swarm init`, the command did a lot of things during that time, some of them are:

- It created a root **certificate authority** (**CA**)
- It created a key-value store that is used to store the state of the whole swarm

Now, in the preceding output, we can see a command that can be used to join other nodes to the swarm that we just created. The command is as follows:

```
$ docker swarm join --token <join-token> <IP address>:2377
```

Here:

- `<join-token>` is a token generated by the swarm leader at the time the swarm was initialized
- `<IP address>` is the IP address of the leader

Although our cluster remains simple, as it consists of only one member, we can still ask the Docker CLI to list all the nodes of the swarm. This will look similar to the following screenshot:

Listing the nodes of the Docker Swarm

In this output we first see the ID that was given to the node. The star (*) that follows the ID indicates that this is the node on which the `docker node ls` was executed; basically, saying that this is the active node. Then we have the (human-readable) name of the node, its status, availability, and manager status. As mentioned earlier, this very first node of the swarm automatically became the leader, which is indicated in the preceding screenshot. Lastly, we see which version of the Docker engine we're using.

To get even more information about a node we can use the `docker node inspect` command, as shown in the following screenshot:

```
$ docker node inspect mc07c43kp8v8d4ofnl5i9skb2
[
    {
        "ID": "mc07c43kp8v8d4ofnl5i9skb2",
        "Version": {
            "Index": 9
        },
        "CreatedAt": "2018-03-06T01:48:57.625002322Z",
        "UpdatedAt": "2018-03-06T01:48:58.235847341Z",
        "Spec": {
            "Labels": {},
            "Role": "manager",
            "Availability": "active"
        },
        "Description": {
            "Hostname": "linuxkit-025000000001",
            "Platform": {
                "Architecture": "x86_64",
                "OS": "linux"
            },
            "Resources": {
                "NanoCPUs": 4000000000,
                "MemoryBytes": 2095788032
            },
            "Engine": {
                "EngineVersion": "18.03.0-ce-rc1",
                "Plugins": [
                    {
                        "Type": "Log",
                        "Name": "awslogs"
                    },
```

Truncated output of the command docker node inspect

There is a lot of information generated by this command, so we only present a truncated version of the output. This output can be useful, for example, when one needs to troubleshoot a misbehaving cluster node.

Creating a local swarm in VirtualBox or Hyper-V

Sometimes a single node swarm is not enough, but we don't have or don't want to use an account to create a swarm in the cloud. In this case, we can create a local swarm in either VirtualBox or Hyper-V. Creating the swarm in VirtualBox is slightly easier than creating it in Hyper-V, but if you're using Windows 10 and have Docker for Windows running then you cannot use VirtualBox at the same time. The two hypervisors are mutually exclusive.

Let's assume we have VirtualBox and `docker-machine` installed on our laptop. We can then use `docker-machine` to list all Docker hosts that are currently defined and may be running in VirtualBox:

```
$ docker-machine ls
NAME       ACTIVE    DRIVER       STATE       URL    SWARM    DOCKER
ERRORS
default    -         virtualbox   Stopped                     Unknown
```

In my case, I have one VM called `default` defined, which is currently stopped. I can easily start the VM by issuing the `docker-machine start default` command. This command takes a while and will result in the following (shortened) output:

```
$ docker-machine start default
Starting "default"...
(default) Check network to re-create if needed...
(default) Waiting for an IP...
Machine "default" was started.
Waiting for SSH to be available...
Detecting the provisioner...
Started machines may have new IP addresses. You may need to re-run the
`docker-machine env` command.
```

Now, if I list my VMs again I should see the following screenshot:

List of all VMs running in VirtualBox

If we do not have a VM called `default` yet, we can easily create one using the `create` command:

```
docker-machine create --driver virtualbox default
```

This results in the following output:

Output of docker-machine create

We can see in the preceding output how `docker-machine` creates the VM from an ISO image, defines SSH keys and certificates, and copies them to the VM and to the local `~/.docker/machine` directory, where we will use it later when we want to remotely access this VM through the Docker CLI. It also provisions an IP address for the new VM.

We're using the `docker-machine create` command with the parameter `--driver virtualbox`. Docker machine can also work with other drivers such as Hyper-V, AWS, Azure, DigitalOcean, and many more. Please see the documentation of docker-machine for more information. By default, a new VM gets 1 GB of memory associated, which is enough to use this VM as a node for a development or test swarm.

Now let's create five VMs for a five-node swarm. We can use a bit of scripting to reduce the manual work:

```
$ for NODE in `seq 1 5`; do
    docker-machine create --driver virtualbox "node-${NODE}"
done
```

Docker machine will now create five VMs with the names `node-1` to `node-5`. This might take a few moments, so this is a good time to get yourself a hot cup of tea. After the VMs are created we can list them:

```
$ docker-machine ls
NAME      ACTIVE   DRIVER       STATE      URL                          SWARM   DOCKER      ERRORS
default   -        virtualbox   Running    tcp://197.168.99.188:7376            v17.17.1-ce
node-1    -        virtualbox   Running    tcp://192.168.99.181:2376            v17.12.1-ce
node-2    -        virtualbox   Running    tcp://197.168.99.187:7376            v17.17.1-ce
node-3    -        virtualbox   Running    tcp://192.168.99.183:2376            v17.12.1-ce
node-4    -        virtualbox   Running    tcp://197.168.99.184:7376            v17.17.1-ce
node-5    -        virtualbox   Running    tcp://192.168.99.185:2376            v17.12.1-ce
$
```

List of all VMs we need for the swarm

Now we're ready to build a swarm. Technically, we could SSH into the first VM `node-1` and initialize a swarm and then SSH into all the other VMs and join them to the swarm leader. But this is not efficient. Let's again use a script that does all the hard work:

```
# get IP of Swarm leader
$ export IP=$(docker-machine ip node-1)
# init the Swarm
$ docker-machine ssh node-1 docker swarm init --advertise-addr $IP
# Get the Swarm join-token
$ export JOIN_TOKEN=$(docker-machine ssh node-1 \
    docker swarm join-token worker -q)
```

Now that we have the join token and the IP address of the swarm leader, we can ask the other nodes to join the swarm as follows:

```
$ for NODE in `seq 2 5`; do
  NODE_NAME="node-${NODE}"
  docker-machine ssh $NODE_NAME docker swarm join \
      --token $JOIN_TOKEN $IP:2377
done
```

To make the swarm highly available we can now promote, for example, `node-2` and `node-3` to become managers:

```
$ docker-machine ssh node-1 docker node promote node-2 node-3
Node node-2 promoted to a manager in the swarm.
Node node-3 promoted to a manager in the swarm.
```

Finally, we can list all the nodes of the swarm:

```
$ docker-machine ssh node-1 docker node ls
```

We should see the following screenshot:

List of all the nodes of the Docker Swarm on VirtualBox

This is the proof that we have just created a highly available Docker Swarm locally on our laptop or workstation. Let's pull all our code snippets together and make the whole thing a bit more robust. The script will look as follows:

```
alias dm="docker-machine"
for NODE in `seq 1 5`; do
  NODE_NAME=node-${NODE}
  dm rm --force $NODE_NAME
  dm create --driver virtualbox $NODE_NAME
done
alias dms="docker-machine ssh"
export IP=$(docker-machine ip node-1)
dms node-1 docker swarm init --advertise-addr $IP;
export JOIN_TOKEN=$(dms node-1 docker swarm join-token worker -q);
for NODE in `seq 2 5`; do
  NODE_NAME="node-${NODE}"
  dms $NODE_NAME docker swarm join --token $JOIN_TOKEN $IP:2377
done;
dms node-1 docker node promote node-2 node-3
```

The preceding script first deletes (if present) and then recreates five VMs called node-1 to node-5, and then initializes a Swarm on node-1. After that, the remaining four VMs are added to the swarm, and finally, node-2 and node-3 are promoted to manager status to make the swarm highly available. The whole script will take less than 5 minutes to execute and can be repeated as many times as desired. The complete script can be found in the repository, in the subfolder docker-swarm; it is called create-swarm.sh

It is a highly recommended best practice to always script and thus automate operations.

Using Play with Docker (PWD) to generate a Swarm

To experiment with Docker Swarm without having to install or configure anything locally on our computer, we can use PWD. PWD is a website that can be accessed with a browser and which offers us the ability to create a Docker Swarm consisting of up to five nodes. It is definitely a playground, as the name implies, and the time for which we can use it is limited to four hours per session. We can open as many sessions as we want, but each session automatically ends after four hours. Other than that, it is a fully functional Docker environment that is ideal for tinkering with Docker or to demonstrate some features.

Let's access the site now. In your browser, navigate to the website `https://labs.play-with-docker.com`. You will be presented a welcome and login screen. Use your Docker ID to log in. After successfully logging in you will be presented with a screen that looks like the following screenshot:

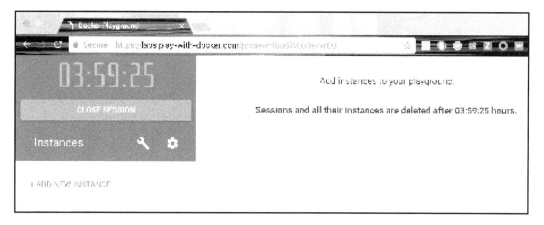

Play with Docker window

As we can see immediately, there is a big timer counting down from four hours. That's how much time we have left to play in this session. Furthermore, we see an **+ ADD NEW INSTANCE** link. Click it to create a new Docker host. When you do that, your screen should look like the following screenshot:

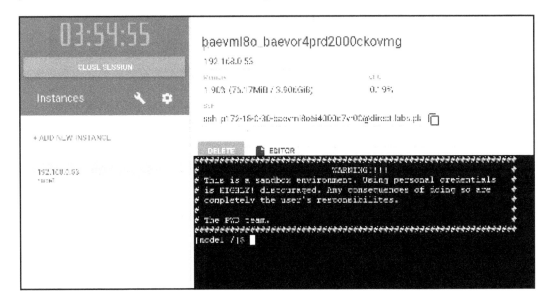

PWD with one new node

On the left-hand side we see the newly-created node with its IP address (192.168.0.53) and its name (node1). On the right-hand side, we have some additional information about this new node in the upper half of the screen and a terminal in the lower half. Yes, this terminal is used to execute commands on this node that we just created. This node has the Docker CLI installed, and thus we can execute all the familiar Docker commands on it such as docker version. Try it out.

But now we want to create a Docker Swarm. Execute the following command in the terminal in your browser:

```
$ docker swarm init --advertise-addr=eth0
```

The output generated by the preceding command corresponds to what we already know from our previous trials with the one-node cluster on our workstation and the local cluster using VirtualBox or Hyper-V. The important information, once again, is the join command that we want to use to join additional nodes to the cluster we just created.

You might have noted that this time we specified the parameter `--advertise-addr` in the swarm `init` command. *Why is that necessary here?* The reason is that the nodes generated by PWD have more than one IP address associated with them. One can easily verify that by executing the command `ip a` on the node. This command will show us that there are indeed two endpoints, `eth0` and `eth1`, present. We thus have to specify explicitly to the new to-be-swarm manager which one we want to use. In our case, it is `eth0`.

Create four additional nodes in PWD by clicking four times on the **+ ADD NEW INSTANCE** link. The new nodes will be called `node2`, `node3`, `node4`, and `node5` and will all be listed on the left-hand side. If you click on one of the nodes on the left-hand side, then the right-hand side shows the details of the respective node and a terminal window for that node.

Select each node (2 to 5) and execute the `docker swarm join` command that you have copied from the leader node (`node1`) in the respective terminal:

Joining a node to the swarm in PWD

Once you have joined all four nodes to the swarm, switch back to `node1` and list all nodes, which, unsurprisingly, results in this:

List of all the nodes of the swarm in PWD

Still on `node1`, we can now promote, say, `node2` and `node3`, to make the swarm highly available:

```
$ docker node promote node2 node3
Node node2 promoted to a manager in the swarm.
Node node3 promoted to a manager in the swarm.
```

With this, our swarm on PWD is ready to accept a workload. We have created a highly available Docker Swarm with three manager nodes that form a Raft consensus group and two worker nodes.

Creating a Docker Swarm in the cloud

All the Docker Swarms we have created so far are wonderful to use in development or to experiment or for demonstration purposes. If we want to create a swarm that can be used as a production environment where we run our mission critical applications, though, then we need to create a, I'm tempted to say, real swarm in the cloud or on-premise. In this book, we are going to demonstrate how to create a Docker Swarm in Amazon AWS.

One way to create a swarm is by using **Docker machine** (**DM**). DM has a driver for Amazon AWS. If we have an account on AWS, we need the AWS access key ID and the AWS secret access key. We can add those two values to a file called `~/.aws/configuration`. It should look like the following:

```
[default]
aws_access_key_id = AKID1234567890
aws_secret_access_key = MY-SECRET-KEY
```

Every time we run `docker-machine create`, DM will look up those values in that file. For more in-depth information on how to get an AWS account and how to obtain the two secret keys, please consult this link: `http://dockr.ly/2FFelyT`.

Once we have an AWS account in place and have stored the access keys in the configuration file, we can start building our swarm. The necessary code looks exactly the same as the one we used to create a swarm on our local machine in VirtualBox. Let's start with the first node:

```
$ docker-machine create --driver amazonec2 \
    --amazonec2-region us-east-1 aws-node-1
```

This will create an EC2 instance called `aws-node-1` in the requested region (`us-east-1` in my case). The output of the preceding command looks like the following screenshot:

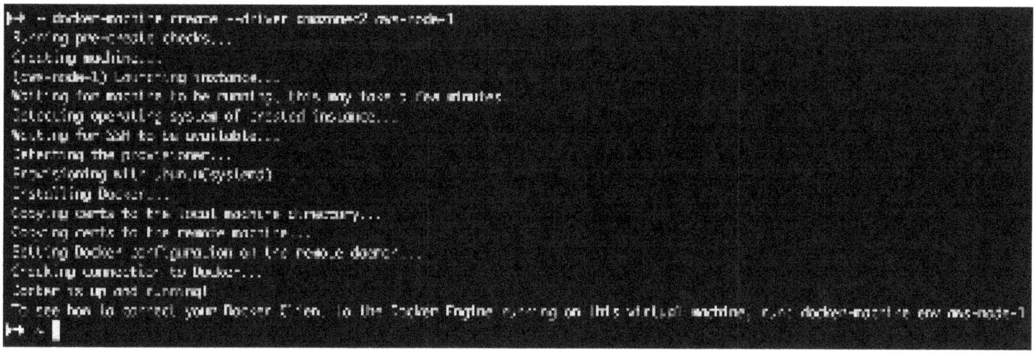

Creating a swarm node on AWS with Docker machine

It looks very similar to the output we already know from working with VirtualBox. We can now configure our terminal for remote access to that EC2 instance:

```
$ eval $(docker-machine env aws-node-1)
```

This will configure the environment variables used by the Docker CLI accordingly:

```
↳ ~ export | grep DOCKER
DOCKER_CERT_PATH=/Users/gabriel/.docker/machine/machines/aws-node-1
DOCKER_HOST=tcp://35.172.240.127:2376
DOCKER_MACHINE_NAME=aws-node-1
DOCKER_TLS_VERIFY=1
↳ ~ █
```

Environment variables used by Docker to enable remote access to the AWS EC2 node

For security reasons, **transport layer security (TLS)** is used for the communication between our CLI and the remote node. The certificates necessary for that were copied by DM to the path we assigned to the environment variable DOCKER_CERT_PATH.

All Docker commands that we now execute in our Terminal will be remotely executed in Amazon AWS on our EC2 instance. Let's try to run Nginx on this node:

```
$ docker container run -d -p 8000:80 nginx:alpine
```

We can use docker container ls to verify that the container is running. If so, then let's test it using curl:

```
$ curl -4 <IP address>:8000
```

Here, <IP address> is the public IP address of the AWS node; in my case it would be 35.172.240.127. Sadly this doesn't work; the preceding command times out:

```
↳ ~ curl -4 35.172.240.127:8000
curl: (7) Failed to connect to 35.172.240.127 port 8000: Operation timed out
↳ ~ █
```

Accessing Nginx on the AWS node times out

The reason for this is that our node is part of an AWS **security group (SG)**. By default, access to objects inside this SG is denied. Thus, we have to find out to which SG our instance belongs and configure access explicitly. For this, we typically use the AWS console. Go to the EC2 dashboard and select instances on the left-hand side. Locate the EC2 instance called aws-node-1 and select it. In the details view, under **Security groups,** click on the link **docker-machine** as shown in the following screenshot:

Locating the SG to which our swarm node belongs

This will lead us to the SG page with the SG `docker-machine` pre-selected. In the details section under the tab **Inbound**, add a new rule for your IP address (the IP address of workstation):

Open access to SG for our computer

In the preceding screenshot, the IP address `70.113.114.234` happens to be the one assigned to my personal workstation. I have enabled all inbound traffic coming from this IP address to the `docker-machine` SG. Note that in a production system you should be very careful about which ports of the SG to open to the public. Usually, it is ports `80` and `443` for HTTP and HTTPS access. Everything else is a potential invitation to hackers.

You can get your own IP address through a service like `https://www.whatismyip.com/`. Now, if we execute the `curl` command again, the greeting page of Nginx is returned.

Before we leave the SG we should add another rule to it. The swarm nodes need to be able to freely communicate on ports `7946` and `4789` through TCP and UDP and on port `2377` through TCP. We could now add five rules with these requirements where the source is the SG itself, or we just define a more crud rule that allows all inbound traffic inside the SG (`sg-c14f4db3` in my case):

Type	Protocol	Port Range	Source	Description
All traffic	All	A	TCP 1 14324I3	personal access
All traffic	All	*	sg-c14f4d... de... da...	intra-swarm comm...
SSH	TCP	Y	0.0.0.0	
Custom TCP Rule	TCP	2377	0.0.0.0	

SG rule to enable intra-swarm communication

Now, let's continue with the creation of the remaining four nodes. Once again, we can use a script to ease the process:

```
$ for NODE in `seq 2 5`; do
    docker-machine create --driver amazonec2 \
        --amazonec2-region us-east-1 aws-node-${NODE}
done
```

After the provisioning of the nodes is done we can list all nodes with DM. In my case, I see this:

```
▶ ~ docker-machine ls
NAME        ACTIVE   DRIVER       STATE     URL                          SWARM   DOCKER        ERRORS
aws-node-1  *        amazonec2    Running   tcp://35.177.248.177:7376            v18.07.8-ce
aws-node-2  -        amazonec2    Running   tcp://54.236.48.1:2376              v18.02.8-ce
aws-node-3  -        amazonec2    Running   tcp://34.785.171.56:7376            v18.07.8-ce
aws-node-4  -        amazonec2    Running   tcp://34.239.93.22:2376             v18.02.8-ce
aws-node-5  -        amazonec2    Running   tcp://57.785.76.718:7376            v18.07.8-ce
node-1      -        virtualbox   Running   tcp://192.160.99.188:2376           v17.12.1-ce
node-2      -        virtualbox   Running   tcp://192.168.99.181:7376           v17.12.1-ce
node-3      -        virtualbox   Running   tcp://192.160.99.182:2376           v17.12.1-ce
node-4      -        virtualbox   Running   tcp://192.168.99.183:7376           v17.12.1-ce
node-5      -        virtualbox   Running   tcp://192.160.99.184:2376           v17.12.1-ce
▶ ~
```

List of all the nodes created by Docker Machine

In the preceding screenshot, we can see the five nodes that we originally created in VirtualBox and the five new nodes that we have created in AWS. Apparently, the nodes on AWS are using a new version of Docker; here the version is `18.02.0-ce`. The IP addresses we see in the column `URL` are the public IP addresses of my EC2 instances.

Due to the fact that our CLI is still configured for remote access to the node `aws-node-1`, we can just run the `swarm init` command as follows:

```
$ docker swarm init
```

We then need the `join-token`:

```
$ export JOIN_TOKEN=$(docker swarm join-token -q worker)
```

The address of the leader with the following command:

```
$ export LEADER_ADDR=$(docker node inspect \
    --format "{{.ManagerStatus.Addr}}" self)
```

With this information, we can now join the other four nodes to the swarm leader:

```
$ for NODE in `seq 2 5`; do
  docker-machine ssh aws-node-${NODE} \
    sudo docker swarm join --token ${JOIN_TOKEN} ${LEADER_ADDR}
done
```

An alternative way to achieve the same without needing to SSH into the individual nodes would be to reconfigure our client CLI every time we want to access a different node:

```
$ for NODE in `seq 2 5`; do
    eval $(docker-machine env aws-node-${NODE})
    docker swarm join --token ${JOIN_TOKEN} ${LEADER_ADDR}
done
```

As a last step, we want to promote nodes 2 and 3 to manager:

```
$ eval $(docker-machine env node-1)
$ docker node promote aws-node-2 aws-node-3
```

We can then list all the swarm nodes, as shown in the following screenshot:

List of all nodes of our swarm in the cloud

And thus do we have a highly available Docker Swarm running in the cloud. To clean up the swarm in the cloud and avoid incurring unnecessary costs, we can use the following command:

```
$ for NODE in `seq 1 5`; do
    docker-machine rm -f aws-node-${NODE}
done
```

Deploying a first application

We have created a few Docker Swarms on various platforms. Once created, a swarm behaves the same way on any platform. The way we deploy and update applications on a swarm is not platform-dependent. It has been one of Docker's main goals to avoid a vendor lock-in when using a swarm. Swarm-ready applications can be effortlessly migrated from, say, a swarm running on-premise to a cloud based swarm. It is even technically possible to run part of a swarm on-premise and another part in the cloud. It works, yet one has of course to consider possible side effects due to the higher latency between nodes in geographically distant areas.

Now that we have a highly available Docker Swarm up and running, it is time to run some workloads on it. I'm using a local swarm created with Docker Machine. We'll start by first creating a single service. For this we need to SSH into one of the manager nodes. I select `node-1`:

```
$ docker-machine ssh node-1
```

Creating a service

A service can be either created as part of a stack, or directly using the Docker CLI. Let's first look at a sample stack file that defines a single service:

```
version: "3.5"
services:
  whoami:
    image: training/whoami:latest
    networks:
      - test-net
    ports:
      - 81:8000
    deploy:
      replicas: 6
      update_config:
        parallelism: 2
        delay: 10s
      labels:
        app: sample-app
        environment: prod-south

networks:
  test-net:
    driver: overlay
```

In the preceding example we see what the desired state of a service called `whoami` is:

- It is based on the image `training/whoami:latest`
- Containers of the service are attached to the network `test-net`
- The container port `8000` is published to port `81`
- It is running with six replicas (or tasks)

- During a rolling update, the individual tasks are updated in batches of two, with a delay of 10 seconds between each successful batch
- The service (and its tasks and containers) is assigned the two labels `app` and `environment`, with the values `sample-app` and `prod-south` respectively

There are many more settings that we could define for a service, but the preceding ones are some of the more important ones. Most settings have meaningful default values. If, for example, we do not specify the number of replicas, then Docker defaults it to `1`. The name and image of a service are of course mandatory. Note that the name of the service must be unique in the swarm.

To create the preceding service, we use the `docker stack deploy` command. Assuming that the file in which the preceding content is stored is called `stack.yaml`, we have:

```
$ docker stack deploy -c stack.yaml sample-stack
```

Here, we have created a stack called `sample-stack` that consists of one service, `whoami`. We can list all stacks on our swarm, whereupon we should get this:

```
$ docker stack ls
NAME              SERVICES
sample-stack      1
```

If we list the services defined in our swarm, we get the following output:

List of all services running in the swarm

In the output, we can see that currently we have only one service running, which was to be expected. The service has an ID. The format of the ID, contrary, what you have used so far for containers, networks, or volumes, is alphanumeric. We can also see that the name of the service is a combination of the service name we defined in the stack file and the name of the stack, which is used as a prefix. This makes sense, since we want to be able to deploy multiple stacks (with different names) using the same stack file into our swarm. To make sure that service names are unique, Docker decided to combine service name and stack name.

In the third column we see the mode, which is `replicated`. The number of replicas is shown as `6/6`. This tells us that six out of the six requested replicas are running. This corresponds to the desired state. In the output we also see the image that the service uses and the port mappings of the service.

Inspecting the service and its tasks

In the preceding output, we cannot see the details of the `6` replicas that have been created. To get some deeper insight into that, we can use the `docker service ps` command. If we execute this command for our service, we will get the following output:

Details of the whoami service

In the preceding output, we can see the list of six tasks that correspond to the requested six replicas of our `whoami` service. In the `NODE` column, we can also see the node to which each task has been deployed. The name of each task is a combination of the service name plus an increasing index. Also note that, similar to the service itself, each task gets an alphanumeric ID assigned.

In my case, apparently task 2, with the name `sample-stack_whoami.2`, has been deployed to `node-1`, which is the leader of our swarm. Thus, I should find a container running on this node. Let's see what we get if we list all containers running on `node-1`:

List of containers on node-1

As expected, we find a container running from
the `training/whoami:latest` image with a name that is a combination of its parent
task name and ID. We can try to visualize the whole hierarchy of objects that we
generated when deploying our sample stack:

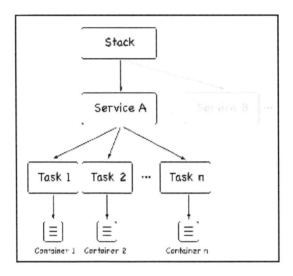

Object hierarchy of a Docker Swarm stack

A stack can consist of one to many services. Each service has a collection of tasks.
Each task has a one-to-one association with a container. Stacks and services are
created and stored on the Swarm manager nodes. Tasks are then scheduled to swarm
worker nodes, where the worker node creates the corresponding container. We can
also get some more information about our service by inspecting it. Execute the
following command:

```
$ docker service inspect sample-stack_whoami
```

This provides a wealth of information about all the relevant settings of the service.
This includes those we have explicitly defined in our `stack.yaml` file, but also those
which we didn't specify and which therefore got their default values assigned. We're
not going to list the whole output here, as it is too long, but I encourage the reader to
inspect it on their own machine. We will discuss part of the information in more
detail in the *The Swarm Routing Mesh* section.

Logs of a service

In an earlier chapter we worked with the logs produced by a container. Here we're concentrating on a service. Remember that, ultimately, a service with many replicas has many containers running. Thus, we would expect that, if we ask the service for its logs, that Docker returns an aggregate of all logs of those containers belonging to the service. And indeed, that's what we get if we use the `docker service logs` command:

Logs of the whoami service

There is not much information in the logs at this point, but it is enough to discuss what we get. The first part of each line in the log always contains the name of the container combined with the node name from which the log entry originates. Then, separated by the vertical bar (|), we get the actual log entry. So if we would, say, ask for the logs of the first container in the list directly, we would only get a single entry, and the value we would see in this case would be `Listening on :8000`.

The aggregated logs that we get with the `docker service logs` command are not sorted in any particular way. So, if correlation of events is happening in different containers you should add information to your log output that makes this correlation possible. Typically, this is a timestamp for each log entry. But this has to be done at the source; for example, the application that produces a log entry needs to also make sure a timestamp is added.

We can also query the logs of an individual task of the service by providing the task ID instead of the service ID or name. So, querying the logs from task 2 gives us the following screenshot:

Logs of an individual task of the whoami service

Reconciling the desired state

We have learned that a swarm service is a description or manifest of the desired state that we want an application or application service to run in. Now, let's see how Docker Swarm reconciles this desired state if we do something that causes the actual state of the service to be different from the desired state. The easiest way to do this is to forcibly kill one of the tasks or containers of the service.

Let's do this with the container that has been scheduled on `node-1`:

```
$ docker container rm -f sample-
stack_whoami.2.n21e7ktyvo4b2sufalk0aibzy
```

If we do that and then do a `docker service ps` right thereafter, we will see the following output:

Docker Swarm reconciling the desired state after one task failed

We see that task 2 failed with exit code `137` and that the swarm immediately reconciled the desired state by rescheduling the failed task on a node with free resources. In this case, the scheduler selected the same node as the failed tasks, but this is not always the case. So, without us intervening, the swarm completely fixed the problem, and since the service is running in multiple replicas, at no time was the service down.

Let's try another failure scenario. This time we're going to shut down an entire node and are going to see how the swarm reacts. Let's take `node-2` for this, as it has two tasks (tasks 3 and 4) running on it. For this we need to open a new terminal window and use Docker machine to stop `node-2`:

```
$ docker-machine stop node-2
```

Back on `node-1`, we can now again run `docker service ps` to see what happened:

Swarm reschedules all tasks of a failed node

In the preceding screenshot, we can see that immediately task 3 was rescheduled on `node-1` whilst task 4 was rescheduled on `node-3`. Even this more radical failure is handled gracefully by Docker Swarm.

It is important to note though that if `node-2` ever comes back online in the swarm, the tasks that had previously been running on it will not automatically be transferred back to it. But the node is now ready for a new workload.

Deleting a service or a stack

If we want to remove a particular service from the swarm, we can use the `docker service rm` command. If on the other hand we want to remove a stack from the swarm, we analogously use the `docker stack rm` command. This command removes all services that are part of the stack definition. In the case of the `whoami` service, it was created by using a stack file and thus we're going to use the latter command:

```
docker@node-1:~$ docker stack rm sample-stack
Removing service sample-stack_whoami
Removing network sample-stack_test-net
docker@node-1:~$
```

Removing a stack

The preceding command will make sure that all tasks of each service of the stack are terminated, and the corresponding containers are stopped by first sending a `SIGTERM`, and then, if not successful, a `SIGKILL` after 10 seconds of timeout.

It is important to note that the stopped containers are not removed from the Docker host. Thus, it is advised to purge containers from time to time on worker nodes to reclaim unused resources. Use `docker container purge -f` for this purpose.

Deploying a multi-service stack

In Chapter 8, *Docker Compose,* we used an application consisting of two services that were declaratively described in a Docker compose file. We can use this compose file as a template to create a stack file that allows us to deploy the same application into a swarm. The content of our stack file called `pet-stack.yaml` looks like this:

```
version: "3.5"
services:
  web:
    image: fundamentalsofdocker/ch08-web:1.0
    networks:
      - pets-net
    ports:
      - 3000:3000
    deploy:
      replicas: 3
  db:
    image: fundamentalsofdocker/ch08-db:1.0
    networks:
      - pets-net
    volumes:
      - pets-data:/var/lib/postgresql/data

volumes:
  pets-data:

networks:
  pets-net:
    driver: overlay
```

We request that the service `web` has three replicas, and both services are attached to the overlay network `pets-net`. We can deploy this application using the `docker stack deploy` command:

Deploy the pets stack

Docker creates the `pets_pets-net` overlay network and then the two services `pets_web` and `pets_db`. We can then list all the tasks in the `pets` stack:

List of all the tasks in the pets stack

Finally, let's test the application using `curl`. And, indeed, the application works as expected:

Testing the pets application using curl

The container ID is in the output, where it says `Delivered to you by container c9aa9dacd9b2`. If you run the `curl` command multiple times, the ID should cycle between three different values. These are the ID's of the three containers (or replicas) that we have requested for the service `web`.

Once we're done, we can remove the stack with `docker stack rm pets`.

The swarm routing mesh

If you have been paying attention, then you might have noticed something interesting in the last section. We had the pets application deployed and it resulted in the fact that an instance of the service **web** was installed on the three nodes node-3, node-4, and node-5. Yet, we were able to access the **web** service on node-1 with localhost and we reached each container from there. *How is that possible?* Well, this is due to the so-called swarm routing mesh. The routing mesh makes sure that when we publish a port of a service, that port is then published on all nodes of the swarm. Thus, network traffic that hits any node of the swarm and requests to use the specific port, will be forwarded to one of the service containers by routing the mesh. Let's look at the following figure to see how that works:

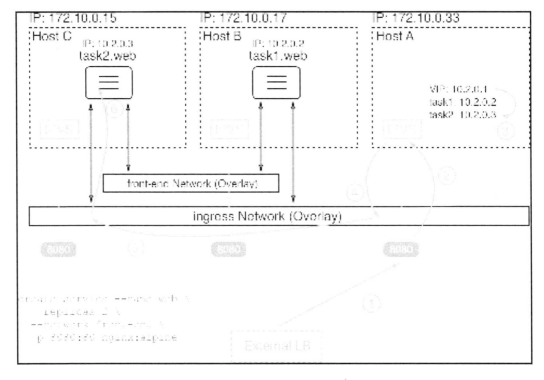

Docker Swarm routing mesh

In this situation we have three nodes, called **Host A** to **Host C**, with the IP addresses `172.10.0.15`, `172.10.0.17`, and `172.10.0.33`. In the lower left-corner of the figure, we see the command that created a service **web** with two replicas. The corresponding tasks have been scheduled on **Host B** and **Host C**. Task 1 landed on host B while task 2 landed on host C.

When a service is created on Docker Swarm it automatically gets a **virtual IP** (**VIP**) address assigned. This IP address is stable and reserved during the whole life cycle of the service. Let's assume that in our case the VIP is `10.2.0.1`.

If now a request for port `8080` coming from an external **load balancer** (**LB**) is targeted at one of the nodes of our swarm, then this request is handled by the Linux **IP Virtual Server** (**IPVS**) service on that node. This service makes a lookup with the given port `8080` in the IP table and will find that this corresponds to the VIP of service **web**. Now, since the VIP is not a real target, the IPVS service will load balance the IP addresses of the tasks that are associated with this service. In our case it picked task 2, with the IP address `10.2.0.3`. Finally, the **ingress** overlay network is used to forward the request to the target container on host C.

It is important to note that it doesn't matter which swarm node the external request is forwarded to by the external LB. The routing mesh will always handle the request correctly and forward it to one of the tasks of the targeted service.

Summary

In this chapter, we have introduced Docker Swarm, which, next to Kubernetes, is the second most popular orchestrator for containers. We have looked into the architecture of a swarm, discussed all the types of resources running in a swarm, such as services, tasks, and more, and we have created services in the swarm and deployed an application that consists of multiple related services.

In the next chapter, we are going to explore how to deploy services or applications onto a Docker Swarm with zero downtime and automatic rollback capabilities. We are also going to introduce secrets as a means to protect sensitive information.

Questions

To assess your learning progress please answer the following questions:

1. How do you initialize a new Docker Swarm?
    1. docker init swarm
    2. docker swarm init --advertise-addr <IP address>
    3. docker swarm join --token <join token>
2. You want to remove a worker node from a Docker Swarm. What steps are necessary?
3. How do you create an overlay network called `front-tier`? Make the network attachable.
4. How will you create a service called `web` from the `nginx:alpine` image with five replicas, which exposes port 3000 on the ingress network and is attached to the `front-tier` network?
5. How will you scale the web service down to three instances?

Further reading

Please consult the following link for more in-depth information about selected topics:

- *Amazon AWS EC2 example* at `http://dockr.ly/2FFelyT`

11
Zero Downtime Deployments and Secrets

In the last chapter, we explored Docker Swarm and its resources in detail. We learned how to build a highly available swarm locally, and in the cloud. Then, we discussed swarm services and stacks in depth. Finally, we created services and stacks in the swarm.

In this chapter, we will show you how we can update services and stacks running in Docker Swarm without interrupting their availability. This is called **zero downtime deployment**. We are also going to introduce swarm secrets as a means to securely provide sensitive information to containers of a service using those secrets.

The topics of this chapter are:

- Zero downtime deployment
- Secrets

After finishing this chapter, you will be able to:

- List two to three different deployment strategies commonly used to update a service without downtime
- Update a service in batches without causing a service interruption
- Define a rollback strategy for a service that is used if an update fails
- Use a secret with a service
- Update the value of a secret without causing downtime

Zero downtime deployment

One of the most important aspects of a mission-critical application that needs frequent updates is the ability to do updates in a fashion that requires no outage at all. We call this a zero downtime deployment. At all times, the application which is updated is fully operational.

Popular deployment strategies

There are various ways how this can be achieved. Some of them are as follows:

- Rolling updates
- Blue-green deployments
- Canary releases

Docker Swarm supports rolling updates out of the box. The other two types of deployments can be achieved with some extra effort from our side.

Rolling updates

In a mission-critical application, each application service has to run in multiple replicas. Depending on the load, that can be as few as two to three instances and as many as dozens, hundreds, or thousands of instances. At any given time, we want to have a clear majority of all service instances running. So, if we have three replicas, we want to have at least two of them up and running all the time. If we have 100 replicas, we can content ourselves with a minimum of, say 90 replicas, that need to be available. We can then define a batch size of replicas that we may take down to upgrade. In the first case, the batch size would be 1 and in the second case, it would be 10.

When we take replicas down, Docker Swarm will automatically take those instances out of the load balancing pool and all traffic will be load balanced across the remaining active instances. Those remaining instances will thus experience a slight increase in traffic. In the following diagram, prior to the start of the rolling update, if **Task A3** wanted to access **Service B,** it could have been load balanced to any of the three tasks of service B by SwarmKit. Once the rolling update had started, SwarmKit took down **Task B1** for updates. Automatically, this task is then taken out of the pool of targets. So, if **Task A3** now requests to connect to **Service B**, the load balancing will only select from the remaining tasks B2 and B3. Thus, those two tasks might experience a higher load temporarily:

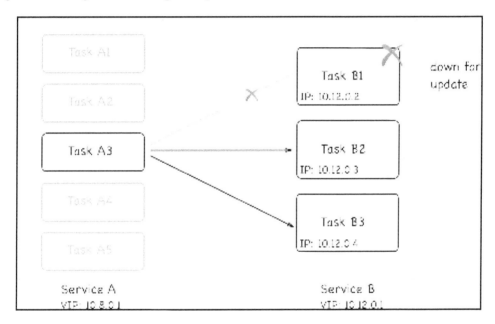

Task B1 is taken down for update

The stopped instances are then replaced by an equivalent number of new instances of the new version of the application service. Once the new instances are up and running, we can have the swarm observe them for a given period of time and make sure they're healthy. If all is good, then we can continue by taking down the next batch of instances and replacing them with instances of the new version. This process is repeated until all instances of the application service are replaced.

In the the following diagram, we see that **Task B1** of **Service B** has been updated to version 2. The container of **Task B1** got a new IP address assigned, and it got deployed to another worker node with free resources:

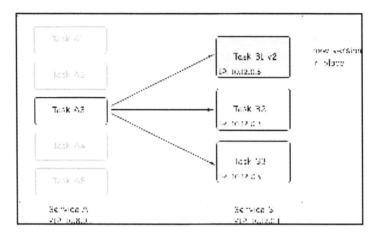

First batch updated in a rolling update

It is important to understand that when a task of a service is updated, it, in most cases, gets deployed to a different worker node than the one it used to live on. But that should be fine as long as the corresponding service is stateless. If we have a stateful service that is location or node aware and we'd like to update it, then we have to adjust our approach, but this is outside of the scope of this book.

Now, let's look into how we can actually instruct the swarm to perform a rolling update of an application service. When we declare a service in a stack file, we can define multiple options that are relevant in this context. Let's look at a snippet of a typical stack file:

```
version: "3.5"
services:
 web:
   image: nginx:alpine
   deploy:
     replicas: 10
     update_config:
       parallelism: 2
       delay: 10s
...
```

In this snippet, we see a section, `update_config`, with the properties `parallelism` and `delay`. Parallelism defines the batch size of how many replicas are going to be updated at a time during a rolling update. Delay defines how long Docker Swarm is going to wait between the update of individual batches. In the preceding case, we have `10` replicas that are updated in two instances at a time and, between each successful update, Docker Swarm waits for `10` seconds.

Let's test such a rolling update. We navigate to subfolder `ch11` of our `labs` folder and use the file `stack.yaml` to create a web service configured for a rolling update. The service uses the Alpine-based Nginx image with version `1.12-alpine`. We will then later update the service to a newer version `1.13-alpine`.

We will deploy this service to our swarm that we created locally in VirtualBox. First, we make sure we have our Terminal window configured to access one of the master nodes of our cluster. We can take the leader `node-1`:

```
$ eval $(docker-machine env node-1)
```

Now, we can deploy the service using the stack file:

```
$ docker stack deploy -c stack.yaml web
```

The output of the preceding command looks like this:

Deployment of the stack called web

Once the service is deployed, we can monitor it using the following command:

```
$ watch docker stack ps web
```

And we will see the following output:

Service web of stack web running in swarm with 10 replicas

If you're working on a Mac, you need to make sure your watch tool is installed. Use this command to do so: `brew install watch`.

The previous command will continuously update the output and provide us with a good overview on what's happening during the rolling update.

Now, we need to open a second Terminal and also configure it for remote access to a manager node of our swarm. Once we have done that, we can execute the `docker` command that will update the image of the `web` service of the stack also called `web`:

```
$ docker service update --image nginx:1.13-alpine web_web
```

The preceding command leads to the following output, indicating the progress of the rolling update:

```
overall progress: 4 out of 10 tasks
1/10: running   [================================================>]
2/10: running   [================================================>]
3/10: running   [================================================>]
4/10: running   [================================================>]
5/10: preparing [=========================>                        ]
6/10: preparing [=========================>                        ]
7/10:
8/10:
9/10:
10/10:
```

Screen showing progress of rolling update

The output indicates that the first two batches with each two tasks have been successful and that the third batch is preparing.

In the first terminal window, where we're watching the stack, we should now see how Docker Swarm updates the service batch by batch with an interval of 10 seconds. After the first batch, it should look like the following screenshot:

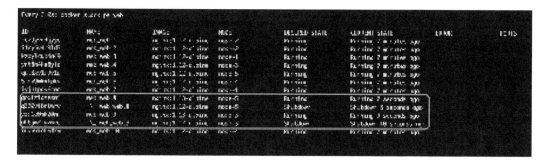

Rolling update of a service in Docker Swarm

In the preceding screenshot, we can see that the first batch of the two tasks, 8 and 9, has been updated. Docker Swarm is waiting for 10 seconds to proceed with the next batch.

> It is interesting to note that in this particular case, SwarmKit deploys the new version of the task to the same node as the previous version. This is accidental since we have five nodes and two tasks on each node. SwarmKit always tries to balance the workload evenly across the nodes. So, when SwarmKit takes down a task, then the corresponding node has less workload than all the others and thus gets the new instance scheduled. Normally, you cannot expect to find the new instance of a task on the same node. Just try it out yourself by deleting the stack with docker stack rm web and changing the number of replicas to say, seven, and then redeploy and update.

Once all the tasks are updated, the output of our watch `docker stack ps web` command looks similar to the following screenshot:

All tasks have been updated successfully

Please note that SwarmKit does not immediately remove the containers of the previous versions of the tasks from the corresponding nodes. This makes sense as we might want to, for example, retrieve the logs from those containers for debugging purposes, or we might want to retrieve their metadata using `docker container inspect`. SwarmKit keeps the four latest terminated task instances around before it purges older ones to not clog the system with unused resources.

Once we're done, we can tear down the stack using the following command:

```
$ docker stack rm web
```

Although using stack files to define and deploy applications is the recommended best practice, we can also define the update behavior in a service `create` statement. If we just want to deploy a single service, this might be the preferred way. Let's look at such a `create` command:

```
$ docker service create --name web \
    --replicas 10 \
    --update-parallelism 2 \
    --update-delay 10s \
    nginx:alpine
```

This command defines the same desired state as the preceding stack file. We want the service to run with 10 replicas and we want a rolling update to happen in batches of 2 tasks at a time, with a 10 second interval between consecutive batches.

Health checks

To make informed decisions, for example, during a rolling update of a swarm service whether or not the just-installed batch of new service instances is running OK or if a rollback is needed, the SwarmKit needs a way to know about the overall health of the system. On its own, SwarmKit (and Docker) can collect quite a bit of information. But there is a limit. Imagine a container containing an application. The container, as seen from outside, can look absolutely healthy and chuckle away just fine. But that doesn't necessarily mean that the application running inside the container is also doing well. The application could, for example, be in an infinite loop or be in a corrupt state, yet still running. But, as long as the application runs, the container runs and from outside, everything looks perfect.

Thus, SwarmKit provides a seam where we can provide it with some help. We, the authors of the application services running inside the containers in the swarm, know best whether or not our service is in a healthy state. SwarmKit gives us the opportunity to define a command that is executed against our application service to test its health. *What exactly this command does is not important to Swarm*, the command just needs to return OK or NOT OK or time out. The latter two situations, namely NOT OK or timeout, will tell SwarmKit that the task it is investigating is potentially unhealthy. Here, I am writing *potentially* on purpose and later, we will see why:

```
FROM alpine:3.6
...
HEALTHCHECK --interval=30s \
    --timeout=10s
    --retries=3
    --start-period=60s
    CMD curl -f http://localhost:3000/health || exit 1
...
```

In the preceding snippet from a Dockerfile, we see the keyword `HEALTHCHECK`. It has a few options or parameters and an actual command `CMD`. Let's first discuss the options:

- `--interval` defines the wait time between health checks. Thus, in our case the orchestrator executes a check every `30` seconds.
- The `--timeout` parameter defines how long Docker should wait if the health check does not respond until it times out with an error. In our sample, this is `10` seconds. Now, if one health check fails, the SwarmKit retries a couple of times until it gives up and declares the corresponding task as unhealthy and opens the door for Docker to kill this task and replace it by a new instance.

- The number of retries is defined with the parameter `--retries`. In the preceding code, we want to have three retries.
- Next, we have the start period. Some containers need some time to start up (not that this is a recommended pattern, but sometimes it is inevitable). During this start up time, the service instance might not be able to respond to health checks. With the start period, we can define how long the SwarmKit should wait before it executes the very first health check and thus give the application time to initialize. To define the start up time, we use the `--start-period` parameter. In our case, we do the first check after `60` seconds. How long this start period needs to be totally depends on the application and its start up behavior. The recommendation is to start with a relatively low value and if you have a lot of false positives and tasks that are restarted many times, you might want to increase the time interval.
- Finally, we define the actual probing command on the last line with the `CMD` keyword. In our case, we are defining a request to the `/health` endpoint of `localhost` at port `3000` as a probing command. This call is expected to have three possible outcomes:
    - The command succeeds
    - The command fails
    - The command times out

The latter two are treated the same way by SwarmKit. It is an indication to the orchestrator that the corresponding task might be unhealthy. I did say *might* with intent since SwarmKit does not immediately assume the worst case scenario but assumes that this might just be a temporary fluke of the task and that it will recover from it. This is the reason why we have a `--retries` parameter. There, we can define how many times SwarmKit should retry before it can assume that the task is indeed unhealthy, and consequently kill it and reschedule another instance of this task on another free node to reconcile the desired state of the service.

Why can we use localhost in our probing command? This is a very good question, and the reason is because SwarmKit, when probing a container running in the swarm, executes this `probing` command inside the container (that is, it does something like `docker container exec <containerID> <probing command>`). Thus, the command executes in the same network namespace as the application running inside the container. In the following diagram, we see the life cycle of a service task from its beginning:

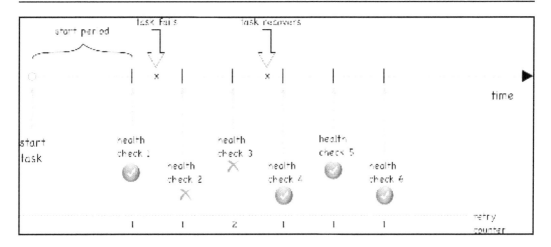

Service task with transient health failure

First, SwarmKit waits with probing until the start period is over. Then, we have a first health check. Shortly thereafter, the task fails when probed. It fails two consecutive times but then it recovers. Thus, health check number 4 is again successful and SwarmKit leaves the task running.

Here, we, see a task that is permanently failing:

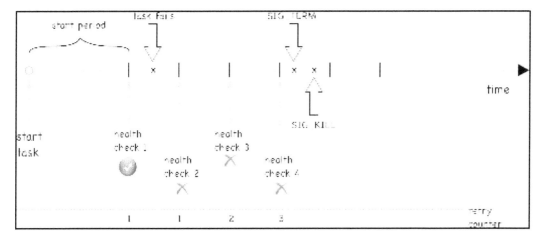

Permanent failure of task

If the task does not recover and after having three retries (or as many as you have defined), then SwarmKit first sends a SIGTERM to the container of the task, and if that times out after 10 seconds, it sends a SIGKILL signal.

We have just learned how we can define a health check for a service in the Dockerfile of its image. But this is not the only way. We can also define the health check in a stack file that we use to deploy our application into a Docker Swarm. Here is a short snippet of what such a stack file would look like:

```
version: "3.5"
services:
  web:
    image: example/web:1.0
    healthcheck:
      test: ["CMD", "curl", "-f", "http://localhost:3000/health"]
      interval: 30s
      timeout: 10s
      retries: 3
      start_period: 60s
...
```

In this snippet, we see how the health check-related information is defined in the stack file. First and foremost, it is important to realize that we have to define a health check for every service individually. There is no health check on an application or global level.

Similar to what we have defined previously in the Dockerfile, the command that is used to execute the health check by the SwarmKit is `curl -f http://localhost:3000/health`. We also have definitions for `interval`, `timeout`, `retries`, and `start_period`. These latter four key-value pairs have the same meaning as the corresponding parameters we used in the Dockerfile. If there are health check-related settings defined in the image, then the ones defined in the stack file override the ones from the Dockerfile.

Now, let's try to use a service that has a health check defined. In our `lab` folder, we have a file called `stack-health.yaml` with the following content:

```
version: "3.5"
services:
  web:
    image: nginx:alpine
    healthcheck:
      test: ["CMD", "wget", "-qO", "-", "http://localhost"]
      interval: 5s
      timeout: 2s
      retries: 3
      start_period: 15s
```

That we're going to deploy now:

```
$ docker stack deploy -c stack-health.yaml myapp
```

We can find out where the single task got deployed to by using `docker stack ps myapp`. On that particular node, we can list all containers to find the one of our stack. In my example, the task had been deployed to `node-3`:

Displaying the health status of a running task instance

The interesting thing in this screenshot is the `STATUS` column. Docker, or more precisely SwarmKit, has recognized that the service has a health check function defined and is using it to determine the health of each task of the service.

Rollback

Sometimes, things don't go as expected. A last minute fix in an application release inadvertently introduced a new bug, or the new version significantly decreases the throughput of the component, and so on. In such cases, we need to have a plan B which in most cases means the ability to roll back the update to the previous good version.

As with the update, the rollback has to happen in a such a way that it does not cause any outages of the application; it needs to cause zero downtime. In that sense, a rollback can be looked at as a reverse update. We are installing a new version, yet this new version is actually the previous version.

As with the update behavior, we can declare, either in our stack files or in the Docker service `create` command, how the system should behave in case it needs to execute a rollback. Here, we have the stack file that we used before, but this time with some rollback-relevant attributes:

```
version: "3.5"
services:
  web:
    image: nginx:1.12-alpine
    ports:
      - 80:80
    deploy:
```

```
    replicas: 10
    update_config:
      parallelism: 2
      delay: 10s

      failure_action: rollback
      monitor: 10s

  healthcheck:
    test: ["CMD", "wget", "-qO", "-", "http://localhost"]
    interval: 2s
    timeout: 2s
    retries: 3
    start_period: 2s
```

In this stack file, which is available in our lab as `stack-rollback.yaml`, we have defined the details about the rolling update, the health checks, and the behavior during rollback. The health check is defined so that after an initial wait time of 2 seconds, the orchestrator starts to poll the service on `http://localhost` every 2 seconds and it retries 3 times before it considers a task as unhealthy. If we do the math, then it takes at least 8 seconds until a task will be stopped if it is unhealthy due to a bug. So, now under deploy, we have a new entry `monitor`. This entry defines how long newly deployed tasks should be monitored for health as a decision point whether or not to continue with the next batch in the rolling update. Here, in this sample, we have given it 10 seconds. This is slightly more than the 8 seconds we calculated it takes to discover that a defective service has been deployed. So this is good.

We also have a new entry, `failure_action`, which defines what the orchestrator will do if it encounters a failure during the rolling update such as that the service is unhealthy. By default, the action is just to stop the whole update process and leave the system in an intermediate state. The system is not down since it is a rolling update and at least some healthy instances of the service are still operational, but some operations engineer better at taking a look and fixing the problem.

In our case, we have defined the action to be `rollback`. Thus, in case of failure, SwarmKit will automatically revert all tasks that have been updated back to their previous version.

Blue–green deployments

We have discussed in Chapter 6, *Distributed Application Architecture,* what blue–green deployments are, in an abstract way. It turns out that on Docker Swarm we cannot really implement blue–green deployments for arbitrary services. The service discovery and load balancing between two services running in Docker Swarm are part of the swarm routing mesh and cannot be (easily) customized. If **Service A** wants to call **Service B**, then Docker does it all implicitly. Docker, given the name of the target service, will use the Docker DNS service to resolve this name to a **virtual IP** (**VIP**) address. When the request is then targeted at the VIP, the Linux IPVS service will do another lookup in the Linux kernel IP tables with the VIP and load balances the request to one of the physical IP addresses of the tasks of the service represented by the VIP, as shown in the following figure:

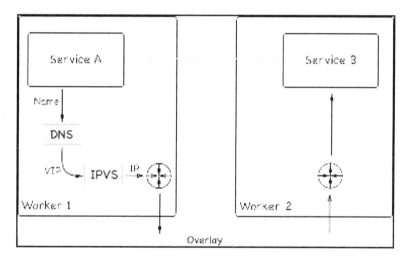

How service discovery and load balancing work in Docker Swarm

Unfortunately, there is no easy way to intercept this mechanism and replace it with a custom behavior. But this would be needed to allow for a true blue–green deployment of **Service B**, which is the target service in our example.

That said, we can always deploy the public-facing services in a blue–green fashion. We can use interlock 2 and its layer 7 routing mechanism to allow for a true blue–green deployment.

Canary releases

Technically, rolling updates are a kind of canary release. But due to their lack of seams, where you could plug customized logic into the system, rolling updates are only a very limited version of canary releases.

True canary releases require us to have more fine-grained control about the update process. Also, true canary releases do not take down the old version of the service until 100% of the traffic has been funneled through the new version. In that regard, they are treated like blue–green deployments.

In a canary release scenario, we want to not just use things such as health checks as deciding factors whether or not to funnel more and more traffic through the new version of the service, but we also want to consider external input in the decision making, such as metrics collected and aggregated by a log aggregator or tracing information. Examples that could be used as decision makers are the conformance to **service level agreements** (**SLAs**), namely if the new version of the service shows response times that are outside of the tolerance band. This can happen if we add new functionality to an existing service, yet this new functionality degrades the response time.

Secrets

Secrets are used to work with confidential data in a secure way. Swarm secrets are secure at rest and in transit. That is, when a new secret is created on a manager node, and it can only be created on a manager node, its value is encrypted and stored in the raft consensus storage. This is why it is secure at rest. If a service gets a secret assigned to it, then the manager reads the secret from storage, decrypts it, and forwards it to all the containers who are instances of the Swarm service that requests the secret. Since the node-to-node communication in swarm is using mutual **transport layer security** (**TLS**), the secret value, although decrypted, is still secure in transit. The manager forwards the secret only to the worker nodes on which a service instance is running. Secrets are then mounted as files into the target container. Each secret corresponds to a file. The name of the secret will be the name of the file inside the container, and the value of the secret is the content of the respective file. Secrets are never stored on the filesystem of a worker node but are mounted using `tmpFS` into the container. By default, secrets are mounted into the container at `/run/secrets`, but you can change that to any custom folder.

Creating secrets

First let's see how we can actually create a secret:

```
$ echo "sample secret value" | docker secret create sample-secret -
```

This command creates a secret called `sample-secret` with the value `sample secret value`. Please note the hyphen at the end of the `docker secret create` command. This means that Docker expects the value of the secret from standard input. This is exactly what we're doing by piping the value, `sample secret value` into the `create` command.

Alternatively, we can use a file as the source for the secret value:

```
$ docker secret create other-secret ~/my-secrets/secret-value.txt
```

Here, the value of the secret with the name `other-secret` is read from a file, `~/my-secrets/secret-value.txt`. Once a secret has been created, there is no way to access the value of it. We can, for example, list all our secrets and we will get the following screenshot:

List of all secrets

In this list, we only see the ID and name of the secret plus some other metadata, but the actual value of the secret is not visible. We can also use inspect on a secret, for example, to get more information about the `other-secret`:

```
$ docker secret inspect other-secret
[
    {
        "ID": "axykb7msipit1g5so63ef02it",
        "Version": {
            "Index": 135
        },
        "CreatedAt": "2018-03-16T01:29:14.367872931Z",
        "UpdatedAt": "2018-03-16T01:29:14.367872931Z",
        "Spec": {
            "Name": "other-secret",
            "Labels": {}
        }
    }
]
$
```

Inspecting a swarm secret

Even here, we do not get the value of the secret back. This is of course intentional, a secret is a secret and thus needs to remain confidential. We can assign labels to secrets if we want and we can even use a different driver to encrypt and decrypt the secret, if we're not happy with what Docker delivers out of the box.

Using a secret

Secrets are used by services that run in the swarm. Usually, secrets are assigned to a service at creation time. Thus, if we want to run a service called `web` and assign it a secret, `api-secret-key`, the syntax would look like the following command:

```
$ docker service create --name web \
    --secret api-secret-key \
    --publish 8000:8000 \
    fundamentalsofdocker/whoami:latest
```

This command creates a service called `web` based on the image `fundamentalsofdocker/whoami:latest`, publishes the container port `8000` to port `8000` on all swarm nodes, and assigns it the secret, `api-secret-key`.

This will only work if the secret called `api-secret-key` is defined in the swarm, otherwise an error will be generated with the text `secret not found: api-secret-key`. Thus, let's create this secret now:

```
$ echo "my secret key" | docker secret create api-secret-key -
```

And now, if we rerun the service `create` command, it will succeed:

Creating a service with a secret

We can now do a `docker service ps web` to find out on which node the sole service instance has been deployed, and then exec into this container. In my case, the instance has been deployed to `node-3`, thus I SSH into that node:

```
$ docker-machine ssh node-3
```

And then I list all my containers on that node to find the one instance belonging to my service and copy its container ID. We can then run the following command to make sure that the secret is indeed available inside the container under the expected filename containing the secret value in clear text:

```
$ docker exec -it <container ID> cat /run/secrets/api-secret-key
```

Once again, in my case, this looks like this:

A secret as a container sees it

If, for some reason, the default location where Docker mounts the secrets inside the container is not acceptable to you, you can define a custom location. In the following command, we mount the secret to `/app/my-secrets`:

```
$ docker service create --name web \
```

```
     --name web \
     -p 8000:8000 \
     --secret source=api-secret-key,target=/run/my-secrets/api-secret-
key \
     fundamentalsofdocker/whoami:latest
```

In this command, we are using the extended syntax to define a secret which includes the destination folder.

Simulating secrets in a development environment

When working in development, we usually don't have a local swarm on our machine. But secrets only work in a swarm. So, *what can we do*? Well, luckily it is really simple. Due to the fact that secrets are treated as files, we can easily mount a volume that contains the secrets into the container to the expected location, which by default is at /run/secrets.

Assume that we have a folder ./dev-secrets on our local workstation. For each secret, we have a file called the same way as the secret name and with the un-encrypted value of the secret as content of the file. For example, we can simulate a secret called demo-secret with a secret value demo secret value by executing the following command on our workstation:

```
$ echo "demo secret value" > ./dev-secrets/sample-secret
```

We can then create a container that mounts this folder like this:

```
$ docker container run -d --name whoami \
    -p 8000:8000 \
    -v $(pwd)/dev-secrets:/run/secrets \
    fundamentalsofdocker/whoami:latest
```

And the process running inside the container will not be able to distinguish these mounted files from ones originating from a secret. So, for example, the demo-secret is available as file /run/secrets/demo-secret inside the container and has the expected value demo secret value.

To test this, we can exec a shell inside the preceding container:

```
$ docker container exec -it whoami /bin/bash
```

And then navigate to the folder, /run/secrets and display the content of the file demo-secret:

```
/# cd /run/secrets
/# cat demo-secret
demo secret value
```

Secrets and legacy applications

Sometimes, we want to containerize a legacy application that we cannot easily, or do not want to, change. This legacy application might expect a secret value to be available as an environment variable. *How are we going to deal with this now?* Docker presents us with the secrets as files but the application is expecting them in the form of environment variables.

In this situation, it is helpful to define a script that runs when the container is started (a so-called entrypoint or start up script). This script will read the secret value from the respective file and define an environment variable with the same name as the file, assigning the new variable the value read from the file. In the case of a secret called demo-secret whose value should be available in an environment variable called DEMO_SECRET, the necessary code snippet in this start up script could look like this:

```
export DEMO_SECRET=`cat /run/secrets/demo-secret`
```

Similarly, if the legacy application expects the secret values to be present as an entry in say, a YAML configuration file located in the /app/bin folder, and called app.config whose relevant part looks like this:

```
...
secrets:
  demo-secret: "<<demo-secret-value>>"
  other-secret: "<<other-secret-value>>"
  yet-another-secret: "<<yet-another-secret-value>>"
...
```

Our initialization script now needs to read the secret value from the secret file and replace the corresponding placeholder in the config file with the secret value. For the demo-secret, this could look like this:

```
file=/app/bin/app.conf
demo_secret=`cat /run/secret/demo-secret`
sed -i "s/<<demo-secret-value>>/$demo_secret/g" "$file"
```

In this snippet, we're using the `sed` tool to replace a placeholder with a value in place. We can use the same technique for the other two secrets in the config file.

We put all the initialization logic into a file called `entrypoint.sh`, make this file executable and, for example, add it to the root of the container's filesystem, and then we define this file as `ENTRYPOINT` in the Dockerfile, or we can override the existing `ENTRYPOINT` of an image in the `docker container run` command.

Let's make a sample. Assume that we have a legacy application running inside a container defined by the image `fundamentalsofdocker/whoami:latest` that expects a secret `db_password` to be defined in a file, `whoami.conf`, in the application folder. We can define a file, `whoami.conf`, on our local machine with this content:

```
database:
  name: demo
  db_password: "<<db_password_value>>"
others:
  val1=123
  val2="hello world"
```

The important part is line 3 of this snippet. It defines where the secret value has to be put by the start up script. Let's add a file called `entrypoint.sh` to the local folder with the following content:

```
file=/app/whoami.conf
db_pwd=`cat /run/secret/db-password`
sed -i "s/<<db_password_value>>/$db_pwd/g" "$file"

/app/http
```

The last line in this script stems from the fact that this is the start command used in the original Dockerfile. Now, change the mode of this file to be executable:

```
$ sudo chmod +x ./entrypoint.sh
```

Now, we define a Dockerfile which inherits from the image `fundamentalsofdocker/whoami:latest`. Add a file called `Dockerfile` to the current folder with the following content:

```
FROM fundamentalsofdocker/whoami:latest
COPY ./whoami.conf /app/
COPY ./entrypoint.sh /
CMD ["/entrypoint.sh"]
```

```
$ docker image build -t secrets-demo:1.0 .
```

Once the image is built, we can run a service from it. But before we can do that, we need to define the secret in the swarm:

```
$ echo "passw0rD123" | docker secret create demo-secret -
```

And now we can create the service that uses the following secret:

```
$ docker service create --name demo \
    --secret demo-secret \
    secrets-demo:1.0
```

Updating secrets

At times, we need to update a secret in a running service, the reason being that secrets could be leaked out to the public or be stolen by malicious people, such a hackers. In this case, we need to change our confidential data since the moment it has leaked to a non-trusted entity, it has to be considered as insecure.

The updating of secrets, like any other update, has to happen in a way which requires zero downtime. SwarmKit supports us in this regard.

First, we create the new secret in the Swarm. It is recommended to use a versioning strategy when doing so. In our example, we use a version as a postfix of the secret name. We originally started with the secret named db-password and now the new version of this secret is called db-password-v2:

```
$ echo "newPassw0rD" | docker secret create db-password-v2 -
```

Assume that the original service that used the secret had been created like this:

```
$ docker service create --name web \
    --publish 80:80 \
    --secret db-password
    nginx:alpine
```

The application running inside the container was able to access the secret at `/run/secrets/db-password`. Now, SwarmKit does not allow us to update an existing secret in a running service, thus we have to first remove the now obsolete version of the secret and then add the new one. Let's start with the removal with the following command:

```
$ docker service update --secret-rm db-password web
```

And then we can add the new secret with the following command:

```
$ docker service update \
    --secret-add source=db-password-v2, target=db-password \
    web
```

Summary

In this chapter, we learned how SwarmKit allows us to update services without requiring downtime. We also discussed the current limits of SwarmKit in regards to zero downtime deployments. In the second part of the chapter, we introduced secrets as a means to provide confidential data to services in a highly secure way.

Questions

To assess your understanding of the topics discussed in this chapter, please answer the following questions:

1. Explain to an interested layman in a few simple sentences what *zero downtime deployment* means.
2. How does SwarmKit achieve zero downtime deployments?
3. Contrary to traditional (non-containerized) systems, why does a rollback in Docker Swarm *just work*? Explain in a few short sentences.
4. Describe two to three characteristics of a Docker secret.

5. You need to roll out a new version of the `inventory` service. What does your command look like? Here is some more information:
    1. The new image is called `acme/inventory:2.1`.
    2. We want to use a rolling update strategy with a batch size of two tasks.
    3. We want the system to wait for one minute after each batch.

6. You need to update an existing service named `inventory` with a new password that is provided through a Docker secret. The new secret is called `MYSQL_PASSWORD_V2`. The code in the service expects the secret to be called `MYSQL_PASSWORD`. What does the update command look like? (Note: we do not want the code of the service to be changed!)

Further reading

Here are some links to external sources:

- *Apply rolling updates to a service* at `https://dockr.ly/2HfGj1D`
- *Manage sensitive data with Docker secrets* at `https://dockr.ly/2vUNbuH`
- *Introducing Docker secrets management* at `https://dockr.ly/2k7zwzE`
- *From env variables to Docker secrets* at `https://bit.ly/2GY3UUB`

12
Building Your Own Kubernetes Cluster

In this chapter, we will cover the following recipes:

- Exploring the Kubernetes architecture
- Setting up a Kubernetes cluster on macOS by minikube
- Setting up a Kubernetes cluster on Windows by minikube
- Setting up a Kubernetes cluster on Linux by kubeadm
- Setting up a Kubernetes cluster on Linux by Ansible (kubespray)
- Running your first container in Kubernetes

Introduction

Welcome to your journey into Kubernetes! In this very first section, you will learn how to build your own Kubernetes cluster. Along with understanding each component and connecting them together, you will learn how to run your first container on Kubernetes. Having a Kubernetes cluster will help you continue your studies in the chapters ahead.

Exploring the Kubernetes architecture

Kubernetes is an open source container management tool. It is a Go language-based (https://golang.org), lightweight and portable application. You can set up a Kubernetes cluster on a Linux-based OS to deploy, manage, and scale Docker container applications on multiple hosts.

Getting ready

Kubernetes is made up of the following components:

- Kubernetes master
- Kubernetes nodes
- etcd
- Kubernetes network

These components are connected via a network, as shown in the following diagram:

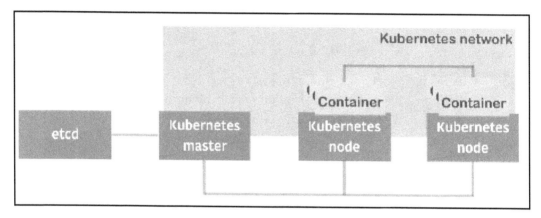

The preceding diagram can be summarized as follows:

- **Kubernetes master**: It connects to etcd via HTTP or HTTPS to store the data
- **Kubernetes nodes**: It connect to the Kubernetes master via HTTP or HTTPS to get a command and report the status
- **Kubernetes network**: It L2, L3 or overlay make a connection of their container applications

How to do it...

In this section, we are going to explain how to use the Kubernetes master and nodes to realize the main functions of the Kubernetes system.

Kubernetes master

The Kubernetes master is the main component of the Kubernetes cluster. It serves several functionalities, such as the following:

- Authorization and authentication
- RESTful API entry point
- Container deployment scheduler to Kubernetes nodes
- Scaling and replicating controllers
- Reading the configuration to set up a cluster

The following diagram shows how master daemons work together to fulfill the aforementioned functionalities:

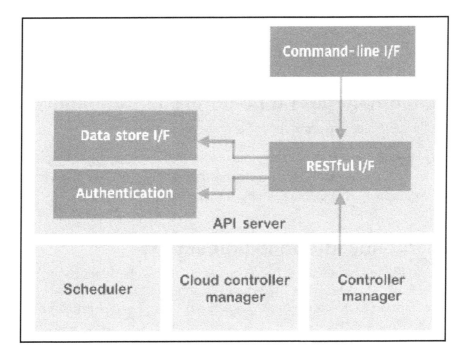

There are several daemon processes that form the Kubernetes master's functionality, such as `kube-apiserver`, `kube-scheduler` and `kube-controller-manager`. Hypercube, the wrapper binary, can launch all these daemons.

In addition, the Kubernetes command-line interface, kubect can control the Kubernetes master functionality.

API server (kube-apiserver)

The API server provides an HTTP- or HTTPS-based RESTful API, which is the hub between Kubernetes components, such as kubectl, the scheduler, the replication controller, the etcd data store, the kubelet and kube-proxy, which runs on Kubernetes nodes, and so on.

Scheduler (kube-scheduler)

The scheduler helps to choose which container runs on which nodes. It is a simple algorithm that defines the priority for dispatching and binding containers to nodes. For example:

- CPU
- Memory
- How many containers are running?

Controller manager (kube-controller-manager)

The controller manager performs cluster operations. For example:

- Manages Kubernetes nodes
- Creates and updates the Kubernetes internal information
- Attempts to change the current status to the desired status

Command-line interface (kubectl)

After you install the Kubernetes master, you can use the Kubernetes command-line interface, kubectl, to control the Kubernetes cluster. For example, kubectl get cs returns the status of each component. Also, kubectl get nodes returns a list of Kubernetes nodes:

```
//see the Component Statuses
# kubectl get cs
NAME                  STATUS    MESSAGE               ERROR
controller-manager    Healthy   ok                    nil
scheduler             Healthy   ok                    nil
etcd-0                Healthy   {"health": "true"}    nil


//see the nodes
```

```
# kubectl get nodes
NAME            LABELS                                  STATUS      AGE
kub-node1       kubernetes.io/hostname=kub-node1        Ready       26d
kub-node2       kubernetes.io/hostname=kub-node2        Ready       26d
```

Kubernetes node

The Kubernetes node is a slave node in the Kubernetes cluster. It is controlled by the Kubernetes master to run container applications using Docker (`http://docker.com`) or rkt (`http://coreos.com/rkt/docs/latest/`). In this book, we will use the Docker container runtime as the default engine.

Node or slave?

The term slave is used in the computer industry to represent the cluster worker node; however, it is also associated with discrimination. The Kubernetes project uses minion in the early version and node in the current version.

The following diagram displays the role and tasks of daemon processes in the node:

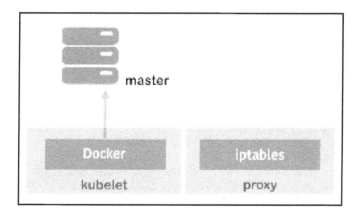

The node also has two daemon processes, named kubelet and kube-proxy, to support its functionalities.

kubelet

kubelet is the main process on the Kubernetes node that communicates with the Kubernetes master to handle the following operations:

- Periodically accesses the API controller to check and report
- Performs container operations
- Runs the HTTP server to provide simple APIs

Proxy (kube-proxy)

The proxy handles the network proxy and load balancer for each container. It changes Linux iptables rules (nat table) to control TCP and UDP packets across the containers.

After starting the kube-proxy daemon, it configures iptables rules; you can use `iptables -t nat -L` or `iptables -t nat -S` to check the nat table rules, as follows:

```
//the result will be vary and dynamically changed by kube-proxy
# sudo iptables -t nat -S
-P PREROUTING ACCEPT
-P INPUT ACCEPT
-P OUTPUT ACCEPT
-P POSTROUTING ACCEPT
-N DOCKER
-N FLANNEL
-N KUBE-NODEPORT-CONTAINER
-N KUBE-NODEPORT-HOST
-N KUBE-PORTALS-CONTAINER
-N KUBE-PORTALS-HOST
-A PREROUTING -m comment --comment "handle ClusterIPs; NOTE: this must
be before the NodePort rules" -j KUBE-PORTALS-CONTAINER
-A PREROUTING -m addrtype --dst-type LOCAL -m comment --comment
"handle service NodePorts; NOTE: this must be the last rule in the
chain" -j KUBE-NODEPORT-CONTAINER
-A PREROUTING -m addrtype --dst-type LOCAL -j DOCKER
-A OUTPUT -m comment --comment "handle ClusterIPs; NOTE: this must be
before the NodePort rules" -j KUBE-PORTALS-HOST
-A OUTPUT -m addrtype --dst-type LOCAL -m comment --comment "handle
service NodePorts; NOTE: this must be the last rule in the chain" -j
KUBE-NODEPORT-HOST
-A OUTPUT ! -d 127.0.0.0/8 -m addrtype --dst-type LOCAL -j DOCKER
-A POSTROUTING -s 192.168.90.0/24 ! -o docker0 -j MASQUERADE
-A POSTROUTING -s 192.168.0.0/16 -j FLANNEL
```

```
-A FLANNEL -d 192.168.0.0/16 -j ACCEPT
-A FLANNEL ! -d 224.0.0.0/4 -j MASQUERADE
```

How it works...

There are two more components to complement Kubernetes node functionalities, the data store etcd and the inter-container network. You can learn how they support the Kubernetes system in the following subsections.

etcd

etcd (`https://coreos.com/etcd/`) is the distributed key-value data store. It can be accessed via the RESTful API to perform CRUD operations over the network. Kubernetes uses etcd as the main data store.

You can explore the Kubernetes configuration and status in etcd (`/registry`) using the `curl` command, as follows:

```
//example: etcd server is localhost and default port is 4001
# curl -L http://127.0.0.1:4001/v2/keys/registry
{"action":"get","node":{"key":"/registry","dir":true,"nodes":[{"key":"
/registry/namespaces","dir":true,"modifiedIndex":6,"createdIndex":6},{
"key":"/registry/pods","dir":true,"modifiedIndex":187,"createdIndex":1
87},{"key":"/registry/clusterroles","dir":true,"modifiedIndex":196,"cr
eatedIndex":196},{"key":"/registry/replicasets","dir":true,"modifiedIn
dex":178,"createdIndex":178},{"key":"/registry/limitranges","dir":true
,"modifiedIndex":202,"createdIndex":202},{"key":"/registry/storageclas
ses","dir":true,"modifiedIndex":215,"createdIndex":215},{"key":"/regis
try/apiregistration.k8s.io","dir":true,"modifiedIndex":7,"createdIndex
":7},{"key":"/registry/serviceaccounts","dir":true,"modifiedIndex":70,
"createdIndex":70},{"key":"/registry/secrets","dir":true,"modifiedInde
x":71,"createdIndex":71},{"key":"/registry/deployments","dir":true,"mo
difiedIndex":177,"createdIndex":177},{"key":"/registry/services","dir"
:true,"modifiedIndex":13,"createdIndex":13},{"key":"/registry/configma
ps","dir":true,"modifiedIndex":52,"createdIndex":52},{"key":"/registry
/ranges","dir":true,"modifiedIndex":4,"createdIndex":4},{"key":"/regis
try/minions","dir":true,"modifiedIndex":58,"createdIndex":58},{"key":"
/registry/clusterrolebindings","dir":true,"modifiedIndex":171,"created
Index":171}],"modifiedIndex":4,"createdIndex":4}}
```

Kubernetes network

Network communication between containers is the most difficult part. Because Kubernetes manages multiple nodes (hosts) running several containers, those containers on different nodes may need to communicate with each other.

If the container's network communication is only within a single node, you can use Docker network or Docker compose to discover the peer. However, along with multiple nodes, Kubernetes uses an overlay network or **container network interface** (**CNI**) to achieve multiple container communication.

See also

This recipe describes the basic architecture and methodology of Kubernetes and the related components. Understanding Kubernetes is not easy, but a step-by-step learning process on how to set up, configure, and manage Kubernetes is really fun.

Setting up the Kubernetes cluster on macOS by minikube

Kubernetes consists of combination of multiple open source components. These are developed by different parties, making it difficult to find and download all the related packages and install, configure, and make them work from scratch.

Fortunately, there are some different solutions and tools that have been developed to set up Kubernetes clusters effortlessly. Therefore, it is highly recommended you use such a tool to set up Kubernetes on your environment.

The following tools are categorized by different types of solution to build your own Kubernetes:

- Self-managed solutions that include:
    - minikube
    - kubeadm
    - kubespray
    - kops

- Enterprise solutions that include:
    - OpenShift (`https://www.openshift.com`)
    - Tectonic (`https://coreos.com/tectonic/`)
- Cloud-hosted solutions that include:
    - Google Kubernetes engine (`https://cloud.google.com/kubernetes-engine/`)
    - Amazon elastic container service for Kubernetes (Amazon EKS, `https://aws.amazon.com/eks/`)
    - Azure Container Service (AKS, `https://azure.microsoft.com/en-us/services/container-service/`)

A self-managed solution is suitable if we just want to build a development environment or do a proof of concept quickly.

By using minikube (`https://github.com/kubernetes/minikube`) and kubeadm (`https://kubernetes.io/docs/admin/kubeadm/`), we can easily build the desired environment on our machine locally; however, it is not practical if we want to build a production environment.

By using kubespray (`https://github.com/kubernetes-incubator/kubespray`) and kops (`https://github.com/kubernetes/kops`), we can also build a production-grade environment quickly from scratch.

An enterprise solution or cloud-hosted solution is the easiest starting point if we want to create a production environment. In particular, the **Google Kubernetes Engine** (**GKE**), which has been used by Google for many years, comes with comprehensive management, meaning that users don't need to care much about the installation and settings. Also, Amazon EKS is a new service that was introduced at AWS re: Invent 2017, which is managed by the Kubernetes service on AWS.

Kubernetes can also run on different clouds and on-premise VMs by custom solutions. To get started, we will build Kubernetes using minikube on macOS desktop machines in this chapter.

Getting ready

minikube runs Kubernetes on the Linux VM on macOS. It relies on a hypervisor (virtualization technology), such as VirtualBox (`https://www.virtualbox.org`), VMWare fusion (`https://www.vmware.com/products/fusion.html`), or hyperkit (`https://github.com/moby/hyperkit`) In addition, we will need to have the Kubernetes **command-line interface** (**CLI**) `kubectl`, which is used to connect through the hypervisor, to control Kubernetes.

With minikube, you can run the entire suite of the Kubernetes stack on your macOS, including the Kubernetes master, node, and CLI. It is recommended that macOS has enough memory to run Kubernetes. By default, minikube uses VirtualBox as the hypervisor.

In this chapter, however, we will demonstrate how to use hyperkit, which is the most lightweight solution. As Linux VM consumes 2 GB of memory, at least 4 GB of memory is recommended. Note that hyperkit is built on the top of the hypervisor framework (`https://developer.apple.com/documentation/hypervisor`) on macOS; therefore, macOS 10.10 Yosemite or later is required.

The following diagram shows the relationship between kubectl, the hypervisor, minikube, and macOS:

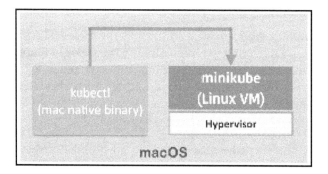

How to do it...

macOS doesn't have an official package management tool, such as yum and apt-get on Linux. But there are some useful tools available for macOS. Homebrew (`https://brew.sh`) is the most popular package management tool and manages many open source tools, including minikube.

In order to install `Homebrew` on macOS, perform the following steps:

1. Open the Terminal and then type the following command:

```
$ /usr/bin/ruby -e "$(curl -fsSL
https://raw.githubusercontent.com/Homebrew/install/master/
install)"
```

2. Once installation is completed, you can type `/usr/local/bin/brew help` to see the available command options.

 If you just install or upgrade Xcode on your macOS, the `Homebrew` installation may stop. In that case, open Xcode to accept the license agreement or type `sudo xcodebuild -license` beforehand.

3. Next, install the `hyperkit driver` for minikube. At the time of writing (February 2018), HomeBrew does not support hyperkit; therefore type the following command to install it:

```
$ curl -LO
https://storage.googleapis.com/minikube/releases/latest/do
cker-machine-driver-hyperkit \
&& chmod +x docker-machine-driver-hyperkit \
&& sudo mv docker-machine-driver-hyperkit /usr/local/bin/
\
&& sudo chown root:wheel /usr/local/bin/docker-machine-
driver-hyperkit \
&& sudo chmod u+s /usr/local/bin/docker-machine-driver-
hyperkit
```

4. Next, let's install the Kubernetes CLI. Use Homebrew with the following comment to install the `kubectl` command on your macOS:

```
//install kubectl command by "kubernetes-cli" package
$ brew install kubernetes-cli
```

Finally, you can install minikube. It is not managed by Homebrew; however, Homebrew has an extension called `homebrew-cask` (`https://github.com/caskroom/homebrew-cask`) that supports minikube.

5. In order to install minikube by `homebrew-cask`, just simply type the following command:

```
//add "cask" option
$ brew cask install minikube
```

6. If you have never installed **Docker for Mac** on your machine, you need to install it via `homebrew-cask` as well

```
//only if you don't have a Docker for Mac
$ brew cask install docker

//start Docker
$ open -a Docker.app
```

7. Now you are all set! The following command shows whether the required packages have been installed on your macOS or not:

```
//check installed package by homebrew
$ brew list
kubernetes-cli


//check installed package by homebrew-cask
$ brew cask list
minikube
```

How it works...

minikube is suitable for setting up Kubernetes on your macOS with the following command, which downloads and starts a Kubernetes VM stet, and then configures the kubectl configuration (`~/.kube/config`):

```
//use --vm-driver=hyperkit to specify to use hyperkit
$ /usr/local/bin/minikube start --vm-driver=hyperkit
Starting local Kubernetes v1.10.0 cluster...
Starting VM...
Downloading Minikube ISO
 150.53 MB / 150.53 MB [===============================================]
100.00% 0s
Getting VM IP address...
Moving files into cluster...
Downloading kubeadm v1.10.0
Downloading kubelet v1.10.0
Finished Downloading kubelet v1.10.0
Finished Downloading kubeadm v1.10.0
Setting up certs...
Connecting to cluster...
Setting up kubeconfig...
Starting cluster components...
Kubectl is now configured to use the cluster.
Loading cached images from config file.
```

```
//check whether .kube/config is configured or not
$ cat ~/.kube/config
apiVersion: v1
clusters:
- cluster:
    certificate-authority: /Users/saito/.minikube/ca.crt
    server: https://192.168.64.26:8443
  name: minikube
contexts:
- context:
    cluster: minikube
    user: minikube
  name: minikube
current-context: minikube
kind: Config
preferences: {}
users:
- name: minikube
  user:
    as-user-extra: {}
    client-certificate: /Users/saito/.minikube/client.crt
    client-key: /Users/saito/.minikube/client.key
```

After getting all the necessary packages, perform the following steps:

1. Wait for a few minutes for the Kubernetes cluster setup to complete.
2. Use `kubectl version` to check the Kubernetes master version and `kubectl get cs` to see the component status.
3. Also, use the `kubectl get nodes` command to check whether the Kubernetes node is ready or not:

```
//it shows kubectl (Client) is 1.10.1, and Kubernetes
master (Server) is 1.10.0
$ /usr/local/bin/kubectl version --short
Client Version: v1.10.1
Server Version: v1.10.0


//get cs will shows Component Status
$ kubectl get cs
NAME                 STATUS    MESSAGE              ERROR
controller-manager   Healthy   ok
scheduler            Healthy   ok
etcd-0               Healthy   {"health": "true"}


//Kubernetes node (minikube) is ready
```

```
$ /usr/local/bin/kubectl get nodes
NAME        STATUS    ROLES     AGE     VERSION
minikube    Ready     master    2m      v1.10.0
```

4. Now you can start to use Kubernetes on your machine. The following sections describe how to use the kubectl command to manipulate Docker containers.

5. Note that, in some cases, you may need to maintain the Kubernetes cluster, such as starting/stopping the VM or completely deleting it. The following commands maintain the minikube environment:

Command	Purpose
minikube start --vm-driver=hyperkit	Starts the Kubernetes VM using the hyperkit driver
minikube stop	Stops the Kubernetes VM
minikube delete	Deletes a Kubernetes VM image
minikube ssh	ssh to the Kubernetes VM guest
minikube ip	Shows the Kubernetes VM (node) IP address
minikube update-context	Checks and updates ~/.kube/config if the VM IP address is changed
minikube dashboard	Opens the web browser to connect the Kubernetes UI

For example, minikube starts a dashboard (the Kubernetes UI) by the default. If you want to access the dashboard, type minikube dashboard; it then opens your default browser and connects the Kubernetes UI, as illustrated in the following screenshot:

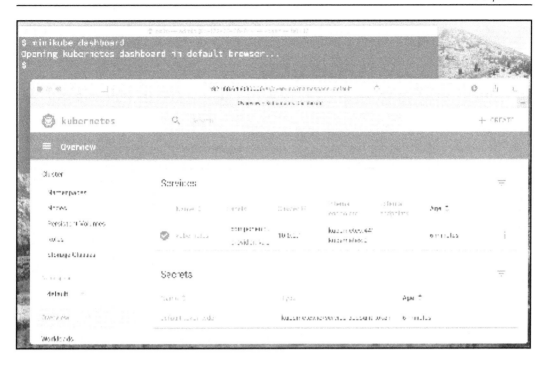

See also

This recipe describes how to set up a Kubernetes cluster on your macOS using minikube. It is the easiest way to start using Kubernetes. We also learned how to use kubectl, the Kubernetes command-line interface tool, which is the entry point to control our Kubernetes cluster!

Setting up the Kubernetes cluster on Windows by minikube

By nature, Docker and Kubernetes are based on a Linux-based OS. Although it is not ideal to use the Windows OS to explore Kubernetes, many people are using the Windows OS as their desktop or laptop machine. Luckily, there are a lot of ways to run the Linux OS on Windows using virtualization technologies, which makes running a Kubernetes cluster on Windows machines possible. Then, we can build a development environment or do a proof of concept on our local Windows machine.

You can run the Linux VM by using any hypervisor on Windows to set up Kubernetes from scratch, but using minikube (`https://github.com/kubernetes/minikube`) is the fastest way to build a Kubernetes cluster on Windows. Note that this recipe is not ideal for a production environment because it will set up a Kubernetes on Linux VM on Windows.

Getting ready

To set up minikube on Windows requires a hypervisor, either VirtualBox (`https://www.virtualbox.org`) or Hyper-V, because, again, minikube uses the Linux VM on Windows. This means that you cannot use the Windows virtual machine (for example, running the Windows VM on macOS by parallels).

However, `kubectl`, the Kubernetes CLI, supports a Windows native binary that can connect to Kubernetes over a network. So, you can set up a portable suite of Kubernetes stacks on your Windows machine.

The following diagram shows the relationship between kubectl, Hypervisor, minikube, and Windows:

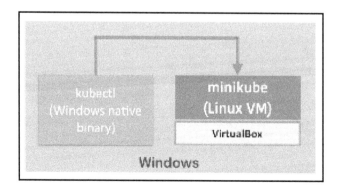

Hyper-V is required for Windows 8 Pro or later. While many users still use Windows 7, we will use VirtualBox as the minikube hypervisor in this recipe.

How to do it...

First of all, VirtualBox for Windows is required:

1. Go to the VirtualBox website (`https://www.virtualbox.org/wiki/Downloads`) to download the Windows installer.

2. Installation is straightforward, so we can just choose the default options and click **Next**:

3. Next, create the `Kubernetes` folder, which is used to store the minikube and kubectl binaries. Let's create the `k8s` folder on top of the `C:` drive, as shown in the following screenshot:

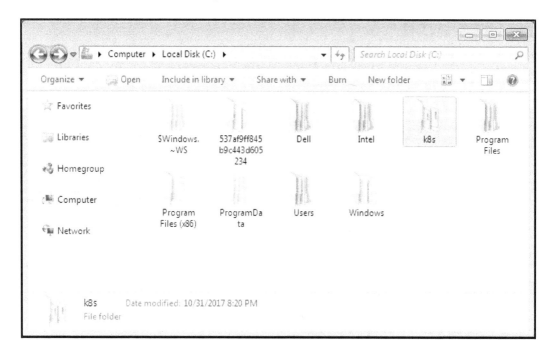

4. This folder must be in the command search path, so open **System Properties**, then move to the **Advanced** tab.
5. Click the **Environment Variables...** button, then choose **Path** , and then click the **Edit...** button, as shown in the following screenshot:

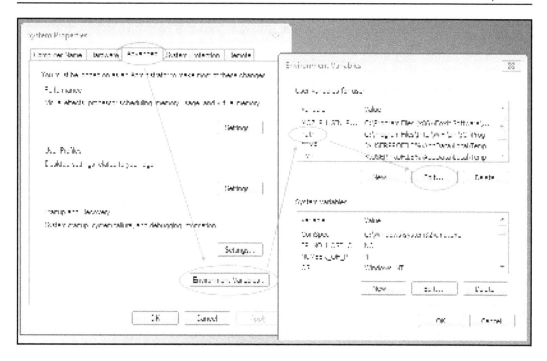

6. Then, append `c:\k8s` , as follows:

7. After clicking the **OK** button, log off and logo on to Windows again (or reboot) to apply this change.

8. Next, download minikube for Windows. It is a single binary, so use any web browser to download `https://github.com/kubernetes/minikube/releases/download/v0.26.1/minikube-windows-amd64` and then copy it to the `c:\k8s` folder, but change the filename to `minikube.exe`.

9. Next, download kubectl for Windows, which can communicate with Kubernetes. It is also single binary like minikube. So, download `https://storage.googleapis.com/kubernetes-release/release/v1.10.2/bin/windows/amd64/kubectl.exe` and then copy it to the `c:\k8s` folder as well.

10. Eventually, you will see two binaries in the `c:\k8s` folder, as shown in the following screenshot:

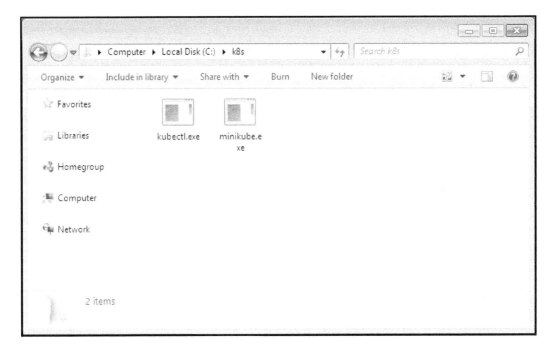

 If you are running anti-virus software, it may prevent you from running `kubectl.exe` and `minikube.exe`. If so, please update your anti-virus software setting that allows running these two binaries.

How it works...

Let's get started!

1. Open Command Prompt and then type `minikube start`, as shown in the following screenshot:

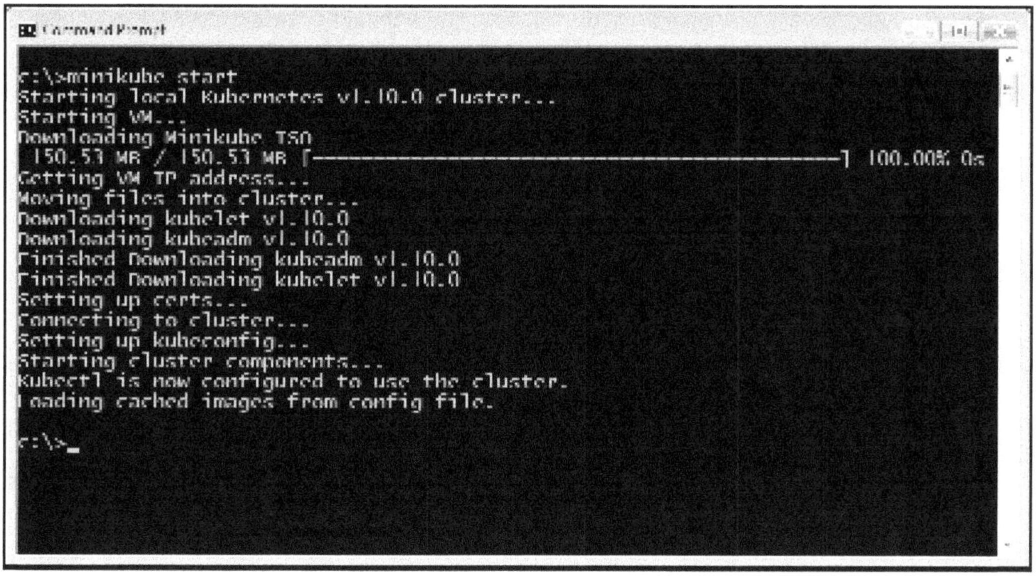

2. minikube downloads the Linux VM image and then sets up Kubernetes on the Linux VM; now if you open VirtualBox, you can see that the minikube guest has been registered, as illustrated in the following screenshot:

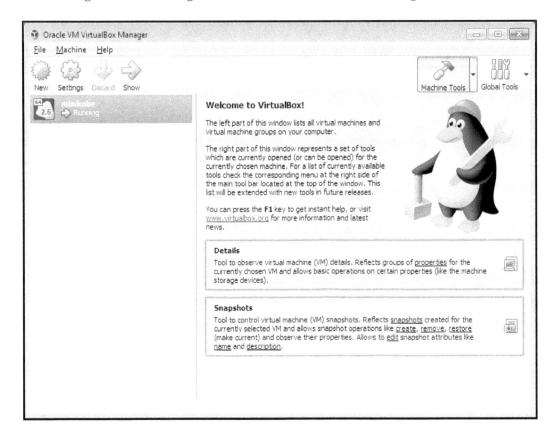

3. Wait for a few minutes to complete the setup of the Kubernetes cluster.

4. As per the following screenshot, type `kubectl version` to check the Kubernetes master version.

5. Use the `kubectl get nodes` command to check whether the Kubernetes node is ready or not:

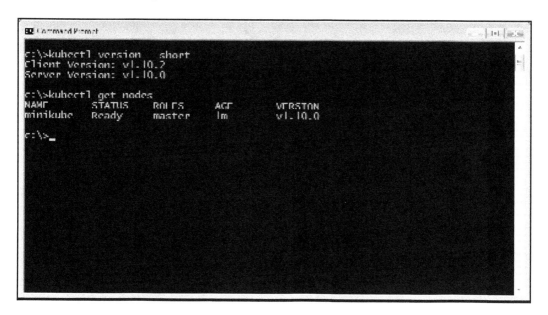

6. Now you can start to use Kubernetes on your machine! Again, Kubernetes is running on the Linux VM, as shown in the next screenshot.

7. Using `minikube ssh` allows you to access the Linux VM that runs Kubernetes:

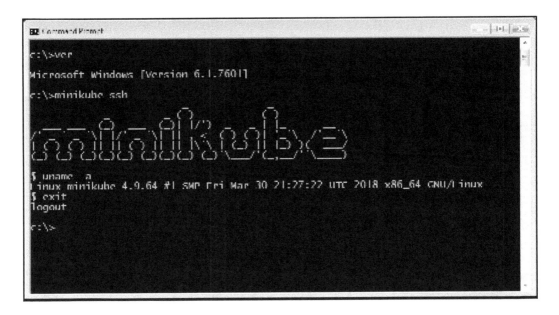

Therefore, any Linux-based Docker image is capable of running on your Windows machine.

8. Type `minikube ip` to verify which IP address the Linux VM uses and also `minikube dashboard`, to open your default web browser and navigate to the Kubernetes UI ,as shown in the following screenshot:

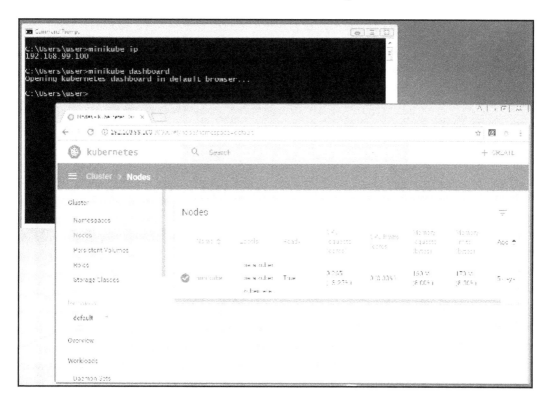

9. If you don't need to use Kubernetes anymore, type `minikube stop` or
   open VirtualBox to stop the Linux guest and release the resource, as shown
   in the following screenshot:

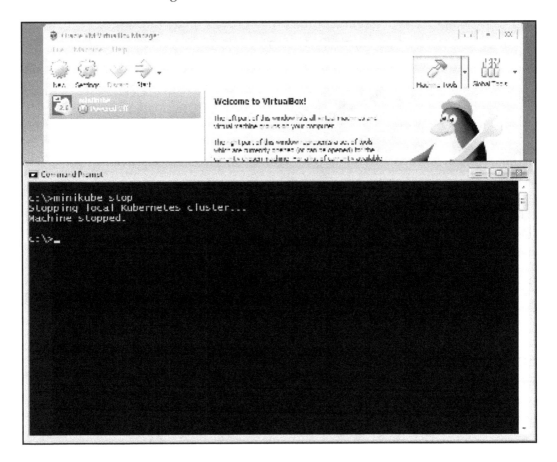

See also

This recipe describes how to set up a Kubernetes cluster on your Windows OS using
minikube. It is the easiest way to start using Kubernetes. It also describes kubectl, the
Kubernetes command-line interface tool, which is the entry point form which to
control your Kubernetes.

Setting up the Kubernetes cluster on Linux via kubeadm

In this recipe, we are going to show how to create a Kubernetes cluster along with kubeadm (`https://github.com/kubernetes/kubeadm`) on Linux servers. Kubeadm is a command-line tool that simplifies the procedure of creating and managing a Kubernetes cluster. Kubeadm leverages the fast deployment feature of Docker, running the system services of the Kubernetes master and the etcd server as containers. When triggered by the `kubeadm` command, the container services will contact kubelet on the Kubernetes node directly; kubeadm also checks whether every component is healthy. Through the kubeadm setup steps, you can avoid having a bunch of installation and configuration commands when you build everything from scratch.

Getting ready

We will provide instructions of two types of OS:

- Ubuntu Xenial 16.04 (LTS)
- CentOS 7.4

Make sure the OS version is matched before continuing. Furthermore, the software dependency and network settings should be also verified before you proceed to thecd cd next step. Check the following items to prepare the environment:

- **Every node has a unique MAC address and product UUID**: Some plugins use the MAC address or product UUID as a unique machine ID to identify nodes (for example, `kube-dns`). If they are duplicated in the cluster, kubeadm may not work while starting the plugin:

  ```
  // check MAC address of your NIC
  $ ifconfig -a
  // check the product UUID on your host
  $ sudo cat /sys/class/dmi/id/product_uuid
  ```

- **Every node has a different hostname**: If the hostname is duplicated, the Kubernetes system may collect logs or statuses from multiple nodes into the same one.

- **Docker is installed**: As mentioned previously, the Kubernetes master will run its daemon as a container, and every node in the cluster should get Docker installed. For how to perform the Docker installation, you can follow the steps on the official website: (Ubuntu: `https://docs.docker.com/engine/installation/linux/docker-ce/ubuntu/`, and CentOS: `https://docs.docker.com/engine/installation/linux/docker-ce/centos/`) Here we have Docker CE 17.06 installed on our machines; however, only Docker versions 1.11.2 to 1.13.1, and 17.03.x are verified with Kubernetes version 1.10.
- **Network ports are available**: The Kubernetes system services need network ports for communication. The ports in the following table should now be occupied according to the role of the node:

Node role	Ports	System service
Master	`6443`	Kubernetes API server
	`10248/10250/10255`	kubelet local healthz endpoint/Kubelet API/Heapster (read-only)
	`10251`	kube-scheduler
	`10252`	kube-controller-manager
	`10249/10256`	kube-proxy
	`2379/2380`	etcd client/etcd server communication
Node	`10250/10255`	Kubelet API/Heapster (read-only)
	`30000~32767`	Port range reserved for exposing container service to outside world

- The Linux command, `netstat`, can help to check if the port is in use or not:

```
// list every listening port
$ sudo netstat -tulpn | grep LISTEN
```

- Network tool packages are installed. `ethtool` and `ebtables` are two required utilities for kubeadm. They can be download and installed by the `apt-get` or `yum` package managing tools.

How to do it...

The installation procedures for two Linux OSes, Ubuntu and CentOS, are going to be introduced separately in this recipe as they have different setups.

Package installation

Let's get the Kubernetes packages first! The repository for downloading needs to be set in the source list of the package management system. Then, we are able to get them installed easily through the command-line.

Ubuntu

To install Kubernetes packages in Ubuntu perform the following steps:

1. Some repositories are URL with HTTPS. The `apt-transport-https` package must be installed to access the HTTPS endpoint:

   ```
   $ sudo apt-get update && sudo apt-get install -y apt-transport-https
   ```

2. Download the public key for accessing packages on Google Cloud, and add it as follows:

   ```
   $ curl -s
   https://packages.cloud.google.com/apt/doc/apt-key.gpg |
   sudo apt-key add -
   OK
   ```

3. Next, add a new source list for the Kubernetes packages:

   ```
   $ sudo bash -c 'echo "deb http://apt.kubernetes.io/
   kubernetes-xenial main" >
   /etc/apt/sources.list.d/kubernetes.list'
   ```

3. Finally, it is good to install the Kubernetes packages:

   ```
   // on Kubernetes master
   $ sudo apt-get update && sudo apt-get install -y kubelet
   kubeadm kubectl
   // on Kubernetes node
   $ sudo apt-get update && sudo apt-get install -y kubelet
   ```

CentOS

To install Kubernetes packages in CentOS perform the following steps:

1. As with Ubuntu, new repository information needs to be added:

   ```
   $ sudo vim /etc/yum.repos.d/kubernetes.repo
   [kubernetes]
   ```

```
name=Kubernetes
baseurl=https://packages.cloud.google.com/yum/repos/kubern
etes-el7-x86_64
enabled=1
gpgcheck=1
repo_gpgcheck=1
gpgkey=https://packages.cloud.google.com/yum/doc/yum-key.g
pg
https://packages.cloud.google.com/yum/doc/rpm-package-key.
gpg
```

2. Now, we are ready to pull the packages from the Kubernetes source base via the yum command:

```
// on Kubernetes master
$ sudo yum install -y kubelet kubeadm kubectl
// on Kubernetes node
$ sudo yum install -y kubelet
```

3. No matter what OS it is, check the version of the package you get!

```
// take it easy! server connection failed since there is
not server running
$ kubectl version
Client Version: version.Info{Major:"1", Minor:"10",
GitVersion:"v1.10.2",
GitCommit:"81753b10df112992bf51bbc2c2f85208aad78335",
GitTreeState:"clean", BuildDate:"2018-04-27T09:22:21Z",
GoVersion:"go1.9.3", Compiler:"gc",
Platform:"linux/amd64"}
The connection to the server 192.168.122.101:6443 was
refused - did you specify the right host or port?
```

System configuration prerequisites

Before running up the whole system by kubeadm, please check that Docker is running on your machine for Kubernetes. Moreover, in order to avoid critical errors while executing kubeadm, we will show the necessary service configuration on both the system and kubelet. As well as the master, please set the following configurations on the Kubernetes nodes to get kubelet to work fine with kubeadm.

CentOS system settings

There are other additional settings in CentOS to make Kubernetes behave correctly. Be aware that, even if we are not using kubeadm to manage the Kubernetes cluster, the following setup should be considered while running kubelet:

1. Disable SELinux, since kubelet does not support SELinux completely:

```
// check the state of SELinux, if it has already been
disabled, bypass below commands
$ sestatus
```

We can `disable SELinux` through the following command, or by `modifying the configuration file`:

```
// disable SELinux through command
$   sudo setenforce 0
// or modify the configuration file
$ sudo sed -I 's/ SELINUX=enforcing/SELINUX=disabled/g'
/etc/sysconfig/selinux
```

Then we'll need to `reboot` the machine:

```
// reboot is required
$ sudo reboot
```

2. Enable the usage of iptables. To prevent some routing errors happening, add runtime parameters:

```
// enable the parameters by setting them to 1
$ sudo bash -c 'echo "net.bridge.bridge-nf-call-ip6tables
= 1" > /etc/sysctl.d/k8s.conf'
$ sudo bash -c 'echo "net.bridge.bridge-nf-call-iptables =
1" >> /etc/sysctl.d/k8s.conf'
// reload the configuration
$ sudo sysctl --system
```

Booting up the service

Now we can start the service. First enable and then start kubelet on your Kubernetes master machine:

```
$ sudo systemctl enable kubelet && sudo systemctl start kubelet
```

While checking the status of kubelet, you may be worried to see the status displaying activating (`auto-restart`); and you may get further frustrated to see the detail logs by the `journalctl` command, as follows:

```
error: unable to load client CA file /etc/kubernetes/pki/ca.crt:
open /etc/kubernetes/pki/ca.crt: no such file or directory
```

Don't worry. kubeadm takes care of creating the certificate authorities file. It is defined in the service configuration file, `/etc/systemd/system/kubelet.service.d/10-kubeadm.conf` by argument `KUBELET_AUTHZ_ARGS`. The kubelet service won't be a healthy without this file, so keep trying to restart the daemon by itself.

Go ahead and start all the master daemons via kubeadm. It is worth noting that using kubeadm requires the root permission to achieve a service level privilege. For any sudoer, each kubeadm would go after the `sudo` command:

```
$ sudo kubeadm init
```

Find preflight checking error while firing command `kubeadm init`? Using following one to disable running swap as description.

```
$ sudo kubeadm init --ignore-preflight-errors=Swap
```

And you will see the sentence `Your Kubernetes master has initialized successfully!` showing on the screen. Congratulations! You are almost done! Just follow the information about the user environment setup below the greeting message:

```
$ mkdir -p $HOME/.kube
$ sudo cp -i /etc/kubernetes/admin.conf $HOME/.kube/config
$ sudo chown $(id -u):$(id -g) $HOME/.kube/config
```

The preceding commands ensure every Kubernetes instruction is fired by your account execute with the proper credentials and connects to the correct server portal:

```
// Your kubectl command works great now
$ kubectl version
Client Version: version.Info{Major:"1", Minor:"10",
GitVersion:"v1.10.2",
GitCommit:"81753b10df112992bf51bbc2c2f85208aad78335",
GitTreeState:"clean", BuildDate:"2018-04-27T09:22:21Z",
GoVersion:"go1.9.3", Compiler:"gc", Platform:"linux/amd64"}
Server Version: version.Info{Major:"1", Minor:"10",
GitVersion:"v1.10.2",
GitCommit:"81753b10df112992bf51bbc2c2f85208aad78335",
```

```
GitTreeState:"clean", BuildDate:"2018-04-27T09:10:24Z",
GoVersion:"go1.9.3", Compiler:"gc", Platform:"linux/amd64"}
```

More than that, kubelet goes into a healthy state now:

```
// check the status of kubelet
$ sudo systemctl status kubelet
...
Active: active (running) Mon 2018-04-30 18:46:58 EDT; 2min 43s ago
...
```

Network configurations for containers

After the master of the cluster is ready to handle jobs and the services are running, for the purpose of making containers accessible to each other through networking, we need to set up the network for container communication. It is even more important initially while building up a Kubernetes cluster with kubeadm, since the master daemons are all running as containers. kubeadm supports the CNI (https://github. com/containernetworking/cni). We are going to attach the CNI via a Kubernetes network add-on.

There are many third-party CNI solutions that supply secured and reliable container network environments. Calico (https://www.projectcalico.org), one CNI provide stable container networking. Calico is light and simple, but still well implemented by the CNI standard and integrated with Kubernetes:

```
$ kubectl apply -f
https://docs.projectcalico.org/v2.6/getting-started/kubernetes/install
ation/hosted/kubeadm/1.6/calico.yaml
```

Here, whatever your host OS is, the command kubectl can fire any sub command for utilizing resources and managing systems. We use kubectl to apply the configuration of Calico to our new-born Kubernetes.

Getting a node involved

Let's log in to your Kubernetes node to join the group controlled by kubeadm:

1. First, enable and start the service, `kubelet`. Every Kubernetes machine should have `kubelet` running on it:

   ```
   $ sudo systemctl enable kubelet && sudo systemctl start
   kubelet
   ```

2. After that, fire the `kubeadm` join command with an input flag token and the IP address of the master, notifying the master that it is a secured and authorized node. You can get the token on the master node via the `kubeadm` command:

   ```
   // on master node, list the token you have in the cluster
   $ sudo kubeadm token list
   TOKEN                    TTL        EXPIRES
   USAGES                   DESCRIPTION
   EXTRA GROUPS
   da3a90.9a119695a933a867    6h
   2018-05-01T18:47:10-04:00    authentication,signing    The
   default bootstrap token generated by 'kubeadm init'.
   system:bootstrappers:kubeadm:default-node-token
   ```

3. In the preceding output, if `kubeadm init` succeeds, the default token will be generated. Copy the token and paste it onto the node, and then compose the following command:

   ```
   // The master IP is 192.168.122.101, token is
   da3a90.9a119695a933a867, 6443 is the port of api server.
   $ sudo kubeadm join --token da3a90.9a119695a933a867
   192.168.122.101:6443 --discovery-token-unsafe-skip-ca-
   verification
   ```

    What if you call `kubeadm token list` to list the tokens, and see they are all expired? You can create a new one manually by this command: `kubeadm token create`.

4. Please make sure that the master's firewall doesn't block any traffic to port `6443`, which is for API server communication. Once you see the words `Successfully established connection` showing on the screen, it is time to check with the master if the group got the new member:

   ```
   // fire kubectl subcommand on master
   ```

```
$ kubectl get nodes
NAME        STATUS    ROLES     AGE       VERSION
ubuntu01    Ready     master    11h       v1.10.2
ubuntu02    Ready     <none>    26s       v1.10.2
```

Well done! No matter if whether your OS is Ubuntu or CentOS, kubeadm is installed and kubelet is running. You can easily go through the preceding steps to build your Kubernetes cluster.

You may be wondering about the flag `discovery-token-unsafe-skip-ca-verification` used while joining the cluster. Remember the kubelet log that says the certificate file is not found? That's it, since our Kubernetes node is brand new and clean, and has never connected with the master before. There is no certificate file to find for verification. But now, because the node has shaken hands with the master, the file exists. We may join in this way (in some situation requiring rejoining the same cluster):

```
kubeadm join --token $TOKEN $MASTER_IPADDR:6443 --discovery-token-
ca-cert-hash sha256:$HASH
```

The hash value can be obtained by the `openssl` command:

```
// rejoining the same cluster
$ HASH=$(openssl x509 -pubkey -in /etc/kubernetes/pki/ca.crt | openssl
rsa -pubin -outform der 2>/dev/null | openssl dgst -sha256 -hex | sed
's/^.* //')
$ sudo kubeadm join --token da3a90.9a119695a933a867
192.168.122.101:6443 --discovery-token-ca-cert-hash sha256:$HASH
```

How it works...

When kubeadm init sets up the master, there are six stages:

1. **Generating certificate files and keys for services**: Certificated files and keys are used for security management during cross-node communications. They are located in the `/etc/kubernetes/pki` directory. Take kubelet, for example. It cannot access the Kubernetes API server without passing the identity verification.
2. **Writing kubeconfig files**: The `kubeconfig` files define permissions, authentication, and configurations for kubectl actions. In this case, the Kubernetes controller manager and scheduler have related `kubeconfig` files to fulfill any API requests.

3. **Creating service daemon YAML files**: The service daemons under kubeadm's control are just like computing components running on the master. As with setting deployment configurations on disk, kubelet will make sure each daemon is active.

4. **Waiting for kubelet to be alive, running the daemons as pods**: When kubelet is alive, it will boot up the service pods described in the files under the `/etc/kubernetes/manifests` directory. Moreover, kubelet guarantees to keep them activated, restarting the pod automatically if it crashes.

5. **Setting post-configuration for the cluster**: Some cluster configurations still need to be set, such as configuring **role-based accessing control** (**RBAC**) rules, creating a namespace, and tagging the resources.

6. **Applying add-ons**: DNS and proxy services can be added along with the kubeadm system.

While the user enters kubeadm and joins the Kubernetes node, kubeadm will complete the first two stages like the master.

If you have faced a heavy and complicated set up procedure in earlier versions of Kubernetes, it is quite a relief to set up a Kubernetes cluster with kubeadm. kubeadm reduces the overhead of configuring each daemon and starting them one by one. Users can still do customization on kubelet and master services, by just modifying a familiar file, `10-kubeadm.conf` and the YAML files under `/etc/kubernetes/manifests`. Kubeadm not only helps to establish the cluster but also enhances security and availability, saving you time.

See also

We talked about how to build a Kubernetes cluster. If you're ready to run your first application on it, check the last recipe in this chapter and run the container! And for advanced management of your cluster, you can also look at Chapter 18, *Advanced Cluster Administration*, of this book:

- *Advanced settings in kubeconfig*, in Chapter 18, *Advanced Cluster Administration*

Setting up the Kubernetes cluster on Linux via Ansible (kubespray)

If you are familiar with configuration management, such as Puppet, Chef and Ansible, kubespray (`https://github.com/kubernetes-incubator/kubespray`) is the best choice to set up a Kubernetes cluster from scratch. It provides the Ansible playbook that supports the majority of Linux distributions and public clouds, such as AWS and GCP.

Ansible (`https://www.ansible.com`) is a Python-based SSH automation tool that can configure Linux as your desired state based on the configuration, which is called playbook. This cookbook describes how to use kubespray to set up Kubernetes on Linux.

Getting ready

As of May 2018, the latest version of kubespray is 2.5.0, which supports the following operation systems to install Kubernetes:

- RHEL/CentOS 7
- Ubuntu 16.04 LTS

According to the kubespray documentation, it also supports CoreOS and debian distributions. However, those distributions may need some additional steps or have technical difficulties. This cookbook uses CentOS 7 and Ubuntu 16.04 LTS.

In addition, you need to install Ansible on your machine. Ansible works on Python 2.6, 2.7, and 3.5 or higher. macOS and Linux might be the best choice to install Ansible because Python is preinstalled by most of macOS and Linux distributions by default. In order to check which version of Python you have, open a Terminal and type the following command:

```
//Use capital V
$ python -V
Python 2.7.5
```

Overall, you need at least three machines, as mentioned in the following table:

Type of host	Recommended OS/Distribution
Ansible	macOS or any Linux which has Python 2.6, 2.7, or 3.5
Kubernetes master	RHEL/CentOS 7 or Ubuntu 16.04 LTS
Kubernetes node	RHEL/CentOS 7 or Ubuntu 16.04 LTS

There are some network communicating with each other, so you need to at least open a network port (for example, AWS Security Group or GCP Firewall rule) as:

- **TCP/22 (ssh)**: Ansible to Kubernetes master/node host
- **TCP/6443 (Kubernetes API server)**: Kubernetes node to master
- **Protocol 4 (IP encapsulated in IP)**: Kubernetes master and node to each other by Calico

 In Protocol 4 (IP encapsulated in IP), if you are using AWS, set an ingress rule to specify `aws ec2 authorize-security-group-ingress --group-id <your SG ID> --cidr <network CIDR> --protocol 4`. In addition, if you are using GCP, set the firewall rule to specify as `cloud compute firewall-rules create allow-calico --allow 4 --network <your network name> --source-ranges <network CIDR>`.

Installing pip

The easiest way to install Ansible, is to use pip, the Python package manager. Some of newer versions of Python have `pip` already (Python 2.7.9 or later and Python 3.4 or later):

1. To confirm whether `pip` is installed or not, similar to the Python command, use `-V`:

```
//use capital V
$ pip -V
pip 9.0.1 from /Library/Python/2.7/site-packages (python
2.7)
```

2. On the other hand, if you see the following result, you need to install `pip`:

```
//this result shows you don't have pip yet
$ pip -V
-bash: pip: command not found
```

3. In order to install pip, download `get-pip.py` and install by using the following command:

```
//download pip install script
$ curl -LO https://bootstrap.pypa.io/get-pip.py


//run get-pip.py by privileged user (sudo)
$ sudo python get-pip.py
Collecting pip
  Downloading pip-9.0.1-py2.py3-none-any.whl (1.3MB)
    100% |###############################| 1.3MB 779kB/s
Collecting wheel
  Downloading wheel-0.30.0-py2.py3-none-any.whl (49kB)
    100% |###############################| 51kB 1.5MB/s
Installing collected packages: pip, wheel
Successfully installed pip-9.0.1 wheel-0.30.0


//now you have pip command
$ pip -V
pip 9.0.1 from /usr/lib/python2.7/site-packages (python
2.7)
```

Installing Ansible

Perform the following steps to install Ansible:

1. Once you have installed `pip`, you can install Ansible with the following command:

```
//ran by privileged user (sudo)
$ sudo pip install ansible
```

 `pip` scans your Python and installs the necessary libraries for Ansible, so it may take a few minutes to complete.

2. Once you have successfully installed Ansible by `pip`, you can verify it with the following command and see output as this:

```
$ which ansible
/usr/bin/ansible
```

```
$ ansible --version
ansible 2.4.1.0
```

Installing python-netaddr

Next, according to kubespray's documentation (https://github.com/kubernetes-incubator/kubespray#requirements), it needs the python-netaddr package. This package can also be installed by pip, as shown in the following code:

```
$ sudo pip install netaddr
```

Setting up ssh public key authentication

One more thing, as mentioned previously, Ansible is actually the ssh automation tool. If you log on to host via ssh, you have to have an appropriate credential (user/password or ssh public key) to the target machines. In this case, the target machines mean the Kubernetes master and nodes.

Due to security reasons, especially in the public cloud, Kubernetes uses only the ssh public key authentication instead of ID/password authentication.

To follow the best practice, let's copy the ssh public key from your Ansible machine to the Kubernetes master/node machines:

 If you've already set up ssh public key authentication between the Ansible machine to Kubernetes candidate machines, you can skip this step.

1. In order to create an ssh public/private key pair from your Ansible machine, type the following command:

   ```
   //with -q means, quiet output
   $ ssh-keygen -q
   ```

2. It will ask you to set a passphrase. You may set or skip (empty) this, but you have to remember it.
3. Once you have successfully created a key pair, you can see the private key as ~/.ssh/id_rsa and public key as ~/.ssh/id_rsa.pub. You need to append the public key to the target machine under ~/.ssh/authorized_keys, as shown in the following screenshot:

4. You need to copy and paste your public key to all Kubernetes master and node candidate machines.

5. To make sure your ssh public key authentication works, just ssh from the Ansible machine to the target host that won't ask for your logon password, as here:

```
//use ssh-agent to remember your private key and
passphrase (if you set)
ansible_machine$ ssh-agent bash
ansible_machine$ ssh-add
Enter passphrase for /home/saito/.ssh/id_rsa: Identity
added: /home/saito/.ssh/id_rsa (/home/saito/.ssh/id_rsa)


//logon from ansible machine to k8s machine which you
copied public key
ansible_machine$ ssh 10.128.0.2
Last login: Sun Nov  5 17:05:32 2017 from
133.172.188.35.bc.googleusercontent.com
k8s-master-1$
```

Now you are all set! Let's set up Kubernetes using kubespray (Ansible) from scratch.

How to do it...

kubespray is provided through the GitHub repository (`https://github.com/kubernetes-incubator/kubespray/tags`), as shown in the following screenshot:

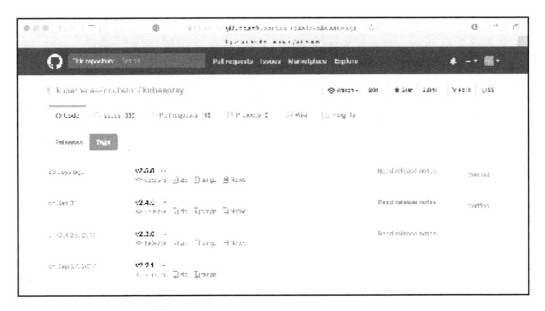

Because kubespray is an Ansible playbook, not a binary, you can download the latest version (as of May 2018, version 2.5.0 is the latest) of the `zip` or `tar.gz` to your Ansible machine directly and unarchive it with the following command:

```
//download tar.gz format
ansible_machine$ curl -LO
https://github.com/kubernetes-incubator/kubespray/archive/v2.5.0.tar.g
z


//untar
ansible_machine$ tar zxvf v2.5.0.tar.gz


//it unarchives under kubespray-2.5.0 directory
ansible_machine$ ls -F
get-pip.py  kubespray-2.5.0/  v2.5.0.tar.gz


//change to kubespray-2.5.0 directory
ansible_machine$ cd kubespray-2.5.0/
```

Maintaining the Ansible inventory

In order to perform the Ansible playbook, you need to maintain your own inventory file, which contains target machine IP addresses:

1. There is a sample inventory file under the inventory directory, so you can copy it by using the following:

    ```
    //copy sample to mycluster
    ansible_machine$ cp -rfp inventory/sample
    inventory/mycluster

    //edit hosts.ini
    ansible_machine$ vi inventory/mycluster/hosts.ini
    ```

2. In this cookbook, we are using target machines that have the following IP addresses:
    *   Kubernetes master : 10.128.0.2
    *   Kubernetes node : 10.128.0.4

3. In this case, hosts.ini should be in the following format:

```
 1  my-master-1 ansible_ssh_host=10.128.0.2
 2  my-node-1 ansible_ssh_host=10.128.0.4
 3
 4
 5  [kube-master]
 6  my-master-1
 7
 8  [etcd]
 9  my-master-1
10
11  [kube-node]
12  my-master-1
13  my-node-1
14
15  [k8s-cluster:children]
16  kube-node
17  kube-master
```

4. Please change the IP address to match your environment.

Note that hostname (my-master-1 and my-node-1) will be set by the kubespray playbook based on this hosts.ini, so feel free to assign a meaningful hostname.

Running the Ansible ad hoc command to test your environment

Before running the kubespray playbook, let's check whether `hosts.ini` and Ansible itself work properly or not:

1. To do that, use the Ansible ad hoc command, using the ping module, as shown in the following screenshot:

2. This result indicates SUCCESS. But if you see the following error, probably the IP address is wrong or the target machine is down, so please the check target machine first:

3. Next, check your authority whether you can escalate a privilege on the target machine or not. In other words, whether you can run `sudo` or not. This is because you will need to install Kubernetes, Docker, and some related binaries, and configurations that need a root privilege. To confirm that, add the `-b` (become) option, as shown in the following screenshot:

```
kubespray-2.5.0 — bash — 90×12
ansible_machine$ ansible -b -i inventory/mycluster/hosts.ini -m ping all
my-master-1 | SUCCESS => {
    "changed": false,
    "ping": "pong"
}
my-node-1 | SUCCESS => {
    "changed": false,
    "ping": "pong"
}
ansible_machine$
```

4. With the `-b` option, it actually tries to perform sudo on the target machine. If you see SUCCESS, you are all set! Go to the *How it works...* section to run kubespray.

If you're unfortunate enough to see some errors, please refer to the following section to solve Ansible issues.

Ansible troubleshooting

The ideal situation would be to use the same Linux distribution, version, settings, and logon user. However, the environment will be different based on policy, compatibility, and other reasons. Ansible is flexible and can support many use cases to run `ssh` and `sudo`.

Need to specify a sudo password

Based on your Linux machine setting, you may see the following error when adding the −b option. In this case, you need to type your password while running the sudo command:

```
ansible_machine$ ansible -b -i inventory/mycluster/hosts.ini -m ping all
my-master-1 | FAILED! => {
    "changed": false,
    "module_stderr": "sudo: a password is required\n",
    "module_stdout": "",
    "msg": "MODULE FAILURE",
    "rc": 1
}
my-node-1 | FAILED! => {
    "changed": false,
    "module_stderr": "sudo: a password is required\n",
    "module_stdout": "",
    "msg": "MODULE FAILURE",
    "rc": 1
}
ansible_machine$
```

In this case, add −K (ask for the sudo password) and run again. It will ask for your sudo password when running the Ansible command, as shown in the following screenshot:

```
ansible_machine$ ansible -b -K -i inventory/mycluster/hosts.ini -m ping all
SUDO password:
```

> If your Linux uses the su command instead of sudo, adding --become-method=su to run the Ansible command could help. Please read the Ansible documentation for more details : http://docs.ansible.com/ansible/latest/become.html

Need to specify different ssh logon user

Sometimes you may need to ssh to target machines using a different logon user. In this case, you can append the `ansible_user` parameter to an individual host in `hosts.ini`. For example:

- Use the username `kirito` to `ssh` to `my-master-1`
- Use the username `asuna` to `ssh` to `my-node-1`

In this case, change `hosts.ini`, as shown in the following code:

```
my-master-1 ansible_ssh_host=10.128.0.2 ansible_user=kirito
my-node-1 ansible_ssh_host=10.128.0.4 ansible_user=asuna
```

Need to change ssh port

Another scenario is where you may need to run the ssh daemon on some specific port number rather than the default port number `22`. Ansible also supports this scenario and uses the `ansible_port` parameter to the individual host in `hosts.ini`, as shown in the following code (in the example, the `ssh` daemon is running at `10022` on `my-node-1`):

```
my-master-1 ansible_ssh_host=10.128.0.2
my-node-1 ansible_ssh_host=10.128.0.4 ansible_port=10022
```

Common ansible issue

Ansible is flexible enough to support any other situations. If you need any specific parameters to customize the ssh logon for the target host, read the Ansible inventory documentation to find a specific parameter: `http://docs.ansible.com/ansible/latest/intro_inventory.html`

In addition, Ansible has a configuration file, `ansible.cfg`, on top of the `kubespray` directory. It defines common settings for Ansible. For example, if you are using a very long username that usually causes an Ansible error, change `ansible.cfg` to set `control_path` to solve the issue, as shown in the following code:

```
[ssh_connection]
control_path = %(directory)s/%%h-%%r
```

If you plan to set up more than 10 nodes, you may need to increase ssh simultaneous sessions. In this case, adding the forks parameter also requires you to increase the ssh timeout from 10 seconds to 30 seconds by adding the timeout parameter, as shown in the following code:

```
[ssh_connection]
forks = 50
timeout = 30
```

The following screenshot contains all of the preceding configurations in ansible.cfg:

For more details, please visit the Ansible configuration documentation at http://docs.ansible.com/ansible/latest/intro_configuration.html

How it works...

Now you can start to run the kubepray playbook:

1. You've already created an inventory file as inventory/mycluster/hosts.ini. Other than hosts.ini, you need to check and update global variable configuration files at inventory/mycluster/group_vars/all.yml.

2. There are a lot of variables defined, but at least one variable, bootstrap_os , needs to be changed from none to your target Linux machine. If you are using RHEL/CentOS7, set bootstrap_os as centos. If you are using Ubuntu 16.04 LTS, set bootstrap_os as ubuntu as shown in the following screenshot:

```
                     kubespray-2.0.0 — vim inventory/mycluster/group_vars/all.yml — 80×11
1 # Valid bootstrap options (required): ubuntu, coreos, centos, none
2 bootstrap_os  ubuntu
3
4 #Directory where etcd data stored
5 etcd_data_dir  /var/lib/etcd
6
7 # Directory where the binaries will be installed
8 bin_dir  /usr/local/bin
9
10 ## The access_ip variable is used to define how other nodes should access
```

You can also update other variables, such as kube_version, to change or install a Kubernetes version. For more details, read the documentation at https://github.com/kubernetes-incubator/kubespray/blob/master/docs/vars.md.

3. Finally, you can execute the playbook. Use the ansible-playbook command instead of the Ansible command. Ansible-playbook runs multiple Ansible modules based on tasks and roles that are defined in the playbook.

4. To run the kubespray playbook, type the ansible-playbook command with the following parameters:

```
//use -b (become), -i (inventory) and specify cluster.yml
as playbook
$ ansible-playbook -b -i inventory/mycluster/hosts.ini
cluster.yml
```

The ansible-playbook argument parameter is the same as the Ansible command. So, if you need to use -K (ask for the `sudo` password) or --become-method=su, you need to specify for ansible-playbook as well.

5. It takes around 5 to 10 minutes to complete based on the machine spec and network bandwidth. But eventually you can see PLAY RECAP, as shown in the following screenshot, to see whether it has succeeded or not:

6. If you see `failed=0` like in the preceding screenshot, you have been successful in setting up a Kubernetes cluster. You can ssh to the Kubernetes master machine and run the `/usr/local/bin/kubectl` command to see the status, as shown in the following screenshot:

```
ansible_machine$ ssh 10.128.0.2
The authenticity of host '10.128.0.2 (10.128.0.2)' can't be established.
ECDSA key fingerprint is SHA256:zv4pnlQkatti8pPuBBreAPiZdl14s/dTlrgOrY2m49s.
ECDSA key fingerprint is MD5:2a:91:5b:dd:6c:34:31:c5:fc:e7:bb:d7:4a:f7:34:bf.
Are you sure you want to continue connecting (yes/no)? yes
Warning: Permanently added '10.128.0.2' (ECDSA) to the list of known hosts.
Last login: Tue May  8 22:08:28 2018 from 209.194.91.4
[saito@my-master-1 ~]$ /usr/local/bin/kubectl get nodes
NAME          STATUS    ROLES        AGE       VERSION
my-master-1   Ready     master,node  5m        v1.10.2
my-node-1     Ready     node         5m        v1.10.2
[saito@my-master-1 ~]$ /usr/local/bin/kubectl version --short
Client Version: v1.10.2
Server Version: v1.10.2
[saito@my-master-1 ~]$
```

7. The preceding screenshot shows that you have been successful in setting up the Kubernetes version 1.10.2 master and node. You can continue to use the `kubectl` command to configure you Kubernetes cluster in the following chapters.

8. Unfortunately, if you see a failed count of more than 0, the Kubernetes cluster has probably not been set up correctly. Because failure is caused by many reasons, there is no single solution. It is recommended that you append the verbose option `-v` to see more detailed output from Ansible, as shown in the following code:

```
//use –b (become), –i (inventory) and –v (verbose)
$ ansible-playbook –v –b –i inventory/mycluster/hosts.ini
cluster.yml
```

9. If the failure is timeout, just retrying the ansible-playbook command again may solve it. Because Ansible is designed as an idempotency, if you re-perform the ansible-playbook command twice or more, Ansible still can configure correctly.

10. If the failure is change target IP address after you run ansible-playbook (for example, re-using the Ansible machine to set up another Kubernetes cluster), you need to clean up the fact cache file. It is located under /tmp directory, so you just delete this file, as shown in the following screenshot:

See also

This section describes how to set up the Kubernetes cluster on the Linux OS using kubespray. It is the Ansible playbook that supports major Linux distribution. Ansible is simple, but due to supporting any situation and environment, you need to care about some different use cases. Especially with ssh and sudo-related configurations, you need to understand Ansible deeper to fit it with your environment.

Running your first container in Kubernetes

Congratulations! You've built your own Kubernetes cluster in the previous recipes. Now, let's get on with running your very first container, nginx (http://nginx.org/), which is an open source reverse proxy server, load balancer, and web server. Along with this recipe, you will create a simple nginx application and expose it to the outside world.

Getting ready

Before you start to run your first container in Kubernetes, it's better to check if your cluster is in a healthy mode. A checklist showing the following items would make your kubectl sub commands stable and successful, without unknown errors caused by background services:

1. Checking the master daemons. Check whether the Kubernetes components are running:

```
// get the components status
$ kubectl get cs
NAME                 STATUS    MESSAGE               ERROR
controller-manager   Healthy   ok
scheduler            Healthy   ok
etcd-0               Healthy   {"health": "true"}
```

2. Check the status of the Kubernetes master:

```
// check if the master is running
$ kubectl cluster-info
Kubernetes master is running at
https://192.168.122.101:6443
KubeDNS is running at
https://192.168.122.101:6443/api/v1/namespaces/kube-system
/services/kube-dns/proxy

To further debug and diagnose cluster problems, use
'kubectl cluster-info dump'.
```

3. Check whether all the nodes are ready:

```
$ kubectl get nodes
NAME       STATUS   ROLES    AGE   VERSION
ubuntu01   Ready    master   20m   v1.10.2
ubuntu02   Ready    <none>   2m    v1.10.2
```

Ideal results should look like the preceding outputs. You can successfully fire the kubectl command and get the response without errors. If any one of the checked items failed to meet the expectation, check out the settings in the previous recipes based on the management tool you used.

4. Check the access permission of the Docker registry, as we will use the official free image as an example. If you want to run your own application, be sure to dockerize it first! What you need to do for your custom application is to write a Dockerfile (`https://docs.docker.com/engine/reference/builder/`), and build and push it into the public or private Docker registry.

Test your node connectivity with the public/private Docker registry

On your node, try the Docker pull nginx command to test whether you can pull the image from the Docker Hub. If you're behind a proxy, please add `HTTP_PROXY` into your Docker configuration file(`https://docs.docker.com/engine/admin/systemd/#httphttps-proxy`). If you want to run the image from the private repository in the Docker Hub, or the image from the private Docker registry, a Kubernetes secret is required.

How to do it...

We will use the official Docker image of nginx as an example. The image is provided in the Docker Hub (`https://store.docker.com/images/nginx`), and also the Docker Store (`https://hub.docker.com/_/nginx/`).

Many of the official and public images are available on the Docker Hub or Docker Store so that you do not need to build them from scratch. Just pull them and set up your custom setting on top of them.

Docker Store versus Docker Hub

As you may be aware, there is a more familiar official repository, Docker Hub, which was launched for the community for sharing the based image. Compared with the Docker Hub, the Docker Store is focused on enterprise applications. It provides a place for enterprise-level Docker images, which could be free or paid for software. You may feel more confident in using a more reliable image on the Docker Store.

Running a HTTP server (nginx)

On the Kubernetes master, we can use `kubectl run` to create a certain number of containers. The Kubernetes master will then schedule the pods for the nodes to run, with general command formatting, as follows:

```
$ kubectl run <replication controller name> --image=<image name> --
replicas=<number of replicas> [--port=<exposing port>]
```

The following example will create two replicas with the name `my-first-nginx` from the nginx image and expose port `80`. We can deploy one or more containers in what is referred to as a pod. In this case, we will deploy one container per pod. Just like a normal Docker behavior, if the nginx image doesn't exist locally, it will pull it from the Docker Hub by default:

```
// run a deployment with 2 replicas for the image nginx and expose the
container port 80
$ kubectl run my-first-nginx --image=nginx --replicas=2 --port=80
deployment "my-first-nginx" created
```

The name of deployment <my-first-nginx> cannot be duplicated

The resource (pods, services, deployment, and so on) in one Kubernetes namespace cannot be duplicated. If you run the preceding command twice, the following error will pop up:

```
Error from server (AlreadyExists):
deployments.extensions "my-first-nginx" already exists
```

Let's move on and see the current status of all the pods by `kubectl get pods`. Normally the status of the pods will hold on Pending for a while, since it takes some time for the nodes to pull the image from the registry:

```
// get all pods
$ kubectl get pods
NAME                              READY   STATUS    RESTARTS   AGE
my-first-nginx-7dcd87d4bf-jp572   1/1     Running   0          7m
my-first-nginx-7dcd87d4bf-ns7h4   1/1     Running   0          7m
```

If the pod status is not running for a long time

You could always use kubectl get pods to check the current status of the pods, and kubectl describe pods $pod_name to check the detailed information in a pod. If you make a typo of the image name, you might get the ErrImagePull error message, and if you are pulling the images from a private repository or registry without proper credentials, you might get the ImagePullBackOff message. If you get the Pending status for a long time and check out the node capacity, make sure you don't run too many replicas that exceed the node capacity. If there are other unexpected error messages, you could either stop the pods or the entire replication controller to force the master to schedule the tasks again.

You can also check the details about the deployment to see whether all the pods are ready:

```
// check the status of your deployment
$ kubectl get deployment
NAME            DESIRED   CURRENT   UP-TO-DATE   AVAILABLE   AGE
my-first-nginx  2         2         2            2           2m
```

Exposing the port for external access

We might also want to create an external IP address for the nginx deployment. On cloud providers that support an external load balancer (such as Google compute engine), using the LoadBalancer type will provision a load balancer for external access. On the other hand, you can still expose the port by creating a Kubernetes service as follows, even though you're not running on platforms that support an external load balancer. We'll describe how to access this externally later:

```
// expose port 80 for replication controller named my-first-nginx
$ kubectl expose deployment my-first-nginx --port=80 --
type=LoadBalancer
service "my-first-nginx" exposed
```

We can see the service status we just created:

```
// get all services
$ kubectl get service
NAME            TYPE        CLUSTER-IP   EXTERNAL-IP   PORT(S)
AGE
kubernetes      ClusterIP   10.96.0.1    <none>        443/TCP
```

```
2h
my-first-nginx    LoadBalancer    10.102.141.22    <pending>
80:31620/TCP    3m
```

You may find an additional service named `kubernetes` if the service daemon run as a container (for example, using kubeadm as a management tool). It is for exposing the REST API of the Kubernetes API server internally. The pending state of `my-first-nginx` service's external IP indicates that it is waiting for a specific public IP from cloud provider. Take a look at `Chapter 17`, *Building Kubernetes on AWS* for more details.

Congratulations! You just ran your first container with a Kubernetes pod and exposed port `80` with the Kubernetes service.

Stopping the application

We can stop the application using commands such as the delete deployment and service. Before this, we suggest you read through the following code first to understand more about how it works:

```
// stop deployment named my-first-nginx
$ kubectl delete deployment my-first-nginx
deployment.extensions "my-first-nginx" deleted

// stop service named my-first-nginx
$ kubectl delete service my-first-nginx
service "my-first-nginx" deleted
```

How it works...

Let's take a look at the insight of the service using describe in the `kubectl` command. We will create one Kubernetes service with the type `LoadBalancer`, which will dispatch the traffic into two endpoints, `192.168.79.9` and `192.168.79.10` with port `80`:

```
$ kubectl describe service my-first-nginx
Name:              my-first-nginx
Namespace:         default
Labels:            run=my-first-nginx
Annotations:       <none>
Selector:          run=my-first-nginx
Type:              LoadBalancer
IP:                10.103.85.175
```

```
Port:                      <unset>  80/TCP
TargetPort:                80/TCP
NodePort:                  <unset>  31723/TCP
Endpoints:                 192.168.79.10:80,192.168.79.9:80
Session Affinity:          None
External Traffic Policy:   Cluster
Events:                    <none>
```

The port here is an abstract service port, which will allow any other resources to access the service within the cluster. The `nodePort` will be indicating the external port to allow external access. The `targetPort` is the port the container allows traffic into; by default, it will be the same port.

In the following diagram, external access will access the service with `nodePort`. The service acts as a load balancer to dispatch the traffic to the pod using port `80`. The pod will then pass through the traffic into the corresponding container using `targetPort` `80`:

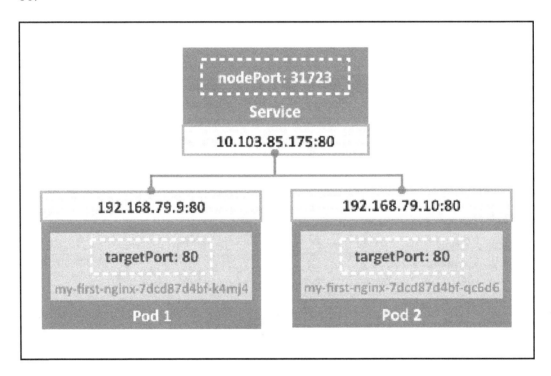

In any nodes or master, once the inter-connection network is set up, you should be able to access the nginx service using `ClusterIP 192.168.61.150` with port `80`:

```
// curl from service IP
$ curl 10.103.85.175:80
<!DOCTYPE html>
<html>
<head>
<title>Welcome to nginx!</title>
<style>
    body {
        width: 35em;
        margin: 0 auto;
        font-family: Tahoma, Verdana, Arial, sans-serif;
    }
</style>
</head>
<body>
<h1>Welcome to nginx!</h1>
<p>If you see this page, the nginx web server is successfully
installed and
working. Further configuration is required.</p>
<p>For online documentation and support please refer to
<a href="http://nginx.org/">nginx.org</a>.<br/>
Commercial support is available at
<a href="http://nginx.com/">nginx.com</a>.</p>
<p><em>Thank you for using nginx.</em></p>
</body>
</html>
```

It will be the same result if we `curl` to the target port of the pod directly:

```
// curl from endpoint, the content is the same as previous nginx html
$ curl 192.168.79.10:80
<!DOCTYPE html>
<html>
...
```

If you'd like to try out external access, use your browser to access the external IP address. Please note that the external IP address depends on which environment you're running in.

In the Google compute engine, you could access it via a `ClusterIP` with a proper rewall rules setting:

```
$ curl http://<clusterIP>
```

In a custom environment, such as on-premise data center, you could go through the IP address of nodes to access :

```
$ curl http://<nodeIP>:<nodePort>
```

You should be able to see the following page using a web browser:

See also

We have run our very first container in this section. Go ahead and read the next chapter to aquire more knowledge about Kubernetes:

- `Chapter 13`, *Walking through Kubernetes Concepts*

13
Walking through Kubernetes Concepts

In this chapter, we will cover the following recipes:

- Linking Pods and containers
- Managing Pods with ReplicaSets
- Deployment API
- Working with Services
- Working with Volumes
- Working with Secrets
- Working with names
- Working with Namespaces
- Working with labels and selectors

Introduction

In this chapter, we will start by creating different kinds of resources on the Kubernetes system. In order to realize your application in a microservices structure, reading the recipes in this chapter will be a good start towards understanding the concepts of the Kubernetes resources and consolidating them. After you deploy applications in Kubernetes, you can work on its scalable and efficient container management, and also fulfill the DevOps delivering procedure of microservices.

An overview of Kubernetes

Working with Kubernetes is quite easy, using either a **Command Line Interface** (CLI) or API (RESTful). This section will describe Kubernetes control by CLI. The CLI we use in this chapter is version 1.10.2.

After you install Kubernetes master, you can run a `kubectl` command as follows. It shows the kubectl and Kubernetes master versions (both the API Server and CLI are v1.10.2):

```
$ kubectl version --short
Client Version: v1.10.2
Server Version: v1.10.2
```

`kubectl` connects the Kubernetes API server using the RESTful API. By default, it attempts to access the localhost if `.kube/config` is not configured, otherwise you need to specify the API server address using the `--server` parameter. Therefore, it is recommended to use `kubectl` on the API server machine for practice.

 If you use kubectl over the network, you need to consider authentication and authorization for the API server.

`kubectl` is the only command for Kubernetes clusters, and it controls the Kubernetes cluster manager. Find more information at `http://kubernetes.io/docs/user-guide/kubectl-overview/`. Any container, or Kubernetes cluster operation, can be performed by a `kubectl` command.

In addition, kubectl allows the inputting of information via either the command line's optional arguments or a file (use the `-f` option); it is highly recommended to use a file, because you can maintain Kubernetes configuration as code. This will be described in detail in this chapter.

Here is a typical `kubectl` command-line argument:

```
kubectl [command] [TYPE] [NAME] [flags]
```

The attributes of the preceding command are as follows:

- `command`: Specifies the operation that you want to perform on one or more resources.
- `TYPE`: Specifies the resource type. Resource types are case-sensitive and you can specify the singular, plural, or abbreviated forms.

- NAME: Specifies the name of the resource. Names are case-sensitive. If the name is omitted, details for all resources are displayed.
- flags: Specifies optional flags.

For example, if you want to launch nginx, you can use either the kubectl run command or the kubectl create -f command with the YAML file as follows:

1. Use the run command:

   ```
   $ kubectl run my-first-nginx --image=nginx "my-first-
   nginx"
   ```

2. Use the create -f command with the YAML file:

   ```
   $ cat nginx.yaml
   apiVersion: apps/v1
   kind: Deployment
   metadata:
     name: my-first-nginx
     labels:
       app: nginx
   spec:
     replicas: 1
     selector:
       matchLabels:
         app: nginx
     template:
       metadata:
         labels:
           app: nginx
       spec:
         containers:
         - name: nginx
           image: nginx

   //specify -f (filename)
   $ kubectl create -f nginx.yaml
   deployment.apps "my-first-nginx" created
   ```

3. If you want to see the status of the Deployment, type the kubectl get command as follows:

   ```
   $ kubectl get deployment
   NAME              DESIRED   CURRENT   UP-TO-DATE
   AVAILABLE   AGE
   my-first-nginx    1         1         1            1
   4s
   ```

4. If you also want the support abbreviation, type the following:

```
$ kubectl get deploy
NAME               DESIRED   CURRENT   UP-TO-DATE
AVAILABLE    AGE
my-first-nginx   1         1         1                1
38s
```

5. If you want to delete these resources, type the `kubectl delete` command as follows:

```
$ kubectl delete deploy my-first-nginx
deployment.extensions "my-first-nginx" deleted
```

6. The `kubectl` command supports many kinds of sub-commands; use the `-h` option to see the details, for example:

```
//display whole sub command options
$ kubectl -h


//display sub command "get" options
$ kubectl get -h


//display sub command "run" options
$ kubectl run -h
```

This section describes how to use the `kubectl` command to control the Kubernetes cluster. The following recipes describe how to set up Kubernetes components:

- *Setting up a Kubernetes cluster on macOS using minikube* and *Set up a Kubernetes cluster on Windows using minikube* in `Chapter 12`, *Building Your Own Kubernetes Cluster*
- *Setting up a Kubernetes cluster on Linux using kubeadm* in `Chapter 12`, *Building Your Own Kubernetes Cluster*
- *Setting up a Kubernetes cluster on Linux using kubespray (Ansible)* in `Chapter 12`, *Building Your Own Kubernetes Cluster*

Linking Pods and containers

The Pod is a group of one or more containers and the smallest deployable unit in Kubernetes. Pods are always co-located and co-scheduled, and run in a shared context. Each Pod is isolated by the following Linux namespaces:

- The **process ID** (**PID**) namespace
- The network namespace
- The **interprocess communication** (**IPC**) namespace
- The **unix time sharing** (**UTS**) namespace

In a pre-container world, they would have been executed on the same physical or virtual machine.

It is useful to construct your own application stack Pod (for example, web server and database) that are mixed by different Docker images.

Getting ready

You must have a Kubernetes cluster and make sure that the Kubernetes node has accessibility to the Docker Hub (`https://hub.docker.com`) in order to download Docker images.

 If you are running minikube, use `minikube ssh` to log on to the minikube VM first, then run the `docker pull` command.

You can simulate downloading a Docker image by using the `docker pull` command as follows:

```
//this step only if you are using minikube
$ minikube ssh

                     _             _
         _ _ ( ) ( )
   ___ ___ (_) ___ (_)| |/')  _ _ | |_  __
 /' _ ` _ `\| |/' _ `\| || , < ( ) ( )| '_`\ /'__`\
 | ( ) ( ) || || ( ) || || |\`\ | (_) || |_) ) ( ___/
 (_) (_) (_)(_)(_) (_)(_)(_) (_)`\___/'(_,__/'`\____)


//run docker pull to download CentOS docker image
$ docker pull centos
```

```
Using default tag: latest
latest: Pulling from library/centos
d9aaf4d82f24: Pull complete
Digest:
sha256:4565fe2dd7f4770e825d4bd9c761a81b26e49cc9e3c9631c58cfc3188be9505
a
Status: Downloaded newer image for centos:latest
```

How to do it...

The following are the steps to create a Pod has 2 containers:

1. Log on to the Kubernetes machine (no need to log on if using minikube) and prepare the following YAML file. It defines the launch `nginx` container and the CentOS container.

2. The `nginx` container opens the HTTP port (TCP/80). On the other hand, the CentOS container attempts to access the `localhost:80` every three seconds using the `curl` command:

```
$ cat my-first-pod.yaml
apiVersion: v1
kind: Pod
metadata:
  name: my-first-pod
spec:
  containers:
  - name: my-nginx
    image: nginx
  - name: my-centos
    image: centos
    command: ["/bin/sh", "-c", "while : ;do curl
http://localhost:80/; sleep 10; done"]
```

3. Then, execute the `kubectl create` command to launch `my-first-pod` as follows:

```
$ kubectl create -f my-first-pod.yaml
pod "my-first-pod" created
```

It takes between a few seconds and a few minutes, depending on the network bandwidth of the Docker Hub and Kubernetes node's spec.

4. You can check `kubectl get pods` to see the status, as follows:

```
//still downloading Docker images (0/2)
$ kubectl get pods
NAME              READY      STATUS               RESTARTS
AGE
my-first-pod      0/2        ContainerCreating    0
14s


//my-first-pod is running (2/2)
$ kubectl get pods
NAME              READY      STATUS     RESTARTS    AGE
my-first-pod      2/2        Running    0           1m
```

Now both the nginx container (`my-nginx`) and the CentOS container (`my-centos`) are ready.

5. Let's check whether the CentOS container can access `nginx` or not. You can run the `kubectl exec` command to run bash on the CentOS container, then run the `curl` command to access the `nginx`, as follows:

```
//run bash on my-centos container
//then access to TCP/80 using curl
$ kubectl exec my-first-pod -it -c my-centos -- /bin/bash
[root@my-first-pod /]#
[root@my-first-pod /]# curl -L http://localhost:80
<!DOCTYPE html>
<html>
<head>
<title>Welcome to nginx!</title>
<style>
    body {
        width: 35em;
        margin: 0 auto;
        font-family: Tahoma, Verdana, Arial, sans-serif;
    }
</style>
</head>
<body>
<h1>Welcome to nginx!</h1>
<p>If you see this page, the nginx web server is
successfully installed and
working. Further configuration is required.</p>

<p>For online documentation and support please refer to
<a href="http://nginx.org/">nginx.org</a>.<br/>
```

```
Commercial support is available at
<a href="http://nginx.com/">nginx.com</a>.</p>

<p><em>Thank you for using nginx.</em></p>
</body>
</html>
```

As you can see, the Pod links two different containers, `nginx` and `CentOS`, into the same Linux network namespace.

How it works...

When launching a Pod, the Kubernetes scheduler dispatches to the kubelet process to handle all the operations to launch both `nginx` and `CentOS` containers on one Kubernetes node.

The following diagram illustrates these two containers and the Pod; these two containers can communicate via the localhost network, because within the Pod containers, it share the network interface:

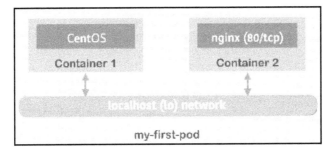

A Pod has two containers, which can communicate via localhost

If you have two or more nodes, you can check the `-o wide` option to find a node which runs a Pod:

```
//it indicates Node "minikube" runs my-first-pod
$ kubectl get pods -o wide
NAME            READY    STATUS      RESTARTS    AGE      IP
NODE
my-first-pod    2/2      Running     0           43m      172.17.0.2
minikube
```

Log in to that node, then you can check the `docker ps | grep my-first-pod` command to see the running containers as follows:

List of containers that belong to my-first-pod

You may notice that `my-first-pod` contains three containers; `centos`, `nginx`, and `pause` are running instead of two. Because each Pod we need to keep belongs to a particular Linux namespace, if both the CentOS and nginx containers die, the namespace will also destroyed. Therefore, the pause container just remains in the Pod to maintain Linux namespaces.

Let's launch a second Pod, rename it as `my-second-pod`, and run the `kubectl` create command as follows:

```
//just replace the name from my-first-pod to my-second-pod
$ cat my-first-pod.yaml | sed -e 's/my-first-pod/my-second-pod/' > my-
second-pod.yaml


//metadata.name has been changed to my-second-pod
$ cat my-second-pod.yaml
apiVersion: v1
kind: Pod
metadata:
  name: my-second-pod
spec:
  containers:
  - name: my-nginx
    image: nginx
```

```
    - name: my-centos
      image: centos
      command: ["/bin/sh", "-c", "while : ;do curl
http://localhost:80/; sleep 10; done"]


//create second pod
$ kubectl create -f my-second-pod.yaml
pod "my-second-pod" created


//2 pods are running
$ kubectl get pods
NAME            READY   STATUS    RESTARTS   AGE
my-first-pod    2/2     Running   0          1h
my-second-pod   2/2     Running   0          43s
```

Now you have two Pods; each Pod has two containers, `centos` and `nginx`. So a total of four containers are running on your Kubernetes cluster as in the following diagram:

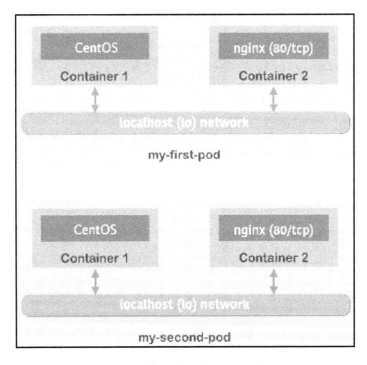

Duplicate Pod from my-first-pod to my-second-pod

If you would like to deploy more of the same Pod, consider using a Deployment (ReplicaSet) instead.

After your testing, you can run the `kubectl` delete command to delete your Pod from the Kubernetes cluster:

```
//specify --all option to delete all pods
$ kubectl delete pods --all
pod "my-first-pod" deleted
pod "my-second-pod" deleted


//pods are terminating
$ kubectl get pods
NAME             READY    STATUS        RESTARTS    AGE
my-first-pod     2/2      Terminating   0           1h
my-second-pod    2/2      Terminating   0           3m
```

See also

This recipe from this chapter described how to control Pods. They are the basic components of Kubernetes operation. The following recipes will describe the advanced operation of Pods using Deployments, Services, and so on:

- *Managing Pods with ReplicaSets*
- *Deployment API*
- *Working with Services*
- *Working with labels and selectors*

Managing Pods with ReplicaSets

A ReplicaSet is a term for API objects in Kubernetes that refer to Pod replicas. The idea is to be able to control a set of Pods' behaviors. The ReplicaSet ensures that the Pods, in the amount of a user-specified number, are running all the time. If some Pods in the ReplicaSet crash and terminate, the system will recreate Pods with the original configurations on healthy nodes automatically, and keep a certain number of processes continuously running. While changing the size of set, users can scale the application out or down easily. According to this feature, no matter whether you need replicas of Pods or not, you can always rely on ReplicaSet for auto-recovery and scalability. In this recipe, you're going to learn how to manage your Pods with ReplicaSet:

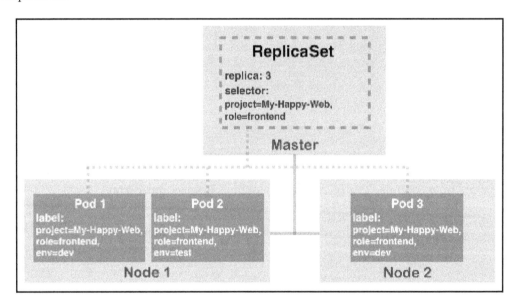

ReplicaSet and their Pods on two nodes

The ReplicaSet usually handles a tier of applications. As you can see in the preceding diagram, we launch a ReplicaSet with three Pod replicas. Some mechanism details are listed as follows:

- The **kube-controller-manager** daemon helps to maintain the resource running in its desired state. For example, the desired state of ReplicaSet in the diagram is three Pod replicas.

- The **kube-scheduler** daemon on master, the scheduler of Kubernetes, takes charge of assigning tasks to healthy nodes.
- The selector of the **ReplicaSet** is used for deciding which Pods it covers. If the key-value pairs in the Pod's label include all items in the selector of the ReplicaSet, this Pod belongs to this ReplicaSet. As you will see, the diagram shows three Pods are under the charge of the ReplicaSet. Even though Pod 2 has a different label of `env`, it is selected since the other two labels, `role` and `project`, match the ReplicaSet's selector.

ReplicationController? ReplicaSet?

For experienced Kubernetes players, you may notice ReplicaSet looks quite similar to the ReplicationController. Since version 1.2 of Kubernetes, in order to concentrate on different features, the ReplicationController's functionality has been covered by ReplicaSet and Deployment. ReplicaSet focuses on the Pod replica, keeping certain Pods running in healthy states. On the other hand, Deployment is a higher-level API, which can manage the ReplicaSet, perform application rolling updates, and expose the services. In Kubernetes v1.8.3, users can still create replication controllers. However, using Deployment with ReplicaSet is more recommended because these are up to date and have finer granularity of configuration.

Getting ready

Creating a ReplicaSet is the same as creating any Kubernetes resource; we fire the `kubectl` command on the Kubernetes master. Therefore, we ensure your Kubernetes environment is ready to accept your order. More than that, the Kubernetes node should be able to access the Docker Hub. For the demonstration in the following few pages, we would take official `nginx` docker image for example, which stores in public docker registry as well.

The evaluation of a prepared Kubernetes system
You can verify whether your Kuberenetes master is a practical one through checking the items here:

- **Check whether the daemons are running or no**t: There should be three working daemon processes on the master node: `apiserver`, `scheduler`, and `controller-manager`.
- **Check whether the command kubectl exists and is workable**: Try the command `kubectl get cs` to cover this bullet point and the first one. You can verify not only the status of components but also the feasibility of `kubectl`.
- **Check whether the nodes are ready to work**: You can check them by using the command `kubectl get nodes` to get their status.

In the case that some items listed here are invalid, please refer to `Chapter 12`, *Building Your Own Kubernetes Cluster,* for proper guidelines based on the installation you chose.

How to do it...

In this section, we will demonstrate the life cycle of a ReplicaSet from creation to destruction.

Creating a ReplicaSet

When trying to use the command line to launch a Kubernetes Service immediately, we usually fire `kubectl run`. However, it would creates a Deployment by default, and not only taking care of the Pod replica but also providing a container-updating mechanism. To simply create a standalone ReplicaSet, we can exploit a configuration YAML file and run it:

```
$ cat my-first-replicaset.yaml
apiVersion: extensions/v1beta1
kind: ReplicaSet
metadata:
  name: my-first-replicaset
  labels:
```

```
      version: 0.0.1
spec:
  replicas: 3
  selector:
    matchLabels:
      project: My-Happy-Web
      role: frontend
  template:
    metadata:
      labels:
        project: My-Happy-Web
        role: frontend
        env: dev
    spec:
      containers:
      - name: happy-web
        image: nginx:latest
```

The preceding file is the YAML for our first ReplicaSet. It defines a ReplicaSet named `my-first-replicaset`, which has three replicas for its Pods. Labels and the selector are the most characteristic settings of ReplicaSet. There are two sets of labels: one for ReplicaSet, the other for Pods. The first label for ReplicaSet is under the metadata of this resource, right beneath the name, which is simply used for description. However, the other label value under the template's metadata, the one for Pods, is also used for identification. ReplicaSet takes charge of the Pods which have the labels covered by its selector.

In our example configuration file, the selector of ReplicaSet looks for Pods with `project: My-Happy-Web` and `role: frontend` tags. Since we initiate Pods under control of this ReplicaSet, the Pods' labels should definitely include what selector cares. You may get following error message while creating a ReplicaSet with incorrectly labeled Pods: `` `selector` does not match template `labels` ``.

Now, let's create ReplicaSet through this file:

```
$ kubectl create -f my-first-replicaset.yaml
replicaset.extensions "my-first-replicaset" created
```

The API version of ReplicaSet in Kubernetes v1.9

While this book is under construction, Kubernetes v1.9 is released. The API version of ReplicaSet turns to a stable version `apps/v1` instead of `apps/v1beta2`. If you have an older version Kubernetes, please change the value of `apiVersion` to `apps/v1beta2`, or you can just update your Kubernetes system.

Getting the details of a ReplicaSet

After we create the ReplicaSet, the subcommands `get` and `describe` can help us to capture its information and the status of Pods. In the CLI of Kubernetes, we are able to use the abbreviation rs for resource type, instead of the full name ReplicaSet:

```
// use subcommand "get" to list all ReplicaSets
$ kubectl get rs
NAME                DESIRED   CURRENT   READY   AGE
my-first-replicaset 3         3         3       4s
```

This result shows roughly that the Pod replicas of `my-first-replicaset` are all running successfully; currently running Pods are of the desired number and all of them are ready for serving requests.

For detailed information, check by using the subcommand `describe`:

```
// specify that we want to check ReplicaSet called my-first-replicaset
$ kubectl describe rs my-first-replicaset
Name:        my-first-replicaset
Namespace:   default
Selector:    project=My-Happy-Web,role=frontend
Labels:      version=0.0.1
Annotations: <none>
Replicas:    3 current / 3 desired
Pods Status: 3 Running / 0 Waiting / 0 Succeeded / 0 Failed
Pod Template:
  Labels:  env=dev
           project=My-Happy-Web
           role=frontend
  Containers:
   happy-web:
    Image:        nginx:latest
    Port:         <none>
    Host Port:    <none>
    Environment:  <none>
    Mounts:       <none>
   Volumes:       <none>
Events:
  Type    Reason          Age   From                   Message
  ----    ------          ----  ----                   -------
  Normal  SuccessfulCreate 9s    replicaset-controller  Created pod:
my-first-replicaset-8hg55
  Normal  SuccessfulCreate 9s    replicaset-controller  Created pod:
my-first-replicaset-wtphz
  Normal  SuccessfulCreate 9s    replicaset-controller  Created pod:
my-first-replicaset-xcrws
```

You can see that the output lists ReplicaSet's particulars of the configuration, just like what we requested in the YAML file. Furthermore, the logs for the creation of Pods are shown as part of ReplicaSet, which confirms that the Pod replicas are successfully created and designated with unique names. You can also check Pods by name:

```
// get the description according the name of Pod, please look at the
Pod name shown on your screen, which should be different from this
book.
$ kubectl describe pod my-first-replicaset-xcrws
```

Changing the configuration of a ReplicaSet

The subcommands known as `edit`, `patch`, and `replace` can help to update live Kubernetes resources. All these functionalities change the settings by way of modifying a configuration file. Here we just take `edit`, for example.

The subcommand edit lets users modify resource configuration through the editor. Try to update your ReplicaSet through the command `kubectl edit rs $REPLICASET_NAME`; you will access this resource via the default editor with a YAML configuration file:

```
// demonstrate to change the number of Pod replicas.
$ kubectl get rs
NAME                    DESIRED   CURRENT   READY   AGE
my-first-replicaset     3         3         3       2m

// get in the editor, modify the replica number, then save and leave
$ kubectl edit rs my-first-replicaset
# Please edit the object below. Lines beginning with a '#' will be
ignored,
# and an empty file will abort the edit. If an error occurs while
saving this file will be
# reopened with the relevant failures.
#
apiVersion: extensions/v1beta1
kind: ReplicaSet
metadata:
  creationTimestamp: 2018-05-05T20:48:38Z
  generation: 1
  labels:
    version: 0.0.1
  name: my-first-replicaset
  namespace: default
  resourceVersion: "1255241"
  selfLink:
```

```
/apis/extensions/v1beta1/namespaces/default/replicasets/my-first-
replicaset
  uid: 18330fa8-cd55-11e7-a4de-525400a9d353
spec:
  replicas: 4
  selector:
    matchLabels:
...
replicaset "my-first-replicaset" edited
$ kubectl get rs
NAME                     DESIRED    CURRENT    READY     AGE
my-first-replicaset      4          4          4         4m
```

In the demonstration, we succeed to add one Pod in the set, yet this is not the best practice for auto-scaling the Pod. Take a look at the *Working with configuration files* recipe in `Chapter 14`, *Playing with Containers*, for Reference, and try to change the other values.

Deleting a ReplicaSet

In order to remove the ReplicaSet from the Kubernetes system, you can rely on the subcommand `delete`. When we fire `delete` to remove the resource, it removes the target objects forcefully:

```
$ time kubectl delete rs my-first-replicaset && kubectl get pod
replicaset.extensions "my-first-replicaset" deleted
real   0m2.492s
user   0m0.188s
sys    0m0.048s
NAME                          READY    STATUS        RESTARTS    AGE
my-first-replicaset-8hg55     0/1      Terminating   0           53m
my-first-replicaset-b6kr2     1/1      Terminating   0           48m
my-first-replicaset-wtphz     0/1      Terminating   0           53m
my-first-replicaset-xcrws     1/1      Terminating   0           53m
```

We find that the response time is quite short and the effect is also instantaneous.

Removing the Pod under ReplicaSet

As we mentioned previously, it is impossible to scale down the ReplicaSet by deleting the Pod, because while a Pod is removed, the ReplicaSet is out of stable status: if the desired number of Pods is not met, and the controller manager will ask ReplicaSet to create another one. The concept is shown in the following commands:

```
// check ReplicaSet and the Pods
$ kubectl get rs,pod
NAME DESIRED CURRENT READY AGE
rs/my-first-replicaset 3 3 3 14s
NAME READY STATUS RESTARTS AGE
po/my-first-replicaset-bxf45 1/1 Running 0 14s
po/my-first-replicaset-r6wpx 1/1 Running 0 14s
po/my-first-replicaset-vt6fd 1/1 Running 0 14s

// remove certain Pod and check what happened
$ kubectl delete pod my-first-replicaset-bxf45
pod "my-first-replicaset-bxf45" deleted
$ kubectl get rs,pod
NAME DESIRED CURRENT READY AGE
rs/my-first-replicaset 3 3 3 2m
NAME READY STATUS RESTARTS AGE
po/my-first-replicaset-dvbpg 1/1 Running 0 6s
po/my-first-replicaset-r6wpx 1/1 Running 0 2m
po/my-first-replicaset-vt6fd 1/1 Running 0 2m
```

```
// check the event log as well
$ kubectl describe rs my-first-replicaset
(ignored)
:
Events:
Type Reason Age From Message
---- ------ ---- ---- -------
Normal SuccessfulCreate 2m replicaset-controller
Created pod: my-first-replicaset-bxf45
Normal SuccessfulCreate 2m replicaset-controller
Created pod: my-first-replicaset-r6wpx
Normal SuccessfulCreate 2m replicaset-controller
Created pod: my-first-replicaset-vt6fd
Normal SuccessfulCreate 37s replicaset-controller
Created pod: my-first-replicaset-dvbpg
```

You will find that although the `my-first-replicaset-bxf45` Pod is removed, the `my-first-replicaset-dvbpg` Pod is created automatically and attached to this ReplicaSet.

How it works...

The ReplicaSet defines a set of Pods by using a Pod template and labels. As in the ideas from previous sections, the ReplicaSet only manages the Pods via their labels. It is possible that the Pod template and the configuration of the Pod are different. This also means that standalone Pods can be added into a set by using label modification.

Let's evaluate this concept of selectors and labels by creating a ReplicaSet similar to the diagram at the beginning of this recipe:

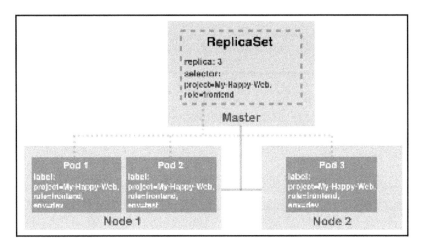

The ReplicaSet would cover Pods which have the same labels describing in its selector

First, we are going to create a CentOS Pod with the labels project: `My-Happy-Web`, `role: frontend,` and `env: test`:

```
// use subcommand "run" with tag restart=Never to create a Pod
$ kubectl run standalone-pod --image=centos --labels="project=My-
Happy-Web,role=frontend,env=test" --restart=Never --command sleep 3600
pod "standalone-pod" created

// check Pod along with the labels
$ kubectl get pod -L project -L role -L env
NAME             READY     STATUS    RESTARTS   AGE        PROJECT
ROLE        ENV
standalone-pod   1/1       Running   0          3m         My-Happy-Web
frontend    test
```

After adding this command, a standalone Pod runs with the labels we specified.

Next, go create your first ReplicaSet example by using the YAML file again:

```
$ kubectl create -f my-first-replicaset.yaml
replicaset.apps "my-first-replicaset" created

// check the Pod again
$ kubectl get pod -L project -L role -L env
NAME                          READY     STATUS     RESTARTS    AGE
PROJECT         ROLE        ENV
my-first-replicaset-fgdc8   1/1       Running    0           14s
My-Happy-Web    frontend    dev
my-first-replicaset-flc9m   1/1       Running    0           14s
My-Happy-Web    frontend    dev
standalone-pod                1/1       Running    0           6m
My-Happy-Web    frontend    test
```

As in the preceding result, only two Pods are created. It is because the Pod `standalone-pod` is considered one of the sets taken by `my-first-replicaset`. Remember that `my-first-replicaset` takes care of the Pods labeled with project: `My-Happy-Web` and `role:frontend` (ignore the `env` tag). Go check the standalone Pod; you will find it belongs to a member of the ReplicaSet as well:

```
$ kubectl describe pod standalone-pod
Name:          standalone-pod
Namespace:     default
Node:          ubuntu02/192.168.122.102
Start Time:    Sat, 05 May 2018 16:57:14 -0400
Labels:        env=test
               project=My-Happy-Web
               role=frontend
Annotations:   <none>
Status:        Running
IP:            192.168.79.57
Controlled By: ReplicaSet/my-first-replicaset
...
```

Similarly, once we delete the set, the standalone Pod will be removed with the group:

```
// remove the ReplicaSet and check pods immediately
$ kubectl delete rs my-first-replicaset && kubectl get pod
replicaset.extensions "my-first-replicaset" deleted
NAME                          READY     STATUS        RESTARTS    AGE
my-first-replicaset-fgdc8   0/1       Terminating   0           1m
my-first-replicaset-flc9m   0/1       Terminating   0           1m
standalone-pod                0/1       Terminating   0           7m
```

There's more...

There are multiple Kubernetes resources for Pod management. Users are encouraged to leverage various types of resources to meet different purposes. Let's comparing the resource types listed below with ReplicaSet:

- **Deployment**: In general cases, Kubernetes Deployments are used together with ReplicaSet for complete Pod management: container rolling updates, load balancing, and service exposing.
- **Job**: Sometimes, we want the Pods run as a job instead of a service. A Kubernetes job is suitable for this situation. You can consider it a ReplicaSet with the constraint of termination.
- **DaemonSet**: More than ReplicaSet, the Kubernetes DaemonSet guarantees that the specified set is running on every node in the cluster. That said, a subset of ReplicaSet on every node.

To get more idea and instruction, you can check the recipe *Ensuring flexible usage of your containers* in `Chapter 14`, *Playing with Containers*.

See also

Now you understand the idea of ReplicaSet. Continue to look up the following recipes in this chapter for more Kubernetes resources, which will allow you to explore the magical effects of ReplicaSet:

- *Deployment API*
- *Working with Services*
- *Working with labels an selectors*

Moreover, since you have built a simple ReplicaSet by using a configuration file, refer to more details about creating your own configuration files for Kubernetes resources:

- *Working with configuration files* section in `Chapter 14`, *Playing with Containers*

Deployment API

The Deployment API was introduced in Kubernetes version 1.2. It is replacing the replication controller. The functionalities of rolling-update and rollback by replication controller, it was achieved with client side (`kubectl` command and `REST API`), that `kubectl` need to keep connect while updating a replication controller. On the other hand, Deployments takes care of the process of rolling-update and rollback at the server side. Once that request is accepted, the client can disconnect immediately.

Therefore, the Deployments API is designed as a higher-level API to manage ReplicaSet objects. This section will explore how to use the Deployments API to manage ReplicaSets.

Getting ready

In order to create Deployment objects, as usual, use the `kubectl run` command or prepare the YAML/JSON file that describe Deployment configuration. This example is using the `kubectl run` command to create a `my-nginx` Deployment object:

```
//create my-nginx Deployment (specify 3 replicas and nginx version
1.11.0)
$ kubectl run my-nginx --image=nginx:1.11.0 --port=80 --replicas=3
deployment.apps "my-nginx" created


//see status of my-nginx Deployment
$ kubectl get deploy
NAME          DESIRED    CURRENT    UP-TO-DATE    AVAILABLE    AGE
my-nginx      3          3          3             3            8s


//see status of ReplicaSet
$ kubectl get rs
NAME                   DESIRED    CURRENT    READY     AGE
my-nginx-5d69b5ff7     3          3          3         11s


//see status of Pod
$ kubectl get pods
NAME                        READY    STATUS     RESTARTS    AGE
my-nginx-5d69b5ff7-9mhbc    1/1      Running    0           14s
my-nginx-5d69b5ff7-mt6z7    1/1      Running    0           14s
my-nginx-5d69b5ff7-rdl2k    1/1      Running    0           14s
```

As you can see, a Deployment object `my-nginx` creates one `ReplicaSet`, which has an identifier: `<Deployment name>-<hex decimal hash>`. And then ReplicaSet creates three Pods which have an identifier: `<ReplicaSet id>-<random id>`.

 Until Kubernetes version 1.8, `<Deployment name>-<pod-template-hash value (number)>` was used as a ReplicaSet identifier instead of a hex decimal hash.

For more details, look at pull request: `https://github.com/kubernetes/kubernetes/pull/51538`.

This diagram illustrates the **Deployment**, **ReplicaSet**, and **Pod** relationship:

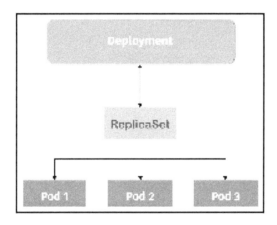

Relationship diagram for Deployments, ReplicaSets, and Pods

Because of this relationship, if you perform `delete` on a `my-nginx` Deployment object, it will also attempt to delete ReplicaSet and Pods respectively:

```
//delete my-nginx Deployment
$ kubectl delete deploy my-nginx
deployment.extensions "my-nginx" deleted


//see status of ReplicaSet
$ kubectl get rs
No resources found.


//see status of Pod, it has been terminated
$ kubectl get pods
```

```
NAME                          READY    STATUS          RESTARTS   AGE
my-nginx-5d69b5ff7-9mhbc      0/1      Terminating     0          2m
my-nginx-5d69b5ff7-mt6z7      0/1      Terminating     0          2m
my-nginx-5d69b5ff7-rdl2k      0/1      Terminating     0          2m
```

This example is just a simple `create` and `delete`, that easy to understand Deployment object and ReplicaSet object 1:1 relationship at this moment. However, a Deployment object can manage many ReplicaSets to preserve as a history. So the actual relationship is 1:N, as in the following diagram:

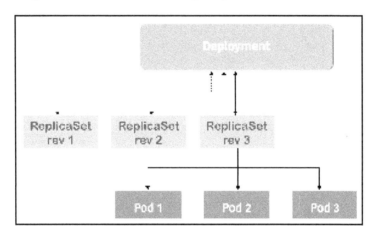

Deployments maintain ReplicaSet history

To understand the 1:N relationship, let's recreate this Deployment object again and perform to make some changes to see how Deployment manages ReplicaSet history.

How to do it...

You may run the `kubectl run` command to recreate `my-nginx`, or write a Deployments configuration file that produces the same result. This is a great opportunity to learn about the Deployment configuration file.

This example is an equivalent of `kubectl run my-nginx --image=nginx:1.11.0 --port=80 --replicas=3`:

```
$ cat deploy.yaml
apiVersion: apps/v1
kind: Deployment
metadata:
  name: my-nginx
spec:
  replicas: 3
  selector:
    matchLabels:
      run: my-nginx
  template:
    metadata:
      labels:
        run: my-nginx
    spec:
      containers:
      - name: my-nginx
        image: nginx:1.11.0
        ports:
        - containerPort: 80
```

These parameters, sorted by key and value, are described here:

Key	Value	Description
`apiVersion`	`apps/v1`	Until Kubernetes v1.8, it had been used apps/v1Beta1, v1.8 used apps/v1Beta2, then v1.9 or later use apps/v1
`kind`	`deployment`	Indicates that this is a set of Deployment configurations
`metadata.name`	`my-nginx`	Name of Deployment
`spec.replicas`	3	Desire to have three Pods
`spec.selector.matchLabels`	`run:my-nginx`	Control ReplicaSet/Pods which have this label
`spec.template.metadata.labels`	`run:my-nginx`	Assigns this label when creating a ReplicaSet/Pod; it must match `spec.selector.matchLabels`

	name: my-nginx image: nginx:1.11.0 port: — containerPort:80	ReplicaSet creates and manages Pods which have: • name as my-nginx • Container image as nginx version 1.11.0 • Publish port number 80
spec.template.spec.containers		

If you use this YAML file to create a Deployment, use the kubectl create command instead of kubectl run.

Note that, this time, you should also specify --save-config, which allows you to update the resource using the kubectl apply command in the future. In addition, specify --record which can store the command line history. Those two options are not mandatory to manage ReplicaSet history but help you to preserve better information:

```
//use -f to specify YAML file
$ kubectl create -f deploy.yaml --save-config --record
deployment.apps "my-nginx" created


//check my-nginx Deployment
$ kubectl get deploy
NAME        DESIRED    CURRENT    UP-TO-DATE    AVAILABLE    AGE
my-nginx    3          3          3             3            5s


$ kubectl describe deploy my-nginx
Name:                   my-nginx
Namespace:              default
CreationTimestamp:      Wed, 09 May 2018 03:40:09 +0000
Labels:                 <none>
Annotations:            deployment.kubernetes.io/revision=1
                        kubectl.kubernetes.io/last-applied-
configuration={"apiVersion":"apps/v1","kind":"Deployment","metadata":{
"annotations":{},"name":"my-
nginx","namespace":"default"},"spec":{"replicas":3,"selector":{"mat...
                        kubernetes.io/change-cause=kubectl create --
filename=deploy.yaml --save-config=true --record=true
Selector:               run=my-nginx
Replicas:               3 desired | 3 updated | 3 total | 3 available
| 0 unavailable
StrategyType:           RollingUpdate
MinReadySeconds:        0
RollingUpdateStrategy:  25% max unavailable, 25% max surge
Pod Template:
```

```
      Labels:    run=my-nginx
      Containers:
       my-nginx:
        Image:          nginx:1.11.0
        Port:           80/TCP
        Host Port:      0/TCP
        Environment:    <none>
        Mounts:         <none>
       Volumes:         <none>
      Conditions:
        Type            Status   Reason
        ----            ------   ------
        Available       True     MinimumReplicasAvailable
        Progressing     True     NewReplicaSetAvailable
      OldReplicaSets:   <none>
      NewReplicaSet:    my-nginx-54bb7bbcf9 (3/3 replicas created)
      Events:
        Type      Reason               Age    From                  Message
        ----      ------               ----   ----                  -------
        Normal    ScalingReplicaSet    34s    deployment-controller   Scaled up
      replica set my-nginx-54bb7bbcf9 to 3
```

You can see a property OldReplicaSets and NewReplicaSet in the preceding code, which are some association between Deployment and ReplicaSet.

Whenever you update a definition of a container template, for example, changing the nginx image version from 1.11.0 to 1.12.0, then Deployment my-nginx will create a new ReplicaSet. Then the property NewReplicaSet will point to the new ReplicaSet which has nginx version 1.12.0.

On the other hand, the OldReplicaSets property points to an old ReplicaSet which has nginx version 1.11.0 until new ReplicaSet is complete to setup new Pod.

These old/new ReplicaSet associations between Deployment, Kubernetes administrator can easy to achieve rollback operation in case new ReplicaSet has any issues.

In addition, Deployment can keep preserves the history of ReplicaSet which were associated with it before. Therefore, Deployment can anytime to change back (rollback) to any point of older ReplicaSet.

How it works...

As mentioned earlier, let's bump the nginx image version from 1.11.0 to 1.12.0. There are two ways to change the container image: use the `kubectl set` command, or update YAML then use the `kubectl apply` command.

Using the `kubectl set` command is quicker and there is better visibility when using the `--record` option.

On the other hand, updating YAML and using the `kubectl apply` command is better to preserve the entire Deployment YAML configuration file, which is better when using a version control system such as `git`.

Using kubectl set to update the container image

Use the `kubectl set` command allows us to overwrite the `spec.template.spec.containers[].image` property that is similar to using the `kubectl run` command to specify the image file. The following example specifies `my-nginx` deployment to set the container `my-nginx` to change the image to nginx version 1.12.0:

```
$ kubectl set image deployment my-nginx my-nginx=nginx:1.12.0 --record
deployment.apps "my-nginx" image updated


$ kubectl describe deploy my-nginx
Name:                   my-nginx
...
...
Conditions:
  Type            Status   Reason
  ----            ------   ------
  Available       True     MinimumReplicasAvailable
  Progressing     True     ReplicaSetUpdated
OldReplicaSets:   my-nginx-54bb7bbcf9 (3/3 replicas created)
NewReplicaSet:    my-nginx-77769b7666 (1/1 replicas created)
Events:
  Type     Reason             Age   From                   Message
  ----     ------             ----  ----                   -------
  Normal   ScalingReplicaSet  27s   deployment-controller  Scaled up
replica set my-nginx-54bb7bbcf9 to 3
  Normal   ScalingReplicaSet  2s    deployment-controller  Scaled up
replica set my-nginx-77769b7666 to 1
```

As you can see, OldReplicaSets becomes the previous ReplicaSet (my-nginx-54bb7bbcf9) and NewReplicaSet becomes my-nginx-77769b7666. Note that you can see the OldReplicaSets property until NewReplicaSet is ready, so once the new ReplicaSet is successfully launched, OldReplicaSet becomes <none>, as follows:

```
$ kubectl describe deploy my-nginx
Name:                   my-nginx
...
...
  Type           Status  Reason
  ----           ------  ------
  Available      True    MinimumReplicasAvailable
  Progressing    True    NewReplicaSetAvailable
OldReplicaSets:    <none>
NewReplicaSet:     my-nginx-77769b7666 (3/3 replicas created)
```

If you can see the ReplicaSet list by kubectl get rs, you can see two ReplicaSet, as follows:

```
$ kubectl get rs
NAME                     DESIRED   CURRENT   READY   AGE
my-nginx-54bb7bbcf9      0         0         0       3m
my-nginx-77769b7666      3         3         3       3m
```

As you can see, in the old ReplicaSet (my-nginx-54bb7bbcf9), the numbers of DESIRED/CURRENT/READY pods are all zero.

In addition, because the preceding example uses the --record option, you can see the history of the Deployment my-nginx rollout with the kubectl rollout history command, as follows:

```
$ kubectl rollout history deployment my-nginx
deployments "my-nginx"
REVISION   CHANGE-CAUSE
1          kubectl create --filename=deploy.yaml --save-config=true --
record=true
2          kubectl set image deployment/my-nginx my-nginx=nginx:1.12.0
--record=true
```

Updating the YAML and using kubectl apply

For demo purposes, copy `deploy.yaml` to `deploy_1.12.2.yaml` and change the `nginx` version to `1.12.2`, as follows:

```
image: nginx:1.12.2
```

Then run the `kubectl apply` command with the `--record` option:

```
$ kubectl apply -f deploy_1.12.2.yaml --record
deployment.apps "my-nginx" configured
```

This will perform the same thing as the `kubectl set` image command, so you can see that the nginx image version has been bumped up to `1.12.2`; also, the `OldReplicaSets/NewReplicaSet` combination has been changed as follows:

```
$ kubectl describe deploy my-nginx
Name:                  my-nginx
...
...
Pod Template:
  Labels: run=my-nginx
  Containers:
   my-nginx:
    Image: nginx:1.12.2
...
...
Conditions:
  Type           Status   Reason
  ----           ------   ------
  Available      True     MinimumReplicasAvailable
  Progressing    True     ReplicaSetUpdated
OldReplicaSets: my-nginx-77769b7666 (3/3 replicas created)
NewReplicaSet: my-nginx-69fbc98fd4 (1/1 replicas created)
```

After a few moments, `NewReplicaSet` will be ready. Then there will be a total of three `ReplicaSets` existing on your system:

```
$ kubectl get rs
NAME                  DESIRED   CURRENT   READY   AGE
my-nginx-54bb7bbcf9   0         0         0       7m
my-nginx-69fbc98fd4   3         3         3       1m
my-nginx-77769b7666   0         0         0       6m
```

You can also see the rollout history:

```
$ kubectl rollout history deployment my-nginx
deployments "my-nginx"
REVISION   CHANGE-CAUSE
1          kubectl create --filename=deploy.yaml --save-config=true --
record=true
2          kubectl set image deployment/my-nginx my-nginx=nginx:1.12.0
--record=true
3          kubectl apply --filename=deploy_1.12.2.yaml --record=true
```

Whenever you want to revert to a previous `ReplicaSet`, which means rolling back to the previous nginx version, you can use `kubectl rollout undo` with the `--to-revision` option. For example, if you want to roll back to revision 2 in your history (`kubectl set image deployment/my-nginx my-nginx=nginx:1.12.0 --record=true`), specify `--to-revision=2`:

```
$ kubectl rollout undo deployment my-nginx --to-revision=2
deployment.apps "my-nginx" rolled back'
```

A few moments later, Deployment will deactivate the current `ReplicaSet`, which uses the Pod template with `nginx` version `1.12.2`, and will then activate the `ReplicaSet` which uses `nginx` version `1.12`, as follows:

```
$ kubectl get rs
NAME                    DESIRED   CURRENT   READY   AGE
my-nginx-54bb7bbcf9     0         0         0       8m
my-nginx-69fbc98fd4     0         0         0       2m
my-nginx-77769b7666     3         3         3       7m
```

See also

In this section, you learned about the concept of Deployment. It is an important core feature in Kubernetes ReplicaSet life cycle management. It allows us to achieve rollout and rollback functionalities, and can integrate to CI/CD. In the following chapter you will see detailed operations of rollout and rollback:

- *Updating live containers* section in `Chapter 14`, *Playing with Containers*
- *Setting up a continuous delivery pipeline* section in `Chapter 16`, *Building Continuous Delivery Pipelines*

Working with Services

The network service is an application that receives requests and provides a solution. Clients access the service by a network connection. They don't have to know the architecture of the service or how it runs. The only thing that clients have to verify is whether the endpoint of the service can be accessed, and then follow its usage policy to get the response of the server. The Kubernetes Service has similar ideas. It is not necessary to understand every Pod before reaching their functionalities. For components outside the Kubernetes system, they just access the Kubernetes Service with an exposed network port to communicate with running Pods. It is not necessary to be aware of the containers' IPs and ports. Behind Kubernetes Services, we can fulfill a zero-downtime update for our container programs without struggling:

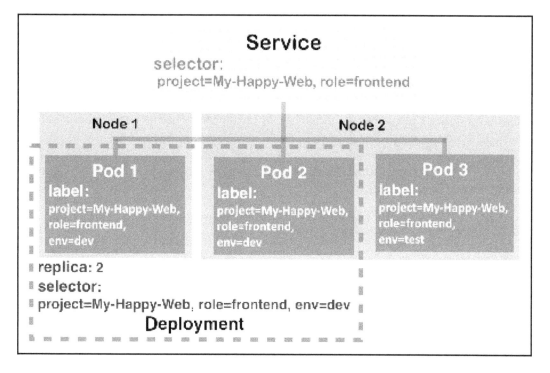

Kubernetes Service-covered Pods by labels of Pods and their selectors

The preceding diagram shows the basic structure of the **Service** and realizes the following concepts:

- As with the **Deployment**, the **Service** directs requests to Pods that have labels containing the Service's selector. In other words, the Pods selected by the **Service** are based on their labels.
- The load of requests sent to the Services will distribute to three Pods.
- The **Deployment**, along with ReplicaSet, ensures that the number of running Pods meets its desired state. It monitors the Pods for the **Service**, making sure they will be healthy for taking over duties from the **Service**.
- **Service** is an abstraction layer for grouping Pods, which allows for Pods scaling across nodes.

In this recipe, you will learn how to create Services in front of your Pods for the requests.

Getting ready

Prior to applying Kubernetes Services, it is important to verify whether all nodes in the system are running `kube-proxy`. The daemon `kube-proxy` works as a network proxy in a node. It helps to reflect Service settings, such as IPs or ports on each node, and to do network forwarding. To check if `kube-proxy` is running or not, we take a look at network connections:

```
// check by command netstat with proper tags for showing the
information we need, t:tcp, u:udp, l:listening, p:program, n:numeric
address
// use root privilege for grabbing all processes
$ sudo netstat -tulpn | grep kube-proxy
tcp        0      0 127.0.0.1:10249         0.0.0.0:*
LISTEN      2326/kube-proxy
tcp6       0      0 :::31723                :::*
LISTEN      2326/kube-proxy
tcp6       0      0 :::10256                :::*
LISTEN      2326/kube-proxy
```

Once you see the output, the process ID `2326`, `kube-proxy`, listening on port `10249` on localhost, the node is ready for Kubernetes Services. Go ahead and verify whether all of your nodes in the Kubernetes cluster having `kube-proxy` running on them.

How to do it...

As mentioned in the previous section, the Kubernetes Service exposes Pods by selecting them through corresponding labels. However, there is another configuration we have to take care of: the network port. As the following diagram indicates, the Service and Pod have their own key-value pair labels and ports:

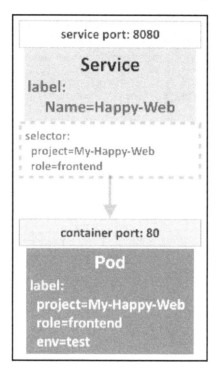

Network port mapping between Service and Pod

Therefore, setting the selector of Service and binding the service exposed port to the container port are required to be carried out while creating Services. If either of them fail to be set properly, clients won't get responses or will get connection-refused errors.

We can define and create a new Kubernetes Service through the CLI or a configuration file. Here, we are going to explain how to deploy the Services by command. The subcommands `expose` and `describe` are utilized in the following commands for various scenarios. For file-format creation, it is recommended to read the *Working with configuration files* recipe in `Chapter 14`, *Playing with Containers*, for a detailed discussion.

Creating a Service for different resources

You can attach a Service to a Pod, a Deployment, an endpoint outside the Kubernetes system, or even another Service. We will show you these, one by one, in this section. The creation of the Kubernetes Service looks similar to these command formats: `kubectl expose $RESOURCE_TYPE $RESOURCE_NAME [OTHER TAGS]` or `kubectl expose -f $CONFIG_FILE`. The resource types (Pod, Deployment, and Service) are supported by the subcommand `expose`. So is the configuration file, which follows the limitation type. Accordingly, for a later demonstration we will attach the newly created Service to the endpoint by the configuration file.

Creating a Service for a Pod

Kubernetes Pods covered by Service require labels, so that Service can recognize who is the one it should take charge of. In the following commands, we create a Pod with labels first, and attach a Service on it:

```
// using subcommand "run" with "never" restart policy, and without
replica, you can get a Pod
// here we create a nginx container with port 80 exposed to outside
world of Pod
$ kubectl run nginx-pod --image=nginx --port=80 --restart="Never" --
labels="project=My-Happy-Web,role=frontend,env=test"
pod "nginx-pod" created

// expose Pod "nginx-pod" with a Service officially with port 8080,
target port would be the exposed port of pod
$ kubectl expose pod nginx-pod --port=8080 --target-port=80 --
name="nginx-service"
service "nginx-service" exposed
```

You may find that, based on the preceding command, we did not assign any selector to this Service. Nonetheless, since Service `nginx-service` takes the port forwarding task of Pod `nginx-pod`, it will take the labels of the Pod as its selector. Go ahead and check the details of the Service with the subcommand `describe`:

```
// "svc" is the abbreviate of Service, for the description's resource
type
$ kubectl describe svc nginx-service
Name:            nginx-service
Namespace:       default
Labels:          env=test
                 project=My-Happy-Web
                 role=frontend
Annotations:     <none>
```

```
Selector:            env=test,project=My-Happy-Web,role=frontend
Type:                ClusterIP
IP:                  10.96.107.213
Port:                <unset>  8080/TCP
TargetPort:          80/TCP
Endpoints:           192.168.79.24:80
Session Affinity:    None
Events:              <none>
```

Now you can see that, for guaranteeing the responsibility, this successfully exposed Service just copied the labels of the Pod as its selector. The value list after `Endpoints` was the IP of the Pod and its exposed port `80`. Furthermore, the Service took the Pod's labels as its own. According to this example, the Pod can be accessed through Service by surfing `10.96.107.213:8080`.

Except for the selector of Service, some parameters can be automatically configured if they are bypassed by users. One parameter is the labels of the Pod; another is the name of the Service; and the other is the exposed port of the Service. Let's take a look at how this simple set of Pod and Service can be managed:

```
// create a Pod and a Service for it
$ kubectl run nginx-no-label --image=nginx --port=80 --restart="Never"
&& kubectl expose pod nginx-no-label
pod "nginx-no-label" created
service "nginx-no-label" exposed
// take a lookat the configurations of the Service
$ kubectl describe svc nginx-no-label
Name:                nginx-no-label
Namespace:           default
Labels:              run=nginx-no-label
Annotations:         <none>
Selector:            run=nginx-no-label
Type:                ClusterIP
IP:                  10.105.96.243
Port:                <unset>  80/TCP
TargetPort:          80/TCP
Endpoints:           192.168.79.10:80
Session Affinity:    None
Events:              <none>
```

Here, we can see that the Service inherited the name, label, and port from the Pod. The selector was assigned the dummy label with the key named `run` and the value named as Pod's name, which is just the same dummy one of Pod `nginx-no-label`. Users should access the Service through port `80`, as well. For such simple settings, you can alternatively try the following command to create the Pods and Service at the same time:

```
// through leveraging tag "--expose", create the Service along with
Pod
$ kubectl run another-nginx-no-label --image=nginx --port=80 --
restart="Never" --expose
service "another-nginx-no-label" created
pod "another-nginx-no-label" created
```

Creating a Service for a Deployment with an external IP

Kubernetes Deployment is the ideal resource type for a Service. For Pods supervised by the ReplicaSet and Deployment, the Kubernetes system has a controller manager to look over the their life cycles. It is also helpful for updating the version or state of the program by binding the existing Services to another Deployment. For the following commands, we create a Deployment first, and attach a Service with an external IP:

```
// using subcommand "run" and assign 2 replicas
$ kubectl run nginx-deployment --image=nginx --port=80 --replicas=2 --
labels="env=dev,project=My-Happy-Web,role=frontend"
deployment.apps "nginx-deployment" created
// explicitly indicate the selector of Service by tag "--selector",
and assign the Service an external IP by tag "--external-ip"
// the IP 192.168.122.102 demonstrated here is the IP of one of the
Kubernetes node in system
$ kubectl expose deployment nginx-deployment --port=8080 --target-
port=80 --name="another-nginx-service" --selector="project=My-Happy-
Web,role=frontend" --external-ip="192.168.122.102"
service "another-nginx-service" exposed
```

Let's go ahead and check the details of the newly created Service, `another-nginx-service`:

```
$ kubectl describe svc another-nginx-service
Name:              another-nginx-service
Namespace:         default
Labels:            env=dev
                   project=My-Happy-Web
                   role=frontend
Annotations:       <none>
```

```
Selector:              project=My-Happy-Web,role=frontend
Type:                  ClusterIP
IP:                    10.100.109.230
External IPs:          192.168.122.102
Port:                  <unset>  8080/TCP
TargetPort:            80/TCP
Endpoints:             192.168.79.15:80,192.168.79.21:80,192.168.79.24:80
Session Affinity:      None
Events:                <none>
```

Apart from the Service IP (in the case of the preceding command, `10.100.109.230`), which can be accessed within the Kubernetes system, the Service can now be connected through an external one (`192.168.122.102`, for example) beyond the Kubernetes system. While the Kubernetes master is able to communicate with every node, in this case, we can fire a request to the Service such as the following command:

```
$ curl 192.168.122.102:8080
<!DOCTYPE html>
<html>
<head>
<title>Welcome to nginx!</title>
...
```

Creating a Service for an Endpoint without a selector

First, we are going to create an Endpoint directing the external service. A Kubernetes Endpoint is an abstraction, making components beyond Kubernetes (for instance, a database in other system) become a part of Kubernetes resources. It provides a feasible use case for a hybrid environment. To create an endpoint, an IP address, along with a port, is required. Please take a look at the following template:

```
$ cat k8s-endpoint.yaml
apiVersion: v1
kind: Endpoints
metadata:
  name: k8s-ep
subsets:
  - addresses:
      - hostname: kubernetes-io
        ip: 45.54.44.100
    ports:
      - port: 80
```

The template defines an Endpoint named `k8s-ep`, which points to the IP of the host of the official Kubernetes website (`https://kubernetes.io`). Never mind that this Endpoint forwards to a plain HTML; we just take this Endpoint as an example. As mentioned, Endpoint is not a resource supported by the Kubernetes API for exposing:

```
// Give it a try!
$ kubectl expose -f k8s-endpoint.yaml
error: cannot expose a { Endpoints}
```

In Kubernetes, an Endpoint not only represents an external service; an internal Kubernetes Service is also a Kubernetes Endpoint. You can check Endpoint resources with the command `kubectl get endpoints`. You will find that there is not a single endpoint `k8s-ep` (which you just created), but many endpoints named the same as the Services in previous pages. When a Service is created with a selector and exposes certain resources (such as a Pod, Deployment, or other Service), a corresponding Endpoint with the same name is created at the same time.

Therefore, we still can create a Service associated with the Endpoint using an identical name, as in the following template:

```
$ cat endpoint-service.yaml
apiVersion: v1
kind: Service
metadata:
  name: k8s-ep
spec:
  ports:
    - protocol: TCP
      port: 8080
      targetPort: 80
```

The relationship between the Endpoints and the Service is built up with the resource name. For the Service `k8s-ep`, we didn't indicate the selector, since it did not actually take any Pod in responsibility:

```
// go create the Service and the endpoint
$ kubectl create -f endpoint-service.yaml && kubectl create -f k8s-
endpoint.yaml
service "k8s-ep" created
endpoints "k8s-ep" created
// verify the Service k8s-ep
$ kubectl describe svc k8s-ep
Name:            k8s-ep
Namespace:       default
Labels:          <none>
Annotations:     <none>
```

```
Selector:           <none>
Type:               ClusterIP
IP:                 10.105.232.226
Port:               <unset>  8080/TCP
TargetPort:         80/TCP
Endpoints:          45.54.44.100:80
Session Affinity:   None
Events:             <none>
```

Now you can see that the endpoint of the Service is just the one defined in `k8s-endpoint.yaml`. It is good for us to access the outside world through the Kubernetes Service! In the case earlier, we can verify the result with the following command:

```
$ curl 10.105.232.226:8080
```

Creating a Service for another Service with session affinity

While building a Service over another, we may think of multiple layers for port forwarding. In spite of redirecting traffic from one port to another, the action of exposing a Service is actually copying the setting of one Service to another. This scenario could be utilized as updating the Service setting, without causing headaches to current clients and servers:

```
// create a Service by expose an existed one
// take the one we created for Deployment for example
$ kubectl expose svc another-nginx-service --port=8081 --target-
port=80 --name=yet-another-nginx-service --session-affinity="ClientIP"
service "yet-another-nginx-service" exposed
// check the newly created Service
$ kubectl describe svc yet-another-nginx-service
Name:               yet-another-nginx-service
Namespace:          default
Labels:             env=dev
                    project=My-Happy-Web
                    role=frontend
Annotations:        <none>
Selector:           project=My-Happy-Web,role=frontend
Type:               ClusterIP
IP:                 10.110.218.136
Port:               <unset>  8081/TCP
TargetPort:         80/TCP
Endpoints:          192.168.79.15:80,192.168.79.21:80,192.168.79.24:80
Session Affinity:   ClientIP
Events:             <none>
```

Here we are! We successfully exposed another Service with similar settings to the Service `another-nginx-service`. The commands and output can be summarized as follows:

- **A new Service name is required**: Although we can copy the configurations from another Service, the name of the resource type should always be unique. When exposing a Service without the tag `--name`, you will get the error message: `Error from server (AlreadyExists): services "another-nginx-service" already exists.`
- **Adding or updating the configuration is workable**: We are able to add a new configuration, like adding session affinity; or we can update the port of the Service, like here, where we change to open port `8081` instead of `8080`.
- **Avoid changing target port**: Because the target port is along with the IP of the Pods, once the Service exposing changes the target port, the newly copied Service cannot forward traffic to the same endpoints. In the preceding example, since the new target port is defined, we should point out the container port again. It prevented the new Service from using the target port as the container port and turned out a misleading transaction.

With session affinity, the list of description tags session affinity as `ClientIP`. For the current Kubernetes version, the client IP is the only option for session affinity. It takes the action as a hash function: with the same IP address, the request will always send to the identical Pod. However, this could be a problem if there is a load balancer or ingress controller in front of the Kubernetes Service: the requests would be considered to come from the same source, and the traffic forwarded to a single Pod. Users have to handle this issue on their own, for example, by building an HA proxy server instead of using the Kubernetes Service.

Deleting a Service

If you go through every command in this section, there are definitely some demonstrated Kubernetes Services (we counted six of them) that should be removed. To delete a Service, the same as with any other Kubernetes resource, you can remove the Service with the name or the configuration file through the subcommand `delete`. When you try to remove the Service and the Endpoint at the same time, the following situation will happen:

```
// the resource abbreviation of endpoint is "ep", separate different
resource types by comma
$ kubectl delete svc,ep k8s-ep
```

```
service "k8s-ep" deleted
Error from server (NotFound): endpoints "k8s-ep" not found
```

This is because a Service is also a Kubernetes Endpoint. That's why, although we created the Service and the endpoint separately, once they are considered to work as a unit, the Endpoint is going to be removed when the Service is removed. Thus, the error message expresses that there is no endpoint called `k8s-ep`, since it was already removed with the Service deletion.

How it works...

On the network protocol stack, the Kubernetes Service relies on the transport layer, working together with the **overlay network** and `kube-proxy`. The overlay network of Kubernetes builds up a cluster network by allocating a subnet lease out of a pre-configured address space and storing the network configuration in `etcd`; on the other hand, `kube-proxy` helps to forward traffic from the endpoints of Services to the Pods through `iptables` settings.

Proxy-mode and Service `kube-proxy` currently has three modes with different implementation methods: `userspace`, `iptables`, and `ipvs`. The modes affect how the requests of clients reach to certain Pods through the Kubernete Service:

- `userspace`: `kube-proxy` opens a random port, called a proxy port, for each Service on the local node, then updates the `iptables` rules, which capture any request sent to the Service and forward it to the proxy port. In the end, any message sent to the proxy port will be passed to the Pods covered by the Service. It is less efficient, since the traffic is required to go to `kube-proxy` for routing to the Pod.
- `iptables`: As with the `userspace` mode, there are also required `iptables` rules for redirecting the client traffic. But there is no proxy port as mediator. Faster but need to take care the liveness of Pod. By default, there is no way for a request to retry another Pod if the target one fails. To avoid accessing the unhealthy Pod, health-checking Pods and updating `iptables` in time is necessary.

- ipvs: ipvs is the beta feature in Kubernetes v1.9. In this mode, kube-proxy builds up the interface called netlink between the Service and its backend set. The ipvs mode takes care of the downside in both userspace and iptables; it is even faster, since the routing rules stored a hash table structure in the kernel space, and even reliable that kube-proxy keeps checking the consistency of netlinks. ipvs even provides multiple load balancing options.

The system picks the optimal and stable one as the default setting for kube-proxy. Currently, it is the mode iptables.

When a Pod tries to communicate with a Service, it can find the Service through environment variables or a DNS host lookup. Let's give it a try in the following scenario of accessing a service in a Pod:

```
// run a Pod first, and ask it to be alive 600 seconds
$ kubectl run my-1st-centos --image=centos --restart=Never sleep 600
pod "my-1st-centos" created
// run a Deployment of nginx and its Service exposing port 8080 for
nginx
$ kubectl run my-nginx --image=nginx --port=80
deployment.apps "my-nginx" created
$ kubectl expose deployment my-nginx --port=8080 --target-port=80 --
name="my-nginx-service"
service "my-nginx-service" exposed
// run another pod
$ kubectl run my-2nd-centos --image=centos --restart=Never sleep 600
pod "my-2nd-centos" created
//Go check the environment variables on both pods.
$ kubectl exec my-1st-centos -- /bin/sh -c export
$ kubectl exec my-2nd-centos -- /bin/sh -c export
```

You will find that the Pod my-2nd-centos comes out with additional variables showing information for the Service my-nginx-service, as follows:

```
export MY_NGINX_SERVICE_PORT="tcp://10.104.218.20:8080"
export MY_NGINX_SERVICE_PORT_8080_TCP="tcp://10.104.218.20:8080"
export MY_NGINX_SERVICE_PORT_8080_TCP_ADDR="10.104.218.20"
export MY_NGINX_SERVICE_PORT_8080_TCP_PORT="8080"
export MY_NGINX_SERVICE_PORT_8080_TCP_PROTO="tcp"
export MY_NGINX_SERVICE_SERVICE_HOST="10.104.218.20"
export MY_NGINX_SERVICE_SERVICE_PORT="8080"
```

This is because the system failed to do a real-time update for Services; only the Pods created subsequently can be applied to accessing the Service through environment variables. With this ordering-dependent constraint, pay attention to running your Kubernetes resources in a proper sequence if they have to interact with each other in this way. The keys of the environment variables representing the Service host are formed as `<SERVICE NAME>_SERVICE_HOST`, and the Service port is like `<SERVICE NAME>_SERVICE_PORT`. In the preceding example, the dash in the name is also transferred to the underscore:

```
// For my-2nd-centos, getting information of Service by environment
variables
$ kubectl exec my-2nd-centos -- /bin/sh -c 'curl
$MY_NGINX_SERVICE_SERVICE_HOST:$MY_NGINX_SERVICE_SERVICE_PORT'
<!DOCTYPE html>
<html>
<head>
<title>Welcome to nginx!</title>
...
```

Nevertheless, if the `kube-dns` add-on is installed, which is a DNS server in the Kubernetes system, any Pod in the same Namespace can access the Service, no matter when the Service was created. The hostname of the Service would be formed as `<SERVICE NAME>.<NAMESPACE>.svc.cluster.local`. `cluster.local` is the default cluster domain defined in booting `kube-dns`:

```
// go accessing my-nginx-service by A record provided by kube-dns
$ kubectl exec my-1st-centos -- /bin/sh -c 'curl my-nginx-
service.default.svc.cluster.local:8080'
$ kubectl exec my-2nd-centos -- /bin/sh -c 'curl my-nginx-
service.default.svc.cluster.local:8080'
```

There's more...

The Kubernetes Service has four types: `ClusterIP`, `NodePort`, `LoadBalancer`, and `ExternalName`. In the *How to do it...* section in this recipe, we only demonstrate the default type, `ClusterIP`. The type `ClusterIP` indicates that the Kubernetes Service is assigned a unique virtual IP in the overlay network, which also means the identity in this Kubernetes cluster. `ClusterIP` guarantees that the Service is accessible internally.

The following diagram expresses the availability coverage of the types, and their entry points:

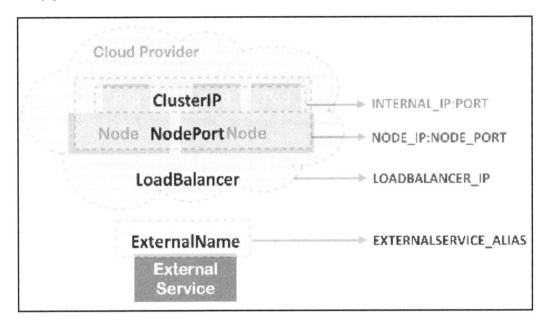

Four Service types and their entry points

For the `NodePort` type, it covers the `ClusterIP`'s features, has a peer-accessible virtual IP, and also allows the user to expose Services on each node with the same port. The type `LoadBalancer` is on the top of the other two types. The `LoadBalancer` Service would be exposed internally and on the node. More than that, if your cloud provider supports external load balancing servers, you can bind the load balancer IP to the Service, and this will become another exposing point. On the other hand, the type `ExternalName` is used for the endpoint out of your Kubernetes system. It is similar to the Endpoint we created with the configuration file in a previous section; moreover, a single `ExternalName` Service can provide this feature.

We can use the subcommand `create` to create Services in different types:

```
// create a NodePort Service
// the tag "tcp" is for indicating port configuration:
SERVICE_PORT:TARGET_PORT
$ kubectl create service nodeport my-nginx --tcp=8080:80
service "my-nginx" created
$ kubectl describe svc my-nginx
Name:                   my-nginx
```

```
Namespace:                default
Labels:                   app=my-nginx
Annotations:              <none>
Selector:                 app=my-nginx
Type:                     NodePort
IP:                       10.105.106.134
Port:                     8080-80  8080/TCP
TargetPort:               80/TCP
NodePort:                 8080-80  31336/TCP
Endpoints:                <none>
Session Affinity:         None
External Traffic Policy:  Cluster
Events:                   <none>
```

In this example of the `NodePort` Service, you can see that it still has the virtual IP (`10.105.106.134`) in the cluster, and can be accessed through port `31336` of any Kubernetes node:

```
// run an nginx Deployment with the label as NodePort Service my-
nginx's selector
$ kubectl run test-nodeport --image=nginx --labels="app=my-nginx"
deployment.apps "test-nodeport" created
// check the Kubernetes node with Service port on the node
$ curl ubuntu02:31336
<!DOCTYPE html>
<html>
<head>
<title>Welcome to nginx!</title>
...
```

In the case here, we demonstrate creating an `ExternalName` Service which exposes the CNAME `kubernetes.io`:

```
$ kubectl create service externalname k8s-website --external-name
kubernetes.io
service "k8s-website" created
// create a CentOS Pod for testing the Service availability
$ kubectl run my-centos --image=centos --restart=Never sleep 600
pod "my-centos" created
//now you can check the Service by Service's DNS name
$ kubectl exec -it my-centos -- /bin/sh -c 'curl k8s-
website.default.svc.cluster.local '
//Check all the Services we created in this section
//ExternalName Service has no cluster IP as defined
$ kubectl get svc
NAME                  TYPE         CLUSTER-IP    EXTERNAL-IP
PORT(S)          AGE
k8s-website           ExternalName  <none>       kubernetes.io
```

`<none>`	`31m`				
`kubernetes`		`ClusterIP`	`10.96.0.1`	`<none>`	
`443/TCP`	`14d`				
`my-nginx`		`NodePort`	`10.105.106.134`	`<none>`	
`8080:31336/TCP`	`1h`				

Yet, we cannot build an `ExternalName` Service in CLI with the subcommand `expose`, because `expose` works on exposing the Kubernetes resources, while the `ExternalName` Service is for the resources in the outside world. Then, it is also reasonable that the `ExternalName` Service doesn't need to be defined with the selector.

Using the subcommand "create" to create Services

While using the subcommand `create` on Service creation, the command line would look like this: `kubectl create service <SERVICE TYPE> <SERVICE NAME> [OPTIONS]`. And we can put the Service types at `<SERVICE TYPE>`, such as `clusterip`, `nodeport`, `loadbalancer`, and `externalname`. With this method, we cannot specify the selector of the Service. As with the `NodePort` Service we created in that section, only a default selector, `app: my-nginx`, is created, and we have to assign this label to a later created Deployment `test-nodeport`. Except for the type `ExternalName`, Service types can be created with the subcommand `expose` with the tag `type`. Try to create the `NodePort` service with `kubectl expose` for existing resources!

See also

To get the best practices of Kubernetes Services, the following recipes in Chapter 13, *Walking though Kubernetes Concepts*, are suggested reading:

- *Deployment API*
- *Working with Secrets*
- *Working with labels and selectors*

There is more advanced knowledge to make your service more functional and flexible. Stay tuned:

- *Forwarding container ports* section in `Chapter 14`, *Playing with Containers*
- *Ensuring flexible usage of your containers* section in `Chapter 14`, *Playing with Containers*

Working with volumes

Files in a container are ephemeral. When the container is terminated, the files are gone. Docker has introduced data volumes to help us persist data (`https://docs.docker.com/engine/admin/volumes/volumes`). However, when it comes to multiple hosts, as a container cluster, it is hard to manage volumes across all the containers and hosts for file sharing or provisioning volume dynamically. Kubernetes introduces volume, which lives with a Pod across a container life cycle. It supports various types of volumes, including popular network disk solutions and storage services in different public clouds. Here are a few:

Volume type	Storage provider
emptyDir	Localhost
hostPath	Localhost
glusterfs	GlusterFS cluster
downwardAPI	Kubernetes Pod information
nfs	NFS server
awsElasticBlockStore	Amazon Web Service Amazon Elastic Block Store
gcePersistentDisk	Google Compute Engine persistent disk
azureDisk	Azure disk storage
projected	Kubernetes resources; currently supports `secret`, `downwardAPI`, and `configMap`
secret	Kubernetes Secret resource
vSphereVolume	vSphere VMDK volume
gitRepo	Git repository

Getting ready

Storage providers are required when you start to use volume in Kubernetes, except for `emptyDir`, which will be erased when the Pod is removed. For other storage providers, folders, servers, or clusters have to be built before using them in the Pod definition. Dynamic provisioning was promoted to stable in Kubernetes version 1.6, which allows you to provision storage based on the supported cloud provider.

In this section, we'll walk through the details of `emptyDir`, `hostPath`, `nfs`, `glusterfs`, `downwardAPI`, and `gitRepo`. `Secret`, which is used to store credentials, will be introduced in the next section. `Projected`, on the other hand, is a way one could group other volume resources under one single mount point. As it only supports `secret`, `downwardAPI`, and `configMap`, we'll be introducing this in the Secret section, as well. The rest of the volume types have similar Kubernetes syntax, just with different backend volume implementations.

How to do it...

Volumes are defined in the volumes section of the pod definition with unique names. Each type of volume has a different configuration to be set. Once you define the volumes, you can mount them in the `volumeMounts` section in the container specs. `volumeMounts.name` and `volumeMounts.mountPath` are required, which indicate the name of the volumes you defined and the mount path inside the container, respectively.

We'll use the Kubernetes configuration file with the YAML format to create a Pod with volumes in the following examples.

emptyDir

`emptyDir` is the simplest volume type, which will create an empty volume for containers in the same Pod to share. When the Pod is removed, the files in `emptyDir` will be erased, as well. `emptyDir` is created when a Pod is created. In the following configuration file, we'll create a Pod running Ubuntu with commands to sleep for `3600` seconds. As you can see, one volume is defined in the volumes section with name data, and the volumes will be mounted under the `/data-mount` path in the Ubuntu container:

```
// configuration file of emptyDir volume
# cat 2-6-1_emptyDir.yaml
```

```
apiVersion: v1
kind: Pod
metadata:
  name: ubuntu
  labels:
    name: ubuntu
spec:
  containers:
    - image: ubuntu
      command:
        - sleep
        - "3600"
      imagePullPolicy: IfNotPresent
      name: ubuntu
      volumeMounts:
        - mountPath: /data-mount
          name: data
      volumes:
        - name: data
          emptyDir: {}

// create pod by configuration file emptyDir.yaml
# kubectl create -f 2-6-1_emptyDir.yaml
pod "ubuntu" created
```

 Check which node the Pod is running on
By using the `kubectl describe pod <Pod name> | grep Node`
command, you can check which node the Pod is running on.

After the Pod is running, you can use `docker inspect <container ID>` on the
target node and you can see the detailed mount points inside your container:

```
"Mounts": [
    ...
  {
            "Type": "bind",
            "Source": "/var/lib/kubelet/pods/98c7c676-
e9bd-11e7-9e8d-080027ac331c/volumes/kubernetes.io~empty-dir/data",
            "Destination": "/data-mount",
            "Mode": "",
            "RW": true,
            "Propagation": "rprivate"
        }
    ...
]
```

Kubernetes mounts
`/var/lib/kubelet/pods/<id>/volumes/kubernetes.io~empty-dir/<volumeMount name>` to `/data-mount` for the Pod to use. If you create a Pod with more than one container, all of them will mount the same destination `/data-mount` with the same source. The default mount propagation is `rprivate`, which means any mount points on the host are invisible in the container, and vice versa.

`emptyDir` could be mounted as `tmpfs` by setting `emptyDir.medium` as `Memory`.

Taking the previous configuration file `2-6-1_emptyDir_mem.yaml` as an example, it would be as follows:

```
volumes:
    -
        name: data
        emptyDir:
            medium: Memory
```

We could verify whether it's successfully mounted with the `kubectl exec <pod_name> <commands>` command. We'll run the `df` command in this container:

```
# kubectl exec ubuntu df
Filesystem 1K-blocks Used Available Use% Mounted on
...
tmpfs 1024036 0 1024036 0% /data-mount
...
```

Note that `tmpfs` is stored in memory instead of in the filesystem. No file will be created, and it'll be flushed in every reboot. In addition, it is constrained by memory limits in Kubernetes. For more information about container resource constraint, refer to *Working with Namespace* in this chapter.

If you have more than one container inside a Pod, the `Kubectl exec` command will be `kubectl exec <pod_name> <container_name> <commands>`.

hostPath

hostPath acts as data volume in Docker. The local folder on a node listed in hostPath will be mounted into the Pod. Since the Pod can run on any nodes, read/write functions happening in the volume could explicitly exist in the node on which the Pod is running. In Kubernetes, however, the Pod should not be node-aware. Please note that the configuration and files might be different on different nodes when using hostPath. Therefore, the same Pod, created by the same command or configuration file, might act differently on different nodes.

By using hostPath, you're able to read and write the files between containers and localhost disks of nodes. What we need for volume definition is for hostPath.path to specify the target mounted folder on the node:

```
apiVersion: v1
# cat 2-6-2_hostPath.yaml
kind: Pod
metadata:
  name: ubuntu
spec:
  containers:
    -
      image: ubuntu
      command:
        - sleep
        - "3600"
      imagePullPolicy: IfNotPresent
      name: ubuntu
      volumeMounts:
        -
          mountPath: /data-mount
          name: data
  volumes:
    -
      name: data
      hostPath:
        path: /tmp/data
```

Using docker inspect to check the volume details, you will see the volume on the host is mounted in the /data-mount destination:

```
"Mounts": [
        {
            "Type": "bind",
            "Source": "/tmp/data",
            "Destination": "/data-mount",
```

```
        "Mode": "",
        "RW": true,
        "Propagation": "rprivate"
    },
            ...
]
```

If we run `kubectl exec ubuntu touch /data-mount/sample`, we should be able to see one empty file, named `sample under /tmp/data`, on the host.

NFS

You can mount an **network filesystem (NFS)** to your Pod as `nfs volume`. Multiple Pods can mount and share the files in the same `nfs volume`. The data stored into `nfs volume` will be persistent across the Pod lifetime. You have to create your own NFS server before using `nfs volume`, and make sure the `nfs-utils` package is installed on Kubernetes minions.

 Check whether your NFS server works before you go. You should check out the `/etc/exports` file with a proper sharing parameter and directory, and use the `mount -t nfs <nfs server>:<share name> <local mounted point>` command to check whether it could be mounted locally.

The configuration file of the volume type with NFS is similar to others, but `nfs.server` and `nfs.path` are required in the volume definition to specify NFS server information and the path mounted from. `nfs.readOnly` is an optional field for specifying whether the volume is read-only or not (the default is `false`):

```
# configuration file of nfs volume
$ cat 2-6-3_nfs.yaml
apiVersion: v1
kind: Pod
metadata:
  name: nfs
spec:
  containers:
    -
      name: nfs
      image: ubuntu
      volumeMounts:
        - name: nfs
          mountPath: "/data-mount"
  volumes:
```

```
    - name: nfs
      nfs:
        server: <your nfs server>
        path: "/"
```

After you run `kubectl create -f 2-6-3_nfs.yaml`, you can describe your Pod with `kubectl describe <pod name>` to check the mounting status. If it's mounted successfully, it should show conditions. Ready as true and the target `nfs` you mount:

```
Conditions:
  Type Status
  Ready True
Volumes:
  nfs:
    Type: NFS (an NFS mount that lasts the lifetime of a pod)
    Server: <your nfs server>
    Path: /
    ReadOnly: false
```

If we inspect the container with the `docker` command, we can see the volume information in the `Mounts` section:

```
"Mounts": [
 {
         "Source":
"/var/lib/kubelet/pods/<id>/volumes/kubernetes.io~nfs/nfs",
         "Destination": "/data-mount",
         "Mode": "",
         "RW": true
     },

                     . . .

     ]
```

Actually, Kubernetes just mounts your `<nfs server>:<share name>` into `/var/lib/kubelet/pods/<id>/volumes/kubernetes.io~nfs/nfs`, and then mounts it into the container as the destination in `/data-mount`. You could also use `kubectl exec` to touch the file, to test whether it's perfectly mounted.

glusterfs

GlusterFS (`https://www.gluster.org`) is a scalable, network-attached storage filesystem. The `glusterfs` volume type allows you to mount GlusterFS volume into your Pod. Just like NFS volume, the data in `glusterfs` volume is persistent across the Pod lifetime. If the Pod is terminated, the data is still accessible in `glusterfs` volume. You should build the GlusterFS system before using `glusterfs` volume.

 Check whether `glusterfs` works before you go. By using `glusterfs` volume information on GlusterFS servers, you can see currently available volumes. By using `mount -t glusterfs <glusterfs server>:/<volume name> <local mounted point>` on local, you can check whether the GlusterFS system can be successfully mounted.

Since the volume replica in GlusterFS must be greater than 1, let's assume we have two replicas in the servers `gfs1` and `gfs2`, and the volume name is `gvol`.

First, we need to create an endpoint acting as a bridge for `gfs1` and `gfs2`:

```
$ cat 2-6-4_gfs-endpoint.yaml
kind: Endpoints
apiVersion: v1
metadata:
  name: glusterfs-cluster
subsets:
  -
    addresses:
      -
        ip: <gfs1 server ip>
    ports:
      -
        port: 1
  -
    addresses:
      -
        ip: <gfs2 server ip>
    ports:
      -
        port: 1

# create endpoints
$ kubectl create -f 2-6-4_gfs-endpoint.yaml
```

Then, we can use `kubectl get endpoints` to check the endpoint was created properly:

```
$kubectl get endpoints
NAME ENDPOINTS AGE
glusterfs-cluster <gfs1>:1,<gfs2>:1 12m
```

After that, we should be able to create the Pod with `glusterfs` volume by `glusterfs.yaml`. The parameters of the `glusterfs` volume definition are `glusterfs.endpoints`, which specify the endpoint name we just created, and `glusterfs.path`, which is the volume name `gvol`. `glusterfs.readOnly` is used to set whether the volume is mounted in read-only mode:

```
$ cat 2-6-4_glusterfs.yaml
apiVersion: v1
kind: Pod
metadata:
  name: ubuntu
spec:
  containers:
    -
      image: ubuntu
      command:
        - sleep
        - "3600"
      imagePullPolicy: IfNotPresent
      name: ubuntu
      volumeMounts:
        -
          mountPath: /data-mount
          name: data
  volumes:
    -
      name: data
      glusterfs:
        endpoints: glusterfs-cluster
        path: gvol
```

Let's check the volume setting with `kubectl describle`:

```
Volumes:
  data:
    Type: Glusterfs (a Glusterfs mount on the host that shares a pod's
lifetime)
    EndpointsName: glusterfs-cluster
    Path: gvol
    ReadOnly: false
```

Using `docker inspect`, you should be able to see that the mounted source is `/var/lib/kubelet/pods/<id>/volumes/kubernetes.io~glusterfs/data` to the destination `/data-mount`.

downwardAPI

`downwardAPI` volume is used to expose Pod information into a container. The definition of `downwardAPI` is a list of items. An item contains a path and `fieldRef`. Kubernetes will dump the specified metadata listed in `fieldRef` to a file named `path` under `mountPath` and mount the `<volume name>` into the destination you specified. Currently supported metadata for `downwardAPI` volume includes:

Field path	Scope	Definition
`spec.nodeName`	Pod	The node that the Pod is running on
`spec.serviceAccountName`	Pod	The service account associating with the current Pod
`metadata.name`	Pod	The name of the Pod
`metadata.namespace`	Pod	The Namespace that the Pod belongs to
`metadata.annotations`	Pod	The annotations of the Pod
`metadata.labels`	Pod	The labels of the Pod
`status.podIP`	Pod	The ip of the Pod
`limits.cpu`	Container	The CPU limits of the container
`requests.cpu`	Container	The CPU requests of the container
`limits.memory`	Container	The memory limits of the container
`requests.memory`	Container	The memory requests of the container
`limits.ephemeral-storage`	Container	The ephemeral storage limits of the container
`requests.ephemeral-storage`	Container	The ephemeral storage requests of the container

We use `fieldRef.fieldPath` if the scope is with a Pod; `resourceFieldRef` is used when the scope is with a container. For example, the following configuration file could expose `metadata.labels` in `/data-mount` volume in an Ubuntu container:

```
// pod scope example
# cat 2-6-5_downward_api.yaml
apiVersion: v1
kind: Pod
metadata:
```

```
    name: downwardapi
    labels:
       env: demo
spec:
    containers:
       -
          name: downwardapi
          image: ubuntu
          command:
             - sleep
             - "3600"
          volumeMounts:
             - name: podinfo
               mountPath: "/data-mount"
    volumes:
       - name: podinfo
         downwardAPI:
            items:
               - path: metadata
                 fieldRef:
                    fieldPath: metadata.labels
```

By describing the pod, we could check that the volume is mounted successfully to /data-mount, and metadata.labels is pointed to the metadata file:

```
// describe the pod
# kubectl describe pod downwardapi
...
    Mounts:
       /data-mount from podinfo (rw)
...
Volumes:
  podinfo:
    Type: DownwardAPI (a volume populated by information about the
pod)
    Items:
       metadata.labels -> metadata
```

We could check the file inside the container with kubectl exec downwardapi cat /data-mount/metadata, and you should be able to see env="example" presents.

If it's in the container scope, we'll have to specify the container name:

```
# cat 2-6-5_downward_api_container.yaml
apiVersion: v1
kind: Pod
metadata:
  name: downwardapi-container
```

```
spec:
  containers:
    -
      name: downwardapi
      image: ubuntu
      command:
        - sleep
        - "3600"
      volumeMounts:
          - name: podinfo
            mountPath: "/data-mount"
  volumes:
    - name: podinfo
      downwardAPI:
        items:
          - path: "cpu_limit"
            resourceFieldRef:
              containerName: downwardapi
              resource: limits.cpu
```

We could use the `docker inspect <container_name>` command inside a node to check the implementation:

```
{
        "Source":
"/var/lib/kubelet/pods/<id>/volumes/kubernetes.io~downward-api/<volume
name>",
        "Destination": "/data-mount",
        "Mode": "",
        "RW": true
}
```

Kubernetes exposes `pod` information in source volume, and mounts it to `/data-mount`.

For the IP of the Pod, using environment variable to propagate in Pod spec would be must easier:

```
spec:
  containers:
    - name: envsample-pod-info
      env:
        - name: MY_POD_IP
          valueFrom:
            fieldRef:
              fieldPath: status.podIP
```

The sample folder in the Kubernetes GitHub (`https://kubernetes.io/docs/tasks/ inject-data-application/downward-api-volume-expose-pod-information`) contains more examples for both environment variables and `downwardAPI` volume.

gitRepo

`gitRepo` is a convenient volume type that clones your existing Git repository into a container:

```
// an example of how to use gitRepo volume type
# cat 2-6-6_gitRepo.yaml
apiVersion: v1
kind: Pod
metadata:
  name: gitrepo
spec:
  containers:
  - image: ubuntu
    name: ubuntu
    command:
      - sleep
      - "3600"
    volumeMounts:
    - mountPath: /app
      name: app-git
  volumes:
  - name: app-git
    gitRepo:
      repository:
"https://github.com/kubernetes-cookbook/second-edition.git"
      revision: "9d8e845e2f55a5c65da01ac4235da6d88ef6bcd0"

# kubectl create -f 2-6-6_gitRepo.yaml
pod "gitrepo" created
```

In the preceding example, the volume plugin mounts an empty directory and runs the git clone `<gitRepo.repolist>` to clone the repository into it. Then the Ubuntu container will be able to access it.

There's more...

In the previous cases, the user needs to know the details of the storage provider. Kubernetes provides `PersistentVolumes` and `PersistentVolumeClaim` to abstract the details of the storage provider and storage consumer.

PersistentVolumes

An illustration of `PersistentVolume` is shown in the following graph. First, the administrator provisions the specification of a `PersistentVolume`. Then the consumer requests for storage with `PersistentVolumeClaim`. Finally, the Pod mounts the volume with the reference of `PersistentVolumeClaim`:

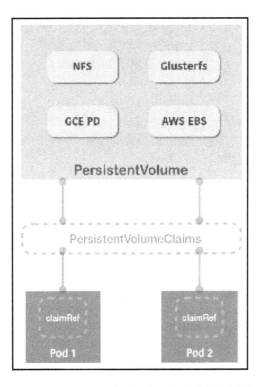

PersistentVolumeClaims is an abstract layer to decouple volumes for a Pod and physical volume resource

Here is an example using `NFS`. The administrator needs to provision and allocate `PersistentVolume` first:

```
# example of PV with NFS
```

```
$ cat 2-6-7_pv.yaml
  apiVersion: "v1"
  kind: "PersistentVolume"
  metadata:
    name: "pvnfs01"
  spec:
    capacity:
      storage: "3Gi"
    accessModes:
      - "ReadWriteOnce"
    nfs:
      path: "/"
      server: "<your nfs server>"
    persistentVolumeReclaimPolicy: "Recycle"

# create the pv
$ kubectl create -f 2-6-7_pv.yaml
persistentvolume "pvnfs01" created
```

We can see that there are three parameters here: capacity, accessModes, and persistentVolumeReclaimPolicy. capacity is the size of this PersistentVolume. Now, accessModes is based on the capability of the storage provider and can be set to a specific mode during provision. For example, NFS supports multiple readers and writers simultaneously—then we can specify the accessModes as one of ReadWriteOnce, ReadOnlyMany, or ReadWriteMany. Now, persistentVolumeReclaimPolicy is used to define the behavior when PersistentVolume is released. The currently supported policy is retain and recycle for nfs and hostPath. You have to clean the volume by yourself in retain mode; on the other hand, Kubernetes will scrub the volume in recycle mode.

PV is a resource like a node. We could use kubectl get pv to see current provisioned PVs:

```
# list current PVs
$ kubectl get pv
NAME LABELS CAPACITY ACCESSMODES STATUS CLAIM REASON AGE
pvnfs01 <none> 3Gi RWO Bound default/pvclaim01 37m
```

Next, we will need to bind PersistentVolume with PersistentVolumeClaim in order to mount it as volume into the pod:

```
# example of PersistentVolumeClaim
$ cat claim.yaml
apiVersion: "v1"
kind: "PersistentVolumeClaim"
metadata:
```

```
    name: "pvclaim01"
spec:
  accessModes:
    - ReadWriteOnce
  resources:
    requests:
      storage: 1Gi

# create the claim
$ kubectl create -f claim.yaml
persistentvolumeclaim "pvclaim01" created

# list the PersistentVolumeClaim (pvc)
$ kubectl get pvc
NAME LABELS STATUS VOLUME CAPACITY ACCESSMODES AGE
pvclaim01 <none> Bound pvnfs01 3Gi RWO 59m
```

The constraints of `accessModes` and storage can be set in `PersistentVolumeClaim`. If the claim is bound successfully, its status will turn to `Bound`; on the other hand, if the status is `Unbound`, it means there is no PV currently matching the requests.

Then we are able to mount the PV as volume with the reference of `PersistentVolumeClaim`:

```
# example of mounting into Pod
$ cat nginx.yaml
apiVersion: v1
kind: Pod
metadata:
  name: nginx
  labels:
    project: pilot
    environment: staging
    tier: frontend
spec:
  containers:
    -
      image: nginx
      imagePullPolicy: IfNotPresent
      name: nginx
      volumeMounts:
      - name: pv
        mountPath: "/usr/share/nginx/html"
      ports:
      - containerPort: 80
  volumes:
    - name: pv
```

```
    persistentVolumeClaim:
      claimName: "pvclaim01"

# create the pod
$ kubectl create -f nginx.yaml
pod "nginx" created
```

It will be similar syntax to other volume types. Just add the `claimName` of `persistentVolumeClaim` in the volume definition. We are all set! Let's check the details to see whether we mounted it successfully:

```
# check the details of a pod
$ kubectl describe pod nginx
...
Volumes:
  pv:
    Type: PersistentVolumeClaim (a reference to a
PersistentVolumeClaim in the same namespace)
    ClaimName: pvclaim01
    ReadOnly: false
...
```

We can see we have a volume mounted in the Pod `nginx` with the type `pv` `pvclaim01`. Use `docker inspect` to see how it is mounted:

```
"Mounts": [
        {
            "Source":
"/var/lib/kubelet/pods/<id>/volumes/kubernetes.io~nfs/pvnfs01",
            "Destination": "/usr/share/nginx/html",
            "Mode": "",
            "RW": true
        },
            ...
    ]
```

Kubernetes mounts `/var/lib/kubelet/pods/<id>/volumes/kubernetes.io~nfs/<persistentvolume name>` into the destination in the Pod.

Using storage classes

In the cloud world, people provision storage or data volume dynamically. While `PersistentVolumeClaim` is based on existing static `PersistentVolume` that is provisioned by administrators, it might be really beneficial if the cloud volume could be requested dynamically when it needs to be. Storage classes are designed to resolve this problem. To make storage classes available in your cluster, three conditions need to be met. First, the `DefaultStorageClass` admission controller has to be enabled. Then `PersistentVolumeClaim` needs to request a storage class. The last condition is trivial; administrators have to configure a storage class in order to make dynamic provisioning work:

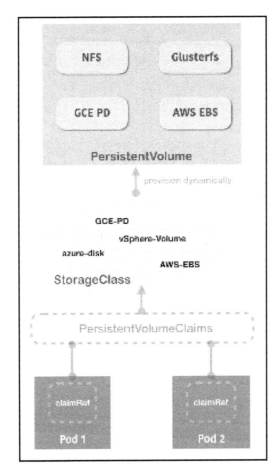

StorageClass dynamically allocates a PV and associates it with a PVC

The default storage classes are various, basically based on your underlying cloud provider. Storage classes are the abstract way to define underlying storage providers. They have different syntax based on different types of providers. Default storage classes can be changed, but cannot be deleted. The default storage class has an annotation `storageclass.beta.kubernetes.io/is-default-class=true` on. Removing that annotation can disable the dynamic provisioning. Moving the annotation to another storage class can switch the default storage class. If no storage classes have that annotation, dynamic provisioning will not be triggered when there is a new `PersistentVolumeClaim`.

gcePersistentDisk

`gcePersistentDisk` volume mounts a **Google Compute Engine (GCE) Persistent Disk (PD)** into a Pod. If you provision it statically, you'll have to create it first with the `gcloud` command or in the GCE console. The following is an example:

```
# cat 2-6-8_gce/static_mount.yaml
apiVersion: v1
kind: Pod
metadata:
  name: gce-pd-pod
spec:
  containers:
  - image: nginx
    name: gce-pd-example
    volumeMounts:
    - mountPath: /mount-path
      name: gce-pd
      ports:
        - containerPort: 80
  volumes:
  - name: gce-pd
    gcePersistentDisk:
      pdName: example
      fsType: ext4
```

Alternatively, and more cost-effectively, we could use dynamic provisioning. Then we don't need to provision PD beforehand. For enabling dynamic provisioning, the `DefaultStorageClass` admission controller has to be enabled on the API server. In some Kubernetes environments, it has been enabled by default, such as in GCE. We could explicitly disable it by setting the `storageClassName: ""` in `Pod/Deployment/ReplicaSet` configuration file.

Next, we'll introduce how to create a non-default `StorageClass`:

```
// list storageclasses (sc)
# kubectl get sc
NAME PROVISIONER
standard (default) kubernetes.io/gce-pd
```

We can see we have a default storage class named `standard`. If that's the desired provider, then you don't need to create your own storage classes. In the following example, we'll create a new storage class named `example`:

```
// gce storage class
# cat 2-6-8_gce/storageclass.yaml
kind: StorageClass
apiVersion: storage.k8s.io/v1
metadata:
  name: example
provisioner: kubernetes.io/gce-pd
parameters:
  type: pd-standard
  zones: us-central1-a
// create storage class
# kubectl create -f storageclass.yaml
    storageclass "example" created

// check current storage classes
# kubectl get sc
NAME PROVISIONER
example kubernetes.io/gce-pd
    standard (default) kubernetes.io/gce-pd
```

For the type, you can specify any storage type that GCE supports, such as `pd-ssd`. You can specify zones by changing zone parameters, too. Next, we'll add a `PersistentVolumeClaim` for using this storage class:

```
# 2-6-8_gce/pvc.yaml
apiVersion: v1
kind: PersistentVolumeClaim
metadata:
  name: gce-example
spec:
  accessModes:
    - ReadWriteOnce
  storageClassName: example
  resources:
    requests:
      storage: 5Gi
```

```
// create pvc
# kubectl create -f pvc.yaml
persistentvolumeclaim "gce-example" created

// check pvc status
# kubectl get pvc
NAME STATUS VOLUME CAPACITY ACCESS MODES STORAGECLASS AGE
gce-example Bound pvc-d04218e3-ede5-11e7-aef7-42010a8001f4 5Gi RWO
example 1h
```

This configuration file will create a PVC by specifying the storage class named example. A PV will be created by the claim. When a PVC is in Bound status, Kubernetes will always bind that PV to the matching PVC. Then, let's have a Pod using this PVC:

```
# cat 2-6-8_gce/pod.yaml
kind: Pod
apiVersion: v1
metadata:
  name: gce-pd-pod
spec:
  volumes:
    - name: gce-pd
      persistentVolumeClaim:
       claimName: gce-example
  containers:
    - name: gce-pd-example
      image: nginx
      ports:
        - containerPort: 80
      volumeMounts:
        - mountPath: /mount-path
          name: gce-pd

// create a pod
# kubectl create -f pod.yaml
pod "gce-pd-pod" created

// check the volume setting in pod
# kubectl describe pod gce-pd-pod
...
Containers:
  gce-pd-example:
    Container ID:
    Mounts:
      /mount-path from gce-pd (rw)
...
Volumes:
```

```
gce-pd:
   Type: PersistentVolumeClaim (a reference to a
PersistentVolumeClaim in the same namespace)
   ClaimName: gce-example
   ReadOnly: false
```

We can see that `gce-pd` is mounted under `/mount-path`. Let's see if the volume has been provisioned dynamically.

Alternatively, you could use `gcloud compute disks list`. `gcloud` in a command-line tool in GCE.

awsElasticBlockStore

`awsElasticBlockStore` volume mounts an **Amazon Web Service Elastic Block Store** (**AWS EBS**) volume. It's a service that provides persistent block storage for Amazon EC2. Just like the GCE persistent disk, we can provision it statically or dynamically.

To provision it statically, administrators have to create an EBS volume by the AWS console or AWS CLI beforehand. The following is an example of how to mount an existing EBS volume to the containers in a Deployment:

```
// example of how we used pre-created EBS volume.
# cat 2-6-8_aws/static_mount.yaml
kind: Deployment
apiVersion: apps/v1
metadata:
  name: aws-ebs-deployment
spec:
  replicas: 2
  selector:
    matchLabels:
      run: nginx
  template:
    metadata:
      labels:
        run: nginx
    spec:
      volumes:
        - name: aws-ebs
          awsElasticBlockStore:
            volumeID: <ebs volume ID>
            fsType: ext4
      containers:
      - name: aws-ebs-example
```

```
image: nginx
ports:
  - containerPort: 80
volumeMounts:
  - mountPath: /mount-path
    name: aws-ebs
```

To provision it dynamically, on the other hand, just like how we demonstrated in the GCE persistent disk, we first create a non-default storage class; you're free to use a default storage class as well. Here, our environment is provisioned by kops (https://github.com/kubernetes/kops; for more information, please refer to Chapter 17, *Building Kubernetes on AWS*). The environment has been bound with the required IAM policies, such as ec2:AttachVolume, ec2:CreateVolume, ec2:DetachVolume, and ec2:DeleteVolume. If you provision it from scratch, be sure that you have required policies attaching to the masters:

```
// declare a storage class
# cat 2-6-8_aws/storageclass.yaml
kind: StorageClass
apiVersion: storage.k8s.io/v1
metadata:
  name: example-ebs
provisioner: kubernetes.io/aws-ebs
parameters:
  type: io1
  zones: us-east-1a

// create storage class
# kubectl create -f storageclass.yaml
storageclass "example-ebs" created

// check if example-ebs sc is created
# kubectl get sc
NAME PROVISIONER
default kubernetes.io/aws-ebs
example-ebs kubernetes.io/aws-ebs
gp2 (default) kubernetes.io/aws-ebs
```

Next, we create a PVC with the storage class name we just created:

```
// declare a PVC
# cat 2-6-8_aws/pvc.yaml
apiVersion: v1
kind: PersistentVolumeClaim
metadata:
  name: aws-example
spec:
```

```
    accessModes:
      - ReadWriteOnce
    storageClassName: example-ebs
    resources:
      requests:
        storage: 5Gi
```

```
// create a PVC
# kubectl create -f pvc.yaml
persistentvolumeclaim "aws-example" created
```

```
// check if PVC has been created
# kubectl get pvc
NAME STATUS VOLUME CAPACITY ACCESS MODES STORAGECLASS AGE
aws-example Bound pvc-d1cddc08-ee31-11e7-8582-022bb4c3719e 5Gi RWO
example-ebs 5s
```

When Kubernetes receives the request of `PersistentVolumeClaim`, it'll try to allocate a new `PersistentVolume`, or bind to an existing PV, if possible:

```
// check if a PV is created by a PVC.
# kubectl get pv
NAME CAPACITY ACCESS MODES RECLAIM POLICY STATUS CLAIM STORAGECLASS
REASON AGE
pvc-d1cddc08-ee31-11e7-8582-022bb4c3719e 5Gi RWO Delete Bound
default/aws-example example-ebs 36m
```

We can check the corresponding PV in the AWS console, as well.

At the end, we create a Deployment with this volume by specifying `persistentVolumeClaim` in the spec:

```
// create a deployment
# cat 2-6-8_aws/deployment.yaml
kind: Deployment
apiVersion: apps/v1
metadata:
  name: aws-ebs-deployment
spec:
  replicas: 2
  selector:
    matchLabels:
      run: nginx
  template:
    metadata:
      labels:
        run: nginx
    spec:
```

```
        volumes:
        - name: aws-ebs
          persistentVolumeClaim:
            claimName: aws-example
        containers:
        - name: aws-ebs-example
          image: nginx
          ports:
            - containerPort: 80
          volumeMounts:
            - mountPath: /mount-path
              name: aws-ebs
```

By specifying `claimName` as `aws-example`, it'll then use the EBS volume we just create by PVC, which is requested to AWS dynamically. If we take a look at the Pod description with `kubectl describe pod <pod_name>`, we can see the details of the volumes:

```
// kubectl describe pod <pod_name>
# kubectl describe pod aws-ebs-deployment-68bdc6f546-246s7
Containers:
  aws-ebs-example:
    ...
    Mounts:
      /mount-path from aws-ebs (rw)
Volumes:
  aws-ebs:
    Type: AWSElasticBlockStore (a Persistent Disk resource in AWS)
    VolumeID: vol-0fccc3b0af8c17727
    FSType: ext4
    Partition: 0
    ReadOnly: false
  ...
```

EBS volume `vol-0fccc3b0af8c17727` is mounted under `/mount-path` inside the container.

If the volume was dynamically provisioned, the default reclaim policy is set to `delete`. Set it to `retain` if you want to keep them, even if a PVC is deleted.

The StorageObjectInUseProtection admission controller

A PVC might be deleted accidentally by user even if it's used by a Pod. In Kubernetes v1.10, a new admission controller is added to prevent this from happening. `kubernetes.io/pv-protection` or `kubernetes.io/pvc-protection` finalizer will be added into PV or PVC by `StorageObjectInUseProtection` admission controller. Then when object deletion request is sent, admission controller will do pre-delete check and see if there is any Pod are using it. This will prevent data loss.

See also

Volumes can be mounted on the Pods by declaring in Pods or ReplicaSet spec. Check out the following recipes to jog your memory:

- *Working with Pods* section in `Chapter 13`, *Walking through Kubernetes Concepts*
- *Working with replica sets* section in `Chapter 13`, *Walking through Kubernetes Concepts*
- *Working with Secrets* section in `Chapter 13`, *Walking through Kubernetes Concepts*
- *Setting resource in nodes* section in `Chapter 18`, *Advanced Cluster Administration*
- *Authentication and authorization* section in `Chapter 18`, *Advanced Cluster Administration*

Working with Secrets

Kubernetes Secrets manage information in key-value formats with the value encoded. It can be a password, access key, or token. With Secrets, users don't have to expose sensitive data in the configuration file. Secrets can reduce the risk of credential leaks and make our resource configurations more organized.

Currently, there are three types of Secrets:

- Generic/Opaque: `https://en.wikipedia.org/wiki/Opaque_data_type`
- Docker registry
- TLS

Generic/Opaque is the default type that we're using in our application. Docker registry is used to store the credential of a private Docker registry. TLS Secret is used to store the CA certificate bundle for cluster administration.

Kubernetes creates built-in Secrets for the credentials that using to access API server.

Getting ready

Before using Secrets, we have to keep in mind that Secret should be always created before dependent Pods, so dependent Pods can reference it properly. In addition, Secrets have a 1 MB size limitation. It works properly for defining a bunch of information in a single Secret. However, Secret is not designed for storing large amounts of data. For configuration data, consider using `ConfigMaps`. For large amounts of non-sensitive data, consider using volumes instead.

How to do it...

In the following example, we'll walk through how to create a Generic/Opaque Secret and use it in your Pods by assuming that we have an access token that needs to be used inside a Pod.

Creating a Secret

There are two ways to create a Secret. The first one is with `kubectl create secret` in the command line, and the other one is with direct resource creation in the configuration file.

Working with kubectl create command line

By using `kubectl create secret` command line, you can create a Secret from a file, directory, or literal value. With this method, you don't need to encode the Secret by yourself. Kubernetes will do that for you:

From a file

1. If a file is the source of Secret, we'll have to create a text file which contains our sensitive data first:

```
// assume we have a sensitive credential named access
```

```
token.
# cat 2-7-1_access-token
9S!g0U61699r
```

2. Next, we could use `kubectl create secret` in the command line to create the Secret. The syntax is:

```
Kubectl create secret <secret-type> --from-file <file1> (-
-from-file <file2> ...)
```

3. In our case, we use generic Secret type, since the access token is neither the Docker registry image pull Secrets nor TLS information:

```
# kubectl create secret generic access-token --from-file
2-7-1_access-token
secret "access-token" created
```

4. You can check the detailed Secret information with the `kubectl get secret` command:

```
// get the detailed information for a Secret.
# kubectl get secret access-token -o yaml
apiVersion: v1
data:
  2-7-1_access-token: OVMhZzBVNjE2OTlyCg==
kind: Secret
metadata:
  creationTimestamp: 2018-01-01T20:26:24Z
  name: access-token
  namespace: default
  resourceVersion: "127883"
  selfLink: /api/v1/namespaces/default/secrets/access-
token
  uid: 0987ec7d-ef32-11e7-ac53-080027ac331c
type: Opaque
```

5. You can use the `base64` command (`https://linux.die.net/man/1/base64`) in Linux to decode the encoded Secret:

```
// decode encoded Secret
# echo "OVMhZzBVNjE2OTlyCg==" | base64 --decode
9S!g0U61699r
```

From a directory

Creating a Secret from a directory is similar to creating from a file, using the same command, but with `directory`. Kubernetes will iterate all the files inside that directory and create a Secret for you:

```
// show directory structure
# tree
.
├── 2-7-1_access-token-dir
│   └── 2-7-1_access-token

// create Secrets from a directory
# kubectl create secret generic access-token --from-file 2-7-1_access-token-dir/
secret "access-token" created
```

You can check the Secret with the `kubectl get secret access-token -o yaml` command again and see if they're identical to the ones from the file.

From a literal value

Kubernetes supports creating a Secret with a single command line, as well:

```
// create a Secret via plain text in command line
# kubectl create secret generic access-token --from-literal=2-7-1_access-token=9S\!g0U61699r
secret "access-token" created
```

Then we can use the `get secret` command to check if they're identical to the previous method:

```
// check the details of a Secret
# kubectl get secret access-token -o yaml
apiVersion: v1
data:
  2-7-1_access-token: OVMhZzBVNjE2OTlyCg==
kind: Secret
metadata:
  creationTimestamp: 2018-01-01T21:44:32Z
  name: access-token
  ...
type: Opaque
```

Via configuration file

A Secret can also be created directly through the configuration file; however, you'll have to encode the Secret manually. Just use the kind of Secret:

```
// encode Secret manually
# echo '9S!g0U61699r' | base64
OVMhZzBVNjE2OTlyCg==

// create a Secret via configuration file, put encoded Secret into the
file
# cat 2-7-1_secret.yaml
apiVersion: v1
kind: Secret
metadata:
  name: access-token
type: Opaque
data:
  2-7-1_access-token: OVMhZzBVNjE2OTlyCg==

// create the resource
# kubectl create -f 2-7-1_secret.yaml
secret "access-token" created
```

Using Secrets in Pods

To use Secrets inside Pods, we can choose to expose them in environment variables or mount the Secrets as volumes.

By environment variables

In terms of accessing Secrets inside a Pod, add `env section` inside the container spec as follows:

```
// using access-token Secret inside a Pod
# cat 2-7-2_env.yaml
apiVersion: v1
kind: Pod
metadata:
  name: secret-example-env
spec:
  containers:
  - name: ubuntu
    image: ubuntu
    command: ["/bin/sh", "-c", "while : ;do echo $ACCESS_TOKEN; sleep
10; done"]
```

```
env:
    - name: ACCESS_TOKEN
      valueFrom:
        secretKeyRef:
          name: access-token
          key: 2-7-1_access-token

// create a pod
# kubectl create -f 2-7-2_env.yaml
pod "secret-example-env" created
```

In the preceding example, we expose `2-7-1_access-token` key in access-token Secret as `ACCESS_TOKEN` environment variable, and print it out through a while infinite loop. Check the `stdout via kubectl` log command:

```
// check stdout logs
# kubectl logs -f secret-example-env
9S!g0U61699r
```

Note that the environment variable was exposed during Pod creation. If a new value of Secret is pushed, you'll have to re-launch/rolling-update a Pod or Deployment to reflect that.

If we describe the `secret-example-env` Pod, we can see that an environment variable was set to a Secret:

```
# kubectl describe pods secret-example-env
Name: secret-example-env
...
Environment:
      ACCESS_TOKEN: <set to the key '2-7-1_access-token' in secret
'access-token'>
```

By volumes

A Secret can be also mounted as volume by using the Secret type of the volume. The following is an example of how to use it:

```
// example of using Secret volume
# cat 2-7-3_volumes.yaml
apiVersion: v1
kind: Pod
metadata:
  name: secret-example-volume
spec:
  containers:
  - name: ubuntu
```

```
    image: ubuntu
    command: ["/bin/sh", "-c", "while : ;do cat /secret/token; sleep
10; done"]
    volumeMounts:
      - name: secret-volume
        mountPath: /secret
        readOnly: true
  volumes:
    - name: secret-volume
      secret:
        secretName: access-token
        items:
        - key: 2-7-1_access-token
          path: token

// create the Pod
kubectl create -f 2-7-3_volumes.yaml
pod "secret-example-volume" created
```

The preceding example will mount `secret-volume` into the `/secret mount` point inside the Pod. `/secret` will contain a file with the name token, which contains our access token. If we check the Pod details, it'll show that we mounted a read-only Secret volume:

```
// check the Pod details
# kubectl describe pods secret-example-volume
Name: secret-example-volume
...
Containers:
  ubuntu:
    ...
    Mounts:
      /secret from secret-volume (ro)
      ...
Volumes:
  secret-volume:
    Type: Secret (a volume populated by a Secret)
    SecretName: access-token
    Optional: false
...
```

If we check the `stdout`, it'll show the Pod can properly retrieve the expected value:

```
# kubectl logs -f secret-example-volume
9S!g0U61699r
```

The same as with the environment variable, the files in the mounted volume are created upon Pod creation time. It won't change dynamically when the Secret value is updated after the Pod creation time.

Deleting a Secret

To delete a Secret, simply use the `kubectl delete secret` command:

```
# kubectl delete secret access-token
secret "access-token" deleted
```

If a Secret is deleted when a Secret volume is attached, it'll show an error message whenever the volume reference disappears:

```
# kubectl describe pods secret-example-volume
...
Events:
  Warning FailedMount 53s (x8 over 1m) kubelet, minikube
MountVolume.SetUp failed for volume "secret-volume" : secrets "access-
token" not found
```

How it works...

In order to reduce the risk of leaking the Secrets' content, Secret is not landed to the disk. Instead, kubelet creates a `tmpfs` filesystem on the node to store the Secret. The Kubernetes API server pushes the Secret to the node on which the demanded container is running. The data will be flashed when the container is destroyed.

There's more...

Secrets hold small amounts of sensitive data. For application configuration, consider using `ConfigMaps` to hold non-sensitive information.

Using ConfigMaps

Here is an example of using `ConfigMaps`:

```
# cat configmap/2-7-4_configmap.yaml
apiVersion: v1
kind: ConfigMap
metadata:
```

```
    name: config-example
data:
  app.properties: |
    name=kubernetes-cookbook
    port=443

// create configmap
# kubectl create -f configmap/2-7-4_configmap.yaml
configmap "config-example" created
```

Similar to Secret, `ConfigMaps` can be retrieved with environment variables or volumes:

```
# cat configmap/2-7-4_env.yaml
apiVersion: v1
kind: Pod
metadata:
  name: configmap-env
spec:
  containers:
    - name: configmap
      image: ubuntu
      command: ["/bin/sh", "-c", "while : ;do echo $APP_NAME; sleep
10; done"]
      env:
        - name: APP_NAME
          valueFrom:
            configMapKeyRef:
              name: config-example
              key: app.properties

// create the pod
#kubectl create -f configmap/2-7-4_env.yaml
pod "configmap-env" created
```

Alternatively, you can use `ConfigMaps` volume to retrieve the configuration information:

```
// using configmap in a pod
# cat configmap/2-7-4_volumes.yaml
apiVersion: v1
kind: Pod
metadata:
  name: configmap-volume
spec:
  containers:
    - name: configmap
      image: ubuntu
```

```
      command: ["/bin/sh", "-c", "while : ;do cat
/src/app/config/app.properties; sleep 10; done"]
      volumeMounts:
      - name: config-volume
        mountPath: /src/app/config
  volumes:
    - name: config-volume
      configMap:
        name: config-example
```

Mounting Secrets and ConfigMap in the same volume

Projected volume is a way to group multiple volume sources into the same mount point. Currently, it supports Secrets, ConfigMap, and downwardAPI.

The following is an example of how we group the examples of Secrets and ConfigMaps that we used in this chapter:

```
// using projected volume
# cat 2-7-5_projected_volume.yaml
apiVersion: v1
kind: Pod
metadata:
  name: projected-volume-example
spec:
  containers:
  - name: container-tes
    image: ubuntu
    command: ["/bin/sh", "-c", "while : ;do cat /projected-
volume/configmap && cat /projected-volume/token; sleep 10; done"]
    volumeMounts:
    - name: projected-volume
      mountPath: "/projected-volume"
  volumes:
  - name: projected-volume
    projected:
      sources:
      - secret:
          name: access-token
          items:
            - key: 2-7-1_access-token
              path: token
      - configMap:
          name: config-example
          items:
```

```
        - key: app.properties
          path: configmap

// create projected volume
# kubectl create -f 2-7-5_projected_volume.yaml
pod "projected-volume-example" created
```

Let's check `stdout` to see if it works properly:

```
# kubectl logs -f projected-volume-example
name=kubernetes-cookbook
port=443
9S!g0U61699r
```

Working with names

When you create any Kubernetes object, such as a Pod, Deployment, and Service, you can assign a name to it. The names in Kubernetes are spatially unique, which means you cannot assign the same name in the Pods.

Getting ready

Kubernetes allows us to assign a name with the following restrictions:

- Up to 253 characters
- Lowercase of alphabet and numeric characters
- May contain special characters in the middle, but only dashs (-) and dots (.)

How to do it...

For assigning a name to the Pod, follow the following steps:

1. The following example is the Pod YAML configuration that assigns the Pod name as `my-pod` to the container name as `my-container`; you can successfully create it as follows:

```
# cat my-pod.yaml
apiVersion: v1
kind: Pod
metadata:
  name: my-pod
spec:
  containers:
  - name: my-container
    image: nginx


# kubectl create -f my-pod.yaml
pod "my-pod" created


# kubectl get pods
NAME       READY    STATUS    RESTARTS   AGE
my-pod     0/1      Running   0          4s
```

2. You can use the `kubectl describe` command to see the container named `my-container` as follows:

```
$ kubectl describe pod my-pod
Name:          my-pod
Namespace:     default
Node:          minikube/192.168.64.12
Start Time:    Sat, 16 Dec 2017 10:53:38 -0800
Labels:        <none>
Annotations:   <none>
Status:        Running
IP:            172.17.0.3
Containers:
  my-container:
    Container ID:
docker://fcf36d0a96a49c5a08eb6de1ef27ca761b4ca1c6b4a3a4312df836cb8e0a5
304
    Image:           nginx
    Image ID:        docker-
```

```
pullable://nginx@sha256:2ffc60a51c9d658594b63ef5acfac9d92f4e1550f633a3
a16d898925c4e7f5a7
    Port:           <none>
    State:          Running
      Started:      Sat, 16 Dec 2017 10:54:43 -0800
    Ready:          True
    Restart Count:  0
    Environment:    <none>
    Mounts:
      /var/run/secrets/kubernetes.io/serviceaccount from default-
token-lmd62 (ro)
Conditions:
  Type           Status
  Initialized    True
  Ready          True
  PodScheduled   True
Volumes:
  default-token-lmd62:
    Type:          Secret (a volume populated by a Secret)
    SecretName:    default-token-lmd62
    Optional:      false
QoS Class:         BestEffort
Node-Selectors:    <none>
Tolerations:       <none>
Events:
  Type     Reason                Age    From             Message
  ----     ------                ----   ----             -------
  Normal   Scheduled             1m     default-scheduler Successfully
assigned my-pod to minikube
  Normal   SuccessfulMountVolume 1m     kubelet, minikube
MountVolume.SetUp succeeded for volume "default-token-lmd62"
  Normal   Pulling               1m     kubelet, minikube pulling
image "nginx"
  Normal   Pulled                50s    kubelet, minikube Successfully
pulled image "nginx"
  Normal   Created               50s    kubelet, minikube Created
container
  Normal   Started               50s    kubelet, minikube Started
container
```

3. On the other hand, the following example contains two containers, but assigns the same name, `my-container`; therefore, the `kubectl create` command returns an error and can't create the Pod:

```
//delete previous Pod
$ kubectl delete pod --all
pod "my-pod" deleted
```

```
$ cat duplicate.yaml
apiVersion: v1
kind: Pod
metadata:
  name: my-pod
spec:
  containers:
  - name: my-container
    image: nginx
  - name: my-container
    image: centos
    command: ["/bin/sh", "-c", "while : ;do curl
http://localhost:80/; sleep 3; done"]


$ kubectl create -f duplicate.yaml
The Pod "my-pod" is invalid: spec.containers[1].name:
Duplicate value: "my-container"
```

 You can add the `--validate` flag.
For example, the command `kubectl create -f`
`duplicate.yaml --validate` uses a schema to validate the input
before sending it.

In another example, the YAML contains a ReplicationController and Service, both of which are using the same name, `my-nginx`, but it is successfully created because the Deployment and Service are different objects:

```
$ cat my-nginx.yaml
apiVersion: apps/v1
kind: Deployment
metadata:
  name: my-nginx
spec:
  replicas: 3
  selector:
    matchLabels:
      run: my-label
  template:
    metadata:
      labels:
        run: my-label
    spec:
      containers:
      - name: my-container
        image: nginx
```

```
        ports:
        - containerPort: 80
---
apiVersion: v1
kind: Service
metadata:
  name: my-nginx
spec:
  ports:
    - protocol: TCP
      port: 80
  type: NodePort
  selector:
    run: my-label


//create Deployment and Service
$ kubectl create -f my-nginx.yaml
deployment.apps "my-nginx" created
service "my-nginx" created


//Deployment "my-nginx" is created
$ kubectl get deploy
NAME        DESIRED    CURRENT    UP-TO-DATE    AVAILABLE    AGE
my-nginx    3          3          3             3            1m

//Service "my-nginx" is also created
$ kubectl get svc
NAME TYPE CLUSTER-IP EXTERNAL-IP PORT(S) AGE
kubernetes ClusterIP 10.0.0.1 <none> 443/TCP 13d
my-nginx NodePort 10.0.0.246 <none> 80:31168/TCP 1m
```

How it works...

A name is just a unique identifier, and all naming conventions are good; however, it is recommended to look up and identify the container image. For example:

- `memcached-pod1`
- `haproxy.us-west`
- `my-project1.mysql`

On the other hand, the following examples do not work because of Kubernetes restrictions:

- `Memcache-pod1` (contains uppercase)
- `haproxy.us_west` (contains underscore)
- `my-project1.mysql.` (dot in the last)

Note that Kubernetes supports a label that allows assigning a `key=value` style identifier. It also allows duplication. Therefore, if you want to assign something like the following information, use a label instead:

- Environment (for example: staging, production)
- Version (for example: v1.2)
- Application role (for example: frontend, worker)

In addition, Kubernetes also supports names that have different Namespaces. This means that you can use the same name in different Namespaces (for example: `nginx`). Therefore, if you want to assign just an application name, use Namespaces instead.

See also

This section from the chapter described how to assign and find the name of objects. This is just a basic methodology, but Kubernetes has more powerful naming tools, such as Namespace and selectors, to manage clusters:

- *Working with Pods*
- *Deployment API*
- *Working with Services*
- *Working with Namespaces*
- *Working with labels and selectors*

Working with Namespaces

In a Kubernetes cluster, the name of a resource is a unique identifier within a Namespace. Using a Kubernetes Namespace could separate user spaces for different environments in the same cluster. It gives you the flexibility of creating an isolated environment and partitioning resources to different projects and teams. You may consider Namespace as a virtual cluster. Pods, Services, and Deployments are contained in a certain Namespace. Some low-level resources, such as nodes and `persistentVolumes`, do not belong to any Namespace.

Before we dig into the resource Namespace, let's understand `kubeconfig` and some keywords first:

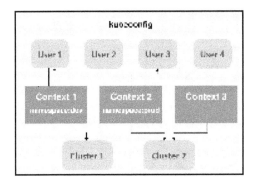

The relationship of kubeconfig components

`kubeconfig` is used to call the file which configures the access permission of Kubernetes clusters. As the original configuration of the system, Kubernetes takes `$HOME/.kube/config` as a `kubeconfig` file. Some concepts that are illustrated by the preceding diagram are as follows:

- **kubeconfig defines user, cluster, and context**: `kubeconfig` lists multiple users for defining authentication, and multiple clusters for indicating the Kubernetes API server. Also, the context in `kubeconfig` is the combination of a user and a cluster: accessing a certain Kubernetes cluster with what kind of authentication.
- **Users and clusters are sharable between contexts**: In the previous diagram, both **Context 1** and **Context 3** take **User 1** as their user content. However, each context can only have a single user and single cluster definition.

- **Namespace can be attached to context**: Every context can be assigned to an existing Namespace. If there are none, like **Context 3**, it is along with the default Namespace, named `default`, as well.
- **The current context is the default environment for client**: We may have several contexts in `kubeconfig`, but only one for the current context. The current context and the Namespace attached on it will construct the default computing environment for users.

Now you will get the idea that, as Namespace works with `kubeconfig`, users can easily switch default resources for usage by switching the current context in `kubeconfig`. Nevertheless, users can still start any resource in a different Namespace with a specified one. In this recipe, you will learn how to create your own Namespace and how to work with it.

Getting ready

By default, Kubernetes has created a Namespace named `default`. All the objects created without specifying Namespaces will be put into the `default` Namespace. Kubernetes will also create another initial Namespace called `kube-system` for locating Kubernetes system objects, such as an add-on or overlay network. Try to list all the Namespaces:

```
// check all Namespaces, "ns" is the resource abbreviation of
Namespace
$ kubectl get ns
NAME           STATUS     AGE
default        Active     15d
kube-public    Active     15d
kube-system    Active     15d
```

You may find an additional Namespace, `kube-public`, listed at the initial stage. It is designed for presenting some public configurations for even users without permission to access the Kubernetes system. Both of the provisioning tools, minikube and kubeadm, will create it while booting the system up.

The name of a Namespace must be a DNS label and follow the following rules:

- At most, 63 characters
- Matching regex [a-z0-9]([-a-z0-9]*[a-z0-9])

How to do it...

In this section, we will demonstrate how to create a Namespace, change the default Namespace, and delete the Namespace.

Creating a Namespace

For creating a Namespace, following are the steps:

1. After deciding on our desired name for Namespace, let's create it with a configuration file:

```
$ cat my-first-namespace.yaml
apiVersion: v1
kind: Namespace
metadata:
  name: my-namespace

// create the resource by subcommand "create"
$ kubectl create -f my-first-namespace.yaml
namespace "my-namespace" created
// list the namespaces again
$ kubectl get ns
NAME            STATUS      AGE
default         Active      16d
kube-public     Active      16d
kube-system     Active      16d
my-namespace    Active      6s
```

2. You can now see that we have an additional namespace called my-namespace. Next, let's run a Kubernetes Deployment in this new Namespace:

```
// run a Deployment with a flag specifying Namespace
$ kubectl run my-nginx --image=nginx --namespace=my-namespace
deployment.apps "my-nginx" created
```

3. While trying to check the newly created resource, we cannot easily find them as usual:

```
$ kubectl get deployment
No resources found.
```

4. Instead, the Deployment is shown with a flag related to the Namespace:

```
// list any Deployment in all Namespaces
$ kubectl get deployment --all-namespaces
NAMESPACE       NAME                         DESIRED
CURRENT    UP-TO-DATE    AVAILABLE    AGE
kube-system     calico-kube-controllers    1            1
1             1              16d
kube-system     calico-policy-controller   0            0
0             0              16d
kube-system     kube-dns                               1            1
1             1              16d
my-namespace    my-nginx                               1            1
1             1              1m

// get Deployments from my-namespace
$ kubectl get deployment --namespace=my-namespace
NAME          DESIRED     CURRENT    UP-TO-DATE     AVAILABLE
AGE
my-nginx    1           1          1              1            1m
```

Now you can find the resource that was just created.

Changing the default Namespace

As in the previous introduction, we can change the default Namespace by switching
the current context in `kubeconfig` to another one:

1. First, we may check the current context with the subcommand `config`:

```
// check the current context in kubeconfig
$ kubectl config current-context
kubernetes-admin@kubernetes
```

You may feel unfamiliar with the output when checking the current context.
The value of the preceding current context is defined and created by
`kubeadm`. You could get `minikube` shown on screen if you leveraged
`minikube` as your Kubernetes system management tool.

2. No matter what you got from checking the current context in `kubeconfig`,
use the subcommand `config set-context` to create a new context:

```
// create a new context called "my-context"
// the new context is going to follow the cluster and the
user of current context, but attached with new Namespace
//This is for kubeadm environment
```

```
$ kubectl config set-context my-context --namespace=my-
namespace --cluster=kubernetes --user=kubernetes-admin
Context "my-context" created.
```

3. The preceding command is based on `kubeadm` managed Kubernetes; you may fire a similar one for `minikube`, with the names of the default cluster and user in `kubeconfig`:

```
// for minikube environemt
$ kubectl config set-context my-context --namespace=my-
namespace --cluster=minikube --user=minikube
```

4. Next, check `kubeconfig` to verify the changes:

```
//check kubectlconfig for the new context
$ kubectl config view
apiVersion: v1
clusters:
- cluster:
    certificate-authority-data: REDACTED
    server: https://192.168.122.101:6443
  name: kubernetes
contexts:
- context:
    cluster: kubernetes
    user: kubernetes-admin
  name: kubernetes-admin@kubernetes
- context:
    cluster: kubernetes
    namespace: my-namespace
    user: kubernetes-admin
  name: my-context
current-context: kubernetes-admin@kubernetes
kind: Config
preferences: {}
users:
- name: kubernetes-admin
  user:
    client-certificate-data: REDACTED
    client-key-data: REDACTED
```

When checking the configuration of `kubeconfig`, in the section of contexts, you can find a context named exactly as what we defined and which also takes our newly created Namespace.

5. Fire the following command to switch to using the new context:

```
$ kubectl config use-context my-context
Switched to context "my-context".
// check current context
$ kubectl config current-context
my-context
```

Now the current context is our customized one, which is along with the Namespace my-namespace.

6. Since the default Namespace is changed to my-namespace, it is possible that we can get the Deployment without specifying the Namespace:

```
$ kubectl get deployment
NAME         DESIRED   CURRENT   UP-TO-DATE   AVAILABLE
AGE
my-nginx     1         1         1            1
20m

//double check the namespace of resource
$ kubectl describe deployment my-nginx
Name:                  my-nginx
Namespace:             my-namespace
CreationTimestamp:     Mon, 18 Dec 2017 15:39:46 -0500
Labels:                run=my-nginx
:
(ignored)
```

Deleting a Namespace

If you followed the previous pages for the Kubernetes resource, you may have gotten the idea that the subcommand delete is used to remove resources. It is workable in the case of removing a Namespace. At the same time, if we try to delete a Namespace, the resources under it will be removed, as well:

```
// first, go ahead to remove the Namespace "my-namespace"
$ kubectl delete ns my-namespace
namespace "my-namespace" deleted
// check the Deployment again, the exited "my-nginx" is terminated
$ kubectl get deployment
No resources found.
```

```
// while trying to create anything, the error message showing the
default Namespace is not existed
$ kubectl run my-alpine --image=alpine
Error from server (NotFound): namespaces "my-namespace" not found
```

To solve this issue, you may attach another Namespace to the current context, or just change your current context to the previous one:

```
// first solution: use set-context to update the Namespace
// here we just leave Namespace empty, which means to use default
Namespace
$ kubectl config set-context my-context --namespace=""
Context "my-context" modified.

// second solution: switch current context to another context
// in this case, it is kubeadm environment
$ kubectl config use-context kubernetes-admin@kubernetes
Switched to context "kubernetes-admin@kubernetes".
```

How it works...

Although we discussed the Namespaces and context of kubeconfig together, they are independent objects in the Kubernetes system. The context of kubeconfig is a client concept which can only be controlled by certain users, and it makes it easier to work with Namespaces and clusters. On the other hand, Namespace is the concept of the server side, working for resource isolation in clusters, and it is able to be shared between clients.

There's more...

We not only leverage Namespace to separate our resources, but also to realize finer computing resource provisioning. By restricting the usage amount of the computing power of a Namespace, the system manager can avoid the client creating too many resources and making servers overload.

Creating a LimitRange

To set the resource limitation of each Namespace, the admission controller LimitRanger should be added in the Kubernetes API server. Do not worry about this setting if you have minikube or kubeadm as your system manager.

The admission controller in the Kubernetes API server

Admission controller is a setting in the Kubernetes API server which defines more advanced functionality in the API server. There are several functions that can be set in the admission controller. Users can add the functions when starting the API server through the configuration file or using CLI with the flag `--admission-control`. Relying on `minikube` or `kubeadm` for system management, they have their own initial settings in the admission controller:

- **Default admission controller in kubeadm**:
  `Initializers, NamespaceLifecycle, LimitRanger, ServiceAccount, PersistentVolumeLabel, DefaultStorageClass, DefaultTolerationSeconds, NodeRestriction, ResourceQuota`

- **Default admission controller in minikube**:
  `NamespaceLifecycle, LimitRanger, ServiceAccount, DefaultStorageClass, ResourceQuota`

Based on the version of your API server, there is a recommended list in an official document at `https://kubernetes.io/docs/admin/admission-controllers/#is-there-a-recommended-set-of-admission-controllers-to-use`. Check for more ideas!

A plain new Namespace has no limitation on the resource quota. At the beginning, we start a Namespace and take a look at its initial settings:

```
// create a Namespace by YAML file
$ kubectl create -f my-first-namespace.yaml
namespace "my-namespace" created

$ kubectl describe ns my-namespace
Name:         my-namespace
Labels:       <none>
Annotations:  <none>
Status:       Active

No resource quota.

No resource limits.
```

After that, we create a resource called `LimitRange` for specifying the resource limitation of a Namespace. The following is a good example of creating a limit in a Namespace:

```
$ cat my-first-limitrange.yaml
apiVersion: v1
kind: LimitRange
metadata:
  name: my-limitrange
spec:
  limits:
  - type: Pod
    max:
      cpu: 2
      memory: 1Gi
    min:
      cpu: 200m
      memory: 6Mi
  - type: Container
    default:
      cpu: 300m
      memory: 200Mi
    defaultRequest:
      cpu: 200m
      memory: 100Mi
    max:
      cpu: 2
      memory: 1Gi
    min:
      cpu: 100m
      memory: 3Mi
```

We will then limit the resources in a Pod with the values of 2 as `max` and `200m` as a `min` for CPU, and `1Gi` as max and `6Mi` as a min for memory. For the container, the CPU is limited between `100m – 2` and the memory is between `3Mi` - `1Gi`. If the max is set, then you have to specify the limit in the Pod/container spec during the resource creation; if the min is set, then the request has to be specified during the Pod/container creation. The `default` and `defaultRequest` section in LimitRange is used to specify the default limit and request in the container spec.

The value of CPU limitation in LimitRange

What do the values of 2 and 200m mean in the Pod limitation in the file `my-first-limitrange.yaml`? The integer value means the number of CPU; the "m" in the value means millicpu, so 200m means 0.2 CPU (200 * 0.001). Similarly, the default CPU limitation of the container is 0.2 to 0.3, and the real limitation is 0.1 to 2.

Afterwards, we create the LimitRange in our plain Namespace and check what will happen:

```
// create the limitrange by file with the flag of Namespace
// the flag --namespace can be abbreviated to "n"
$ kubectl create -f my-first-limitrange.yaml -n my-namespace
limitrange "my-limitrange" created

// check the resource by subcommand "get"
$ kubectl get limitrange -n my-namespace
NAME              AGE
my-limitrange     23s

// check the customized Namespace
$ kubectl describe ns my-namespace
Name:         my-namespace
Labels:       <none>
Annotations:  <none>
Status:       Active

No resource quota.

Resource Limits
 Type        Resource   Min   Max   Default Request   Default Limit   Max
Limit/Request Ratio
 ----        --------   ---   ---   ---------------   -------------   -----
-----------------
 Pod         cpu        200m  2     -                 -               -
 Pod         memory     6Mi   1Gi   -                 -               -
 Container   memory     3Mi   1Gi   100Mi             200Mi           -
 Container   cpu        100m  2     200m              300m            -
```

When you query the detail description of `my-namespace`, you will see the constraint attached to the Namespace directly. There is not any requirement to add the LimitRange. Now, all the Pods and containers created in this Namespace have to follow the resource limits listed here. If the definitions violate the rule, a validation error will be thrown accordingly:

```
// Try to request an overcommitted Pod, check the error message
$ kubectl run my-greedy-nginx --image=nginx --namespace=my-namespace -
-restart=Never --requests="cpu=4"
The Pod "my-greedy-nginx" is invalid:
spec.containers[0].resources.requests: Invalid value: "4": must be
less than or equal to cpu limit
```

Deleting a LimitRange

We can delete the LimitRange resource with the subcommand `delete`. Like creating the `LimitRange`, deleting a `LimitRange` in a Namespace would remove the constraints in the Namespace automatically:

```
$ kubectl delete -f my-first-limitrange.yaml -n=my-namespace
limitrange "my-limitrange" deleted
$ kubectl describe ns my-namespace
Name:          my-namespace
Labels:        <none>
Annotations:   <none>
Status:        Active

No resource quota.

No resource limits.
```

See also

Many Kubernetes resources are able to run under a Namespace. To achieve good resource management, check out the following recipes:

- *Working with Pods*
- *Deployment API*
- *Working with names*

Working with labels and selectors

Labels are a set of key/value pairs, which are attached to object metadata. We could use labels to select, organize, and group objects, such as Pods, ReplicaSets, and Services. Labels are not necessarily unique. Objects could carry the same set of labels.

Label selectors are used to query objects with labels of the following types:

- Equality-based:
  - Use equal (= or ==) or not-equal (!=) operators
- Set-based:
  - Use in or notin operators

Getting ready

Before you get to setting labels in the objects, you should consider the valid naming convention of key and value.

A valid key should follow these rules:

- A name with an optional prefix, separated by a slash.
- A prefix must be a DNS subdomain, separated by dots, no longer than 253 characters.
- A name must be less than 63 characters with the combination of [a-z0-9A-Z] and dashes, underscores, and dots. Note that symbols are illegal if put at the beginning and the end.

A valid value should follow the following rules:

- A name must be less than 63 characters with the combination of [a-z0-9A-Z] and dashes, underscores, and dots. Note that symbols are illegal if put at the beginning and the end.

You should also consider the purpose, too. For example, there are two projects, `pilot` and `poc`. Also, those projects are under different environments, such as `develop` and `production`. In addition, some contain multiple tiers, such as `frontend`, `cache`, and `backend`. We can make our labels key and value pair combination like follows:

```
labels:
  project: pilot
  environment: develop
  tier: frontend
```

How to do it...

1. Let's try to create several Pods with the previous labels to distinguish different projects, environments, and tiers, as follows:

YAML Filename	Pod Image	Project	Environment	Tier
pilot-dev.yaml	nginx	pilot	develop	frontend
pilot-dev.yaml	memcached			cache
pilot-prod.yaml	nginx		production	frontend
pilot-prod.yaml	memcached			cache
poc-dev.yaml	httpd	poc	develop	frontend
poc-dev.yaml	memcached			cache

2. For convenience, we will prepare three YAML files that contain two Pods each, with a `YAML separator` `---` between Pods:

- `pilot-dev.yaml`:

```yaml
apiVersion: v1
kind: Pod
metadata:
  name: pilot.dev.nginx
  labels:
    project: pilot
    environment: develop
    tier: frontend
spec:
  containers:
    - name: nginx
      image: nginx
---
apiVersion: v1
```

```
kind: Pod
metadata:
  name: pilot.dev.memcached
  labels:
    project: pilot
    environment: develop
    tier: cache
spec:
  containers:
    - name: memcached
      image: memcached
```

* `pilot-prod.yaml`:

```
apiVersion: v1
kind: Pod
metadata:
  name: pilot.prod.nginx
  labels:
    project: pilot
    environment: production
    tier: frontend
spec:
  containers:
    - name : nginx
      image: nginx
---
apiVersion: v1
kind: Pod
metadata:
  name: pilot.prod.memcached
  labels:
    project: pilot
    environment: production
    tier: cache
spec:
  containers:
    - name: memcached
      image: memcached
```

* `poc-dev.yaml`:

```
apiVersion: v1
kind: Pod
metadata:
  name: poc.dev.httpd
  labels:
    project: poc
```

```
      environment: develop
      tier: frontend
  spec:
    containers:
      - name: httpd
        image: httpd
  ---
  apiVersion: v1
  kind: Pod
  metadata:
    name: poc.dev.memcached
    labels:
      project: poc
      environment: develop
      tier: cache
  spec:
    containers:
      - name: memcached
        image: memcached
```

3. Create those six Pods with the `kubectl create` command, as follows, to see how labels are defined:

```
$ kubectl create -f pilot-dev.yaml
pod "pilot.dev.nginx" created
pod "pilot.dev.memcached" created


$ kubectl create -f pilot-prod.yaml
pod "pilot.prod.nginx" created
pod "pilot.prod.memcached" created


$ kubectl create -f poc-dev.yaml
pod "poc.dev.httpd" created
pod "poc.dev.memcached" created
```

4. Run `kubectl describe <Pod name>` to check labels, as follows. It looks good, so let's use the label selector to query these Pods by different criteria:

```
$ kubectl describe pod poc.dev.memcache
Name: poc.dev.memcached
Namespace: default
Node: minikube/192.168.99.100
Start Time: Sun, 17 Dec 2017 17:23:15 -0800
Labels: environment=develop
                project=poc
```

```
                        tier=cache
Annotations: <none>
Status: Running
...
```

How it works...

As mentioned earlier in this section, there are two types of label selectors: either equality-based or set-based. Those types have different operators to specify criteria.

Equality-based label selector

The equality-based selector can specify equal or not equal, and also uses commas to add more criteria. Use the `-l` or `--selector` option to specify these criteria to filter the name of the object; for example:

- Query Pods which belong to the pilot project:

```
$ kubectl get pods -l "project=pilot"
NAME READY STATUS RESTARTS AGE
pilot.dev.memcached 1/1 Running 0 21m
pilot.dev.nginx 1/1 Running 0 21m
pilot.prod.memcached 1/1 Running 0 21m
pilot.prod.nginx 1/1 Running 0 21m
```

- Query Pods which belong to the frontend tier:

```
$ kubectl get pods -l "tier=frontend"
NAME READY STATUS RESTARTS AGE
pilot.dev.nginx 1/1 Running 0 21m
pilot.prod.nginx 1/1 Running 0 21m
poc.dev.httpd 1/1 Running 0 21m
```

- Query Pods which belong to the frontend tier AND the under develop environment:

```
$ kubectl get pods -l "tier=frontend,environment=develop"
NAME READY STATUS RESTARTS AGE
pilot.dev.nginx 1/1 Running 0 22m
poc.dev.httpd 1/1 Running 0 21m
```

- Query Pods which belong to the frontend tier and NOT the under develop environment:

```
$ kubectl get pods -l "tier=frontend,environment!=develop"
```

```
NAME READY STATUS RESTARTS AGE
pilot.prod.nginx 1/1 Running 0 29m
```

Set-based label selector

With the set-based selector, you can use either the `in` or `notin` operator, which is similar to the `SQL IN` clause that can specify multiple keywords, as in the following examples:

- Query `Pods` which belong to the `pilot` project:

```
$ kubectl get pods -l "project in (pilot)"
NAME READY STATUS RESTARTS AGE
pilot.dev.memcached 1/1 Running 0 36m
pilot.dev.nginx 1/1 Running 0 36m
pilot.prod.memcached 1/1 Running 0 36m
pilot.prod.nginx 1/1 Running 0 36m
```

- Query `Pods` which belong to the pilot project and `frontend` tier:

```
$ kubectl get pods -l "project in (pilot), tier in
(frontend)"
NAME READY STATUS RESTARTS AGE
pilot.dev.nginx 1/1 Running 0 37m
pilot.prod.nginx 1/1 Running 0 37m
```

- Query `Pods` which belong to the pilot project and either the `frontend` or cache tier:

```
$ kubectl get pods -l "project in (pilot), tier in
(frontend,cache)"
NAME READY STATUS RESTARTS AGE
pilot.dev.memcached 1/1 Running 0 37m
pilot.dev.nginx 1/1 Running 0 37m
pilot.prod.memcached 1/1 Running 0 37m
pilot.prod.nginx 1/1 Running 0 37m
```

- Query `Pods` which belong to the pilot project and not the `frontend` or backend tier (note, we didn't create the `backend` tier object):

```
$ kubectl get pods -l "project in (pilot), tier notin
(frontend, backend)"
NAME READY STATUS RESTARTS AGE
pilot.dev.memcached 1/1 Running 0 50m
pilot.prod.memcached 1/1 Running 0 50m
```

As you can see in the preceding examples for both the equality-based and set-based label selector, equality-based is simpler and set-based is more expressive. Note that you can mix both operator as follows:

- Query Pods which do not belong to the pilot project and develop environment:

```
$ kubectl get pods -l "project notin (pilot),
environment=develop"
NAME READY STATUS RESTARTS AGE
poc.dev.httpd 1/1 Running 0 2m
poc.dev.memcached 1/1 Running 0 2m
```

So, you can use the most efficient way to filter out the Kubernetes objects. In addition, you can also use either or both types of selectors to configure the Kubernetes Service, Deployments, and so on. However, some objects support the equality-based selector and some objects support both. So, let's take a look at how to define it.

There's more...

Label selectors are useful to not only list an object, but also to specify the Kubernetes Service and Deployment to bind objects.

Linking Service to Pods or ReplicaSets using label selectors

As of Kubernetes version 1.9, Service only supports the equality-based selector to bind to Pods or ReplicaSet.

Let's create one Service that binds to `nginx`, which belongs to the production environment and the pilot project. Remember that `nginx` also belongs to the frontend tier:

```
//check your selector filter is correct or not
$ kubectl get pods -l
'environment=production,project=pilot,tier=frontend'
NAME READY STATUS RESTARTS AGE
pilot.prod.nginx 1/1 Running 0 19m


//create Service yaml that specify selector
$ cat pilot-nginx-svc.yaml
apiVersion: v1
```

```
kind: Service
metadata:
  name: pilot-nginx-svc
spec:
  type: NodePort
  ports:
    - protocol: TCP
      port: 80
  selector:
    project: pilot
    environment: production
    tier: frontend


//create pilot-nginx-svc
$ kubectl create -f pilot-nginx-svc.yaml
service "pilot-nginx-svc" created
```

Here is the equivalent, where you can use the `kubectl expose` command to specify the label selector:

```
$ kubectl expose pod pilot.prod.nginx --name=pilot-nginx-svc2 --
type=NodePort --port=80 --
selector="project=pilot,environment=develop,tier=frontend"
service "pilot-nginx-svc2" exposed
```

Based on your Kubernetes environment, if you are using minikube, it is easier to check your Service with `minikube service <Service name>`, as in the following screenshot. If you are not using minikube, access to any Kubernetes node and assigned Service port number. For the following screenshot, it would be `<node ip>:31981` or `<node ip>:31820`:

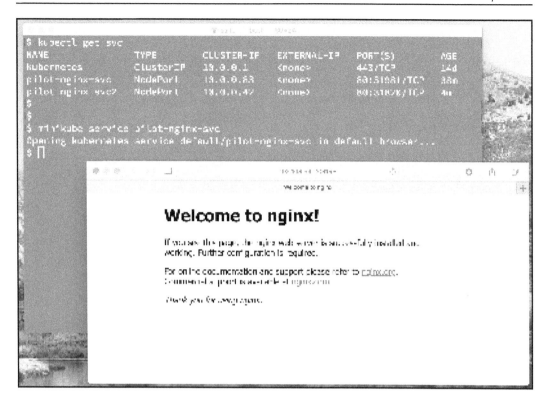

Access to Service which is running on minikube

Linking Deployment to ReplicaSet using the set-based selector

Deployment supports not only the equality-based selector, but also the set-based selector, to specify `ReplicaSet`. To do that, you can write `spec.selector.matchExpressions[]` to specify the key and `in/notin` operator. For example, if you want to specify `project in (poc)`, `environment in (staging)`, `tier notn (backend,cache)`, then `matchExpressions` would be as follows:

```
$ cat deploy_set_selector.yaml
apiVersion: apps/v1
kind: Deployment
metadata:
  name: my-nginx
spec:
```

```
replicas: 3
selector:
  matchExpressions:
    - {key: project, operator: In, values: [poc]}
    - {key: environment, operator: In, values: [staging]}
    - {key: tier, operator: NotIn, values: [backend,cache]}
template:
  metadata:
    labels:
      project: poc
      environment: staging
      tier: frontend
  spec:
    containers:
    - name: my-nginx
      image: nginx
      ports:
      - containerPort: 80
```

As you can see, the YAML array is represented as –, and the map object as { }, to specify the key, operator, and values. Note that values would also be an array, so use the square bracket [] to specify one or more values.

One thing you need to aware of is one label, called the `pod-template-hash` label, which is created by Deployment. When you create a Deployment, it will also create a `ReplicaSet` object. At this time, Deployment will also assign the `pod-template-hash` label to the `ReplicaSet`. Let's see how it works:

```
$ kubectl create -f deploy_set_selector.yaml
deployment.apps "my-nginx" created

$ kubectl get rs
NAME                   DESIRED   CURRENT   READY   AGE
my-nginx2-764d7cfff    3         3         3       19s

$ kubectl describe rs my-nginx2-764d7cfff
Name:          my-nginx2-764d7cfff
Namespace:     default
Selector:      environment in (staging),pod-template-
hash=320837999,project in (poc),tier notin (backend,cache)
...
...
Pod Template:
  Labels:  environment=staging
           pod-template-hash=320837999
           project=poc
           tier=frontend
```

```
. . .
. . .
```

As you can see, the `ReplicaSet my-nginx2-764d7cfff` has an equality-based selector, as `pod-template-hash=320837999` is appended to the Selector and Pod template. It will be used to generate a `ReplicaSet` and Pod name with a particular hash function (for example, `my-nginx2-764d7cfff`).

See also

In this section, you learned how flexible it is to assign a label to your Kubernetes object. In addition, equality-based and set-based selectors allow us to filter out an object by label. Selector is important that loosely couple an object such as Service and ReplicaSet/Pod as well as Deployment and ReplicaSet.

Playing with Containers

14

In this chapter, we will cover the following topics:

- Scaling your containers
- Updating live containers
- Forwarding container ports
- Ensuring flexible usage of your containers
- Submitting Jobs on Kubernetes
- Working with configuration files

Introduction

When talking about container management, you need to know some of the differences compared to application package management, such as rpm/dpkg, because you can run multiple containers on the same machine. You also need to care about network port conflicts. This chapter covers how to update, scale, and launch a container application using Kubernetes.

Scaling your containers

Scaling up and down the application or service based on predefined criteria is a common way to utilize the most compute resources in most efficient way. In Kubernetes, you can scale up and down manually or use a **Horizontal Pod Autoscaler** (**HPA**) to do autoscaling. In this section, we'll describe how to perform both operations.

Getting ready

Prepare the following YAML file, which is a simple Deployment that launches two
`nginx` containers. Also, a NodePort service with TCP—30080 exposed:

```
# cat 3-1-1_deployment.yaml
apiVersion: apps/v1
kind: Deployment
metadata:
  name: my-nginx
spec:
  replicas: 2
  selector:
    matchLabels:
      service : nginx
  template:
    metadata:
      labels:
        service : nginx
    spec:
      containers:
        - name: my-container
          image: nginx
---
apiVersion: v1
kind: Service
metadata:
  name: my-nginx
spec:
  ports:
    - protocol: TCP
      port: 80
      nodePort: 30080
  type: NodePort
  selector:
    service: nginx
```

 NodePort will bind to all the Kubernetes nodes (port range: `30000`
to `32767`); therefore, make sure `NodePort` is not used by other
processes.

Let's use `kubectl` to create the resources used by the preceding configuration file:

```
// create deployment and service
# kubectl create -f 3-1-1_deployment.yaml
deployment "my-nginx" created
service "my-nginx" created
```

After a few seconds, we should see that the `pods` are scheduled and up and running:

```
# kubectl get pods
NAME READY STATUS RESTARTS AGE
my-nginx-6484b5fc4c-9v7dc 1/1 Running 0 7s
my-nginx-6484b5fc4c-krd7p 1/1 Running 0 7s
```

The service is up, too:

```
# kubectl get services
NAME TYPE CLUSTER-IP EXTERNAL-IP PORT(S) AGE
kubernetes ClusterIP 10.96.0.1 <none> 443/TCP 20d
my-nginx NodePort 10.105.9.153 <none> 80:30080/TCP 59s
```

How to do it...

Assume our services are expected to have a traffic spike at a certain of time. As a DevOps, you might want to scale it up manually, and scale it down after the peak time. In Kubernetes, we can use the `kubectl scale` command to do so. Alternatively, we could leverage a HPA to scale up and down automatically based on compute resource conditions or custom metrics.

Let's see how to do it manually and automatically in Kubernetes.

Scale up and down manually with the kubectl scale command

Assume that today we'd like to scale our `nginx` Pods from two to four:

```
// kubectl scale --replicas=<expected_replica_num> deployment
<deployment_name>
# kubectl scale --replicas=4 deployment my-nginx
deployment "my-nginx" scaled
```

Let's check how many `pods` we have now:

```
# kubectl get pods
NAME READY STATUS RESTARTS AGE
my-nginx-6484b5fc4c-9v7dc 1/1 Running 0 1m
my-nginx-6484b5fc4c-krd7p 1/1 Running 0 1m
my-nginx-6484b5fc4c-nsvzt 0/1 ContainerCreating 0 2s
my-nginx-6484b5fc4c-v68dr 1/1 Running 0 2s
```

We could find two more Pods are scheduled. One is already running and another one is creating. Eventually, we will have four Pods up and running if we have enough compute resources.

Kubectl scale (also kubectl autoscale!) supports **Replication Controller** (**RC**) and **Replica Set** (**RS**), too. However, deployment is the recommended way to deploy Pods.

We could also scale down with the same `kubectl` command, just by setting the `replicas` parameter lower:

```
// kubectl scale –replicas=<expected_replica_num> deployment
<deployment_name>
# kubectl scale --replicas=2 deployment my-nginx
deployment "my-nginx" scaled
```

Now, we'll see two Pods are scheduled to be terminated:

```
# kubectl get pods
NAME READY STATUS RESTARTS AGE
my-nginx-6484b5fc4c-9v7dc 1/1 Running 0 1m
my-nginx-6484b5fc4c-krd7p 1/1 Running 0 1m
my-nginx-6484b5fc4c-nsvzt 0/1 Terminating 0 23s
my-nginx-6484b5fc4c-v68dr 0/1 Terminating 0 23s
```

There is an option, `--current-replicas`, which specifies the expected current replicas. If it doesn't match, Kubernetes doesn't perform the scale function as follows:

```
// adding –-current-replicas to precheck the condistion for scaling.
# kubectl scale --current-replicas=3 --replicas=4 deployment my-nginx
error: Expected replicas to be 3, was 2
```

Horizontal Pod Autoscaler (HPA)

An HPA queries the source of metrics periodically and determines whether scaling is required by a controller based on the metrics it gets. There are two types of metrics that could be fetched; one is from Heapster (`https://github.com/kubernetes/heapster`), another is from RESTful client access. In the following example, we'll show you how to use Heapster to monitor Pods and expose the metrics to an HPA.

First, Heapster has to be deployed in the cluster:

 If you're running minikube, use the `minikube addons enable heapster` command to enable heapster in your cluster. Note that `minikube logs | grep heapster` command could also be used to check the logs of heapster.

```
// at the time we're writing this book, the latest configuration file
of heapster in kops is 1.7.0. Check out
https://github.com/kubernetes/kops/tree/master/addons/monitoring-stand
alone for the latest version when you use it.
# kubectl create -f
https://raw.githubusercontent.com/kubernetes/kops/master/addons/monito
ring-standalone/v1.7.0.yaml
deployment "heapster" created
service "heapster" created
serviceaccount "heapster" created
clusterrolebinding "heapster" created
rolebinding "heapster-binding" created
```

Check if the `heapster pods` are up and running:

```
# kubectl get pods --all-namespaces | grep heapster
kube-system heapster-56d577b559-dnjvn 2/2 Running 0 26m
kube-system heapster-v1.4.3-6947497b4-jrczl 3/3 Running 0 5d
```

Assuming we continue right after the *Getting Ready* section, we will have two `my-nginx` Pods running in our cluster:

```
# kubectl get pods
NAME READY STATUS RESTARTS AGE
my-nginx-6484b5fc4c-9v7dc 1/1 Running 0 40m
my-nginx-6484b5fc4c-krd7p 1/1 Running 0 40m
```

Then, we can use the `kubectl autoscale` command to deploy an HPA:

```
# kubectl autoscale deployment my-nginx --cpu-percent=50 --min=2 --
max=5
deployment "my-nginx" autoscaled
```

```
# cat 3-1-2_hpa.yaml
apiVersion: autoscaling/v1
kind: HorizontalPodAutoscaler
metadata:
  name: my-nginx
spec:
  scaleTargetRef:
    kind: Deployment
    name: my-nginx
  minReplicas: 2
  maxReplicas: 5
  targetCPUUtilizationPercentage: 50
```

To check if it's running as expected:

```
// check horizontal pod autoscaler (HPA)
# kubectl get hpa
NAME REFERENCE TARGETS MINPODS MAXPODS REPLICAS AGE
my-nginx Deployment/my-nginx <unknown> / 50% 2 5 0 3s
```

We find the target shows as unknown and replicas are 0. Why is this? the runs as a control loop, at a default interval of 30 seconds. There might be a delay before it reflects the real metrics.

 The default sync period of an HPA can be altered by changing the following parameter in control manager: `--horizontal-pod-autoscaler-sync-period`.

After waiting a couple of seconds, we will find the current metrics are there now. The number showed in the target column presents (`current / target`). It means the load is currently `0%`, and scale target is `50%`:

```
# kubectl get hpa
NAME REFERENCE TARGETS MINPODS MAXPODS REPLICAS AGE
my-nginx Deployment/my-nginx 0% / 50% 2 5 2 48m

// check details of a hpa
# kubectl describe hpa my-nginx
Name: my-nginx
Namespace: default
Labels: <none>
Annotations: <none>
CreationTimestamp: Mon, 15 Jan 2018 22:48:28 -0500
Reference: Deployment/my-nginx
Metrics: ( current / target )
  resource cpu on pods (as a percentage of request): 0% (0) / 50%
```

```
Min replicas: 2
Max replicas: 5
```

To test if HPA can scale the Pod properly, we'll manually generate some loads to `my-nginx` service:

```
// generate the load
# kubectl run -it --rm --restart=Never <pod_name> --image=busybox --
sh -c "while true; do wget -O - -q http://my-nginx; done"
```

In the preceding command, we ran a `busybox` image which allowed us to run a simple command on it. We used the –c parameter to specify the default command, which is an infinite loop, to query `my-nginx` service.

After about one minute, you can see that the current value is changing:

```
// check current value — it's 43% now. not exceeding scaling condition
yet.
# kubectl get hpa
NAME REFERENCE TARGETS MINPODS MAXPODS REPLICAS AGE
my-nginx Deployment/my-nginx 43% / 50% 2 5 2 56m
```

With the same command, we can run more loads with different Pod names repeatedly. Finally, we see that the condition has been met. It's scaling up to 3 replicas, and up to 4 replicas afterwards:

```
# kubectl get hpa
NAME REFERENCE TARGETS MINPODS MAXPODS REPLICAS AGE
my-nginx Deployment/my-nginx 73% / 50% 2 5 3 1h

# kubectl get hpa
NAME REFERENCE TARGETS MINPODS MAXPODS REPLICAS AGE
my-nginx Deployment/my-nginx 87% / 50% 2 5 4 15m
Keeping observing it and deleting some busybox we deployed. It will
eventually cool down and scale down without manual operation involved.
# kubectl get hpa
NAME REFERENCE TARGETS MINPODS MAXPODS REPLICAS AGE
my-nginx Deployment/my-nginx 40% / 50% 2 5 2 27m
```

We can see that HPA just scaled our Pods from 4 to 2.

How it works...

Note that cAdvisor acts as a container resource utilization monitoring service, which is running inside kubelet on each node. The CPU utilizations we just monitored are collected by cAdvisor and aggregated by Heapster. Heapster is a service running in the cluster that monitors and aggregates the metrics. It queries the metrics from each cAdvisor. When HPA is deployed, the controller will keep observing the metrics which are reported by Heapster, and scale up and down accordingly. An illustration of the process is as follows:

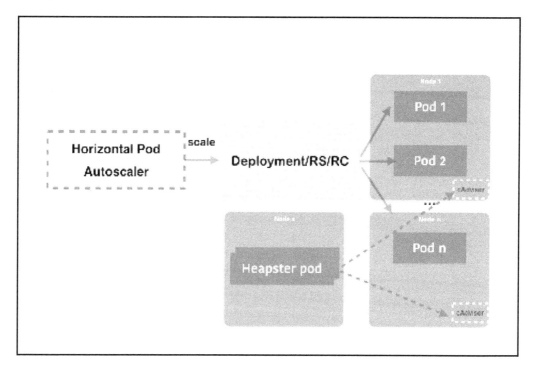

Based on the specified metrics, HPA determines whether scaling is required

There is more...

Alternatively, you could use custom metrics, such as Pod metrics or object metrics, to determine if it's time to scale up or down. Kubernetes also supports multiple metrics. HPA will consider each metric sequentially. Check out `https://kubernetes.io/docs/tasks/run-application/horizontal-pod-autoscale` for more examples.

See also

This recipe described how to change the number of Pods using the scaling option of the deployment. It is useful to scale up and scale down your application quickly. To know more about how to update your container, refer to the following recipes:

- *Updating live containers* in `Chapter 14`, *Playing with Containers*
- *Ensuring flexible usage of your containers* in `Chapter 14`, *Playing with Containers*

Updating live containers

For the benefit of containers, we can easily publish new programs by executing the latest image, and reduce the headache of environment setup. But, what about publishing the program on running containers? While managing a container natively, we have to stop the running containers prior to booting up new ones with the latest images and the same configurations. There are some simple and efficient methods for updating your program in the Kubernetes system. One is called rolling-update, which means Deployment can update its Pods without downtime to clients. The other method is called *recreate*, which just terminates all Pods then create a new set. We will demonstrate how these solutions are applied in this recipe.

Rolling-update in Docker swarm
To achieve zero downtime application updating, there is a similar managing function in Docker swarm. In Docker swarm, you can leverage the command docker service update with the flag `--update-delay`, `--update-parallelism` and `--update-failure-action`. Check the official website for more details about Docker swarm's rolling-update: `https://docs.docker.com/engine/swarm/swarm-tutorial/rolling-update/`.

Getting ready

For a later demonstration, we are going to update `nginx` Pods . Please make sure all Kubernetes nodes and components are working healthily:

```
// check components
$ kubectl get cs
// check nodes
$ kubectl get node
```

Furthermore, to well understand the relationship between ReplicaSet and Deployment, please check *Deployment API* section in `Chapter 13`, *Walking through Kubernetes Concepts*.

To illustrate the updating of the containers in Kubernetes system, we will create a Deployment, change its configurations of application, and then check how the updating mechanism handles it. Let's get all our resources ready:

```
// create a simple nginx Deployment with specified labels
$ kubectl run simple-nginx --image=nginx --port=80 --replicas=5 --
labels="project=My-Happy-Web,role=frontend,env=test"
deployment.apps "simple-nginx" created
```

This Deployment is created with 5 replicas. It is good for us to discover the updating procedure with multiple numbers of Pods:

```
// expose the Deployment, and named the service "nginx-service"
$ kubectl expose deployment simple-nginx --port=8080 --target-port=80
--name="nginx-service"
service "nginx-service" exposed
// For minikube environment only, since Kubernetes is installed in a
VM, add Service type as NodePort for accessing outside the VM.
$ kubectl expose deployment simple-nginx --port=8080 --target-port=80
--name="nginx-service" --type=NodePort
service "nginx-service" exposed
```

Attaching a Service on the Deployment will help to simulate the real experience of clients.

How to do it...

At the beginning, take a look at the Deployment you just created and its ReplicaSet by executing the following code block:

```
$ kubectl describe deployment simple-nginx
Name:                   simple-nginx
Namespace:              default
CreationTimestamp:      Fri, 04 May 2018 12:14:21 -0400
Labels:                 env=test
                        project=My-Happy-Web
                        role=frontend
Annotations:            deployment.kubernetes.io/revision=1
Selector:               env=test,project=My-Happy-Web,role=frontend
Replicas:               5 desired | 5 updated | 5 total | 5 available
| 0 unavailable
```

```
StrategyType:              RollingUpdate
MinReadySeconds:           0
RollingUpdateStrategy:     1 max unavailable, 1 max surge
Pod Template:
  Labels:  env=test
           project=My-Happy-Web
           role=frontend
  Containers:
   simple-nginx:
    Image:          nginx
    Port:           80/TCP
    Environment:    <none>
    Mounts:         <none>
  Volumes:          <none>
Conditions:
  Type           Status   Reason
  ----           ------   ------
  Available      True     MinimumReplicasAvailable
  Progressing    True     NewReplicaSetAvailable
OldReplicaSets:  <none>
NewReplicaSet:   simple-nginx-585f6cddcd (5/5 replicas created)
Events:
  Type     Reason           Age    From                   Message
  ----     ------           ----   ----                   -------
  Normal   ScalingReplicaSet 1h    deployment-controller  Scaled up
replica set simple-nginx-585f6cddcd to 5
// rs is the abbreviated resource key of replicaset
$ kubectl get rs
NAME                        DESIRED   CURRENT   READY   AGE
simple-nginx-585f6cddcd     5         5         5       1h
```

Based on the preceding output, we know that the default updating strategy of deployment is rolling-update. Also, there is a single ReplicaSet named <Deployment Name>-<hex decimal hash> that is created along with the Deployment.

Next, check the content of the current Service endpoint for the sake of verifying our update later:

```
// record the cluster IP of Service "nginx-service"
$ export SERVICE_URL=$(kubectl get svc | grep nginx-service | awk
'{print $3}'):8080

// For minikube environment only, record the VM host IP and port for
the service
$ export SERVICE_URL=$(minikube service nginx-service --url)
$ curl $SERVICE_URL | grep "title"
<title>Welcome to nginx!</title>
```

We will get the welcome message in the title of the HTML response with the original `nginx` image.

Deployment update strategy – rolling-update

The following will introduce the subcommands `edit` and `set`, for the purpose of updating the containers under Deployment:

1. First, let's update the Pods in Deployment with a new command:

```
// get into editor mode with the command below
// the flag "--record" is for recording the update
// add the command argument as below and save the change
$ kubectl edit deployment simple-nginx --record
spec:
  replicas: 5
  ...
  template:
    ...
    spec:
      containers:
      - image: nginx
        command:
          - sh
          - -c
          - echo "Happy Programming with Kubernetes!" >
/usr/share/nginx/html/index.html && service nginx stop &&
nginx -g "daemon off;"
        imagePullPolicy: Always
      ...
deployment.extensions "simple-nginx" edited
```

We are not only doing the update; we record this change as well. With the flag `--record`, we keep the command line as a tag in revision.

2. After editing the Deployment, check the status of rolling-update with the subcommand `rollout` right away:

```
// you may see different output on your screen, but
definitely has the last line showing update successfully
$ kubectl rollout status deployment simple-nginx
Waiting for rollout to finish: 4 out of 5 new replicas
have been updated...
Waiting for rollout to finish: 4 out of 5 new replicas
have been updated...
Waiting for rollout to finish: 4 out of 5 new replicas
```

```
have been updated...
Waiting for rollout to finish: 4 out of 5 new replicas
have been updated...
Waiting for rollout to finish: 1 old replicas are pending
termination...
Waiting for rollout to finish: 1 old replicas are pending
termination...
Waiting for rollout to finish: 1 old replicas are pending
termination...
Waiting for rollout to finish: 4 of 5 updated replicas are
available...
deployment "simple-nginx" successfully rolled out
```

It is possible that you get several `Waiting for` ... lines, as shown in the preceding code. They are the standard output showing the status of the update.

3. For whole updating procedures, check the details of the Deployment to list its events:

```
// describe the Deployment again
$ kubectl describe deployment simple-nginx
Name:                   simple-nginx
...
Events:
  Type     Reason           Age   From
Message
  ----     ------           ----  ----
-------
  Normal   ScalingReplicaSet 1h    deployment-controller
Scaled up replica set simple-nginx-585f6cddcd to 5
  Normal   ScalingReplicaSet 1h    deployment-controller
Scaled up replica set simple-nginx-694f94f77d to 1
  Normal   ScalingReplicaSet 1h    deployment-controller
Scaled down replica set simple-nginx-585f6cddcd to 4
  Normal   ScalingReplicaSet 1h    deployment-controller
Scaled up replica set simple-nginx-694f94f77d to 2
  Normal   ScalingReplicaSet 1h    deployment-controller
Scaled down replica set simple-nginx-585f6cddcd to 3
  Normal   ScalingReplicaSet 1h    deployment-controller
Scaled up replica set simple-nginx-694f94f77d to 3
  Normal   ScalingReplicaSet 1h    deployment-controller
Scaled down replica set simple-nginx-585f6cddcd to 2
  Normal   ScalingReplicaSet 1h    deployment-controller
Scaled up replica set simple-nginx-694f94f77d to 4
  Normal   ScalingReplicaSet 1h    deployment-controller
Scaled down replica set simple-nginx-585f6cddcd to
  Normal   ScalingReplicaSet 1h    deployment-controller
```

```
Scaled up replica set simple-nginx-694f94f77d to 5
  Normal  ScalingReplicaSet  1h   deployment-controller
(combined from similar events): Scaled down replica set
simple-nginx-585f6cddcd to 0
```

As you see, a new `replica set simple-nginx-694f94f77d` is created in the Deployment `simple-nginx`. Each time the new ReplicaSet scales one Pod up successfully, the old ReplicaSet will scale one Pod down. The scaling process finishes at the moment that the new ReplicaSet meets the original desired Pod number (as said, 5 Pods), and the old ReplicaSet has zero Pods.

4. Go ahead and check the new ReplicaSet and existing Service for this update:

```
// look at the new ReplicaSet in detail, you will find it
copied the labels of the old one
$ kubectl describe rs simple-nginx-694f94f77d
Name:          simple-nginx-694f94f77d
Namespace:     default
Selector:      env=test,pod-template-
hash=2509509338,project=My-Happy-Web,role=frontend
Labels:        env=test
               pod-template-hash=2509509338
               project=My-Happy-Web
               role=frontend
...
// send request to the same endpoint of Service.
$ curl $SERVICE_URL
Happy Programming with Kubernetes!
```

5. Let's make another update! This time, use the subcommand `set` to modify a specific configuration of a Pod.

6. To set a new image to certain containers in a Deployment, the subcommand format would look like this: `kubectl set image deployment <Deployment name> <Container name>=<image name>`:

```
// change the image version with the subcommand "set"
// when describing the deployment, we can know that the
container name is the same as the name of the Deployment
// record this change as well
$ kubectl set image deployment simple-nginx simple-
nginx=nginx:stable --record
deployment.apps "simple-nginx" image updated
```

What else could the subcommand "set" help to configure?
The subcommand set helps to define the configuration of the application. Until version 1.9, CLI with set could assign or update the following resources:

Subcommand after set	Acting resource	Updating item
env	Pod	Environment variables
image	Pod	Container image
resources	Pod	Computing resource requirement or limitation
selector	Any resource	Selector
serviceaccount	Any resource	ServiceAccount
subject	RoleBinding or ClusterRoleBinding	User, group, or ServiceAccount

7. Now, check if the update has finished and whether the image is changed:

```
// check update status by rollout
$ kubectl rollout status deployment simple-nginx
...
deployment "simple-nginx" successfully rolled out
// check the image of Pod in simple-nginx
$ kubectl describe deployment simple-nginx
Name:                  simple-nginx
...
Pod Template:
  Labels:  env=test
           project=My-Happy-Web
           role=frontend
  Containers:
   simple-nginx:
    Image:  nginx:stable
    Port:    80/TCP
    Host Port:  0/TCP
...
```

8. You can also check out the ReplicaSets. There should be another one taking responsibility of the Pods for Deployment:

```
$ kubectl get rs
NAME                       DESIRED   CURRENT   READY
AGE
simple-nginx-585f6cddcd    0         0         0         1h
simple-nginx-694f94f77d    0         0         0         1h
simple-nginx-b549cc75c     5         5         5         1h
```

Rollback the update

Kubernetes system records every update for Deployment:

1. We can list all of the revisions with the subcommand `rollout`:

```
// check the rollout history
$ kubectl rollout history deployment simple-nginx
deployments "simple-nginx"
REVISION   CHANGE-CAUSE
1          <none>
2          kubectl edit deployment simple-nginx --
record=true
3          kubectl set image deployment simple-nginx
simple-nginx=nginx:stable --record=true
```

You will get three revisions, as in the preceding lines, for the Deployment `simple-nginx`. For Kubernetes Deployment, each revision has a matched `ReplicaSet` and represents a stage of running an update command. The first revision is the initial state of `simple-nginx`. Although there is no command tag for indication, Kubernetes takes its creation as its first version. However, you could still record the command when you create the Deployment.

2. Add the flag `--record` after the subcommand `create` or `run`.

3. With the revisions, we can easily resume the change, which means rolling back the update. Use the following commands to rollback to previous revisions:

```
// let's jump back to initial Deployment!
// with flag --to-revision, we can specify which revision
for rollback processing
$ kubectl rollout undo deployment simple-nginx --to-
revision=1
deployment.apps "simple-nginx"
// check if the rollback update is finished
$ kubectl rollout status deployment simple-nginx
...
deployment "simple-nginx" successfully rolled out
// take a look at ReplicaSets, you will find that the old
ReplicaSet takes charge of the business now
$ kubectl get rs
NAME                        DESIRED   CURRENT   READY
AGE
simple-nginx-585f6cddcd     5         5         5        4h
simple-nginx-694f94f77d     0         0         0        4h
```

```
simple-nginx-b549cc75c     0          0          0          3h
// go ahead and check the nginx webpage or the details of
Deployment
$ curl $SERVICE_URL
$ kubectl describe deployment simple-nginx
```

4. Without specifying the revision number, the rollback process will simply jump back to previous version:

```
// just go back to previous status
$ kubectl rollout undo deployment simple-nginx
deployment.apps "simple-nginx"
// look at the ReplicaSets agin, now the latest one takes
the job again
$ kubectl get rs
NAME                      DESIRED   CURRENT   READY
AGE
simple-nginx-585f6cddcd   0         0         0         4h
simple-nginx-694f94f77d   0         0         0         4h
simple-nginx-b549cc75c    5         5         5         4h
```

Deployment update strategy – recreate

Next, we are going to introduce the other update strategy, `recreate`, for Deployment. Although there is no subcommand or flag to create a recreate-strategy deployment, users could fulfill this creation by overriding the default element with the specified configuration:

```
// create a new Deployment, and override the update strategy.
$ kubectl run recreate-nginx --image=nginx --port=80 --replicas=5 --
overrides='{"apiVersion": "apps/v1", "spec": {"strategy": {"type":
"Recreate"}}}'
deployment.apps "recreate-nginx" created
// verify our new Deployment
$ kubectl describe deployment recreate-nginx
Name:                recreate-nginx
Namespace:           default
CreationTimestamp:   Sat, 05 May 2018 18:17:07 -0400
Labels:              run=recreate-nginx
Annotations:         deployment.kubernetes.io/revision=1
Selector:            run=recreate-nginx
Replicas:            5 desired | 5 updated | 5 total | 0 available | 5
unavailable
StrategyType:        Recreate
...
```

In our understanding, the `recreate` mode is good for an application under development. With `recreate`, Kubernetes just scales the current ReplicaSet down to zero Pods, and creates a new ReplicaSet with the full desired number of Pods. Therefore, recreate has a shorter total updating time than rolling-update because it scales ReplicaSets up or down simply, once for all. Since a developing Deployment doesn't need to take care of any user experience, it is acceptable to have downtime while updating and enjoy faster updates:

```
// try to update recreate-strategy Deployment
$ kubectl set image deployment recreate-nginx recreate-
nginx=nginx:stable
deployment.apps "recreate-nginx" image updated
// check both the rollout status and the events of Deployment
$ kubectl rollout status deployment recreate-nginx
$ kubectl describe deployment recreate-nginx
...
Events:
  Type      Reason          Age     From              Message
  ----      ------          ----    ----              -------
  Normal    ScalingReplicaSet   3h      deployment-controller  Scaled up
replica set recreate-nginx-9d5b69986 to 5
  Normal    ScalingReplicaSet   2h      deployment-controller  Scaled down
replica set recreate-nginx-9d5b69986 to 0
  Normal    ScalingReplicaSet   2h      deployment-controller  Scaled up
replica set recreate-nginx-674d7f9c7f to 5
```

How it works...

Rolling-update works on the units of the ReplicaSet in a Deployment. The effect is to create a new ReplicaSet to replace the old one. Then, the new ReplicaSet is scaling up to meet the desired numbers, while the old ReplicaSet is scaling down to terminate all the Pods in it. The Pods in the new ReplicaSet are attached to the original labels. Therefore, if any service exposes this Deployment, it will take over the newly created Pods directly.

An experienced Kubernetes user may know that the resource ReplicationController can be rolling-update as well. So, what are the differences of rolling-update between ReplicationController and deployment? The scaling processing uses the combination of ReplicationController and a client such as `kubectl`. A new ReplicationController will be created to replace the previous one. Clients don't feel any interruption since the service is in front of ReplicationController while doing replacement. However, it is hard for developers to roll back to previous ReplicationControllers (they have been removed), because there is no built-in mechanism that records the history of updates.

In addition, rolling-update might fail if the client connection is disconnected while rolling-update is working. Most important of all, Deployment with ReplicaSet is the most recommended deploying resource than ReplicationController or standalone ReplicaSet.

While paying close attention to the history of update in deployment, be aware that it is not always listed in sequence. The algorithm of adding revisions could be clarified as the following bullet points show:

- Take the number of last revision as N
- When a new rollout update comes, it would be $N+1$
- Roll back to a specific revision number X, X would be removed and it would become $N+1$
- Roll back to the previous version, which means $N-1$, then $N-1$ would be removed and it would become $N+1$

With this revision management, no stale and overlapped updates occupy the rollout history.

There's more...

Taking Deployment update into consideration is a good step towards building a CI/CD (continuous integration and continuous delivery) pipeline. For a more common usage, developers don't exploit command lines to update the Deployment. They may prefer to fire some API calls from CI/CD platform, or update from a previous configuration file. Here comes an example working with the subcommand `apply`:

```
// A simple nginx Kubernetes configuration file
$ cat my-update-nginx.yaml
apiVersion: apps/v1
kind: Deployment
metadata:
  name: my-update-nginx
spec:
  replicas: 5
  selector:
    matchLabels:
      run: simple-nginx
  template:
    metadata:
      labels:
        run: simple-nginx
```

```
    spec:
      containers:
      - name: simple-nginx
        image: nginx
        ports:
        - containerPort: 80

// create the Deployment by file and recording the command in the
revision tag
$ kubectl create -f my-update-nginx.yaml --record
deployment.apps "my-update-nginx" created
```

As a demonstration, modifying the container image from `nginx` to `nginx:stable` (you may check the code bundle `my-update-nginx-updated.yaml` for the modification). Then, we can use the changed file to update with the subcommand `apply`:

```
$ kubectl apply -f my-update-nginx-updated.yaml --record
Warning: kubectl apply should be used on resource created by either
kubectl create --save-config or kubectl apply
deployment.apps "my-update-nginx" configured
// check the update revisions and status
$ kubectl rollout history deployment my-update-nginx
deployments "my-update-nginx"
REVISION   CHANGE-CAUSE
1          kubectl create --filename=my-update-nginx.yaml --record=true
2          kubectl apply --filename=my-update-nginx-updated.yaml --
record=true
$ kubectl rollout status deployment my-update-nginx
deployment "my-update-nginx" successfully rolled out
```

Now, you can learn another way to update your Deployment.

Digging deeper into rolling-update on Deployment, there are some parameters we may leverage when doing updates:

- `minReadySeconds`: After a Pod is considered to be ready, the system still waits for a period of time for going on to the next step. This time slot is the minimum ready seconds, which will be helpful when waiting for the application to complete post-configuration.
- `maxUnavailable`: The maximum number of Pods that can be unavailable during updating. The value could be a percentage (the default is 25%) or an integer. If the value of `maxSurge` is 0, which means no tolerance of the number of Pods over the desired number, the value of `maxUnavailable` cannot be 0.

- `maxSurge`: The maximum number of Pods that can be created over the desired number of ReplicaSet during updating. The value could be a percentage (the default is 25%) or an integer. If the value of `maxUnavailable` is 0, which means the number of serving Pods should always meet the desired number, the value of `maxSurge` cannot be 0.

Based on the configuration file `my-update-nginx-advanced.yaml` in the code bundle, try playing with these parameters by yourself and see if you can feel the ideas at work.

See also

You could continue studying the following recipes to learn more ideas about deploying Kubernetes resources efficiently:

- Scaling your containers
- Working with configuration files

Forwarding container ports

In previous chapters, you have learned how to work with the Kubernetes Services to forward the container port internally and externally. Now, it's time to take it a step further to see how it works.

There are four networking models in Kubernetes, and we'll explore the details in the following sections:

- Container-to-container communications
- Pod-to-pod communications
- Pod-to-service communications
- External-to-internal communications

Getting ready

Before we go digging into Kubernetes networking, let's study the networking of Docker to understand the basic concept. Each container will have a network namespace with its own routing table and routing policy. By default, the network bridge docker0 connects the physical network interface and virtual network interfaces of containers, and the virtual network interface is the bidirectional cable for the container network namespace and the host one. As a result, there is a pair of virtual network interfaces for a single container: the Ethernet interface (**eth0**) on the container and the virtual Ethernet interface (**veth-**) on the host.

The network structure can be expressed as in the following image:

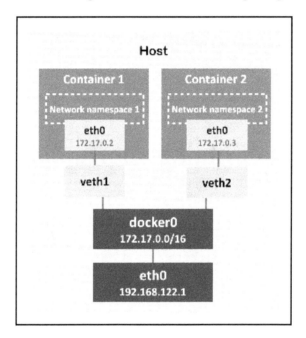

Container network interfaces on host

What is a network namespace?
A network namespace is the technique provided by Linux kernel. With this feature, the operating system can fulfill network virtualization by separating the network capability into independent resources. Each network namespace has its own iptable setup and network devices.

How to do it...

A Pod contains one or more containers, which run on the same host. Each Pod has their own IP address on an overlay network; all the containers inside a Pod see each other as on the same host. Containers inside a Pod will be created, deployed, and deleted almost at the same time. We will illustrate four communication models between container, Pod, and Service.

Container-to-container communication

In this scenario, we would focus on the communications between containers within single Pod:

1. Let's create two containers in one Pod: a nginx web application and a CentOS, which checks port 80 on localhost:

```
// configuration file of creating two containers within a
pod
$ cat two-container-pod.yaml
apiVersion: v1
kind: Pod
metadata:
  name: two-container
spec:
  containers:
    - name: web
      image: nginx
      ports:
        - containerPort: 80
          hostPort: 80
    - name: centos
      image: centos
      command: ["/bin/sh", "-c", "while : ;do curl
http://localhost:80/; sleep 30; done"]

// create the pod
$ kubectl create -f two-container-pod.yaml
pod "two-container" created
// check the status of the newly-created Pod
$ kubectl get pod two-container
NAME            READY     STATUS    RESTARTS   AGE
two-container   2/2       Running   0          5s
```

We see the count in the READY column becomes 2/2, since there are two containers inside this Pod.

2. Using the kubectl describe command, we may see the details of the Pod:

```
$ kubectl describe pod two-container
Name:          two-container
Namespace:     default
Node:          ubuntu02/192.168.122.102
Start Time:    Sat, 05 May 2018 18:28:22 -0400
Labels:        <none>
Annotations:   <none>
Status:        Running
IP:            192.168.79.198
Containers:
  web:
    Container ID:
docker://e832d294f176f643d604445096439d485d94780faf60eab7a
e5d3849cbf15d75
...
  centos:
    Container ID:
docker://9e35275934c1acdcfac4017963dc046f9517a8c1fc972df56
ca37e69d7389a72
...
```

We can see that the Pod is run on node ubuntu02 and that its IP is 192.168.79.198.

3. Also, we may find that the Centos container can access the nginx on localhost:

```
$ kubectl logs two-container centos | grep "title"
<title>Welcome to nginx!</title>
...
```

4. Let's log in to node ubuntu02 to check the network setting of these two containers:

```
// list containers of the Pod
$ docker ps | grep "two-container"
9e35275934c1          centos
"/bin/sh -c 'while...'"   11 hours ago        Up 11 hours
k8s_centos_two-container_default_113e727f-f440-11e7-
ac3f-525400a9d353_0
e832d294f176          nginx
```

```
"nginx -g 'daemon ..."    11 hours ago        Up 11 hours
k8s_web_two-container_default_113e727f-f440-11e7-
ac3f-525400a9d353_0
9b3e9caf5149         gcr.io/google_containers/pause-
amd64:3.1    "/pause"                 11 hours ago
Up 11 hours                          k8s_POD_two-
container_default_113e727f-f440-11e7-ac3f-525400a9d353_0
```

Now, we know that the two containers created are 9e35275934c1 and e832d294f176. On the other hand, there is another container, 9b3e9caf5149, that is created by Kubernetes with the Docker image gcr.io/google_containers/pause-amd64. We will introduce it later. Thereafter, we may get a detailed inspection of the containers with the command docker inspect, and by adding the command jq (https://stedolan.github.io/jq/) as a pipeline, we can parse the output information to show network settings only.

5. Taking a look at both containers covered in the same Pod:

```
// inspect the nginx container, and use jq to parse it
$ docker inspect e832d294f176 | jq '.[]| {NetworkMode:
.HostConfig.NetworkMode, NetworkSettings:
.NetworkSettings}'
{
  "NetworkMode":
"container:9b3e9caf5149ffb0ec14c1ffc36f94b2dd55b223d0d20e4
d48c4e33228103723",
  "NetworkSettings": {
    "Bridge": "",
    "SandboxID": "",
    "HairpinMode": false,
    "LinkLocalIPv6Address": "",
    "LinkLocalIPv6PrefixLen": 0,
    "Ports": {},
    "SandboxKey": "",
    "SecondaryIPAddresses": null,
    "SecondaryIPv6Addresses": null,
    "EndpointID": "",
    "Gateway": "",
    "GlobalIPv6Address": "",
    "GlobalIPv6PrefixLen": 0,
    "IPAddress": "",
    "IPPrefixLen": 0,
    "IPv6Gateway": "",
    "MacAddress": "",
    "Networks": {}
  }
```

```
}
// then inspect the centos one
$ docker inspect 9e35275934c1 | jq '.[]| {NetworkMode:
.HostConfig.NetworkMode, NetworkSettings:
.NetworkSettings}'
{
  "NetworkMode":
"container:9b3e9caf5149ffb0ec14c1ffc36f94b2dd55b223d0d20e4
d48c4e33228103723",
  ...
```

We can see that both containers have identical network settings; the network mode is set to mapped container mode, leaving the other configurations cleaned. The network bridge container is `container:9b3e9caf5149ffb0ec14c1ffc36f94b2dd55b223d0d20e4d48c4e332 28103723`. What is this container? It is the one created by Kubernetes, container ID `9b3e9caf5149`, with the image `gcr.io/google_containers/pause-amd64`.

What does the container "pause" do?

Just as its name suggests, this container does nothing but "pause". However, it preserves the network settings, and the Linux network namespace, for the Pod. Anytime the container shutdowns and restarts, the network configuration will still be the same and not need to be recreated, because the "pause" container holds it. You can check its code and Dockerfile at `https://github.com/kubernetes/ kubernetes/tree/master/build/pause` for more information.

The "pause" container is a network container, which is created when a Pod

is created and used to handle the route of the Pod network. Then, two containers will share the network namespace with pause; that's why they see each other as localhost.

Create a network container in Docker

In Docker, you can easily make a container into a network container, sharing its network namespace with another container. Use the command line: `$ docker run -- network=container:<CONTAINER_ID or CONTAINER_NAME> [other options]`. Then, you will be able to start a container which uses the network namespace of the assigned container.

Pod-to-Pod communication

As mentioned, containers in a Pod share the same network namespace. And a Pod is the basic computing unit in Kubernetes. Kubernetes assigns an IP to a Pod in its world. Every Pod can see every other with the virtual IP in Kubernetes network. While talking about the communication between Pods , we can separate into two scenarios: Pods that communicate within a node, or Pods that communicate across nodes. For Pods in single node, since they have separate IPs, their transmissions can be held by bridge, same as containers in a Docker node. However, for communication between Pods across nodes, how would be the package routing work while Pod doesn't have the host information (the host IP)?

Kubernetes uses the CNI to handle cluster networking. CNI is a framework for managing connective containers, for assigning or deleting the network resource on a container. While Kubernetes takes CNI as a plugin, users can choose the implementation of CNI on demand. Commonly, there are the following types of CNI:

- **Overlay**: With the technique of packet encapsulation. Every data is wrapped with host IP, so it is routable in the internet. An example is flannel (`https://github.com/coreos/flannel`).
- **L3 gateway**: Transmission between containers pass to a gateway node first. The gateway will maintain the routing table to map the container subnet and host IP. An example is Project Calico (`https://www.projectcalico.org/`).
- **L2 adjacency**: Happening on L2 switching. In Ethernet, two nodes have adjacency if the package can be transmitted directly from source to destination, without passing by other nodes. An example is Cisco ACI (`https://www.cisco.com/c/en/us/td/docs/switches/datacenter/aci/apic/sw/kb/b_Kubernetes_Integration_with_ACI.html`).

There are pros and cons to every type of CNI. The former type within the bullet points has better scalability but bad performance, while the latter one has a shorter latency but requires complex and customized setup. Some CNIs cover all three types in different modes, for example, Contiv (`https://github.com/contiv/netplugin`). You can get more information about CNI while checking its spec at: `https://github.com/containernetworking/cni`. Additionally, look at the CNI list on official website of Kubernetes to try out these CNIs: `https://kubernetes.io/docs/concepts/cluster-administration/networking/#how-to-achieve-this`.

After introducing the basic knowledge of the packet transaction between Pods , we will continue to bring you a Kubernetes API, `NetworkPolicy`, which provides advanced management between the communication of Pods .

Working with NetworkPolicy

As a resource of Kubernetes, NetworkPolicy uses label selectors to configure the firewall of Pods from infrastructure level. Without a specified NetworkPolicy, any Pod in the same cluster can communicate with each other by default. On the other hand, once a NetworkPolicy with rules is attached to a Pod, either it is for ingress or egress, or both, and all traffic that doesn't follow the rules will be blocked.

Before demonstrating how to build a NetworkPolicy, we should make sure the network plugin in Kubernetes cluster supports it. There are several CNIs that support NetworkPolicy: Calico, Contive, Romana (`https://github.com/romana/kube`), Weave Net (`https://github.com/weaveworks/weave`), Trireme (`https://github.com/aporeto-inc/trireme-kubernetes`), and others.

Enable CNI with NetworkPolicy support as network plugin in minikube

While working on minikube, users will not need to attach a CNI specifically, since it is designed as a single local Kubernetes node. However, to enable the functionality of NetworkPolicy, it is necessary to start a NetworkPolicy-supported CNI. Be careful, as, while you configure the minikube with CNI, the configuration options and procedures could be quite different to various CNI implementations. The following steps show you how to start minikube with CNI, Calico:

1. We take this issue `https://github.com/projectcalico/calico/issues/1013#issuecomment-325689943` as reference for these building steps.
2. The minikube used here is the latest version, 0.24.1.
3. Reboot your minikube: `minikube start --network-plugin=cni \`
   `--host-only-cidr 172.17.17.1/24 \`
   `--extra-config=kubelet.PodCIDR=192.168.0.0/16 \`
   `--extra-config=proxy.ClusterCIDR=192.168.0.0/16 \`
   `--extra-config=controller-manager.ClusterCIDR=192.168.0.0/16.`
4. Create Calico with the configuration file "minikube-calico.yaml" from the code bundle `kubectl create -f minikue-calico.yaml`.

To illustrate the functionality of NetworkPolicy, we are going to create a Pod and expose it as a service, then attach a NetworkPolicy on the Pod to see what happens:

```
// start a pod of our favourite example, nginx
$ kubectl run nginx-pod --image=nginx --port=80 --restart=Never
pod "nginx-pod" created
//expose the pod as a service listening on port 8080
$ kubectl expose pod nginx-pod --port=8080 --target-port=80
service "nginx-pod" exposed
// check the service IP
$ kubectl get svc
NAME          TYPE        CLUSTER-IP       EXTERNAL-IP   PORT(S)     AGE
kubernetes    ClusterIP   10.96.0.1        <none>        443/TCP     1h
nginx-pod     ClusterIP   10.102.153.182   <none>        8080/TCP    1m
```

Now, we can go ahead and check the Pod's connection from a simple Deployment, busybox, using the command wget with --spider flag to verify the existence of endpoint:

```
// check the accessibility of the service
// create busybox and open standard input and independent terminal by
flag "i" and "t", similar to docker command
$ kubectl run busybox -it --image=busybox /bin/sh
If you don't see a command prompt, try pressing enter.
/ # wget --spider 10.102.153.182:8080
Connecting to 10.102.153.182:8080 (10.102.153.182:8080)
```

As shown in the preceding result, we know that the nginx service can be accessed without any constraints. Later, let's run a NetworkPolicy that restricts that only the Pod tagging <test: inbound> can access nginx service:

```
// a configuration file defining NetworkPolicy of pod nginx-pod
$ cat networkpolicy.yaml
kind: NetworkPolicy
apiVersion: networking.k8s.io/v1
metadata:
  name: nginx-networkpolicy
spec:
  podSelector:
    matchLabels:
      run: nginx-pod
  ingress:
    - from:
      - podSelector:
          matchLabels:
            test: inbound
```

As you can see, in the spec of NeworkPolicy, it is configured to apply to Pods with the label <run: nginx-pod>, which is the one we have on the pod nginx-pod. Also, a rule of ingress is attached in the policy, which indicates that only Pods with a specific label can access nginx-pod:

```
// create the NetworkPolicy
$ kubectl create -f networkpolicy.yaml
networkpolicy.networking.k8s.io "nginx-networkpolicy" created
// check the details of NetworkPolicy
$ kubectl describe networkpolicy nginx-networkpolicy
Name:          nginx-networkpolicy
Namespace:     default
Created on:    2018-05-05 18:36:56 -0400 EDT
Labels:        <none>
Annotations:   <none>
```

```
Spec:
  PodSelector:      run=nginx-pod
  Allowing ingress traffic:
    To Port: <any> (traffic allowed to all ports)
    From PodSelector: test=inbound
  Allowing egress traffic:
    <none> (Selected pods are isolated for egress connectivity)
  Policy Types: Ingress
```

Great, everything is looking just like what we expected. Next, check the same service endpoint on our previous `busybox` Pod:

```
// if you turned off the terminal, resume it with the subcommand
attach
$ kubectl attach busybox-598b87455b-s2mfq -c busybox -i -t
// we add flag to specify timeout interval, otherwise it will just
keep hanging on wget
/ # wget --spider 10.102.153.182:8080 --timeout=3
wget: download timed out
```

As expected again, now we cannot access the `nginx-pod` service after NetworkPolicy is attached. The `nginx-pod` can only be touched by Pod labelled with <test: inbound>:

```
// verify the connection by yourself with new busybox
$ kubectl run busybox-labelled --labels="test=inbound" -it --
image=busybox /bin/sh
```

Catch up with the concept of label and selector in the recipe *Working with labels and selectors* in `Chapter 13`, *Walking through Kubernetes Concepts*.

In this case, you have learned how to create a NetworkPolicy with ingress restriction by Pod selector. Still, there are other settings you may like to build on your Pod:

- **Egress restriction**: Egress rules can be applied by `.spec.egress`, which has similar settings to ingress.
- **Port restriction**: Each ingress and egress rule can point out what port, and with what kind of port protocol, is to be accepted or blocked. Port configuration can be applied through `.spec.ingress.ports` or `.spec.egress.ports`.

- **Namespace selector**: We can also make limitations on certain Namespaces. For example, Pods for the system daemon might only allow access to others in the Namespace `kube-system`. Namespace selector can be applied with `.spec.ingress.from.namespaceSelector` or `.spec.egress.to.namespaceSelector`.
- **IP block**: A more customized configuration is to set rules on certain CIDR ranges, which come out as similar ideas to what we work with iptables. We may utilize this configuration through `.spec.ingress.from.ipBlock` or `.spec.egress.to.ipBlock`.

It is recommended to check more details in the API document: `https://kubernetes.io/docs/reference/generated/kubernetes-api/v1.10/#networkpolicyspec-v1-networking`. Furthermore, we would like to show you some more interesting setups to fulfill general situations:

- **Apply to all Pod**: A NetworkPolicy can be easily pushed to every Pod by setting `.spec.podSelector` with an empty value.
- **Allow all traffic**: We may allow all incoming traffic by assigning `.spec.ingress` with empty value, an empty array; accordingly, outgoing traffic could be set without any restriction by assigning `.spec.egress` with empty value.
- **Deny all traffic**: We may deny all incoming or outgoing traffic by simply indicating the type of NetworkPolicy without setting any rule. The type of the NetworkPolicy can be set at `.spec.policyTypes`. At the same time, do not set `.spec.ingress or .spec.egress`.

Go check the code bundle for the example files `networkpolicy-allow-all.yaml` and `networkpolicy-deny-all.yaml`.

Pod-to-Service communication

In the ordinary course of events, Pods can be stopped accidentally. Then, the IP of the Pod can be changed. When we expose the port for a Pod or a Deployment, we create a Kubernetes Service that acts as a proxy or a load balancer. Kubernetes would create a virtual IP, which receives the request from clients and proxies the traffic to the Pods in a service. Let's review how to do this:

1. First, we would create a Deployment and expose it to a Service:

```
$ cat nodeport-deployment.yaml
apiVersion: apps/v1
```

```
kind: Deployment
metadata:
  name: nodeport-deploy
spec:
  replicas: 2
  selector:
    matchLabels:
      app: nginx
  template:
    metadata:
      labels:
        app: nginx
    spec:
      containers:
      - name: my-nginx
        image: nginx
---
apiVersion: v1
kind: Service
metadata:
  name: nodeport-svc
spec:
  type: NodePort
  selector:
    app: nginx
  ports:
    - protocol: TCP
      port: 8080
      targetPort: 80
$ kubectl create -f nodeport-deployment.yaml
deployment.apps "nodeport-deploy" created
service "nodeport-svc" created
```

2. At this moment, check the details of the Service with the subcommand
   `describe`:

```
$ kubectl describe service nodeport-svc
Name:                   nodeport-svc
Namespace:              default
Labels:                 <none>
Annotations:            <none>
Selector:               app=nginx
Type:                   NodePort
IP:                     10.101.160.245
Port:                   <unset>  8080/TCP
TargetPort:             80/TCP
NodePort:               <unset>  30615/TCP
Endpoints:              192.168.80.5:80,192.168.80.6:80
```

```
Session Affinity:        None
External Traffic Policy: Cluster
Events:                  <none>
```

The virtual IP of the Service is 10.101.160.245, which exposes the port 8080. The Service would then dispatch the traffic into the two endpoints 192.168.80.5:80 and 192.168.80.6:80. Moreover, because the Service is created in NodePort type, clients can access this Service on every Kubernetes node at <NODE_IP>:30615. As with our understanding of the recipe *Working with Services* in Chapter 13, *Walking through Kubernetes Concepts*, it is the Kubernetes daemon kube-proxy that helps to maintain and update routing policy on every node.

3. Continue on, checking the iptable on any Kubernetes node:

 Attention! If you are in minikube environment, you should jump into the node with the command minikube ssh.

```
// Take a look at following marked "Chain"
$ sudo iptables -t nat -nL
...
Chain KUBE-NODEPORTS (1 references)
target      prot opt source              destination
KUBE-MARK-MASQ  tcp  --  0.0.0.0/0            0.0.0.0/0
/* default/nodeport-svc: */ tcp dpt:30615
KUBE-SVC-GFPAJ7EGCNM4QF4H  tcp  --  0.0.0.0/0
0.0.0.0/0            /* default/nodeport-svc: */ tcp
dpt:30615
...
Chain KUBE-SEP-DIS6NYZTQKZ5ALQS (1 references)
target      prot opt source              destination
KUBE-MARK-MASQ  all  --  192.168.80.6        0.0.0.0/0
/* default/nodeport-svc: */
DNAT        tcp  --  0.0.0.0/0            0.0.0.0/0
/* default/nodeport-svc: */ tcp to:192.168.80.6:80
...
Chain KUBE-SEP-TC6HXYYMMLGUSFNZ (1 references)
target      prot opt source              destination
KUBE-MARK-MASQ  all  --  192.168.80.5        0.0.0.0/0
/* default/nodeport-svc: */
DNAT        tcp  --  0.0.0.0/0            0.0.0.0/0
/* default/nodeport-svc: */ tcp to:192.168.80.5:80
Chain KUBE-SERVICES (2 references)
target      prot opt source              destination
```

```
...
KUBE-SVC-GFPAJ7EGCNM4QF4H  tcp  --  0.0.0.0/0
10.101.160.245       /* default/nodeport-svc: cluster IP
*/ tcp dpt:8080
...
KUBE-NODEPORTS  all  --  0.0.0.0/0              0.0.0.0/0
/* kubernetes service nodeports; NOTE: this must be the
last rule in this chain */ ADDRTYPE match dst-type LOCAL
...
Chain KUBE-SVC-GFPAJ7EGCNM4QF4H (2 references)
target      prot opt source               destination
KUBE-SEP-TC6HXYYMMLGUSFNZ  all  --  0.0.0.0/0
0.0.0.0/0            /* default/nodeport-svc: */ statistic
mode random probability 0.50000000000
KUBE-SEP-DIS6NYZTQKZ5ALQS  all  --  0.0.0.0/0
0.0.0.0/0            /* default/nodeport-svc: */
...
```

There will be a lot of rules showing out. To focus on policies related to the Service nodeport-svc, go through the following steps for checking them all. The output on your screen may not be listed in the expected order:

1. Find targets under chain KUBE-NODEPORTS with the comment mentioned nodeport-svc. One target will be named with the prefix KUBE-SVC-. In the preceding output, it is the one named KUBE-SVC-GFPAJ7EGCNM4QF4H. Along with the other target KUBE-MARK-MASQ, they work on passing traffics at port 30615 to the Service.

2. Find a specific target named KUBE-SVC-XXX under Chain KUBE-SERVICES. In this case, it is the target named KUBE-SVC-GFPAJ7EGCNM4QF4H, ruled as allowing traffics from "everywhere" to the endpoint of nodeport-svc, 10.160.245:8080.

3. Find targets under the specific Chain KUBE-SVC-XXX. In this case, it is Chain KUBE-SVC-GFPAJ7EGCNM4QF4H. Under the Service chain, you will have number of targets based on the according Pods with the prefix KUBE-SEP-. In the preceding output, they are KUBE-SEP-TC6HXYYMMLGUSFNZ and KUBE-SEP-DIS6NYZTQKZ5ALQS.

4. Find targets under specific `Chain KUBE-SEP-YYY`. In this case, the two chains required to take a look are `Chain KUBE-SEP-TC6HXYYMMLGUSFNZ` and `Chain KUBE-SEP-DIS6NYZTQKZ5ALQS`. Each of them covers two targets, `KUBE-MARK-MASQ` and `DNAT`, for incoming and outgoing traffics between "everywhere" to the endpoint of Pod, `192.168.80.5:80` or `192.168.80.6:80`.

One key point here is that the Service target `KUBE-SVC-GFPAJ7EGCNM4QF4H` exposing its cluster IP to outside world will dispatch the traffic to chain `KUBE-SEP-TC6HXYYMMLGUSFNZ` and `KUBE-SEP-DIS6NYZTQKZ5ALQS` with a statistic mode random probability of 0.5. Both chains have DNAT targets that work on changing the destination IP of the packets to the private subnet one, the one of a specific Pod.

External-to-internal communication

To publish applications in Kubernetes, we can leverage either Kubernetes Service, with type `NodePort` or `LoadBalancer`, or Kubernetes Ingress. For NodePort service, as introduced in previous section, the port number of the node will be a pair with the Service. Like the following diagram, port `30361` on both node 1 and node 2 points to Service A, which dispatch the traffics to Pod1 and a Pod with static probability.

LoadBalancer Service, as you may have learned from the recipe *Working with Services* in `Chapter 13`, *Walking through Kubernetes Concepts*, includes the configurations of NodePort. Moreover, a LoadBalancer Service can work with an external load balancer, providing users with the functionality to integrate load balancing procedures between cloud infrastructure and Kubernetes resource, such as the settings `healthCheckNodePort` and `externalTrafficPolicy`. **Service B** in the following image is a LoadBalancer Service. Internally, **Service B** works the same as **Service A**, relying on **iptables** to redirect packets to Pod; Externally, cloud load balancer doesn't realize Pod or container, it only dispatches the traffic by the number of nodes. No matter which node is chosen to get the request, it would still be able to pass packets to the right Pod:

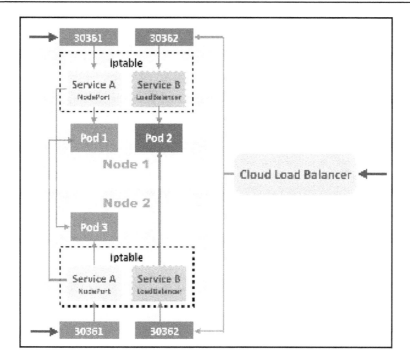

Kubernetes Services with type NodePort and type LoadBalancer

Working with Ingress

Walking through the journey of Kubernetes networking, users get the idea that each Pod and Service has its private IP and corresponding port to listen on request. In practice, developers may deliver the endpoint of service, the private IP or Kubernetes DNS name, for internal clients; or, developers may expose Services externally by type of NodePort or LoadBalancer. Although the endpoint of Service is more stable than Pod, the Services are offered separately, and clients should record the IPs without much meaning to them. In this section, we will introduce `Ingress`, a resource that makes your Services work as a group. More than that, we could easily pack our service union as an API server while we set Ingress rules to recognize the different URLs, and then ingress controller works for passing the request to specific Services based on the rules.

Before we try on Kubernetes Ingress, we should create an ingress controller in cluster. Different from other controllers in `kube-controller-manager` (`https://kubernetes.io/docs/reference/generated/kube-controller-manager/`), ingress controller is run by custom implementation instead of working as a daemon. In the latest Kubernetes version, 1.10, nginx ingress controller is the most stable one and also generally supports many platforms. Check the official documents for the details of deployment: `https://github.com/kubernetes/ingress-nginx/blob/master/README.md`. We will only demonstrate our example on minikube; please see the following information box for the setup of the ingress controller.

Enable Ingress functionality in minikube
Ingress in minikube is an add-on function. Follow these steps to start this feature in your environment:

1. Check if the add-on ingress is enabled or not: Fire the command `minikube addons list` on your terminal. If it is not enabled, means it shows `ingress: disabled`, you should keep follow below steps.
2. Enable ingress: Enter the command `minikube addons enable ingress`, you will see an output like `ingress was successfully enabled`.
3. Check the add-on list again to verify that the last step does work. We expect that the field ingress shows as `enabled`.

Here comes an example to demonstrate how to work with Ingress. We would run up two Deployments and their Services, and an additional Ingress to expose them as a union. In the beginning, we would add a new hostname in the host file of Kubernetes master. It is a simple way for our demonstration. If you work on the production environment, a general use case is that the hostname should be added as a record in the DNS server:

```
// add a dummy hostname in local host file
$ sudo sh -c "echo `minikube ip` happy.k8s.io >> /etc/hosts"
```

Our first Kubernetes Deployment and Service would be `echoserver`, a dummy Service showing server and request information. For the other pair of Deployment and Service, we would reuse the NodePort Service example from the previous section:

```
$ cat echoserver.yaml
apiVersion: apps/v1
```

```
kind: Deployment
metadata:
  name: echoserver-deploy
spec:
  replicas: 2
  selector:
    matchLabels:
      app: echo
  template:
    metadata:
      labels:
        app: echo
    spec:
      containers:
        - name: my-echo
          image: gcr.io/google_containers/echoserver:1.8
---
apiVersion: v1
kind: Service
metadata:
  name: echoserver-svc
spec:
  selector:
    app: echo
  ports:
    - protocol: TCP
      port: 8080
      targetPort: 8080
```

Go ahead and create both set of resources through configuration files:

```
$ kubectl create -f echoserver.yaml
deployment.apps "echoserver-deploy" created
service "echoserver-svc" created
$ kubectl create -f nodeport-deployment.yaml
deployment.apps "nodeport-deploy" created
service "nodeport-svc" created
```

Our first Ingress makes two Services that listen at the separate URLs /nginx and /echoserver, with the hostname happy.k8s.io, the dummy one we added in the local host file. We use annotation rewrite-target to guarantee that traffic redirection starts from root, /. Otherwise, the client may get page not found because of surfing the wrong path. More annotations we may play with are listed at https:// github.com/kubernetes/ingress-nginx/blob/master/docs/user-guide/nginx-configuration/annotations.md:

```
$ cat ingress.yaml
```

```
apiVersion: extensions/v1beta1
kind: Ingress
metadata:
  name: happy-ingress
  annotations:
    nginx.ingress.kubernetes.io/rewrite-target:
spec:
  rules:
    - host: happy.k8s.io
      http:
        paths:
          - path: /nginx
            backend:
              serviceName: nodeport-svc
              servicePort: 8080
          - path: /echoserver
            backend:
              serviceName: echoserver-svc
              servicePort: 8080
```

Then, just create the Ingress and check its information right away:

```
$ kubectl create -f ingress.yaml
ingress.extensions "happy-ingress" created
// "ing" is the abbreviation of "ingress"
$ kubectl describe ing happy-ingress
Name:             happy-ingress
Namespace:        default
Address:
Default backend:  default-http-backend:80 (172.17.0.3:8080)
Rules:
  Host            Path  Backends
  ----            ----  --------
  happy.k8s.io
                  /nginx          nodeport-svc:8080 (<none>)
                  /echoserver     echoserver-svc:8080 (<none>)
Annotations:
  nginx.ingress.kubernetes.io/rewrite-target
Events:
  Type    Reason  Age   From                    Message
  ----    ------  ----  ----                    -------
  Normal  CREATE  14s   ingress-controller      Ingress default/happy-
ingress
```

You may find that there is no IP address in the field of description. It will be attached after the first DNS lookup:

```
// verify the URL set in ingress rules
```

```
$ curl http://happy.k8s.io/nginx
...
<title>Welcome to nginx!</title>
...
$ curl http://happy.k8s.io/echoserver
Hostname: echoserver-deploy-5598f5796f-d8cr4
Pod Information:
    -no pod information available-
Server values:
    server_version=nginx: 1.13.3 - lua: 10008
...
// the IP address would be added after connection
$ kubectl get ing
NAME            HOSTS         ADDRESS        PORTS    AGE
happy-ingress   happy.k8s.io  192.168.64.4   80       1m
```

Although working with Ingress is not as straightforward as other resources, as you have to start an ingress controller implementation by yourself, it still makes our application exposed and flexible. There are many network features coming that are more stable and user friendly. Keep up with the latest updates and have fun!

There's more...

In the last part of external-to-internal communication, we learned about Kubernetes Ingress, the resource that makes services work as a union and dispatches requests to target services. Does any similar idea jump into your mind? It sounds like a microservice, the application structure with several loosely coupled services. A complicated application would be distributed to multiple lighter services. Each service is developed independently while all of them can cover original functions. Numerous working units, such as Pods in Kubernetes, run volatile and can be dynamically scheduled on Services by the system controller. However, such a multi-layered structure increases the complexity of networking and also suffers potential overhead costs.

External load balancers are not aware the existence of Pods; they only balance the workload to hosts. A host without any served Pod running would then redirect the loading to other hosts. This situation comes out of a user's expectation for fair load balancing. Moreover, a Pod may crash accidentally, in which case it is difficult to do failover and complete the request.

To make up the shortcomings, the idea of a service mesh focus on the networking management of microservice was born, dedicated to delivering more reliable and performant communications on orchestration like Kubernetes:

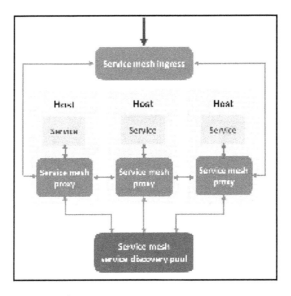

Simpe service mesh structure

The preceding diagram illustrates the main components in a service mesh. They work together to achieve features as follows:

- **Service mesh ingress**: Using applied Ingress rules to decide which Service should handle the incoming requests. It could also be a proxy that is able to check the runtime policies.
- **Service mesh proxy**: Proxies on every node not only direct the packets, but can also be used as an advisory agent reporting the overall status of the Services.
- **Service mesh service discovery pool**: Serving the central management for mesh and pushing controls over proxies. Its responsibility includes procedures of network capability, authentication, failover, and load balancing.

Although well-known service mesh implementations such as Linkerd (`https://linkerd.io`) and Istio (`https://istio.io`) are not mature enough for production usage, the idea of service mesh is not ignorable.

See also

Kubernetes forwards ports based on the overlay network. In this chapter, we also run Pods and Services with nginx. Reviewing the previous sections will help you to understand more about how to manipulate it. Also, look at the following recipes:

- The *Creating an overlay network* and *Running your first container in Kubernetes* recipes in `Chapter 12`, *Building Your Own Kubernetes Cluster*
- The *Working with Pods* and *Working with Services* recipes in `Chapter 13`, *Walking through Kubernetes Concepts*
- The *Moving monolithic to microservices* recipe in `Chapter 16`, *Building Continuous Delivery Pipelines*

Ensuring flexible usage of your containers

Pod, in Kubernetes, means a set of containers, which is also the smallest computing unit. You may have know about the basic usage of Pod in the previous recipes. Pods are usually managed by deployments and exposed by services; they work as applications with this scenario.

In this recipe, we will discuss two new features: **DaemonSets** and **StatefulSets**. These two features can manage Pods with more specific purpose.

Getting ready

What are **Daemon-like Pod** and **Stateful Pod**? The regular Pods in Kubernetes will determine and dispatch to particular Kubernetes nodes based on current node resource usage and your configuration.

However, a **Daemon-like Pod** will be created in each node. For example, if you have three nodes, three daemon-like Pods will be created and deployed to each node. Whenever a new node is added, DaemonSets Pod will be deployed to the new node automatically. Therefore, it will be useful to use node level monitoring or log correction.

On the other hand, a **Stateful Pod** will stick to some resources such as network identifier (Pod name and DNS) and **persistent volume** (**PV**). This also guarantees an order during deployment of multiple Pods and during rolling update. For example, if you deploy a Pod named `my-pod`, and set the scale to **4**, then Pod name will be assigned as `my-pod-0`, `my-pod-1`, `my-pod-2`, and `my-pod-3`. Not only Pod name but also DNS and persistent volume are preserved. For example, when `my-pod-2` is recreated due to resource shortages or application crash, those names and volumes are taken over by a new Pod which is also named `my-pod-2`. It is useful for some cluster based applications such as HDFS and ElasticSearch.

In this recipe, we will demonstrate how to use DaemonSets and StatefulSet; however, to have a better understanding, it should use multiple Kubernetes Nodes environment. To do this, minikube is not ideal, so instead, use either kubeadm/kubespray to create a multiple Node environment.

Using kubeadm or kubespray to set up Kubernetes cluster was described in `Chapter 12`, *Build Your Own Kubernetes Cluster*.

To confirm whether that has **2** or more nodes, type `kubectl get nodes` as follows to check how many nodes you have:

```
//this result indicates you have 2 nodes
$ kubectl get nodes
NAME           STATUS    ROLES         AGE     VERSION
node1          Ready     master, node  6h      v1.10.2
node2          Ready     node          6h      v1.10.2
```

In addition, if you want to execute the StatefulSet recipe later in this chapter, you need a StorageClass to set up a dynamic provisioning environment. It was described in *Working with volumes* section in `Chapter 13`, *Walking through Kubernetes Concepts*.

To check whether `StorageClass` is configured or not, use `kubectl get sc`:

```
//in Google Kubernetes Engine Environment
$ kubectl get sc
NAME                PROVISIONER
standard (default)  kubernetes.io/gce-pd
```

How to do it...

There is no CLI for us to create DaemonSets or StatefulSets. Therefore, we will build these two resource types by writing all the configurations in a YAML file.

Pod as DaemonSets

If a Kubernetes DaemonSet is created, the defined Pod will be deployed in every single node. It is guaranteed that the running containers occupy equal resources in each node. In this scenario, the container usually works as the daemon process.

For example, the following template has an Ubuntu image container that keeps checking its memory usage half a minute at a time:

1. To build it as a DaemonSet, execute the following code block:

```
$ cat daemonset-free.yaml
apiVersion: apps/v1
kind: DaemonSet
metadata:
  name: ram-check
spec:
  selector:
    matchLabels:
      name: checkRam
  template:
    metadata:
      labels:
        name: checkRam
    spec:
      containers:
      - name: ubuntu-free
        image: ubuntu
        command: ["/bin/bash","-c","while true; do free;
sleep 30; done"]
        restartPolicy: Always
```

As the Job, the selector could be ignored, but it takes the values of the labels. We will always configure the restart policy of the DaemonSet as Always, which makes sure that every node has a Pod running.

2. The abbreviation of the `daemonset` is `ds` in `kubectl` command, use this shorter one in the CLI for convenience:

```
$ kubectl create -f daemonset-free.yaml
daemonset.apps "ram-check" created

$ kubectl get ds
NAME         DESIRED   CURRENT   READY      UP-TO-DATE
AVAILABLE    NODE SELECTOR    AGE
ram-check    2            2        2          2          2
<none>           5m
```

3. Here, we have two Pods running in separated nodes. They can still be recognized in the channel of the `pod`:

```
$ kubectl get pods -o wide
NAME                  READY       STATUS    RESTARTS    AGE
IP                    NODE
ram-check-6ldng       1/1         Running   0           9m
10.233.102.130        node1
ram-check-ddpdb       1/1         Running   0           9m
10.233.75.4           node2
```

4. It is good for you to evaluate the result using the subcommand `kubectl logs`:

```
$ kubectl logs ram-check-6ldng
              total         used        free        shared
buff/cache    available
Mem:          3623848       790144      329076      9128
2504628       2416976
Swap:         0             0           0
              total         used        free        shared
buff/cache    available
Mem:          3623848       786304      328028      9160
2509516       2420524
Swap:         0             0           0
              total         used        free        shared
buff/cache    available
Mem:          3623848       786344      323332      9160
2514172       2415944
Swap:         0             0           0
.
.
```

Whenever, you add a Kubernetes node onto your existing cluster, DaemonSets will recognize and deploy a Pod automatically.

5. Let's check again current status of DaemonSets, there are two Pods that have been deployed due to having two nodes as follows:

```
$ kubectl get ds
NAME          DESIRED    CURRENT     READY      UP-TO-DATE
AVAILABLE     NODE SELECTOR     AGE
ram-check     2          2           2          2               2
<none>             14m

$ kubectl get nodes
NAME          STATUS     ROLES          AGE       VERSION
node1         Ready      master,node    6h        v1.10.2
node2         Ready      node           6h        v1.10.2
```

6. So, now we are adding one more node onto the cluster through either `kubespray` or `kubeadm`, based on your setup:

```
$ kubectl get nodes
NAME          STATUS     ROLES          AGE       VERSION
node1         Ready      master,node    6h        v1.10.2
node2         Ready      node           6h        v1.10.2
node3         Ready      node           3m        v1.10.2
```

7. A few moments later, without any operation, the DaemonSet's size become 3 automatically, which aligns to the number of nodes:

```
$ kubectl get ds
NAME          DESIRED    CURRENT     READY      UP-TO-DATE
AVAILABLE     NODE SELECTOR     AGE
ram-check     3          3           3          3               3
<none>             18m


$ kubectl get pods -o wide
NAME              READY      STATUS      RESTARTS   AGE
IP                NODE
ram-check-6ldng   1/1        Running     0          18m
10.233.102.130    node1
ram-check-ddpdb   1/1        Running     0          18m
10.233.75.4       node2
ram-check-dpdmt   1/1        Running     0          3m
10.233.71.0       node3
```

Running a stateful Pod

Let's see another use case. We used Deployments/ReplicaSets to replicate the Pods. It scales well and is easy to maintain and Kubernetes assigns a DNS to the Pod using the Pod's IP address, such as `<Pod IP address>.<namespace>.pod.cluster.local`.

The following example demonstrates how the Pod DNS will be assigned:

```
$ kubectl run apache2 --image=httpd --replicas=3
deployment "apache2" created


//one of Pod has an IP address as 10.52.1.8
$ kubectl get pods -o wide
NAME                         READY      STATUS      RESTARTS    AGE      IP
NODE
apache2-55c684c66b-7m5zq   1/1        Running   0           5s
10.52.1.8   gke-chap7-default-pool-64212da9-z96q
apache2-55c684c66b-cjkcz   1/1        Running   0           1m
10.52.0.7   gke-chap7-default-pool-64212da9-8gzm
apache2-55c684c66b-v78tq   1/1        Running   0           1m
10.52.2.5   gke-chap7-default-pool-64212da9-bbs6


//another Pod can reach to 10-52-1-8.default.pod.cluster.local
$ kubectl exec apache2-55c684c66b-cjkcz -- ping -c 2
10-52-1-8.default.pod.cluster.local
PING 10-52-1-8.default.pod.cluster.local (10.52.1.8): 56 data bytes
64 bytes from 10.52.1.8: icmp_seq=0 ttl=62 time=1.642 ms
64 bytes from 10.52.1.8: icmp_seq=1 ttl=62 time=0.322 ms
--- 10-52-1-8.default.pod.cluster.local ping statistics ---
2 packets transmitted, 2 packets received, 0% packet loss
round-trip min/avg/max/stddev = 0.322/0.982/1.642/0.660 ms
```

However, this DNS entry is not guaranteed to stay in use for this Pod, because the Pod might crash due to an application error or node resource shortage. In such a case, the IP address will possibly be changed:

```
$ kubectl delete pod apache2-55c684c66b-7m5zq
pod "apache2-55c684c66b-7m5zq" deleted


//Pod IP address has been changed to 10.52.0.7
$ kubectl get pods -o wide
NAME                         READY      STATUS      RESTARTS    AGE
IP           NODE
```

```
apache2-55c684c66b-7m5zq   0/1       Terminating   0        1m
<none>     gke-chap7-default-pool-64212da9-z96q
apache2-55c684c66b-cjkcz   1/1       Running       0        2m
10.52.0.7  gke-chap7-default-pool-64212da9-8gzm
apache2-55c684c66b-l9vqt   1/1       Running       0        7s
10.52.1.9  gke-chap7-default-pool-64212da9-z96q
apache2-55c684c66b-v78tq   1/1       Running       0        2m
10.52.2.5  gke-chap7-default-pool-64212da9-bbs6
```

```
//DNS entry also changed
$ kubectl exec apache2-55c684c66b-cjkcz -- ping -c 2
10-52-1-8.default.pod.cluster.local
PING 10-52-1-8.default.pod.cluster.local (10.52.1.8): 56 data bytes
92 bytes from gke-chap7-default-pool-64212da9-z96q.c.kubernetes-
cookbook.internal (192.168.2.4): Destination Host Unreachable
92 bytes from gke-chap7-default-pool-64212da9-z96q.c.kubernetes-
cookbook.internal (192.168.2.4): Destination Host Unreachable
--- 10-52-1-8.default.pod.cluster.local ping statistics ---
2 packets transmitted, 0 packets received, 100% packet loss
```

For some applications, this will cause an issue; for example, if you manage a cluster application that needs to be managed by DNS or IP address. As of the current Kubernetes implementation, IP addresses can't be preserved for Pods . How about we use Kubernetes Service? Service preserves a DNS name. Unfortunately, it's not realistic to create the same amount of service with Pod. In the previous case, create three Services that bind to three Pods one to one.

Kubernetes has a solution for this kind of use case that uses StatefulSet. It preserves not only the DNS but also the persistent volume to keep a bind to the same Pod. Even if Pod is crashed, StatefulSet guarantees the binding of the same DNS and persistent volume to the new Pod. Note that the IP address is not preserved due to the current Kubernetes implementation.

To demonstrate, use **Hadoop Distributed File System** (**HDFS**) to launch one NameNode and three DataNodes. To perform this, use a Docker image from https://hub.docker.com/r/uhopper/hadoop/ that has NameNode and DataNode images. In addition, borrow the YAML configuration files namenode.yaml and datanode.yaml from https://gist.github.com/polvi/34ef498a967de563dc4252a7bfb7d582 and change a little bit:

1. Let's launch a Service and StatefulSet for namenode and datanode:

```
//create NameNode
$ kubectl create -f
https://raw.githubusercontent.com/PacktPublishing/Getting-
```

```
Started-with-
Containerization/master/Chapter14/14-4/namenode.yaml
service "hdfs-namenode-svc" created
statefulset "hdfs-namenode" created

$ kubectl get statefulset
NAME              DESIRED     CURRENT     AGE
hdfs-namenode     1           1           19s

$ kubectl get pods
NAME              READY       STATUS      RESTARTS    AGE
hdfs-namenode-0   1/1         Running     0           26s


//create DataNodes
$ kubectl create -f
https://raw.githubusercontent.com/PacktPublishing/Getting-
Started-with-
Containerization/master/Chapter14/14-4/datanode.yaml
statefulset "hdfs-datanode" created

$ kubectl get statefulset
NAME              DESIRED     CURRENT     AGE
hdfs-datanode     3           3           50s
hdfs-namenode     1           1           5m

$ kubectl get pods
NAME              READY       STATUS      RESTARTS    AGE
hdfs-datanode-0   1/1         Running     0           9m
hdfs-datanode-1   1/1         Running     0           9m
hdfs-datanode-2   1/1         Running     0           9m
hdfs-namenode-0   1/1         Running     0           9m
```

As you can see, the Pod naming convention is `<StatefulSet-name>-`
`<sequence number>`. For example, NameNode Pod's name is `hdfs-`
`namenode-0`. Also DataNode Pod's names are `hdfs-datanode-0`, `hdfs-`
`datanode-1` and `hdfs-datanode-2`.

In addition, both NameNode and DataNode have a service that is
configured as Headless mode (by `spec.clusterIP: None`). Therefore,
you can access these Pods using DNS as `<pod-name>.<service-`
`name>.<namespace>.svc.cluster.local`. In this case, this NameNode
DNS entry could be `hdfs-namenode-0.hdfs-namenode-`
`svc.default.svc.cluster.local`.

2. Let's check what NameNode Pod's IP address is, you can get this using `kubectl get pods -o wide` as follows:

```
//Pod hdfs-namenode-0 has an IP address as 10.52.2.8
$ kubectl get pods hdfs-namenode-0 -o wide
NAME            READY    STATUS    RESTARTS    AGE
IP          NODE
hdfs-namenode-0  1/1      Running   0           9m
10.52.2.8    gke-chapter14-default-pool-97d2e17c-0dr5
```

3. Next, log in (run `/bin/bash`) to one of the DataNodes using `kubectl exec` to resolve this DNS name and check whether the IP address is `10.52.2.8` or not:

```
$ kubectl exec hdfs-datanode-1 -it -- /bin/bash
root@hdfs-datanode-1:/#
root@hdfs-datanode-1:/# ping -c 1 hdfs-namenode-0.hdfs-
namenode-svc.default.svc.cluster.local
PING hdfs-namenode-0.hdfs-namenode-
svc.default.svc.cluster.local (10.52.2.8): 56 data bytes
...
...
```

Looks all good! For demonstration purposes, let's access the HDFS web console to see DataNode's status.

4. To do that, use `kubectl port-forward` to access to the NameNode web port (tcp/`50070`):

```
//check the status by HDFS web console
$ kubectl port-forward hdfs-namenode-0 :50070
Forwarding from 127.0.0.1:60107 -> 50070
```

5. The preceding result indicates that your local machine TCP port `60107` (you result will vary) has been forwarded to NameNode Pod TCP port `50070`. Therefore, use a web browser to access `http://127.0.0.1:60107/` as follows:

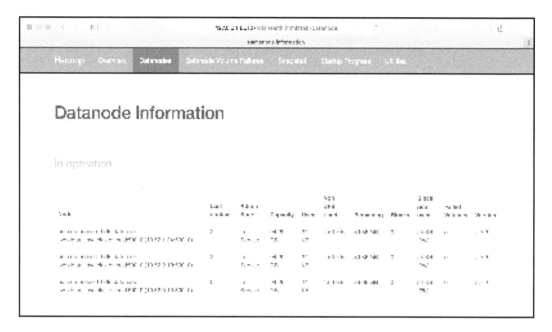

HDFS Web console shows three DataNodes

As you may see, three DataNodes have been registered to NameNode successfully. The DataNodes are also using the Headless Service so that same name convention assigns DNS names for DataNode as well.

How it works...

DaemonSets and StatefulSets; both concepts are similar but behave differently, especially when Pod is crashed. Let's take a look at how it works.

Pod recovery by DaemonSets

DaemonSets keep monitoring every Kubernetes node, so when one of the Pods crashes, DaemonSets recreates it on the same Kubernetes node.

To simulate this, go back to the DaemonSets example and use `kubectl delete pods` to delete an existing Pod from `node1` manually, as follows:

```
$ kubectl delete pod ram-check-6ldng
pod "ram-check-6ldng" deleted

$ kubectl get pods -o wide
NAME                READY    STATUS        RESTARTS    AGE       IP
NODE
ram-check-6ldng     1/1      Terminating   0           29m
10.233.102.132      node1
ram-check-ddpdb     1/1      Running       0           29m
10.233.75.5         node2
ram-check-dpdmt     1/1      Running       0           13m
10.233.71.0         node3

$ kubectl get pods -o wide
NAME                READY    STATUS     RESTARTS    AGE        IP
NODE
ram-check-ddpdb     1/1      Running    0           30m        10.233.75.5
node2
ram-check-dh5hq     1/1      Running    0           24s
10.233.102.135      node1
ram-check-dpdmt     1/1      Running    0           14m        10.233.71.0
node3
```

As you can see, a new Pod has been created automatically to recover the Pod in `node1`. Note that the Pod name has been changed from `ram-check-6ldng` to `ram-check-dh5hq`—it has been assigned a random suffix name. In this use case, Pod name doesn't matter, because we don't use hostname or DNS to manage this application.

Pod recovery by StatefulSet

StatefulSet behaves differently to DaemonSet during Pod recreation. In StatefulSet managed Pods, the Pod name is always consisted to assign an ordered number such as `hdfs-datanode-0`, `hdfs-datanode-1` and `hdfs-datanode-2`, and if you delete one of them, a new Pod will take over the same Pod name.

To simulate this, let's delete one DataNode (`hdfs-datanode-1`) to see how StatefulSet recreates a Pod:

```
$ kubectl get pods
NAME                READY   STATUS    RESTARTS   AGE
hdfs-datanode-0     1/1     Running   0          3m
hdfs-datanode-1     1/1     Running   0          2m
hdfs-datanode-2     1/1     Running   0          2m
hdfs-namenode-0     1/1     Running   0          23m

//delete DataNode-1
$ kubectl delete pod hdfs-datanode-1
pod "hdfs-datanode-1" deleted

//DataNode-1 is Terminating
$ kubectl get pods
NAME                READY   STATUS        RESTARTS   AGE
hdfs-datanode-0     1/1     Running       0          3m
hdfs-datanode-1     1/1     Terminating   0          3m
hdfs-datanode-2     1/1     Running       0          2m
hdfs-namenode-0     1/1     Running       0          23m

//DataNode-1 is recreating automatically by statefulset
$ kubectl get pods
NAME                READY   STATUS              RESTARTS   AGE
hdfs-datanode-0     1/1     Running             0          4m
hdfs-datanode-1     0/1     ContainerCreating   0          16s
hdfs-datanode-2     1/1     Running             0          3m
hdfs-namenode-0     1/1     Running             0          24m

//DataNode-1 is recovered
$ kubectl get pods
NAME                READY   STATUS    RESTARTS   AGE
hdfs-datanode-0     1/1     Running   0          4m
hdfs-datanode-1     1/1     Running   0          22s
hdfs-datanode-2     1/1     Running   0          3m
hdfs-namenode-0     1/1     Running   0          24m
```

As you see, the same Pod name (`hdfs-datanode-1`) has been assigned. Approximately after 10 minutes (due to HDFS's heart beat interval), HDFS web console shows that the old Pod has been marked as dead and the new Pod has the in service state, shown as follows:

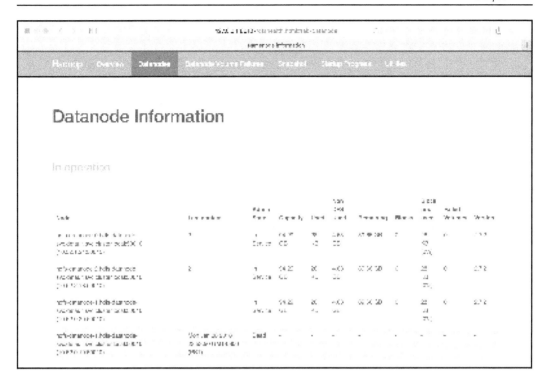

Status when one DataNode is dead

Note that this is not a perfect ideal case for HDFS, because DataNode-1 lost data and expects to re-sync from other DataNodes. If the data size is bigger, it may take a long time to complete re-sync.

Fortunately, StatefulSets has an capability that preserve a persistent volume while replacing a Pod. Let's see how HDFS DataNode can preserve data during Pod recreation.

There's more...

StatefulSet with persistent volume; it requires a `StorageClass` that provisions a volume dynamically. Because each Pod is created by StatefulSets, it will create a **persistent volume claim** (**PVC**) with a different identifier. If your StatefulSets specify a static name of PVC, there will be trouble if multiple Pods try to attach the same PVC.

If you have `StorageClass` on your cluster, update `datanode.yaml` to add `spec.volumeClaimTemplates` as follows:

```
$ curl
https://raw.githubusercontent.com/PacktPublishing/Getting-Started-with
-Containerization/master/Chapter14/14-4/datanode-pv.yaml
...
  volumeClaimTemplates:
  - metadata:
      name: hdfs-data
    spec:
      accessModes: [ "ReadWriteOnce" ]
      resources:
        requests:
          storage: 10Gi
```

This tells Kubernetes to create a PVC and PV when a new Pod is created by StatefulSet. So, that Pod template (`spec.template.spec.containers.volumeMounts`) should specify `hdfs-data`, as follows:

```
$ curl
https://raw.githubusercontent.com/PacktPublishing/Getting-Started-with
-Containerization/master/Chapter14/14-4/datanode-pv.yaml
...
          volumeMounts:
          - mountPath: /hadoop/dfs/data
            name: hdfs-data
```

Let's recreate HDFS cluster again:

```
//delete DataNodes
$ kubectl delete -f
https://raw.githubusercontent.com/PacktPublishing/Getting-Started-with
-Containerization/master/Chapter14/14-4/datanode.yaml
service "hdfs-datanode-svc" deleted
statefulset "hdfs-datanode" deleted

//delete NameNode
$ kubectl delete -f
https://raw.githubusercontent.com/PacktPublishing/Getting-Started-with
-Containerization/master/Chapter14/14-4/namenode.yaml
service "hdfs-namenode-svc" deleted
statefulset "hdfs-namenode" deleted


//create NameNode again
$ kubectl create -f
```

```
https://raw.githubusercontent.com/PacktPublishing/Getting-Started-with
-Containerization/master/Chapter14/14-4/namenode.yaml
service "hdfs-namenode-svc" created
statefulset "hdfs-namenode" created

//create DataNode which uses Persistent Volume (datanode-pv.yaml)
$ kubectl create -f
https://raw.githubusercontent.com/PacktPublishing/Getting-Started-with
-Containerization/master/Chapter14/14-4/datanode-pv.yaml
service "hdfs-datanode-svc" created
statefulset "hdfs-datanode" created

//3 PVC has been created automatically
$ kubectl get pvc
NAME STATUS VOLUME CAPACITY ACCESS MODES STORAGECLASS AGE
hdfs-data-hdfs-datanode-0 Bound pvc-bc79975d-f5bd-11e7-
ac7a-42010a8a00ef 10Gi RWO standard 53s
hdfs-data-hdfs-datanode-1 Bound pvc-c753a336-f5bd-11e7-
ac7a-42010a8a00ef 10Gi RWO standard 35s
hdfs-data-hdfs-datanode-2 Bound pvc-d1e10587-f5bd-11e7-
ac7a-42010a8a00ef 10Gi RWO standard 17s
```

To demonstrate, use `kubectl exec` to access the NameNode, then copy some dummy files to HDFS:

```
$ kubectl exec -it hdfs-namenode-0 -- /bin/bash
root@hdfs-namenode-0:/# hadoop fs -put /lib/x86_64-linux-gnu/* /
root@hdfs-namenode-0:/# exit
command terminated with exit code 255

//delete DataNode-1
$ kubectl delete pod hdfs-datanode-1
pod "hdfs-datanode-1" deleted
```

At this moment, `DataNode-1` is restarting, as shown in the following image. However, the data directory of `DataNode-1` is kept by PVC as `hdfs-data-hdfs-datanode-1`. The new Pod `hdfs-datanode-1` will take over this PVC again:

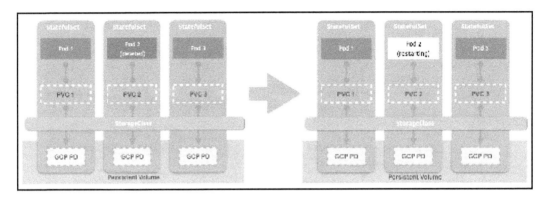

StatefulSet keeps PVC/PV while restarting

Therefore, when you access HDFS after `hdfs-datanode-1` has recovered, you don't see any data loss or re-sync processes:

```
$ kubectl exec -it hdfs-namenode-0 -- /bin/bash
root@hdfs-namenode-0:/# hdfs fsck /
Connecting to namenode via
http://hdfs-namenode-0.hdfs-namenode-svc.default.svc.cluster.local:500
70/fsck?ugi=root&path=%2F
FSCK started by root (auth:SIMPLE) from /10.52.1.13 for path / at Wed
Jan 10 04:32:30 UTC 2018
.................................................................
...................................
...........................................................Statu
s: HEALTHY
 Total size: 22045160 B
 Total dirs: 2
 Total files: 165
 Total symlinks: 0
 Total blocks (validated): 165 (avg. block size 133607 B)
 Minimally replicated blocks: 165 (100.0 %)
 Over-replicated blocks: 0 (0.0 %)
 Under-replicated blocks: 0 (0.0 %)
 Mis-replicated blocks: 0 (0.0 %)
 Default replication factor: 3
 Average block replication: 3.0
 Corrupt blocks: 0
 Missing replicas: 0 (0.0 %)
 Number of data-nodes: 3
```

```
 Number of racks: 1
FSCK ended at Wed Jan 10 04:32:30 UTC 2018 in 85 milliseconds


The filesystem under path '/' is HEALTHY
```

As you see, the Pod and PV pair is fully managed by StatefulSets. It is convenient if you want to scale more HDFS DataNode using just the kubectl scale command to make it double or hundreds—whatever you need:

```
//make double size of HDFS DataNodes
$ kubectl scale statefulset hdfs-datanode --replicas=6
statefulset "hdfs-datanode" scaled

$ kubectl get pods
NAME READY STATUS RESTARTS AGE
hdfs-datanode-0 1/1 Running 0 20m
hdfs-datanode-1 1/1 Running 0 13m
hdfs-datanode-2 1/1 Running 0 20m
hdfs-datanode-3 1/1 Running 0 56s
hdfs-datanode-4 1/1 Running 0 38s
hdfs-datanode-5 1/1 Running 0 21s
hdfs-namenode-0 1/1 Running 0 21m

$ kubectl get pvc
NAME STATUS VOLUME CAPACITY ACCESS MODES STORAGECLASS AGE
hdfs-data-hdfs-datanode-0 Bound pvc-bc79975d-f5bd-11e7-
ac7a-42010a8a00ef 10Gi RWO standard 21m
hdfs-data-hdfs-datanode-1 Bound pvc-c753a336-f5bd-11e7-
ac7a-42010a8a00ef 10Gi RWO standard 21m
hdfs-data-hdfs-datanode-2 Bound pvc-d1e10587-f5bd-11e7-
ac7a-42010a8a00ef 10Gi RWO standard 21m
hdfs-data-hdfs-datanode-3 Bound pvc-888b6e0d-f5c0-11e7-
ac7a-42010a8a00ef 10Gi RWO standard 1m
hdfs-data-hdfs-datanode-4 Bound pvc-932e6148-f5c0-11e7-
ac7a-42010a8a00ef 10Gi RWO standard 1m
hdfs-data-hdfs-datanode-5 Bound pvc-9dd71bf5-f5c0-11e7-
ac7a-42010a8a00ef 10Gi RWO standard 1m
```

You can also use PV to NameNode to persist metadata. However, kubectl scale does not work well due to HDFS architecture. In order to have high availability or scale out HDFS NameNode, please visit the HDFS Federation document at : https://hadoop.apache. org/docs/stable/hadoop-project-dist/hadoop-hdfs/Federation. html.

See also

In this recipe, we went deeply into Kubernetes Pod management through DaemonSets and StatefulSet. It manages Pod in a particular way, such as Pod per node and consistent Pod names. It is useful when the Deployments/ReplicaSets stateless Pod management style can't cover your application use cases. For further information, consider the following:

- The *Working with Pods* recipe in `Chapter 12`, *Walking through Kubernetes Concepts*
- Working with configuration files

Submitting Jobs on Kubernetes

Your container application is designed not only for daemon processes such as nginx, but also for some batch Jobs which eventually exit when the task is complete. Kubernetes supports this scenario; you can submit a container as a Job and Kubernetes will dispatch to an appropriate node and execute your Job.

In this recipe, we will discuss two new features: **Jobs** and **CronJob**. These two features can make another usage of Pods to utilize your resources.

Getting ready

Since Kubernetes version 1.2, Kubernetes Jobs has been introduced as a stable feature (`apiVersion: batch/v1`). In addition, CronJob is a beta feature (`apiVersion: batch/v1beta1`) as of Kubernetes version 1.10.

Both work well on **minikube,** which was introduced at `Chapter 12`, *Building Your Own Kubernetes Cluster.* Therefore, this recipe will use minikube version 0.24.1.

How to do it...

When submitting a Job to Kubernetes, you have three types of Job that you can define:

- Single Job
- Repeat Job
- Parallel Job

Pod as a single Job

A Job-like Pod is suitable for testing your containers, which can be used for unit test or integration test; alternatively, it can be used for batch programs:

1. In the following example, we will write a Job template to check the packages installed in image Ubuntu:

```
$ cat job-dpkg.yaml
apiVersion: batch/v1
kind: Job
metadata:
  name: package-check
spec:
  template:
    spec:
      containers:
      - name: package-check
        image: ubuntu
        command: ["dpkg-query", "-l"]
      restartPolicy: Never
```

Note that restart policy for Pods created in a Job should be set to Never or OnFailure, since a Job goes to termination once it is completed successfully.

2. Now, you are ready to create a job using your template:

```
$ kubectl create -f job-dpkg.yaml
job.batch "package-check" created
```

3. After creating a `job` object, it is possible to verify the status of both the Pod and Job:

```
$ kubectl get jobs
NAME            DESIRED    SUCCESSFUL    AGE
package-check   1          1             26s
```

4. This result indicates that Job is already done, executed (by `SUCCESSFUL = 1`) in `26` seconds. In this case, Pod has already disappeared:

```
$ kubectl get pods
No resources found, use --show-all to see completed
objects.
```

5. As you can see, the `kubectl` command hints to us that we can use `--show-all` or `-a` option to find the completed Pod, as follows:

```
$ kubectl get pods --show-all
NAME                 READY      STATUS        RESTARTS    AGE
package-check-hmjxj  0/1        Completed     0           3m
```

Here you go. So why does the `Completed` Pod object remain? Because you may want to see the result after your program has ended. You will find that a Pod is booting up for handling this task. This Pod is going to be stopped very soon at the end of the process.

6. Use the subcommand `kubectl logs` to get the result:

```
$ kubectl logs package-check-hmjxj
Desired=Unknown/Install/Remove/Purge/Hold
| Status=Not/Inst/Conf-files/Unpacked/halF-conf/Half-
inst/trig-aWait/Trig-pend
|/ Err?=(none)/Reinst-required (Status,Err: uppercase=bad)
||/ Name                      Version
Architecture Description
+++-=========================-
==============================-=============-
============================================================
============
ii  adduser                   3.113+nmu3ubuntu4
all           add and remove users and groups
ii  apt                       1.2.24
amd64         commandline package manager
ii  base-files                9.4ubuntu4.5
amd64         Debian base system miscellaneous files
ii  base-passwd               3.5.39
amd64         Debian base system master password and group
```

```
files
ii   bash                          4.3-14ubuntu1.2
amd64          GNU Bourne Again SHell
.
.
.
```

7. Please go ahead and check the `job package-check` using the subcommand `kubectl describe`; the confirmation for Pod completion and other messages are shown as system information:

```
$ kubectl describe job package-check
Name:            package-check
Namespace:       default
Selector:        controller-uid=9dfd1857-f5d1-11e7-8233-
ae782244bd54
Labels:          controller-uid=9dfd1857-f5d1-11e7-8233-
ae782244bd54
                 job-name=package-check
Annotations:     <none>
Parallelism:     1
Completions:     1
Start Time:      Tue, 09 Jan 2018 22:43:50 -0800
Pods Statuses:   0 Running / 1 Succeeded / 0 Failed
.
.
.
```

8. Later, to remove the `job` you just created, delete it with the name. This also removes the completed Pod as well:

```
$ kubectl delete jobs package-check
job.batch "package-check" deleted

$ kubectl get pods --show-all
No resources found.
```

Create a repeatable Job

Users can also decide the number of tasks that should be finished in a single Job. It is helpful to solve some random and sampling problems. Let's try it on the same template in the previous example:

1. Add the `spec.completions` item to indicate the Pod number:

```
$ cat job-dpkg-repeat.yaml
apiVersion: batch/v1
kind: Job
metadata:
  name: package-check
spec:
  completions: 3
  template:
    spec:
      containers:
      - name: package-check
        image: ubuntu
        command: ["dpkg-query", "-l"]
      restartPolicy: Never
```

2. After creating this Job, check how the Pod looks with the subcommand `kubectl describe`:

```
$ kubectl create -f job-dpkg-repeat.yaml
job.batch "package-check" created

$ kubectl describe jobs package-check
Name:          package-check
Namespace:     default
...
...
Annotations:   <none>
Parallelism:   1
Completions:   3
Start Time:    Tue, 09 Jan 2018 22:58:09 -0800
Pods Statuses: 0 Running / 3 Succeeded / 0 Failed
...
...
Events:
  Type    Reason            Age   From             Message
  ----    ------            ----  ----             -------
  Normal  SuccessfulCreate  42s   job-controller   Created
pod: package-check-f72wk
  Normal  SuccessfulCreate  32s   job-controller   Created
```

```
pod: package-check-2mnw8
  Normal  SuccessfulCreate  27s   job-controller  Created
pod: package-check-whbr6
```

As you can see, three Pods are created to complete this Job. This is useful if you need to run your program repeatedly at particular times. However, as you may have noticed from the `Age` column in preceding result, these Pods ran sequentially, one by one. This means that the 2nd Job was started after the 1st Job was completed, and the 3rd Job was started after the 2nd Job was completed.

Create a parallel Job

If your batch Job doesn't have a state or dependency between Jobs, you may consider submitting Jobs in parallel. Similar to the `spec.completions` parameter, the Job template has a `spec.parallelism` parameter to specify how many Jobs you want to run in parallel:

1. Re-use a repeatable Job but change it to specify `spec.parallelism: 3` as follows:

```
$ cat job-dpkg-parallel.yaml
apiVersion: batch/v1
kind: Job
metadata:
  name: package-check
spec:
  parallelism: 3
  template:
    spec:
      containers:
      - name: package-check
        image: ubuntu
        command: ["dpkg-query", "-l"]
      restartPolicy: Never
```

2. The result is similar to `spec.completions=3`, which made 3 Pods to run your application:

```
$ kubectl get pods --show-all
NAME                   READY   STATUS      RESTARTS   AGE
package-check-5jhr8    0/1     Completed   0          1m
package-check-5zlmx    0/1     Completed   0          1m
package-check-glkpc    0/1     Completed   0          1m
```

3. However, if you see an `Age` column through the `kubectl describe` command, it indicates that 3 Pods ran at the same time:

```
$ kubectl describe jobs package-check
Name:           package-check
Namespace:      default
Selector:       controller-uid=de41164e-f5d6-11e7-8233-
ae782244bd54
Labels:         controller-uid=de41164e-f5d6-11e7-8233-
ae782244bd54

                job-name=package-check
Annotations:    <none>
Parallelism:    3
Completions:    <unset>
...
Events:
  Type      Reason          Age   From            Message
  ----      ------          ----  ----            -------
  Normal    SuccessfulCreate  24s   job-controller  Created
pod: package-check-5jhr8
  Normal    SuccessfulCreate  24s   job-controller  Created
pod: package-check-glkpc
  Normal    SuccessfulCreate  24s   job-controller  Created
pod: package-check-5zlmx
```

In this setting, Kubernetes can dispatch to an available node to run your application and that easily scale your Jobs. It is useful if you want to run something like a worker application to distribute a bunch of Pods to different nodes.

Schedule to run Job using CronJob

If you are familiar with **UNIX CronJob** or **Java Quartz** (http://www.quartz-scheduler.org), Kubernetes CronJob is a very straightforward tool that you can define a particular timing to run your Kubernetes Job repeatedly.

The scheduling format is very simple; it specifies the following five items:

- Minutes (0 – 59)
- Hours (0 – 23)
- Day of Month (1 – 31)
- Month (1 – 12)
- Day of week (0: Sunday – 6: Saturday)

For example, if you want to run your Job only at 9:00am on November 12th, every year, to send a birthday greeting to me :-), the schedule format could be `0 9 12 11 *`.

You may also use slash (/) to specify a step value; a `run every 5 minutes` interval for the previous Job example would have the following schedule format: `*/5 * * * *`.

In addition, there is an optional parameter, `spec.concurrencyPolicy`, that you can specify a behavior if the previous Job is not finished but the next Job schedule is approaching, to determine how the next Job runs. You can set either:

- **Allow**: Allow execution of the next Job
- **Forbid**: Skip execution of the next Job
- **Replace**: Delete the current Job, then execute the next Job

If you set as `Allow`, there might be a potential risk of accumulating some unfinished Jobs in the Kubernetes cluster. Therefore, during the testing phase, you should set either `Forbid` or `Replace` to monitor Job execution and completion:

```
$ cat cron-job.yaml
apiVersion: batch/v1beta1
kind: CronJob
metadata:
  name: package-check
spec:
  schedule: "*/5 * * * *"
  concurrencyPolicy: "Forbid"
  jobTemplate:
    spec:
      template:
        spec:
          containers:
          - name: package-check
            image: ubuntu
            command: ["dpkg-query", "-l"]
```

```
        restartPolicy: Never

//create CronJob
$ kubectl create -f cron-job.yaml
cronjob.batch "package-check" created

$ kubectl get cronjob
NAME            SCHEDULE      SUSPEND   ACTIVE    LAST SCHEDULE   AGE
package-check   */5 * * * *   False     0         <none>
```

After a few moments, the Job will be triggered by your desired timing—in this case, every 5 minutes. You may then see the Job entry through the kubectl get jobs and kubectl get pods -a commands, as follows:

```
//around 9 minutes later, 2 jobs have been submitted already
$ kubectl get jobs
NAME                        DESIRED   SUCCESSFUL   AGE
package-check-1515571800    1         1            7m
package-check-1515572100    1         1            2m


//correspond Pod are remain and find by -a option
$ kubectl get pods -a
NAME                              READY   STATUS      RESTARTS   AGE
package-check-1515571800-jbzbr    0/1     Completed   0          7m
package-check-1515572100-bp5fz    0/1     Completed   0          2m
```

CronJob will keep remaining until you delete; this means that, every 5 minutes, CronJob will create a new Job entry and related Pods will also keep getting created. This will impact the consumption of Kubernetes resources. Therefore, by default, CronJob will keep up to 3 successful Jobs (by spec.successfulJobsHistoryLimit) and one failed Job (by spec.failedJobsHistoryLimit). You can change these parameters based on your requirements.

Overall, CronJob supplement allows Jobs to automatically to run in your application with the desired timing. You can utilize CronJob to run some report generation Jobs, daily or weekly batch Jobs, and so on.

How it works...

Although Jobs and CronJob are the special utilities of Pods, the Kubernetes system has different management systems between them and Pods.

For Job, its selector cannot point to an existing pod. It is a bad idea to take a Pod controlled by the deployment/ReplicaSets as a Job. The deployment/ReplicaSets have a desired number of Pods running, which is against Job's ideal situation: Pods should be deleted once they finish their tasks. The Pod in the Deployments/ReplicaSets won't reach the state of end.

See also

In this recipe, we executed Jobs and CronJob, demonstrating another usage of Kubernetes Pod that has a completion state. Even once a Pod is completed, Kubernetes can preserve the logs and Pod object so that you can retrieve the result easily. For further information, consider:

- The *Working with Pods* recipe in `Chapter 13`, *Walking through Kubernetes Concepts*
- *Working with configuration files*

Working with configuration files

Kubernetes supports two different file formats, *YAML* and *JSON*. Each format can describe the same function of Kubernetes.

Getting ready

Before we study how to write a Kubernetes configuration file, learning how to write a correct template format is important. We can learn the standard format of both YAML and JSON from their official websites.

YAML

The YAML format is very simple, with few syntax rules; therefore, it is easy to read and write, even for users. To know more about YAML, you can refer to the following website link: `http://www.yaml.org/spec/1.2/spec.html`. The following example uses the YAML format to set up the `nginx` Pod:

```
$ cat nginx-pod.yaml
apiVersion: v1
kind: Pod
metadata:
  name: my-nginx
  labels:
    env: dev
spec:
  containers:
  - name: my-nginx
    image: nginx
    ports:
    - containerPort: 80
```

JSON

The JSON format is also simple and easy to read for users, but more program-friendly. Because it has data types (number, string, Boolean, and object), it is popular to exchange the data between systems. Technically, YAML is a superset of JSON, so JSON is a valid YAML, but not the other way around. To know more about JSON, you can refer to the following website link: `http://json.org/`.

The following example of the Pod is the same as the preceding YAML format, but using the JSON format:

```
$ cat nginx-pod.json
{
  "apiVersion": "v1",
  "kind": "Pod",
  "metadata": {
      "name": "my-nginx",
      "labels": {
              "env": "dev"
      }
  },
  "spec": {
    "containers": [
      {
```

```
            "name": "my-nginx",
            "image": "nginx",
            "ports": [
              {
                "containerPort": 80
              }
            ]
          }
        ]
      }
    }
```

How to do it...

Kubernetes has a schema that is defined using a verify configuration format; schema can be generated after the first instance of running the subcommand create with a configuration file. The cached schema will be stored under the .kube/cache/discovery/<SERVICE_IP>_<PORT>, based on the version of API server you run:

```
// create the resource by either YAML or JSON file introduced before
$ kubectl create -f nginx-pod.yaml
// or
$ kubectl create -f nginx-pod.json
// as an example of v1.10.0, the content of schema directory may look
like following
// you would have different endpoint of server
ll ~/.kube/cache/discovery/192.168.99.100_8443/
total 76
drwxr-xr-x 18 nosus nosus 4096 May 6 10:10 ./
drwxr-xr-x 4 nosus nosus 4096 May 6 10:00 ../
drwxr-xr-x 3 nosus nosus 4096 May 6 10:00
admissionregistration.k8s.io/
drwxr-xr-x 3 nosus nosus 4096 May 6 10:00 apiextensions.k8s.io/
drwxr-xr-x 4 nosus nosus 4096 May 6 10:00 apiregistration.k8s.io/
drwxr-xr-x 5 nosus nosus 4096 May 6 10:00 apps/
drwxr-xr-x 4 nosus nosus 4096 May 6 10:00 authentication.k8s.io/
drwxr-xr-x 4 nosus nosus 4096 May 6 10:00 authorization.k8s.io/
drwxr-xr-x 4 nosus nosus 4096 May 6 10:00 autoscaling/
drwxr-xr-x 4 nosus nosus 4096 May 6 10:00 batch/
drwxr-xr-x 3 nosus nosus 4096 May 6 10:00 certificates.k8s.io/
drwxr-xr-x 3 nosus nosus 4096 May 6 10:00 events.k8s.io/
drwxr-xr-x 3 nosus nosus 4096 May 6 10:00 extensions/
drwxr-xr-x 3 nosus nosus 4096 May 6 10:00 networking.k8s.io/
drwxr-xr-x 3 nosus nosus 4096 May 6 10:00 policy/
drwxr-xr-x 4 nosus nosus 4096 May 6 10:00 rbac.authorization.k8s.io/
```

```
-rwxr-xr-x 1 nosus nosus 3898 May 6 10:10 servergroups.json*
drwxr-xr-x 4 nosus nosus 4096 May 6 10:00 storage.k8s.io/
drwxr-xr-x 2 nosus nosus 4096 May 6 10:10 v1/
```

Each directory listed represents an API category. You will see a file named `serverresources.json` under the last layer of each directory, which clearly defines every resource covered by this API category. However, there are some alternative and easier ways to check the schema. From the website of Kubernetes, we can get any details of how to write a configuration file of specific resources. Go ahead and check the official API documentation of the latest version: `https://kubernetes.io/docs/reference/generated/kubernetes-api/v1.10/`. In the webpage, there are three panels: from left to right, they are the resource list, description, and the input and output of HTTP requests or the command kubectl. Taking Deployment as an example, you may click **Deployment v1 app** at the resource list, the leftmost panel, and the following screenshot will show up:

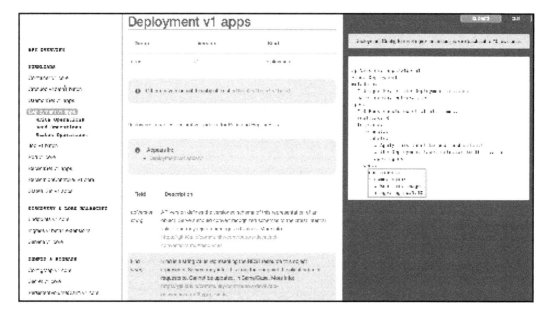

Documentation of Kubernetes Deployment API

But, how do we know the details of setting the container part at the marked place on the preceding image? In the field part of object description, there are two values. The first one, like **apiVersion**, means the name, and the second one, like **string**, is the type. Type could be integer, string, array, or the other resource object. Therefore, for searching the containers configuration of deployment, we need to know the structure of layers of objects. First, according to the example configuration file on web page, the layer of objects to containers is `spec.template.spec.containers`. So, start by clicking the hyperlink **spec DeploymentSpec** under Deployment's fields, which is the type of resource object, and go searching hierarchically. Finally, you can find the details listed on this page: `https://kubernetes.io/docs/reference/generated/kubernetes-api/v1.10/#container-v1-core`.

Solution for tracing the configuration of containers of Deployment
Here comes the solution for the preceding example:

- Click **spec DeploymentSpec**
- Click **template PodTemplateSpec**
- Click **spec PodSpec**
- Click **containers Container array**

Now you got it!

Taking a careful look at the definition of container configuration. The following are some common descriptions you should pay attention to:

- **Type**: The user should always set the corresponding type for an item.
- **Optional or not**: Some items are indicated as optional, which means not necessary, and can be applied as a default value, or not set if you don't specify it.
- **Cannot be updated**: If the item is indicated as failed to be updated, it is fixed when the resource is created. You need to recreate a new one instead of updating it.
- **Read-only**: Some of the items are indicated as `read-only`, such as UID. Kubernetes generates these items. If you specify this in the configuration file, it will be ignored.

Another method for checking the schema is through swagger UI. Kubernetes uses swagger (`https://swagger.io/`) and OpenAPI (`https://www.openapis.org`) to generate the REST API. Nevertheless, the web console for swagger is by default disabled in the API server. To enable the swagger UI of your own Kubernetes API server, just add the flag `--enable-swagger-ui=ture` when you start the API server. Then, by accessing the endpoint `https://<KUBERNETES_MASTER>:<API_SERVER_PORT>/swagger-ui`, you can successfully browse the API document through the web console:

The swagger web console of Kubernetes API

How it works...

Let's introduce some necessary items in configuration files for creating Pod, Deployment, and Service.

Pod

Item	Type	Example
apiVersion	String	v1
kind	String	Pod
metadata.name	String	my-nginx-pod
spec	v1.PodSpec	
v1.PodSpec.containers	Array[v1.Container]	
v1.Container.name	String	my-nginx
v1.Container.image	String	nginx

Deployment

Item	Type	Example
apiVersion	String	apps/v1beta1
kind	String	Deployment
metadata.name	String	my-nginx-deploy
spec	v1.DeploymentSpec	
v1.DeploymentSpec.template	v1.PodTemplateSpec	
v1.PodTemplateSpec.metadata.labels	Map of string	env: test
v1.PodTemplateSpec.spec	v1.PodSpec	my-nginx
v1.PodSpec.containers	Array[v1.Container]	As same as Pod

Service

Item	Type	Example
apiVersion	String	v1
kind	String	Service
metadata.name	String	my-nginx-svc
spec	v1.ServiceSpec	
v1.ServiceSpec.selector	Map of string	env: test
v1.ServiceSpec.ports	Array[v1.ServicePort]	
v1.ServicePort.protocol	String	TCP
v1.ServicePort.port	Integer	80

Please check the code bundle file `minimal-conf-resource.yaml` to find these three resources with minimal configuration.

See also

This recipe described how to find and understand a configuration syntax. Kubernetes has some detailed options to define containers and components. For more details, the following recipes will describe how to define Pods, Deployments, and Services:

- The *Working with Pods*, *Deployment API*, and *Working with Services* recipes in `Chapter 13`, *Walking through Kubernetes Concepts*

15
Building High-Availability Clusters

In this chapter, we will cover the following recipes:

- Clustering etcd
- Building multiple masters

Introduction

Avoiding a single point of failure is a concept we need to always keep in mind. In this chapter, you will learn how to build components in Kubernetes with high availability. We will also go through the steps to build a three-node etcd cluster and masters with multinodes.

Clustering etcd

etcd stores network information and states in Kubernetes. Any data loss could be crucial. Clustering etcd is strongly recommended in a production environment. etcd comes with support for clustering; a cluster of N members can tolerate up to (N-1)/2 failures. Typically, there are three mechanisms for creating an etcd cluster. They are as follows:

- Static
- etcd discovery
- DNS discovery

Static is a simple way to bootstrap an etcd cluster if we have all etcd members provisioned before starting. However, it's more common if we use an existing etcd cluster to bootstrap a new member. Then, the discovery method comes into play. The discovery service uses an existing cluster to bootstrap itself. It allows a new member in an etcd cluster to find other existing members. In this recipe, we will discuss how to bootstrap an etcd cluster via static and etcd discovery manually.

We learned how to use kubeadm and kubespray in `Chapter 12`, *Building Your Own Kubernetes Cluster*. At the time of writing, HA work in kubeadm is still in progress. Regularly backing up your etcd node is recommended in the official documentation. The other tool we introduced, kubespray, on the other hand, supports multi-nodes etcd natively. In this chapter, we'll also describe how to configure etcd in kubespray.

Getting ready

Before we learn a more flexible way to set up an etcd cluster, we should know etcd comes with two major versions so far, which are v2 and v3. etcd3 is a newer version that aims to be more stable, efficient, and reliable. Here is a simple comparison to introduce the major differences in their implementation:

	etcd2	etcd3
Protocol	http	gRPC
Key expiration	TTL mechanism	Leases
Watchers	Long polling over HTTP	Via a bidirectional gRPC stream

etcd3 aims to be the next generation of etcd2 . etcd3 supports the gRPC protocol by default. gRPC uses HTTP2, which allows multiple RPC streams over a TCP connection. In etcd2, however, a HTTP request must establish a connection in every request it makes. For dealing with key expiration, in etcd2, a TTL attaches to a key; the client should periodically refresh the keys to see if any keys have expired. This will establish lots of connections.

In etcd3, the lease concept was introduced. A lease can attach multiple keys; when a lease expires, it'll delete all attached keys. For the watcher, the etcd2 client creates long polling over HTTP—this means a TCP connection is opened per watch. However, etcd3 uses bidirectional gRPC stream implementation, which allows multiple steams to share the same connection.

Although etcd3 is preferred. However, some deployments still use etcd2. We'll still introduce how to use those tools to achieve clustering, since data migration in etcd is well-documented and smooth. For more information, please refer to the upgrade migration steps at `https://coreos.com/blog/migrating-applications-etcd-v3.html`.

Before we start building an etcd cluster, we have to decide how many members we need. How big the etcd cluster should be really depends on the environment you want to create. In the production environment, at least three members are recommended. Then, the cluster can tolerate at least one permanent failure. In this recipe, we will use three members as an example of a development environment:

Name/hostname	IP address
ip-172-31-3-80	172.31.3.80
ip-172-31-14-133	172.31.14.133
ip-172-31-13-239	172.31.13.239

Secondly, the etcd service requires `port 2379` (`4001` for legacy uses) for etcd client communication and `port 2380` for peer communication. These ports have to be exposed in your environment.

How to do it...

There are plenty of ways to provision an etcd cluster. Normally, you'll use kubespray, kops (in AWS), or other provisioning tools.

Here, we'll simply show you how to perform a manual install. It's fairly easy as well:

```
// etcd installation script
$ cat install-etcd.sh
ETCD_VER=v3.3.0

# ${DOWNLOAD_URL} could be ${GOOGLE_URL} or ${GITHUB_URL}
GOOGLE_URL=https://storage.googleapis.com/etcd
GITHUB_URL=https://github.com/coreos/etcd/releases/download
DOWNLOAD_URL=${GOOGLE_URL}

# delete tmp files
rm -f /tmp/etcd-${ETCD_VER}-linux-amd64.tar.gz
rm -rf /tmp/etcd && rm -rf /etc/etcd && mkdir -p /etc/etcd

curl -L ${DOWNLOAD_URL}/${ETCD_VER}/etcd-${ETCD_VER}-linux-amd64.tar.gz -o /tmp/etcd-${ETCD_VER}-linux-amd64.tar.gz
```

```
tar xzvf /tmp/etcd-${ETCD_VER}-linux-amd64.tar.gz -C /etc/etcd --
strip-components=1
rm -f /tmp/etcd-${ETCD_VER}-linux-amd64.tar.gz

# check etcd version
/etc/etcd/etcd --version
```

This script will put `etcd` binary under `/etc/etcd` folder. You're free to put them in different place. We'll need `sudo` in order to put them under `/etc` in this case:

```
// install etcd on linux
# sudo sh install-etcd.sh
...
etcd Version: 3.3.0
Git SHA: c23606781
Go Version: go1.9.3
Go OS/Arch: linux/amd64
```

The version we're using now is 3.3.0. After we check the `etcd` binary work on your machine, we can attach it to the default `$PATH` as follows. Then we don't need to include the `/etc/etcd` path every time we execute the `etcd` command:

```
$ export PATH=/etc/etcd:$PATH
$ export ETCDCTL_API=3
```

You also can put it into your `.bashrc` or `.bash_profile` to let it set by default.

After we have at least three etcd servers provisioned, it's time to make them pair together.

Static mechanism

A static mechanism is the easiest way to set up a cluster. However, the IP address of every member should be known beforehand. This means that if you bootstrap an etcd cluster in a cloud provider environment, the static mechanism might not be so practical. Therefore, etcd also provides a discovery mechanism to bootstrap itself from the existing cluster.

To make etcd communications secure, etcd supports TLS channels to encrypt the communication between peers, and also clients and servers. Each member needs to have a unique key pair. In this section, we'll show you how to use automatically generated certificates to build a cluster.

In CoreOs GitHub, there is a handy tool we can use to generate self-signed certificates (https://github.com/coreos/etcd/tree/v3.2.15/hack/tls-setup). After cloning the repo, we have to modify a configuration file under config/req-csr.json. Here is an example:

```
// sample config, put under $repo/config/req-csr.json
$ cat config/req-csr.json
{
  "CN": "etcd",
  "hosts": [
    "172.31.3.80",
    "172.31.14.133",
    "172.31.13.239"
  ],
  "key": {
    "algo": "ecdsa",
    "size": 384
  },
  "names": [
    {
      "O": "autogenerated",
      "OU": "etcd cluster",
      "L": "the internet"
    }
  ]
}
```

In the next step we'll need to have Go (https://golang.org/) installed and set up $GOPATH:

```
$ export GOPATH=$HOME/go
$ make
```

Then the certs will be generated under ./certs/.

First, we'll have to set a bootstrap configuration to declare what members will be inside the cluster:

```
// set as environment variables, or alternatively, passing by --
initial-cluster and --initial-cluster-state parameters inside launch
command.
#
ETCD_INITIAL_CLUSTER="etcd0=http://172.31.3.80:2380,etcd1=http://172.3
1.14.133:2380,etcd2=http://172.31.13.239:2380"
ETCD_INITIAL_CLUSTER_STATE=new
```

In all three nodes, we'll have to launch the etcd server separately:

```
// first node: 172.31.3.80
# etcd --name etcd0 --initial-advertise-peer-urls
https://172.31.3.80:2380 \
  --listen-peer-urls https://172.31.3.80:2380 \
  --listen-client-urls https://172.31.3.80:2379,https://127.0.0.1:2379
\
  --advertise-client-urls https://172.31.3.80:2379 \
  --initial-cluster-token etcd-cluster-1 \
  --initial-cluster
etcd0=https://172.31.3.80:2380,etcd1=https://172.31.14.133:2380,etcd2=
https://172.31.13.239:2380 \
  --initial-cluster-state new \
  --auto-tls \
  --peer-auto-tls
```

Then, you'll see the following output:

```
2018-02-06 22:15:20.508687 I | etcdmain: etcd Version: 3.3.0
2018-02-06 22:15:20.508726 I | etcdmain: Git SHA: c23606781
2018-02-06 22:15:20.508794 I | etcdmain: Go Version: go1.9.3
2018-02-06 22:15:20.508824 I | etcdmain: Go OS/Arch: linux/amd64
...
2018-02-06 22:15:21.439067 N | etcdserver/membership: set the initial
cluster version to 3.0
2018-02-06 22:15:21.439134 I | etcdserver/api: enabled capabilities
for version 3.0
```

Let's wake up the second `etcd` service:

```
// second node: 172.31.14.133
$ etcd --name etcd1 --initial-advertise-peer-urls
https://172.31.14.133:2380 \
   --listen-peer-urls https://172.31.14.133:2380 \
   --listen-client-urls
https://172.31.14.133:2379,https://127.0.0.1:2379 \
   --advertise-client-urls https://172.31.14.133:2379 \
   --initial-cluster-token etcd-cluster-1 \
   --initial-cluster
etcd0=https://172.31.3.80:2380,etcd1=https://172.31.14.133:2380,etcd2=
https://172.31.13.239:2380 \
   --initial-cluster-state new \
   --auto-tls \
   --peer-auto-tls
```

You'll see similar logs in the console:

```
2018-02-06 22:15:20.646320 I | etcdserver: starting member
ce7c9e3024722f01 in cluster a7e82f7083dba2c1
2018-02-06 22:15:20.646384 I | raft: ce7c9e3024722f01 became follower
at term 0
2018-02-06 22:15:20.646397 I | raft: newRaft ce7c9e3024722f01 [peers:
[], term: 0, commit: 0, applied: 0, lastindex: 0, lastterm: 0]
2018-02-06 22:15:20.646403 I | raft: ce7c9e3024722f01 became follower
at term 1
...
2018-02-06 22:15:20.675928 I | rafthttp: starting peer
25654e0e7ea045f8...
2018-02-06 22:15:20.676024 I | rafthttp: started HTTP pipelining with
peer 25654e0e7ea045f8
2018-02-06 22:15:20.678515 I | rafthttp: started streaming with peer
25654e0e7ea045f8 (writer)
2018-02-06 22:15:20.678717 I | rafthttp: started streaming with peer
25654e0e7ea045f8 (writer)
```

It starts pairing with our previous node (`25654e0e7ea045f8`). Let's trigger the following command in the third node:

```
// third node: 172.31.13.239
$ etcd --name etcd2 --initial-advertise-peer-urls
https://172.31.13.239:2380 \
   --listen-peer-urls https://172.31.13.239:2380 \
   --listen-client-urls
https://172.31.13.239:2379,https://127.0.0.1:2379 \
   --advertise-client-urls https://172.31.13.239:2379 \
   --initial-cluster-token etcd-cluster-1 \
```

```
  --initial-cluster
etcd0=https://172.31.3.80:2380,etcd1=https://172.31.14.133:2380,etcd2=
https://172.31.13.239:2380 \
  --initial-cluster-state new \
  --auto-tls \
  --peer-auto-tls

// in node2 console, it listens and receives new member
(4834416c2c1e751e) added.
2018-02-06 22:15:20.679548 I | rafthttp: starting peer
4834416c2c1e751e...
2018-02-06 22:15:20.679642 I | rafthttp: started HTTP pipelining with
peer 4834416c2c1e751e
2018-02-06 22:15:20.679923 I | rafthttp: started streaming with peer
25654e0e7ea045f8 (stream Message reader)
2018-02-06 22:15:20.680190 I | rafthttp: started streaming with peer
25654e0e7ea045f8 (stream MsgApp v2 reader)
2018-02-06 22:15:20.680364 I | rafthttp: started streaming with peer
4834416c2c1e751e (writer)
2018-02-06 22:15:20.681880 I | rafthttp: started peer 4834416c2c1e751e
2018-02-06 22:15:20.681909 I | rafthttp: added peer 4834416c2c1e751e
After all nodes are in, it'll start to elect the leader inside the
cluster, we could find it in the logs:
2018-02-06 22:15:21.334985 I | raft: raft.node: ce7c9e3024722f01
elected leader 4834416c2c1e751e at term 27
...
2018-02-06 22:17:21.510271 N | etcdserver/membership: updated the
cluster version from 3.0 to 3.3
2018-02-06 22:17:21.510343 I | etcdserver/api: enabled capabilities
for version 3.3
```

And the cluster is set. We should check to see if it works properly:

```
$ etcdctl cluster-health
member 25654e0e7ea045f8is healthy: got healthy result from
http://172.31.3.80:2379
member ce7c9e3024722f01 is healthy: got healthy result from
http://172.31.14.133:2379
member 4834416c2c1e751e is healthy: got healthy result from
http://172.31.13.239:2379
```

Discovery mechanism

Discovery provides a more flexible way to create a cluster. It doesn't need to know other peer IPs beforehand. It uses an existing etcd cluster to bootstrap one. In this section, we'll demonstrate how to leverage that to launch a three-node etcd cluster:

1. Firstly, we'll need to have an existing cluster with three-node configuration. Luckily, the `etcd` official website provides a discovery service (`https://discovery.etcd.io/new?size=n`); n will be the number of nodes in your `etcd` cluster, which is ready to use:

```
// get a request URL
# curl -w "n" 'https://discovery.etcd.io/new?size=3'
https://discovery.etcd.io/f6a3fb54b3fd1bb02e26a89fd40df0e8
```

2. Then we are able to use the URL to bootstrap a cluster easily. The command line is pretty much the same as in the static mechanism. What we need to do is change `–initial-cluster` to `–discovery`, which is used to specify the discovery service URL:

```
// in node1, 127.0.0.1 is used for internal client
listeneretcd –name ip-172-31-3-80 –initial-advertise-peer-
urls http://172.31.3.80:2380  –listen-peer-urls
http://172.31.3.80:2380  –listen-client-urls
http://172.31.3.80:2379,http://127.0.0.1:2379  –advertise-
client-urls http://172.31.3.80:2379  –discovery
https://discovery.etcd.io/f6a3fb54b3fd1bb02e26a89fd40df0e8

// in node2, 127.0.0.1 is used for internal client
listener
etcd –name ip-172-31-14-133 –initial-advertise-peer-urls
http://172.31.14.133:2380  –listen-peer-urls
http://172.31.14.133:2380  –listen-client-urls
http://172.31.14.133:2379,http://127.0.0.1:2379  –
advertise-client-urls http://172.31.14.133:2379  –
discovery
https://discovery.etcd.io/f6a3fb54b3fd1bb02e26a89fd40df0e8

// in node3, 127.0.0.1 is used for internal client
listener
etcd –name ip-172-31-13-239 –initial-advertise-peer-urls
http://172.31.13.239:2380  –listen-peer-urls
http://172.31.13.239:2380  –listen-client-urls
http://172.31.13.239:2379,http://127.0.0.1:2379  –
advertise-client-urls http://172.31.13.239:2379  –
discovery
```

```
https://discovery.etcd.io/f6a3fb54b3fd1bb02e26a89fd40df0e8
```

3. Let's take a closer look at node1's log:

```
2018-02-10 04:58:03.819963 I | etcdmain: etcd Version:
3.3.0
...
2018-02-10 04:58:03.820400 I | embed: listening for peers
on http://172.31.3.80:2380
2018-02-10 04:58:03.820427 I | embed: listening for client
requests on
127.0.0.1:2379
2018-02-10 04:58:03.820444 I | embed: listening for client
requests on 172.31.3.80:2379
2018-02-10 04:58:03.947753 N | discovery: found self
f60c98e749d41d1b in the cluster
2018-02-10 04:58:03.947771 N | discovery: found 1 peer(s),
waiting for 2 more
2018-02-10 04:58:22.289571 N | discovery: found peer
6645fe871c820573 in the cluster
2018-02-10 04:58:22.289628 N | discovery: found 2 peer(s),
waiting for 1 more
2018-02-10 04:58:36.907165 N | discovery: found peer
1ce61c15bdbb20b2 in the cluster
2018-02-10 04:58:36.907192 N | discovery: found 3 needed
peer(s)
...
2018-02-10 04:58:36.931319 I | etcdserver/membership:
added member 1ce61c15bdbb20b2 [http://172.31.13.239:2380]
to cluster 29c0e2579c2f9563
2018-02-10 04:58:36.931422 I | etcdserver/membership:
added member 6645fe871c820573 [http://172.31.14.133:2380]
to cluster 29c0e2579c2f9563
2018-02-10 04:58:36.931494 I | etcdserver/membership:
added member f60c98e749d41d1b [http://172.31.3.80:2380] to
cluster 29c0e2579c2f9563
2018-02-10 04:58:37.116189 I | raft: f60c98e749d41d1b
became leader at term 2
```

We can see that the first node waited for the other two members to join, and added member to cluster, became the leader in the election at term 2:

4. If you check the other server's log, you might find a clue to the effect that some members voted for the current leader:

```
// in node 2
2018-02-10 04:58:37.118601 I | raft: raft.node:
6645fe871c820573 elected leader f60c98e749d41d1b at term 2
```

5. We can also use member lists to check the current leader:

```
# etcdctl member list
1ce61c15bdbb20b2: name=ip-172-31-13-239
peerURLs=http://172.31.13.239:2380
clientURLs=http://172.31.13.239:2379 isLeader=false
6645fe871c820573: name=ip-172-31-14-133
peerURLs=http://172.31.14.133:2380
clientURLs=http://172.31.14.133:2379 isLeader=false
f60c98e749d41d1b: name=ip-172-31-3-80
peerURLs=http://172.31.3.80:2380
clientURLs=http://172.31.3.80:2379 isLeader=true
```

6. Then we can confirm the current leader is 172.31.3.80. We can also use etcdctl to check cluster health:

```
# etcdctl cluster-health
member 1ce61c15bdbb20b2 is healthy: got healthy result
from http://172.31.13.239:2379
member 6645fe871c820573 is healthy: got healthy result
from http://172.31.14.133:2379
member f60c98e749d41d1b is healthy: got healthy result
from http://172.31.3.80:2379
cluster is healthy
```

7. If we remove the current leader by etcdctl command:

```
# etcdctl member remove f60c98e749d41d1b
```

8. We may find that the current leader has been changed:

```
# etcdctl member list
1ce61c15bdbb20b2: name=ip-172-31-13-239
peerURLs=http://172.31.13.239:2380
clientURLs=http://172.31.13.239:2379 isLeader=false
6645fe871c820573: name=ip-172-31-14-133
peerURLs=http://172.31.14.133:2380
clientURLs=http://172.31.14.133:2379 isLeader=true
```

By using `etcd` discovery, we can set up a cluster painlessly `etcd` also provides lots of APIs for us to use. We can leverage it to check cluster statistics:

9. For example, use `/stats/leader` to check the current cluster view:

```
# curl http://127.0.0.1:2379/v2/stats/leader
{"leader":"6645fe871c820573","followers":{"1ce61c15bdbb20b
2":{"latency":{"current":0.002463,"average":0.0038775,"sta
ndardDeviation":0.0014144999999999997,"minimum":0.002463,"
maximum":0.005292},"counts":{"fail":0,"success":2}}}}
```

For more information about APIs, check out the official API document: `https://coreos.com/etcd/docs/latest/v2/api.html`.

Building a cluster in EC2
CoreOS builds CloudFormation in AWS to help you bootstrap your cluster in AWS dynamically. What we have to do is just launch a CloudFormation template and set the parameters, and we're good to go. The resources in the template contain AutoScaling settings and network ingress (security group). Note that these etcds are running on CoreOS. To log in to the server, firstly you'll have to set your keypair name in the KeyPair parameter, then use the command `ssh -i $your_keypair core@$ip` to log in to the server.

kubeadm

If you're using kubeadm (`https://github.com/kubernetes/kubeadm`) to bootstrap your Kubernetes cluster, unfortunately, at the time of writing, HA support is still in progress (v.1.10). The cluster is created as a single master with a single etcd configured. You'll have to back up etcd regularly to secure your data. Refer to the kubeadm limitations at the official Kubernetes website for more information (`https://kubernetes.io/docs/setup/independent/create-cluster-kubeadm/#limitations`).

kubespray

On the other hand, if you're using kubespray to provision your servers, kubespray supports multi-node etcd natively. What you need to do is add multiple nodes in the etcd section in the configuration file (`inventory.cfg`):

```
# cat inventory/inventory.cfg
my-master-1 ansible_ssh_host=<master_ip>
my-node-1 ansible_ssh_host=<node_ip>
my-etcd-1 ansible_ssh_host=<etcd1_ip>
my-etcd-2 ansible_ssh_host=<etcd2_ip>
my-etcd-3 ansible_ssh_host=<etcd3_ip>

[kube-master]
my-master-1

[etcd]
my-etcd-1
my-etcd-2
my-etcd-3

[kube-node]
my-master-1
my-node-1
```

Then you are good to provision a cluster with three-node etcd:

```
// provision a cluster
$ ansible-playbook -b -i inventory/inventory.cfg cluster.yml
```

After the ansible playbook is launched, it will configure the role, create the user, check if all certs have already been generated in the first master, and generate and distribute the certs. At the end of the deployment, ansible will check if every component is in a healthy state.

Kops

Kops is the most efficient way to create Kubernetes clusters in AWS. Via the kops configuration file, you can easily launch a custom cluster on the cloud. To build an etcd multi-node cluster, you could use the following section inside the kops configuration file:

```
etcdClusters:
  - etcdMembers:
    - instanceGroup: my-master-us-east-1a
      name: my-etcd-1
    - instanceGroup: my-master-us-east-1b
      name: my-etcd-2
    - instanceGroup: my-master-us-east-1c
      name: my-etcd-3
```

Normally, an instanceGroup means an auto-scaling group. You'll have to declare a related `intanceGroup my-master-us-east-1x` in the configuration file as well. We'll learn more about it in `Chapter 17`, *Building Kubernetes on AWS*. By default, kops still uses etcd2 at the time this book is being written; you could add a version key inside the kops configuration file, such as **version: 3.3.0**, under each `instanceGroup`.

Building multiple masters

The master node serves as a kernel component in the Kubernetes system. Its duties include the following:

1. Pushing and pulling information from etcd servers
2. Acting as the portal for requests
3. Assigning tasks to nodes
4. Monitoring the running tasks

Three major daemons enable the master to fulfill the preceding duties; the following diagram indicates the activities of the aforementioned bullet points:

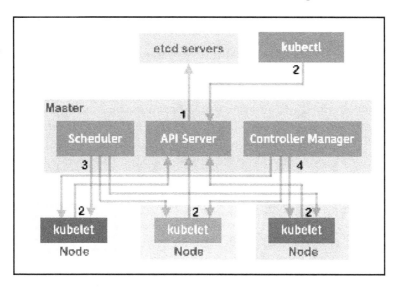

The interaction between the Kubernetes master and other components

As you can see, the master is the communicator between workers and clients. Therefore, it will be a problem if the master crashes. A multiple-master Kubernetes system is not only fault tolerant, but also workload-balanced. It would not be an issue if one of them crashed, since other masters would still handle the jobs. We call this infrastructure design *high availability*, abbreviated to HA. In order to support HA structures, there will no longer be only one API server for accessing datastores and handling requests. Several API servers in separated master nodes would help to solve tasks simultaneously and shorten the response time.

Getting ready

There are some brief ideas you should understand about building a multiple-master system:

- Add a load balancer server in front of the masters. The load balancer will become the new endpoint accessed by nodes and clients.
- Every master runs its own API server.
- Only one scheduler and one controller manager are eligible to work in the system, which can avoid conflicting directions from different daemons while managing containers. To achieve this setup, we enable the `--leader-elect` flag in the scheduler and controller manager. Only the one getting the lease can take duties.

In this recipe, we are going to build a two-master system via *kubeadm*, which has similar methods while scaling more masters. Users may also use other tools to build up HA Kubernetes clusters. Our target is to illustrate the general concepts.

Before starting, in addition to master nodes, you should prepare other necessary components in the systems:

- Two Linux hosts, which will be set up as master nodes later. These machines should be configured as kubeadm masters. Please refer to the *Setting up Kubernetes clusters on Linux by kubeadm recipe* in `Chapter 12`, *Building Your Own Kubernetes Cluster*. You should finish the *Package installation and System configuring prerequisites* parts on both hosts.
- A LoadBalancer for masters. It would be much easier if you worked on the public cloud, that's said ELB of AWS and Load balancing of GCE.
- An etcd cluster. Please check the *Clustering etcd* recipe in this chapter.

How to do it...

We will use a configuration file to run kubeadm for customized daemon execution. Please follow the next sections to make multiple master nodes as a group.

Setting up the first master

First, we are going to set up a master, ready for the HA environment. Like the initial step, running a cluster by using kubeadm, it is important to enable and start kubelet on the master at the beginning. It can then take daemons running as pods in the kube-system namespace:

```
// you are now in the terminal of host for first master
$ sudo systemctl enable kubelet && sudo systemctl start kubelet
```

Next, let's start the master services with the custom kubeadm configuration file:

```
$ cat custom-init-1st.conf
apiVersion: kubeadm.k8s.io/v1alpha1
kind: MasterConfiguration
api:
  advertiseAddress: "<FIRST_MASTER_IP>"
etcd:
  endpoints:
  - "<ETCD_CLUSTER_ENDPOINT>"
apiServerCertSANs:
- "<FIRST_MASTER_IP>"
- "<SECOND_MASTER_IP>"
- "<LOAD_BALANCER_IP>"
- "127.0.0.1"
token: "<CUSTOM_TOKEN: [a-z0-9]{6}.[a-z0-9]{16}>"
tokenTTL: "0"
apiServerExtraArgs:
  endpoint-reconciler-type: "lease"
```

This configuration file has multiple values required to match your environment settings. The IP ones are straightforward. Be aware that you are now setting the first master; the <FIRST_MASTER_IP> variable will be the physical IP of your current location. <ETCD_CLUSTER_ENDPOINT> will be in a format like "http://<IP>:<PORT>", which will be the load balancer of the etcd cluster. <CUSTOM_TOKEN> should be valid in the specified format (for example, 123456.aaaabbbbccccdddd). After you allocate all variables aligning to your system, you can run it now:

```
$ sudo kubeadm init --config=custom-init-1st.conf
```

 You may get the Swap is not supported error message. Add an additional --ignore-preflight-errors=Swap flag with kubeadm init to avoid this interruption.

Make sure to update in both files of the masters.

We need to complete client functionality via the following commands:

```
$ mkdir -p $HOME/.kube
$ sudo cp -i /etc/kubernetes/admin.conf $HOME/.kube/config
$ sudo chown $(id -u):$(id -g) $HOME/.kube/config
```

Like when running a single master cluster via kubeadm, without a container network interface the add-on `kube-dns` will always have a pending status. We will use CNI Calico for our demonstration. It is fine to apply the other CNI which is suitable to kubeadm:

```
$ kubectl apply -f
https://docs.projectcalico.org/v2.6/getting-started/kubernetes/install
ation/hosted/kubeadm/1.6/calico.yaml
```

Now it is OK for you to add more master nodes.

Setting up the other master with existing certifications

Similar to the last session, let's start and enable `kubelet` first:

```
// now you're in the second master
$ sudo systemctl enable kubelet && sudo systemctl start kubelet
```

After we have set up the first master, we should share newly generated certificates and keys with the whole system. It makes sure that the masters are secured in the same manner:

```
$ sudo scp -r root@$FIRST_MASTER_IP:/etc/kubernetes/pki/*
/etc/kubernetes/pki/
```

You will have found that several files such as certificates or keys are copied to the `/etc/kubernetes/pki/` directly, where they can only be accessed by the root. However, we are going to remove the files `apiserver.crt` and `apiserver.key`. It is because these files should be generated in line with the hostname and IP of the second master, but the shared client certificate `ca.crt` is also involved in the generating process:

```
$ sudo rm /etc/kubernetes/pki/apiserver.*
```

Next, before we fire the master initialization command, please change the API advertise address in the configuration file for the second master. It should be the IP of the second master, your current host. The configuration file of the second master is quite similar to the first master's.

The difference is that we should indicate the information of `etcd` server and avoid creating a new set of them:

```
// Please modify the change by your case
$ cat custom-init-2nd.conf
apiVersion: kubeadm.k8s.io/v1alpha1
kind: MasterConfiguration
api:
  advertiseAddress: "<SECOND_MASTER_IP>"
...
```

Go ahead and fire the `kubeadm init` command, record the `kubeadm join` command shown in the last line of the `init` command to add the node later, and enable the client API permission:

```
$ sudo kubeadm init --config custom-init-2nd.conf
// copy the "kubeadm join" command showing in the output
$ mkdir -p $HOME/.kube
$ sudo cp -i /etc/kubernetes/admin.conf $HOME/.kube/config
$ sudo chown $(id -u):$(id -g) $HOME/.kube/config
```

Then, check the current nodes; you will find there are two master :

```
$ kubectl get nodes
NAME       STATUS   ROLES    AGE   VERSION
master01   Ready    master   8m    v1.10.2
master02   Ready    master   1m    v1.10.2
```

Adding nodes in a HA cluster

Once the masters are ready, you can add nodes into the system. This node should be finished with the prerequisite configuration as a worker node in the kubeadm cluster. And, in the beginning, you should start kubelet as the master ones:

```
// now you're in the second master
$ sudo systemctl enable kubelet && sudo systemctl start kubelet
```

After that, you can go ahead and push the join command you copied. However, please change the master IP to the load balancer one:

```
// your join command should look similar to following one
$ sudo kubeadm join --token <CUSTOM_TOKEN> <LOAD_BALANCER_IP>:6443 --
discovery-token-ca-cert-hash sha256:<HEX_STRING>
```

You can then jump to the first master or second master to check the nodes' status:

```
// you can see the node is added
$ kubectl get nodes
NAME        STATUS    ROLES     AGE       VERSION
master01    Ready     master    4h        v1.10.2
master02    Ready     master    3h        v1.10.2
node01      Ready     <none>    22s       v1.10.2
```

How it works...

To verify our HA cluster, take a look at the pods in the namespace `kube-system`:

```
$ kubectl get pod -n kube-system
NAME                                         READY     STATUS     RESTARTS
AGE
calico-etcd-6bnrk                            1/1       Running    0
1d
calico-etcd-p7lpv                            1/1       Running    0
1d
calico-kube-controllers-d554689d5-qjht2      1/1       Running    0
1d
calico-node-2r2zs                            2/2       Running    0
1d
calico-node-97fjk                            2/2       Running    0
1d
calico-node-t55l8                            2/2       Running    0
1d
kube-apiserver-master01                      1/1       Running    0
1d
kube-apiserver-master02                      1/1       Running    0
1d
kube-controller-manager-master01             1/1       Running    0
1d
kube-controller-manager-master02             1/1       Running    0
1d
kube-dns-6f4fd4bdf-xbfvp                      3/3       Running    0
1d
kube-proxy-8jk69                             1/1       Running    0
```

```
1d
kube-proxy-qbt7q                    1/1        Running   0
1d
kube-proxy-rkxwp                    1/1        Running   0
1d
kube-scheduler-master01             1/1        Running   0
1d
kube-scheduler-master02             1/1        Running   0
1d
```

These pods are working as system daemons: Kubernetes system services such as the API server, Kubernetes add-ons such as the DNS server, and CNI ones; here we used Calico. But wait! As you take a closer look at the pods, you may be curious about why the controller manager and scheduler runs on both masters. Isn't there just single one in the HA cluster?

As we understood in the previous section, we should avoid running multiple controller managers and multiple schedulers in the Kubernetes system. This is because they may try to take over requests at the same time, which not only creates conflict but is also a waste of computing power. Actually, while booting up the whole system by using kubeadm, the controller manager and scheduler are started with the leader-elect flag enabled by default:

```
// check flag leader-elect on master node
$ sudo cat /etc/kubernetes/manifests/kube-controller-manager.yaml
apiVersion: v1
kind: Pod
metadata:
  annotations:
    scheduler.alpha.kubernetes.io/critical-pod: ""
  creationTimestamp: null
  labels:
    component: kube-controller-manager
    tier: control-plane
  name: kube-controller-manager
  namespace: kube-system
spec:
  containers:
  - command:
    - kube-controller-manager
...
    - --leader-elect=true
...
```

You may find that the scheduler has also been set with `leader-elect`. Nevertheless, why is there still more than one pod? The truth is, one of the pods with the same role is idle. We can get detailed information by looking at system endpoints:

```
// ep is the abbreviation of resource type "endpoints"
$ kubectl get ep -n kube-system
NAME                        ENDPOINTS
AGE
calico-etcd                 192.168.122.201:6666,192.168.122.202:6666
1d
kube-controller-manager     <none>
1d
kube-dns                    192.168.241.67:53,192.168.241.67:53
1d
kube-scheduler              <none>
1d

// check endpoint of controller-manager with YAML output format
$ kubectl get ep kube-controller-manager -n kube-system -o yaml
apiVersion: v1
kind: Endpoints
metadata:
  annotations:
    control-plane.alpha.kubernetes.io/leader:
'{"holderIdentity":"master01_bf4e22f7-4f56-11e8-
aee3-52540048ed9b","leaseDurationSeconds":15,"acquireTime":"2018-05-04
T04:51:11Z","renewTime":"2018-05-04T05:28:34Z","leaderTransitions":0}'
  creationTimestamp: 2018-05-04T04:51:11Z
  name: kube-controller-manager
  namespace: kube-system
  resourceVersion: "3717"
  selfLink: /api/v1/namespaces/kube-system/endpoints/kube-controller-
manager
  uid: 5e2717b0-0609-11e8-b36f-52540048ed9b
```

Take the endpoint for `kube-controller-manager`, for example: there is no virtual IP of a pod or service attached to it (the same as `kube-scheduler`). If we dig deeper into this endpoint, we find that the endpoint for `kube-controller-manager` relies on `annotations` to record lease information; it also relies on `resourceVersion` for pod mapping and to pass traffic. According to the annotation of the `kube-controller-manager` endpoint, it is our first master that took control. Let's check the controller manager on both masters:

```
// your pod should be named as kube-controller-manager-<HOSTNAME OF
MASTER>
$ kubectl logs kube-controller-manager-master01 -n kube-system | grep
```

```
"leader"
I0504 04:51:03.015151 1 leaderelection.go:175] attempting to acquire
leader lease kube-system/kube-controller-manager...
...
I0504 04:51:11.627737 1 event.go:218]
Event(v1.ObjectReference{Kind:"Endpoints", Namespace:"kube-system",
Name:"kube-controller-manager", UID:"5e2717b0-0609-11e8-
b36f-52540048ed9b", APIVersion:"v1", ResourceVersion:"187",
FieldPath:""}): type: 'Normal' reason: 'LeaderElection'
master01_bf4e22f7-4f56-11e8-aee3-52540048ed9b became leader
```

As you can see, only one master works as a leader and handles the requests, while the other one persists, acquires the lease, and does nothing.

For a further test, we are trying to remove our current leader pod, to see what happens. While deleting the deployment of system pods by a `kubectl` request, a kubeadm Kubernetes would create a new one since it's guaranteed to boot up any application under the `/etc/kubernetes/manifests` directory. Therefore, avoid the automatic recovery by kubeadm, we remove the configuration file out of the manifest directory instead. It makes the downtime long enough to give away the leadership:

```
// jump into the master node of leader
// temporary move the configuration file out of kubeadm's control
$ sudo mv /etc/kubernetes/manifests/kube-controller-manager.yaml ./
// check the endpoint
$ kubectl get ep kube-controller-manager -n kube-system -o yaml
apiVersion: v1
kind: Endpoints
metadata:
  annotations:
    control-plane.alpha.kubernetes.io/leader:
'{"holderIdentity":"master02_4faf95c7-4f5b-11e8-
bda3-525400b06612","leaseDurationSeconds":15,"acquireTime":"2018-05-04
T05:37:03Z","renewTime":"2018-05-04T05:37:47Z","leaderTransitions":1}'
  creationTimestamp: 2018-05-04T04:51:11Z
  name: kube-controller-manager
  namespace: kube-system
  resourceVersion: "4485"
  selfLink: /api/v1/namespaces/kube-system/endpoints/kube-controller-
manager
  uid: 5e2717b0-0609-11e8-b36f-52540048ed9b
subsets: null
```

The /etc/kubernetes/manifests directory is defined in kubelet by --pod-manifest-path flag. Check /etc/systemd/system/kubelet.service.d/10-kubeadm.conf, which is the system daemon configuration file for kubelet, and the help messages of kubelet for more details.

Now, it is the other node's turn to wake up its controller manager and put it to work. Once you put back the configuration file for the controller manager, you find the old leader is now waiting for the lease:

```
$ kubectl logs kube-controller-manager-master01 -n kube-system
I0504 05:40:10.218946 1 controllermanager.go:116] Version: v1.10.2
W0504 05:40:10.219688 1 authentication.go:55] Authentication is
disabled
I0504 05:40:10.219702 1 insecure_serving.go:44] Serving insecurely on
127.0.0.1:10252
I0504 05:40:10.219965 1 leaderelection.go:175] attempting to acquire
leader lease kube-system/kube-controller-manager...
```

See also

Before you read this recipe, you should have mastered the basic concept of single master installation by kubeadm. Refer to the related recipes mentioned here to get an idea for how to build a multiple-master system automatically:

- Setting up a Kubernetes cluster on Linux by kubeadm in Chapter 12, *Building Your Own Kubernetes Cluster*
- Clustering etcd

16
Building Continuous Delivery Pipelines

In this chapter, we will cover the following recipes:

- Moving monolithic to microservices
- Working with the private Docker registry
- Integrating with Jenkins

Introduction

Kubernetes is a perfect match for applications featuring the microservices architecture. However, most of the old applications are built in the monolithic style. We will give you an idea about how to move from the monolithic to the microservices world. As for microservices, deployment will become a burden if you are doing it manually. We will learn how to build up our own continuous delivery pipeline by coordinating Jenkins, the Docker registry, and Kubernetes.

Moving monolithic to microservices

Typically, application architecture is the monolithic design that contains a **Model-View- Controller** (**MVC**) and every component within a single, big binary. A monolithic design has some benefits, such as less latency within components, being all in one straightforward package, and being easy to deploy and test.

However, a monolithic design has some downsides because the binary will be getting bigger and bigger. You always need to take care of the side effects when adding or modifying the code, therefore making release cycles longer.

Containers and Kubernetes give more flexibility when using microservices for your application. The microservices architecture is very simple and can be divided into some modules or some service classes together with MVC:

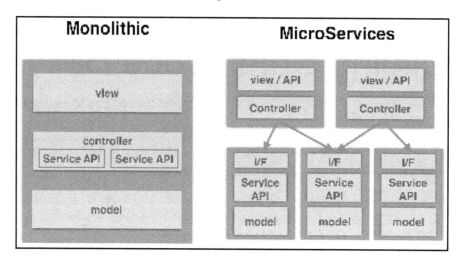

Monolithic and microservices design

Each microservice provides a **Remote Procedure Call** (**RPC**) using RESTful or some standard network APIs to other microservices. The benefit is that each microservice is independent. There are minimal side effects when adding or modifying the code. Release the cycle independently, so it perfectly ties in with the Agile software development methodology and allows for the reuse of these microservices to construct another application that builds the microservices ecosystem.

Getting ready

Prepare the simple microservices program. In order to push and pull your microservices, please register to Docker hub (`https://hub.docker.com/`) to create your free Docker ID in advance.

If you push the Docker image to Docker hub, it will be public; anyone can pull your image. Therefore, don't put any confidential information into the image.

Once you successfully log in to your Docker ID, you will be redirected to your **Dashboard** page as follows:

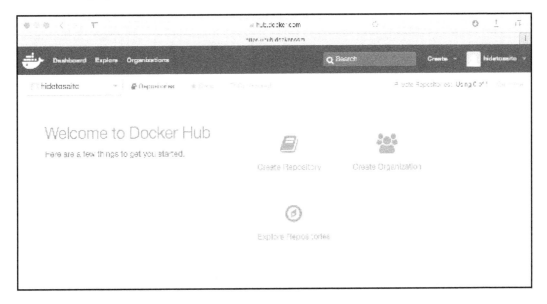

After logging in to Docker hub

How to do it...

Prepare both microservices and the frontend WebUI as a Docker image. Then, deploy them using the Kubernetes replication controller and service.

Microservices

Build a microservice which provides a simple math function by using following steps:

1. Here is the simple microservice using Python Flask (http://flask.pocoo.org/):

```
$ cat entry.py
from flask import Flask, request
app = Flask(__name__)

@app.route("/")
def hello():
    return "Hello World!"
```

```
@app.route("/power/<int:base>/<int:index>")
def power(base, index):
    return "%d" % (base ** index)

@app.route("/addition/<int:x>/<int:y>")
def add(x, y):
    return "%d" % (x+y)

@app.route("/substraction/<int:x>/<int:y>")
def substract(x, y):
    return "%d" % (x-y)

if __name__ == "__main__":
    app.run(host='0.0.0.0')
```

2. Prepare a `Dockerfile` as follows in order to build the Docker image:

```
$ cat Dockerfile
FROM ubuntu:14.04

# Update packages
RUN apt-get update -y

# Install Python Setuptools
RUN apt-get install -y python-setuptools git telnet curl

# Install pip
RUN easy_install pip

# Bundle app source
ADD . /src
WORKDIR /src

# Add and install Python modules
RUN pip install Flask

# Expose
EXPOSE 5000

# Run
CMD ["python", "entry.py"]
```

3. Then, use the `docker build` command to build the Docker image as follows:

```
//name as "your_docker_hub_id/my-calc"
$ sudo docker build -t hidetosaito/my-calc .
Sending build context to Docker daemon 3.072 kB
```

```
Step 1 : FROM ubuntu:14.04
 ---> 6cc0fc2a5ee3
Step 2 : RUN apt-get update -y
 ---> Using cache


(snip)


Step 8 : EXPOSE 5000
 ---> Running in 7c52f4bfe373
 ---> 28f79bb7481f
Removing intermediate container 7c52f4bfe373
Step 9 : CMD python entry.py
 ---> Running in 86b39c727572
 ---> 20ae465bf036
Removing intermediate container 86b39c727572
Successfully built 20ae465bf036


//verity your image
$ sudo docker images
REPOSITORY            TAG              IMAGE ID
CREATED             VIRTUAL SIZE
hidetosaito/my-calc   latest           20ae465bf036
19 seconds ago      284 MB
ubuntu                14.04            6cc0fc2a5ee3
3 weeks ago         187.9 MB
```

4. Then, use the `docker login` command to log in to Docker hub:

```
//type your username, password and e-mail address in
Docker hub
$ sudo docker login
Username: hidetosaito
Password:
Email: hideto.saito@yahoo.com
WARNING: login credentials saved in /home/ec2-
user/.docker/config.json
Login Succeeded
```

5. Finally, use the `docker push` command to register to your Docker hub repository as follows:

```
//push to your docker index
$ sudo docker push hidetosaito/my-calc
The push refers to a repository [docker.io/hidetosaito/my-
calc] (len: 1)
20ae465bf036: Pushed

(snip)

92ec6d044cb3: Pushed
latest: digest:
sha256:203b81c5a238e228c154e0b53a58e60e6eb3d1563293483ce58
f48351031a474 size: 19151
```

6. Upon access to Docker hub, you can see your microservice in the repository:

Your microservice Docker image on Docker hub

Frontend WebUI

Build WebUI that uses preceding microservice by following steps:

1. Here is the simple frontend WebUI that also uses Python `Flask`:

```
$ cat entry.py
import os
import httplib
from flask import Flask, request, render_template

app = Flask(__name__)

@app.route("/")
def index():
    return render_template('index.html')


@app.route("/add", methods=['POST'])
def add():
    #
    # from POST parameters
    #
    x = int(request.form['x'])
    y = int(request.form['y'])

    #
    # from Kubernetes Service(environment variables)
    #
    my_calc_host =
os.environ['MY_CALC_SERVICE_SERVICE_HOST']
    my_calc_port =
os.environ['MY_CALC_SERVICE_SERVICE_PORT']

    #
    # REST call to MicroService(my-calc)
    #
    client = httplib.HTTPConnection(my_calc_host,
my_calc_port)
    client.request("GET", "/addition/%d/%d" % (x, y))
    response = client.getresponse()
    result = response.read()
    return render_template('index.html', add_x=x, add_y=y,
add_result=result)

if __name__ == "__main__":
    app.debug = True
    app.run(host='0.0.0.0')
```

Kubernetes service generates the Kubernetes service name and port number as an environment variable to the other pods. Therefore, the environment variable's name and the Kubernetes service name must be consistent. In this scenario, the `my-calc` service name must be `my-calc-service`.

2. The frontend WebUI uses the `Flask` HTML template; it is similar to PHP and JSP in that `entry.py` will pass the parameter to the template (`index.html`) to render the HTML:

```
$ cat templates/index.html
<html>
   <body>
   <div>
        <form method="post" action="/add">
            <input type="text" name="x" size="2"/>
            <input type="text" name="y" size="2"/>
            <input type="submit" value="addition"/>
        </form>
        {% if add_result %}
        <p>Answer : {{ add_x }} + {{ add_y }} = {{
add_result }}</p>
        {% endif %}
   </div>
   </body>
</html>
```

3. `Dockerfile` is exactly the same as the microservice `my-calc`. So, eventually, the file structure will be as follows. Note that `index.html` is a jinja2 template file; therefore, put it under the `/templates` directory:

```
/Dockerfile
/entry.py
/templates/index.html
```

4. Then, build a Docker image and push to Docker hub as follows:

In order to push your image to Docker hub, you need to log in using the Docker login command. It is needed only once; the system checks `~/.docker/config.json` to read from there.

```
//build frontend Webui image
$ sudo docker build -t hidetosaito/my-frontend .

//login to docker hub
```

```
$ sudo docker login

//push frontend webui image
$ sudo docker push hidetosaito/my-frontend
```

5. Upon access to Docker hub, you can see your WebUI application in the repository:

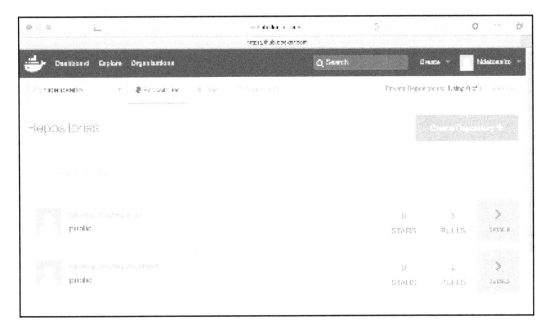

Microservices and frontend WebUI image on Docker Hub

How it works...

Let's prepare two YAML configurations to launch a microservice container and frontend WebUI container using Kubernetes.

Microservices

Microservices (`my-calc`) uses the Kubernetes deployment and service, but it needs to communicate to other pods only. In other words, there's no need to expose it to the outside Kubernetes network. Therefore, the service type is set as `ClusterIP`:

```
$ cat my-calc.yaml
apiVersion: apps/v1
kind: Deployment
metadata:
  name: my-calc-deploy
spec:
  replicas: 2
  selector:
    matchLabels:
      run: my-calc
  template:
    metadata:
      labels:
        run: my-calc
    spec:
      containers:
      - name: my-calc
        image: hidetosaito/my-calc
---
apiVersion: v1
kind: Service
metadata:
  name: my-calc-service
spec:
  ports:
    - protocol: TCP
      port: 5000
  type: ClusterIP
  selector:
      run: my-calc
```

Use the `kubectl` command to load the `my-calc` pods as follows:

```
$ kubectl create -f my-calc.yaml
deployment.apps "my-calc-deploy" created
service "my-calc-service" created
```

Frontend WebUI

Frontend WebUI also uses the deployment and service, but it exposes the port (TCP port 30080) in order to access it from an external web browser:

```
$ cat my-frontend.yaml
apiVersion: apps/v1
kind: Deployment
metadata:
  name: my-frontend-deploy
spec:
  replicas: 2
  selector:
    matchLabels:
      run: my-frontend
  template:
    metadata:
      labels:
        run: my-frontend
    spec:
      containers:
      - name: my-frontend
        image: hidetosaito/my-frontend
---
apiVersion: v1
kind: Service
metadata:
  name: my-frontend-service
spec:
  ports:
    - protocol: TCP
      port: 5000
      nodePort: 30080
  type: NodePort
  selector:
      run: my-frontend


$ kubectl create -f my-frontend.yaml
deployment.apps "my-frontend-deploy" created
service "my-frontend-service" created
```

Let's try to access `my-frontend-service` using a web browser. You can access any Kubernetes node's IP address; specify the port number 30080. If you are using minikube, simply type `minikube service my-frontend-service` to access. Then you can see the `my-frontend` application as follows:

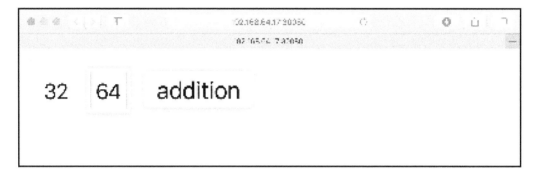

Access to the frontend WebUI

When you click on the **addition** button, it will forward a parameter to microservices (`my-calc`). Microservices compute the addition (yes, just an addition!) and then return the result back to the frontend WebUI as follows:

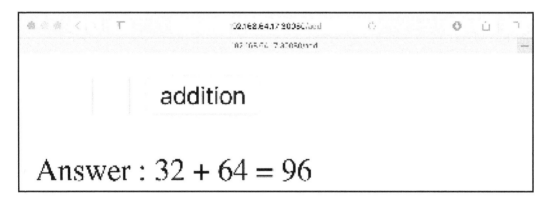

Getting a result from microservices and rendering the HTML

So now, it is easy to scale the pod for the frontend WebUI and microservices independently. For example, scale WebUI pod from `2` to `8` and microservice pod from `2` to `16`, as shown:

```
$ kubectl get deploy
NAME              DESIRED   CURRENT   UP-TO-DATE   AVAILABLE   AGE
my-calc-deploy    2         2         2            2           30m
```

```
my-frontend-deploy    2          2          2                   2              28m

$ kubectl scale deploy my-frontend-deploy --replicas=8
deployment "my-frontend-deploy" scaled

$ kubectl scale deploy my-calc-deploy --replicas=16
deployment "my-calc-deploy" scaled

$ kubectl get deploy
NAME                  DESIRED    CURRENT    UP-TO-DATE    AVAILABLE    AGE
my-calc-deploy        16         16         16            16           31m
my-frontend-deploy    8          8          8             8            29m
```

Also, if there's a need to fix some bugs, for example, if there's a frontend need to validate
the input parameter to check whether it is numeric or a string (yes, if you type string and
then submit, it will show an error!), it will not affect the build and deploy the cycle against
microservices:

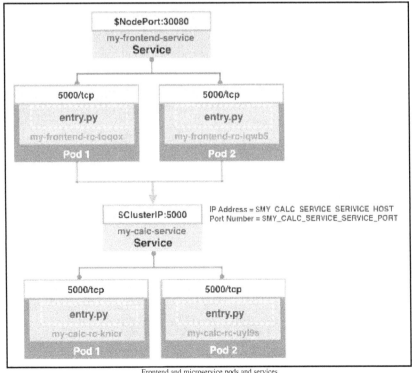

Frontend and microservice pods and services

In addition, if you want to add another microservice, for example, subtraction microservices, you may need to create another Docker image and deploy with another deployments and service, so it will be independent from the current microservices. Then, you can keep accumulating your own microservice ecosystem to reuse in another application.

Working with the private Docker registry

Once you start to build your microservice application via Docker, you'll need to have a Docker registry to put your container image in. Docker hub offers you free public repositories, however, in some cases you might want to make your image private due to business needs or organization policy.

Docker hub offers the **private repository**, which only allows authenticated users to push and pull your images, and is not visible to other users. However, there is only one quota (repository) for a free plan. You may pay to increase the number of private repositories, but if you adopt the microservices architecture, you will need a large number of private repositories:

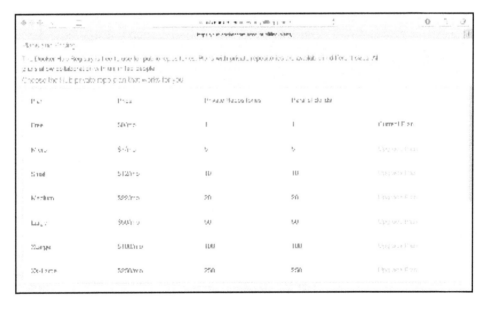

Docker hub private repositories price list

Docker hub with a paid plan is the easiest way to set up your private registry, but there are some other ways to set up your own private Docker registry, which the unlimited Docker image quota locates inside your network. In addition, you can also use other cloud-provided registry services to manage your private registry.

Getting ready

In this recipe, we will show you three different ways to set up your own private registries:

- Using Kubernetes to run a private registry image (`https://hub.docker.com/_/registry/`)
- Using Amazon elastic container registry (`https://aws.amazon.com/ecr/`)
- Using Google container registry (`https://cloud.google.com/container-registry/`)

When using a Kubernetes to set up a private registry, you may use your own Kubernetes cluster on the private or public cloud, which allows you to have full control and utilize most of your physical resources.

On the other hand, when using a public cloud-provided service, such as AWS or GCP, you can be relieved of the management of servers and storage. Whatever you need, those public clouds provide you with elastic resources. We'll just have to set the credentials to Kubernetes and let the nodes know. The following recipes will go through these three different options.

Using Kubernetes to run a Docker registry server

If you want to launch a private registry server using Kubernetes, you need your own Kubernetes cluster. You will have set up your own Kubernetes while exploring this book. If you haven't done yet, please read `Chapter 12`, *Building Your Own Kubernetes Cluster*, to choose the easiest way.

Please note that Docker registry will store some of your Docker images. You must have a `PersistentVolume` to manage your storage via Kubernetes. In addition, we should expect that multiple pods will read and write to the same `PersistentVolume` due to scalability. Therefore, you must have the **ReadWriteMany** (**RWX**) access mode of `PersistentVolume`, such as GlusterFS or NFS.

Details of `PersistentVolume` are described in the *Working with volumes* section in Chapter 13, *Walking through Kubernetes Concepts*. Let's create a `PersistentVolume` that uses NFS and the name `pvnfs01` to allocate `100` GB:

```
//my NFS server(10.138.0.5) shares /nfs directory
$ showmount -e 10.138.0.5
Export list for 10.138.0.5:
/nfs *


//please change spec.nfs.path and spec.nfs.server to yours
$ cat pv_nfs.yaml
apiVersion: "v1"
kind: "PersistentVolume"
metadata:
  name: pvnfs01
spec:
  capacity:
    storage: "100Gi"
  accessModes:
    - "ReadWriteMany"
  nfs:
    path: "/nfs"
    server: "10.138.0.5"


$ kubectl create -f pv_nfs.yaml
persistentvolume "pvnfs01" created

$ kubectl get pv
NAME      CAPACITY ACCESS MODES RECLAIM POLICY STATUS     CLAIM
STORAGECLASS REASON AGE
pvnfs01 100Gi     RWX          Retain          Available
5s
```

If you can't prepare RWX `PersistentVolume`, you may still be able to set up Docker registry by Kubernetes, but you can launch only one pod (replicas: one). As an alternative, you may use AWS S3 or GCP PD as private registry backend storage; please visit `https://docs.docker.com/registry/configuration/` to learn how to configure backend storage for your registry.

Next, create `PersistentVolumeClaim` that decouples NFS `PersistentVolume` and pod configuration. Let's create one `PersistentVolumeClaim` named `pvc-1`. Make sure `accessModes` is `ReadWriteMany` and that `STATUS` became `Bound` after creation:

```
$ cat pvc-1.yml
apiVersion: v1
kind: PersistentVolumeClaim
metadata:
    name: pvc-1
spec:
  storageClassName: ""
  accessModes:
    - ReadWriteMany
  resources:
    requests:
      storage: 100Gi

$ kubectl create -f pvc-1.yml
persistentvolumeclaim "pvc-1" created

$ kubectl get pvc
NAME STATUS VOLUME CAPACITY ACCESS MODES STORAGECLASS AGE
pvc-1 Bound pvnfs01 100Gi RWX 5s
```

This is enough to set up your private registry. It has some prerequisites; alternatively, using the public cloud is much simpler.

Using Amazon elastic container registry

Amazon **elastic container registry** (ECR) was introduced as a part of Amazon **elastic container service** (ECS). This recipe won't touch on ECS itself; instead, just use ECR as a private registry.

In order to use Amazon ECR, you have to have an AWS account and install AWS CLI on your machine. It will be described in more detail in Chapter 17, *Building Kubernetes on AWS*. You'll have to create an IAM user with `ACCESS KEY ID` and `SECRET ACCESS KEY`, and associated `AmazonEC2ContainerRegistryFullAccess` policies, which allow full administrator access to Amazon ECR:

```
{
  "Version": "2012-10-17",
  "Statement": [
    {
      "Effect": "Allow",
```

```
      "Action": [
        "ecr:*"
      ],
      "Resource": "*"
    }
  ]
}
```

Then configure the default settings in AWS CLI via the `aws configure` command:

```
$ aws configure
AWS Access Key ID [None]: <Your AWS ACCESS KEY ID>
AWS Secret Access Key [None]: <Your AWS SECRET ACCESS KEY>
Default region name [None]: us-east-1
Default output format [None]:
```

Then we can start to play with Amazon ECR.

Using Google cloud registry

Google container registry (`https://cloud.google.com/container-registry/`) is a part of the GCP. Similar to AWS, having a GCP account is required, as well as Cloud SDK (`https://cloud.google.com/sdk/`), which is the command-line interface in GCP.

On GCP, we'll just need to create a project and enable billing and the container registry API for our project. Otherwise, any operation in `gcloud` will display an error:

```
$ gcloud container images list
ERROR: (gcloud.container.images.list) Bad status during token
exchange: 403
```

In order to enable billing and container registry API, visit the GCP web console (`https://console.cloud.google.com`), navigate to the billing page and container registry page, then just enable those. Once activation is done, you can use the `gcloud container` command:

```
$ gcloud container images list
Listed 0 items.
```

Now we can start to use Google container registry.

How to do it...

We have set up the preparation steps. Let's see how to configure your private registry step by step.

Launching a private registry server using Kubernetes

In order to launch a private registry, it is necessary to configure these files in order to configure a private registry with appropriate security settings:

- SSL certificate
- HTTP secret
- HTTP basic authentication file

Creating a self-signed SSL certificate

There is a pitfall—people tend to set up a plain HTTP (disable TLS) registry without authentication in the beginning. Then it also needs to configure a Docker client (Kubernetes node) to allow an insecure registry and so on. It is a bad practice that requires many steps to set up an insecure environment.

The best practice is always using the official SSL certificate that is issued by the certificate authority. However, a self-signed certificate is always handy, especially in the testing phase. An official certificate can wait until we have FQDN defined. Therefore, this recipe will show you how to use OpenSSL to create a self-signed SSL certificate via the following steps:

1. Create a `secrets` directory:

   ```
   $ mkdir secrets
   ```

2. Run the `openssl` command to specify the options to generate a certificate (`domain.crt`) and a private key (`domain.key`) under the **secrets** directory. Note that you may type `.` to skip to input location and email info:

   ```
   $ openssl req -newkey rsa:4096 -nodes -sha256 -keyout
   secrets/domain.key -x509 -days 365 -out secrets/domain.crt
   Generating a 4096 bit RSA private key
   ...........................................++
   ...........................................................
   .++
   ```

```
writing new private key to 'secrets/domain.key'
-----
You are about to be asked to enter information that will
be incorporated
into your certificate request.
What you are about to enter is what is called a
Distinguished Name or a DN.
There are quite a few fields but you can leave some blank
For some fields there will be a default value,
If you enter '.', the field will be left blank.
-----
Country Name (2 letter code) []:us
State or Province Name (full name) []:California
Locality Name (eg, city) []:Cupertino
Organization Name (eg, company) []:packtpub
Organizational Unit Name (eg, section) []:chapter5
Common Name (eg, fully qualified host name) []:.
Email Address []:.
```

3. Check whether both certificate and private keys are generated under the secrets directory:

```
$ ls secrets/
domain.crt domain.key
```

Creating HTTP secret

Regarding HTTP secret, it will be randomly generated by the private registry instance upon startup by default. However, it is a problem if you run multiple pods, because each pod may have a different HTTP secret that occur an error when Docker client push or pull the image. So we explicitly state that all pods will use the same HTTP secret, via the following steps:

1. Use the openssl command to create a http.secret file under the secrets directory:

```
//create 8 byte random HEX string by OpenSSL
$ openssl rand -hex -out secrets/http.secret 8
```

2. Check the secrets directory, which has three files now:

```
$ ls secrets/
domain.crt domain.key http.secret
```

Creating the HTTP basic authentication file

Finally, regarding the HTTP basic authentication file, if you set up a private registry, authentication is needed when you interact with the Docker registry. You'll have to do `docker login` to get a token when pushing and pulling images. In order to create an HTTP basic authentication file, use the `htpasswd` command that is provided by Apache2 as this is easiest. Let's create a HTTP basic authentication file via the following steps:

1. Run Docker with Apache2 Docker image (`httpd`) to run the `htpasswd` command with the `bcrypt` (`-B`) option and generate a basic authentication file (`registry_passwd`) under the `secrets` directory:

   ```
   //set user=user01, passwd=my-super-secure-password
   $ docker run -i httpd /bin/bash -c 'echo my-super-secure-
   password | /usr/local/apache2/bin/htpasswd -nBi user01' >
   secrets/registry_passwd
   ```

2. Check the `secrets` directory so that now you have four files:

   ```
   $ ls secrets/
   domain.crt domain.key http.secret registry_passwd
   ```

Creating a Kubernetes secret to store security files

There are four files. We use **Kubernetes Secret** so that all pods can access it via an environment variable or mount a volume and access as a file. For more details about secrets, please refer to the *Working with secrets* section in `Chapter 13`, *Walking through Kubernetes Concepts*. You can use the `kubectl` command to load these four files to store to the Kubernetes secret via the following steps:

1. Run the `kubectl create` command with the `--from-file` parameter to specify the secrets directory:

   ```
   $ kubectl create secret generic registry-secrets --from-
   file secrets/
   secret "registry-secrets" created
   ```

2. Check the status via the `kubectl describe` command:

   ```
   $ kubectl describe secret registry-secrets
   Name:         registry-secrets
   Namespace:    default
   Labels:       <none>
   Annotations:  <none>
   ```

```
Type:    Opaque
Data
====
domain.key:       3243 bytes
http.secret:      17 bytes
registry_passwd:  69 bytes
domain.crt:       1899 bytes
```

Configuring a private registry to load a Kubernetes secret

On the other hand, the private registry itself supports reading the HTTP secret as an environment variable in string format. It also can support specifying the file path for the SSL certificate and HTTP basic authentication file as environment variables:

Environment variable name	Description	Sample value

REGISTRY_HTTP_SECRET	HTTP secret string	`valueFrom:`
		`  secretKeyRef:`
		`    name:`
		`registry-secrets`
		`    key:`
		`http.secret`

REGISTRY_HTTP_TLS_CERTIFICATE	File path for certificate (`domain.crt`)	`/mnt/domain.crt`
REGISTRY_HTTP_TLS_KEY	File path for private key (`domain.key`)	`/mnt/domain.key`
REGISTRY_AUTH_HTPASSWD_REALM	The realm in which the registry server authenticates	`basic-realm`
REGISTRY_AUTH_HTPASSWD_PATH	File path for `htpasswd` file (`registry_passwd`)	`/mnt/registry_passwd`
REGISTRY_HTTP_HOST	Specify one of Kubernetes node IP and `nodePort`	`10.138.0.3:30500`

Ideally, you should have a load balancer and set up a Kubernetes Service type as `LoadBalancer`. And then `REGISTRY_HTTP_HOST` could be the load balancer IP and port number. For simplicity, we'll just use `NodePort` in this recipe.

We'll conduct a deployment to a Kubernetes YAML file for creating a registry, and include the preceding variables inside it, so the registry pods can use them. Now we have `PersistentVolumeClaim` as `pvc-1` that supplies the container image store, and mounts SSL certificate files (`domain.crt` and `domain.key`) and an HTTP basic authentication file (`registry_passwd`) via Secret `registry-secrets`. As well as reading the HTTP Secret string as an environment variable by Secret `registry-secrets`. The entire YAML configuration is as follows:

```
$ cat private_registry.yaml
apiVersion: apps/v1
kind: Deployment
metadata:
  name: my-private-registry
spec:
  replicas: 1
  selector:
    matchLabels:
      run: my-registry
  template:
    metadata:
      labels:
        run: my-registry
    spec:
      containers:
      - name: my-registry
        image: registry
        env:
          - name: REGISTRY_HTTP_HOST
            value: 10.138.0.3:30500
          - name: REGISTRY_HTTP_SECRET
            valueFrom:
              secretKeyRef:
                name: registry-secrets
                key: http.secret
          - name: REGISTRY_HTTP_TLS_CERTIFICATE
            value: /mnt/domain.crt
          - name: REGISTRY_HTTP_TLS_KEY
            value: /mnt/domain.key
          - name: REGISTRY_AUTH_HTPASSWD_REALM
            value: basic-realm
          - name: REGISTRY_AUTH_HTPASSWD_PATH
            value: /mnt/registry_passwd
        ports:
          - containerPort: 5000
        volumeMounts:
          - mountPath: /var/lib/registry
            name: registry-storage
```

```
              - mountPath: /mnt
                name: certs
          volumes:
          - name: registry-storage
            persistentVolumeClaim:
              claimName: "pvc-1"
          - name: certs
            secret:
              secretName: registry-secrets
              items:
              - key: domain.key
                path: domain.key
              - key: domain.crt
                path: domain.crt
              - key: registry_passwd
                path: registry_passwd
---
apiVersion: v1
kind: Service
metadata:
  name: private-registry-svc
spec:
  ports:
    - protocol: TCP
      port: 5000
      nodePort: 30500
  type: NodePort
  selector:
    run: my-registry


$ kubectl create -f private_registry.yaml
deployment.apps "my-private-registry" created
service "private-registry-svc" created


//can scale to multiple Pod (if you have RWX PV set)
$ kubectl scale deploy my-private-registry --replicas=3
deployment "my-private-registry" scaled


$ kubectl get deploy
NAME                   DESIRED   CURRENT   UP-TO-DATE   AVAILABLE   AGE
my-private-registry    3         3         3            3           2m
```

Now your own private registry is ready to use!

Create a repository on the AWS elastic container registry

In order to push a container image to Amazon ECR, you need to create a repository beforehand. Unlike Docker hub or private registry, Amazon ECR doesn't create a repository automatically when it is the first time to push the image. Therefore, if you want to push three container images, you have to create three repositories in advance:

It is simple to type the `aws ecr create-repository` command to specify the repository name:

```
$ aws ecr create-repository --repository-name my-nginx
{
    "repository": {
        "registryId": "************",
        "repositoryName": "my-nginx",
        "repositoryArn": "arn:aws:ecr:us-
east-1:************:repository/my-nginx",
        "createdAt": 1516608220.0,
        "repositoryUri": "************.dkr.ecr.us-
east-1.amazonaws.com/my-nginx"
    }
}
```

That's it! You need to remember the `repositoryUri` (in the previous case, `************.dkr.ecr.us-east-1.amazonaws.com/my-nginx`) that will be used as the private image URL.

> The previous URL is masked as an ID as `************`. It is tied with your AWS account ID.

On the other hand, if you see something like the following error message, your IAM user doesn't have the permission of the `CreateRepository` operation. In this case, you need to attach an IAM policy from `AmazonEC2ContainerRegistryFullAccess`:

```
$ aws ecr create-repository --repository-name chapter5
An error occurred (AccessDeniedException) when calling the
CreateRepository operation: User: arn:aws:iam::***********:user/ecr-
user is not authorized to perform: ecr:CreateRepository on resource: *
```

Determining your repository URL on Google container registry

In order to push a container image to Google container registry, there is an important consideration regarding the repository URL. First of all, there are several Google container registry region hosts available:

- `gcr.io` (currently USA region)
- `us.gcr.io` (USA region)
- `eu.gcr.io` (Europe region)
- `asia.gcr.io` (Asia region)

 Note that these region hosts are network latency purpose, doesn't mean to restrict to a particular region. They are still accessible worldwide.

Second of all, while you tag the container image, you also need to specify your `project-id` on which you've enabled billing and API. Therefore, the entire repository URL could be:

```
<gcr region>/<project-id>/<image name>:tag
```

In my case, I used the region USA default, the project ID is `kubernetes-cookbook`, and the image name is `my-nginx`; therefore, my repository URL is:

```
gcr.io/kubernetes-cookbook/my-nginx:latest
```

Other than that, Google container registry is ready to use now!

How it works...

When you start to use private registry with Kubernetes, you must configure a credential properly. Amazon ECR and Google cloud registry need special consideration. Let's configure a credential for private registry, Amazon ECR and Google cloud registry.

Push and pull an image from your private registry

Now you can push your container image to your private registry. Because we have set up an HTTP basic authentication, you need to do docker login first. Otherwise you get a no basic auth credentials error:

```
//just tag nginx to your own private image
$ docker tag nginx 10.138.0.3:30500/my-nginx

//will be failed when push without login information. using complete
image name with private registry as prefix
$ docker push 10.138.0.3:30500/my-nginx
The push refers to a repository [10.138.0.3:30500/my-nginx]
a103d141fc98: Preparing
73e2bd445514: Preparing
2ec5c0a4cb57: Preparing
no basic auth credentials
```

Therefore, you need docker login to specify the username and password, which you set onto the registry_passwd file:

```
//docker login
$ docker login 10.138.0.3:30500
Username: user01
Password:
Login Succeeded

//successfully to push
$ docker push 10.138.0.3:30500/my-nginx
The push refers to a repository [10.138.0.3:30500/my-nginx]
a103d141fc98: Pushed
73e2bd445514: Pushed
2ec5c0a4cb57: Pushed
latest: digest:
sha256:926b086e1234b6ae9a11589c4cece66b267890d24d1da388c96dd8795b2ffcf
b size: 948
```

On the other hand, as for pulling an image from a private registry, Kubernetes nodes also needs to have a credential for your private registry. But using the `docker login` command on every node is not realistic. Instead, Kubernetes supports storing this credential as a Kubernetes secret and each node will use this credential while pulling an image.

To do that, we need to create a `docker-registry` resource that needs to specify:

- `--docker-server`: In this example, `10.138.0.3:30500`
- `--docker-username`: In this example, `user01`
- `--docker-password`: In this example, `my-super-secure-password`
- `--docker-email`: Your email address

```
//create secret named "my-private-credential"
$ kubectl create secret docker-registry my-private-credential \
> --docker-server=10.138.0.3:30500 \
> --docker-username=user01 \
> --docker-password=my-super-secure-password \
> --docker-email=hideto.saito@example.com
secret "my-private-credential" created

//successfully to created
$ kubectl get secret my-private-credential
NAME TYPE DATA AGE
my-private-credential kubernetes.io/dockerconfigjson 1 18s
```

Finally, you can pull your private image from the private registry that is specifying the `my-private-credential` secret. To do that, set `spec.imagePullSecrets` as follows:

```
$ cat private-nginx.yaml
apiVersion: v1
kind: Pod
metadata:
  name: private-nginx
spec:
  containers:
  - name: private-nginx
    image: 10.138.0.3:30500/my-nginx
  imagePullSecrets:
  - name: my-private-credential

$ kubectl create -f private-nginx.yaml
pod "private-nginx" created

//successfully to launch your Pod using private image
```

```
$ kubectl get pods private-nginx
NAME             READY      STATUS      RESTARTS     AGE
private-nginx    1/1        Running     0            10s
```

Congratulations! Now you can feel free to push your private images to your private registry run by Kubernetes. Also, pull an image from Kubernetes too. At any time, you can scale out based on client traffic.

Push and pull an image from Amazon ECR

Amazon ECR has an authentication mechanism to provide access to your private repositories. AWS CLI has a functionality to generate an access token using the `aws ecr get-login` command:

```
$ aws ecr get-login --no-include-email
```

It outputs the `docker login` command with the ID and password:

```
docker login -u AWS -p eyJwYXlsb2FkIjoiNy(very long strings)...
https://************.dkr.ecr.us-east-1.amazonaws.com
```

Therefore, just copy and paste to your terminal to acquire a token from AWS. Then try `docker push` to upload your Docker image to ECR:

```
$ docker tag nginx ************.dkr.ecr.us-east-1.amazonaws.com/my-
nginx

$ docker push ************.dkr.ecr.us-east-1.amazonaws.com/my-nginx
The push refers to repository [************.dkr.ecr.us-
east-1.amazonaws.com/my-nginx]
a103d141fc98: Pushed
73e2bd445514: Pushing 8.783MB/53.23MB
2ec5c0a4cb57: Pushing 4.333MB/55.26MB
```

On the other hand, pulling an image from ECR to Kubernetes follows exactly the same steps as the private registry that uses a Kubernetes secret to store the token:

```
$ kubectl create secret docker-registry my-ecr-secret \
> --docker-server=https://************.dkr.ecr.us-east-1.amazonaws.com
\
> --docker-email=hideto.saito@example.com \
> --docker-username=AWS \
> --docker-password=eyJwYXlsb2FkIjoiS...
secret "my-ecr-secret" created
```

```
$ kubectl get secret my-ecr-secret
NAME                TYPE                              DATA    AGE
my-ecr-secret       kubernetes.io/dockerconfigjson    1      10s
```

Now, `spec.imagePullSecrets` needs to specify `my-ecr-secret`. As well as the image URL, it also specifies the ECR repository:

```
$ cat private-nginx-ecr.yaml
apiVersion: v1
kind: Pod
metadata:
  name: private-nginx-ecr
spec:
  containers:
  - name: private-nginx-ecr
    image: ***********.dkr.ecr.us-east-1.amazonaws.com/my-nginx
  imagePullSecrets:
  - name: my-ecr-secret


$ kubectl create -f private-nginx-ecr.yaml
pod "private-nginx-ecr" created


$ kubectl get pods private-nginx-ecr
NAME                 READY    STATUS     RESTARTS    AGE
private-nginx-ecr    1/1      Running    0           1m
```

Note that this token is short-lived: it's valid up to 12 hours. So, 12 hours later, you need to run `aws ecr get-login` again to acquire a new token, then update the secret `my-ecr-secret`. It is absolutely not ideal to do this.

The good news is that Kubernetes supports the updating of the ECR token automatically via `CloudProvider`. However, it requires that your Kubernetes runs on an AWS environment such as EC2. In addition, the EC2 instance has to have an IAM role that is equivalent or higher than the `AmazonEC2ContainerRegistryReadOnly` policy.

If you really want to use your Kubernetes cluster outside of AWS by pulling an image from the ECR repository, there is a challenge in that you need to update the ECR token every 12 hours. Maybe you can do this using a cron job or by adopting some automation tools.

For more detail, please visit the AWS online document at `https://docs.aws.amazon.com/AmazonECR/latest/userguide/Registries.html`.

Push and pull an image from Google cloud registry

According to GCP documentation (`https://cloud.google.com/container-registry/docs/advanced-authentication`), there are several way to push/pull to a container registry.

Using gcloud to wrap the Docker command

The `gcloud` command has a wrapper function to run a `docker` command to push and pull. For example, if you want to push the image `gcr.io/kubernetes-cookbook/my-nginx`, use the `gcloud` command:

```
$ gcloud docker -- push gcr.io/kubernetes-cookbook/my-nginx
```

It is sufficient to push the image from your machine, however, it is not ideal if you integrate with Kubernetes. This is because it is not easy to wrap the `gcloud` command on the Kubernetes node.

Fortunately, there is a solution that creates a GCP service account and grants a permission (role) to it.

Using the GCP service account to grant a long-lived credential

We need to integrate to pull an image from the Kubernetes node, which requires a long-lived credential that can be stored to the Kubernetes secret. To do that, perform the following steps:

1. Create a GCP service account (`container-sa`):

```
$ gcloud iam service-accounts create container-sa
Created service account [container-sa].

//full name is as below
$ gcloud iam service-accounts list | grep container
container-sa@kubernetes-cookbook.iam.gserviceaccount.com
```

2. Assign `container-sa` (use full name) to the `roles/storage.admin` role:

```
$ gcloud projects add-iam-policy-binding kubernetes-
cookbook \
> --member serviceAccount:container-sa@kubernetes-
cookbook.iam.gserviceaccount.com \
> --role=roles/storage.admin
```

3. Generate a key file (`container-sa.json`) for `container-sa`:

```
$ gcloud iam service-accounts keys create container-
sa.json \
> --iam-account container-sa@kubernetes-
cookbook.iam.gserviceaccount.com

created key [f60a81235a1ed9fbce881639f621470cb087149c] of
type [json] as [container-sa.json] for [container-
sa@kubernetes-cookbook.iam.gserviceaccount.com]
```

4. Use `docker login` to check whether the key file is working or not:

```
//note that username must be _json_key
$ cat container-sa.json | docker login --username
_json_key --password-stdin gcr.io
Login Succeeded
```

5. Use `docker pull` to check whether you can pull from container registry or not:

```
$ docker pull gcr.io/kubernetes-cookbook/my-nginx
Using default tag: latest
latest: Pulling from kubernetes-cookbook/my-nginx
e7bb522d92ff: Pulling fs layer
6edc05228666: Pulling fs layer
...
```

Looks all fine! Now you can use the Kubernetes secret the exact same way with the private registry or AWS ECR.

6. Create a Kubernetes secret (`my-gcr-secret`) to specify `_json_key` and `container-sa.json`:

```
$ kubectl create secret docker-registry my-gcr-secret \
> --docker-server=gcr.io \
> --docker-username=_json_key \
> --docker-password=`cat container-sa.json` \
> --docker-email=hideto.saito@example.com
secret "my-gcr-secret" created
```

7. Specify `my-gcr-secret` to `imagePullSecrets` to launch a pod:

```
$ cat private-nginx-gcr.yaml
apiVersion: v1
kind: Pod
metadata:
  name: private-nginx-gcr
spec:
  containers:
  - name: private-nginx-gcr
    image: gcr.io/kubernetes-cookbook/my-nginx
  imagePullSecrets:
  - name: my-gcr-secret


$ kubectl create -f private-nginx-gcr.yaml
pod "private-nginx-gcr" created


$ kubectl get pods
NAME                READY    STATUS     RESTARTS   AGE
private-nginx-gcr   1/1      Running    0          47s
```

Congratulations! Now you can use Google container registry for your private registry that is fully managed by GCP. And Kubernetes can pull your private image from there.

Integrating with Jenkins

In software engineering, **continuous integration (CI)** (https://en.wikipedia.org/wiki/Continuous_integration) and **continuous delivery (CD)** (https://en.wikipedia.org/wiki/Continuous_delivery), abbreviated as CI/CD, have the ability to simplify the procedure of the traditional development process with continuous developing, testing, and delivering mechanisms in order to reduce the panic of serious conflict, namely, to deliver small changes one at a time and to narrow down the problems immediately, if any. Furthermore, through automatic tools, a product delivered by the CI/CD system can achieve better efficiency and shorten time-to-market.

Jenkins is one of the well-known CI systems, which can be configured as a continuous delivery system. Jenkins can pull your project codes from the source code control system, run the tests, and then deploy based on your configuration. In this recipe, we will show you how to integrate Jenkins to Kubernetes to achieve continuous delivery.

Getting ready

Before you start this recipe, prepare a Docker hub account (https://hub.docker.com) or you may use your private registry that is described in the previous section. But the important part is you must have a credential to pull and push to the registry. If you use Docker hub, make sure `docker login` with your credentials works.

Next, make sure your Kubernetes is ready. But we will use RBAC authentication for access from the Jenkins pod to the Kubernetes master API. If you use `minikube`, you need to add the `--extra-config=apiserver.Authorization.Mode=RBAC` option when starting a minikube:

```
//enable RBAC and allocate 8G memory
$ minikube start --memory=8192 --extra-
config=apiserver.Authorization.Mode=RBAC
```

Then, you can set up your own Jenkins server through Kubernetes as well; the details are in this section.

Some minikube versions have a `kube-dns` issue that can't resolve the external domain name, such as `https://github.com/` and `https://jenkins.io/`, that can't process this recipe. Replacing the `kube-dns` add-on with the `coredns` add-on could resolve the issue after launching `minikube` with the following command:

```
$ minikube addons disable kube-dns
$ minikube addons enable coredns
```

How to do it...

There are two important parts to go through in the Jenkins setup:

1. Jenkins needs to run a `docker` command to build your application to compose your container image
2. Jenkins need to communicate with the Kubernetes master to control deployment

To achieve step 1, there is a tricky part that needs something like a **Docker-in-Docker (dind)**. This is because Jenkins is run by Kubernetes as a pod (Docker container), and Jenkins also needs to invoke a `docker` command to build your application. It can be achieved by mounting `/var/run/docker.sock` from the Kubernetes node to the Jenkins pod that can communicate with Jenkins, the Kubernetes node, and the Docker daemon.

Docker-in-Docker and mounting `/var/run/docker.sock` have been described at `https://blog.docker.com/2013/09/docker-can-now-run-within-docker/` and `http://jpetazzo.github.io/2015/09/03/do-not-use-docker-in-docker-for-ci/`.

In order to achieve step 2, we will set up a Kubernetes service account and assign one `ClusterRole` so that the Jenkins service account can have a necessary privilege.

Let's do it step by step.

Setting up a custom Jenkins image

Run Jenkins by Kubernetes, we use an official image (`https://hub.docker.com/u/jenkins/`) but customize it to install the following applications on it:

- Docker CE
- kubectl binary
- Jenkins Docker plugin

To do that, prepare `Dockerfile` to maintain your own Jenkins image:

```
$ cat Dockerfile
FROM jenkins/jenkins:lts

EXPOSE 8080 50000

# install Docker CE for Debian :
https://docs.docker.com/engine/installation/linux/docker-ce/debian/
USER root
RUN apt-get update
RUN apt-get install -y sudo apt-transport-https ca-certificates curl
gnupg2 software-properties-common
RUN curl -fsSL https://download.docker.com/linux/$(. /etc/os-release;
echo "$ID")/gpg | apt-key add -
RUN add-apt-repository "deb [arch=amd64]
https://download.docker.com/linux/$(. /etc/os-release; echo "$ID")
$(lsb_release -cs) stable"
RUN apt-get update && apt-get install -y docker-ce

# install kubectl binary
RUN curl -LO
https://storage.googleapis.com/kubernetes-release/release/v1.9.2/bin/l
inux/amd64/kubectl
RUN chmod +x ./kubectl
RUN mv ./kubectl /usr/local/bin/kubectl

# setup Jenkins plubins :
https://github.com/jenkinsci/docker#script-usage
RUN /usr/local/bin/install-plugins.sh docker
```

Use `docker build` to build your Jenkins image and then `docker push` command to upload to your own registry in Docker hub, as shown:

```
//build your own Jenkins image
$ docker build -t <your-docker-hub-account>/my-jenkins .

//push to Docker Hub
$ docker push <your-docker-hub-account>/my-jenkins
```

Or, alternatively, you could upload that to your private registry or any other cloud-provided registry.

Hurray! We have our build system image ready now.

Setting up Kubernetes service account and ClusterRole

Imagine that after using Jenkins successfully to build your application container, you then use `kubectl` to update deployment to roll out a new binary. To do that, invoke a `kubectl` command from the inside of a Jenkins pod. In this scenario, we need a credential to communicate to the Kubernetes master.

Fortunately, Kubernetes supports this kind of scenario, which uses a service account. It is described in detail in `Chapter 18`, *Advanced Cluster Administration*. So, this recipe will use the simplest way, which uses the `default` namespace and `cluster-admin` ClusterRole.

To check whether RBAC is enabled and also if the `cluster-admin` ClusterRole exists or not, type the `kubectl get clusterrole` command:

```
$ kubectl get clusterrole cluster-admin
NAME            AGE
cluster-admin   42m
```

Next, create a service account, `jenkins-sa`, which will be used by a Jenkins pod. Prepare the following YAML configuration, and type the `kubectl create` command to create it:

```
$ cat jenkins-serviceaccount.yaml
apiVersion: v1
kind: ServiceAccount
metadata:
  name: jenkins-sa
  namespace: default
```

```
$ kubectl create -f jenkins-serviceaccount.yaml
serviceaccount "jenkins-sa" created
```

Now we can associate the `jenkins-sa` service account with a `cluster-admin` `ClusterRole`. Prepare a `ClusterRoleBinding` configuration and run the `kubectl create` command:

```
$ cat jenkins-cluteradmin.yaml
apiVersion: rbac.authorization.k8s.io/v1
kind: ClusterRoleBinding
metadata:
  name: jenkins-cluster-admin
roleRef:
  apiGroup: rbac.authorization.k8s.io
  kind: ClusterRole
  name: cluster-admin
subjects:
- kind: ServiceAccount
  name: jenkins-sa
  namespace: default


$ kubectl create -f jenkins-cluster-admin.yaml
clusterrolebinding.rbac.authorization.k8s.io "jenkins-cluster-admin"
created
```

In the result, if a pod is launched with the service account `jenkins-sa`, this Pod has the privilege to control a Kubernetes cluster because of the `cluster-admin` `ClusterRole`.

 It should create a custom `ClusterRole` that has minimal privilege for Jenkins usage. But this recipe is to focus on the Jenkins setup itself. If you want to create a custom `ClusterRole`, please go to `Chapter 18`, *Advanced Cluster Administration*.

Launching the Jenkins server via Kubernetes deployment

Based on the previous recipes, now you have:

- A custom Jenkins container image
- A service account

Finally, you can launch your custom Jenkins server on your Kubernetes cluster. Remember that we need to run a `docker` command in the Docker environment, which needs to mount `/var/run/docker.sock` from the local Kubernetes node.

In addition, we need to use a `jenkins-sa` service account to launch a Jenkins pod. It needs to specify `spec.template.spec.serviceAccountName: jenkins-sa` in the deployment configuration.

It is also recommended to have a `PersistentVolume` to preserve Jenkins home (`/var/jenkins_home`), in case a pod is restarted. We just simply use the `hostPath` `/data/jenkins-data` directory (assuming you use minikube). You may change to another path or other types of `PersistentVolume` to fit with your environment.

Overall, the deployments YAML configuration for Jenkins is as follows:

```
$ cat jenkins.yaml
apiVersion: apps/v1
kind: Deployment
...
    spec:
      serviceAccountName: jenkins-sa
      containers:
      - name: my-jenkins
        image: hidetosaito/my-jenkins
        readinessProbe:
          initialDelaySeconds: 40
          tcpSocket:
            port: 8080
        volumeMounts:
        - mountPath: /var/run/docker.sock
          name: docker-sock
        - mountPath: /var/jenkins_home
          name: jenkins-data
      volumes:
      - name: docker-sock
        hostPath:
          path: /var/run/docker.sock
```

```
        - name: jenkins-data
          hostPath:
            path: /data/jenkins-data
...


$ kubectl create -f jenkins.yaml
deployment.apps "my-jenkins" created
service "my-jenkins-service" created
```

After a few minutes, Kubernetes pulls your custom Jenkins image and runs a Jenkins pod which is capable of running a `docker` command and a `kubectl` command without any configuration due to mounting the `/var/run/docker.sock` and `jenkins-sa` service account:

```
//check Jenkins Pod status
$ kubectl get pods
NAME                          READY     STATUS     RESTARTS    AGE
my-jenkins-758b89849c-t2sm9   1/1       Running    0           17m


//access to Jenkins Pod
$ kubectl exec -it my-jenkins-758b89849c-t2sm9 -- /bin/bash


//within Jenkins Pod, you can run docker command
root@my-jenkins-758b89849c-t2sm9:/# docker pull nginx
Using default tag: latest
latest: Pulling from library/nginx
e7bb522d92ff: Pull complete
6edc05228666: Pull complete
cd866a17e81f: Pull complete
Digest:
sha256:926b086e1234b6ae9a11589c4cece66b267890d24d1da388c96dd8795b2ffcf
b
Status: Downloaded newer image for nginx:latest


//within Jenkins Pod, you can run kubectl command
root@my-jenkins-758b89849c-t2sm9:/# kubectl get nodes
NAME                                     STATUS    ROLES     AGE
VERSION
gke-chapter5-default-pool-97f6cad9-19vm  Ready     <none>    1h
v1.8.6-gke.0
gke-chapter5-default-pool-97f6cad9-1qxc  Ready     <none>    1h
v1.8.6-gke.0
gke-chapter5-default-pool-97f6cad9-cglm  Ready     <none>    1h
v1.8.6-gke.0
```

```
//go back to your terminal
root@my-jenkins-758b89849c-t2sm9:/# exit
exit
```

You are all set! Now you can configure a Jenkins job to build your application, build a container, and deploy to Kubernetes.

How it works...

Now we start to configure Jenkins to build your application. However, to access the WebUI of your custom Jenkins, you need to access the Kubernetes service that binds to your Jenkins pod. It is easier to use `kubectl port-forward` to access remotely to configure Jenkins:

```
//check pod name
$ kubectl get pods
NAME                          READY   STATUS    RESTARTS   AGE
my-jenkins-cbdd6446d-ttxj5    1/1     Running   0          1m

//port forward from your machine :58080 to Jenkins :8080
$ kubectl port-forward my-jenkins-cbdd6446d-ttxj5 58080:8080
Forwarding from 127.0.0.1:58080 -> 8080
```

The initial configuration of Jenkins is done via the following steps:

1. Access the `http://127.0.0.1:58080` Jenkins WebUI; it asks you to input `initialAdminPassword`.

2. Use `kubectl exec` to acquire the `initialAdminPassword`. Then copy and paste to the Jenkins WebUI to proceed with the initial configuration to install the suggested plugin and create an admin user:

   ```
   $ kubectl get pods
   NAME                          READY   STATUS    RESTARTS
   AGE
   my-jenkins-cbdd6446d-ttxj5    1/1     Running   0
   1m

   //now you see initialAdminPassword
   $ kubectl exec my-jenkins-cbdd6446d-ttxj5 -- /bin/bash -c
   'cat /var/jenkins_home/secrets/initialAdminPassword'
   47e236f0bf334f838c33f80aac206c22
   ```

3. You will see a Jenkins top page. Then click **Manage Jenkins**, then **Configure System**:

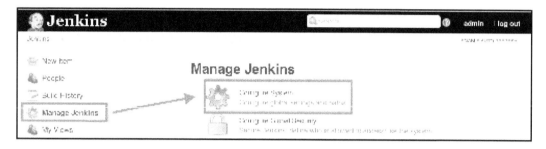

Navigate to Jenkins configuration

4. Scroll to the bottom and find a **Cloud** section. Click **Add a new cloud** to select **Docker**:

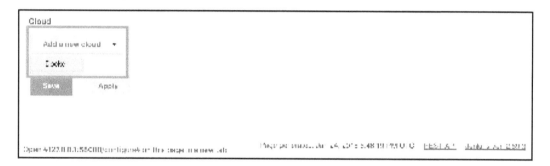

Adding a Docker setting

5. Put **Name** as your desired name (example: `my-docker`) and specify the **Docker Host URI** and Docker domain socket as `unix:///var/run/docker.sock`:

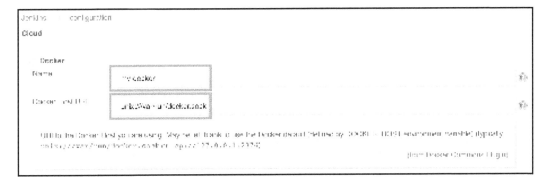

Configure Docker on Jenkins

Using Jenkins to build a Docker image

Let's configure a Jenkins job to build a sample microservice application, which was introduced in the previous recipe (`my-calc`). Perform the following steps to configure and build a Docker image:

1. On the left navigation, click **New Item**:

Navigating to create a new item

2. Put your in desired item name (example: `my-calc`), select **Freestyle project**, then click **OK**:

Creating a new Jenkins Job

3. In the **Source Code Management** tab, select **Git** and set the **Repository URL** as `https://github.com/kubernetes-cookbook/my-calc.git`, or you may use your own repository which has a `Dockerfile`:

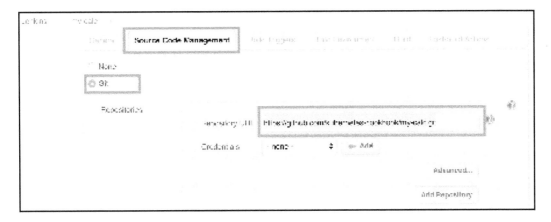

Source Code Management settings

4. On the **Build Environment** tab, click **Add build step** to add **Build / Publish Docker Image**:

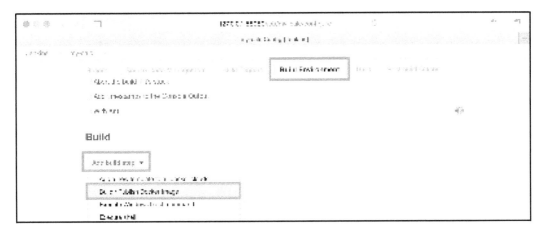

Build Environment settings

5. In the **Build / Publish Docker Image** panel:
    1. Directory for `Dockerfile` as current (`.`)
    2. Choose **my-docker** in the **Cloud** that we've set up
    3. Put image as your Docker repository, but append `:${BUILD_NUMBER}` (example: `hidetosaito/my-calc:${BUILD_NUMBER}`)
    4. Enable **Push image**
    5. Click **Add** to add your Docker hub ID credential
    6. Then, click **Save**:

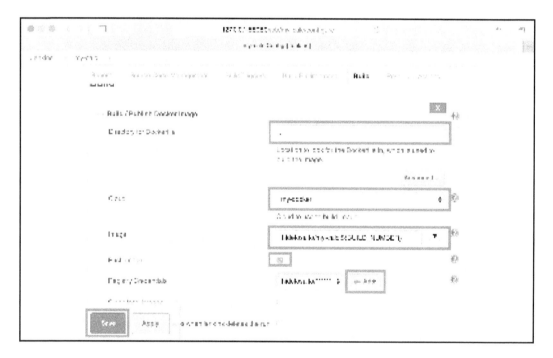

Docker build/publish settings

6. Finally, you can click **Build Now** to trigger a build; for testing purposes you can click five times to see how it works:

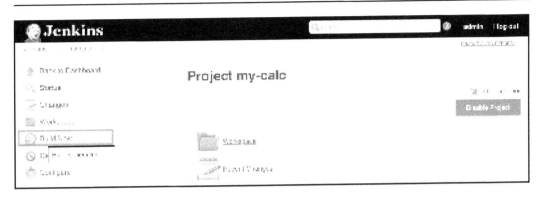

Trigger a build

7. Note that you can see a **Console** that knows it performs a Docker build and push:

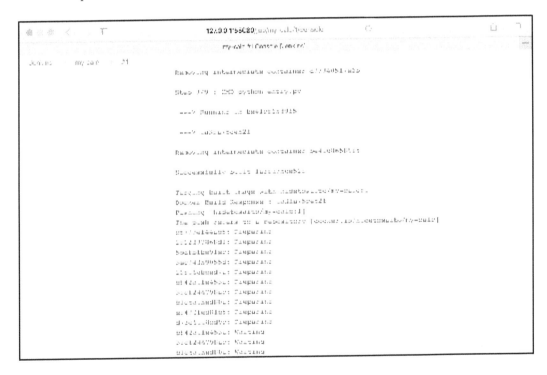

Showing a build log

8. Access your Docker hub repository; it has been pushed five times (because of clicking on **build** five times):

Docker hub repository

That's it! You can achieve continuous integration to build a Docker image so that when you update a source in GitHub, you can continuously build and push the latest image to your Docker hub repository by Jenkins.

Deploying the latest container image to Kubernetes

After each build, Jenkins keeps pushing your container image on your Docker hub repository at the end of the CI process. Next, update the Jenkins job configuration to use the latest image to deploy to Kubernetes, via the following steps:

1. The first time, we pre-deploy microservice application manually via `kubectl deploy --record`. Note that you may change `spec.template.spec.containers.image: hidetosaito/my-calc` to your repository:

```
$ cat my-calc.yaml
apiVersion: apps/v1
kind: Deployment
metadata:
  name: my-calc-deploy
spec:
  replicas: 2
  selector:
    matchLabels:
      run: my-calc
  template:
    metadata:
      labels:
        run: my-calc
    spec:
      containers:
      - name: my-calc
        image: hidetosaito/my-calc


//use --record to trace the history
$ kubectl create -f my-calc-deploy.yaml --record
deployment.apps "my-calc-deploy" created
```

2. Open Jenkins Job configuration; on the **Build** tab, right after the **Docker build settings**, click **Add build step** and choose **Execute shell**:

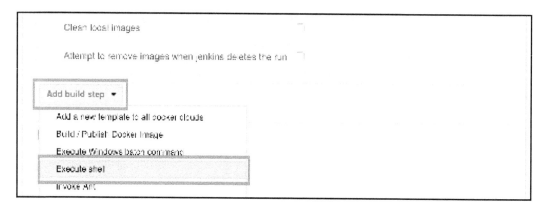

Adding a build step

3. Add this shell script and click **Save**:

```
#!/bin/sh

set +x

# These 2 are defined in Deployment YAML
DEPLOYMENT_NAME=my-calc-deploy
CONTAINER_NAME=my-calc

# change to your Docker Hub repository
REPOSITORY=hidetosaito/my-calc


echo "********************"
echo "*** before deploy ***"
echo "********************"
kubectl rollout history deployment $DEPLOYMENT_NAME
kubectl set image deployment $DEPLOYMENT_NAME
$CONTAINER_NAME=$REPOSITORY:$BUILD_NUMBER


echo "******************************************"
echo "*** waiting to complete rolling update ***"
echo "******************************************"
kubectl rollout status --watch=true deployment
$DEPLOYMENT_NAME
```

```
echo "********************"
echo "*** after deploy ***"
echo "********************"
kubectl rollout history deployment $DEPLOYMENT_NAME
```

4. Trigger a new build; you can see that after Docker push, it runs the preceding script:

Kubernetes rollout result

Now you can extend continuous integration to continuous delivery! You may extend to add a unit test or integration test and roll back mechanisms onto the above script to make your CI/CD work stronger.

Building Kubernetes on AWS

17

The following recipes are covered in this chapter:

- Playing with Amazon Web Services
- Setting up Kubernetes by kops
- Using AWS as Kubernetes Cloud Provider
- Managing Kubernete cluster on AWS by kops

Introduction

Based on a recent survey of the Cloud Native Computing Foundation, CNCF, **Amazon Web Services** (**AWS**) is a dominant solution for production-level Kubernetes systems (`https://www.cncf.io/blog/2017/12/06/cloud-native-technologies-scaling-production-applications/`). In this chapter, you will learn about the cloud services of AWS, and how these services work together to deliver a robust Kubernetes system. We will also introduce how kops works, a tool for Kubernetes operation, which helps us manage the Kubernetes cluster. Let's explore the world of Kubernetes in AWS!

Playing with Amazon Web Services

Amazon Web Services (`https://aws.amazon.com`) is the most popular public cloud service. It provides the online service for Virtual Server (EC2), Software Defined Network (VPC), Object Store (S3), and so on. It is a suitable infrastructure to set up a Kubernetes cluster. We will explore AWS to understand the fundamental function of AWS.

Getting ready

First of all, you need to sign up to AWS. AWS gives a free tier that allows you to use some amount of AWS resources, free for 12 months. Go to `https://aws.amazon.com/free/` to register your information and credit card. It may take 24 hours to verify and activate your account.

Once your AWS account is activated, we need to create one **Identity and Access Management** (**IAM**) user, which will control your AWS infrastructure via APIs. Then, install the AWS CLI on to your computer.

Creating an IAM user

Perform the following steps to create an IAM user:

1. Go to AWS Web console `https://console.aws.amazon.com`.
2. Click on **IAM** (use the search box, which makes it easier to find):

Access to IAM console

3. Click on **Users** in the left navigation and then click on **Add user**:

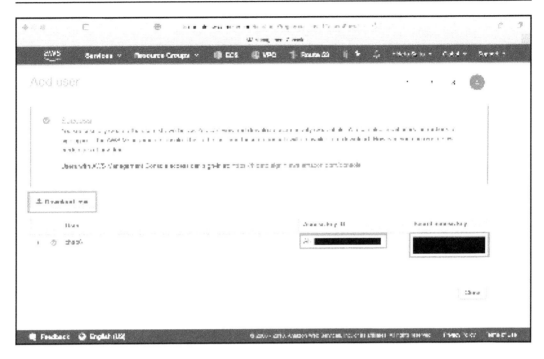

Downloading Access key ID and Secret access key

Installing AWS CLI on macOS

Install `awscli` to macOS using HomeBrew (`https://brew.sh`); this is the easiest way. HomeBrew has already been introduced in `Chapter 12`, *Building your own Kubernetes Cluster*, while installing minikube.

To install awscli by HomeBrew on your Mac, perform the following steps:

1. Type the following command to update the latest formula:

```
$ brew update
```

2. Specify `awscli` to install:

```
$ brew install awscli
```

3. Verify the `aws` command using the `--version` option:

```
$ aws --version
aws-cli/1.15.0 Python/3.6.5 Darwin/17.5.0 botocore/1.10.0
```

Installing AWS CLI on Windows

Install awscli on Windows; there is a Windows installer package, which is the easiest way to install awscli on to your Windows:

1. Go to AWS Command Line Interface page (https://aws.amazon.com/cli/).
2. Download Windows installer 64 bit (https://s3.amazonaws.com/aws-cli/AWSCLI64.msi) or 32 bit (https://s3.amazonaws.com/aws-cli/AWSCLI32.msi), based on your Windows OS.
3. Launch AWS CLI installer, and then choose the default option to proceed with the installation:

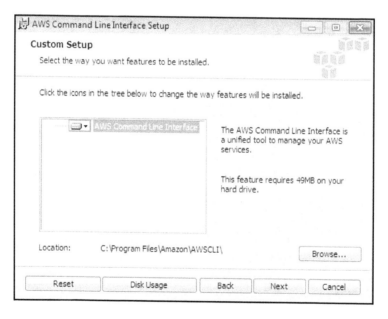

Installing AWS CLI for Windows

4. After complete installation, launch Command Prompt. Then, type the `aws` command with the `--version` option to verify:

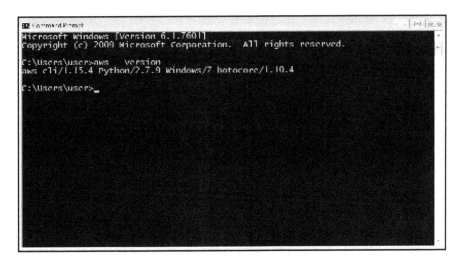

Showing aws command on Windows

How to do it...

First of all, you need to set your **AWS Access Key ID** and **AWS Secret Access Key** for awscli. We've already acquired `chap6` for the IAM user. We will use this user's Access Key ID and Secret Access Key.

1. Launch terminal (Command Prompt for Windows), and then use the `aws` command to set `Access Key ID` and `Secret Access Key`. Also, set the default region as `us-east-1`:

```
$ aws configure
AWS Access Key ID [None]: <Your Access KeyID>
AWS Secret Access Key [None]: <Your Secret Access Key>
Default region name [None]: us-east-1
Default output format [None]:
```

2. Check `chap6` IAM user using the following command:

```
$ aws iam get-user
{
    "User": {
        "Path": "/",
        "UserName": "chap6",
        "UserId": "*********************",
        "Arn": "arn:aws:iam::**************:user/chap6",
        "CreateDate": "2018-04-14T04:22:21Z"
    }
}
```

That's it! Now you can start using AWS to launch your own network and instances.

How it works...

Let's explorer AWS to launch a typical infrastructure. Using awscli to build your own VPC, Subnet, Gateway, and Security group. Then, launch the EC2 instance to understand the basic usage of AWS.

Creating VPC and Subnets

Virtual Private Cloud (**VPC**) is a Software-Defined Network. You can configure a virtual network on AWS. Subnets are inside of VPC that define network block (**Classless Inter Domain Routing** (**CIDR**)) such as `192.168.1.0/24`.

Let's create one VPC and two subnets using the following steps:

1. Create a new VPC that has `192.168.0.0/16` CIDR block (IP range: `192.168.0.0 − 192.168.255.255`). Then, capture `VpcId`:

```
$ aws ec2 create-vpc --cidr-block 192.168.0.0/16
{
    "Vpc": {
        "CidrBlock": "192.168.0.0/16",
        "DhcpOptionsId": "dopt-3d901958",
        "State": "pending",
        "VpcId": "vpc-69cfbd12",
        "InstanceTenancy": "default",
        "Ipv6CidrBlockAssociationSet": [],
        "CidrBlockAssociationSet": [
            {
                "AssociationId": "vpc-cidr-assoc-
```

```
                c35411ae",
                            "CidrBlock": "192.168.0.0/16",
                            "CidrBlockState": {
                                "State": "associated"
                            }
                        }
                    ],
                    "IsDefault": false,
                    "Tags": []
                }
            }
```

2. Create the first subnet under the VPC (vpc-69cfbd12) that has
   192.168.0.0/24 CIDR block (IP range: 192.168.0.0 − 192.168.0.255)
   and specify the availability zone as us-east-1a. Then, capture SubnetId:

```
$ aws ec2 create-subnet --vpc-id vpc-69cfbd12 --cidr-block
192.168.0.0/24 --availability-zone us-east-1a
{
    "Subnet": {
        "AvailabilityZone": "us-east-1a",
        "AvailableIpAddressCount": 251,
        "CidrBlock": "192.168.0.0/24",
        "DefaultForAz": false,
        "MapPublicIpOnLaunch": false,
        "State": "pending",
        "SubnetId": "subnet-6296863f",
        "VpcId": "vpc-69cfbd12",
        "AssignIpv6AddressOnCreation": false,
        "Ipv6CidrBlockAssociationSet": []
    }
}
```

3. Create the second subnet on us-east-1b, which has 192.168.1.0/24
   CIDR block (IP range: 192.168.1.0 − 192.168.1.255). Then, capture
   SubnetId:

```
$ aws ec2 create-subnet --vpc-id vpc-69cfbd12 --cidr-block
192.168.1.0/24 --availability-zone us-east-1b
{
    "Subnet": {
        "AvailabilityZone": "us-east-1b",
        "AvailableIpAddressCount": 251,
        "CidrBlock": "192.168.1.0/24",
        "DefaultForAz": false,
        "MapPublicIpOnLaunch": false,
        "State": "pending",
```

```
            "SubnetId": "subnet-ce947da9",
            "VpcId": "vpc-69cfbd12",
           "AssignIpv6AddressOnCreation": false,
           "Ipv6CidrBlockAssociationSet": []
        }
    }
```

4. Check the subnet list under VPC (vpc-69cfbd12) using the following command:

```
$ aws ec2 describe-subnets --filters "Name=vpc-
id,Values=vpc-69cfbd12" --query
"Subnets[*].{Vpc:VpcId,CIDR:CidrBlock,AZ:AvailabilityZone,
Id:SubnetId}" --output=table
-------------------------------------------------------
-----------
|                       DescribeSubnets
|
+-----------+----------------+------------------+-----
----------+
|    AZ     |     CIDR       |       Id         |
Vpc        |
+-----------+----------------+------------------+-----
----------+
|  us-east-1a|  192.168.0.0/24  |   subnet-6296863f  |
vpc-69cfbd12 |
|  us-east-1b|  192.168.1.0/24  |   subnet-ce947da9  |
vpc-69cfbd12 |
+-----------+----------------+------------------+-----
----------+
```

This looks good!

Internet gateway

To access your VPC network, you need to have a gateway that accesses it from the internet. **Internet Gateway** (**IGW**) is the one that connects the internet to your VPC.

Then, in the subnets under VPC, you can set the default route to go to IGW or not. If it routes to IGW, the subnet is classified as the public subnet. Then, you can assign the global IP address on the public subnet.

Let's configure the first subnet (`192.168.0.0/24`) as the public subnet that routes to IGW using the following steps:

1. Create IGW and capture `InternetGatewayId`:

```
$ aws ec2 create-internet-gateway
{
    "InternetGateway": {
        "Attachments": [],
        "InternetGatewayId": "igw-e50b849d",
        "Tags": []
    }
}
```

2. Attach IGW (`igw-e50b849d`) to your VPC (`vpc-69cfbd12`):

```
$ aws ec2 attach-internet-gateway --vpc-id vpc-69cfbd12 --internet-gateway-id igw-e50b849d
```

3. Create a routing table on VPC (`vpc-69cfbd12`) and then capture `RouteTableId`:

```
$ aws ec2 create-route-table --vpc-id vpc-69cfbd12
{
    "RouteTable": {
        "Associations": [],
        "PropagatingVgws": [],
        "RouteTableId": "rtb-a9e791d5",
        "Routes": [
            {
                "DestinationCidrBlock": "192.168.0.0/16",
                "GatewayId": "local",
                "Origin": "CreateRouteTable",
                "State": "active"
            }
        ],
        "Tags": [],
        "VpcId": "vpc-69cfbd12"
    }
}
```

4. Set the default route (0.0.0.0/0) for route table (rtb-a9e791d5) as IGW
(igw-e50b849d):

```
$ aws ec2 create-route --route-table-id rtb-a9e791d5 --
gateway-id igw-e50b849d --destination-cidr-block 0.0.0.0/0
```

5. Associate route table (rtb-a9e791d5) to public subnet
(subnet-6296863f):

```
$ aws ec2 associate-route-table --route-table-id rtb-
a9e791d5 --subnet-id subnet-6296863f
```

6. Enable autoassign public IP on the public subnet (subnet-6296863f):

```
$ aws ec2 modify-subnet-attribute --subnet-id
subnet-6296863f --map-public-ip-on-launch
```

NAT-GW

What happens if the subnet default route is not pointing to IGW? The subnet is
classified as a private subnet with no connectivity to the internet. However, some of
situation, your VM in private subnet needs to access to the Internet. For example,
download some security patch.

In this case, you can setup NAT-GW. It allows you access to the internet from the
private subnet. However, it allows outgoing traffic only, so you cannot assign public
IP address for a private subnet. Therefore, it is suitable for backend instances, such as
the database.

Let's create NAT-GW and configure a second subnet (192.168.1.0/24) as a private
subnet that routes to NAT-GW using the following steps:

1. NAT-GW needs a Global IP address, so create **Elastic IP (EIP)**:

```
$ aws ec2 allocate-address
{
  "PublicIp": "18.232.18.38",
  "AllocationId": "eipalloc-bad28bb3",
  "Domain": "vpc"
}
```

2. Create NAT-GW on the public subnet (subnet-6296863f) and assign EIP
(eipalloc-bad28bb3). Then, capture NatGatewayId.

Since NAT-GW needs to access the internet, it must be located on the public subnet instead of the private subnet.

Input the following command:

```
$ aws ec2 create-nat-gateway --subnet-id subnet-6296863f -
-allocation-id eipalloc-bad28bb3
{
    "NatGateway": {
        "CreateTime": "2018-04-14T18:49:36.000Z",
        "NatGatewayAddresses": [
            {
                "AllocationId": "eipalloc-bad28bb3"
            }
        ],
        "NatGatewayId": "nat-0b12be42c575bba43",
        "State": "pending",
        "SubnetId": "subnet-6296863f",
        "VpcId": "vpc-69cfbd12"
    }
}
```

3. Create the route table and capture `RouteTableId`:

```
$ aws ec2 create-route-table --vpc-id vpc-69cfbd12
{
    "RouteTable": {
        "Associations": [],
        "PropagatingVgws": [],
        "RouteTableId": "rtb-70f1870c",
        "Routes": [
            {
                "DestinationCidrBlock": "192.168.0.0/16",
                "GatewayId": "local",
                "Origin": "CreateRouteTable",
                "State": "active"
            }
        ],
        "Tags": [],
        "VpcId": "vpc-69cfbd12"
    }
}
```

4. Set the default route (0.0.0.0/0) of the route table (rtb-70f1870c) to NAT-GW (nat-0b12be42c575bba43):

```
$ aws ec2 create-route --route-table-id rtb-70f1870c --
nat-gateway-id nat-0b12be42c575bba43 --destination-cidr-
block 0.0.0.0/0
```

5. Associate route table (rtb-70f1870c) to private subnet (subnet-ce947da**9**):

```
$ aws ec2 associate-route-table --route-table-id
rtb-70f1870c --subnet-id subnet-ce947da9
```

Security group

Before launching your Virtual Server (EC2), you need to create a Security Group that has an appropriate security rule. Now, we have two subnets, public and private. Let's set public subnet such that it allows ssh (22/tcp) and http (80/tcp) from the internet. Then, set the private subnet such that it allows ssh from the public subnet:

1. Create one security group for the public subnet on VPC (vpc-69cfbd12):

```
$ aws ec2 create-security-group --vpc-id vpc-69cfbd12 --
group-name public --description "public facing host"
{
    "GroupId": "sg-dd8a3f94"
}
```

2. Add the ssh allow rule to the public security group (sg-dd8a3f94):

```
$ aws ec2 authorize-security-group-ingress --group-id sg-
dd8a3f94 --protocol tcp --port 22 --cidr 0.0.0.0/0
```

3. Add the http allow rule to the public security group (sg-dd8a3f94):

```
$ aws ec2 authorize-security-group-ingress --group-id sg-
dd8a3f94 --protocol tcp --port 80 --cidr 0.0.0.0/0
```

4. Create a second security group for the private subnet on VPC (vpc-69cfbd12):

```
$ aws ec2 create-security-group --vpc-id vpc-69cfbd12 --
group-name private --description "private subnet host"
{
    "GroupId": "sg-a18c39e8"
}
```

5. Add an `ssh` allow rule to the private security group (`sg-a18c39e8`):

```
$ aws ec2 authorize-security-group-ingress --group-id sg-
a18c39e8 --protocol tcp --port 22 --source-group sg-
dd8a3f94
```

6. Check the Security Group list using the following command:

```
$ aws ec2 describe-security-groups --filters "Name=vpc-id,
Values=vpc-69cfbd12" --query
"SecurityGroups[*].{id:GroupId,name:GroupName}" --output
table
---------------------------
|   DescribeSecurityGroups  |
+--------------+----------+
|      id      |   name   |
+--------------+----------+
|  sg-2ed56067 |  default |
|  sg-a18c39e8 |  private |
|  sg-dd8a3f94 |  public  |
+--------------+----------+
```

EC2

Now you need to upload your ssh public key and then launch the EC2 instance on both the public subnet and the private subnet:

1. Upload your ssh public key (assume you have a public key that is located at `~/.ssh/id_rsa.pub`):

```
$ aws ec2 import-key-pair --key-name=chap6-key --public-
key-material "`cat ~/.ssh/id_rsa.pub`"
```

2. Launch the first EC2 instance with the following parameters:
   - Use Amazon Linux image: `ami-1853ac65` (Amazon Linux)
   - T2.nano instance type: `t2.nano`
   - Ssh key: `chap6-key`
   - Public Subnet: `subnet-6296863f`
   - Public Security Group: `sg-dd8a3f94`

```
$ aws ec2 run-instances --image-id ami-1853ac65 --
instance-type t2.nano --key-name chap6-key --security-
group-ids sg-dd8a3f94 --subnet-id subnet-6296863f
```

3. Launch the second EC2 instance with the following parameters:
   - Use Amazon Linux image: `ami-1853ac65`
   - T2.nano instance type: `t2.nano`
   - Ssh key: `chap6-key`
   - Private subnet: `subnet-ce947da9`
   - Private Secuity Group: `sg-a18c39e8`

```
$ aws ec2 run-instances --image-id ami-1853ac65 --
instance-type t2.nano --key-name chap6-key --security-
group-ids sg-a18c39e8 --subnet-id subnet-ce947da9
```

4. Check the status of the EC2 instances:

```
$ aws ec2 describe-instances --filters "Name=vpc-
id,Values=vpc-69cfbd12" --query
"Reservations[*].Instances[*].{id:InstanceId,PublicIP:Publ
icIpAddress,PrivateIP:PrivateIpAddress,Subnet:SubnetId}" -
-output=table
--------------------------------------------------------------
--------------------
|                         DescribeInstances                  |
|                                                            |
+--------------+-----------------+-----------------+----
--------------------+
|   PrivateIP  |    PublicIP     |     Subnet      |
id            |
+--------------+-----------------+-----------------+----
--------------------+
|  192.168.0.206|  34.228.228.140|  subnet-6296863f|
i-03a0e49d26a2dafa4   |
|  192.168.1.218|  None          |  subnet-ce947da9|
i-063080766d2f2f520   |
+--------------+-----------------+-----------------+----
--------------------+
```

5. SSH (use the `-A` option to forward your authentication info) to the public EC2 host from your computer:

```
$ ssh -A ec2-user@34.228.228.140
The authenticity of host '34.228.228.140 (34.228.228.140)'
can't be established.
ECDSA key fingerprint is
SHA256:1E7hoBhHntVDvRItnasqyHRynajn2iuHJ7U3nsWySRU.
Are you sure you want to continue connecting (yes/no)? yes
Warning: Permanently added '34.228.228.140' (ECDSA) to the
list of known hosts.
```

```
  __|  __|_  )
  _|  (     /   Amazon Linux AMI
  ___|\___|___|
https://aws.amazon.com/amazon-linux-ami/2017.09-release-no
tes/
8 package(s) needed for security, out of 13 available
Run "sudo yum update" to apply all updates.
[ec2-user@ip-192-168-0-206 ~]$
```

6. Install and launch nginx to the public EC2 host:

```
[ec2-user@ip-192-168-0-206 ~]$ sudo yum -y install nginx
[ec2-user@ip-192-168-0-206 ~]$ sudo service nginx start
Starting nginx:
[ OK  ]
```

7. Make sure you can access the nginx server from your machine (see the following screenshot):

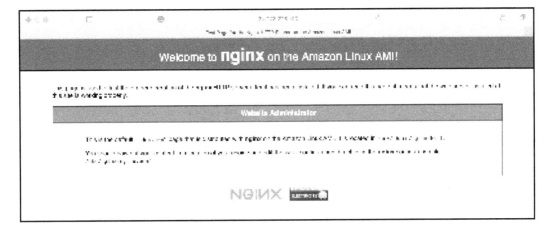

Accessing nginx web server on public host

8. SSH from the public host to the private host (you must use a private IP address):

```
$ ssh 192.168.1.218
```

9. Make sure the private host can perform yum update via NAT-GW:

```
[ec2-user@ip-192-168-1-218 ~]$ sudo yum -y update
```

Congratulations! You can set up your own infrastructure on AWS, as shown in the following diagram, which has the following:

- One VPC with CIDR `192.168.0.0/16`
- IGW
- NAT-GW
- Two Subnets
    - public subnet: `192.168.0.0/24` route to IGW
    - private subnet: 192.168.1.0/24 route to NAT-GW
- Two EC2 instances (public and private)
- Two Security Groups (allow public http/ssh and private ssh)

Now, take a look at the diagram:

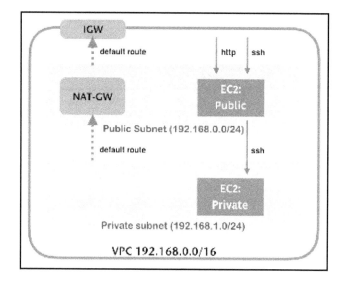

AWS components diagram

In this section, you have learned how to use AWS from scratch. We have covered its basic uses, but it is important to know while setup Kubernetes on AWS. Next, we will explore how to set up Kubernetes on AWS.

Setting up Kubernetes with kops

What is kops? It is the abbreviated term of Kubernetes Operation (`https://github.com/kubernetes/kops`). Similar to kubeadm, minikube, and kubespray, kops reduces the heavy duty of building up a Kubernetes cluster by ourselves. It helps in creation, and provides an interface to users for managing the clusters. Furthermore, kops achieves a more automatic installing procedure and delivers a production-level system. It targets to support dominate cloud platforms, such as AWS, GCE, and VMware vSphere. In this recipe, we will talk about how to run a Kubernetes cluster with kops.

Getting ready

Before our major tutorial, we will need to install kops on to your local host. It is a straightforward step for downloading the binary file and moving it to the system directory of the execution file:

```
// download the latest stable kops binary
$ curl -LO https://github.com/kubernetes/kops/releases/download/$(curl
-s https://api.github.com/repos/kubernetes/kops/releases/latest | grep
tag_name | cut -d '"' -f 4)/kops-linux-amd64
$ chmod +x kops-linux-amd64
$ sudo mv kops-linux-amd64 /usr/local/bin/kops
// verify the command is workable
$ kops version
Version 1.9.0 (git-cccd71e67)
```

Next, we have to prepare some AWS configuration on your host and required services for cluster. Refer to the following items and make sure that they are ready:

- **IAM user**: Since kops would create and build several AWS service components together for you, you must have an IAM user with kops required permissions. We've created an IAM user named **chap6** in the previous section that has the following policies with the necessary permissions for kops:
  - AmazonEC2FullAccess
  - AmazonRoute53FullAccess
  - AmazonS3FullAccess
  - IAMFullAccess
  - AmazonVPCFullAccess

Then, exposing the AWS access key ID and secret key as environment variables can make this role applied on host while firing `kops` commands:

```
$ export AWS_ACCESS_KEY_ID=${string of 20 capital
character combination}
$ export AWS_SECRET_ACCESS_KEY=${string of 40 character
and number combination}
```

- **Prepare an S3 bucket for storing cluster configuration**: In our demonstration later, the S3 bucket name will be `kubernetes-cookbook`.
- **Prepare a Route53 DNS domain for accessing points of cluster**: In our demonstration later, the domain name we use will be `k8s-cookbook.net`.

How to do it...

We can easily run up a Kubernetes cluster using a single command with parameters containing complete configurations. These parameters are described in the following table:

Parameter	Description	Value in example
--name	This is the name of the cluster. It will also be the domain name of the cluster's entry point. So you can utilize your Route53 DNS domain with a customized name, for example, `{your cluster name}.{your Route53 domain name}`.	`my-cluster.k8s-cookbook.net`
--state	This indicates the S3 bucket that stores the status of the cluster in the format `s3://{bucket name}`.	`s3://kubernetes-cookbook`
--zones	This is the availability zone where you need to build your cluster.	`us-east-1a`
--cloud	This is the cloud provider.	`aws`

`--network-cidr`	Here, kops helps to create independent CIDR range for the new VPC.	`10.0.0.0/16`
`--master-size`	This is the instance size of Kubernetes master.	`t2.large`
`--node-size`	This is the instance size of Kubernetes nodes.	`t2.medium`
`--node-count`	This is the number of nodes in the cluster.	`2`
`--network`	This is the overlay network used in this cluster.	`calico`
`--topology`	This helps you decide whether the cluster is public facing.	`private`
`--ssh-public-key`	This helps you assign an SSH public key for bastion server, then we may log in through the private key.	`~/.ssh/id_rsa.pub`
`--bastion`	This gives you an indication to create the bastion server.	N/A
`--yes`	This gives you the confirmation for executing immediately.	N/A

Now we are ready to compose the configurations into a command and fire it:

```
$ kops create cluster --name my-cluster.k8s-cookbook.net --
state=s3://kubernetes-cookbook --zones us-east-1a --cloud aws --
network-cidr 10.0.0.0/16 --master-size t2.large --node-size t2.medium
--node-count 2 --networking calico --topology private --ssh-public-key
~/.ssh/id_rsa.pub --bastion --yes
...
I0408 15:19:21.794035    13144 executor.go:91] Tasks: 105 done / 105
total; 0 can run
I0408 15:19:21.794111    13144 dns.go:153] Pre-creating DNS records
I0408 15:19:22.420077    13144 update_cluster.go:248] Exporting kubecfg
for cluster
kops has set your kubectl context to my-cluster.k8s-cookbook.net
Cluster is starting.  It should be ready in a few minutes.
...
```

After a few minutes, the command takes out the preceding logs showing what AWS services have been created and served for you kops-built Kubernetes cluster. You can even check your AWS console to verify their relationships, which will look similar to the following diagram:

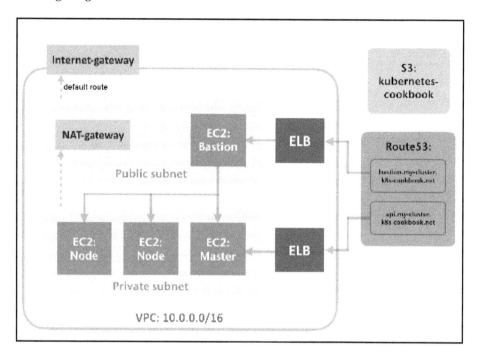

The components of Kubernetes cluster in AWS created by kops

How it works...

From localhost, users can interact with the cluster on AWS using the kops command:

```
//check the cluster
$ kops get cluster --state s3://kubernetes-cookbook
NAME                       CLOUD   ZONES
my-cluster.k8s-cookbook.net  aws     us-east-1a
```

Working with kops-built AWS cluster

Furthermore, as you can see in the previous section, the last few logs of kops cluster creation shows that the environment of the client is also ready. It means that kops helps to bind the API server to our host securely as well. We may use the `kubectl` command like we were in Kubernetes master. What we need to do is install kubectl manually. It would be as simple as installing kops; just download the binary file:

```
// install kubectl on local
$ curl -LO
https://storage.googleapis.com/kubernetes-release/release/$(curl -s
https://storage.googleapis.com/kubernetes-release/release/stable.txt)/
bin/linux/amd64/kubectl
$ chmod +x kubectl
$ sudo mv kubectl /usr/local/bin/
// check the nodes in cluster on AWS
$ kubectl get nodes
NAME                        STATUS    ROLES     AGE       VERSION
ip-10-0-39-216.ec2.internal Ready     master    2m        v1.8.7
ip-10-0-40-26.ec2.internal  Ready     node      31s       v1.8.7
ip-10-0-50-147.ec2.internal Ready     node      33s       v1.8.7
```

However, you can still access the nodes in the cluster. Since the cluster is set down in a private network, we will require to login to the bastion server first, and jump to the nodes for the next:

```
//add private key to ssh authentication agent
$ ssh-add ~/.ssh/id_rsa

//use your private key with flag "-i"
//we avoid it since the private key is in default location,
~/.ssh/id_rsa
//also use -A option to forward an authentication agent
$ ssh -A admin@bastion.my-cluster.k8s-cookbook.net

The programs included with the Debian GNU/Linux system are free
software;
the exact distribution terms for each program are described in the
individual files in /usr/share/doc/*/copyright.

Debian GNU/Linux comes with ABSOLUTELY NO WARRANTY, to the extent
permitted by applicable law.
Last login: Sun Apr  8 19:37:31 2018 from 10.0.2.167
// access the master node with its private IP
admin@ip-10-0-0-70:~$ ssh 10.0.39.216

The programs included with the Debian GNU/Linux system are free
```

```
software;
the exact distribution terms for each program are described in the
individual files in /usr/share/doc/*/copyright.

Debian GNU/Linux comes with ABSOLUTELY NO WARRANTY, to the extent
permitted by applicable law.
Last login: Sun Apr  8 19:36:22 2018 from 10.0.0.70
admin@ip-10-0-39-216:~$
```

Deleting kops-built AWS cluster

We can simply remove our cluster using the kops command as follows:

```
$ kops delete cluster --name my-cluster.k8s-cookbook.net --state
s3://kubernetes-cookbook --yes
Deleted cluster: "my-cluster.k8s-cookbook.net"
```

It will clean the AWS services for you. But some other services created by yourself: S3 bucket, IAM role with powerful authorization, and Route53 domain name; kops will not remove them on user's behavior. Remember to delete the no used AWS services on your side.

See also

- *Playing with Amazon Web Services*
- *Using AWS as Kubernetes Cloud Provider*
- *Managing Kubernetes cluster on AWS by kops*
- *Setting up the Kubernetes cluster on Linux by kubeadm* in Chapter 12, *Building your own Kubernetes Cluster*
- *Setting up Kubernetes cluster on Linux by kubespray* in Chapter 12, *Building your own Kubernetes Cluster*

Using AWS as Kubernetes Cloud Provider

From Kubernetes 1.6, **Cloud Controller Manager** (**CCM**) was introduced, which defines a set of interfaces so that different cloud providers could evolve their own implementations out of the Kubernetes release cycle. Talking to the cloud providers, you can't ignore the biggest player: Amazon Web Service. According to the Cloud Native Computing Foundation, in 2017, 63% of Kubernetes workloads run on AWS. AWS CloudProvider supports Service as **Elastic Load Balancer** (**ELB**) and Amazon **Elastic Block Store** (**EBS**) as StorageClass.

At the time this book was written, Amazon Elastic Container Service for Kubernetes (Amazon EKS) was under preview, which is a hosted Kubernetes service in AWS. Ideally, it'll have better integration with Kubernetes, such as **Application Load Balancer** (**ALB**) for Ingress, authorization, and networking. Currently in AWS, the limitation of routes per route tables in VPC is 50; it could be up to 100 as requested. However, network performance may be impacted if the routes exceed 50 according to the official documentation of AWS. While kops uses kubenet networking by default, which allocates a/24 CIDR to each node and configures the routes in route table in AWS VPC. This might lead to the performance hit if the cluster has more than 50 nodes. Using a CNI network could address this problem.

Getting ready

For following along with the examples in this recipe, you'll need to create a Kubernetes cluster in AWS. The following example is using kops to provision a Kubernetes cluster named `k8s-cookbook.net` in AWS; as the preceding recipes show, set `$KOPS_STATE_STORE` as a s3 bucket to store your kops configuration and metadata:

```
# kops create cluster --master-count 1 --node-count 2 --zones us-
east-1a,us-east-1b,us-east-1c --node-size t2.micro --master-size
t2.small --topology private --networking calico --authorization=rbac -
-cloud-labels "Environment=dev" --state $KOPS_STATE_STORE --name k8s-
cookbook.net
I0408 16:10:12.212571 34744 create_cluster.go:1318] Using SSH public
key: /Users/k8s/.ssh/id_rsa.pub I0408 16:10:13.959274 34744
create_cluster.go:472] Inferred --cloud=aws from zone "us-east-1a"
I0408 16:10:14.418739 34744 subnets.go:184] Assigned CIDR
172.20.32.0/19 to subnet us-east-1a
I0408 16:10:14.418769 34744 subnets.go:184] Assigned CIDR
```

```
172.20.64.0/19 to subnet us-east-1b I0408 16:10:14.418777 34744
subnets.go:184] Assigned CIDR 172.20.96.0/19 to subnet us-east-1c
I0408 16:10:14.418785 34744 subnets.go:198] Assigned CIDR
172.20.0.0/22 to subnet utility-us-east-1a I0408 16:10:14.418793 34744
subnets.go:198] Assigned CIDR 172.20.4.0/22 to subnet utility-us-
east-1b
I0408 16:10:14.418801 34744 subnets.go:198] Assigned CIDR
172.20.8.0/22 to subnet utility-us-east-1c ...
Finally configure your cluster with: kops update cluster k8s-
cookbook.net --yes
```

Once we run the recommended kops update cluster `<cluster_name>` `--yes` command, after a few minutes, the cluster is up and running. We can use the kops validate cluster to check whether the cluster components are all up:

```
# kops validate cluster
Using cluster from kubectl context: k8s-cookbook.net
Validating cluster k8s-cookbook.net
INSTANCE GROUPS
NAME                    ROLE    MACHINETYPE   MIN   MAX   SUBNETS
master-us-east-1a       Master  t2.small      1     1     us-east-1a
nodes                   Node    t2.micro      2     2     us-
east-1a,us-east-1b,us-east-1c
NODE STATUS
NAME                            ROLE    READY
ip-172-20-44-140.ec2.internal   node    True
ip-172-20-62-204.ec2.internal   master  True
ip-172-20-87-38.ec2.internal    node    True
Your cluster k8s-cookbook.net is ready
```

We're good to go!

How to do it...

When running Kubernetes in AWS, there are two possible integrations we could use: ELB as Service with `LoadBalancer` Type and Amazon Elastic Block Store as `StorageClass`.

Elastic load balancer as LoadBalancer service

Let's create a `LoadBalancer` Service with Pods underneath, which is what we learned in `Chapter 14`, *Playing with Containers*:

```
# cat aws-service.yaml
apiVersion: apps/v1
kind: Deployment
metadata:
  name: nginx
spec:
  replicas: 3
  selector:
    matchLabels:
      run: nginx
  template:
    metadata:
      labels:
        run: nginx
    spec:
      containers:
        - image: nginx
          name: nginx
          ports:
            - containerPort: 80
---
apiVersion: v1
kind: Service
metadata:
  name: nginx
spec:
  ports:
    - port: 80
      targetPort: 80
  type: LoadBalancer
  selector:
    run: nginx
```

In the preceding template, we declared one nginx Pod and associated it with the `LoadBalancer` service. The service will direct the packet to container port `80`:

```
# kubectl create -f aws-service.yaml
deployment.apps "nginx" created
service "nginx" created
```

Let's describe our `nginx` Service:

```
# kubectl describe svc nginx
Name:                   nginx
Namespace:              default
Labels:                 <none>
Annotations:            <none>
Selector:               run=nginx
Type:                   LoadBalancer
IP:                     100.68.35.30
LoadBalancer Ingress:
a9da4ef1d402211e8b1240ef0c7f25d3-1251329976.us-
east-1.elb.amazonaws.com
Port:                   <unset>  80/TCP
TargetPort:             80/TCP
NodePort:               <unset>  31384/TCP
Endpoints:
100.124.40.196:80,100.99.102.130:80,100.99.102.131:80
Session Affinity:       None
External Traffic Policy: Cluster
Events:
  Type     Reason                Age    From               Message
  ----     ------                ----   ----               -------
  Normal   EnsuringLoadBalancer  2m     service-controller  Ensuring
load balancer
  Normal   EnsuredLoadBalancer   2m     service-controller  Ensured load
balancer
```

After the service is created, we will find out that the AWS CloudProvider will provision a classic load balancer with the endpoint `adb576a05401911e8b1240ef0c7f25d3-1637943008.us-east-1.elb.amazonaws.com`. We can check its detailed settings via the aws command-line interface (`https://aws.amazon.com/cli/`).

To install aws CLI, you can use pip to install in Mac or Linux (`pip install awscli`); for Windows users, you'll have to download the installer from the official website.

The combination of AWS CLI commands is `aws [options] <command> <subcommand> [<subcommand> ...] [parameters]`. For listing load balancers, we'll use `aws elb describe-load-balancers` as the major command. Using the `--load-balancer-names` parameter will filter load balancers by name, and for the `--output` parameter, you can choose text, JSON, or table:

```
# aws elb describe-load-balancers --load-balancer-names
a9da4ef1d402211e8b1240ef0c7f25d3 --output text
LOADBALANCERDESCRIPTIONS
a9da4ef1d402211e8b1240ef0c7f25d3-1251329976.us-
east-1.elb.amazonaws.com Z35SXDOTRQ7X7K 2018-04-14T20:30:45.990Z
a9da4ef1d402211e8b1240ef0c7f25d3-1251329976.us-
east-1.elb.amazonaws.com a9da4ef1d402211e8b1240ef0c7f25d3     internet-
facing       vpc-07374a7c
AVAILABILITYZONES      us-east-1a
AVAILABILITYZONES      us-east-1b
AVAILABILITYZONES      us-east-1c
HEALTHCHECK    2       10      TCP:31384       5       6
INSTANCES      i-03cafedc27dca591b
INSTANCES      i-060f9d17d9b473074
LISTENER       31384   TCP     80      TCP
SECURITYGROUPS sg-3b4efb72
SOURCESECURITYGROUP    k8s-elb-a9da4ef1d402211e8b1240ef0c7f25d3
516726565417
SUBNETS subnet-088f9d27
SUBNETS subnet-e7ec0580
SUBNETS subnet-f38191ae
```

If we access this ELB endpoint port 80, we'll see the nginx welcome page:

Access ELB endpoint to access LoadBalancer Service

Behind the scene, AWS CloudProvider creates a AWS elastic load balancer and configures its ingress rules and listeners by the Service we just defined. The following is a diagram of how the traffic gets into the Pods:

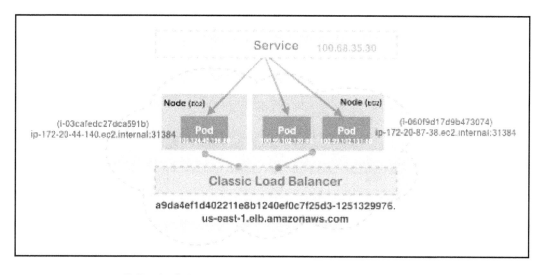

The illustration of Kubernetes resources and AWS resources for Service with LoadBalancer type

The external load balancer receives the requests and forwards them to EC2 instances using a round-robin algorithm. For Kubernetes, the traffic gets into the Service via NodePort and starts a Service-to-Pod communication.

Elastic Block Store as StorageClass

We've learned about Volumes in Chapter 13, *Walking through Kubernetes Concepts*. We know PersistentVolumeClaims is used to abstract storage resources from users. It can dynamically provision the PersistentVolume via StorageClass. The default provisioner in StorageClass in **AWS CloudProvider is Elastic Block Storage Service (aws-ebs)**. Whenever you request a PVC, aws-ebs provisioner will create a volume in AWS EBS.

Let's check the storage class in our cluster:

```
// list all storageclass
# kubectl get storageclass
NAME             PROVISIONER           AGE
default          kubernetes.io/aws-ebs  2h
gp2 (default)    kubernetes.io/aws-ebs  2h
In this recipe, we'll reuse the PVC example we mentioned in Chapter
2-6:
# cat chapter2/2-6_volumes/2-6-7_pvc.yaml
apiVersion: "v1"
kind: "PersistentVolumeClaim"
metadata:
  name: "pvclaim01"
spec:
  accessModes:
    - ReadWriteOnce
  resources:
    requests:
      storage: 1Gi
// create pvc
# kubectl create -f chapter2/2-6_volumes/2-6-7_pvc.yaml
persistentvolumeclaim "pvclaim01" created
// check pvc is created successfully.
# kubectl get pvc
NAME             STATUS    VOLUME
CAPACITY
pvclaim01   Bound     pvc-e3d881d4-402e-11e8-b124-0ef0c7f25d36   1Gi
ACCESS     MODES   STORAGECLASS    AGE
RWO            gp2            16m
```

After PVC is created, an associated PV will be created:

```
# kubectl get pv
NAME                                        CAPACITY   ACCESS MODES
pvc-e3d881d4-402e-11e8-b124-0ef0c7f25d36    1Gi        RWO
RECLAIM POLICY   STATUS    CLAIM                STORAGECLASS   REASON
AGE
Delete           Bound     default/pvclaim01    gp2
16m
```

You can take a closer look at PV here:

```
# kubectl describe pv pvc-e3d881d4-402e-11e8-b124-0ef0c7f25d36
Name:           pvc-e3d881d4-402e-11e8-b124-0ef0c7f25d36
Labels:         failure-domain.beta.kubernetes.io/region=us-east-1
                failure-domain.beta.kubernetes.io/zone=us-east-1a
Annotations:    kubernetes.io/createdby=aws-ebs-dynamic-provisioner
                pv.kubernetes.io/bound-by-controller=yes
                pv.kubernetes.io/provisioned-by=kubernetes.io/aws-ebs
Claim:          default/pvclaim01
...
Source:
    Type:       AWSElasticBlockStore (a Persistent Disk resource in
AWS)
    VolumeID:   aws://us-east-1a/vol-035ca31b9cc1820d7
    FSType:     ext4
    Partition:  0
    ReadOnly:   false
```

We can find that it's associated with the claim we just created `pvclaim01` and the source type is `AWSElasticBlockStore`, as expected.

We can use AWS CLI to inspect the volume we created in EBS. Using the `--filter Name=tag-value` we can filter the volumes in EBS:

```
// aws ec2 describe-volumes --filter Name=tag-value,Values=$PV_NAME
# aws ec2 describe-volumes --filter Name=tag-value,Values="pvc-
e3d881d4-402e-11e8-b124-0ef0c7f25d36"{
    "Volumes": [
        {
            "AvailabilityZone": "us-east-1a",
            "Tags": [
                {   "Value": "k8s-cookbook.net",
                    "Key": "KubernetesCluster" },
                {   "Value": "default",
                    "Key": "kubernetes.io/created-for/pvc/namespace"
},
                {   "Value": "k8s-cookbook.net-dynamic-pvc-
```

```
e3d881d4-402e-11e8-b124-0ef0c7f25d36",
                        "Key": "Name" },
              {    "Value": "pvclaim01",
                   "Key": "kubernetes.io/created-for/pvc/name" },
              {    "Value": "owned",
                   "Key": "kubernetes.io/cluster/k8s-cookbook.net" },
              {    "Value": "pvc-e3d881d4-402e-11e8-
b124-0ef0c7f25d36",
                   "Key": "kubernetes.io/created-for/pv/name" }],
           "VolumeType": "gp2",
           "VolumeId": "vol-035ca31b9cc1820d7",
        ...
      }
   ]
}
```

We can see that the EBS resource has been tagged with lots of different values: by observing these tags, we can know which Kubernetes cluster, namespace, PVC, and PV are associated with this EBS volume.

Thanks to dynamic provisioning that StorageClass and CloudProvider support, Volume management is no longer a huge pain. We can create and destroy PV on the fly.

There's more...

At the time of writing this book, there is no native way in Kubernetes 1.10 to support Ingress integration in AWS CloudProvider yet (ideally with application load balancer). Alternatively, kops provides addons that allow you to do so. The first one is ingress-nginx (`https://github.com/kubernetes/kops/tree/master/addons/ingress-nginx`), which is powered by nginx (`https://nginx.org`) and AWS Elastic Load Balancer. The requests will go through ELB to nginx, and nginx will dispatch the requests, based on the path definition in Ingress. Another alternative is running skipper as kubernetes-ingress-controller (`https://zalando.github.io/skipper/dataclients/kubernetes`). Kops also provides add-ons to help you deploy and leverage skipper and AWS Application Load Balancer (`https://github.com/kubernetes/kops/tree/master/addons/kube-ingress-aws-controller`).

We're expecting CCM and Amazon EKS (`https://aws.amazon.com/eks/`) to provide more native integration for Ingress via AWS Application Load Balancer, and there will be more to come!

Managing Kubernetes cluster on AWS by kops

In kops, both Kubernetes masters and nodes are running as auto-scaling groups in AWS. In kops, the concept is called **instance groups (ig)**, which indicate the same type of instances in your cluster. Similar to nodes across zones, or masters in each availability zone, we could check it via the kops command line:

```
// kops get instancegroups or kops get ig
# kops get instancegroups --name k8s-cookbook.net
NAME ROLE MACHINETYPE MIN MAX ZONES
master-us-east-1a Master t2.small 1 1 us-east-1a
nodes Node t2.micro 2 2 us-east-1a,us-east-1b,us-east-1c
```

With kops, you can change the instance type, resize instance groups (masters and nodes), rolling-update, and upgrade cluster. Kops also supports configuration for specific AWS features, such as enable AWS detailed monitoring for the instances in the cluster.

Getting ready

For performing this recipe, you'll need a Kubernetes cluster deployed by kops in AWS. You will need to follow the previous recipes in this chapter to launch a cluster. Here, we'll use the same cluster we created in the previous recipe:

```
# kops validate cluster
Using cluster from kubectl context: k8s-cookbook.net
Validating cluster k8s-cookbook.net
INSTANCE GROUPS
NAME                    ROLE    MACHINETYPE   MIN    MAX    SUBNETS
master-us-east-1a       Master t2.small       1      1      us-east-1a
nodes                   Node    t2.micro       2      2      us-
east-1a,us-east-1b,us-east-1c
NODE STATUS
NAME                         ROLE     READY
ip-172-20-44-140.ec2.internal        node    True
ip-172-20-62-204.ec2.internal        master True
ip-172-20-87-38.ec2.internal node    True
Your cluster k8s-cookbook.net is ready
```

In the previous recipe, we've had the `KOPS_STATE_STORE` environment variable set as one of our S3 bucket names by the format `s3://<bucket_name>` to store the kops configuration and metadata.

How to do it...

The upcoming subsections cover some common operational examples that cluster administrators may run into.

Modifying and resizing instance groups

Modifying instance groups may be cumbersome if you deploy all instances manually. You'll need to update instances one by one or relaunch them. By kops, we can easily perform the update without pain.

Updating nodes

Using the kops edit command, we can modify the instance type and the node count:

```
// kops edit ig nodes
# kops edit instancegroups nodes --name k8s-cookbook.net
apiVersion: kops/v1alpha2
kind: InstanceGroup
metadata:
  creationTimestamp: 2018-04-14T19:06:47Z
  labels:
    kops.k8s.io/cluster: k8s-cookbook.net
  name: nodes
spec:
  image: kope.io/k8s-1.8-debian-jessie-amd64-hvm-ebs-2018-02-08
  machineType: t2.micro
  maxSize: 2
  minSize: 2
  nodeLabels:
    kops.k8s.io/instancegroup: nodes
  role: Node
  subnets:
  - us-east-1a
  - us-east-1b
  - us-east-1c
```

In this example, we modify both minSize and maxSize from 2 to 3. After the modification, we'll need to run the kops update to see it take effect:

```
# kops update cluster k8s-cookbook.net --yes
...
I0414 21:23:52.505171   16291 update_cluster.go:291] Exporting kubecfg
for cluster
kops has set your kubectl context to k8s-cookbook.net
Cluster changes have been applied to the cloud.
Changes may require instances to restart: kops rolling-update cluster
```

Some updates will need a rolling-update cluster. In this example, kops has updated the configuration in the AWS auto scaling group. AWS will then launch a new instance to accommodate the change. The following is a screenshot from AWS Auto Scaling Group's console:

nodes_in_AWS_Auto_Scaling_Groups

We can see that the configuration has been updated, and AWS is scaling a new instance. After few minutes, we can check cluster status via `kops validate` or `kubectl get nodes`:

```
# kops validate cluster
Using cluster from kubectl context: k8s-cookbook.net
Validating cluster k8s-cookbook.net
INSTANCE GROUPS
NAME                   ROLE     MACHINETYPE    MIN    MAX    SUBNETS
master-us-east-1a      Master   t2.small       1      1      us-east-1a
nodes                  Node     t2.micro       3      3      us-
east-1a,us-east-1b,us-east-1c
NODE STATUS
NAME                            ROLE     READY
ip-172-20-119-170.ec2.internal  node     True
ip-172-20-44-140.ec2.internal   node     True
ip-172-20-62-204.ec2.internal   master   True
ip-172-20-87-38.ec2.internal node True
```

Everything looks good!

Updating masters

Updating masters is the same as updating nodes. Note that masters in the same availability zone are in one instance group. This means that you can't add additional subnets into the master instance group. In the following example, we'll resize the master count from 1 to 2.

 In this recipe, we only make the master count 1. In the real world, the recommended way is to deploy masters to at least two availability zones and have three masters per zone (one kops instance group). You can achieve that via the `--master-count` and `--master-zones` parameters when launching the cluster.

Now take a look at the following command:

```
# kops edit ig master-us-east-1a
apiVersion: kops/v1alpha2
kind: InstanceGroup
metadata:
  creationTimestamp: 2018-04-14T19:06:47Z
  labels:
    kops.k8s.io/cluster: k8s-cookbook.net
  name: master-us-east-1a
spec:
  image: kope.io/k8s-1.8-debian-jessie-amd64-hvm-ebs-2018-02-08
  machineType: t2.small
  maxSize: 1
  minSize: 1
  nodeLabels:
    kops.k8s.io/instancegroup: master-us-east-1a
  role: Master
  subnets:
  - us-east-1a
```

Before applying the change, we can run the update cluster command without `--yes` in the dry run mode:

```
# kops update cluster k8s-cookbook.net
...
Will modify resources:
  AutoscalingGroup/master-us-east-1a.masters.k8s-cookbook.net
        MinSize                 1 -> 2
        MaxSize                 1 -> 2
Must specify --yes to apply changes
```

After we verify the dry run message as expected, we can perform the update as follows. In this case, we'll have to perform a rolling update.

How to know whether a rolling update is needed
If we didn't run a kops rolling update in the preceding example, kops will show a validation error when running the kops validate cluster:

VALIDATION ERRORS
KIND   NAME   MESSAGE
InstanceGroup `master-us-east-1a` InstanceGroup `master-us-east-1a` did not have enough nodes 1 vs 2

Remember to replace k8s-cookbook.net with your cluster name.

```
# kops update cluster k8s-cookbook.net --yes && kops rolling-update
cluster
...
Using cluster from kubectl context: k8s-cookbook.net
NAME                STATUS NEEDUPDATE   READY  MIN   MAX    NODES
master-us-east-1a   Ready  0            2      2     2      1
nodes               Ready  0            3      3     3      3
No rolling-update required.
```

Just like modifying nodes, we can use both `kubectl get nodes` and `kops validate cluster` to check whether the new master has joined the cluster.

Upgrading a cluster

For demonstrating how we upgrade the Kubernetes version, we'll first launch the cluster with the 1.8.7 version. For detailed instructions of parameters, refer to the previous recipes in this chapter. Input the following command:

```
// launch a cluster with additional parameter --kubernetes-version
1.8.7 # kops create cluster --master-count 1 --node-count 2 --zones
us-east-1a,us-east-1b,us-east-1c --node-size t2.micro --master-size
t2.small --topology private --networking calico --authorization=rbac -
-cloud-labels "Environment=dev" --state $KOPS_STATE_STORE --
kubernetes-version 1.8.7 --name k8s-cookbook.net --yes
```

After few minutes, we can see that the master and the nodes are up with version 1.8.7:

```
# kubectl get nodes
NAME STATUS ROLES AGE VERSION
ip-172-20-44-128.ec2.internal Ready master 3m v1.8.7
ip-172-20-55-191.ec2.internal Ready node 1m v1.8.7
ip-172-20-64-30.ec2.internal Ready node 1m v1.8.7
```

In the following example, we'll walk through how to upgrade Kubernetes cluster from 1.8.7 to 1.9.3 using kops. Firstly, run the kops upgrade cluster command. Kops will show us the latest version that we could upgrade to:

```
# kops upgrade cluster k8s-cookbook.net --yes
ITEM PROPERTY OLD NEW
Cluster KubernetesVersion 1.8.7 1.9.3
Updates applied to configuration. You can now apply these changes,
using `kops update cluster k8s-cookbook.net`
```

It indicates that the configuration has been updated, and that we'll need to update the cluster now. We run command with the dryrun mode to check what will be modified first:

```
// update cluster
# kops update cluster k8s-cookbook.net
...
Will modify resources:
  LaunchConfiguration/master-us-east-1a.masters.k8s-cookbook.net
      UserData
                              ...
                              +    image: gcr.io/google_containers/kube-
apiserver:v1.9.3
                              -    image: gcr.io/google_containers/kube-
apiserver:v1.8.7
                              ...
                              +    image: gcr.io/google_containers/kube-
controller
manager:v1.9.3
                              -    image: gcr.io/google_containers/kube-
controller-manager:v1.8.7
                              ...
                                   hostnameOverride: '@aws'
                              +    image: gcr.io/google_containers/kube-
proxy:v1.9.3
                              -    image: gcr.io/google_containers/kube-
proxy:v1.8.7
                                   logLevel: 2
                                 kubeScheduler:
                              +    image: gcr.io/google_containers/kube-
```

```
scheduler:v1.9.3
                                   -    image: gcr.io/google_containers/kube
scheduler:v1.8.7
                         ...
Must specify --yes to apply changes
```

We could see all of the components moved from v1.8.7 to v1.9.3 in Auto Scaling Launch Configuration. After verifying that everything is good, we can run the same command with the --yes parameter:

```
// run the same command with --yes
# kops update cluster k8s-cookbook.net --yes
...
kops has set your kubectl context to k8s-cookbook.net
Cluster changes have been applied to the cloud.
Changes may require instances to restart: kops rolling-update cluster
```

In this case, we need to run the rolling update for the cluster:

```
# kops rolling-update cluster --yes
Using cluster from kubectl context: k8s-cookbook.net
NAME                     STATUS          NEEDUPDATE       READY    MIN    MAX
NODES
master-us-east-1a        NeedsUpdate     1                0        1      1
1
nodes                    NeedsUpdate     2                0        2      2
2
I0414 22:45:05.887024    51333 rollingupdate.go:193] Rolling update
completed for cluster "k8s-cookbook.net"!
```

All the nodes have been upgraded to 1.9.3! When performing the rolling update, kops drains one instance first then cordons the node. The auto-scaling group will bring up another node with the updated user data, which contains the Kubernetes component images with the updates. For avoiding downtime, you should have multiple masters and nodes as the basic deployment.

After a rolling update is completed, we can check the cluster version via `kubectl get nodes`:

```
# kubectl get nodes
NAME                          STATUS   ROLES    AGE    VERSION
ip-172-20-116-81.ec2.internal    Ready    node     14m    v1.9.3
ip-172-20-41-113.ec2.internal    Ready    master   17m    v1.9.3
ip-172-20-56-230.ec2.internal    Ready    node     8m     v1.9.3
```

All the nodes have been upgraded to 1.9.3!

There's more...

In kops, there are lots of useful addons, such as autoscaling nodes (`https://github.com/kubernetes/kops/tree/master/addons/cluster-autoscaler`) and mapping the service to the record in Route53 (`https://github.com/kubernetes/kops/tree/master/addons/route53-mapper`). Refer to the add-ons page to find out more!

See also

- *Deployment API* in `Chapter 13`, *Walking through Kubernetes Concepts*
- *Building multiple masters* in `Chapter 15`, *Building High-Availability Cluster*

18
Advanced Cluster Administration

In this chapter, we will cover the following recipes:

- Advanced settings in kubeconfig
- Setting resources in nodes
- Playing with WebUI
- Working with a RESTful API
- Working with Kubernetes DNS
- Authentication and authorization

Introduction

We will go through some advanced administration topics in this chapter. First, you will learn how to use kubeconfig to manage different clusters. Then, we will work on computing resources in nodes. Kubernetes provides a friendly user interface that illustrates the current status of resources, such as deployments, nodes, and pods. You will learn how to build and administrate it.

Next, you will learn how to work with the RESTful API that Kubernetes exposes. It will be a handy way to integrate with other systems. Finally, we want to build a secure cluster; the last section will go through how to set up authentication and authorization in Kubernetes.

Advanced settings in kubeconfig

kubeconfig is a configuration file that manages cluster, context, and authentication settings in Kubernetes, on the client side. Using the `kubeconfig` file, we are able to set different cluster credentials, users, and namespaces to switch between clusters or contexts within a cluster. It can be configured via the command line using the `kubectl config` subcommand or by updating a configuration file directly. In this section, we'll describe how to use `kubectl config` to manipulate kubeconfig and how to input a kubeconfig file directly.

If you have gone through the *Working with namespace* recipe in `Chapter 13`, *Walking through Kubernetes Concepts*, where we first mentioned kubeconfig, you will know of its basic concepts. Let's review some key points:

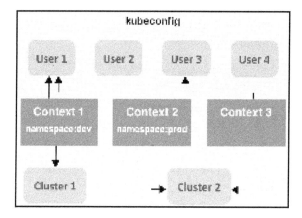

kubeconfig contains three parameters: user, cluster, and context

From the preceding diagram, we can note the following:

- **There are three parameters in kubeconfig**: User, cluster, and context—user has its own authentication, while cluster determines the specific API server with dedicated computing resources. Context is both *user* and cluster.
- **Building multiple contexts for various combinations of settings**: Users and clusters can be shared across different contexts.
- **Namespace can be aligned in one context**: The current context of a namespace sets up the rules. Any requests should follow the mapping user and cluster in the current context.

Getting ready

Please run two Kubernetes clusters and give them the specified host name. You may just update the hostfile (/etc/hosts) on the master nodes. One is under localhost with the API server endpoint http://localhost:8080 and the other is on the remote side with the endpoint http://$REMOTE_MASTER_NODE:8080. We will use these two clusters for our demonstration. The endpoints of the API server here are insecure channels. It is a simple configuration of an API server for the dummy accessing permissions.

Enableing the API server's insecure endpoint on kubeadm

We have to pass additional arguments to the API server while running kubeadm init. In this case, a custom configuration file indicated by flag --config should be applied:

```
// you can also get this file through code bundle
$ cat additional-kubeadm-config
apiVersion: kubeadm.k8s.io/v1alpha1
kind: MasterConfiguration
apiServerExtraArgs:
  insecure-bind-address: "0.0.0.0"
  insecure-port: "8080"
// start cluster with additional system settings
$ sudo kubeadm init --config ./additional-kubeadm-
config
```

After you boot up two clusters that have an insecure-accessing API server endpoint, make sure you can approach them on the localhost cluster:

```
// on localhost cluster, the following commands should be successful
$ curl http://localhost:8080
$ curl http://$REMOTE_MASTER_NODE:8080
```

Please note that the insecure address configuration is just for our upcoming tutorial. Users should be careful to set it properly on a practical system.

Before we start, we should check the default kubeconfig in order to observe the changes after any updates. Fire the command kubectl config view to see your initial kubeconfig:

```
// the settings created by kubeadm
$ kubectl config view
apiVersion: v1
```

```
clusters:
- cluster:
    certificate-authority-data: REDACTED
    server: https://192.168.122.101:6443
  name: kubernetes
contexts:
- context:
    cluster: kubernetes
    user: kubernetes-admin
  name: kubernetes-admin@kubernetes
current-context: kubernetes-admin@kubernetes
kind: Config
preferences: {}
users:
- name: kubernetes-admin
  user:
    client-certificate-data: REDACTED
    client-key-data: REDACTED
```

There will be some different settings based on your installation method. But we may also find a basic context has been initialized by the tool, which is `kubernetes-admin@kubernetes` in kubeadm. Go ahead and copy the physical `kubeconfig` file as the base for later updating, and also for resuming our original environment after our practice.

```
// in default, the kubeconfig used by client is the one under $HOME
$ cp ~/.kube/config ~/original-kubeconfig
```

How to do it...

In this recipe, we'll use localhost cluster as the main console to switch the cluster via context changes. First, run a different number of `nginx` into both the clusters and make sure the pods are all running:

```
// in the terminal of localhost cluster
$ kubectl run local-nginx --image=nginx --replicas=2 --port=80
deployment "local-nginx" created
// check the running pods
$ kubectl get pod
NAME                          READY   STATUS    RESTARTS   AGE
local-nginx-6484bbb57d-xpjp2  1/1     Running   0          1m
local-nginx-6484bbb57d-z4qgp  1/1     Running   0          1m
// in the terminal of remote cluster
$ kubectl run remote-nginx --image=nginx --replicas=4 --port=80
deployment "remote-nginx" created
```

```
$ kubectl get pod
NAME                              READY   STATUS    RESTARTS   AGE
remote-nginx-5dd7b9cb7d-fxr9m     1/1     Running   0          29s
remote-nginx-5dd7b9cb7d-gj2ft     1/1     Running   0          29s
remote-nginx-5dd7b9cb7d-h7lmj     1/1     Running   0          29s
remote-nginx-5dd7b9cb7d-hz766     1/1     Running   0          29s
```

Setting new credentials

Next, we are going to set up two credentials for each cluster. Use the subcommand `set-credentials` as `kubectl config set-credentials <CREDENTIAL_NAME>` to add a credential into kubeconfig. There are different authentication methods supported in Kubernetes. We could use a password, client-certificate, or token. In this example, we'll use HTTP basic authentication to simplify the scenario. Kubernetes also supports client certificate and token authentications. For more information, please fire the `set-credentials` command with the flag `-h` for a detailed introduction to its functionalities:

```
// check the details of setting up credentials
$ kubectl config set-credentials -h
// in localhost cluster, copy the based file into a new one
$ cp ~/original-kubeconfig ~/new-kubeconfig
// add a user "user-local" with credential named "myself@localhost" in
kubeconfig "new-kubeconfig"
$ kubectl config set-credentials myself@localhost --username=user-
local --password=passwordlocal --kubeconfig="new-kubeconfig"
User "myself@local" set.
```

Through the preceding procedures, we successfully add a new credential in the `"new-kubeconfig"` kubeconfig file. The kubeconfig file will be formatted in YAML by default—you may check the file through a text editor. With this method, we are able to customize new configurations without interfering with the current settings. On the other hand, if there is no `--kubeconfig` flag, the update will be directly attached to the `live kubeconfig`:

```
// renew live kubeconfig file with previous update
$ cp ~/new-kubeconfig ~/.kube/config
// add another credential in localhost cluster, this time, let's
update current settings directly
$ kubectl config set-credentials myself@remote --username=user-remote
--password=passwordremote
User "myself@remote" set.
```

At this moment, check your live kubeconfig settings and find out the new credentials:

```
$ kubectl config view
...
users:
- name: myself@local
  user:
    password: passwordlocal
    username: user-local
- name: myself@remote
  user:
    password: passwordremote
    username: user-remote
```

Setting new clusters

To set a new cluster, we use the command `kubectl config set-cluster <CLUSTER_NAME>`. The additional flag `--server` is required to indicate the accessing cluster. Other flags work to define the security level, such as the `--insecure-skip-tls-verify` flag, which bypasses checking the server's certificate. If you are setting up a trusted server with HTTPS, you will need to use `--certificate-authority=$PATH_OF_CERT --embed-certs=true` instead. For more information, fire the command with the `-h` flag for more information. In the following commands, we set up two cluster configurations in our localhost environment:

```
// in localhost cluster, create a cluster information pointing to
itself
$ kubectl config set-cluster local-cluster --insecure-skip-tls-
verify=true --server=http://localhost:8080
Cluster "local-cluster" set.
// another cluster information is about the remote one
$ kubectl config set-cluster remote-cluster --insecure-skip-tls-
verify=true --server=http://$REMOTE_MASTER_NODE:8080
Cluster "remote-cluster" set.
// check kubeconfig in localhost cluster, in this example, the remote
master node has the hostname "node01"
$ kubectl config view
apiVersion: v1
clusters:
...
- cluster:
    insecure-skip-tls-verify: true
    server: http://localhost:8080
  name: local-cluster
- cluster:
```

```
    insecure-skip-tls-verify: true
    server: http://node01:8080
  name: remote-cluster
...
```

> We do not associate anything with **users** and **clusters** yet. We will link them via **context** in the next section.

Setting contexts and changing current-context

One context contains a cluster, namespace, and user. According to the current context, the client will use the specified *user* information and namespace to send requests to the cluster. To set up a context, we will use the `kubectl config set-context <CONTEXT_NAME> --user=<CREDENTIAL_NAME> --namespace=<NAMESPACE> --cluster=<CLUSTER_NAME>` command to create or update it:

```
// in localhost cluster, create a context for accessing local
cluster's default namespace
$ kubectl config set-context default/local/myself --user=myself@local
--namespace=default --cluster=local-cluster
Context "default/local/myself" created.
// furthermore, create another context for remote cluster
$ kubectl config set-context default/remote/myself --
user=myself@remote --namespace=default --cluster=remote-cluster
Context "default/remote/myself" created.
```

Let's check our current kubeconfig. We can find two new contexts:

```
$ kubectl config view
...
contexts:
- context:
    cluster: local-cluster
    namespace: default
    user: myself@local
  name: default/local/myself
- context:
    cluster: remote-cluster
    namespace: default
    user: myself@remote
  name: default/remote/myself
...
```

After creating contexts, we can switch contexts in order to manage different clusters. Here, we will use the `kubectl config use-context <CONTEXT_NAME>` command:

```
// check current context
$ kubectl config current-context
kubernetes-admin@kubernetes

// use the new local context instead
$ kubectl config use-context default/local/myself
Switched to context "default/local/myself".
// check resource for the status of context
$ kubectl get pod
NAME                            READY   STATUS    RESTARTS   AGE
local-nginx-6484bbb57d-xpjp2    1/1     Running   0          2h
local-nginx-6484bbb57d-z4qgp    1/1     Running   0          2h
```

Yes, it looks fine. How about if we switch to the context with the remote cluster setting:

```
// switch to the context of remote cluster
$ kubectl config use-context default/remote/myself
Switched to context "default/remote/myself".
// check the pods
$ kubectl get pod
NAME                             READY   STATUS    RESTARTS   AGE
remote-nginx-5dd7b9cb7d-fxr9m    1/1     Running   0          2h
remote-nginx-5dd7b9cb7d-gj2ft    1/1     Running   0          2h
remote-nginx-5dd7b9cb7d-h7lmj    1/1     Running   0          2h
remote-nginx-5dd7b9cb7d-hz766    1/1     Running   0          2h
```

All the operations we have done are in the localhost cluster. kubeconfig makes the scenario of working on multiple clusters with multiple users easier.

Cleaning up kubeconfig

We can still leverage `kubectl config` to remove configurations in kubeconfig. For cluster sand context, you can delete the neglected one with the subcommands `delete-cluster` and `delete-context`. Alternatively, for these three categories, the `unset` subcommand can complete the deletion:

```
// delete the customized local context
$ kubectl config delete-cluster local-cluster
deleted cluster local-cluster from $HOME/.kube/config
// unset the local user
// to remove cluster, using property clusters.CLUSTER_NAME; to remove
contexts, using property contexts.CONTEXT_NAME
```

```
$ kubectl config unset users.myself@local
Property "users.myself@local" unset.
```

Although the effects of the preceding command would apply to the live kubeconfig right away, an even faster and more reliable way is updating another kubeconfig file for the replacement. A kubeconfig file is the text file `new-kubeconfig`, the one we just updated, or the one we copied from the initial statement, `original-kubeconfig`:

```
// remove all of our practices
$ cp ~/original-kubeconfig ~/.kube/config
// check your kubeconfig to make sure it has been cleaned
$ kubectl config view
```

There's more...

As we mentioned in the previous section, real use cases with credentials and permissions cannot be ignored like walking cross insecure endpoints, just like in our demonstration. To avoid security issues, you may take the official documentation (found at `https://kubernetes.io/docs/admin/authentication/`) while granting permissions to users.

See also

kubeconfig manages cluster, credential, and namespace settings. Check out the following recipes for complete concepts:

- The *Working with Secrets* recipe in `Chapter 13`, *Walking through Kubernetes Concepts*
- The *Working with Namespaces* recipe in `Chapter 13`, *Walking through Kubernetes Concepts*

Setting resources in nodes

Computing resource management is very important in any infrastructure. We should know our application well and preserve enough CPU and memory capacity to avoid running out of resources. In this section, we'll introduce how to manage node capacity in Kubernetes nodes. Furthermore, we'll also describe how to manage pod computing resources.

Kubernetes has the concept of resource **Quality of Service (QoS)**. It allows an administrator to prioritize pods to allocate resources. Based on the pod's setting, Kubernetes classifies each pod as one of the following:

- Guaranteed pod
- Burstable pod
- BestEffort pod

The priority is Guaranteed > Burstable > BestEffort. For example, if a BestEffort pod and a Guaranteed pod exist in the same Kubernetes node, and that node encounters CPU problems or runs out of memory, the Kubernetes master terminates the BestEffort pod first. Let's take a look at how it works.

Getting ready

There are two ways to set a Resource QoS: pod configuration or namespace configuration. If you set a Resource QoS to the Namespace, it will apply to all pods that belong to the same Namespace. If you set a Resource QoS to a pod, it will apply to the pod only. In addition, if you set it to both namespace and pod, it takes a value from the namespace configuration first, and then overwrite it with the pod configuration. Thus, we will set up two Namespaces, one which has a Resource QoS, and one that does not, to see how different they are:

1. Create two namespaces by using the `kubectl` command as follows:

```
$ kubectl create namespace chap8-no-qos
namespace "chap8-no-qos" created

$ kubectl create namespace chap8-qos
namespace "chap8-qos" created
```

2. Prepare a YAML file that sets `spec.limits.defaultRequest.cpu: 0.1` as follows:

```
$ cat resource-request-cpu.yml
apiVersion: v1
kind: LimitRange
metadata:
  name: resource-request-cpu
spec:
  limits:
  - defaultRequest:
      cpu: 0.1
```

```
        type: Container
```

3. Do this by typing the `kubectl` command so that it applies to the `chap8-qos` namespace only:

```
$ kubectl create -f resource-request-cpu.yml --
namespace=chap8-qos
limitrange "resource-request-cpu" created
```

4. Check the resource limit on both `chap8-qos` and `chap8-no-qos` with the `kubectl` command:

```
//chap8-no-qos doesn't have any resource limits value
$ kubectl describe namespaces chap8-no-qos
Name:           chap8-no-qos
Labels:         <none>
Annotations:    <none>
Status:         Active
No resource quota.
No resource limits.


//chap8-qos namespace has a resource limits value
$ kubectl describe namespaces chap8-qos
Name:           chap8-qos
Labels:         <none>
Annotations:    <none>
Status:         Active
No resource quota.
Resource Limits
 Type          Resource  Min  Max  Default Request  Default
Limit  Max Limit/Request Ratio
 ----          --------  ---  ---  ---------------  ---------
----  ----------------------
 Container     cpu       -    -    100m             -
 -
```

How to do it...

Let's configure a BestEffort pod, a Guaranteed pod, and then a Burstable pod step by step.

Configuring a BestEffort pod

The BestEffort pod has the lowest priority in the Resource QoS classes. Therefore, in the case of a resource shortage, this BestEffort pod will be terminated by the Kubernetes scheduler, then will yield CPU and memory resources to other, higher priority pods.

In order to configure a pod as a BestEffort, you need to set the resource limit as 0 (explicit), or specify no resource limit (implicit).

1. Prepare a pod configuration that explicitly sets the `spec.containers.resources.limits` as 0:

```
$ cat besteffort-explicit.yml
apiVersion: v1
kind: Pod
metadata:
  name: besteffort
spec:
  containers:
  - name: nginx
    image: nginx
    resources:
      limits:
        cpu: 0
        memory: 0
```

2. Create the pod on both the `chap8-qos` and `chap8-no-qos` namespaces:

```
$ kubectl create -f besteffort-explicit.yml --
namespace=chap8-qos
pod "besteffort" created


$ kubectl create -f besteffort-explicit.yml --
namespace=chap8-no-qos
pod "besteffort" created
```

3. Check the `QoS` class; both pods have the `BestEffort` class:

```
$ kubectl describe pods besteffort --namespace=chap8-qos |
grep QoS
QoS Class:        BestEffort

$ kubectl describe pods besteffort --namespace=chap8-no-
qos | grep QoS
QoS Class:        BestEffort
```

There is a pitfall : if you don't set any resource settings in the pod configuration, the pod takes a value from the namespace's default settings. Therefore, if you create a pod with no resource settings, the result will be different between `chap8-qos` and `chap8-no-qos`. The following example demonstrates how the namespace settings affect the result:

1. Delete the preceding pods from the `chap8-qos` and `chap8-no-qos` namespaces:

```
$ kubectl delete pod --all --namespace=chap8-qos
pod "besteffort" deleted

$ kubectl delete pod --all --namespace=chap8-no-qos
pod "besteffort" deleted
```

2. Prepare a pod configuration that doesn't have resource settings:

```
$ cat besteffort-implicit.yml
apiVersion: v1
kind: Pod
metadata:
  name: besteffort
spec:
  containers:
  - name: nginx
    image: nginx
```

3. Create the pod on both namespaces:

```
$ kubectl create -f besteffort-implicit.yml --namespace=chap8-qos
pod "besteffort" created

$ kubectl create -f besteffort-implicit.yml --namespace=chap8-no-qos
pod "besteffort" created
```

4. The result of the `QoS` class is different:

```
$ kubectl describe pods besteffort --namespace=chap8-no-qos |grep QoS
QoS Class:        BestEffort

$ kubectl describe pods besteffort --namespace=chap8-qos |grep QoS
QoS Class:        Burstable
```

Because the `chap8-qos` namespace has the default setting `request.cpu: 0.1`, it causes the pod to configure with the `Burstable` class. Therefore, we will use the `chap8-no-qos` namespace, which avoids this unexpected result.

Configuring a Guaranteed pod

The Guaranteed class has the highest priority of resource `QoS` classes. In the case of a resource shortage, the Kubernetes scheduler will try to retain the Guaranteed pod to the last.

In order to configure a pod to have the `guaranteed` class, explicitly set the resource limit and resource request as the same value, or only set the resource limit:

1. Prepare a pod configuration that has the same value for `resources.limit` and `resources.request`:

```
$ cat guaranteed.yml
apiVersion: v1
kind: Pod
metadata:
  name: guaranteed-pod
spec:
  containers:
  - name: nginx
    image: nginx
    resources:
      limits:
        cpu: 0.3
        memory: 350Mi
      requests:
        cpu: 0.3
        memory: 350Mi
```

2. Create the pod on the `chap8-no-qos` namespace:

```
$ kubectl create -f guaranteed.yml --namespace=chap8-no-qos
pod "guaranteed-pod" created
```

3. Check the `QoS class`; it has the `Guaranteed` class:

```
$ kubectl describe pods guaranteed-pod --namespace=chap8-no-qos |grep QoS
QoS Class:        Guaranteed
```

Configuring a Burstable pod

The Burstable pod has a priority that is higher than BestEffort but lower than Guaranteed. In order to configure a pod to be a Burstable Pod, you need to set `resources.request`. `resources.limit` is optional, but the value of `resources.request` and `resources.limit` must not be equal:

1. Prepare a pod configuration that has `resources.request` only:

```
$ cat burstable.yml
apiVersion: v1
kind: Pod
metadata:
  name: burstable-pod
spec:
  containers:
  - name: nginx
    image: nginx
    resources:
      requests:
        cpu: 0.1
        memory: 10Mi
      limits:
        cpu: 0.5
        memory: 300Mi
```

2. Create the pod:

```
$ kubectl create -f burstable.yml --namespace=chap8-no-qos
pod "burstable-pod" created
```

3. Check the `QoS` class; it is `Burstable`:

```
$ kubectl describe pods burstable-pod --namespace=chap8-
no-qos |grep QoS
QoS Class:        Burstable
```

How it works...

Let's see how resource requests/limits affect resource management. A preceding burstable YAML configuration declares both requests and limits by a different threshold as follows:

Type of resource definition	Resource name	Value	Description
requests	CPU	0.1	At least 10% of 1CPU core
	Memory	10Mi	At least 10 Mbytes of memory
limits	CPU	0.5	Maximum 50% of 1 CPU core
	Memory	300Mi	Maximum 300 Mbytes of memory

For the CPU resources, acceptable value expressions are either cores (0.1, 0.2 ... 1.0, 2.0) or millicpu (100 m, 200 m ... 1000 m, 2000 m). 1000 m is equivalent to 1.0 core. For example, if a Kubernetes node has 2 cores CPU (or 1 core with hyperthreading), there are a total of 2.0 cores or 2000 millicpu, as shown in the following figure:

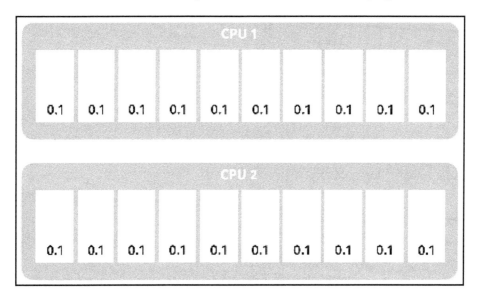

Representing a 2.0 CPU resource

By typing `kubectl describe node <node name>`, you can check what resources are available on the node:

```
//Find a node name
```

```
$ kubectl get nodes
NAME        STATUS    ROLES     AGE       VERSION
minikube    Ready     <none>    22h       v1.9.0


//Specify node name 'minikube'
$ kubectl describe nodes minikube
Name:                   minikube
Roles:                  <none>
Labels:                 beta.kubernetes.io/arch=amd64
...
...
Allocatable:
  cpu:      2
  memory:   1945652Ki
  pods:     110
```

This shows the node `minikube` , which has 2.0 CPU and approximately 1,945 MB memory. If you run the nginx example (`requests.cpu: 0.1`), it occupies at least 0.1 core, as shown in the following figure:

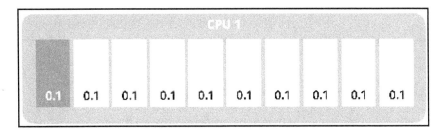

Requesting a 0.1 CPU resource

As long as the CPU has enough spaces, it may occupy up to 0.5 cores (`limits.cpu: 0.5`), as shown in the following figure:

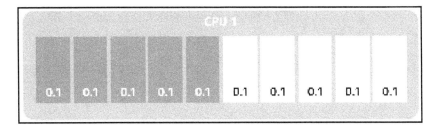

It can occupy up to 0.5 CPU resources

Therefore, if you set `requests.cpu` to be more than 2.0, the pod won't be assigned to this node, because the allocatable CPU is 2.0 and the nginx pod already occupies at least 0.1 CPU.

See also

In this section, you learned how to configure Resource QoS by setting a resource request and limit. The Namespace's default value affects the resulting pod configuration, so you should explicitly specify resource requests and limits.

Please revisit the following chapter to recap how to configure namespaces as well:

- *Working with Namespaces* in `Chapter 13`, *Walking through Kubernetes Concepts*

Playing with WebUI

Kubernetes has a WebUI that visualizes the status of resources and machines, and also works as an additional interface for managing your application without command lines. In this recipe, we are going to introduce Kubernetes dashboard.

Getting ready

Kubernetes dashboard (`https://github.com/kubernetes/dashboard`) is like a server-side application. In the beginning, just make sure you have a healthy Kubernetes cluster running, and we will go through the installation and related setup in the coming pages. Since the dashboard will be accessed by the browser, we can use a minikube-booted, laptop-running Kubernetes system, and reduce procedures for forwarding network ports or setting firewall rules.

For Kubernetes systems booting up by minikube, check that both minikube and the system itself are working:

```
// check if minikube runs well
$ minikube status
minikube: Running
cluster: Running
kubectl: Correctly Configured: pointing to minikube-vm at
192.168.99.100
// check the Kubernetes system by components
$ kubectl get cs
```

```
NAME                 STATUS    MESSAGE              ERROR
scheduler            Healthy   ok
controller-manager   Healthy   ok
etcd-0               Healthy   {"health": "true"}
```

How to do it...

While booting up your Kubernetes system with minikube, it would help to create the dashboard by default. So, we will talk about both scenarios separately.

Relying on the dashboard created by minikube

Because the Kubernetes dashboard has been started, what we have do is to open the web UI with a specific URL. It is convenient; you just need to fire a command on your terminal:

```
$ minikube dashboard
Opening kubernetes dashboard in default browser...
```

Then, you will see your favourite browser opening a new webpage, as we introduced in `Chapter 12`, *Building Your Own Kubernetes Cluster*. Its URL will look like `http://MINIKUBE_VM_IP:30000/#!/overview?namespace=default`. Most of all, we bypass the expected network proxy and authentication procedures.

Creating a dashboard manually on a system using other booting tools

To run Kubernetes dashboard, we simply fire a command to apply a configuration file, and every resource is created automatically:

```
$ kubectl create -f
https://raw.githubusercontent.com/kubernetes/dashboard/master/src/depl
oy/recommended/kubernetes-dashboard.yaml
secret "kubernetes-dashboard-certs" created
serviceaccount "kubernetes-dashboard" created
role "kubernetes-dashboard-minimal" created
rolebinding "kubernetes-dashboard-minimal" created
deployment "kubernetes-dashboard" created
service "kubernetes-dashboard" created
```

Next, let's use the command `kubectl proxy` to open a gateway connecting localhost and the API server. Then, we are good to access the dashboard via a browser:

```
$ kubectl proxy
Starting to serve on 127.0.0.1:8001
```

Once you see a halting result showing, as in the preceding code, you can now access the dashboard by URL: `http://localhost:8001/api/v1/namespaces/kube-system/services/https:kubernetes-dashboard:/proxy/`. There, you will see the following screen in your browser:

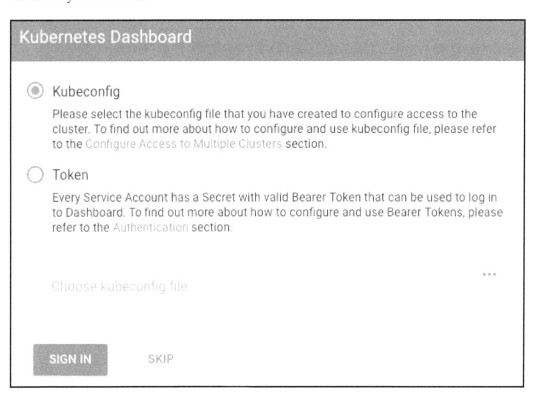

The login portal of Kubernetes dashboard

To step into our demonstration quickly, we will take the token of an existed service account to log in with. No matter what booting tool you use, leveraging the one created by the dashboard is suitable in every case:

```
// check the service account in your system
$ kubectl get secret -n kube-system
NAME                              TYPE
DATA        AGE
default-token-7jfmd               kubernetes.io/service-account-token
3           51d
kubernetes-dashboard-certs        Opaque
0           2d
kubernetes-dashboard-key-holder   Opaque
2           51d
kubernetes-dashboard-token-jw42n  kubernetes.io/service-account-token
3           2d
// grabbing token by checking the detail information of the service
account with prefix "kubernetes-dashboard-token-"
$ kubectl describe secret kubernetes-dashboard-token-jw42n -n kube-
system
Name:        kubernetes-dashboard-token-jw42n
Namespace:   kube-system
Labels:      <none>
Annotations: kubernetes.io/service-account.name=kubernetes-dashboard
             kubernetes.io/service-account.uid=253a1a8f-210b-11e8-
b301-8230b6ac4959
Type:  kubernetes.io/service-account-token
Data
====
ca.crt:      1066 bytes
namespace:   11 bytes
token:
eyJhbGciOiJSUzI1NiIsInR5cCI6IkpXVCJ9.eyJpc3MiOiJrdWJlcm5ldGVzL3NlcnZpY
2VhY2NvdW50Ii....
```

Copy the token and paste it into console on the browser, then, click **SIGN IN**:

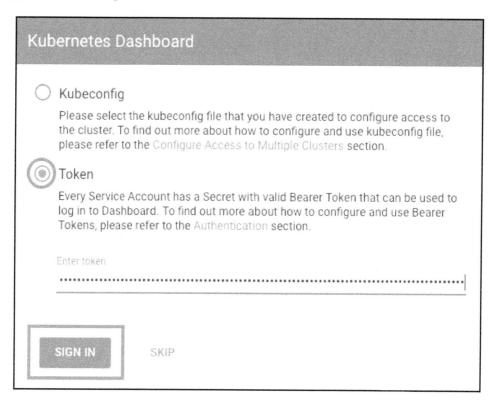

Authentication with the token of a service account

Welcome to the dashboard home page:

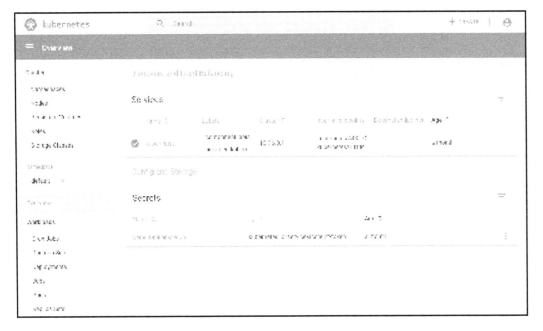

The home page of the Kubernetes dashboard

How it works...

Kubernetes dashboard has two main functions: inspecting the status of resources, and deploying resources. It can cover most of our works in the client terminal using the command `kubectl`, however, the graphic interface is more friendly.

Browsing your resource by dashboard

We can check both hardware and software resources on the dashboard. For example, to take a look at the nodes a cluster, click on **Nodes** under the **Cluster** section in the left-hand menu; every node in the current cluster will be shown on the page, with some basic information:

The status of Kubernetes nodes on the dashboard

Your result on screen may be different from the preceding screenshot, since it will be based on your environment. Go ahead and click on the name of one node; even more details will be shown. Some of them are illustrated in beautiful graphs:

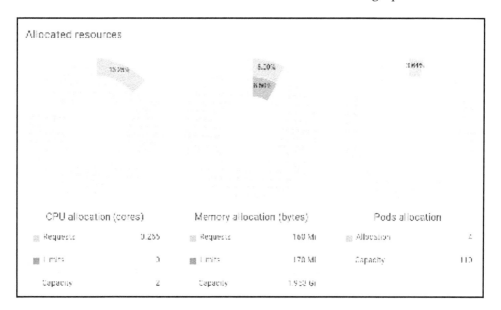

Computing the resource status of a node

To show software resources, let's take a look at the one holding this dashboard. In the left-hand menu, change the Namespace to **kube-system** and click **Overview**, which gathers all the resources under this Namespace. It is easy to find out any issue by putting resources together on a single page with a clear diagram:

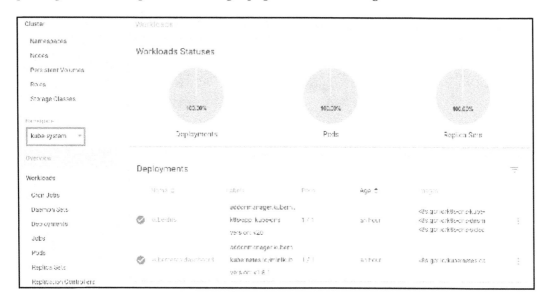

Resource overview of the namespace kube-system

There's more; click on the **Deployments** kubernetes-dashboard, and then click the small text-file icon on the right side of the only pod in the replica set. You can see the logs for the container:

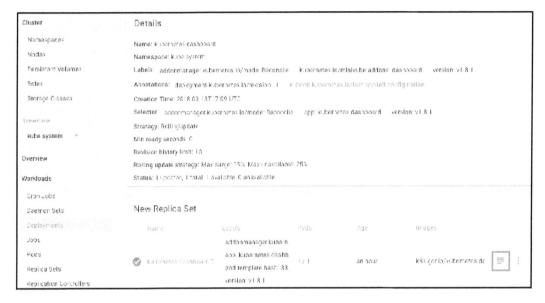

Deployment information of kubernetes-dashboard

Logs of the dashboard application

Now, we have seen that Kubernetes dashboard provides a brilliant interface for displaying resource status, covering nodes, Kubernetes workloads and controllers, and the application log.

Deploying resources by dashboard

Here, we will prepare a YAML configuration file for creating Kubernetes Deployments and related Services under a new Namespace. It will be used to build resources through the dashboard:

```
// the configuration file for creating Deployment and Service on new
Namespace: dashboard-test
$ cat my-nginx.yaml
apiVersion: apps/v1beta2
```

```
kind: Deployment
metadata:
  name: my-nginx
  namespace: dashboard-test
spec:
  replicas: 3
  selector:
    matchLabels:
      run: demo
  template:
    metadata:
      labels:
        run: demo
    spec:
      containers:
      - name: my-container
        image: nginx
        ports:
        - containerPort: 80
---
apiVersion: v1
kind: Service
metadata:
  name: my-nginx
  namespace: dashboard-test
spec:
  ports:
    - protocol: TCP
      port: 80
  type: NodePort
  selector:
    run: demo
```

First, click the **CREATE** button on the top right side of the web page.

There are three methods for deployment. Let's choose the second one and upload the configuration file introduced previously. Click the **UPLOAD** button:

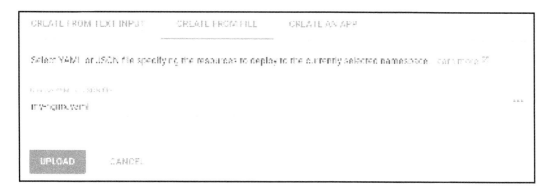

Creating a resource by configuration file

Unfortunately, errors happened:

Deploying file has failed

Your file specifies a namespace that is inconsistent with the namespace currently selected in Dashboard. Either add the namespace entry in your file or select a different namespace in Dashboard to deploy to (eg. 'All namespaces' or the correct namespace provided in the file).

CLOSE

Error message for problems due to bad deployment

Dashboard displays the resource according to a given Namespace, which is picked by *user* on the left-hand menu. This error message popped up and told users that the Namespace mentioned in the file does not match to dashboard one. What we have to do is to create a new Namespace and switch to it.

This time, we are going to create a Namespace using plain text. Click the **CREATE** button again, and pick the **create from text input** method. Paste the following lines for a new Namespace to the web page:

```
apiVersion: v1
kind: Namespace
metadata:
  name: dashboard-test
```

Now, we have a new Namespace, `dashboard-test`. Choose it as the main Namespace on the dashboard, and submit the `my-nginx.yaml` file again:

Picking a correct Namespace before submitting the configuration file

Now you can see the overview of this deployment! Yellow circles mean the pending status. They will turn to green once the pods are ready, or turn to red if they failed, but you will not see red ones if you are following these steps:

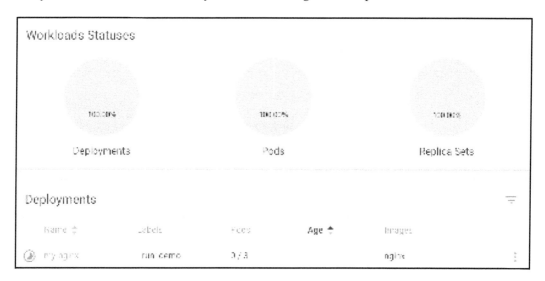

Status graph of creating a resource

Removing resources by dashboard

We can also remove Kubernetes resources through the dashboard. Try to find the Service `my-nginx` we just created by yourself! Perform the following:

- Change the Namespace on the left-hand menu to **dashboard-test**
- Click **Services** under the **Discovery and load balancing** section on left-hand menu
- Click the Service **my-nginx** on the hyperlinked name
- Click **DELETE** at the top right of the page, below the **CREATE** button

That's it! Once you see your screen launching a message for confirmation, just click it. Finally, you have not only created a resource but also removed it from the Kubernetes dashboard.

See also

This recipe described how to launch a web interface that will help with easily exploring and managing Kubernetes instances, such as pods, deployments, and services, without the `kubectl` command. Please refer to the following recipes on how to get detailed information via the `kubectl` command.

- The *Working with Pods, Deployment API*, and *Working with Services* recipes in `Chapter 13`, *Walking through Kubernetes Concepts*

Working with the RESTful API

Users can control Kubernetes clusters via the `kubectl` command; it supports local and remote execution. However, some administrators or operators may need to integrate a program to control the Kubernetes cluster.

Kubernetes has a RESTful API that controls Kubernetes clusters via an API, similar to the `kubectl` command. Let's learn how to manage Kubernetes resources by submitting API requests.

Getting ready

In this recipe, to bypass additional network settings and having to verify permissions, we will demonstrate the a *minikube*-created cluster with a Kubernetes proxy: it is easy to create a Kubernetes cluster on the host, and enable local proximity to an API server with a proxy entry.

First, run up a proxy for fast API request forwarding:

```
//curl by API endpoint
$ kubectl proxy
Starting to serve on 127.0.0.1:8001
```

Having worked with Kubernetes proxy for a while, you may find it is somehow annoying that the command `kubectl proxy` is a halt process on your terminal, forcing you to open a new channel for the following commands. To avoid this, just add & as the last parameter in your command. This & symbol in the shell will make your command run in the background:

```
$ kubectl proxy &
[1] 6372
Starting to serve on 127.0.0.1:8001
```

Be aware that you should kill this process manually if you don't use the proxy:

```
$ kill -j9 6372
```

Then, it is good to try the endpoint with a simple path, /api:

```
$ curl http://127.0.0.1:8001/api
{
  "kind": "APIVersions",
  "versions": [
    "v1"
  ],
  "serverAddressByClientCIDRs": [
    {
      "clientCIDR": "0.0.0.0/0",
      "serverAddress": "10.0.2.15:8443"
    }
  ]
}
```

Once you see some basic API server information showing as in the preceding code, congratulations! You can now play with the kubernetes RESTful API of Kubernetes.

A secured way to access the Kubernetes API server

However, if you consider accessing a more secure API server, likes a kubeadm cluster, the following items should be taken care of:

- The endpoint of the API server
- Token for authentication

We can get the required information through the following commands. And you can successfully fire the API request for the version:

```
$ APISERVER=$(kubectl config view | grep server | cut -
f 2- -d ":" | tr -d " ")
// get the token of default service account
$ TOKEN=$(kubectl get secret --field-selector
type=kubernetes.io/service-account-token -o name | grep
default-token- | head -n 1 | xargs kubectl get -o
'jsonpath={.data.token}' | base64 -d)
$ curl $APISERVER/api -H "Authorization: Bearer $TOKEN"
--insecure
```

On the other hand, you may see a message showing `permission denied` when accessing resources in kubeadm. If so, the solution is to bind the default service account to the role of administrator, that is `cluster-admin` in kubeadm system. We provide the configuration file `rbac.yaml` in the code bundle; please check it out if you need it:

```
$ curl $APISERVER/api/v1/namespaces/default/services -H
"Authorization: Bearer $TOKEN" --insecure
...
 "status": "Failure",
 "message": "services is forbidden: User
\"system:serviceaccount:default:default\" cannot list
services in the namespace \"default\"",
 "reason": "Forbidden",
...
$ kubectl create -f rbac.yaml
clusterrolebinding "fabric8-rbac" created
// now the API request is successful
$ curl $APISERVER/api/v1/namespaces/default/services -H
"Authorization: Bearer $TOKEN" --insecure
{
```

```
        "kind": "ServiceList",
        "apiVersion": "v1",
        "metadata": {
            "selfLink":
    "/api/v1/namespaces/default/services",
            "resourceVersion": "291954"
        },
    ...
```

Be careful of the `--insecure` flags, since the endpoint using HTTPS protocol, and `-H`, add headers with a token. These are the additional ones comparing with our naive demonstration settings.

How to do it...

In this section, we will show you how to manage resources through the RESTful API. Generally, the command line pattern of `curl` will cover the following ideas:

- **The operation**: `curl` without an indicating operation will fire `GET` by default. To specify your operation, add one with the `X` flag.
- **The body data**: Like creating a Kubernetes resource through `kubectl`, we apply resource configuration with the `d` flag. The value with symbol `@` can attach a file. Additionally, the `h` flag helps to add request headers; here we need to add content type in the JSON format.
- **The URL**: There are various paths after the endpoint, based on different functions.

Let's create a deployment using the following JSON configuration file:

```
$ cat nginx-deployment.json
{
  "apiVersion": "apps/v1",
  "kind": "Deployment",
  "metadata": {
    "name": "my-nginx"
  },
  "spec": {
    "replicas": 2,
      "selector": {
      "matchLabels": {
        "app": "nginx"
      }
    },
```

```
    "template": {
      "metadata": {
        "labels": {
          "app": "nginx"
        }
      },
      "spec": {
        "containers": [
          {
            "image": "nginx",
            "name": "my-nginx"
          }
        ]
      }
    }
  }
}
```

We can get every function in the API reference page (`https://kubernetes.io/docs/reference/generated/kubernetes-api/v1.10/`). It is similar to searching for the configuration of a resource while writing up a configuration file. To submit an API request, you should know what kind of resource to work on, and what operation to perform on it. Perform the following procedures to find the corresponding information on the reference webpage:

1. Choose an resource.
2. Choose an operation, for example, read or write.
3. Choose the details of the operation, for example, **Create** or **Delete**.
4. The information will show in the middle panel of the webpage. An optional step is to switch `kubectl` to `curl` on the top right of the console. More details such as command flags will show on the right panel.

To check the information for creating a Deployment, your web console may look as it does in this screenshot:

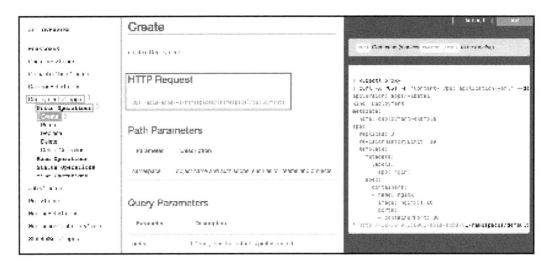

The steps finding the path for API using to create a deployment

Based on the reference page, we can combine a specified `curl` command and fire a request now:

```
$ curl -X POST -H "Content-type: application/json" -d @nginx-
deployment.json
http://localhost:8001/apis/apps/v1/namespaces/default/deployments
{
  "kind": "Deployment",
  "apiVersion": "apps/v1",
  "metadata": {
    "name": "my-nginx",
    "namespace": "default",
    "selfLink": "/apis/apps/v1/namespaces/default/deployments/my-
nginx",
    "uid": "6eca324e-2cc8-11e8-806a-080027b04dc6",
    "resourceVersion": "209",
    "generation": 1,
    "creationTimestamp": "2018-03-21T05:26:39Z",
    "labels": {
      "app": "nginx"
    }
  },
  ...
```

For a successful request, the server returns the status of the resource. Go ahead and check if we can find the new Deployment through the `kubectl` command:

```
$ kubectl get deployment
NAME        DESIRED   CURRENT   UP-TO-DATE   AVAILABLE   AGE
my-nginx    2         2         2            2           1m
```

Of course, it also works while checking it via the RESTful API:

```
// the operation "-X GET" can be ignored, since
$ curl -X GET
http://localhost:8001/apis/apps/v1/namespaces/default/deployments
```

Next, try to delete this new Deployment, `my-nginx`, as well. It is a kind of `write` operation:

```
$ curl -X DELETE
http://localhost:8001/apis/apps/v1/namespaces/default/deployments/my-n
ginx
{
  "kind": "Status",
  "apiVersion": "v1",
  "metadata": {
  },
  "status": "Success",
  "details": {
    "name": "my-nginx",
    "group": "apps",
    "kind": "deployments",
    "uid": "386a3aaa-2d2d-11e8-9843-080027b04dc6"
  }
}
```

How it works...

The RESTful API allows CRUD (**Create**, **Read**, **Update**, and **Delete**) operations, which are the same concepts behind every modern web application. For more details, please refer to https://en.wikipedia.org/wiki/Create,_read,_update_and_delete.

According to the CRUD structure, the Kubernetes RESTful API has the following basic method:

Operation	HTTP Method	Example
Create	POST	POST /api/v1/namespaces/default/pods
Read	GET	GET /api/v1/componentstatuses
Update	PUT	PUT /apis/apps/v1/namespaces/default/deployments/my-nginx
Delete	DELETE	DELETE /api/v1/namespaces/default/services/nginx-service

As we mentioned in the recipe *Working with configuration files* in `Chapter 14`, *Playing with Containers*, Kubernetes builds the RESTful API with *swagger* (`https://swagger.io/`) and OpenAPI (`https://www.openapis.org`). We can open the swagger UI console of your cluster to check the API functions. Nevertheless, it is recommended that you check them through the official website, the one we demonstrated in the last section. The description on the website is more elaborate and user-friendly.

There's more...

An even more programmatic way to utilize Kubernetes API is to use the client library (`https://kubernetes.io/docs/reference/client-libraries/`). Making good use of these client tools not only saves you time in resource management, but also produce a robust and reliable CI/CD environment. Here, we would like to introduce the Kubernetes client library for Python: `https://github.com/kubernetes-client/python`. To start, you should install the Python library for Kubernetes:

```
$ pip install kubernetes
```

Then, please put the following Python file at the same location as the JSON configuration file, `nginx-deployment.json`, where firing `kubectl` does work on the system:

```
$ cat create_deployment.py
from kubernetes import client, config
import json
config.load_kube_config()
resource_config = json.load(open("./nginx-deployment.json"))
api_instance = client.AppsV1Api()
response =
api_instance.create_namespaced_deployment(body=resource_config,
```

```
namespace="default")
print("success, status={}".format(response.status))
```

You don't even enable the Kubernetes proxy now; continue to run this script directly and see what happens:

```
$ python create_deployment.py
```

See also

This recipe described how to use the Kubernetes RESTful API via a program. It is important to integrate this with your automation program remotely. For detailed parameter and security enhancement, please refer to the following recipe:

- The *Working with configuration files* recipe in `Chapter 14`, *Playing with Containers*

Working with Kubernetes DNS

When you deploy many pods to a Kubernetes cluster, service discovery is one of the most important functions, because pods may depend on other pods but the IP address of a pod will be changed when it restarts. You need to have a flexible way to communicate a pod's IP address to other pods. Kubernetes has an add-on feature called `kube-dns` that helps in this scenario. It can register and look up an IP address for pods and Kubernetes Services.

In this section, we will explore how to use `kube-dns`, which gives you a flexible way to configure DNS in your Kubernetes cluster.

Getting ready

Since Kubernetes version 1.3, `kube-dns` has come with Kubernetes and is enabled by default. To check whether `kube-dns` is working or not, check the `kube-system` namespace with the following command:

```
$ kubectl get deploy kube-dns --namespace=kube-system
NAME        DESIRED    CURRENT    UP-TO-DATE    AVAILABLE    AGE
kube-dns    1          1          1             1            1d
```

If you are using minikube, type the following command to see the addon's status:

```
$ minikube addons list |grep kube-dns
- kube-dns: enabled
```

If it shows as disabled, you need to enable it using the following command:

```
$ minikube addons enable kube-dns
```

In addition, prepare two namespaces, chap8-domain1 and chap8-domain2, to demonstrate how kube-dns assigns domain names:

```
$ kubectl create namespace chap8-domain1
namespace "chap8-domain1" created

$ kubectl create namespace chap8-domain2
namespace "chap8-domain2" created

//check chap8-domain1 and chap8-domain2
$ kubectl get namespaces
NAME            STATUS    AGE
chap8-domain1   Active    16s
chap8-domain2   Active    14s
default         Active    4h
kube-public     Active    4h
kube-system     Active    4h
```

How to do it...

kube-dns assigns the **fully qualified domain name** (**FQDN**) to pods and Kubernetes Services. Let's look at some differences.

DNS for pod

Kubernetes assigns the domain name for the pod as <IP address>.<Namespace name>.pod.cluster.local. Because it uses the pod's IP address, FQDN is not guaranteed to be present permanently, but it is nice to have in case an application needs FQDN.

Let's deploy apache2 (httpd) on chap8-domain1 and chap8-domain2, as follows:

```
$ kubectl run my-apache --image=httpd --namespace chap8-domain1
deployment "my-apache" created
```

```
$ kubectl run my-apache --image=httpd --namespace chap8-domain2
deployment "my-apache" created
```

Type `kubectl get pod -o wide` to capture an IP address for those pods:

```
$ kubectl get pods -o wide --namespace=chap8-domain1
NAME                          READY      STATUS      RESTARTS      AGE
IP            NODE
my-apache-55fb679f49-qw58f    1/1        Running     0             27s
172.17.0.4    minikube


$ kubectl get pods -o wide --namespace=chap8-domain2
NAME                          READY      STATUS      RESTARTS      AGE
IP            NODE
my-apache-55fb679f49-z9gsr    1/1        Running     0             26s
172.17.0.5    minikube
```

This shows that `my-apache-55fb679f49-qw58f` on `chap8-domain1` uses `172.17.0.4`. On the other hand, `my-apache-55fb679f49-z9gsr` on `chap8-domain2` uses `172.17.0.5`.

In this case, the FQDN would be:

- `172-17-0-4.chap8-domain1.pod.cluster.local` (`chap8-domain1`)

- `172-17-0-5.chap8-domain2.pod.cluster.local` (`chap8-domain2`)

 Note that the dots (.) in the IP address are changed to hyphens (-). This is because the dot is a delimiter to determine subdomains.

To check whether name resolution works or not, launch the busybox pod in the foreground (using the `-it` option). Then use the `nslookup` command to resolve FQDN to the IP address, as in the following steps:

1. Run `busybox` with the `-it` option:

    ```
    $ kubectl run -it busybox --restart=Never --image=busybox
    ```

2. In the busybox pod, type `nslookup` to resolve the FQDN of apache on `chap8-domain1`:

    ```
    # nslookup 172-17-0-4.chap8-domain1.pod.cluster.local
    ```

```
Server: 10.96.0.10
Address 1: 10.96.0.10 kube-dns.kube-
system.svc.cluster.local

Name: 172-17-0-4.chap8-domain1.pod.cluster.local
Address 1: 172.17.0.4
```

3. Also, type `nslookup` to resolve the FQDN of apache on `chap8-domain2`:

```
# nslookup 172-17-0-5.chap8-domain2.pod.cluster.local
Server: 10.96.0.10
Address 1: 10.96.0.10 kube-dns.kube-
system.svc.cluster.local

Name: 172-17-0-5.chap8-domain2.pod.cluster.local
Address 1: 172.17.0.5
```

4. Exit the busybox pod, then delete it to release a resource:

```
# exit
$ kubectl delete pod busybox
pod "busybox" deleted
```

DNS for Kubernetes Service

First of all, DNS for Kubernetes Service is most important from the service discovery point of view. This is because an application usually connects to Kubernetes Service instead of connecting to the pod. This is why the application looks up the DNS entry for Kubernetes Service more often than for the pod.

Secondly, the DNS entry for Kubernetes Service will use the name of Kubernetes Service instead of an IP address. For instance, it will look like this: `<Service Name>.<Namespace name>.svc.cluster.local`.

Lastly, Kubernetes Service has 2 different behaviors for DNS; either normal service or headless service. Normal service has its own IP address, while headless service uses the pod's IP address(es). Let's go through normal service first.

Normal service is the default Kubernetes Service. It will assign an IP address. Perform the following steps to create a normal service and check how DNS works:

1. Create a normal service for apache on `chap8-domain1` and `chap8-domain2`:

```
$ kubectl expose deploy my-apache --namespace=chap8-
```

```
domain1 --name=my-apache-svc --port=80 --type=ClusterIP
service "my-apache-svc" exposed

$ kubectl expose deploy my-apache --namespace=chap8-
domain2 --name=my-apache-svc --port=80 --type=ClusterIP
service "my-apache-svc" exposed
```

2. Check the IP address for those two services by running the following command:

```
$ kubectl get svc my-apache-svc --namespace=chap8-domain1
NAME            TYPE          CLUSTER-IP      EXTERNAL-IP
PORT(S)    AGE
my-apache-svc   ClusterIP     10.96.117.206   <none>
80/TCP     32s

$ kubectl get svc my-apache-svc --namespace=chap8-domain2
NAME            TYPE          CLUSTER-IP      EXTERNAL-IP
PORT(S)    AGE
my-apache-svc   ClusterIP     10.105.27.49    <none>
80/TCP     49s
```

3. In order to perform name resolution, use the busybox pod in the foreground:

```
$ kubectl run -it busybox --restart=Never --image=busybox
```

4. In the busybox pod, use the `nslookup` command to query the IP address of those two services:

```
//query Normal Service on chap8-domain1
# nslookup my-apache-svc.chap8-domain1.svc.cluster.local
Server: 10.96.0.10
Address 1: 10.96.0.10 kube-dns.kube-
system.svc.cluster.local

Name: my-apache-svc.chap8-domain1.svc.cluster.local
Address 1: 10.96.117.206 my-apache-svc.chap8-
domain1.svc.cluster.local


//query Normal Service on chap8-domain2
# nslookup my-apache-svc.chap8-domain2.svc.cluster.local
Server: 10.96.0.10
Address 1: 10.96.0.10 kube-dns.kube-
system.svc.cluster.local
```

```
Name: my-apache-svc.chap8-domain2.svc.cluster.local
Address 1: 10.105.27.49 my-apache-svc.chap8-
domain2.svc.cluster.local
```

5. Access to service for apache whether traffic can dispatch to the backend apache pod:

```
# wget -q -O - my-apache-svc.chap8-
domain1.svc.cluster.local
<html><body><h1>It works!</h1></body></html>

# wget -q -O - my-apache-svc.chap8-
domain2.svc.cluster.local
<html><body><h1>It works!</h1></body></html>
```

6. Quit the `busybox` pod and delete it:

```
# exit
$ kubectl delete pod busybox
pod "busybox" deleted
```

DNS for a normal service behaves as a proxy; traffic goes to the normal service, then dispatches to the pod. What about the headless service? This will be discussed in the *How it works...* section.

DNS for StatefulSet

StatefulSet was described in `Chapter 14`, *Playing with Containers*. It assigns a pod name with a sequence number—for example, `my-nginx-0`, `my-nginx-1`, `my-nginx-2`. StatefulSet also uses these pod names to assign a DNS entry instead of IP addresses. Because it uses Kubernetes Service, FQDN appear as follows: `<StatefulSet name>-<sequence number>.<Service name>.<Namespace name>.svc.cluster.local`.

Let's create StatefulSet to examine how DNS works in StatefulSet:

1. Prepare StatefulSet and normal service YAML configurations as follows:

```
$ cat nginx-sts.yaml
apiVersion: v1
kind: Service
metadata:
  name: nginx-sts-svc
  labels:
    app: nginx-sts
```

```
spec:
  ports:
  - port: 80
  selector:
    app: nginx-sts
---
apiVersion: apps/v1beta1
kind: StatefulSet
metadata:
  name: nginx-sts
spec:
  serviceName: "nginx-sts-svc"
  replicas: 3
  template:
    metadata:
      labels:
        app: nginx-sts
    spec:
      containers:
        - name: nginx-sts
          image: nginx
          ports:
          - containerPort: 80
        restartPolicy: Always
```

2. Create StatefulSet on `chap8-domain2`:

```
$ kubectl create -f nginx-sts.yaml --namespace=chap8-
domain2
service "nginx-sts-svc" created
statefulset "nginx-sts" created
```

3. Use the `kubectl` command to check the status of the pod and service creation:

```
//check StatefulSet (in short sts)
$ kubectl get sts --namespace=chap8-domain2
NAME          DESIRED   CURRENT   AGE
nginx-sts     3         3         46s


//check Service (in short svc)
$ kubectl get svc nginx-sts-svc --namespace=chap8-domain2
NAME            TYPE        CLUSTER-IP      EXTERNAL-IP
PORT(S)   AGE
nginx-sts-svc   ClusterIP   10.104.63.124   <none>
80/TCP    8m
```

```
//check Pod with "-o wide" to show an IP address
$ kubectl get pods --namespace=chap8-domain2 -o wide
NAME                         READY     STATUS     RESTARTS
AGE        IP             NODE
my-apache-55fb679f49-z9gsr   1/1       Running    1
22h        172.17.0.4     minikube
nginx-sts-0                  1/1       Running    0
2m         172.17.0.2     minikube
nginx-sts-1                  1/1       Running    0
2m         172.17.0.9     minikube
nginx-sts-2                  1/1       Running    0
1m         172.17.0.10    minikube
```

4. Launch the `busybox` pod in the foreground:

```
$ kubectl run -it busybox --restart=Never --image=busybox
```

5. Use the `nslookup` command to query the service's IP address:

```
# nslookup nginx-sts-svc.chap8-domain2.svc.cluster.local
Server:    10.96.0.10
Address 1: 10.96.0.10 kube-dns.kube-
system.svc.cluster.local

Name:       nginx-sts-svc.chap8-domain2.svc.cluster.local
Address 1: 10.104.63.124 nginx-sts-svc.chap8-
domain2.svc.cluster.local
```

6. Use the `nslookup` command to query the individual pod's IP address:

```
# nslookup nginx-sts-0.nginx-sts-svc.chap8-
domain2.svc.cluster.local
Server:    10.96.0.10
Address 1: 10.96.0.10 kube-dns.kube-
system.svc.cluster.local
Name:       nginx-sts-0.nginx-sts-svc.chap8-
domain2.svc.cluster.local
Address 1: 172.17.0.2 nginx-sts-0.nginx-sts-svc.chap8-
domain2.svc.cluster.local


# nslookup nginx-sts-1.nginx-sts-svc.chap8-
domain2.svc.cluster.local
Server:    10.96.0.10
Address 1: 10.96.0.10 kube-dns.kube-
system.svc.cluster.local
Name:       nginx-sts-1.nginx-sts-svc.chap8-
domain2.svc.cluster.local
```

```
Address 1: 172.17.0.9 nginx-sts-1.nginx-sts-svc.chap8-
domain2.svc.cluster.local


# nslookup nginx-sts-2.nginx-sts-svc.chap8-
domain2.svc.cluster.local
Server:    10.96.0.10
Address 1: 10.96.0.10 kube-dns.kube-
system.svc.cluster.local
Name:      nginx-sts-2.nginx-sts-svc.chap8-
domain2.svc.cluster.local
Address 1: 172.17.0.10 nginx-sts-2.nginx-sts-svc.chap8-
domain2.svc.cluster.local
```

7. Clean up the busybox pod:

```
# exit
$ kubectl delete pod busybox
pod "busybox" deleted
```

How it works...

We have set up several components to see how DNS entries are created initially. The Kubernetes Service name is especially important for determining the name of a DNS.

However, Kubernetes Service has 2 modes, either normal service or headless service. Normal service has already been described in the preceding section; it has its own IP address. On the other hand, headless service doesn't have an IP address.

Let's see how to create a headless service and how name resolution works:

1. Create a headless service (specify --cluster-ip=None) for apache on chap8-domain1 and chap8-domain2:

```
$ kubectl expose deploy my-apache --namespace=chap8-
domain1 --name=my-apache-svc-hl --port=80 --type=ClusterIP
--cluster-ip=None
service "my-apache-svc-hl" exposed

$ kubectl expose deploy my-apache --namespace=chap8-
domain2 --name=my-apache-svc-hl --port=80 --type=ClusterIP
--cluster-ip=None
service "my-apache-svc-hl" exposed
```

2. Check there is no IP address for those two headless services with the following command:

```
$ kubectl get svc my-apache-svc-hl --namespace=chap8-
domain1
NAME                  TYPE          CLUSTER-IP    EXTERNAL-IP
PORT(S)    AGE
my-apache-svc-hl    ClusterIP     None           <none>
80/TCP     13m


$ kubectl get svc my-apache-svc-hl --namespace=chap8-
domain2
NAME                  TYPE          CLUSTER-IP    EXTERNAL-IP
PORT(S)    AGE
my-apache-svc-hl    ClusterIP     None           <none>
80/TCP     13m
```

3. Launch the busybox pod in the foreground:

```
$ kubectl run -it busybox --restart=Never --image=busybox
```

4. In the busybox pod, query those two services. It must show the addresses as the pod's address (172.168.0.4 and 172.168.0.5):

```
# nslookup my-apache-svc-hl.chap8-
domain1.svc.cluster.local
Server: 10.96.0.10
Address 1: 10.96.0.10 kube-dns.kube-
system.svc.cluster.local

Name: my-apache-svc-hl.chap8-domain1.svc.cluster.local
Address 1: 172.17.0.4


# nslookup my-apache-svc-hl.chap8-
domain2.svc.cluster.local
Server: 10.96.0.10
Address 1: 10.96.0.10 kube-dns.kube-
system.svc.cluster.local

Name: my-apache-svc-hl.chap8-domain2.svc.cluster.local
Address 1: 172.17.0.5
```

5. Exit the `busybox` pod and delete it:

```
# exit
$ kubectl delete pod busybox
pod "busybox" deleted
```

Headless service when pods scale out

The preceding example shows only one IP address, because we have been setup only one Pod. What happens if you increase an instance using the `kubectl scale` command?

Let's increase the Apache instances on `chap8-domain1` from 1 to 3, then see how the headless service DNS works:

```
//specify --replicas=3
$ kubectl scale deploy my-apache --namespace=chap8-domain1 --
replicas=3
deployment "my-apache" scaled


//Now there are 3 Apache Pods
$ kubectl get pods --namespace=chap8-domain1 -o wide
NAME                         READY     STATUS     RESTARTS     AGE
IP             NODE
my-apache-55fb679f49-c8wg7   1/1       Running    0            1m
172.17.0.7     minikube
my-apache-55fb679f49-cgnj8   1/1       Running    0            1m
172.17.0.8     minikube
my-apache-55fb679f49-qw58f   1/1       Running    0            8h
172.17.0.4     minikube


//launch busybox to run nslookup command
$ kubectl run -it busybox --restart=Never --image=busybox


//query Headless service name
# nslookup my-apache-svc-hl.chap8-domain1.svc.cluster.local
Server: 10.96.0.10

Address 1: 10.96.0.10 kube-dns.kube-system.svc.cluster.local
Name: my-apache-svc-hl.chap8-domain1.svc.cluster.local
Address 1: 172.17.0.4
Address 2: 172.17.0.7
Address 3: 172.17.0.8
```

```
//quit busybox and release it
# exit
$ kubectl delete pod busybox
pod "busybox" deleted
```

The result is straightforward: one DNS entry, `my-apache-svc-hl.chap8-domain1.svc.cluster.local` returns 3 IP addresses. Therefore, when your HTTP client tries to access the Kubernetes Service `my-apache-svc-hl.chap8-domain1.svc.cluster.local`, it gets these 3 IP addresses from `kube-dns`, then accesses one of them directly, as shown in the following diagram:

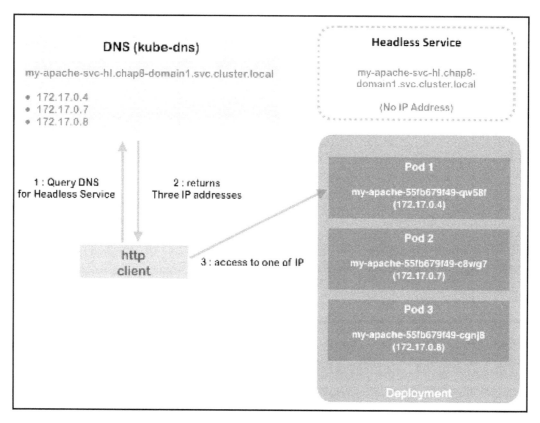

Sequence of accessing to Headless Service and pod

Therefore, Kubernetes headless service doesn't do any traffic dispatches. This is why it is called headless.

See also

This section described how `kube-dns` names pods and services in DNS. It is important to understand the differences between normal service and headless service to understand how to connect to your application. The StatefulSet use case was also described in the following recipe:

- *Ensuring flexible usage of your containers* in `Chapter 14`, *Playing with Containers*

Authentication and authorization

Authentication and authorization are both crucial for a platform such as Kubernetes. Authentication ensures users are who they claim to be. Authorization verifies if users have sufficient permission to perform certain operations. Kubernetes supports various authentication and authorization plugins.

Getting ready

When a request comes to an API server, it firstly establishes a TLS connection by validating the clients' certificate with the **certificate authority** (**CA**) in the API server. The CA in the API server is usually at `/etc/kubernetes/`, and the clients' certificate is usually at `$HOME/.kube/config`. After the handshake, it goes to the authentication stage. In Kubernetes, authentication modules are chain-based. We can use more than one authentication module. When the request comes, Kubernetes will try all the authenticators one by one until it succeeds. If the request fails on all authentication modules, it will be rejected as HTTP 401 unauthorized. Otherwise, one of the authenticators verifies the user's identity, and the requests are authenticated. Then, the Kubernetes authorization modules come into play. They verify if the *user* has the permission to do the action that they requested using a set of policies. Authorization modules are checked one by one. Just like authentication modules, if all modules are failed, the request will be denied. If the user is eligible to make the request, the request will pass through the authentication and authorization modules and go into admission control modules. The request will be checked by various admission controllers one by one. If any admission controller fails the request, the request will be rejected immediately.

The following diagram demonstrates this sequence:

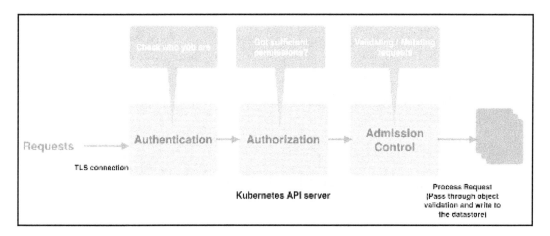

Requests passing through a Kubernetes API server

How to do it...

In Kubernetes, there are two types of account; service accounts and user accounts. The major difference between them is that user accounts are not stored and managed in Kubernetes itself. They cannot be added through API calls. The following table is a simple comparison:

	Service account	User account
Scope	Namespaced	Global
Used by	Processes	Normal user
Created by	API server or via API calls	Administrators, can't be added via API calls
Managed by	API server	Outside the cluster

Service accounts are used by processes inside a Pod to contact the API server. Kubernetes by default will create a service account named **default**. If there is no service account associated with a Pod, it'll be assigned to the default service account:

```
// check default service accoun
# kubectl describe serviceaccount default
Name:           default
Namespace:      default
Labels:         <none>
Annotations:    <none>
```

```
Image pull secrets:    <none>
Mountable secrets:     default-token-q4qdh
Tokens:                default-token-q4qdh
Events:                <none>
```

We may find there is a Secret associated with this service account. This is controlled by the token controller manager. When a new service account is created, the controller will create a token and associate it with the service account with the `kubernetes.io/service-account.name` annotation, allowing API access. Token is in the Secret format in Kubernetes. Anybody with the Secret view permission can see the token. The following is an example of creating a service account:

```
// configuration file of a ServiceAccount named chapter8-
serviceaccount
# cat serviceaccount.yaml
apiVersion: v1
kind: ServiceAccount
metadata:
  name: chapter8-serviceaccount
// create service account
# kubectl create -f serviceaccount.yaml
serviceaccount "chapter8-serviceaccount" created
// describe the service account we just created
# kubectl describe serviceaccount chapter8-serviceaccount
Name:                 chapter8-serviceaccount
Namespace:            default
Labels:               <none>
Annotations:          <none>
Image pull secrets:   <none>
Mountable secrets:    chapter8-serviceaccount-token-nxh47
Tokens:               chapter8-serviceaccount-token-nxh47
Events:               <none>
```

Authentication

There are several account authentication strategies supported in Kuberentes, from client certificates, bearer tokens, and static files to OpenID connect tokens. More than one option could be chosen and combined with others in authentication chains. In this recipe, we'll introduce how to use token, client certs, and OpenID connect token authenticators.

Service account token authentication

We've created a service account in the previous section; now, let's see how to use a service account token to do the authentication. We'll have to retrieve the token first:

```
// check the details of the secret
# kubectl get secret chapter8-serviceaccount-token-nxh47 -o yaml
apiVersion: v1
data:
  ca.crt: <base64 encoded>
  namespace: ZGVmYXVsdA==
  token: <bearer token, base64 encoded>
kind: Secret
metadata:
  annotations:
    kubernetes.io/service-account.name: chapter8-serviceaccount
    name: chapter8-serviceaccount-token-nxh47
  namespace: default
  ...
type: kubernetes.io/service-account-token
```

We can see that the three items under the data are all base64-encoded. We can decode them easily with the `echo "encoded content" | base64 --decode` command in Linux. For example, we can decode encoded namespace content:

```
# echo "ZGVmYXVsdA==" | base64 --decode
default
```

Using the same command we can get the bearer token and use it in a request. The API server expects a HTTP header of `Authorization: Bearer $TOKEN` along with the request. The following is an example of how to use the token to authenticate and make a request directly to the API server.

Firstly, we'll have to get our decoded token:

```
// get the decoded token from secret chapter8-serviceaccount-token-
nxh47
# TOKEN=`echo "<bearer token, base64 encoded>" | base64 --decode`
```

Secondly, we'll have to decode `ca.crt` as well:

```
// get the decoded ca.crt from secret chapter8-serviceaccount-token-
nxh47
# echo "<ca.crt, base64 encoded>" | base64 --decode > cert
```

Next, we'll need to know what the API server is. Using the `kubectl config view` command, we can get a list of servers:

```
# kubectl config view
apiVersion: v1
clusters:
- cluster:
    certificate-authority-data: REDACTED
    server: https://api.demo-k8s.net
  name: demo-k8s.net
- cluster:
    certificate-authority: /Users/chloelee/.minikube/ca.crt
    server: https://192.168.99.100:8443
  name: minikube
...
```

Find the one you're currently using. In this example, we're using minikube. The server is at `https://192.168.99.100:8443`.

 You can use the `kubectl config current-context` command to find the current context.

Then we should be good to go! We'll request the API endpoint directly via `https://$APISERVER/api` with `--cacert` and `--header`

```
# curl --cacert cert https://192.168.99.100:8443/api --header
"Authorization: Bearer $TOKEN"
{
  "kind": "APIVersions",
  "versions": [
    "v1"
  ],
  "serverAddressByClientCIDRs": [
    {
      "clientCIDR": "0.0.0.0/0",
      "serverAddress": "10.0.2.15:8443"
    }
  ]
}
```

We can see that the available version is v1. Let's see what we have in /api/v1 endpoint:

```
# curl --cacert cert https://192.168.99.100:8443/api/v1 --header
"Authorization: Bearer $TOKEN"
{
  "kind": "APIResourceList",
  "groupVersion": "v1",
  "resources": [
    ...
    {
        "name": "configmaps",
        "singularName": "",
        "namespaced": true,
        "kind": "ConfigMap",
        "verbs": [
          "create",
          "delete",
          "deletecollection",
          "get",
          "list",
          "patch",
          "update",
          "watch"
        ],
        "shortNames": ["cm"]
    }
  ], ...
}
```

It will list all the endpoints and verbs we requested. Let's take configmaps as an example and grep the name:

```
# curl --cacert cert https://192.168.99.100:8443/api/v1/configmaps --
header "Authorization: Bearer $TOKEN" |grep \"name\"
          "name": "extension-apiserver-authentication",
          "name": "ingress-controller-leader-nginx",
          "name": "kube-dns",
          "name": "nginx-load-balancer-conf",
```

There are four default configmaps listed in my cluster in this example. We can use `kubectl` to verify this. The result should match the ones we previously got:

```
# kubectl get configmaps --all-namespaces
NAMESPACE       NAME                                    DATA    AGE
kube-system     extension-apiserver-authentication      6       6d
kube-system     ingress-controller-leader-nginx         0       6d
kube-system     kube-dns                                0       6d
kube-system     nginx-load-balancer-conf                1       6d
```

X509 client certs

A common authentication strategy for user accounts is to use client certificates. In the following example, we'll create a user named Linda and generate a client cert for her:

```
// generate a private key for Linda
# openssl genrsa -out linda.key 2048
Generating RSA private key, 2048 bit long modulus
...............+++
...............+++
e is 65537 (0x10001)
// generate a certificate sign request (.csr) for Linda. Make sure /CN
is equal to the username.
# openssl req -new -key linda.key -out linda.csr -subj "/CN=linda"
```

Next, we'll generate a cert for Linda via a private key and sign request files, along with the CA and private key of our cluster:

 In minikube, it's under `~/.minikube/`. For other self-hosted solutions, normally it's under `/etc/kubernetes/`. If you use `kops` to deploy the cluster, the location is under `/srv/kubernetes`, where you can find the path in the`/etc/kubernetes/manifests/kube-apiserver.manifest` file.

```
// generate a cert
# openssl x509 -req -in linda.csr -CA ca.crt -CAkey ca.key -
CAcreateserial -out linda.crt -days 30
Signature ok
subject=/CN=linda
Getting CA Private Key
```

We got Linda signed by our cluster cert; now we can set it into our `kubeconfig` file:

```
# kubectl config set-credentials linda --client-certificate=linda.crt
--client-key=linda.key
User "linda" set.
```

We can use `kubectl config view` to verify the user is set:

```
# kubectl config view
current-context: minikube
kind: Config
users:
  - name: linda
  user:
    client-certificate: /k8s-cookbooks-2e/ch8/linda.crt
    client-key: /k8s-cookbooks-2e/ch8/linda.key
...
```

After the user is created, we can create a context to associate the namespace and cluster with this user:

```
# kubectl config set-context linda-context --cluster=minikube --
user=linda
```

After that, Kubernetes should be able to identify linda and pass it to the authorization stage.

OpenID connect tokens

Another popular authentication strategy is OpenID connect tokens. Delegating the identity verification to OAuth2 providers, is a convenient way to manage users. To enable the feature, two required flags have to be set to the API server: `--oidc-issuer-url`, which indicates the issuer URL that allows the API server to discover public signing keys, and `--oidc-client-id`, which is the client ID of your app to associate with your issuer. For full information, please refer to the official documentation `https://kubernetes.io/docs/admin/authentication/#configuring-the-api-server`. The following is an example of how we set Google OpenID authentication with our minikube cluster. The following steps can be programmed easily for authentication usage.

To start, we'll have to request a set consisting of the client ID, client secret, and redirect URL from Google. The following are the steps for requesting and downloading the secret from Google:

1. In GCP console, go to **APIs & Services** | **Credentials** | **Create credentials** | **OAuth client ID.**
2. Choose Other in application type and click **Create.**
3. Download the JSON file.

After this, the credential is successfully created. We can take a look at the JSON file. The following is the file we got from our example project kubernetes-cookbook:

```
# cat client_secret_140285873781-
f9h7d7bmi6ec1qa0892mk52t3o874j5d.apps.googleusercontent.com.json
{
    "installed":{
        "client_id":"140285873781
f9h7d7bmi6ec1qa0892mk52t3o874j5d.apps.googleusercontent.com",
        "project_id":"kubernetes-cookbook",
        "auth_uri":"https://accounts.google.com/o/oauth2/auth",
        "token_uri":"https://accounts.google.com/o/oauth2/token",
    "auth_provider_x509_cert_url":"https://www.googleapis.com/oauth2/v1/ce
rts",
        "client_secret":"Ez0m1L7436mlJQErhalp3Gda",
        "redirect_uris":[
            "urn:ietf:wg:oauth:2.0:oob",
            "http://localhost"
        ]
    }
}
```

Now, we should be able to start our cluster. Don't forget the OIDC flags have to be passed on. In minikube, this is done via the `--extra-config` parameter:

```
// start minikube cluster and passing oidc parameters.
# minikube start --extra-config=apiserver.Authorization.Mode=RBAC --
extra-
config=apiserver.Authentication.OIDC.IssuerURL=https://accounts.google
.com --extra-config=apiserver.Authentication.OIDC.UsernameClaim=email
--extra-config=apiserver.Authentication.OIDC.ClientID="140285873781-
f9h7d7bmi6ec1qa0892mk52t3o874j5d.apps.googleusercontent.com"
```

After the cluster is started, the user has to log in to the identity provider in order to get `access_token`, `id_token`, and `refresh_token`. In Google, you'll get a code after login, and you pass the code with the request to get the tokens. Then we pass the token to the request to the API server via kubectl. The following is the sequence diagram for this:

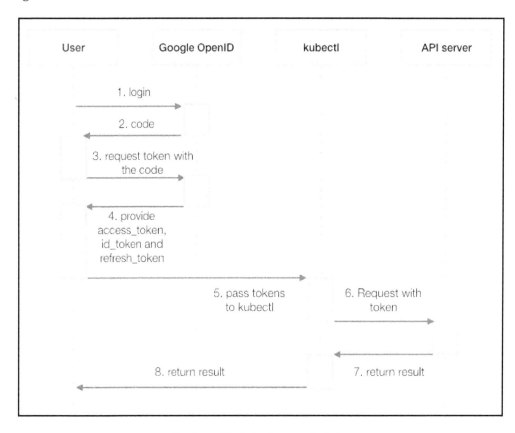

Time diagram of Google OpenID connect authentication

To request the code, your app should send the HTTP request in the following format:

```
//
https://accounts.google.com/o/oauth2/v2/auth?client_id=<client_id>&res
ponse_type=code&scope=openid%20email&redirect_uri=urn:ietf:wg:oauth:2.
0:oob
#
https://accounts.google.com/o/oauth2/v2/auth?client_id=140285873781-f9
h7d7bmi6ec1qa0892mk52t3o874j5d.apps.googleusercontent.com&response_typ
e=code&scope=openid%20email&redirect_uri=urn:ietf:wg:oauth:2.0:oob
```

Then, a browser window will pop out to ask for sign in to Google. After signing in, the code will be shown in the console:

Next, we pass the code for requesting the token to `https://www.googleapis.com/oauth2/v4/token`. Then, we should be able to get `access_token`, `refresh_token`, and `id_token` from the response:

```
// curl -d
"grant_type=authorization_code&client_id=<client_id>&client_secret=<cl
ient_secret>&redirect_uri=urn:ietf:wg:oauth:2.0:oob&code=<code>" -X
POST https://www.googleapis.com/oauth2/v4/token
# curl -d "grant_type=authorization_code&client_id=140285873781-
f9h7d7bmi6ec1qa0892mk52t3o874j5d.apps.googleusercontent.com&client_sec
ret=Ez0m1L7436mlJQErhalp3Gda&redirect_uri=urn:ietf:wg:oauth:2.0:oob&co
de=4/AAAd5nqWFkpKmxo0b_HZGlcAh57zbJzggKmoOG0BH9gJhfgvQK0iu9w" -X POST
https://www.googleapis.com/oauth2/v4/token
{
  "access_token":
"ya29.GluJBQIhJy34vqJl7V6lPF9YSXmKauvvctjUJHwx72gKDDJikiKzQed9iUnmqEv8
gLYg43H6zTSYn1qohkNce1Q3fMl6wbrGMCuXfRlipTcPtZnFt1jNalqMMTCm",
  "token_type": "Bearer",
  "expires_in": 3600,
  "refresh_token": "1/72xFflvdTRdqhjn70Bcar3qyWDiFw-8KoNm6LdFPorQ",
  "id_token": "eyJhbGc...mapQ"
}
```

Assume we'll have the user `chloe-k8scookbook@gmail.com` to associate with this Google account. Let's create it in our cluster. We can append user information into our kubeconfig. The default location of the file is `$HOME/.kube/config`:

```
// append to kubeconfig file.
- name: chloe-k8scookbook@gmail.com
  user:
    auth-provider:
      config:
        client-id: 140285873781-
f9h7d7bmi6ec1qa0892mk52t3o874j5d.apps.googleusercontent.com
        client-secret: Ez0m1L7436mlJQErhalp3Gda
        id-token: eyJhbGc...mapQ
        idp-issuer-url: https://accounts.google.com
        refresh-token: 1/72xFflvdTRdqhjn70Bcar3qyWDiFw-8KoNm6LdFPorQ
      name: oidc
```

After that, let's use the user to list nodes and see if it can pass the authentication:

```
# kubectl --user=chloe-k8scookbook@gmail.com get nodes
Error from server (Forbidden): nodes is forbidden: User "chloe-
k8scookbook@gmail.com" cannot list nodes at the cluster scope
```

We encounter an authorization error! After verifying the identity, the next step will be checking if the user has sufficient rights to perform the request.

Authorization

After passing the authentication phase, authorizers take place. Before we move on to authorization strategies, let's talk about `Role` and `RoleBinding` first.

Role and RoleBinding

`Role` in Kubernetes contains a set of rules. A rule defines a set of permissions for certain operations and resources by specifying `apiGroups`, `resources`, and `verbs`. For example, the following role defines a read-only rule for `configmaps`:

```
# cat role.yaml
kind: Role
apiVersion: rbac.authorization.k8s.io/v1
metadata:
  name: configmap-ro
rules:
  - apiGroups: ["*"]
    resources: ["configmaps"]
```

```
    verbs: ["watch", "get", "list"]
```

A `RoleBinding` is used to associate a role with a list of accounts. The following example shows we assign the `configmap-ro` role to a list of subjects. It only has the user `linda` in this case:

```
# cat rolebinding.yaml
kind: RoleBinding
apiVersion: rbac.authorization.k8s.io/v1
metadata:
  name: devops-role-binding
subjects:
- apiGroup: ""
  kind: User
  name: linda
roleRef:
  apiGroup: ""
  kind: Role
  name: configmap-ro
```

`Role` and `RoleBinding` are namespaced. Their scope is only within a single namespace. For accessing `cluster-wide` resources, we'll need `ClusterRole` and `ClusterRoleBinding`.

For adding namespace into `Role` or `RoleBinding`, simply add a namespace field into the metadata in the configuration file.

ClusterRole and ClusterRoleBinding

`ClusterRole` and `ClusterRoleBinding` are basically similar to `Role` and `RoleBinding`. Unlike how `Role` and `RoleBinding` are scoped into a single namespace, `ClusterRole` and `ClusterRoleBinding` are used to grant cluster-wide resources. Therefore, access to resources across all namespaces, non-namespaced resources, and non-resource endpoints can be granted to `ClusterRole`, and we can use `ClusterRoleBinding` to bind the users and the role.

We can also bind a service account with `ClusterRole`. As a service account is namespaced, we'll have to specify its full name, which includes the namespace it's created in:

```
system:serviceaccount:<namespace>:<serviceaccountname>
```

The following is an example of `ClusterRole` and `ClusterRoleBinding`. In this role, we grant all operations for lots of resources, such as `deployments`, `replicasets`, `ingresses`, `pods`, and `services` to it, and we limit the permission to read-only for namespaces and events:

```
# cat serviceaccount_clusterrole.yaml
apiVersion: rbac.authorization.k8s.io/v1
kind: ClusterRole
metadata:
  name: cd-role
rules:
- apiGroups: ["extensions", "apps"]
  resources:
  - deployments
  - replicasets
  - ingresses
  verbs: ["*"]
- apiGroups: [""]
  resources:
  - namespaces
  - events
  verbs: ["get", "list", "watch"]
- apiGroups: [""]
  resources:
  - pods
  - services
  - secrets
  - replicationcontrollers
  - persistentvolumeclaims
  - jobs
  - cronjobs
  verbs: ["*"]---
apiVersion: rbac.authorization.k8s.io/v1
kind: ClusterRoleBinding
metadata:
  name: cd-role-binding
roleRef:
  apiGroup: rbac.authorization.k8s.io
  kind: ClusterRole
  name: cd-role
subjects:
- apiGroup: rbac.authorization.k8s.io
  kind: User
  name: system:serviceaccount:default:chapter8-serviceaccount
```

Note [""] in `apiGroup`; this indicates the core group in Kubernetes. To see the full list of resources and verbs, check out the Kubernetes API reference site: `https://kubernetes.io/docs/reference/`.

In this case, we create a `cd-role`, which is the role for performing continuous deployment. Also, we create a `ClusterRoleBinding` to associate the service account `chapter8-serviceaccount` with `cd-role`.

Role-based access control (RBAC)

The concept of role-based access control is surrounded by `Role`, `ClusterRole`, `RoleBinding`, and `ClusterRoleBinding`. By `role.yaml` and `rolebinding.yaml`, as we showed previously, Linda should get read-only access to the `configmaps` resource. To apply authorization rules to `chloe-k8scookbook@gmail.com`, simply associate a `ClusterRole` and `ClusterRoleBinding` with it:

```
# cat oidc_clusterrole.yaml
kind: ClusterRole
apiVersion: rbac.authorization.k8s.io/v1
metadata:
  name: oidc-admin-role
rules:
  - apiGroups: ["*"]
    resources: ["*"]
    verbs: ["*"]
---
kind: ClusterRoleBinding
apiVersion: rbac.authorization.k8s.io/v1
metadata:
  name: admin-binding
subjects:
  - kind: User
    name: chloe-k8scookbook@gmail.com
    apiGroup: rbac.authorization.k8s.io
roleRef:
  kind: ClusterRole
  name: oidc-admin-role
  apiGroup: rbac.authorization.k8s.io
```

Then, we should be able to see if we can get nodes with the `chloe-k8scookbook@gmail.com` user:

```
# kubectl --user=chloe-k8scookbook@gmail.com get nodes
NAME STATUS ROLES AGE VERSION minikube Ready <none> 6d v1.9.4
```

It works like a charm. We didn't encounter the Forbidden error anymore.

Before RBAC, Kubernetes provided **Attribute-based access control** (**ABAC**), which allows a cluster administrator to define a set of user authorization polices into a file with one JSON per line format. However, the file has to exist when launching the API server, which makes it unusable in the real world. After RBAC was introduced in Kubernetes 1.6, ABAC became legacy and was deprecated.

Admission control

Admission control modules come into play after Kubernetes verifies who makes requests and whether the requester has sufficient permission to perform them. Unlike authentication and authorization, admission control can see the content of the request, or even have the ability to validate or mutate it. If the request doesn't pass through one of admission controllers, the request will be rejected immediately. For turning on admission controllers in Kubernetes, simply pass `--admission-control` `(version < 1.10)` `--enable-admission-plugins (version >= 1.10)` parameters when starting the API server.

Depending on how you provision your cluster, the method for passing on the `--enable-admission-plugin` parameter may vary. In minikube, adding `--extra-config=apiserver.Admission.PluginNames=` `$ADMISSION_CONTROLLERS` and separate controllers with commas should do the trick.

Different admission controllers are designed for different purposes. In the following recipe, we'll introduce some important admission controllers and those that Kubernetes officially recommends that users have. The recommended list for version >= 1.6.0 is as follows: `NamespaceLifecycle`, `LimitRanger`, `ServiceAccount`, `PersistentVolumeLabel`, `DefaultStorageClass`, `DefaultTolerationSeconds`, `ResourceQuota`.

Please note that the sequence of admission controllers matters since the requests pass one by one in sequence (this is true for versions before 1.10, using the `--admission-control` option; in v1.10, the parameter is replaced by `--enable-admission-plugins` and the sequence no longer matters). We don't want to have `ResourceQuota` checking first and finding out that the resource information is outdated after checking the long chain of admission controllers.

If the version is >= 1.9.0, `MutatingAdmissionWebhook` and `ValidatingAdmissionWebhook` will be added before `ResourceQuota`. For more information about `MutatingAdmissionWebhook` and `ValidatingAdmissionWebhook`, please refer to the *There's more* section in this recipe.

NamespaceLifecycle

When a namespace is deleted, all objects in that namespace will be evicted as well. This plugin ensures no new object creation requests can be made in a namespace that is terminating or non-existent. It also saves Kubernetes native Namespaces from deletion.

LimitRanger

This plugin ensures `LimitRange` can work properly. With `LimitRange`, we can set default requests and limits in a namespace, be used when launching a pod without specifying the requests and limits.

ServiceAccount

The ServiceAccount plugin must be added if you intend to leverage ServiceAccount objects in your use cases. For more information about ServiceAccount, revisit ServiceAccount as we learned it in this recipe.

PersistentVolumeLabel (deprecated from v1.8)

`PersistentVolumeLabel` adds labels to newly-created PV's, based on the labels provided by the underlying cloud provider. This admission controller has been deprecated from 1.8. The function of this controller is now taken care of by cloud controller manager, which defines cloud-specific control logic and runs as a daemon.

DefaultStorageClass

This plugin ensures default storage classes can work as expected if no `StorageClass` is set in a `PersistentVolumeClaim`. Different provisioning tools with different cloud providers will leverage `DefaultStorageClass` (such as GKE, which uses Google Cloud Persistent Disk). Ensure you have this enabled.

DefaultTolerationSeconds

Taints and tolerations are used to prevent a set of pods from scheduling running on some nodes. Taints are applied to nodes, while tolerations are specified for pods. The value of taints could be `NoSchedule` or `NoExecute`. If pods running one tainted node have no matching toleration, the pods will be evicted.

The `DefaultTolerationSeconds` plugin is used to set those pods without any toleration set. It will then apply for the default toleration for the taints `notready:NoExecute` and **unreachable:NoExecute** for 300 s. If a node is not ready or unreachable, wait for 300 seconds before the pod is evicted from the node.

ResourceQuota

Just like `LimitRange`, if you're using the `ResourceQuota` object to administer different levels of QoS, this plugin must be enabled. The `ResourceQuota` should be always be put at the end of the admission control plugin list. As we mentioned in the `ResourceQuota` section, if the used quota is less than the hard quota, resource quota usage will be updated to ensure that clusters have sufficient resources to accept requests. Putting it into the end of ServiceAccount admission controller list could prevent the request from increasing quota usage prematurely if it eventually gets rejected by the following controllers.

DenyEscalatingExec

This plugin denies any kubectl exec and kubectl attach command escalated privilege mode. Pods with privilege mode have access to the host namespace, which could become a security risk.

AlwaysPullImages

The pull policy defines the behavior when kubelet is pulling images. The default pull policy is `IfNotPresent`; that is, it will pull the image if it is not present locally. If this plugin is enabled, the default pull policy will become Always, which is, always pull the latest image. This plugin also provides another benefit if your cluster is shared by different teams. Whenever a pod is scheduled, it'll always pull the latest image whether the image exists locally or not. Then we can ensure pod creation requests always go through an authorization check against the image.

For a full list of admission controllers, visit the official site (`https://kubernetes.io/docs/admin/admission-controllers`) for more information.

There's more...

Before Kubernetes 1.7, admission controllers needed to compile with the API server, and configure before the API server starts. **Dynamic admission control** is designed to break these limitations. As two major components in dynamic admission control are both not GA at the moment we wrote this book, excepting adding them into the admission control chain, additional runtime configuration is required in the API server: `--runtime-config=admissionregistration.k8s.io/v1alpha1`.

 In minikube, ServiceAccount runtime config is set to `api/all`, so it's enabled by default.

Initializers (alpha)

Initializers are a set of tasks during the object initialization stage. They could be a set of checks or mutations to perform force policies or inject defaults. For example, you could implement an initializer to inject a sidecar container or a volume containing test data to a pod. Initializers are configured in `metadata.initializers.pending` for an object. After the corresponding initializer controller (identified by name) performs the task, it'll remove its name from the metadata. If for some reasonsone initializer doesn't work well, all the objects with that initializer will be stuck in ServiceAccount uninitialized stage, and not visible in the API. Use it with caution.

Webhook admission controllers (beta in v1.9)

There are two types of webhook admission controller as of v1.10:

- `ValidatingAdmissionWebhook`: It can do extra customized validation to reject the request
- `MutatingAdmissionWebhooks`: It can mutate the object to force default policies

For more implementation information, please refer to the official documents:
`https://kubernetes.io/docs/admin/extensible-admission-controllers/`

See also

The following recipes are of relevance to this section:

- *Working with Namespaces* in `Chapter 13`, *Walking through Kubernetes Concepts*
- *Setting up continuous delivery pipelines* in `Chapter 16`, *Building Continuous Delivery Pipelines*
- *Advanced settings in kubeconfig* in `Chapter 18`, *Advanced Cluster Administration*
- *Working with ServiceAccount RESTful API* in `Chapter 18`, *Advanced Cluster Administration*

Other Books You May Enjoy

If you enjoyed this book, you may be interested in these other books by Packt:

Mastering Docker - Second Edition
Russ McKendrick, Scott Gallagher

ISBN: 978-1-78728-024-3

- Become fluent in the basic components and concepts of Docker
- Secure your containers and files with Docker's security features
- Extend Docker and solve architectural problems using first- and third-party orchestration tools, service discovery, and plugins
- Leverage the Linux container virtualization paradigm by creating highly scalable applications

Kubernetes Design Patterns and Extensions

Matt Smith

ISBN: 978-1-78961-927-0

- Understand and classify software designs as per the cloud-native paradigm
- Apply best practices in Kubernetes with design patterns
- Set up Kubernetes clusters in managed and unmanaged environments
- Explore Kubernetes extension points
- Extend Kubernetes with custom resources and controllers
- Integrate dynamic admission controllers
- Develop and run custom schedulers in Kubernetes
- Analyze networking models in Kubernetes

Leave a review - let other readers know what you think

Please share your thoughts on this book with others by leaving a review on the site that you bought it from. If you purchased the book from Amazon, please leave us an honest review on this book's Amazon page. This is vital so that other potential readers can see and use your unbiased opinion to make purchasing decisions, we can understand what our customers think about our products, and our authors can see your feedback on the title that they have worked with Packt to create. It will only take a few minutes of your time, but is valuable to other potential customers, our authors, and Packt. Thank you!

Index

executing 41, 42

R

Raft consensus protocol 200
read-only (ro) 102
ReadWriteMany (RWX) 549
redundancy 128
Remote Procedure Call (RPC) 536
repeatable job
  creating 498
Replica Set (RS) 438
  configuration, modifying 339
  creating 336
  deleting 340
  deployment, linking with set-based selector 431
  details, obtaining 338
  Pods, managing 334, 335, 342, 344
  service, linking with label selectors 429
replicated services 179
Replication Controller (RC) 436, 438
resource consumption
  listing 111, 112
ResourceQuota plugin 696
RESTful API
  working with 659, 662, 665, 667
reverse uptime 189
role based access control (RBAC) 568
role-based access control (RBAC) 15
Role-based access control (RBAC) 187
rolling updates 184
Romana
  reference link 462
routing 126, 181

S

scaling 182
scheduler (kube-scheduler) 266
secrets 188
  about 252
  and legacy applications 257, 258
  ConfigMaps, mounting in same volume 405
  ConfigMaps, using 403
  creating 253, 254, 397
  creating, from directory 399

creating, from literal value 399
creating, via configuration file 400
deleting 403
kubectl create command line, working with 397
mounting 405
mounting, as volume 401
simulating, in development environment 256
text file, creating 397
updating 259
using 254, 255
using, in Pods 400
working with 396, 397, 403
security group (SG) 220
security group
  creating 600
security
  about 186
  content trust 189
  cryptographic node identity 186
  network policies, securing 187
  networks, securing 187
  reverse uptime 189
  Role-based access control (RBAC) 187
  secrets 188
  secure communication 186
selectors
  working with 423, 424, 427
self-healing 183
service account token authentication 682
service discovery 124, 125, 180
service level agreement (SLA) 252
service
  scaling 169, 170, 171
ServiceAccount plugin 695
services
  creating, for another service with session affinity 363
  creating, for deployment with external IP 360
  creating, for endpoint without selector 361
  creating, for Pod 358
  creating, for resources 358
  deleting 364
  types 367
  working with 355, 356, 365, 370

W

webhook admission controllers 697
WebUI
  working with 646
Windows
  AWS CLI, installing 592
  Chocolatey, installing 24
  Kubernetes cluster, setting up by minikube
    278, 279, 282, 283, 288
  PowerShell 23
worker node 179, 202, 203
writable container layer 66, 67

X

X509 client certs 685

Y

YAML
  about 504
  reference link 504

Z

zero downtime deployment
  about 184, 238
  blue-green deployments 251
  canary releases 252
  health checks 245, 246, 247, 248
  rollback 249, 250
  rolling updates 238, 239, 240, 241, 242,
    243, 244
  strategies 238

www.ingramcontent.com/pod-product-compliance
Lightning Source LLC
LaVergne TN
LVHW081505050326
832903LV00025B/1390